Cedric J. Robinson

Black Critique
Series editors: Anthony Bogues and Bedour Alagraa

We live in a troubled world. The rise of authoritarianism marks the dominant current political order. The end of colonial empires did not inaugurate a more humane world; rather, the old order reasserted itself.

In opposition, throughout the twentieth century and until today, anti-racist, radical decolonization struggles attempted to create new forms of thought. Figures from Ida B. Wells to W. E. B. Du Bois and Steve Biko, from Claudia Jones to Walter Rodney and Amílcar Cabral produced work which drew from the historical experiences of Africa and the African diaspora. They drew inspiration from the Haitian revolution, radical Black abolitionist thought and practice, and other currents that marked the contours of a Black radical intellectual and political tradition.

The Black Critique series operates squarely within this tradition of ideas and political struggles. It includes books which foreground this rich and complex history. At a time when there is a deep desire for change, Black radicalism is one of the most underexplored traditions that can drive emancipatory change today. This series highlights these critical ideas from anywhere in the Black world, creating a new history of radical thought for our times.

Also available:

Moving Against the System:
The 1968 Congress of Black Writers and the Making of Global Consciousness
Edited and with an Introduction by David Austin

Red International and Black Caribbean Communists in New York City,
Mexico and the West Indies, 1919–1939
Margaret Stevens

A Certain Amount of Madness:
The Life, Politics and Legacies of Thomas Sankara
Edited by Amber Murrey

Cedric J. Robinson

On Racial Capitalism,
Black Internationalism,
and Cultures of Resistance

Edited by H. L. T. Quan

FOREWORD BY RUTH WILSON GILMORE

PLUTO PRESS

First published 2019 by Pluto Press
345 Archway Road, London N6 5AA

www.plutobooks.com

British Library Cataloguing in Publication Data
A catalogue record for this book is available from the British Library

ISBN 978 0 7453 4002 9 Hardback
ISBN 978 0 7453 4003 6 Paperback
ISBN 978 1 7868 0520 1 PDF eBook
ISBN 978 1 7868 0522 5 Kindle eBook
ISBN 978 1 7868 0521 8 EPUB eBook

This book is printed on paper suitable for recycling and made from fully
managed and sustained forest sources. Logging, pulping and manufacturing
processes are expected to conform to the environmental standards of the country of origin.

Typeset by Riverside Publishing Solutions, Salisbury, United Kingdom

Simultaneously printed in the United Kingdom and United States of America

Contents

Acknowledgements   vii

Sources of Original Materials   ix

Foreword by Ruth Wilson Gilmore   xi

Preface by Elizabeth Peters Robinson   xv

Introduction: Looking for Grace in Redemption   1
    H. L. T. Quan

Part I On Africa and Black Internationalism   19

  1 Notes Toward a "Native" Theory of History   21

  2 In Search of a Pan-African Commonwealth   45

  3 The Black Detective and American Memory   54

Part II On Bourgeois Historiography   67

  4 "The First Attack is an Attack on Culture"   69

  5 Oliver Cromwell Cox and the Historiography of the West   75

  6 Fascism and the Intersections of Capitalism, Racialism, and
    Historical Consciousness   87

  7 Ota Benga's Flight Through Geronimo's Eyes: Tales of Science and
    Multiculturalism   110

  8 Slavery and the Platonic Origins of Anti-democracy   127

Part III On World Politics and U.S. Foreign Policy   147

  9 Fascism and the Response of Black Radical *Theorists*   149

 10 Africa: In Hock to History and the Banks   160

 11 The Comedy of Terror   164

 12 Ralph Bunche and *An American Dilemma*   171

Part IV On Reality and Its (Mis)Representations   183

13 White Signs in Black Times: The Politics of Representation in
    Dominant Texts   185

14 The American Press and the Repairing of the Philippines   195

15 On the *Los Angeles Times*, Crack Cocaine, and the Rampart
    Division Scandal   209

16 Micheaux Lynches the Mammy   213

17 Blaxploitation and the Misrepresentation of Liberation   221

18 The Mulatta on Film: From Hollywood to the Mexican
    Revolution   233

19 Ventriloquizing Blackness: Eugene O'Neill and
    Irish-American Racial Performance   251

Part V On Resistance and Redemption   265

20 Malcolm Little as a Charismatic Leader   267

21 The Appropriation of Frantz Fanon   295

22 Amilcar Cabral and the Dialectic of Portuguese Colonialism   308

23 Race, Capitalism, and the Anti-democracy   331

24 David Walker and the Precepts of Black Studies   340

25 The Killing in Ferguson   354

26 On the Truth and Reconciliation Commission   356

Index   359

Acknowledgements

When Cedric J. Robinson died in June 2016, he left behind a rich legacy of learning, teaching, and radical social inquiries, of which this collection is a part. Cedric aimed at and frequently succeeded in supplying his students and the general public with works that are generative – his writings and public lectures sought to open up spaces previously unavailable and/or differently configured. In the process, he made it possible for many of us to join him in a collective journey to radicalize the academy, democratize knowledge, and redeem, in however small measures, our humanity in life and work within this precarious and unjust world order. It is thus a personal privilege for me to partake in this collective endeavor. For this privilege, a three-decade long friendship, and the countless life lessons, I am deeply indebted to Cedric and Elizabeth's generosity and kindred spirit. I am further indebted to Elizabeth who shepherded this project from the earliest stages (more than twenty years ago) through the reassembling of the materials for this acknowledgement, not to mention editorial support and the gentle, persistent urgings ensuring the final publication of this collection.

Elizabeth and I are grateful to a number of individuals whose contributions were invaluable to the making of this collection. Kofi Buenor Hadjor initiated the idea of a collection of essays to compliment Cedric's books, and Africa World Press publisher Kassahun Checole expressed early enthusiasm and support for it. Stephen Ward found and shared the complete draft of the previously unpublished, "David Walker and the Precepts of Black Studies." Luz Maria Cabral co-authored "The Mulatta on Film: From Hollywood to the Mexican Revolution," and gave permission for its republication. Ruth Wilson Gilmore graciously agreed to write the foreword, even in difficult circumstances.

We owe special thanks to the journal, *Race & Class* and the Institute of Race Relations, especially Hazel Waters, Jenny Bourne, and the late A. Sivanandan for their deep engagement with Cedric's work and for making it possible for it to receive public, international airings; Sarah Suhail for research assistance, and M. A. Bortner for invaluable feedback. We are also deeply appreciative of the amazing editorial staff at Pluto Press and their dedication to seeing this project a reality, especially David Shulman's vision and patience and Paul Beanie's and Robert Webb's editorial supports.

We thank the following for permissions to reprint: the Fernand Braudel Center (Binghamton University) for "Notes Toward a 'Native' Theory of History"; Taylor & Francis for "In Search of a Pan-African Commonwealth," "Slavery, and the Platonic Origins of Anti-Democracy," "Malcolm Little as a Charismatic Leader", and "Race, Capitalism, and the Anti-democracy"; the University of Minnesota Press for "Oliver Cromwell Cox and the Historiography of the West"; the Center for the Humanities (University of Southern California) for "Fascism and the Intersections of Capitalism, Racialism, and Historical Consciousness"; Wiley-Blackwell Publishing for "Ota Benga through Geronimo's Eyes: Tales of Science and Multiculturalism"; Duke University Press for "The Comedy of Terror"; *The Santa Barbara News & Review* for "Africa: In Hoc to History and the Banks," The Institute of Race Relations for "The American Press and the Repairing of the Philippines," "Blaxploitation and the Misrepresentation of Liberation," "The Mullata on Film: From Hollywood to the Mexican Revolution", and "The Appropriation of Frantz Fanon"; Palgrave MacMillian for "Ventriloquizing Blackness: Eugene O'Neill and Irish-American Racial Performance"; the Department of Political Science (University of Delhi) for "Amilcar Cabral and the Dialectic of Portuguese Colonialism"; and, commonware.org for "Ferguson, Gaza, Iraq. An Outline on the Official Narrative in 'Post-Racial' America".

Finally, Cedric taught and wrote as he lived, cherishing the life and work of those who are decent, kind and generous in spirit, fighting the battles that needed to be fought, laughing in the face of horror, and never conceding that being oppressed is all that we are. In that spirit, we thank Crystal, Najda, and Jacob for their love and friendship.

Sources of Original Materials

1. Notes Toward a "Native" Theory of History: *Review,* Vol. 4, No. 1, Summer 1980, pp. 45–78 (Fernand Braudel Center).

2. In Search of a Pan-African Commonwealth. *Social Identities,* Vol. 2, No. 1, 1996, pp. 161–168 (Routledge – Taylor & Francis).

3. The Black Detective and American Memory. *The American Studies Association Annual Meeting.* San Antonio, TX, November 18–21, 2010. Previously unpublished.

4. "The First Attack is an Attack on Culture". *Afro-Latin Cultural Festival.* SUNY Binghamton. April 29, 1975. Previously unpublished.

5. Oliver Cromwell Cox and the Historiography of the West, *Cultural Critique,* No 17, Winter 1990–91, pp. 5–19 (University of Minnesota Press).

6. Fascism and the Intersections of Capitalism, Racialism, and Historical Consciousness. *Humanities in Society,* Vol. 3, No. 6, Fall 1983, pp. 325–349 (University of Southern California, Center for the Humanities).

7. Ota Benga through Geronimo's Eyes: Tales of Science and Multiculturalism. *Multiculturalism: A Critical Reader,* ed. David Theo Goldberg, 1994, pp. 388–405 (Wiley-Blackwell).

8. Slavery, and the Platonic Origins of Anti-democracy. *The Changing Racial Regime, National Political Science Review* Vol. 5, 1995, pp. 18–35 (Transaction – Taylor & Francis).

9. Fascism and the Response by Black Radical Theorists. *African Studies Association Annual Meeting.* Baltimore, MD, November 1990. Previously unpublished.

10. Africa: In Hoc to History and the Banks. *Santa Barbara News & Review,* 10 January 1985 (Santa Barbara Independence).

11. The Comedy of Terror. *Radical History Review:* 85, Winter 2003, pp. 164–170 (Duke University Press).

12. Ralph Bunche and the American Dilemma. *"Ralph Bunche and the American Experience,"* Conference. Boston University, Boston, MA, March 19, 2004. Previously unpublished.

13. White Signs in Black Times: The Politics of Representation in Dominant Texts. *Conference on Black Theorizing Post-Modernism, and Post-Structuralism.* Center for Black Studies, UC Santa Barbara, May 1989. Previously unpublished.

14. The American Press and the Repairing of the Philippines. *Race & Class*, Vol. 28, No. 1, 1986, pp. 31–44 (Institute of Race Relations).
15. On the Los Angeles Times, Crack Cocaine, and the Ramparts Division Scandal, 1999. Previously unpublished.
16. Micheaux Lynches the Mammy. *Celebrating Black History Month*. Skyline College, San Bruno, CA, February 2003. Previously unpublished.
17. Blaxploitation and the Misrepresentation of Liberation. *Race & Class*. Vol 40, No. 1, 1998, pp. 1–12 (Institute of Race Relations).
18. The Mulatta on Film: From Hollywood to the Mexican Revolution. Co-authored with Luz Maria Cabral. *Race & Class*, Vol. 45, No. 1, 2003, pp. 1–20 (Institute of Race Relations).
19. Ventriloquizing Blackness: Eugene O'Neill and Irish-American Racial Performance, *The Black and Green Atlantic: Cross-Currents of the African and Irish Diasporas*. Eds. Peter O'Neill, and David Lloyd (Palgrave McMillan).
20. Malcolm Little as a Charismatic Leader. *Afro-American Studies*, Vol. 3, 1972, pp. 81–96 (Taylor & Francis).
21. The Appropriation of Frantz Fanon. *Race & Class*, Vol. 35, No. 1 1993, pp. 79–91 (Institute of Race Relations).
22. Amilcar Cabral and the Dialectic of Portuguese Colonialism. *The Indian Political Science Review*, Vol. 16, No. 2, July 1982, pp. 176–196 (University of Delhi, Department of Political Science).
23. Race, Capitalism and the Antidemocracy, *Reading Rodney King/Reading Urban Uprisings*. Robert Gooding-Williams, ed. Routledge, 1993, pp. 73–81 (Taylor & Francis).
24. David Walker and the Precepts of Black Studies. *Black Studies Conference*, Ohio State University, Columbus, OH, 1997. Previously unpublished.
25. The Killing in Ferguson. Co-authored with Elizabeth Robinson. *Commonware: General Intellect Informazione*, 2013 (commonware.org). Published online.
26. On The Truth and Reconciliation Commission, 1999. Previously unpublished.

Also included:
Foreword by Ruth Wilson Gilmore
Preface by Elizabeth Peters Robinson
Introduction by H. L. T. Quan

Foreword

Ruth Wilson Gilmore

Cedric Robinson's distinguished career as a militant academic models the life of an original thinker who committed his substantial intellect to the long battle to end colonialism, imperialism, racism, and inequality. He wrote vividly about how representation, broadly understood, shapes and is shaped by political, cultural, economic, esthetic, and social life. An iconoclast from the start, he early produced a sustained critique of his discipline, political science, demolishing one of its central conceits – leadership – by using anthropology to show an altogether different social embodiment of authority. Indeed, an interdisciplinary imperative extended throughout his research and community work, in tireless effort to perceive and provoke oppositional consciousness in relation to the multiple contours of actual struggle. Robinson refused historiography that made the region that became Europe the start of everything; devastated though the world has been by European expansion and exploitation, he would not begin from defeat even though, with Cabral, he told no lies and eschewed easy victories. His scholarly and political imagination extended through time and across space, and he persuasively argued multiple geographies that can, if carefully examined, show both residual and emergent alternative – or if you will, abolition – life ways at everyday, expressive, resistant, and revolutionary registers.

Robinson was an old-fashioned scholar who always bothered to learn things before he tried to teach them, and he continued to learn by teaching. I suspect most people who pick up this book will do so out of curiosity about a person whose name in the second decade of the twenty-first century is indelibly associated, at least in the Anglophone world, with "The Black Radical Tradition." It's my hope that readers of this collection will see the massive research as well as theoretical commitments that guided his ability to show subtly changing syncretism underlying the work of resistance and liberation. Robinson traced out action rather than a compendium of polemics, because the Black Radical Tradition is a whole way of being – what he famously termed "an ontological totality." To enliven what might otherwise linger as a suffocating abstraction, he demonstrated its dynamic realization in, for example, the portrait of

Richard Wright's transformation – a self-reinvention blossoming from collective rather than individualistic imperatives.

Many who are notionally sympathetic to a Black Radical Tradition mistakenly imagine it to have been birthed by slavery, and only later to square up against racial capitalism. Ha! As Robinson explains in *Black Marxism*, capitalism's requirement for inequality historically coalesced through racial practices that developed between and among people, all of whose descendants may well have become white. Does this mean slavery did not disfigure the world? Hardly. But neither does it mean that all of Black historical geography has its origins in the slave trade, or in the condition of slavery, or in emancipation. By contrast, although neither natural nor static, the Black Radical Tradition is prior to, during, and after capitalism in all of its forms – including capitalist slavery – with a distinctiveness that might seem to disappear into related forms of being without evaporating in influence or effect.

Lately, Black geography has become a lively if loose topic – variously asserted to be scholarly specialty, hiring opportunity, conference theme, enigma to be explained, compendium of oppressions, abolition exemplar. Insofar as the latter might develop into the topic's principal materialization, then efforts to identify and explain forms of freedom in grounded action would well take guidance from Cedric Robinson's breadth and depth of study and lucid analysis. They would also benefit from paying close attention to critical distinctions that matter. In this volume the collected materials repeatedly and resolutely insist on differences that actually point in a direction that seems a bit counterintuitive at first. That is, underlying the work – not all of which I agree with, nor will any reader – is a remarkably internationalist consistency that neither begins nor ends with *the* Black experience.

As a matter of fact, experience is a complexity to be critically addressed rather than a cumulative condition to be described. After the fact, it seems so obvious – that were experience all it took to make the world otherwise, the sum of exploitation would already have produced its own cataclysmic reversal. This mechanical view of Marxism, not shared by the eponymous thinker but thinly spread wide by some epigones, hardly finds confirmation in the great anti-capitalist, anti-colonial revolutions of the nineteenth and twentieth centuries. And yet it persists. Robinson brings to our consideration a comprehensive and subtle appreciation of how revolutionary thinkers developed syncretic modes for planning struggle, approaches that combined analytical energies attuned to the partial systematicity of capitalist dynamics with active understanding of already-existing modalities, what Cabral termed the upward paths.

The final time I shared the stage with Robinson was in 2014 for the keynote plenary of *Confronting Racial Capitalism* – an astonishing symposium conceived in his honor by Christina Heatherton and Jordan T. Camp. During the question and answer period in a packed auditorium I repeated my favorite sentiment from *Capital Vol. 1* about how we change the external world and our own nature by what we do on and with the earth. Cedric hit me – not with his hand, but rather and most firmly with his look and tone. "I've been trying to tell you," he said. "It's consciousness not experience." My consciousness *of* consciousness opened thanks to that experience as, apparently, no other experience in our long friendship had done. And thanks to his impatient persistence, so many of us, tending toward bitter optimism, never give up trying to crack the codes through which we represent ourselves to ourselves, to one another, to our future. Cedric Robinson, *¡presente!*

Preface

Elizabeth Peters Robinson

Will the U.N. understand the pleas of the Blacks in the townships of Makakoba, Mzilikazi, and Mpopoma, outside the city of Bulawayo, where most often three to four families must stay in one room the size of your kitchen, each family with a wall, parents in the bed, children sleeping beneath the bed, the families' belongings stacked on a shelf above the bed, a curtain for privacy from the others in the room? Will the U.N. understand the pleas of the tens of thousands unemployed because they are not educated, uneducated because they are unemployed, both because they are Black? What about the starvation, the malnutrition, the beatings, the humiliation? Will the U.N. appreciate their effect on these people?

Africa understands, Asia understands, you and I and the millions of blacks in the U.S., Brazil and the West Indies understand, not because we are black or brown but because we have lived it and are living it now.

— *Cedric Robinson, December 8, 1962*
On returning from Southern Rhodesia

For the unaware, nothing was amiss.

— *Cedric J. Robinson,*
Black Marxism, *1982*

As so well defined in her introduction to this volume, H. L. T. (HQ) Quan notes that the work herein spanned more than four decades. I'm pushing even farther back with the first quote above not as a corrective but to offer a slightly different perspective, one that visits the quotidian and that I hope will be illustrative of the daily stew that surely led Cedric to the intellectual and theoretical work for which he is more widely known.

In choosing a title for this book, we were insistent that "racial capitalism" was an insufficient description of the work included, that "internationalism" and "cultures of resistance" were essential in filling the gaps that HQ identifies. I would argue that that is so because whatever the intellectual task, Cedric's *raison d'être* was the broader human terrain. Those were the everyday phenomena that could provoke a change of mood in a heartbeat.

By the time that Cedric returned from what is now Zimbabwe in 1962, he had already learned the imperatives of race and resistance from his grandfather, be they the importance of Joe Louis winning a fight, assisting his grandfather in his janitorial rounds, or standing up against overtly oppressive powers. While he may well have seen poverty and racism up close, he also had experienced the fierce protection of over-qualified Black teachers as they insured that he would acquire the skills he needed to survive, even thrive. Cedric had participated in his own generation's acts of resistance against the House Un-American Activities Committee's witch hunts, the discriminatory practices in the Bay Area from Woolworth's to Auto Row with many stops in between. He had found that the University of California at Berkeley would not allow him to bring Malcolm X to campus as a speaker even as the University celebrated the presence of a dictator's wife and a major Christian evangelist. (Fortunately, there were more enlightened community organizations that agreed to host the event in 1961; by 1963, the University had relented and allowed Malcolm to speak on campus.)

Cedric's trip to Southern Rhodesia was his second international experience as he had used the occasion of his suspension from the University to spend some months in Mexico. In both countries, he witnessed both discrimination and resistance and began to draw connections to the realities of Oakland, California. In the piece for *The Sun-Reporter*, he drew attention to these global connections and concluded with an indictment of the media, marking his first of many forays into media criticisms.

As noted in the second epigram, "For the unaware, nothing was amiss."[1] The "unaware", Cedric would argue, were so not necessarily through their own faults, but because so much of the events of the moment and our histories were erased, elided, or simply denied. When perusing the contents of this volume, understand that much was a recuperative project, not simply a theoretical or academic one. When encountering Frantz Fanon, understand that his context, the anti-colonial struggles of the Algerian people and their post-independence experiments such as workers' self-management experiments, were like shining lights as we all were mired in the violence of the efforts to destroy Vietnam. In this same period we were experiencing the dismantling, the destruction of the newly independent African nations. So the brilliant voice of Amilcar Cabral, leading with a new determination, cautioning us all to tell no lies, to claim no easy victories, provided hope as well as instruction. Cedric's impulse to engage with Black anti-fascism was occasioned in part by his encounters with James Yates and Harry Haywood, both African-American members of the Abraham Lincoln Brigade who fought with the Spanish resistance to Franco's fascist regime and who wanted to fight for Ethiopia.

Finally, may we consider the significance of media and its importance in these forty plus years and now. From the 1960s through much of the 1970s, many of us were participating in resistance to war, racism, to the heavy hand of colonialism. We marched, we watched, and we witnessed the gradual closing down of informative journalism. Cedric would maintain that perhaps the most significant outcome of the Nixon forced resignation was a heavy disciplining of mass media. Whether that was the case might be debated, but by 1983 Ben Bagdikian famously documented the ever-shrinking ownership of mass media and its transformation into raw political power in his landmark, *Media Monopoly*. Under the Reagan administration, regulation of ownership was massively reduced and that continues until now.

As Cedric's project was always about casting light in hidden corners, his attention to media mismanagement and malappropriation was a natural. He began documenting the character of media in films from 'Birth of a Nation' to 'blaxploitation', newspapers including the one with the hubris to claim 'all the news that was fit to print' or the one on the other coast which would blithely claim that it was not written for the poor or people of color. Both in written work and on our weekly television program, *Third World News Review*, Cedric exposed the complicity, the duplicity, of U.S. media in creating a palatable version of what had happened in the Philippines, for example. After more than a decade of martial law, corporate media reports only called out Filipino dictator Ferdinand Marcos while soft-soaping or entirely overlooking the U.S. colonial and military presence. Here indeed, "for the unware, nothing was amiss." In many instances the general public was intentionally kept unaware, or failed to appreciate the urgency of conditions beyond their own.

That is what concerns me today when I find too many of us ignorant of or unconcerned with those we consider outside of our ken, be they from other countries, other ethnicities, or even other generations. In the end, this piece is not intended as a praise song for Cedric or his fellows; it is intended, rather, to signal that there is much hard work to be done. In this world of social media, we are often tempted by a clever meme, even a deep one but even the best are inadequate to the many struggles we must engage.

It is fitting that this collection concludes with pieces addressing cultures of resistance that have little respect for the boundaries imposed by nation states, that have brought people together across ethnic, racial, and continental lines, and that have sustained solidarity movements for decades. When we examine police violence, carceral systems, even military adventurism. we can't help but see the similarity between cities that wall people in and out exist and are often modeled on ones that exist in Occupied Palestine, that existed and linger in apartheid and post-apartheid South Africa. And sadly but surely the apparatus of oppression has been passed from the U.S. to South Africa to Palestine and back again to U.S. policing.

While I am always hesitant to speak for Cedric, he can no longer provide a prefatory remark; thus I am being so bold but remind the reader that the remarks come from my sense of things. I think, had Cedric been able to do so, he might have ended each article or book with "And" or "But" as he considered all of his work incomplete, only as fingerposts for next generations, to think expansively and collectively. I've no doubt that he would be thrilled with work that many are doing even as he urged others to join them.

NOTE

1. Thanks to Christina Heatherton for bringing attention to this passage.

Introduction: Looking for Grace in Redemption

H. L. T. Quan

> This is exactly how the music of *jazz* began, and out of the same
> necessity: not only to redeem a history unwritten and despised,
> but to checkmate the European notion of the world.
> For until this hour, when we speak of history, we are speaking only of
> how Europe saw – and sees – the world.
> — *James Baldwin, 1979*[1]

> ... [H]umaness is no longer a noun. Being human is a praxis.
> — *Sylvia Wynter, 2015*[2]

> [i]n the construction of knowledge there is no beginning and no end...
> — *Cedric J. Robinson*[3]

In a beautiful meditation on music and race disguised as a book review, the ever-vigilant, if understated James Baldwin noted that jazz "is produced by, and bears witness to, one of the most obscene adventures in the history of mankind," and yet, the giants of jazz managed to "make of that captivity a song."[4] Not unlike what jazz does to History, Cedric J. Robinson redeemed political theory, not as a "Master Science" as Aristotle would have it, but as a clarion call for radical, democratic thought, and praxis. Moreover, Robinson imbued it with a practical ethos, one that centers on normative sensibilities, particularly the righteousness of moral action.[5] Given the rigidity of disciplinary practices in academia, few American political theorists managed this feat – one that provides aid and comfort to legions of students and activists on multiple continents. Grounded in the historical density of Black lives, Robinson's teaching and publications have made an imprint on scholarship ranging from Black radical thought and the Black Radical Tradition to racial capitalism, police violence, and Black representations in films and music. Equally important, his vision resonates with freedom struggles from the Anti-Apartheid Movements[6] to Movements for Black Lives. If one knew "how it feels to be free," as the redoubtable Ms. Nina Simone quivered, learning political theory from Robinson is like "startin' anew."

Perhaps echoing Baldwin's interrogation of History, in an essay published in 1981, "Coming to Terms," Robinson observed that "the most important issue is conceptualization: how are we to conceptualize what we were, what we are, what we are becoming?" As a witness and a scholar of racial capitalism and not unlike the intellectual praxis that Sylvia Wynter foregrounds,[7] Robinson sought responses to those questions throughout most of his life. Considered one of the deans of Black Studies, his works have been essential texts for deconstructing racial capitalism, learning about the Black Radical Tradition, and inspiring insurgent movements from Ferguson to the West Bank.

In recent years there has been an upsurge of interest in Robinson's work as evidenced by the republication of *The Terms of Order* (2016, University of North Carolina) and *An Anthropology of Marxism* (2019, University of North Carolina), as well as the special journal issue of *African Identities* (Vol. 11, No. 2, 2013), and the edited collection of essays inspired by his work, *Futures of Black Radicalism* (2017, Verso). In addition, and in the two years following his death, there have also been many articles, panels, and conferences organized in the U.S., U.K., and beyond, devoted to his teaching and scholarship. Indeed, the "Black Radical Tradition" is often conflated with Robinson, however ill-advised that might be. Such embellishment notwithstanding, it is apparent that Robinson's influence extends beyond academe.[8]

The genesis of this collection – *Cedric J. Robinson: On Racial Capitalism, Black Internationalism, and Cultures of Resistance* – was more than twenty years in the making, and the materials herein are based on many conversations with Elizabeth and Cedric Robinson and in the areas of Robinson's work that he hoped would be elucidated. In the mid-1990s, the former speechwriter for President Kwame Nkrumah of Ghana, Kofi Buenor Hadjor initially proposed that he edit a collection of Robinson's essays, and Robinson and Hadjor enlisted me to assist in this endeavor. Hadjor was convinced that "people needed to read Cedric," and as it was before the era of widely distributed pdfs, many of these essays were not readily available in print. Significantly, Kassahun Checole graciously committed Africa World Press to this endeavor. Unsurprisingly, life happened, and the project was tabled until nearly two decades later when Cedric, Elizabeth, and I revisited the project. Also, unsurprisingly, there are twice as many pieces to be taken into consideration as there were two decades ago. We hope that the essays contained in this volume extend Robinson's much larger *oeuvre* than *Black Marxism* conveys, however influential it is.[9]

For the first time, this volume engages a wide array of Robinson's essays, reflective of his diverse interests in the interconnections between culture and politics, radical social theory, and classic and modern political philosophy. These essays spanning over four decades include considerations of Africa, Black internationalism, world politics, race and U.S. foreign policy, representations of Blackness in popular culture, and reflections on popular resistance to racial capitalism, white supremacy, and other tyrannies. Each section includes both previously published and unpublished materials, and essays written for an academic and/or informed audience, as well as those written for the general public.

Collectively these writings and reflections embody both a meticulous scholarship grounded in transdisciplinary research and an insurgent moral authority of a philosophy of democratic resistance and rebellion. Not unlike Baldwin when he admonished us to look to "the unprotected," and not "the policemen, the lawyers, the judges, or the protected members of the middleclass" to know "how justice is administered,"[10] Robinson's work forwards a thesis that centers on the belief that a "people in crisis" or the oppressed are more likely to embody a moral authority than the oppressors. Indeed, once "political order" and authoritarianism disguised as leadership are sufficiently dispatched, and their vacuous machinations and promiscuous desires are demystified, Robinson's readers and students are urged to err on the side of the *demos*: the populous majority, be they slaves, indigenous people, women, or Black people.[11] These people are almost always marked as differently vulnerable and are targeted for harm. Just as Sir M. I. Finley long understood, democracy is essentially an exercise of the mob, and as such, political outcomes are rarely guaranteed; so, Robinson recognized democracy as inherently dangerous.[12] He, however, settled on the wisdom that those who are furthest from democratic polity and whose participation is evacuated or eviscerated are necessarily the likeliest to burst that polity wide open, just as those who are furthest away from justice are most likely to instruct us in the meanings of justice. And it is they who will likely be the most passionate advocates of justice. Robinson explained it this way: "Just as Thucydides believed that historical consciousness of people in crisis provided the possibility of more virtuous action, more informed and rational choices, so do I."[13] Beyond the need to dislodge "the terms of order,"[14] Robinson was suggesting a righteousness of the moral authority of a "people in crisis,"[15] and perhaps a symbiotic relationship between epistemic and everyday justice.[16]

What does it mean to assert a moral authority of those who have been marked as vulnerable, *as the other*, who frequently reside on the margins of authority? Conceptually, the term "moral authority" itself is not uncomplicated. In contrast to the idea of moral bankruptcy as being utterly without morals, moral authority is not so easily recognizable. It is certainly the case that when we use the term moral authority we frequently rely on a constellation of transitive meanings, signifying both contingencies and contradictions. On the one hand, authority connotes, among other things, as the OED tells us, the "right to act," and the "power to enforce obedience or compliance," with political supremacy as *a priori*. On the other hand, morality, especially as it relates to principles or rules of conduct, more often than not is concerned with the private behavior of individuals. Put differently, the very term "moral authority" signals collective allegiance to an external order that instructs individuals how to act or how to live.

Moral authority is also necessarily normative. In so far as the goodness or badness of human endeavors are concerned, however, morality is almost always relational and contextualized, and thus contingent. As John Grote observed in *A Treatise on Moral Ideals* (1876), "[A]ll moral words, by frequent complementary use ... have lost much of their warmth and force."[17] As such, when Robinson appealed to the "more virtuous action" of the *demos*, he was conjuring the power of the collective that inherently resides in the very ideals of a moral majority. This moral majority, however, is neither silent nor complicit with the state or capital. Its authority lies in the fact that it belongs to a "people in crisis," who all along have contested the legitimacy and morality of "the terms of order," including the meanings of justice.[18] For Robinson, and unlike a typical jury in countries where police conduct is governed by (not racist laws but) habituated racial supremacy, the victims of violence would almost always be more credible as witnesses than the perpetrators. This normative reasoning reflects what is needed to undo not only past harm but inherent epistemic injustices, when the victims of everyday injustices, including premature deaths, are also denied their credibility as knowers and interpreters of meanings.[19]

When political authority becomes our only regime of truth, moral authority is conflated with the state in all its manifestations, and justice is merely "whatever the powerful say it is." No other better agents of the state or state actors embody this conflation and manifested order than the police. The legitimacy of the state, the *sine qua non* of state authority, thus becomes its moral authority in the embodiment of the police. A police state is thus frequently the most apparent form of authoritarianism, and for this reason, few police officers who killed have been charged or convicted, regardless of circumstances. By asserting the moral righteousness of the protestors, as Robinson did with BLM or the Black South Africans in the struggles against apartheid, for instance, he was reinstating a familiar *oeuvre*, that is, the assertion that there exists a democratic Black political culture that frequently supplants hegemonic moral consciousness with a democratic social ethic of its own, one that is capable of redeeming what has been lost and/or negated.

This double dialectic Robinson derived from positing oppressed people as the more virtuous, hence, those possessing moral righteousness, confronts the facticity of life amidst settler colonialism, racial capitalism, hetero-patriarchy, and white supremacy, among other things, wherein the very meaning of *the other*, especially of Black life, has long been associated with the absence of morality, including morality in the specific form – a redeemable social ethics. Thus, in his quest to redeem political theory as critical theory, Robinson, affectively located emancipatory potentials at the communal, democratic level. In this way, his emphasis on the Black Radical Tradition's quest for ontological wholeness is akin to a secular search for grace, if grace is understood as a defense against dehumanization and an affirmation of Black life.

When gathering materials for this collection, we imagined it as a companion volume to Robinson's books as well as one that fills the gaps between *The Terms of Order* (1980), *Black Marxism* (1983), *Black Movements in American* (1997), *An Anthropology of Marxism* (2001), and *Forgeries of Memory & Meaning* (2007).[20] Given the economics of publishing today, it was a challenge to whittle down the more than 700 pages of work to the current volume. The larger themes of Robinson's *oeuvre* are not difficult to identify: Africa and Black Internationalism, Bourgeois historiography, world politics and U.S. foreign policy, reality and its misrepresentations, and resistance and popular rebellions. Already present in book forms, some more apparent than others, these themes serve as the deep structure of the collection. The essays as organized are not meant to be understood as discreet pieces unencumbered by issues and concerns raised in other sections. For instance, Robinson's preoccupation with the need to interrogate fascism as a form of western, democratic capitalism shows up first in Part II under "On Bourgeois Historiography," then later in Part III under "On World Politics and US Foreign Policy." This is especially true for Parts III and IV where Robinson's extended analysis of the media and its misrepresentations of reality is showcased. Moreover, Africa and the African Diaspora are embedded in each section, either as a subject of inquiry or as an analytic prefiguration.

Finally, the many outlets where Robinson featured his work convey his diverse interests and transdisciplinary approach to social emancipatory scholarship. These forums included academic, peer-reviewed journals and books, local newspapers, and community cultural celebrations, as well as professional meetings and various gatherings at colleges and universities. From the now out of print, *Indian Journal of Political Science*, the Fernand Braudel Center based *Review*, and *Afro-American Studies*, to the always current *Race & Class* and *Radical History Review*, Robinson's work elided orthodoxies, discursive or otherwise. For nearly four decades, *Race & Class*, the U.K. institution for critical scholarship at the intersections of first race and class, and then later, race, class, and gender, was most responsible for publishing the majority of Robinson's writings. The reprints in this volume represent a small sample of this invaluable collaboration between Robinson and the journal.

ON AFRICA AND BLACK INTERNATIONALISM

Black internationalism, a philosophy that approximates the emancipatory power of jazz as Baldwin aspired it to be, grounds many of Robinson's intellectual endeavors and his personal orientation. Part I best captures the promise and depth of the collection, containing both previously published and unpublished materials, including Robinson's most recent research interest – the Black sleuth and the writing of Pauline Hopkins. This section draws attention to one of

Robinson's most enduring thematics: the centrality of Black Internationalism and Africa within the larger discursive frame of Black radicality. "Notes Toward a 'Native Theory' of History," first published in *Review* in 1989, is essential to understanding the importance of the African Diaspora for emancipatory theory building. Here Robinson maintained that the problem with mainstream "Black scholasticism" was that "It does not challenge theft but attempts to reflect it." The production of radical social theories, Robinson argued, requires "coming to terms with the fundamental nature of historical movement," including its organization and social consciousness. For him, recognizing the importance of the Black Diaspora and Black movements necessarily entails "the recreation of Black life," and a new theory of history informed by Black consciousness. So, "In Search of a Pan-African Commonwealth," first appearing in *Social Identities* in 1996, extended Robinson's delineation of Black movements in the forms of a Pan-African Commonwealth. Echoing his wariness of the political as delineated in *Terms*, Robinson insisted that Pan Africanism should be imagined as a thing that includes all "five different spheres of human experience – the prehistorical, the historical, the demographic, the cultural, and the political."

Part I ends with Robinson's most recent research agenda, "The Black Detective and American Memory." It extends his work on racial regimes in *Forgeries* and preoccupation with the African Diaspora as sediments for future Black rebellions. Robinson made use of Black mystery writings as source materials and centered on Pauline Hopkins' work that interrogated an early racial regime in the U.S. and the ways in which she consciously wrote about Black resistance to and liberation from racial oppression. Robinson argued that while Hopkins' "stunning Black radical intellect had so long been assigned to obscurity," her historical fiction embodied "a radical critique of American culture." Hopkins' critique, Robinson maintained, was one intent on the "pursuit of radical solutions for the Black Nation" in the form of "an African diasporic internationalism."

ON BOURGEOIS HISTORIOGRAPHY

Part II signals three of Robinson's most significant contributions to the scholarship on the Black Radical Tradition and emancipatory social theorizing – an emphasis on culture as an analytic resource, the deconstruction of bourgeoisie historiography, and the demystification of leadership. This section also introduces Robinson's exposition and interrogation of fascism as a historical phenomenon, a largely underexplored theme of Robinson's scholarship. An essay on the contemporary attack against multiculturalism and another on Plato's *The Republic* suggest that students of bourgeois historiography might venture further back in time to locate its earlier anti-democratic predispositions.

As part of a series of lectures at SUNY Binghamton in 1975[21] that included luminaries of Black radical theory and revolutionary activism such as Walter Rodney, C. L. R. James, and Imamu Baraka, "The First Attack Is an Attack on Culture" sought to differentiate between "what is an organization and what is revolution." Influenced by Amílcar Cabral,[22] for Robinson, coming to terms with Black internationalism begins with a systematic exploration of culture as an organizing principle for revolutionary change. Robinson extended Marx's observation that "the first attack is an attack on culture"[23] to take up Haiti, Algeria, and Viet Nam – three theaters of wars and rebellions, and delineated the differences between imperialist and revolutionary attacks on culture. He argued that "the dominant paradigms of human organization, social organization, social moments presume the extraordinary leader," from whom "comes organizations, structure, ideology." The demystification of leadership and the unsettling of the political are the main thrusts of Robinson's doctoral dissertation work at Stanford University,[24] which he later elaborated on in *The Terms of Order*, his first major publication. Robinson also made clear the centrality of the collective: "ideas, structures, the organization of a movement … come from the collective, [they do not] come out of the individual."

"Oliver Cromwell Cox and the Historiography of the West" is in some ways an addendum to the work Robinson started in *Black Marxism*. Drawing from Cox and Ray Huang, not unlike what he did with Dubois, James, and Wright, Robinson deconstructed bourgeois historiography, illustrating how Cox (and secondarily Huang) would "reconfigure radically the episteme of the West." The next essay, "Fascism and the Intersections of Capitalism, Racialism, and Historical Consciousness," delineates one of Robinson major historical excavations and analytic commitments – the study of fascism and Black people's resistance to it. It is also one of several essays where Robinson interrogated fascism as a familiar specie of North America. Examining the responses to fascism in the 1920s in the U.S., Robinson argued that the American revisionist history of anti-fascist movements reflects a deep commitment to the erasure of not only the complicity of American capital and European fascism that translated to open support for fascist regimes, but also the fierce anti-fascist responses from Black people in the African Diaspora. Unlike their white counterparts, for many Black people, "the historical significance of fascism was clear: at home it foreshadowed the descent of liberalism … elsewhere it meant the destruction of even the symbols of racial liberation." First appearing in *Humanities in Societies* in 1983, "Fascism at the Intersections" signaled Robinson's sustained interrogation of fascism as a specie and its progenitors, including white supremacy.

First published as a book chapter in *Multiculturalism* edited by David Theo Goldberg in 1994 and within the context of a well-financed backlash against multiculturalism and gender and ethnic studies, "Ota Benga through Geronimo's

Eyes" tells a story of racism and white supremacy masquerading as science. This science, despite itself, reveals a sub-disciplinary research of multiculturalism, that is, "a concomitant to the domestic sites of Western slave economies and female subordination, and imperialism and colonialism in the outlands ..." Because this iteration of multiculturalism has been an aspect of Western social sciences "since their inceptions," Robinson suggested a need to explore "what alternative significations of multiculturalism might presently be embraced by the social sciences and why." One revelation might be that the contemporary anti-democratic attacks against multiculturalism and related fields of studies are the work of the "racial fabulists," so that they may "continue to preserve their systems of knowledge for as long as the social order which they 'legitimate' endures."

Robinson followed up this insightful read of the contemporary attack on multiculturalism as anti-democratic with "Slavery and the Platonic Origins of Anti-democracy," tracing this anti-democracy to one of its earliest origins. Extending Cynthia Farrar's arguments in *The Origins of Democratic Thinking*,[25] Robinson located contemporary, liberal anti-democratic predisposition to Plato – the West's philosophical epiphenomenon and one whose "articulations of a racial social order convalesced the proximity of slavery and liberty." The placement of "freedom *and* injustice," central to Robinson's delineation of early Black and Native American resistance in the U.S.,[26] is traced here to Plato's canon. Interrogating Plato's most influential work, *The Republic*, as a "sustained attack on democracy," Robinson concluded that the contemporary theorizing of democracy "did not so much appropriate Plato but rather mirrored its Plato genealogy."

ON WORLD POLITICS AND U.S. FOREIGN POLICY

As a public intellectual, Robinson drew from his research, teaching, and community engagement, especially in the form of media activism. Indeed, one of the most underexplored areas of Robinson's scholarship is his sustained interest in and commitment to the study of world politics and U.S. foreign policy. In addition to his research and teaching, and for more than three decades, Robinson was also a Regular Correspondent of the longest running community access TV show in the U.S., *Third World News Review*[27] (co-founded and hosted by Elizabeth Robinson, KCSB, and Santa Barbara Channels, 1979) and a regular guest on several long running radio public affairs programs on KCSB FM Santa Barbara (*Viewpoints*, 1980; *No Alibis*, 1996). In these appearances, Robinson provided needed coverage of political developments, largely ignored by the American foreign press, and imbued them with astute and cogent analyses, frequently accompanied by extended historical elaborations. His collaboration with Elizabeth Robinson, a media producer and activist for over four decades, provided a model to counter the corporate media monopoly – the necessity of moving beyond media criticism to media production. This section thus showcases Robinson's meticulous research and his work as a scholar activist, featuring a sample of Robinson's important contributions to a deeper understanding of race, resistance, and U.S. foreign policies.

Advancing a critical theory of fascism, "Fascism and the Response by Black Radical Theorists" extends Robinson's earlier critique of the erasure of ordinary Black people's more radical response against fascism in the African Diaspora. Presenting at the African Studies Association Annual Meeting in 1990, he drew attention to the ways in which fascism implicates Black people and Black political thought. Robinson suggested that with the exception of Dubois, "Black radical intellectuals who have been influenced by Marxism held to a materialist conception of fascism." By not privileging the primacy of class analysis, Dubois in contrast was able to assert a "cultural identity between fascism and the putative democracies." For Robinson, by insisting that "the essence of fascism was racial," Dubois's views approximate those of ordinary Black people who believed "that the West was pathological and fascism an expression of that nature."

"Africa: In Hoc to History and the Banks," a reprint from a local newspaper, *News & Reviews* (1985), typifies Robinson's sustained media analysis made available to the general public through his reporting for various local TV and radio programs.[28] Emblematic of Robinson's systematic critiques of U.S. foreign policies and the media is his keen attention to the historical fictions being manufactured by a complicit, corporate media. This short essay drew attention to the *Los Angeles Times* series on Africa, "Africa – The Harsh Realities Dim Hope," highlights the ways in which political developments in Africa, especially economic and political crises, are typically distorted to mask non-African and neocolonial interests, including international financial institutions, such as the International Monetary Fund.

Robinson's study of terrorism as a phenomenon began well before the advent of "September 11th" and included state-sponsored terrorism. "The Comedy of Terror," published in *Radical History Review* in 2003, pointed to the spectacles of terror against the peoples of Palestine by Israel and against the people of Latin America and elsewhere by the U.S. government. Robinson noted that most people in the world "recognize the American government's hypocrisy on terrorism," even as the American corporate-owned press chronically failed to interrogate state terrorism. This failure, Robinson argued, is part of the larger stratagem of misinforming the American public.

This section ends with "Ralph Bunche and the American Dilemma," a lectured given at Boston University in 1994, illustrating Robinson's larger critique of U.S. foreign policies as a concomitant of racial capitalism and white supremacy.[29] Using the 60th anniversary of the publication of Gunnar Myrdal's *The American Dilemma* as an entry, Robinson drew attention to Ralph Bunche's "collaboration" on the "Negro Study" portion of the book to delineate Bunche's more radical critique of U.S. racism and racial capitalism. Building on Bunche's analytics, Robinson argued that "fascism, imperialism, and racism were intertwined."

ON REALITY AND ITS (MIS)REPRESENTATIONS

This section elaborates Robinson's keen interests in the media, but also reveals his nearly four decades of research and teaching on critical representation studies beyond film studies. This investigation's focus is much broader than *Forgeries* would suggest. Accordingly, this section showcases a rich sample of Robinson's critical representations studies, including print and electronic media as well as film and performance studies. Similar to the previous section, these essays also illustrate Robinson's persistent attention to U.S. foreign policies and his sustained critique of American imperialism and its varied manifestations.

"White Signs in Black Times: The Politics of Representation in Dominant Texts," was written for the "Conference on Black Theorizing Post-Modernism and Post Structuralism," at UC Santa Barbara in 1989, organized by the Center for Black Studies, where Robinson was a Director for many years. In this essay, Robinson investigated the trend that thematically moved away from racial Blackness and replaced it with the codification, "African-American." This new signifier, he argued, was the Black intelligentsia's response to the "peripheralization of the most audacious expression of Black bourgeois political ambition in American history." Using Jesse Jackson's 1988 presidential campaign as an instantiation of the aspirations and investments of that social class, Robinson maintained that "in their eagerness to seize upon a negotiable historical identity the broker intelligentsia has rendered meaningless the relentless litany of instances in American social, cultural and legal history where race marked the boundaries of polity."

"The American Press and the Repairing of the Philippines," published in *Race & Class* in 1986, extended Robinson's critiques of American imperialism and the corporate press. Using a concept from mass communications literature, "journalistic repair," Robinson examined this practice where the news is "fixed up" to fit a desired narrative. This repairing of news or news normalization belies journalistic claims of truth, seeking and refiguring events so that they are not at risk of revealing "ideologically unacceptable meanings of the event, or to lay bare the fact of mediation itself." Pointing to the collapse of the Ferdinand Marcos regime as an example, Robinson illustrated the ways in which the popular revolution in the Philippines was evicted from news account in order to dramatize the "revolving elites" and to provide a "neat drama [that] is almost totally unrelated to real-world occurrences."

The late 1990s, Rampart Scandal, involving widespread corruption by the police, particularly the Community Resources Against Street Hoodlums (CRASH) of the Los Angeles Police Department's Rampart Division, typifies numerous police scandals in the U.S. throughout the next several decades. At the time, the Rampart Scandal was the most notorious, including police violence, torture, and homicide along with planting false evidence, thefts, and drug deals. When the Rampart Scandal broke wide open, Robinson regularly provided cogent news coverage and analyses on *TWNR* and *No Alibis*. These reports anticipated many contemporary critical police and prison studies. "On the Los Angeles Times, Crack Cocaine, and the Ramparts Division Scandal" is an example of such work. Previously unpublished, this 1999 essay briefly examines the failure of the *Los Angeles Times* to adequately cover lethal corruption in its own hometown. The CIA connection to the crack cocaine epidemic in Los Angeles exposed by Gary Webb of the *San Jose Mercury News*, and the soft-soaping of the corruption in the LAPD Ramparts Division are two such instances.

While Robinson mostly avoided the star-driven academic speaking circuit, he was one of the most gracious public intellectuals, and frequently accepted student invitations from smaller venues such as community colleges. As part of the larger Black History Month celebration at Skyline College in San Bruno (CA) in 2003, Robinson's presentation explored the films of an early Black cinema giant, Oscar Micheaux and anticipated Robinson's later interrogation of films and theater in *Forgeries*. Before the advent of video streaming and the "rediscovery" of early Black films, his spotlight on the works of Micheaux and others provided much-needed attention to the largely ignored contributions of early Black filmmakers. "Micheaux Lynches the Mammy" thus explored Micheaux's films as a response to racial violence and the unrelentingly racist and canonical Hollywood films, including D. W. Griffith's *Birth of a Nation*. Using the iconic figure of the mammy, Robinson showed the ways in which Micheaux radically recuperated Black womanhood from Griffith's racialist fantasies. Whereas Griffith's mammy is "a stock character among similarly grotesque Black domestic servants in American films," Micheaux "extracts the *Mammy* from the lore of plantocratic apologetics, establishing her not as some sort of fictional creature ... but as a mother capable of familial love and anguish" whose faith and loyalty are attached to Black people's visions of justice and freedom.

In 1998, nearly a decade before the publication of *Forgeries*, Robinson interrogated Black representations in American films in *Race & Class* essay, "Blaxploitation and the Misrepresentation of Liberation." It centered on

Blaxploitation films as a genre with specific cultural and historical pedagogical functions. Robinson argued that Blaxploitation is "degraded cinema." In constructing a genre of an "urban jungle," the American film industry not only degraded itself, but also everyone involved in the process – the Black actors, writers, directors, and audience. Most detrimental of all, Blaxploitation films caricatured the Black lower classes and made "a mockery of the aspirations of Black liberationists." Robinson leveled a similar critique at the 1990s neo-Blaxploitation films, and maintained that they were not an improvement over their previous incarnations (1969–1975). Instead, these neo-Blaxploitation films were merely "rehearsing the insults of the first."

Tiffany Willoughby Herard and others[30] have testified eloquently to Robinson's pedagogy as a scholar teacher who was always intentional about co-learning and collaboration. Robinson frequently modeled the conduct of research and social inquiries by being transparent about his research techniques and his analytic stratagems. He also did not privilege graduate student research over undergraduate work. "The Mulatta on Film: From Hollywood to the Mexican Revolution," a collaboration with his undergraduate student, Luz Maria Cabral, exemplifies this approach to teaching and mentoring, even as it extended Robinson's focus on Black filmic misrepresentations. It investigated the figure of the Mulatta and provided a rich exposition of the ways in which this figure troubles the popular, filmic, and political imaginaries in the U.S. and Mexico. Robinson and Cabral observed that, "the mulatto has constituted a threat to North American racial hierarchy, property and authority for more than three-hundred years." They maintained that, especially for Hollywood, the Mulatta represents "a narrative or esthetic disturbance." Robinson and Cabral thus turned to Mexican Cinema to glean a more adequate understanding of this trope. Focusing on *La Negra Angustias* (1949) and *Los Angelitos Negros* (1948), they argued that these films diverge "from the standard tragic Mulatta representations of Hollywood," and even to some extent are able to create Black female characters that have fuller "agency and range of emotion and activity that, hitherto, most/Black filmic representations had been denied."

This section ends with a reprint from a difficult to find book, *The Black and Green Atlantic* (2009), edited by Peter O'Neill and David Lloyd. "Ventriloquizing Blackness: Eugene O'Neill and Irish-American Racial Performance" centers on O'Neill's *Emperor Jones* and furthers Robinson's analysis of racial regimes in American film and theater. Eugene O'Neill is considered a singular influence on the emergence of American theater in the twentieth century. This largely uncritical assessment, Robinson argued, has been substantiated mostly by the use of "interior" treatments of O'Neill's works. In contrast, when we take up the "Negro plays" (1914–1924) we find that O'Neill appropriated many of the performative materials developed by Irish-American black-face minstrels in the nineteenth century's antebellum period. Robinson maintained that, "what did distinguish these characters is not so much their novelty in O'Neill's work but that he inserted them into American dramatic theater in a transformative moment in the country's racial regimes." These works (beginning with *Thirst* and concluding with *All God's Chillun*) coincided with social and historical events of critical significance to the (mis)representation of Black people in American popular culture, and remarked on an era which is radically alternative to the "love and theft" relations between Irish-American and Black communities of the previous century. So in the end, O'Neill "gave lie to Black self-governance," Robinson concluded, and "*The Emperor Jones* became the real, and the real was drowned out by O'Neill's voice and his tom-toms."

ON RESISTANCE AND REDEMPTION

The final section spans over four decades of Robinson's uninterrupted attention to the study of popular resistance against racial capitalism, white supremacy, and other big and small tyrannies. Ranging from the 1972, "Malcolm Little as a Charismatic Leader," a rare and difficult to find essay that anticipates his book-length study on order and the myth of leadership, to the unpublished short entry, "On the Truth and Reconciliation Commission" that alludes to his news reporting and analysis, these essays embody Robinson's magnificent analytics to aid us in our quest to conceptualize "what we were, what we are, what we are becoming." Traveling across time and space, they collectively attest to Robinson's unwavering faith in the righteousness of the moral authority of popular resistance against tyranny, and his gracious rendering of the ordinary men and women who people the many chapters of his radical, democratic social philosophy.

In one of his earliest studies of charismatic leadership, Robinson focuses on Malcolm Little (or the making of Malcolm X) to delineate his theory on charisma and political leadership. This analytical framework would be extended in *Terms*. Key to "mass charismatic event," Robinson argued, are two phenomena relating to identity: "political leaders – or men who *need* to lead desperately, and the other with the historical evolution of moments in the lives of members of communities where they require this particular form of leadership." Reading Malcolm X as a mass charismatic event, Robinson suggested that "as important as [Malcolm] was becoming to the lives of those before whom he spoke and for whom he spoke, they were assuming grander proportions in his life," and more cogently, "Malcolm needed them for they were the fulfillment of his vision." In other words, without the collectivity, a leader's vision is for naught.

Turning his attention to "The Appropriation of Frantz Fanon," Robinson eviscerated the *fin de siècle* Fanon Renaissance for its negligence of history, among other things. Published in *Race & Class* in 1993, this essay took postcolonial studies to task by exposing its selective rediscovery of Fanon's *oeuvre*. Robinson's critique of the "appropriation of Fanon," especially the selective few chapters from *Black Skin, White Mask*, by literary theorists centers on these scholars' tendency to erase not only the larger historical context of anti-colonial struggles that animated Fanon's work, but also Fanon's later and deeper understanding of the dialectic of colonialism and liberation. Robinson argued that while Fanon "mistook a racial subject for his own class – those he terms the 'nationalist bourgeoisie,'" the academician theorists of today, as representatives of that class, "have sought selectively to re-appropriate and apportion Fanon for a post-or anti-revolutionary class-specific initiative."

One of Robinson's earliest and influential writings, "Amilcar Cabral and the Dialectic of Portuguese Colonialism" was published in 1982 in the now defunct, *Indian Political Science Journal* out of the University of Delhi. This essay revealed his investment in reading resistance as an informant of history, and drew attention to his analytic facility with culture as mobilizing resources – a critical element in his appreciation of Cabral as a political theorist. Robinson differentiated Cabral's work as one of the foremost radical thinkers in the twentieth century from Cabral's African contemporaries. Here, he also distinguished between revolutionary movements and national independence movements. Through in-depth coverage of the heady events of the years when the African Party for the Independence of Guinea and Cape Verde (PAIGC) waged a revolution against fascistic Portuguese colonialism, Robinson systematically argued that Cabral's revolutionary theory and praxis emerged "from national liberation struggles which were consciously revolutionary" rather than ones merely for political independence. He showed that national independence as a matter of juridical reforms was "an imperialist initiative" in the service of "the imperialist and capitalist camp." Drawing attention to Cabral's emphasis on culture and the idea that "national liberation required the complete destruction of foreign domination," Robinson's analysis of Cabral's revolutionary thought and praxis remains one of the most important studies of Cabral's work today.

In "Race, Capitalism, and the Anti-democracy," a chapter in *Reading Rodney King/Reading Urban Uprising* edited by Robert Gooding Williams, Robinson turned his attention to popular rebellions closer to home. More than twenty-five years after its publication in 1993, and within the context of Movements for Black Lives, Robinson's astute analysis of the urban uprisings in the aftermath of the Simi Valley verdict in the trial of the police beating of Rodney King is both timely and prescient. Robinson insisted then that "the naked images of 'law enforcement' applying civilizing discipline to King appeared seductively familiar to the American audience … [cascading] backward and forward to the recent and not-so-distant past as an inadvertent mimicry of the info-tech-war in the Persian Gulf and prior instances of Pax Americana." It is within this context that Robinson read the campaign of protests associated with the verdict as an "urban uprising" against the anti-democracy that was "as old (and current) as poverty and injustice," and, therefore, "no one living in America had the right to be surprised" by such mobilization.

For Robinson, the study of the history of the modern world is necessarily also a history of Black ontologies, alternative epistemologies, and rebellions. Consistent in much of Robinson's work is also the idea that critical social inquiry must avail itself for emancipatory social action. This scholarly ethos is especially clear in Robinson's recuperation of David Walker as a progenitor of Black radicalism. In "David Walker's and the Precepts of Black Studies," a public address at *The Black Studies Conference* at Ohio State University in 1997, Robinson maintained that Walker should be considered one of the earliest architects of Black Studies and credited him with introducing precepts that make emancipatory Black Studies viable. Robinson provided a systematic reading and an assessment of David Walker's *Appeal* (1829/1830) as "a messianic pamphlet" aimed at emancipating Black people ("slave and free") by "merging Christianity, pan-Africanism, and national birth-right." Despite recent interests and in contrast to foundational texts, Robinson concluded that Walker "cannot be easily appropriated because he is non-modern. He existed within a trans-historically moral and existential universe, which can only be made to partially coincide with either Black nationalism, Black radicalism, or Black liberalism." Rather than relegating him to the margins of the field, Robinson insisted that, Black Studies should take up Walker's precepts "to be emancipatory and populist, employing inquiry for the purpose of mobilizing for deliberate and informed social actions." In short, a Black Studies in the company of the likes of Walker can avail itself for emancipatory, liberationist, social action.

In one of his last publications, Robinson collaborated with Elizabeth Robinson and again, turned their attention to the media to critique mainstream news coverage as well as authoritarian policing. "The Killing in Ferguson" appeared in *Commonware* in 2014,[31] and provided an outline on the official narrative about "post-racial" America. Written in the immediate aftermath of the police murder of Michael Brown, the crime is examined as an ordinary event in the U.S., which at the time counted an average of two such murders a day. Juxtaposing this "domestic" media event with the failure of U.S. media to note the level of violence directed at Palestinians by the Israeli state, Robinson and Robinson pointed toward the militarization of policing that exacerbated the tendency to social control and authoritarian policing.

This collection concludes with a conference paper, "On the Truth and Reconciliation Commission," presented in South Africa in 1999 just as the TRC's work was concluding and being made public. Examining the TRC and its news coverage, Robinson briefly drew attention to the relationship between truth and justice, and maintained that, "Truth can never be exchanged for or even equated with justice for they exist within different knowledge universes."

In the case of the TRC, "justice was sacrificed for some kind of truth … the truth the new South Africa could afford. And the alternative was never really justice." Presciently, Robinson understood that the dismantling of the apartheid regime would only be a temporary victory, if Black people are proffered only a form of justice that has been delimited to mere "rituals and procedures" of justice. With this prudent warning: "in our actual world, justice is merely a conceit and a sham … just as Thrasymachus told Socrates, [justice] is whatever the powerful say it is," Robinson's students and readers would do well to heed his deep investment in the idea, appropriating from Aristotle, that "the many are wiser than the few," and a justice that is grounded in the life of a people in crisis likely will always be more just than its many counterfeits or forgeries. Indeed, and just as Sylvia Wynter observed "The struggle of our new millennium will be one between the ongoing imperative of securing the well-being of our present ethnoclass (i.e., Western bourgeois) conception of the human, Man, which overrepresents itself as if it were the human itself, and that of securing the well-being, and therefore the full cognitive and behavioral autonomy of the human species itself/ourselves,"[32] Robinson seemed to have understood what was really at stake when he laid down his lot with the *demos*, where ever they might be.

In December 2003, twenty years after the publication of *Black Marxism*, I sat down to talk with Cedric Robinson about his *oeuvre*. Among other things, we talked about his intellectual influences and his method of social inquiry. Elsewhere he had noted the considerable influence on him by Amílcar Cabral and Terrance Hopkins – a sociologist who frequently collaborated with Immanuel Wallenstein. On this occasion, aside from his mother and the women in his extended family, he also discussed the work of major feminist scholars. Among them are Angela Y. Davis, Kathy Piess, Jane Gaines, and Caroline Walker Bynum. It seems fitting that these preliminaries end with a snippet from that conversation:

> As indicated already, there are three or four of them that have been particularly important to me. Angela Davis is important to me, a scholar like Elizabeth Higgenbothom is also important to me, and other non-Black feminists are also important to me, like Kathy Peiss and Jane Gaines, and on and on. Partly it's their theoretical imaginations that I appreciate so deeply. Partly, it's because they are very often better wordsmiths than their male counterparts. Sometimes it gets to be a bit much, but I even like mediaevalists like Caroline Walker Bynum. I like the passion in their works. So, it's the company I keep in this sense, people who have a sense of urgency. They are not producing something for tenure promotions or merit increases. They know that if it isn't done, there will be a consequence. And even if they can't do it best, they lay at least part of it down so that someone can do it better. But it has to be done. I recognize, in that sense, a certain kind of company. The feminist scholars that I appreciate and respect the most are the ones who persuaded me that they understand the urgency of the project.

NOTES

1. James Baldwin (2010), 148. *The Cross of Redemption: Uncollected Writings*, edited by Randall Kenan. New York: Pantheon Books.
2. Katherine McKittrick (2015), 23. *Sylvia Wynter: On Being Human as Praxis*, edited by Kathrine McKittrick. Durham: Duke University Press.
3. Cedric J. Robinson 2019, 342.
4. Baldwin (2010), 154.
5. This ethos grounds itself in the idea that those who are resisting tyranny are more likely to behave justly than the tyrants. This is not to say that they are not capable of unjust or immoral action.
6. The initial reprint of *Black Marxism* by the University of North Carolina Press (2005) was in part prompted by a decision of the newly ascended Black-led government of the Republic of South African to include this text as part of the new curriculum for Black students.
7. As Katherine McKittrick astutely observes: This intellectual praxis is "one that enables us to now *both consciously and communally* re-create ourselves in ecumenically inter-altruistically kin-recognizing *species-oriented* terms" (McKittrick 2015, 62).
8. See Robin D. G. Kelley (2017). "Introduction," *Race, Capitalism, Justice: Boston Review* (Forum 1). Edited by Walter Johnson with Robin D. G. Kelley; see also, Robin D. G. Kelly (2016). "Cedric J. Robinson: The Making of a Black Radical Intellectual," *Counter Punch* (June 17, 2016).
9. For further delineation of *Black Marxism*, see for instance, *Cedric Robinson and the Philosophy of Black Resistance, Race & Class* (Special Issue: Vol. 47, No. 2, 2005). As Guest Editor, Darryl C. Thomas noted, the materials in this issue largely came from a special political theory panel organized by the National Conference of Black Political Scientists, "Black Radicalism: A Retrospective on Cedric Robinson's *Black Marxism*" in Chicago, IL (NCOBPS, 2004), and from the "Symposium on Cedric Robinson's Radical Thought: Toward Critical Social Theories and Practice," in November 2004 at UC Santa Barbara, organized by Francois Cromer, C. A. Griffith, Tiffany Willoughby Herard, Marisela Marquez, and H. L. T. Quan. For a more recent perspective see various postings at *Black Perspectives*: https://www.aaihs.org/tag/cedricrobinson/, especially "A Black Left Feminist View on Cedric Robinson's *Black Marxism*" by Carole Boyce Davies (posted November 10, 2016), as part of a four-day roundtable on this work. While acknowledging *Black Marxism*'s considerable contribution to our understanding of radical traditions, Boyce Davies offered a critique from the standpoint of Black left feminism.
10. James Baldwin (1972). *No Name in the Street*. New York: Random House.
11. Moreover, and as he keenly observed in "In Search of a Pan-African Commonwealth" and documented throughout his work: "Those social orders that come closest to just order are those in which community is privileged above the individual."
12. M. I. Finley (1985). *Democracy: Ancient & Modern*. New Brunswick, NJ: Rutgers University Press.
13. As cited in https://viewpointmag.com/2017/02/16/black-sansculottes-and-ambitious-marionettes-cedric-j-robinson-c-l-r-james-and-the-critique-of-political-leadership/#fn4-7352.
14. Robinson (2017). *The Term of Order: Political Science and the Myth of Leadership*. Chapel Hill: University of North Carolina Press.
15. One could argue that this social ethos is what makes Robinson an "organic intellectual"; after all, Robinson and other scholars have long taught us that the Black Radical Tradition has posited an alternative ontology to the existing social order, and movements for freedom are only one verification of such ontology.
16. Miranda Fricker (2007) coined the phrase "epistemic injustice" to delineate a unique form of injustice that is epistemic in nature – those who have been denied credibility as knower and knowledge producer simply because they have been marked as different. *Epistemic Injustice: Power and the Ethics of Knowing*. London: Oxford University Press.
17. John Grote (1876). *A Treatise on Moral Ideals* (180). Moreover, "moral certainty," the negation of reasonable doubt and a transitive phenomenon associating with self-righteousness, is an

impossibility, as Aristotle understood so long ago when he suggested that moral philosophy is qualitatively different from mathematical proofs (*Nicomachean Ethics* 1094, b13).

18. The moral authority of protestors that I am alluding to here has less to do with justifying protest action and more to do with a claim of judgment. So, I am in agreement with Christopher J. Lebron when he suggests that, "it's not especially philosophically interesting to ask the rote question: are violent protests ever justified?" (Christopher J. Lebron (2017), 156. *The Making of Black Lives Matter: A Brief History of an Idea.* New York: Oxford University Press, 2017). Moreover, and within the context of vicious oppressions, not only is tasking the oppressed to justify their responses, violent or otherwise, not philosophically interesting, it is also a misdirection that conceals the immorality and capriciousness of dominions (Lebron 2017).

19. See for instance Robinson's problematization of South Africa's *Truth and Reconciliation Commission.*

20. Hereafter, these books will be referred to respectively as *Terms, Black Marxism, Anthropology,* and *Forgeries.*

21. *Afro-Latin Cultural Festival – SUNY Binghamton. Sunday, April 29, 1975.*

22. Amilcar Cabral (1973). *Return to the Source: Selected Speeches of Amilcar Cabral,* edited by Africa Information Service. New York: Monthly Review Press.

23. Karl Marx (1843). "The Jewish Question." Access at: https://www.marxists.org/archive/marx/works/1844/jewish-question/.

24. Cedric J. Robinson (1975). *Leadership: A Mythic Paradigm* (Dissertation, Ph.D., Political Science, Stanford University).

25. Farrar (1989) advanced a remarkable thesis that much of what we have taken to be democratic thought is in fact a product of classical, aristocratic biases with a distinct anti-democratic predisposition from thinkers such as Plato and Aristotle. Cynthia Farrar (1989). *The Origins of Democratic Thinking: The Invention of Politics in Classical Athens.* Cambridge: Cambridge University Press.

26. Robinson (1997) in *Black Movements in America* observed that "America had been and is still a nation of freedom *and* injustice," and that "this enduring contradiction prevailed in the consciousness of those who led the country into rebellion" where "in the same place, at the same time and in the same minds, the utopian dreams of liberty and justice competed for the right of place with the reality of slavery" (1).

27. Hereafter, *TWNR.*

28. In this era of data overload, sometimes it is tempting to forget that in North America there was a time when foreign news, particular news about Africa and other parts of the Third World or the Global South, was not available to the general public. When available, it was limited to those who had short wave radios, foreign news subscriptions, and/or access to richly endowed, university libraries.

29. This perspective clearly breaks with mainstream international relations specialists, whose dominant views continue to subscribe to the idea that the making of foreign policy is largely a consequence of action by state actors within a larger international system, where domestic politics (or internal factors) play a minimal role.

30. Tiffany Herard (2005). "Writing in Solidarity: The New Generation," *Race & Class* (Vol. 47, No. 2, pp. 88–99). See also, Eric Edwards (2017). "Cedric People," *Futures of Black Radicalism,* edited by Gaye Theresa Johnson and Alex Lubin. Brooklyn: Verso.

31. Also appeared in an Italian e-publication also published by *Commonware,* "*Una razza di class,*" in 2014.

32. Sylvia Wynter (2003), 261. "Unsettling the Coloniality of Being/Power/Truth/Freedom: Towards the Human, After Man, is Overrepresentation – An Argument," *CR: The New Centennial Review* (Vol. 3, No. 3, Fall 2003, pp. 257–337).

PART I

ON AFRICA AND BLACK INTERNATIONALISM

CHAPTER 1

Notes Toward a "Native" Theory of History

The leaders of a revolution are usually those who have been able to
profit by the cultural advantages of the system they are attacking.
— *C. L. R. James*[1]

THE FIRST ATTACK IS AN ATTACK ON CULTURE

The construction of radical social theory requires coming to terms with the
fundamental nature of historical movement; the characters of social
organization and structure and their historical thrust; and the formulation of
social consciousness. Put differently, change, adaptation, and thought are the
boundaries which mark the work of such social theories.

Yet the work of any theorist – the selection, integration, and interpretation
of events – is not separate from his subject. Social theorists are embedded in
sociohistorical matrices. It is imperative, then, that they acquire consciousness
of the significances which their objects of study possess.[2] This is not a simple
task, for many obstacles mediate against it, the most important of which,
perhaps, is the ideological integument of the very analytical, intellectual,
and conceptual tools they have in hand. Thus the analyst must not only be
concerned with the "objective" form in which the subject "presents itself,"
but must also come to a realization that his or her conceptual set may be in
part a result of the "subject's" social and ideational impact.[3]

Moreover, the difficulties multiply when the theorist must pass beyond his or
her situating culture or, alternatively, when the analyst possesses a disparate
psychosocial identity or cultural heritage from the subject. Without a keen
sense of the historical and ideological trappings in mind, much distortion may
result. Indeed, the total deflection of the intentionality of the theorist may
ensue. When the Black American scholar reviews and reconstructs the events
which make up the dispersions, exploitations, adaptations, and reactions of
Black people, he or she must do that *consciously*. Scholasticism, that is, the

addition of new "facts" or the challenge to old ones (revision), is insufficient in itself. These are merely correctives to Western paradigms of history – the same paradigms produced by European intellectuals for the purpose of rationalizing the political and economic dominances of European ruling classes. Already in 1935, W. E. B. DuBois, the radical Black theorist recognized "that with sufficient general agreement and determination among the dominant classes, the truth of history may be utterly distorted and contradicted and changed to any convenient fairy tale that the masters of men wish."[4] It was not by chance that the dominated, whether they be classes (the poor, the peasantry, and the working class), ethnic groups and peoples (the Irish, Slavs, Jews, and Blacks), or civilizations (Africans, Asians, New World Indians, etc.), were "reduced" in those histories to prehuman beings. They could not be destroyed or exploited in the brutal terms in which they were without the concomitant evolution of a justification. This tendency to rationalize was conserved even in the revolutionary traditions of European thought and historiography.[5]

Thus Black scholasticism is a perversion of intellectual work. It "corrects" the facticity defined and determined by theories of history antithetic to the evolution of Black people. It contributes to the ideological traditions of a civilization whose *raison d'être* is violence, domination, and exploitation. Black scholasticism does not challenge theft but attempts to deflect it. (And here I am referring to thefts of consciousness as well as thefts of labor, life, and material well-being.) The result, I would presume, is an honored position for Black thieves.

The true task for Black scholars, however, is an entirely different one. What is required for the African Diaspora to assume its historical significance is a new and different philosophy and a new theory of history. "[T]he foundation for national liberation rests in the inalienable right of every people to have their own history."[6] Such systems and constructs may, indeed, borrow from the defectors from European historiography, a Marx, a Nietzsche, a Kropotkin, an Oppenheimer, a Weber, etc., but they must be built upon the experience and consciousness of the new African people, the Blacks. In a very literal way, these new interpretations must come to terms with the historical force of Africans in the Ancient World, the Old World, and the New World. (I employ these periodicities as conveniences only for the moment, since they too will have to be resolved into the point of view of this new people in formation.) African peoples, as producers of material and cultural wealth, as producers of ideologies and epistemologies, as producers of history, must be accounted for. This can only be done authentically in our own terms.

I believe that the first stage of this development is criticism. In a sense, the first attack is an attack on culture. This can be demonstrated in social, historical, and theoretical terms. The revolutionary social development of dominated peoples, the emergence of social movements of resistance, and the appearance of revolutionary ideology are all evidence of this process through which the negation of oppression occurs. As Amilcar Cabral observed in the midst of the struggle in Guinea-Bissau:

> The study of the history of national liberation struggles shows that generally these struggles are preceded by an increase in expression of culture, consolidated progressively into a successful or unsuccessful attempt to affirm the cultural personality of the dominated people, as a means of negating the oppressor culture ... [I]t is generally within the culture that we find the seed of opposition, which leads to the structuring and development of the liberation movement.[7]

For that purpose, I have chosen here to criticize the work on African movements of liberation of one of the finest non-African historians of Africa, George Shepperson. In the following pages, I will attempt to identify some of the influences which have made the work of Shepperson distinctive, powerful, but ultimately vulnerable. That vulnerability is less to the challenges of the facticity of positive sciences than to those of Black philosophy and theory of history.

THE CONSCIOUSNESS OF GEORGE SHEPPERSON

"Well," said the Quartermaster, dismissing his native assistant brusquely, "I can't let you have a white sheet or any wood. All I can let you have is a blanket – that's good enough for a Wog's body anyway."

I stiffened. All my annoyance at being forced into this unpleasant task at the end of a hot day vanished. I saw only the image of a live, eager little Amidu before my eyes ...

Back in my tent, I changed into some smarter clothing and put on my Sam Browne. My anger was mounting. I was becoming furious at the nonchalant way in which the funeral of this eager little servant of the Crown was being handled. As I flicked away a few specks of the ubiquitious [sic] red dust from the toes of my highly polished brown boots, I became determined that I, at least, would try to add a little dignity to Amidu's funeral ...

I rolled back the sheet, and turned to leave. But before doing so, I did what many would consider needlessly sentimental: I saluted the corpse of Lance-Corporal Amidu, turned about in the correct manner and left. That is what Amidu would have done in my place, I am sure.[8]

For many reasons, these lines from a short story entitled "Obsequies of Lance-Corporal Amidu" seem a most fitting introduction to George Shepperson, Professor of Commonwealth and American History at the University of Edinburgh. They are his lines, written by him in an obvious passion for justice. Yet, in truth, they are more autobiographical than philosophical, for they could, with only slight stretches of the imagination, be used to describe the historical task as George Shepperson perceives it: "to add a little dignity."

This description might at first glance seem to be nothing more than romantic dribble. However, we shall see that there is a constant motive in the man's work manifesting itself in a peculiar form of historical reconstruction. Shepperson's work is quite reminiscent of the effect of those "amateurish" paleontological drawings, crowded with all sorts of bizarre species in close order, all fully adult, all quite unaware of each other's presence. His themes and reconstructions have that kind of life: tall, distant, and distinct – an analyst's world. With him this is fascinating and problematical.

It is clearly inadequate to describe Professor Shepperson, as he is projected through his works, as an analyst of Commonwealth and American history. His concerns are not only much more particular than such a general historical area, but also seem to deny quite fundamentally the bounded legitimacy of the traditional parameters employed in these fields. Shepperson, using his written work as an indicator, has not been concerned with the Commonwealth, but with one particular part of it – British Central Africa (to use the colonial misnomers, Nyasaland, Northern Rhodesia, and Southern Rhodesia) and South Africa. But to be more particular than administrative and pseudo-geographic referents can be when dealing with human society, it would be accurate to say that Shepperson has concerned himself with Black Revolution, African nationalism, and "what H. Richard Niebuhr called 'the churches of the disinherited.'"[9]

His interests in American history are equally particular. Here, too, he has focused primarily on those Africans and Afro-Americans who have been participants in the development of revolutions, revolts, nationalisms, and separatist churches. Yet his major contribution involves going on and above what could have become localized investments, for Shepperson has attempted to trace the various links, associations, interchanges, and interactions which have occurred between these two spatially very disparate "societies." He has put together "Commonwealth" and "American," much to the dignity and integrity of both.

There is too a "hidden" dimension to Shepperson's work, a dimension which is critical to our interest in conscious historiography. Shepperson is an Anglo-Scot.[10] Moreover, he has taught for some years at Edinburgh, a center of Scottish history, academic nationalism, and national consciousness. The implication is that Shepperson's conceptualization of African and Black nationalism has been informed and mediated by that of Scottish nationalism. And there is much to sustain this implication objectively (that is, historically) and analytically. There are parallels between Scottish, African, and Black histories which suggest that, as Shepperson reconstructs the latter, he transfers in part his preoccupations with the former.

ENGLISH COLONIALISM IN SCOTLAND

As a people, the Scots are a relatively new national identity forged in important part by the dynamics of English imperialism.[11] Prior to the one-hundred years of the Scottish Enlightenment dating from the mid-eighteenth century, what has now become the Scottish people was a population roughly divided into two: the Highlanders of the northwest and the Lowlanders of the south.[12]

The Highlanders were a rough, peasant, generally pastoral, Gaelic-speaking people. They were organized by clans whose structures had been influenced by the Teutonic feudalism to their south. Though Christian missionaries had been active among them for centuries, for the most part their beliefs were pre-Christian or a syncretic mixture of Christian and nonChristian elements.[13] The Highlanders, then, possessed their own language, music, dress, religion, and social and economic institutions and structures.

Effectively, this was all destroyed subsequent to the Battle of Culloden in 1745, when the Highlanders were defeated by a British army recruited from Lowlanders and the "English" lower classes under the command of the Duke of Cumberland.[14] The Highlanders were destructured:

> The battle itself was followed by atrocities against the Highlander prisoners intended to make an example to discourage future rebels ... [T]he clansmen were forbidden to carry arms (except for cattle drovers, whose need of self-defence was still recognised); they were also forbidden to wear the kilt or to play the bagpipes, both the dress and the music being considered too barbarous and martial for good citizenship ... [N]ew ... and more strenuous efforts were made to convert the Highland population to Lowland values.
>
> The result, ultimately, was the extirpation of disorder. Deprived of their leaders, their minds benumbed by the defeat at Culloden and their will to resist eroded by the ideological campaign against them, the wilder and more traditional clans succumbed at last to the rule of law.[15]

In contrast to the Highlanders, the Lowlanders, by the beginning of the eighteenth century, had been introduced to the market society. In the towns, on the land, and in the mines, the majority of Lowlanders had been reduced to a proto-working class.[16] The forces maturing in the eighteenth century would complete the process of impoverishment and exploitation by English and lowland Scottish ruling elites. In political, in economic, and for the most part in cultural terms, the Lowlanders had been Anglicized. The most significant exception to this process was in religion.

Lowland resistance to English authority by the seventeenth century had been mediated through religious ideology and institutions. Forms of Calvinism had been introduced earlier to the Lowlands by John Knox and Andrew Melville. The result was the formation of the Church of Scotland (Presbyterianism), an institution opposing both Roman papacy and English religious (and later, political) authority. Though Oliver Cromwell did crush the Presbyterian movement's more ambitious schemes, he and his "successor," Charles II, did allow for its institutionalization in the Lowlands, subject of course to secular authority.

Thus Lowland society, and increasingly the remnants of the defeated Highlanders, were by the end of the eighteenth century proletarianized and Anglicized, but religiously independent. The tribal society of the northwest had been crushed and "integrated" into a politically unified Scotland, which was described, fifty-odd years later, in the London *Times* as a "province" of England.[17] By 1801, the combined population of Scotland was estimated at 1,600,000.

It was from this period on that one can authentically begin speaking of *Scottish* nationalism. Its precondition was the forging into one people what had essentially been two, and prior to that had been divided into Pict, Scot, Gallovidian (Irish), Angle, Briton, and Norsemen tribes.

This nationalism was concomitant to the Scottish Enlightenment, and the Enlightenment had as its peculiar social base the formation of class society in Scotland. Without the gentry and nobility to support them, James Mill (the father of J. S. Mill), Adam Smith, and Robert Burns would have likely been shoemakers, petty bureaucrats, or peasants, like their fathers before them. Even David Hume might have had some difficulty, since he was the *second* son of a laird in a culture characterized traditionally by primogeniture.

The exploitation of the Scottish people by the English ruling class, and its suppression by the English government, catalyzed the development of Scottish consciousness. These also resulted in the Scottish Diaspora, ranging from the "criminal" colonies of Australia (where rebels were transported) to the immigrant settlements in North America.

In Scotland itself, one finds an historical record of heroic but futile resistance from the fourteenth century onward. Military leaders like Sir William Wallace and Robert the Bruce are joined by millennial figures such as Roderick of Skye and the anonymous "mountain preacher" of the Levellers of 1724 (who was, in turn, a disciple of John Hepburn, founder of the Hebronite sect).

In short, the peoples of Scotland were subject to the same historical process, *mutatis mutandis*, under English colonialism which affected British Africa. This, then, is the significant undercurrent in Shepperson's work. It forms his preconsciousness of African response and reaction. It should also inform our consciousness of Shepperson at work.

SHEPPERSON AND JOHN CHILEMBWE

Professor Shepperson's major work is *Independent African*, coauthored with Thomas Price.[18] It is a mammoth treatment (over 500 pages) of John Chilembwe and what British imperial administrators and historians have termed the "Nyasaland Native Rising of 1915."

Nyasaland in 1915, as a political entity, was almost entirely a construct of colonialism. As Roger Tangri has observed, "Africans in colonial Malawi ... possessed little linguistic, ethnic or religious unity."[19] Thus the boundaries of the Nyasaland colony and the political character of present-day Malawi were a consequence of European intrusion and the dynamics of imperialism. But before significant European penetration of the area in the mid-nineteenth century, the chiefly agrarian peoples around Lake Nyasa experienced other disturbing intrusions.

In the 1830s, a Zulu people, the Ngoni, possessing superior military organization and an unusual political structure for the area, had begun to achieve their domination of the western and southern regions of the lake. The indigenous Nyanja (known to various other people as the Mang'anja, Wanyasa, or Maravi) and the Tonga where the main groups brought under Ngoni hegemony. Further south and east from the lake were the lands of the Yao. From the mid-nineteenth century, the Yao, already acting as middlemen for the Zanzibar market of the Arab slave trade in the area, had begun to occupy the Shire Highlands. Again, the Nyanja bore the brunt of a slave trade made more intense and intrusive by Yao migration.[20] It was, indeed, this trade which was to serve as the most popular rationale for European intervention in the region.[21]

European settlement in Central Africa had been initiated by missionaries. David Livingston had trekked through the Central African territory in the later 1850s, and in response to his entreaties, the "largely English" Universities Mission to Central Africa (U.M.C.A.) had become the first missionary settlement in Nyasaland itself. However, the U.M.C.A. mission was abandoned because of "slave-raiding, tribal warfare, and fever"[22] troubles in 1864 (1863?). More enduring settlements were begun in the mid-1870s: the Free Church of Scotland in 1875 and the Church of Scotland in 1876.[23] By the end of the nineteenth century, the U.M.C.A. had returned and several other Christian missions (the Catholic Montfort Mario Fathers, the Dutch Reformed Church, the Seventh-Day Adventists, and the Seventh-Day Baptists) had arrived. These missions constituted the first European political order in the territory:

> [By 1892,] for over two decades the missionaries had had the field to themselves and had successfully combined the functions of both Church and State. They had created stations, schools, transport, training institutions in crafts and light industries and, above all, a body of native converts-some already active evangelists-as the nucleus of an African Church.[24]

Commercial activity had followed closely the development of the first missions. Hunters and prospectors frequented the area, and some planters were already

established by the 1880s. However, the most significant commercial development was the African Lakes Company, a "trading company ... founded by
Evangelical Glasgow businessmen sympathetic to the Scottish missions and ...
aimed at answering Livingstone's call to combat the slave-trade by Christianity
and commerce."[25] By the late 1880s, the African Lakes Company was being
heavily subsidized by Cecil Rhodes and its Glasgow directorate was fighting
"complete absorption by the predominantly English British South Africa
Company."[26] Rhodes, informed by the activities of his elder brother, Herbert,
who had died in the Shire Highlands, had, like other British imperialist, several
reasons for interest in the region: as a necessary element in realizing the vision
of a Cape-to-Cairo Corridor of British domination and exploitation; as access
to the rich mineral deposits of Katanga; as a source of gold, ivory, rubber,
copper, and coal; as a site for coffee cultivation; and, of course, as a source of
African labor.[27] The most immediate threat to these interests were the missions,
Arab traders at Mlozi and Karonga, and Portuguese ambitions for Portuguese
East Africa.[28]

The establishment of the British Protectorate in Nyasaland seems to have
been largely a local settler initiative. The immediate precipitant had been a
"'scientific expedition' of seven hundred Zulu riflemen,"[29] commanded by the
Portuguese Major Serpa Pinto, which had threatened occupation in 1889. John
Buchanan, the British Vice-Consul in the Highlands, had declared the Shire
Valley under British protection, and, along with Harry Johnston, Consul at
Mozambique, had signed treaties with the leaders of peoples living in much
of those territories now known as Zambia and Malawi. Still, official British
intentions were somewhat contradictory. This became evident in 1890 when
Johnston, negotiating with Portugal in Lisbon, had agreed to Portugal's
absorbing the Shire Highlands. In Scotland, campaigns against the agreement,
orchestrated by the organizations and interests behind the several Scottish
missions and the African Lakes Company, succeeded in pressuring the British
government into not ratifying the agreement.[30] In 1891, the British Central
Africa Protectorate was established. In 1892, Johnston was appointed its first
Commissioner.

The Protectorate's administration was subsidized annually by Cecil Rhodes.
Rhodes was also represented by Johnston as the Administrator of the African
Lakes Company.[31] During the first two years of his dual administration, Johnston
resolved the land settlement question by assigning the bulk of land holdings
to private companies. His concessions to the African Lakes Company and its
representatives were far from modest.[32] The pattern of extending European land
holdings laid down by Johnston and followed by his successors became the
basis for the systematic exploitation of African land and labor. The process
resulted in extensive alienation of land from the Africans; several forms of
labor control and systems of compulsive labor organized through elaborate

kinds of African taxation; and the development of racial discrimination. As the European-dominated economy developed, the demand for African labor increased. This demand was met by the creation of new obligations for the African worker which could only be fulfilled by wage-labor or labor time substituted for tax default.[33] Such was the general character of the colony preceding those events which are seen by Shepperson as precipitants to the 1915 "uprising."

On Saturday morning, January 23, 1915, Chilembwe and several hundreds of his followers began the revolt. By Thursday, February 4, Chilembwe had been hunted down and killed. Also dead were three Europeans, approximately fifty Africans, and the myth that "'natives were happy' under British domination."[34]

To Shepperson, John Chilembwe, leader, organizer, and precipitant of the "rising," was neither prophet, messiah, nor fanatic. These are terms which seek to arrest Chilembwe as a primitive and anachronistic figure much in the way that E. J. Hobsbawm accomplishes for others with his notion of "archaic social movements."[35] According to Shepperson, Chilembwe was, instead, a revolutionary in the traditions of England's Oliver Cromwell, America's John Brown at Harper's Ferry, and Virginia's Nat Turner. Shepperson's Chilembwe sought not to protest the old colonial order through revolt but to create a new theocratic order. As such Chilembwe was a revolutionary nationalist, founding and developing a political tradition out of which mid-twentieth century Malawi would emerge.

For Shepperson, Chilembwe's movement could not be classified under "primary resistance"[36] as colonial historians such as Oliver, Fage, Robinson, and Gallagher, Coleman, and Rotberg would have it. Contrary to the analytical framework imposed by functional anthropology (an ideological framework of imperialism),[37] Chilembwe was not a romantic reactionary, his movement was not some passionate protest against the changes imposed and induced by late nineteenth- and early twentieth-century colonialism. Shepperson saw Chilembwe as an amazingly modern and rational rebel moving against an unjust, European-dominated society which sought to reduce the African to an oppressed servitude.[38] Neither was Chilembwe's movement an encapsulated one; it was instead a movement that had been nurtured by external factors and brought to a head by internal and particular demands, what Marxists have called "contradictions."

The relevant external factors were several.[39] First, there was the character of the occupying British colonial power.

[T]he British Empire ... by 1914 encompassed an area of 13,153,712 square miles and about 434,286,650 or more inhabitants. This vast empire ... included an area almost one-quarter of the land surface of the globe and a little more than one-quarter of the population of the world at that time.[40]

Of course, the British ruling class, its state bureaucracy, and its colonial servants could not themselves directly dominate these peoples and their lands. They were consequently compelled to utilize instruments of repression and exploitation emergent from the historical experience of Anglo-Saxon imperialism in the development of Great Britain (particularly Ireland, Scotland, and Wales). Moreover, British imperialism required the organization of colonial subjects for their own subjugation and that of others (e.g., the British Indian Army constituted two-thirds of the entire British Imperial Army).[41] The character of British colonialism was then most often that of "indirect rule," in some instances combined with settler domination (Australia; New Zealand; Canada; East, Central and Southern Africa; and some islands of the West Indies).[42] In Nyasaland, specifically, British colonialism was characterized by "indirect rule," settler arrogance, and the introduction of Scottish culture primarily through Scottish missions.

A second factor was the interdiction of outsiders who inspired native Africans to expect and demand fuller recognition of their personal, social, and political integrity. According to Shepperson, one such figure was Joseph Booth, the militant Scottish missionary who arrived in Nyasaland in 1892:

> In all such "splinter" movements [African separatist churches] there was a common factor: Joseph Booth. He had arrived in British Central Africa when the first generation of Africans educated in the careful, though rigorously disciplined, Scottish missions had produced a number of restless "proto-intellectuals" ready for independence and greater opportunity, and he slipped easily into the leadership of a movement.[43]

Earlier, Shepperson had observed:

> It seems more likely that his role was to bring to a head a much earlier trend.
> It was the timing of Booth's arrival, perhaps, as much as anything else which was responsible for his effects on the established missions and secular interests.[44]

Chilembwe had been one of Booth's first African colleagues. It was through Booth that Chilembwe had come under the influence of the Black American Negro Baptist Convention. This latter association ultimately precipitated the break between Chilembwe and Booth after 1897. In 1901, Booth, too, was instrumental in the establishment of the first Black American missionary in Nyasaland: Thomas Branch (Seventh-Day Adventist). In the same year, Chilembwe, in his turn, had enlisted the aid of two other Black Americans, L. N. Cheek and Emma B. Delany, both Baptists. The presence of these Blacks was a part of the emerging tradition in Central and South Africa that Black Americans were preparing an invasion of Africa to liberate their kin.[45]

Third, there was the exposure consequent to Africans having been abroad in Europe, America, and even elsewhere in Africa, perceiving and experiencing styles of life contradictory to those at home under colonialism. Chilembwe traveled to America (and possibly Europe) and lived there for almost three years while securing a training to become a missionary evangelist.[46] We might also add that immigrant Nyasas had played an important role in the development of the South African National Congress.

A fourth consideration was the cross-fertilization of ideas and organizational impulses between Africans of different areas. Before Chilembwe's movement, Elliot Kamwana had agitated for a movement against mission fees and the hut tax. After visiting the Cape with some of his own people (Tonga) among the South African mine workers, he had returned to Nyasaland to announce the coming of a new order: "We shall build our own ships; make our own powder; import our own guns."[47] He had been deported by the government in 1909. After Kamwana had come Charles Domingo, an African separatist from Portuguese East Africa. Like Kamwana, Domingo had been associated with Joseph Booth. Also like Kamwana, Domingo looked forward to an African state: [The] Nyasa country [is] now thirty-six years old ... and should start to rise up as our fellow country Japan is."[48] This tradition continued beyond Chilembwe's movement to include such figures as Clement Kadalie, also a Tonga. Africans involved in Kadalie's militant trade union, the Industrial and Commercial Workers Union of Africa in South Africa of the 1920s later founded the Nyasaland separatist African National Church.

The fifth factor was the effect of the First World War, an event confronting Africans with the fact of Christian European nations (or tribes) at war, the task of choosing between them, and the consequent loss of life for distant and alien causes. Shepperson and other analysts of Chilembwe (such as Rotberg and Mwase)[49] have argued that the loss of African lives at Karonga on September 8–9, 1914 in a battle between English and German forces precipitated the protest of, and finally the violence of, Chilembwe's movement. Certainly, Chilembwe's letter to the *Nyasaland Times* of November 26, 1914 confirms this view in part.[50] Shepperson also develops an interesting thesis which contradicts the beliefs of many historians of modern twentieth-century Africa by arguing that the First World War had more impact than the Second World War:

> The coming of the 1939 war did not hit Africans with the same force as the 1914 war which brought about a "deep and fundamental change" in the relations of the African people with the great unknown world which suddenly fell upon them and insisted that they must become a part of it, however unwilling and without understanding they might be.[51]

The sixth influence was that of the infusion of what Shepperson calls "foreign ideologies." Indian and Irish nationalism, and Marxism, are obvious and appropriate candidates, but are rather latecomers to the South and Central African scenes. More importantly for the earlier periods, in Shepperson's view, are Scottish nationalism, Christianity (in its European and American variants including the Scottish Methodists, The Watch Tower movement, the American African Methodist Episcopalian Church, and the National Baptist Convention), American Pan-Africanism, and American Negro nationalism as represented by W. E. B. DuBois and Marcus Garvey.[52]

Chilembwe's movement, then, was in many ways and in part a reflection of a world in torment and turmoil. What was previously considered a rather solitary "rising" begins to assume then the posture and position of a world event, a movement in continuity with those some of which were thousands of miles away, crossing an incredible mix of cultural and social boundaries.

As such, by way of Shepperson, the movement is lent a "dignity" which no official or government inquiry would be (or was) willing to allow. The "official" version of the movement was quite different:

> The movement was designed for the massacre of the whites in the Shire Highlands, where they are principally congregated, and for the suppression of white rule, and there can be no doubt that it had been in the course of preparation for some years by John Chelembwe [sic] and the members of the religious fraternity which he had established under the name of the African Baptist Church and Provident Industrial Mission.[53]

In short, it was seen as a violent racial confrontation.

However, this contiguity with what Barbara Ward has called the "revolution of worldliness" does not fully satisfy Shepperson's task. The foregoing is obviously pedestrian history. It lacks satisfactory explanatory force, as it relies primarily on a distant, third man's perception of the event. It is history without the bowels, ticks, and slight irritants which are so much of the consciousness of real human beings. This historian disagrees with a narrative which would deny that stratum of reality.

Shepperson is concerned with the form of explanation of the "rising" which would attend such particularities as the failing eyesight of John Chilembwe, and the man's thoroughly confused identification with the white man as manifested in his severe, ill-fitting European dress; his short, heavily greased, "Pompadoured" hair; his disciplined handwriting; his ambitious, stylized use of English. Chilembwe was a proud, confused, and finally distraught man, searching for some final reconciliation between his senses and the sense of the thing. He finds it not in Christianity – neither in the patience nor in the protest of mission Christianity – but in revolution.

In Shepperson's estimation, Chilembwe's was a revolution which can be traced to the slave revolts of the American South.[54] It is a revolution which addresses itself to the unjustifiable waste of African blood in alien quarrels. But most pointedly, it is a revolution of a man's spirit revolting against a barrage of particular and personal fears and insecurities. Chilembwe is more than a charismatic leader (a term which inexplicably was not a part of Shepperson's analytical vocabulary); he is a man, just as Amidu was more than one of the king's lance-corporals.

However, despite the seductively esthetic wholeness of Shepperson's vision of Chilembwe's movement, there remain some serious analytical and interpretative questions, as well as questions of style and perception. The more minor concerns should be treated first.

SHEPPERSON'S CRITICS

At least one reviewer of *Independent African*, Margery Perham, has commented on the development by Shepperson and Price of Chilembwe's personality:

> It is unfortunate that though the writers give us his background in full, the chief actor remains, for lack of evidence, a shadowy figure, and that many pages have to be given to speculation about what he might, or must have experienced or done.[55]

If we check out Dr. Perham's criticisms, we find in the volume there are five pages given over to speculative reconstructions of the original Chilembwe, his mother, his tribe, his name.[56] Did he designate himself John, or was he called John after John the Baptist? If so, could this not have influenced his self-identification to assume the mantle and identity of one who gives "light to them that sit in darkness"? Does Chilembwe mean "antelope" or "what is written"? Predestination or coincidence? If Chilembwe was a member of the "wandering" Yao people, could not this have influenced his purported decision to leave the Blantyre Mission and join John Booth? Was Chilembwe's mother the woman of great power implied by the native meaning of her name Nyangu?

These questions, though elaborately dwelt on, remain unanswered by Shepperson and Price, since there was little hard evidence available to them at the time of their research and writings. (There is a short volume which purports to be an authentic and *African* biography of Chilembwe but more of this later.) The exercise does seem fruitless in the face of the thunderous silence of evidence. Yet the answers to these questions would be singularly of importance – if obtained – to an historian who seeks a special value of the historical event. Alexander and Juliette George in their *Woodrow Wilson and Colonel House*, Harold Lasswell in his *Power and Personality* and *Psychopathology and Politics*, Erik Erikson in *Young Man Luther* and *Gandhi's Truth*, have all sought the more integral explanation. They have attempted to identify leaders as men and women who proceed through stages of psychosocial development and have their moments of crisis, but in addition, in the background, there are the communities with their own histories and their own moments of unavoidable and final choice-making. This is apparently very close to Shepperson's perception of the dimensions of explanation of the historical phenomenon. It is what Erikson has, perhaps prematurely, termed the "psychohistorical approach."[57] Yet the approach does have weaknesses and disadvantages. For one, it mobilizes serious distress from other historians. Witness, if you will, the resistance indicated by Dr. Perham in her denial that several hundreds of pages of presentation of hard evidence (primary sources including Chilembwe's letters, his photo album, marginalia, writings on him by his contemporaries, friendly as well as hostile), speculation, inference, and theory-building have deposited with her anything more than a "shadowy" image. In this instance "shadowy" might be inferred to mean less a dimly lit figure as one which is kaleidoscopic.

A second problem is perhaps more enduring since it rests with Shepperson rather than his readers. The psychohistorical approach is prone to the discovery by the analyst of a constant parade of ironies and paradoxes. One develops an intensively sensitive appreciation to, almost a celebration of, those contradictions between the man or woman as an individual and the social roles he or she chooses or is forced to play. There is, too, a highly developed sense of when an event begins to mature into "inevitability" and those points in time when a casually made gesture or choice could have quite carelessly frustrated that development. Perham puts it too succinctly: "anticipating the future is used rather too often."

Shepperson does more than "anticipate"; he indulges. The subjunctive clause "if he only knew that several years later"[58] adds nothing to explanation or style. It is more than simply an annoying habit. It is, in effect, the presentation of a theory of history which presumes at base a single-cause analysis for its framework. It inflates the friction between the past and a different future with no advantage from the exercise: "If pacifist Joseph Booth had been warned that the gentle African with his few quiet words of English, who came to seek work from him in the autumn of 1892, was to become the leader of that Rising, he might well have put it down as just another manifestation of European unfriendliness."[59]

The psychohistorical approach insists on recognizing the presence of real men in history but not so they may be used as controlled subjects for fanciful experimentation. Booth did not know Chilembwe's future, nor his own. Such knowledge is denied to use with such constancy as to make the whole proposition of choices for the future as presented by Shepperson absurd. Notwithstanding Hegelian and Marxist historicism, human beings behave differently than our constructs of historical events or perceived acts. The first is phenomenological; the second and third are analytical constructs. These constructs lend greater coherence and logic to a point in time in a human society than is ever there in reality. There is no long, narrow tunnel through which one may peer and see the opening at the other hand. The parameters of an "event" are quite imaginary – the analytical imagination.

Robert Rotberg and George Mwase have, however, presented a more manageable and immediate threat to Shepperson's interpretation of the Chilembwe incident. Mwase, writing around 1932, produced a strange, almost obsequious "Dialogue" concerning Nyasaland/Malawi's more recent past and the contemporary "outlook."[60] What is of most significance for our present concern is the fact that the typescript contained a lengthy biography of John Chilembwe and extensive commentary on the Chilembwe movement itself. The source of this section of the "Dialogue" seems to have been one Wallace Kampingo, one of Chilembwe's lieutenants, who served seventeen years of a life sentence as a consequence of his participation in the rebellion. During his imprisonment, he met Mwase.

Mwase-Kampingo's narrative and reconstruction of the rebellion is so strikingly different from Shepperson's main emphasis that Rotberg (who edited the published version of Mwase's notes) chose to mark the distinction by entitling it *Strike a Blow and Die*. Though Rotberg in his own work on British Central Africa, *The Rise of Nationalism in Central Africa*, has utilized both Shepperson and Mwase for various portions of his Chilembwe account, he clearly relies most heavily on Mwase.

To be more specific, Shepperson and Price characterized the movement in this way:

> Thus the aims of the Rising appear to have been twofold: first, if successful, the creation of an African state in Nyasaland, with strongly theocratic elements and selected European guidance; second, if unsuccessful, a gesture of protest, in the early months of the new and frightening war, against what were conceived as the intolerable aspects of European rule.[61]

Shepperson and Price steadfastly hold to their characterization by tracing evidence which appears to indicate that Chilembwe was quite committed to the establishment of an independent nation. He attempted, they argue, to enlist others beyond the pale of his Providence Industrial Mission, finding coconspirators in Ncheu and Zomba. There is "evidence" too, they maintain, that Chilembwe attempted to communicate with the German colonial administration in Tanganyika in order to construct an alliance against the Nyasaland colonial forces.

For Shepperson, then, Chilembwe's short-lived movement was a thorough going "nationalist" revolution, complete with dog-eared military manual. Yet there is some slight reservation. In addressing themselves to one African's account, they say:

> This story suggests that Chilembwe looked upon himself more as a martyr in the cause of Nyasaland Africans rather than as a sort of "Emperor Jones" over the Protectorate. (There is indeed, apparent here not a little of the psychology of John Brown at Harper's Ferry.) And so, concluded this African witness, "He strengthened [his followers] with these words, 'We ought to suffer persecution.'"[62]

Such an interpretation is less in the tradition of John the Baptist and more in that of Jesus of Nazareth. Chilembwe becomes less a revolutionary leader and more a messiah. Though this symbolic character of the movement is indicated as one purpose of the movement, it is secondary for Shepperson and Price and – it can be accurately stated – de-emphasized. Instead, Chilembwe finds dignity in a very different tradition:

> The comparison with Cromwell is apt in another sense there was a mixture of religion and politics on the whole movement of the Nyasaland independent African churches which culminated in the 1915 Rising that is not unlike the fusion of religious and political ideologies which characterized the English Revolution of the 1640s.[63]

Kampingo's sense of the event is quite different. He reconstructed Chilembwe's last instruction to his followers in terms consciously modeled on the tradition of John Brown, the American rebel.[64] Chilembwe is sacrificial and tragic:

> You are all patriots as you sit ... This very night you are to go and strike a blow and then die. I do not say that you are going to win the war at all. You have no weapons with you and you are not at all trained military men even ... I now encourage you to go and strike a blow bravely and die.
> This is only way to show whitemen, that the treatment they are treating our men and women was most bad and we have determined to strike a first and a last blow, and then all die by the heavy storm of the whiteman's army. The whiteman will then think, after we are dead, that the treatment they are treating our people is almost (most) bad, and they might change ...
> You must not think that with that blow, you are going to defeat white men and then become Kings of your own country, no. If one of you has such an idea in his head "God forbid" ... for it will lead him astray.[65]

Chilembwe thus emerges with a very different sort of dignity. He had been driven to a last and final gesture by the swelter of contradictory forces: Christianity with its revolutionary ideology and its fatalism; oppression by white Christians; "white men's wars"; the death and sickness of colonialism. Absent from the Mwase-Kampingo account are the frustration of a desperate attempt to reconcile his Africanness with his European identification; his pride, ambivalence, and fear. Chilembwe's revolt is a gesture of love not hatred, though it is consummated in blood. He and his people must kill the love-hate object – the white man – in order to celebrate their Christian spirit, in order to establish their right and duty not to kill. Ambivalence is expressed in contradiction:

> Wallace Kampingo was the last Captain of them all. [Those] captured at the end, who were condemned to death were all executed at the K.A.R. [Kings African Rifles]. They all died bravely, singing hymns of their Great God when [they] were escorted towards a scaffold for their last time in the world ...
>
> John when organizing his troops at the first instance, he said, I want you to go and "strike a blow, and then die." He knew at the beginning that his idea of striking a blow on a whiteman meant his death: Death meant destruction of his own life and that of the other people who were to involve themselves in it. Death does not mean to enjoy at large at all, but decay and ruin, yet John hazarded it ...
>
> John knew that whitemen have strong weapons, strong army and that they were trained, yet he went and struck them with a maize stalk. He depended that he would get weapons from the whitemen themselves, and fight them with their own weapons. Is that not absurd? Not only absurd, but wonderful intrepidity.[66]

Yet Price, for one, will have nothing to do with Mwase's report:

> The editor's title for the work is a slogan which appears several times in alleged quotations from Chilembwe's addresses to his people. It has not been recorded hitherto and in view of the looseness of Mwase's rendering of one document (a letter to the local newspaper) by Chilembwe. As the editor notes, it conflicts with the undignified end of the revolt.[67]

There are, however, perhaps two very different aspects of the movement – the instrumental and the ideological. Shepperson has made his case primarily on the instrumental or technical face of the movement. Chilembwe did organize, did plan, and probably did read, his military manual. It is clear that in all probability he did seek allies, African and European. He did, then, conspire.

But the question remains, finally, why? Is it sufficient to characterize a movement by the instruments it adopts to survive? If so, Christianity, in its infancy, can be identified (as some scholars have) as a political revolution since it possessed organizational cells, hidden caves, secret codes, and other conspiratorial and political phenomena in its development. This represents what its adherents were forced to do, and is in conflict with their ideological presentation. Yet, such a characterization would miss the point.

It is obvious that the second aspect of a movement – its expressive or ideological system – is critical to assigning a character to the movement. Yet which of its faces will prove most significant for a society's story-tellers? If history is an art of interpretation, that interpretation will clearly be responsive to two phenomena: objective evidence and the quite differently contextualized perceptions of the scholar. The Chilembwe movement has been characterized by Shepperson largely through circumstantial data – the official reports, the writings of bureaucrats, European newspapers, settlers, missionaries, planters, but of only one student of Chilembwe (Maynard Mbela, 1904–1911) and one follower (Andrew Mkuliehi). This dependency on, for the most part, distant and often hostile primary sources was not a result of Shepperson's intent, but a consequence of what Shepperson termed a seeming "conspiracy" of "time, fire, human error and suspicion."[68] It has, however, marked the analysis, even if it has not rendered it inauthentic.

The second critical fact of interpretation concerns the various capacities of the scholar himself. That Shepperson is an excellent historian with extraordinary analytical tools, there can be little question. His reconstructions are deliberate and fascinating. His chapter on Chilembwe and Booth in America is one of the most exciting analytical castings I have encountered. The mere mention of Virginia appears excuse enough for Shepperson to discover and explore its history of slave revolts, its slave history, and its consequent racial clashes. There is, too, the penetrating study of the American separatist church movements among Blacks – detailing the histories of the African Methodist Episcopalian Church and the National Baptist Convention. After the butchery of men like E. Franklin Frazier,[69] this volume is of immense value for the preceding alone.

Yet Shepperson does finally succumb to the nature of his task in a debilitating fashion. He has sought to dignify Chilembwe by forcing his peculiar and particular movement into a style quite alien to it: European political revolution. Chilembwe was not a Cromwell; he never could be. But most importantly he never had to be. His movement had its own quite special and remarkable integrity.

Now to say this is not to deny that such movements have occurred elsewhere. Chilembwe's movement is clearly one of those which Anthony Wallace has identified as "revitalization movements."[70] Such movements are attempts to salvage meaning out of a disintegrating social and cultural reality incidental to the paradigm of political order and organization. Such was the case in Nyasaland for Europeans as well as Africans. What was unique about the Kamwana, Domingo, and Chilembwe tradition in Nyasaland was that it was a critique of Western civilization which went beyond the internal oppositions. It was a tradition which Julius Nyerere, later, would most succinctly articulate:

> As prayer is to Christianity or to Islam, so civil war (which they call "class war") is to the European version of socialism-a means inseparable from the end … The European socialist cannot think of his socialism without its father-capitalism:
>
> Brought up in tribal socialism, I must say I find this contradiction quite intolerable. It gives capitalism a philosophical status which capitalism neither

claims nor deserves. This glorification of capitalism by the doctrinaire European socialists, I repeat, I find intolerable ...

The true African socialist does not look on one class of men as his brethren and another as his natural enemies. He does not form an alliance with the "brethren" for the extermination of the "non–brethren."[71]

Amilcar Cabral, in his own critique of the class analysis of history and social revolution, came to conclusions which complement Nyerere's position.[72]

Still the parallels and interceptions of the histories of Scottish and African peoples in relation to the English are compelling. Its influence on Shepperson is persistent. For example, once in a quite formidable lecture on the African Diaspora, Shepperson took time to correct another European (and English) Africanist, Basil Davidson, on feudal Scottish attitudes toward Blacks in the early sixteenth century.[73] According to Shepperson, Davidson suggested in his *Black Mother*[74] that the Scottish poet, William Dunbar's "Of one Black-Moir" indicated somewhat broad tastes among the Scottish nobility – "knights jousting for the sexual favors of this negro woman."[75] Shepperson disagreed:

But precisely the reverse could be argued. Dunbar's poem, it could be claimed, shows all the denigratory, sexual predjudices associated with the early European stereotypes of the negro, which unfortunately, still persist in some misguided quarters down to the present day.[76]

Although it is a defense of a somewhat perfidious interpretation, it also makes the point against liberal romanticization of oppressed peoples.

Again, a century later, it is ironic, perhaps, that just as the Scottish parliament was committing the fortunes of its people to the English Queen, that same woman, Elizabeth I, was issuing orders for the transportation of Blacks out of England. It appears that in 1601, the numbers of Blacks in England constituted a threat to English ruling class sensibilities.[77] To the English upper classes of the time, of course, Scots were just as savage as Africans. Such an attitude might explain the predilection of some Scottish historians to find parallels between eighteenth-century Scotland and nineteenth-century Africa.[78]

But it is the phenomenology of diaspora which is the organizing theme in Shepperson's work. The parallels between the Scottish and the African (more specific to the Chilembwe study, the Malawi) diaspora are multiple and complex. They range from the direct and indirect influence on the development of African national identities of Mungo Park's Niger River explorations;[79] David Livingston's effect on East and Central Mrica; Joseph Booth's "Africa for Mricans," and the "Pan-Negroist" activity of Moses de Rocha, the Afro-Brazilian medical student at Edinburgh at the beginning of this century. The putative nationalism of Chilembwe is for Shepperson a confirmation of this process of intersection between Scottish and African nationalisms.

From the time of James Bruce and Mungo Park in the eighteenth century until well into the twentieth, Scottish institutions and Scots have made a mark on Africa which will not easily be erased; and in helping Africans to change, Scots have changed themselves and the land of their birth. Perhaps the most outstanding quality that the Scots brought to Africa was determination ... Determination is a quality which illustrated the view that, for Africa, Scottish influences have been more effective through the individual than through the group. If this is so, then the ending of the British Empire in Africa may not mean their extinction.[80]

Yet, finally, if Shepperson is more concerned here with a personal truth, his failure to root out a more historical authenticity is a brilliant failure. Shepperson has consummated the European historian's task. Could Amidu have done more? This last question is the informing concern of this essay. Shepperson has fulfilled his legacy. It is now time for the Amidus to complete theirs. The recreation of African and diaspora history must become part of the recreation of Black life. In order that this be done, the work must proceed out of the consciousness of the Amid us rather than their allies. This is the only authenticity that history can claim.

NOTES

1. James (1963, 19).
2. See Erikson (1968).
3. For example, too few students of the "Russian Revolution" pay serious attention to the varied implications of this term: territoriality which implicitly excludes concern for contemporary and related revolutionary movements beyond Russia; the blurring of ethnic-national distinctions subsumed by a term, Russian, which for this period might most effectively apply to the Great Russians; the negation of the perception of many professional revolutionists (and counter-revolutionists) that this movement was a socialist revolution only momentarily restricted to the Russian Empire; and finally, the failure to distinguish between, and to characterize independently, political, military, structural, and ideological events and social forces. See Gouldner (1977–1978), Haupt (1979), and Clarence-Smith (1977).
4. DuBois (1962, 726).
5. To cite two: Marx reiterated in his own fashion Hegel's presumption that Africans possessed no history; and, after Marx, Franz Oppenheimer ignored the presence of slavery in excepting the U.S. from the classic state always founded on exploitation of its workers. For the first, see Shlomo Avineri's introduction to his *Karl Marx on Colonialism and Modernization* (1969), and for the second, see Oppenheimer (1926, 17–19).
6. Cabral (1973, 43).
7. Cabral (1973, 43).
8. Shepperson (1951b, 59, 61).
9. Shepperson (1966, 12).
10. Professor Shepperson was kind enough to supply me with some relevant aspects of his family history.
11. See Hanham (1969).
12. The following review closely follows Smout (1970).
13. See Smout (1970, 333–334). The notion of Christianity as a fixed entity is of course quite erroneous. Christianity is a constantly evolving, syncretic ideological system and initially developed as a synthesis of Afro-Egyptian, Hebraic, Greek, and Roman element. Subsequently,

traditions from other peoples were absorbed, peoples usually described by Christo-centric writers as "pagans." In the text, therefore, I do not mean to imply that the Highlanders were confronted with a closed ideological system, but, instead, a complex of concepts ordered around the belief in the divinity of the figure Christ the Messiah. See Sohm (1895), Jackson (1970), and Diop (1974, 6ff).

14. See Smout (1970, Pt. II), Prebble (1953), and the interesting film of the British Broadcasting Company, "The Battle of Culloden" by Peter Watkins in consultation with John Prebble.
15. Smout (1970, 225).
16. See Thompson (1966, chapters VI–VII) and Thomis (1974).
17. *The Times*, Dec. 4, 1856, cited by Hanham (1969, 79–80).
18. Co-authorship ordinarily would present great difficulties to ferreting out a characterization of one of the writers. However, despite the book being a product of an apparently close collaboration, Shepperson's contribution may be identified (by inference) by comparing many of the major themes of the book with those which appear in numerous articles authored singly by Shepperson (1951a, 1952, 1953, 1960, 1961, 1962a, 1962c).
19. Tangri (1968, 145).
20. See Shepperson and Price (1958, chapter II).
21. See Ross (1966), Shepperson and Price (1958, 13), and Robinson, Gallagher, and Denny (1967, chapters 1–11).
22. Shepperson and Price (1958, 13).
23. See Ross (1966, 333).
24. Shepperson (1954, 234).
25. Ross (1966, 333).
26. Shepperson (1958, 23).
27. See Shepperson (1958, 26–27).
28. See Ross (1966, 333, 338–339).
29. Ross (1966, 333).
30. See Ross (1966, 333) and Shepperson and Price (1958, 13).
31. See Ross (1966, 337).
32. See Shepperson (1958, 24–25) and Shepperson and Price (1958, 14–16).
33. See Sanderson (1961, 259–271).
34. Rotberg (1965, 92).
35. See E. Hobsbawm. *Primative Rebels: Studies in Archaic Forms of Social Movements in the 19th and 20th Centuries* (Manchester: Manchester University Press, 1959).
36. See Ranger (1968, 437–453, 631–641).
37. See Gouldner (1971, 125–134) and Evans-Pritchard (1973, 764–765).
38. See Ranger (1968, 438).
39. See Shepperson (1961).
40. Obichere (1977, 2).
41. See Harries-Jenkins (1977, 4–5, 201–210), British Army (1913, VI), and Hamer (1979, 77–92).
42. Shepperson (1958, 25) has some comments on the controversy around the terms "direct" and "indirect" rule.
43. Shepperson (1954, 235).
44. Shepperson (1954, 235).
45. See Shepperson (1962b, 144–146, 151–152).
46. See Shepperson (1962b, 152).
47. As reported by Shepperson (1954, 239).
48. As reported by Shepperson (1954, 240).
49. See Rotberg (1965, 81), Mwase (1967, 32–33).
50. See Shepperson and Price (1958, 234–236).
51. Shepperson (1961, 209). See Hatch (1965, 25–35) for the opposing view.
52. See Shepperson (1954, 1962b).
53. Shepperson and Price (1958, 219).
54. See Shepperson and Price (1958, 418–437).

55. Perham (1960, 506).
56. See Shepperson and Price (1958, 36–37).
57. See Erikson (1950, chapter IX) as well as Erikson (1962, 105–110). Also of relevance is the discussion of psychohistory as reductionism by Coles (1973) and the exchange between Coles and Mazlish (1973).
58. Shepperson and Price (1958, 36–37); for similar constructions sec Shepperson's articles, especially (1954).
59. See Shepperson and Price (1958, 36–37).
60. See Rotberg's "Introduction" to Mwase (1967, ix–x).
61. Shepperson and Price (1958, 255).
62. Shepperson and Price (1958, 239).
63. Shepperson and Price (1958, 262–263).
64. See Mwase (1967, xxiv–xxv, 36).
65. Mwase (1967, 48–49).
66. Mwase (1967, 47, 73).
67. Price (1969, 195).
68. Shepperson and Price (1958, 195).
69. See Frazier (1974).
70. See Wallace (1956, 264–281).
71. Nyerere (1970, 11–12).
72. See Cabral (1969, 95–96).
73. See Shepperson (1968, 152–176).
74. See Davidson (1961).
75. See Shepperson (1968, 154).
76. Shepperson (1968, 154).
77. See Jones (1965).
78. See Smout (1970, 32, 334, 338) for instances. And Shepperson himself: "This was the major problem of the estates at a time of declared economic expansion: how most effectively to organize and discipline their labor force. The labor force also had its own ideas about the process, which was conducted with a rigorous rationalization not unlike that in the Scottish Highlands after the '45, and rival concepts of land tenure of the newer, more sophisticated owners and the more primitive less settled peoples of the areas concerned, clashed with each other as they had done a century and a half before in the Highlands of Scotland." Shepperson and Price (1958, 224). For additional parallels, see the same text, 263, 382.
79. See Shepperson (1971, 277–281).
80. Shepperson (1971, 281).

REFERENCES

Avineri, Shlomo, ed., *Karl Marx on Colonialism and Modernization* (Garden City, NY: Anchor Books, 1969).
British Army in India, Intelligence Branch, *Frontier and Overseas Expeditions from India* (London: British Government, 1913), VI.
Cabral, Amilcar, "The Weapon of Theory," in *Revolution in Guinea* (New York: Monthly Review Press, 1969), 90–111.
Cabral, Amilcar, "National Liberation and Culture," in *Return to the Source* (New York: Monthly Review Press, 1973), 39–56.
Clarence-Smith, W. G., "For Braudel: A Note on the 'Ecole des Annales' and the Historiography of Africa," *History in Africa*, IV, 1977, 275–281.
Coles, Robert, "Shrinking History, Part 1," *New York Review of Books*, XX, 2, Feb. 22, 1973, 15–21; "Shrinking History, Part II," XX, 3, Mar. 8, 1973, 25–29.

Coles, Robert and Bruce Mazlish, "An Exchange on Psychohistory," *New York Review of Books*, XX, 7, May 3, 1973, 36–38.

Davidson, Basil, *Black Mother* (Boston: Little, Brown, 1961). In soft cover, it is entitled *The African Slave Trade* (Boston: Little, Brown, Atlantic Monthly Press Books, 1961).

Diop, Cheikh Anta, *The African Origin of Civilization: Myth or Reality* (New York: Lawrence Hill, 1974).

DuBois, W. E. B., *Black Reconstruction in America* (New York: Atheneum, 1962). Original publication, 1935.

Erikson, Erik, *Childhood and Society* (New York: W. W. Norton, 1950). Erik Erikson, *Young Man Luther* (New York: W. W. Norton, 1962).

Erikson, Erik, "On the Nature of Psycho-Historical Evidence: In Search of Gandhi," *Daedalw*, XCVII, 3, Summer 1968, 695–730.

Evans-Pritchard, E. E., "Fifty Years of British Anthropology," *The Times literary Supplement*, 3722, July 6, 1973.

Franklin, Frazier E. *The Negro Church in America* (New York: Schocken, 1974).

Gouldner, Alvin, *The Coming Crisis of Western Sociology* (New York: Avon, 1971).

Gouldner, Alvin, "Stalinism: A Study of Internal Colonialism," *Telos*, X, 4, Winter 1977–1978, 5–48.

Hamer, W. S., *The British Army* (Oxford: Clarendon Press, 1979).

Hanham, H. J., *Scottish Nationalism* (London: Faber & Faber, 1969).

Harries-Jenkins, Gwyn, *The Army in Victorian Society* (London: Routledge & Kegan Paul, 1977).

Hatch, John, *A History of Post-War Africa* (New York: Praeger, 1965).

Haupt, George, "In What Sense and to What Degree Was the Russian Revolution a Proletarian Revolution?," *Review*, Ill, I, Summer 1979, 21–33.

Hobsbawm, Eric, *Primitive Rebels: Studies in Archaic Forms of Social Movements in the 19th and 20th Centuries* (Manchester: Manchester University Press, 1959).

Jackson, J., *An Introduction to African Civilization* (New York: University Books, 1970).

James, C. L. R., *The Black Jacobins* (New York: Viking, 1963).

Jones, Eldred, *Othello's Countrymen: The African in English Renaissance Drama* (London: Oxford University Press, 1965).

Mwase, George S., *Strike a Blow and Die* (Cambridge: Harvard University Press, 1967).

Nyerere, Julius, "Ujamaa-The Basis of African Socialism," in *Ujamaa. Essays on Socialism* (Dares Salaam: Oxford University Press, 1970), 1–12.

Obichere, Boniface, "African Critics of Victorian Imperialism: An Analysis," *Journal of African Studies*, IV. I, Spr. 1977, 1–20.

Oppenheimer, Franz, *The State* (New York: Vanguard Press, 1926).

Perham, Margery, Review of *Independent African* by George Shepperson and Thomas Price, *English Historical Review*, LXXV, 296, July 1960, 505–506.

Prebble, John, *The Highland Clearances* (London: Seeker & Warburg, 1953).

Price, Thomas, Review of *Strike a Blow and Die* by George Mwase, *Africa*, XXXIX, 2, Apr. 1969, 194–195.

Ranger, Terence, "Connexions Between 'Primary Resistance' Movements and Modem Mass Nationalism in East and Central Africa, Part 1," *Journal of African History*, IX, 3, 1968, 437–453; "Part II," IX, 4, 631–641.

Robinson, Ronald and John Gallagher, with Alice Denny, *Africa and the Victorians* (New York: St. Martin's, 1967).

Ross, Andrew, "The African-A Child or a Man?," in Eric Stokes and Richard Brown, eds, *The Zombesian Past* (Manchester: University of Manchester Press, 1966), 332–351.

Rotberg, Robert, *The Rise of Nationalism in Central Africa* (Cambridge: Harvard University Press, 1965).

Sanderson, F. E., "The Development of Labour Migration from Nyasaland, 1801–1914," *Journal of African History*, II, 2, 1961, 259–271.

Shepperson, George, "The Free Church and American Slavery," *Scottish Historical Review*, XXX, I, Oct. 1951a, 126–143.

Shepperson, George, "The Obsequies of Lance Corporal Amidu," *Phylon*, XII, I, Mar. 1951b, 55–64.

Shepperson, George, "The United States and East Africa," *Phylon*, XIII, I, Mar. 1952, 25–34.

Shepperson, George, "Ethiopianism and African Nationalism," *Phylon*, XIV, I, Mar. 1953, 9–18.

Shepperson, George, "The Politics of African Church Separatist Movements in British Central Africa, 1892–1916," *Africa*, XXIV, 3, July 1954, 233–245.

Shepperson, George, "The Literature of British Central Africa," *The Rhodes-Livingstone Journal*, No. XXIII, June 1958.

Shepperson, George, "Notes on Negro American Influences on the Emergence of African Nationalism," *Journal of African History*, I, 2, 1960, 229–312.

Shepperson, George, "External Factors in the Development of African Nationalism, with Particular Reference to British Central Africa," *Phylon*, XXII, 3, Sept. 1961, 207–225.

Shepperson, George, "The Comparative Study of Millenarian Movements," in Sylvia Thrupp, ed., *Millennia/Dreams in Action* (The Hague: Mouton, 1962a), 44–52.

Shepperson, George, "Nyasaland and the Millennium," in Sylvia Thrupp, ed., *Millennia/Dreams in Action* (The Hague: Mouton, 1962b), 144–159.

Shepperson, George, "Pan-Africanism and 'Pan-Africanism': Some Historical Notes," *Phylon*, XXIII, 4, Dec. 1962c, 346–358.

Shepperson, George, *Myth and Reality in Malawi* (Evanston, IL: Northwestern University Press, 1966).

Shepperson, George, "The African Abroad or the African Diaspora," in T. O. Ranger, ed., *The Emerging Themes of African History* (Nairobi: East Africa Publication House, 1968), 152–176.

Shepperson, George, "Mungo Park and the Scottish Contribution to Africa," *African Affairs*, LXX, 280, July 1971, 277–281.

Shepperson, George and Thomas Price, *Independent African* (Edinburgh: Edinburgh University Press, 1958).

Smout, T. C., *A History of the Scottish People, 1560–1830* (London: Collins, 1970).

Sohm, Rudolf, *Outlines of Church History* (London: Macmillan, 1895).

Tangri, Roger, "The Rise of Nationalism in Colonial Africa: The Case of Colonial Malawi," *Comparative Studies in Society and History*, X, I, Jan. 1968, 142–161.

Thomis, Malcolm, *The Town Labourer and the Industrial Revolution* (London: Batsford, 1974).

Thompson, E. P., *The Making of the English Working Class* (New York: Random House, 1966).

Wallace, Anthony, "Revitalization Movements," *American Anthropologist*, LVIII, 2, Apr. 1956, 264–281.

CHAPTER 2

In Search of a Pan-African Commonwealth

There will be active Africans
— *Patrice Lumumba*

It is important to remind ourselves that in our own times Pan-Africanism has become the signature of five different spheres of human experience: the prehistorical, the historical, the demographic, the cultural, and the political. But because the political is the preternatural register of modernity, and because the Euro-centric and Western-trained Black intelligentsia which derived its origins from the nineteenth and twentieth centuries were the bearers of modernity, the political tends either to appropriate, efface, or conceal the several alternative modalities of Pan-Africanism. "Seek ye first the political kingdom," hardly commenced in the imagined universe with Nkrumah: it was the legacy of the nation-state, a most bourgeois ambition reaching back into the dawn of that class in the medieval Italian city-states. And even there the political was employed to blanket the disparate cultural and unique historical frameworks of the various elements in the Venetian, Florentian, etc. populace. Political Pan-Africanism made similar claims to social sovereignty, obscuring and problematizing what-ever facets of lived, felt, and contemplative experience it could not master outright. It shunted to the side the prehistorical, the historical, the cultural, and the ethnological. We now must retrieve them. These very different and distinct complexes of Pan-Africanism are both of inherent power and useful epistemological platforms from which to begin an evaluation of the imperium of political Pan-Africanism.

Pan-Africanism as prehistory constitutes the most formal anthropology or science of the human species. Presumably aeons before anything which could be construed as race took or did not take place, paleontological fossils testify that the species seems to have first appeared in what we now designate as Africa. The factuality of this prehistory, of course, has been deployed to signify quite radically different meanings in distinct narratives (not the least being the objectivity of science), but its scientific authority is largely uncontested. Nevertheless, the prehistorical Pan-Africanism exists as the faintest of Pan-African discourses, even when appropriated and paraded by nationalist patriots and cultural nationalists. Its primeval ambiguities concerning geography (i.e., the presumption of continents) and subspecies developments (the modern fixtures of race) alter and decompose our present imaginaries of what must be thought and talked about.

The uncontested authority of prehistorical Pan-Africanism cannot be claimed for its narrative successor, historical Pan-Africanism. Since history is always written or imagined back-to-front, from the present to the past, modernity nominated Blacks as the African. Where once, two millennia ago, Ptolemy imagined all sorts of fabulous inhabitants, modernity has substituted one similarly fabulous being. Consequently historical Pan-Africanism has come to mean whatever past experiences accrued to Blacks, particularly beyond the present African continent. Contemporary scholars have only a preliminary catalogue at best of what those vast experiences were or are but adventurist spirits like Martin Bernal have been assured that there are some well-policed limits as to what they might have been. For Solon of Athens, nearly six-hundred years before the Christian era, it had sufficed merely to recall what Egyptian priests had told him to remind his readers of the intercourse between Africa, Greece, and Persia; two and a half millennia later, Bernal has had trouble being heard despite more than three-hundred substantiations in only the first two chapters of his first volume of *Black Athena*. Our present significations of race provide surveillance points for the whole enterprise, but others such as "civilization" and "the West" are confederated with the modern classifications of human variability.

Demographically, tracing Pan-Africanism on the narrowest of terms, the dispersion of Blacks is rather phenomenal. During the past three millennia, the Black diaspora has resulted in the deposit of millions of Blacks in southern Asia and the Pacific; another hundred million or so in the New World, and several millions in Europe. We have only the vaguest understanding of the precivilization, prehistory migrants; and only an episodic record of the Black explorers of the New World, the Mediterranean, and the Near East. Indeed, we have largely been concerned with the dispersion associated with the creation of the modern world-system, beginning some five-hundred years ago. Thus historical agency has largely been voided with the focus on Black slaves (and those of the Atlantic trade rather than the longer and probably larger trades of the Red Sea and Indian Ocean). They were by no means unimportant, since along with Asians and Native Americans, their labors secured much of the early surplus profit which helped to create the modern world-system. Nevertheless, they are only the diaspora's most recent chapter; and it will require an industry of scholars to recover their predecessors from hegemonic concealments of modernity and Western triumphalism.

Cultural Pan-Africanism is similarly patrolled, and from every vantage point. On the presumption that civilizations are geographical, racial, or political expressions, or some other local effluence, we have nominated civilizations and cultures by continent, subcontinent, and by peninsular or national designation. We are all familiar with Chinese civilization, European civilization, American civilization, English culture, and the like. They scorch our thoughts as predictable entities, as if they were as real as the sun. And just as prehistory mocks our historical constructs, history parodies what we take to be the impervious boundaries of civilizations and cultures. Napoleon was so troubled by the ruptures in Egypt of his packet of Western-ness that he bombarded the face of the Sphinx with canon. Despite the desecration of antiquity, we owe him a debt of gratitude: each thunderous volley reminds us not to take to the extreme what we imagine to be us and to be them. Napoleon's futile effort to shoot down the past represents a habit of mind for modernity.

Political Pan-Africanism was concomitant with the emergence of the nation-state. Consequently, it has been implicated in the troubled chronicle of this modern political structure. And it is infected with the confused rationales and sinister ideological associations of statism. The social authority of the nation-state congeals utilitarianism and instrumentalism, the notions which legitimate the nation-state as either an end in itself or a means toward an end. Nation-states are intoxicated with nationalism, and nationalism is almost without exception a cult of one dominant ethnic group since there are rarely nation-states which are not multiethnic. C. L. R. James, one of the most creative founders of cultural Pan-Africanism, raised this specter more than forty years ago. In his *Mariners, Renegades and Castaways,* James observed that

> the madness of both [Hitler and Stalin] was born and nourished in the very deepest soil of Western Civilization. The political organization of Modern Europe has been based upon the creation and consolidation of national states. And the national state, every single national state, had and still has a racial doctrine. This doctrine is that the national race, the national stock, the national blood, is superior to all other national races, national stocks and national bloods. (James 1953, pp. 10–11)

Birth, as the etymology of the word "nation" suggests, deposes judicial citizenship in the nation-state, but this mythical nationality requires a confirmation bestowed by culture, the culture of the majority, or the most powerful ethnic group. For nearly a century we have been informed that this is not the case in nation-states ruled through liberal democracy. In liberal democracies, neutral, mechanical procedures rule, providing the bases for rational, deliberate self-control of individual desires and ambitions (Farrar 1988, p. 4). Yet even a casual glance through our historical era will confirm that the domestic political cultures of nation-states are animated by irrational impulses which tend toward ethnic domination or in the extreme ethnic cleansing; and their most constant external impulse is expansionism. This deceit was the second modernizing mission appropriated by political Pan-Africanism, so it should not be surprising that we can now add the names of numerous African tyrants to the list of their Western counterparts. But it is clear that political Pan-Africanism was an insufficient if not mistaken mission, so no matter the particular perversions of the Charles Taylors of today, more profoundly they are the heirs of a flawed, misconceived past. Our contemporary rapacious hyenas are not blameless but they did not organize the feast.

It may be possible to justify political Pan-Africanism by the times in which it appeared. In Africa, the West Indies and in the exiled communities, imperialism, colonialism, forced labor, and slavery were the most immediate and urgent horrors of the day. Millions had been murdered in the forced labor system in the Congo; almost equal numbers have been consumed in the wars to settle affairs between conflicting European powers; and the mines, plantations, and trade routes from Africa and the West Indies were littered with the broken bodies of workers. An economy of physical and cultural genocide has been imposed on Black peoples. We recite to ourselves that political Pan-Africanism confronted these damnations and bested them. But from this historical distance and in this lamentable present can we still make those claims? Are we not replicating the apologies for fourteenth century European anti-Semitism which mistook the purging of Jews for a cure of the plague? Were, indeed, colonialism, imperialism, forced labor, and slavery vanquished by political Pan-Africanism?

By intruding C. L. R. James into this discussion I have signaled both what was so extraordinarily right and what was so flawed in the generations which marked the foundings of political Pan-Africanism. James was a powerful force in the reinsertion of Black political consciousness into the historiographic matrix of modernism. In both a temporal and ideological consort with W. E. B. DuBois, James achieved an unparalleled disruption of the praise literatures of British, French, and American imperialism. James' *Black Jacobins* with its resurrection of the Haitian revolution and DuBois' *Black Reconstruction* with its narration of Black insurrection drew not merely on Lenin, Jefferson, Sonthonax, and John Brown, but as well on the Black radical tradition articulated by the likes of Denmark Vesey, David Walker, and Nat Turner, and practiced in the maroon societies of Mexico, Jamaica, Palmares (Brazil), Cuba, Florida, South Carolina, Louisiana, and elsewhere. While DuBois' more extreme or more purely political Pan-Africanism led him to succumb to the conceits of American exceptionalism, Americo-Liberian seductions, and an ill-advised campaign against Marcus Garvey, James' greater respect for the significance of cultural Pan-Africanism saved him from similar excesses when such opportunities arose (e.g., during the Italo-Ethiopian War and later in his contest with Eric Williams).[1] They were both, however, mesmerized by aspects of Victorian/Edwardian social and intellectual conceit.

Some of the early founders of cultural Pan-Africanism were not entirely persuaded that the political kingdom was an adequate objective. Fanon was sufficiently troubled to warn us to leave Europe to the Europeans; and James, Amilcar Cabral, and Fanon had recognized that the carriers of modernism, the Black intelligentsia, were destined ultimately to betray liberation (see Cabral 1973; Robinson, 1987). Their forebodings were not intuitive but based on close observations: it was their own emergent class, after all, which distressed them. In Aristotle's day it might have been very well that the *hoi mesoi* could be expected to mediate between the excesses of the poor and the rich, but in our own day the Black middle class has hybridized freedom with material ambition. They possess no cultures grounded in the historical struggles against oppression, only the costume of political independence. They are not authentic to cultural Pan-Africanism, but merely the appropriators of its symbols. In an historical moment which is no longer than an instant, they are necessary to the struggle, but because they are the darker-faced familiars to those forces which extract wealth and life from Africa, the West Indies, and the exiled communities, the Black middle classes have an unnatural duration. When Soyinka poetically nominated them "madmen and specialists," he was as close as that property of language allows (see Gugler 1988, pp. 71–77). For just as the destiny of all nation-states appears to be the descent into militarism and barbarism, the Black modernists seem fated to spawn men and women of insatiable greed.

We must now consider the corrective. Two and a half millennia into the past, Aristotle had argued that it was money that drove desire into an unnatural form of accumulation. Quite wisely, Aristotle had maintained that one can never accumulate enough money. In our own age, we have warranted capitalist accumulation as the principle culprit. Wage-labor generates surplus profit, surplus profit sustains class divisions, class divisions fuel competition, competition precipitates technological and social revolutions, and so on. One could presuppose, however, a certain parochialism (or presentism, as the literati put it) on our part. It might be more comprehensive to conclude from these disparate observations of noncapitalist and capitalist social orders that any economic structure which privileges private property provides a basis for the unnatural, the insatiable. Like the bulk of the cultural Pan-Africanists, I subscribe to this view.[2] Those social orders that come closest to just order are those in which community is privileged above the individual. I am equally not persuaded that the elimination of private property would mean the forfeiture of electricity or the computer. Such logical diversions would be tantamount to insisting that the appearance of republics, historically, required the suspension of cooked food, a practice begun in what Hobbes imagined as a state of nature.

Political Pan-Africanism drew largely on the West (see Okadigbo 1987; Geiss 1974). And on those few occasions when African custom or tradition was evoked, as Jomo Kenyatta's *Facing Mount Kenya* attests, it was proposed that African governance was suspiciously akin to aristocratic privilege. The case was made, in short, that a deserving elite was immediately at hand. The strategy was self-serving, but for its rhetorical power it required a semblance to the justifications already familiar to Western ruling orders. And following the Second World War, when it became increasingly obvious to colonialists and neocolonialists that popular movements in Africa and the Diaspora under Soviet subscription portended a final and absolute dissolution of imperial spheres of influence, a compelling alternative was local governance under a deserving and sympathetic native bourgeoisie. Thus in the vortex of deliberate as well as inadvertent grants of national sovereignty, political Pan-Africanism acquired its external sponsors.

There were, to be sure, some moments of genuine generosity and historical sensibility on the parts of both the metropolitan and the colonized elites, but the vessel, the nation-state, was an undeserving venue. It flattered egos and fattened pockets; and once in place, it facilitated nationalist and neocolonialist resistances which frustrated Nkrumah, Toure, Keita, and later Nyerere. And the Pan-African radicals, lacking an alternative cultural basis for their enterprise, retained a natural dependence on the metropolitan cultures within which they had spawned. Indeed, it was only when the inevitable legitimation crises struck, that they employed native custom and culture in a desperate attempt to retrieve their popular authority. But since this was culture in the service of power, these projects of Africanization or Caribbeanization quite frequently deteriorated into dominant-subordinate ethnic hierarchies and the inevitable emergence of military castes. In my own exiled community, Black America, this alienation of the few from the many was played out in the civil rights movement. Initiated by mostly southern Black veterans returning from the Second World War, the movement was appropriated by the Black professional classes. They employed the poor and working classes as foot-soldiers for a social initiative whose few beneficiaries were actual or potential members of the middling class. There were, of course, renegade revolutionaries, genuine Pan-Africanists, but they were all too often rewarded by political assassinations, firing squads, and prison cells.

Nevertheless, the present paroxysms of the state in Rwanda, Liberia, Sudan, Zaire, Nigeria, Somalia (not to ignore Central America, Central and Eastern Europe, etc.), and elsewhere are taken as significations of the exhaustion of a certain political authority. *Africa Confidential* began this year with the simple declarative, "There are signs everywhere that the era of the nation-state is fading and nowhere is this clearer than in Africa, where its roots are shallowest" (*Africa Confidential*, 1995). Even with the mistaken modernist tag that presupposes somewhere there are nation-states with deeper roots, the judgment is authentic. The global geopolitical landscape has been dramatically transfigured in the last few years, and there are indicators of dissolution in even the most powerful nation-states. In the U.S., race appears as a most desperate device of the pro-nation statists, the imagined expectation that a white republic can be salvaged from the increasingly transparent processes of moral, economic, and social decay. No doubt there is a delicious irony being presently entertained by the ruling strata which imagines that a Black president might be enlisted to achieve for Blacks in America a social degradation and isolation similar to that over which Black mayors presided in their urban redoubts. Notwithstanding, the critical phenomenon is the fragmentation of the nation-state (Kurth 1992, pp. 26–35). For Pan-Africanists, however, this is also an historical moment of enormous potential. But we must marshal the resources of three Pan-Africanisms: the diasporic, the cultural, and the political. Let me suggest one model, one which I will refer to as the 1 percent solution.

We might consider developing a transnational, indeed global, Pan-African Commonwealth. Rather than states, the constituents of this Pan-African Commonwealth would be communities. Rather than armies, the agencies of this Commonwealth would be bureaux of health and education. The purpose of the Commonwealth would be to secure the health and educational well-being of every African on the planet. Like the Scandinavian aid agencies, it would avoid state structures in delivering its assistance to Black communities. Though some state leaders would raise objections and obstacles to the Commonwealth's presence in their political realms, in time these would fade due to practical need, public pressure, and increasing embarrassment in world opinion.

The capital resources for the Pan-African Commonwealth would come from a 1 percent annual contribution from every Black in the world. And like the Commonwealth Secretariat, its technical and organizational resources, its administrative personnel would be drawn from every Black community on the planet. And at its head, its first director, we would nominate the most powerful Pan-African symbol in the present world, Nelson Mandela. Others who have provided evidence of an equal level of integrity and a consciousness of Pan-Africanism (Nyerere, Boutros Boutros-Ghali, Angela Davis, etc.) might be deputized to Mandela, serve as his successors, or head the divisions of the Commonwealth.

The conduct of the Commonwealth would be on four terrains: medical research in field-satellite centers and in a central clinic with a parallel apparatus for the development of educational programs and training; the delivery of medical and educational resources; the disbursement of a slush fund for emergency relief (principally medical and sanitation facilities); and a central facility for the efficient collection of contributions. Each year, the Commonwealth would designate a particular region or group of communities for a deliberate envelope of medical and educational aid designed to meet immediate needs and provide the base for a more constant and long-term development of those resources by the targeted communities.

The contributions and expectations of contributions from the African and the Diaspora community would serve several purposes. On the practical level, the donations would provide a basis for the aid and development work of the Commonwealth; but in the moral and ideological spheres, the act of contribution would rekindle a Pan-African identity.

In the maelstrom of global and regional wars, and the constancies of national assaults against human rights, the failure of the nation-state as an instrument of international and domestic social order has been tacitly admitted in the attempts to construct international associations of states. In the present century, following on the complete collapses of international systems (the First and Second World Wars), new rules of law were proposed through the formation of the League of Nations and the U.N. Nonetheless, since the architects and sponsors of these organizations were in reality state agents and states themselves, the prerogatives of states were preserved. On the political plane, the force of reconciliation was subverted by the impulses of national parochialisms.

Within the interstices of this contradiction, however, authentic movements of supranationalism have germinated. Within one year of the 1945 signing of its charter, for example, the Government of India violated the U.N.'s preserve of domestic jurisdiction by filing a complaint on behalf of South Africa's Indian citizens and residents (Lloyd 1992). Even more subversive have been the health, educational, refugee, and human rights agencies that have flourished under UNESCO and the U.N.'s executive. Constantly in battle with the U.N. Security Council and member states, these agencies necessarily rupture the boundaries drawn by national sovereignty and imperial ambitions.

The Pan-Africanist movement must now collude with these opportune supranational pressures. Drawing on the cultural Pan-Africanism embedded in the revolutionary Pan-Africanism employed and articulated by James, Padmore, Nkrumah, Nyerere, Cabral, Fanon, and more frequently and significantly the anonymous Black masses which confronted slavery, colonialism, and imperialism on the ground in Africa and the Diaspora, the Pan-African Commonwealth must seek to fulfill Sekou Toure's (1974) recognition that "Since revolutionary Pan-Africanism basically refers to an Africa of Peoples, it is in its interest to uphold the primacy of peoples as against States." In such a conspiracy with other supranational forces, Pan-Africanism would continue its journey toward its more faint signification: in prehistory, Africa was the origins of us all.

NOTES

1. For some misjudgments by DuBois, see Robinson (1990). James, it should be remembered, opposed support for Haile Selassie in the 1930s, and in the 1960s was similarly suspicious of Eric Williams – both instances fuelled by his opposition to tyranny.
2. Though opposing international communism, George Padmore affirmed the socialist principle of Pan-Africanism in his *Pan-Africanism or Communism?*

REFERENCES

Africa Confidential, 36 (1, 6 January, 1995).

Cabral, A. (1973) "National Liberation and Culture," in A. Cabral (ed.) *Return to the Source,* New York: Africa Information Service/PAIGC.

Farrar, C. (1988) *The Origins of Democratic Thinking,* New York: Cambridge University Press.

Geiss, I. (1974) *The Pan-African Movement,* London: Methuen.

Gugler, J. (1988) "African Literary Comment on Dictators: Wole Soyinka's Plays and Nuruddin Farah's Novels," *The Journal of Modern African Studies,* 26 (1): 71–77.

James, C. L. R. (1953) *Mariners, Renegades and Castaways,* New York: C. L. R. James.

Kurth, J. (1992) "The Post-Modern State," *The National Interest,* Summer: 26–35.

Lloyd, L. (1992) "'A Family Quarrel': The Development of the Dispute over Indians in South Africa," *The Historical Journal,* 34 (3, September).

Okadigbo, C. (1987) "The Odyssey and Future of Pan-Africanism," *Africa and the World,* 1 (1 October): 44–53.

Robinson, C. J. (1990) "DuBois and Black Sovereignty," *Race and Class,* 32 (2).

—— (1987) "Fanon and the West: Imperialism in the Native Imagination," *Africa and the World,* 1 (1 October): 30–43.

Toure, S. (1974) "Address of Sekou Toure to the Sixth Pan-African Congress," *Black Scholar,* 5 (10, July–August): 27.

CHAPTER 3

The Black Detective and American Memory

> One of the most daring and heroic adventures of the Civil War was successfully accomplished by a party of Negroes, Robert Small commanding, when the rebel gunboat "The Planter" ran by the forts and batteries of Charleston Harbor, and ... was duly received into the service of the United States government.
> — *Pauline Hopkins,* Hagar's Daughter *(1901)*[1]

From its colonial period, this country has been ruled by regimes of race, gender, and class. Though the power of wealth and the displays of privilege may at times appear glaringly transparent, public discourse nominates them as natural hierarchies of color, sex, and nobility. This hegemony necessarily creates its own contradictions in variegated forms. Those who are economically oppressed, politically repressed, and ideologically humiliated are not merely a disquieting spectacle but always sites that generate resistances. The pursuit of social justice is dialectically embedded in the very tapestry of injustice. In the instance of racial oppression, Black folklore contests race science, social movements respond to mobs, renegade orators and intellects take exception to race propagandists, and radical cultures intersect at unpredictable and unanticipated jurisdictions. Here we interrogate one such moment in an earlier racial regime.

In 1996, Stephen Soitos launched into what some critics have characterized as the first comprehensive study of Black detective fiction writing. In *The Blues Detective,* Soitos argued that in the largely unattended intervention of Black subjectivity into the genre of detective fiction, whether of the classic (i.e., "scientific"), morally ambiguous hardboiled or police procedural, provided evidence of a distinctive Black culture in America. On that score he cited what he discerned as hoodoo, double-consciousness, vernacular, and a racial consciousness of community as the singular tropes of Black detective fiction. Referencing Houston Baker and Henry Louis Gates, Jr., Soitos drew the notion of the blues as an outlying imaginary which burgled hegemonic American literature and art.[2] A few years later Maureen Reddy revisited Soitos, remarking that he had inadequately explored the "whiteness" of dominant detective genre. From her vantage point what characterized detective fiction was its ideological commitment to an insistence on a masculine, heterosexual, and bourgeois social order. "To change the voice, to let the Other speak, is to transform the genre by replacing the traditional central consciousness with another that does not share the ideology or the racial (or sexual or gender) identity ..." Necessarily, Reddy proposed, the intrusion of Black male and female authors would disrupt the genre by making visible that racism is "foundational in U.S. society."[3]

In Soitos's interpretation, the uneasy juxtaposition of the detective genre and race exposes the presence of an alternative historical culture; with Reddy, the most powerful thrust of Black detective fiction is to shatter the self-installed "naturalness" of whiteness trumpeted in the governing American public discourse. There is, as well, the subversion of an adjudicating consciousness. Detective fiction patrols evil, allocating it sometimes to personality (a mainstay of the classic genre), and sometimes to class, that is, the wealthy and their subalterns. Mystery/detective fiction functions, then, to contain dystopia by an assortment of closures maneuvers. The threat of social disorder is more soberly managed by the analytical (classic) detective. In contrast, the hardboiled detective is immersed in corruption, abandoned by the methods of deductive inquiry, the certainties of linear causality, and the conceit of the past as something other than a stew of contingencies.[4] Though there are exceptions, the creators of these two kinds of protagonists trend toward a total absence of race or assigning race as a decorative fragment retrieved from the margins of society. But if these appraisals of the social order are premised on an unexamined, transparent whiteness, as Reddy insists, then the distinctiveness of a Black voice (Soitos) in the detective genre offers the possibility of a more profound dimension of interrogation.

Soitos and Reddy, however, have neglected particular dimensions present in some important works of Black detective fiction. Two of those elements are present in Pauline Hopkins's *Hagar's Daughter,* a work which has now been generally nominated as the first Black detective novel. Those materials are national historical memory and its intersection with the inventions of identity by a Black middle class and its intelligentsia. The same project appears a century later in Stephen Carter's novel, *New England White.* Both writers instigate a national cultural trauma, one a Civil War, the other a blatantly unmerited presidency, when a national crisis was inadequately mediated by the confluence of histories, memories, collective identities, and identity formations.

Black detective/mystery writing has itself been shrouded in mystery. For one, there is the question of its origins. One source of misdirection is the popularity

of Black detectives in film in the midst of the Civil Rights era. Sydney Poitier's
Mr. Tibbs was Black (*In the Heat of the Night,* 1967), but his creator, John Ball,
was not. Soon after, Blaxploitation in the late 1960s and early 1970s brought to
public notice the comedic parodies of Chester Himes and his Black detectives,
Coffin Ed Johnson and Grave Digger Jones (*Cotton Comes to Harlem,* 1970);
and of course the franchise spun from Ernest Tidyman's *Shaft* (1971). More
recently, Walter Mosley's Easy Rawlings, brought to the screen by Denzel
Washington (*Devil in a Blue Dress,* 1995), provided the illusion that Black
detectives were largely a post-Second World War creation. Unattended was the
writings of Pauline Hopkins, a figure which controversy had obscured for
decades. Born and raised in New England, Hopkins (1859–1930) possessed
prodigious talent and range. Before the age of twenty, Hopkins had already
played a significant part in what Martha Patterson has signified as "remaking
the minstrel." In 1878/1879, Hopkins had composed three musicals for the Hyers
Sisters's Negro Operatic and Dramatic Company: *Colored Aristocracy, Winona,*
and *Urlina, the African Princess.* Drawing on Errol Hill, Jo Tanner has stipulated
of a performance in San Francisco: "By presenting *Urlina, the African Princess,*
the Hyers Sisters became the 'first black theater company to stage a musical set
in Africa …'"[5] The next confirmed sighting of Hopkins is in Boston in 1880
when she composed (and performed in) her musical, *Slaves' Escape; or, The
Underground Railroad.*[6] Set in the antebellum period, but written during the
national retreat from Reconstruction, the musical narrates a politics of
resistance: slaves escaping to Canada. Subverting the canons of black-face
minstrelsy, the work evokes the impulse for freedom and dignity among the
familiar Black caricatures of the dominant theater: the mammy, the mulatta, the
comedic coons, etc. Though there are only fleeting and fragmentary records of
the four musicals, Patterson's reflections on *Slaves' Escape* may be employed as a
reflection for all of Hopkins's earliest works: "… granting subjectivity and social
mobility to those characters who resist appropriation by the slave master."[7]

There are many approaches to an understanding of Hopkins, but none of
them is likely to be comprehensive since we know so little about her. So far, this
essay has remarked upon her exceptionality, but this is somewhat misleading.
As she is now remembered through her writings and other works, Hopkins was
reiterative. She constantly and quite consciously pursued the subjects of Black
liberation and resistance to racial oppression whether they took place in the
final decades of slavery or in the postbellum era. On that score she shared in
the culture of Black radicalism. Embedded in that culture were the slave
rebellions and revolutions of two centuries. In the consciousness of Blacks and
non-Blacks were the Haitian Revolution and the more domestic mirrors
represented by the Nat Turner rebellion. There, too, were the published slave
narratives of fugitives, a literature which had played a significant role in the
abolitionist movement and inspired romances and plays. Harriet Beecher

Stowe had recited these themes in *Uncle Tom's Cabin* (1851), and *Dred, a Tale of the Dismal Swamp* (1856). Even deeper, among the slave communities themselves were the "sorrow songs," referred to by Frederick Douglass. These were the spirituals where slaves encoded freedom projects derivative from Christian literature and preachings and also embodied tactics of escape. A literary expression of Black resistance, spurred by the writings of David Walker in the late 1820s (*Appeal to the Coloured Citizens of the World*, 1829), was augmented by the pamphlets, newspaper correspondence and published research of Black veterans of the Civil War like George Washington Williams.

Twenty years following the end of the war, Black resistance and agitation was added to the lore of radicalism by the tales of militant activists who attempted to salvage Reconstruction and such mass immigrationist movements as the "exodusters." And of course the crushing of Reconstruction and the onset of Black lynchings and segregation had soured some members of the aristocracy of color. These new radicals rejected the most basic premises of assimilation: that "whiteness" was a form of nobility or that becoming "white" or white-like provided access to social mobility.[8]

We do know that for a fact the precocious, young Hopkins was a party to the consciously disruptive tendencies which are documented in a generation of Black entertainers in the popular culture. Masquerading, off times, as black-face minstrels in the last quarter of the nineteenth century, they proceeded to transform the theater into a platform for the critique of racism. Indeed, Hopkins may have been one of the first to successfully challenge the imaginings and inventions of "Negroes" in the popular culture. Certainly her participation in the subversion of black-face minstrelsy by the substitution of the Black musical genre is rather remarkable. When this new form became more than embryonic in the early 1890s, it displaced function, form, and content in black-face minstrelsy. The manufactured nostalgia for the Old South and plantation slavery was gradually but unevenly countermanded by the introduction of the spiritual themes of actual slave culture, evocations of the Civil War, and euphoria of emancipation. Uniformed Black military marching bands which lampooned and valorized Black soldiers were inserted into minstrel performances. Songsters tripping through biblical conflations of Moses and Abraham Lincoln, heavenly and secular emancipation, were popularized on the stage and in song sheets. Cunning Black characters were smuggled into the semblance of blackness which had dominated performance in black-face minstrelsy. As Robert Toll observed: "In any case, it is clear that black minstrels themselves did not feel the devotion and subservience to white folks that whites chose to believe they did."[9]

Hopkins, for certain, was in the midst of all this rather complex series of progressions in the racial conceits of popular culture. And though she was no longer a participant, the resistance impulses she did contribute to persisted past the turn of the century. One evidence of this is the testimony of George W. Walker, the partner of Bert Williams, the most celebrated coon on the American stage. In 1906 in an article entitled "The Negro on the American Stage," in *Colored American Magazine,* Walker had declared: "We saw that the colored performer would have to get away from the ragtime limitations of the 'darky,' and we decided to make the break, so as to save ourselves and others."[10] The irony is that this was the same journal from which a few years earlier Hopkins had been ousted.

The *Colored American Magazine* first appeared in May 1900. It was originally published by the Colored Co-operative Publishing Company, a cohort based in Boston. The Co-operative and its activities were financially supported by the Colored American League, an organization of some twenty Black activists which Hopkins had co-founded.[11] The objectives of the publishing venture emanated from the crises which had beset Blacks in the country since the ending of Reconstruction. The urgencies of this mission were marked by the times, the nadir as Rayford Logan put it. Black men, women, and children had become the predominant victims of lynching after 1892; an epidemic of mob-rule had been visited on Black "citizens" of numerous towns and villages; Jim Crow segregation had become constitutionally sanctioned in 1896; peonage and share cropping became the dominant forms for Black farm laborers; and Black voting and other civil rights had been savaged. One of Pauline Hopkins's characters puts it succinctly as "... the systematic destruction of the Negro by every device which the fury of enlightened malevolence can invent." (*Contending Forces,* 244) As the hegemonic regime, a new formulation of white superiority had pervaded the country in an ideological blanket which indiscriminately enveloped Blacks, the white poor, and the millions of immigrants who arrived from Europe, Asia, the Caribbean, and the other Americas. Attempting to construct what they termed a "... racial brotherhood, which alone can enable a people, to assert their racial rights as men, and demand their privileges as citizens," the members of the Colored Co-operative launched their journal as a popular vehicle which would promote a revived radical consciousness in this disheartening moment.[12]

Hopkins was a critical part of this project. Having worked as a stenographer for Republican politicians, the Massachusetts Bureau of Statistics, and MIT, for more than a decade, she now resurfaced with a vengeance. At the *Colored American Magazine* over the next four years, according to Hazel Carby, Hopkins would publish "... three novels, seven short stories, two major biographical series of articles on famous black men and women, and numerous political and social commentaries and editorials."[13] This was an extraordinary, prodigious output and it would only be short-circuited when in 1904, Booker T. Washington's Negro Business League purchased the magazine and moved its offices to New York. Washington's well-known patriarchal aversion to Black women as activists, agitating public intellectuals, or as businesswomen put a full stop to Hopkins's participation in the magazine and may have contributed to the long concealment of her historical imprint. One telling incident occurred in 1907 when the Black club woman Mary Church Terrell made public criticisms of Southern racialism. Washington's ideological surrogate, Fred B. Moore, appointed by Washington as editor of the magazine, rebuked Terrell: "While she was talking that way, Southern men were paying many thousand dollars in taxes to support Negro schools. Women employed in white homes know that their best friends are their employers, and that race peace and good feeling prevail throughout the South."[14] August Meier notes that this editorial was calculated, having emanated from the "Considerable commotion ... in the Washington circle ..." precipitated by Terrell's overt renunciation of the accommodationist Washington line. To our eyes Moore's editorial is preposterous and mean. But we should remind ourselves that the times were perilous. The destruction of the Negro, as Hopkins had written, was proceeding in a daunting breadth.

The rhetoric of segregation and Negro inferiorization was fevered and who could know whether lynching and sporadic incidents of ethnic cleansing might crescendo into a more determined genocide. Moore's declaration was hardly the voice of the Black radicals who had spawned the journal and pursued an assertive Black collective identity. In its stead, he posited an alternative vision of Blackness, one of supplication. Moore was also reproaching the radicals for the codicil which had been attached to their search for a racial brotherhood: the struggle for the dignity and security of Black women which had been championed by Hopkins.

In 1900, Hopkins had published her first novel, *Contending Forces*, a romance in form, it nevertheless concerns the intersections and conspiring of racial and gender oppressions. Referencing "Sappho Clark," the Black woman who is the central protagonist of the work, Stephen Knadler has observed that Sappho's tribulations catalogue many of the social, political, and sexual troubles visited upon Black women in slavery and afterward. Knadler comments that "... *Contending Forces* focuses less on Sappho's violation during her abduction and rape than on her violation by a patriarchal inscription of racial memory [i.e., since they are Jezebels, Black women are un-rapable] that did not give her access to her own experience."[15] Knadler, however, spends little time unpacking the dense histories of Blacks in the West Indies, the Deep South, and New England that Hopkins employed in a novel which is initially set in the antebellum and spans decades.

In the first of her serialized novels, *Hagar's Daughter*, Hopkins took advantage of a narrative trope which traces back to abolitionist propaganda: the tragic mulatta. Like many of those earlier plays and novels, the central figure, Hagar, is raised as a member of the planter aristocracy and when orphaned becomes the target of the villain who reveals that her birthmother was a slave. Hagar is married to a planter, Ellis Enson, and they have had an infant daughter.

The central villain who destroys the marriage, is St. Clair Enson, her brother-in-law. What is distinguishing about Hopkins's treatment of this "discovery" and the subsequent enslavement of Hagar is that the occurrence coincides with the historical events of 1860, specifically the Confederate secession. Quite unusual for Black authors, Hopkins assembles her skills as an historian, writer, and orator to re-create the justifications for the rebellion. As a kind of Thucydidean narrator, Hopkins ventriloquizes pro-secessionist arguments with persuasive logic and performative eloquence. The secessionists' nobility is disrupted only by scenes reproducing the brutality and inhumanity of the slave system they so enthusiastically hope to preserve. Two slave voices of significance appear in these initial chapters. The first is a slave at a slave market who refuses to advertise his sales value by dancing for a prospective buyer. The slave excuses himself: "I don't like to dance, massa; I'se got religion" (11). It is a small rebellion, but with it Hopkins introduces agency and implies the existence of a shared Black capacity for manipulation. Indeed, every one of the speech-acts of the "Negro" slaves at the auction hint at an underlying cunning which is unrecognized by their racial "superiors." The second Black voice was invoked at the beginning of this essay. This one is historical rather than one of Hopkins's inventions.

In May 1862, Robert Smalls, the slave pilot, and other slave crewmen had commandeered the Confederate side-wheel steamer, *The Planter,* steering their families to freedom. The boat became a part of the Union fleet. Congress enacted legislation to apportion a percentage of the appraised value of *The Planter* to the Black renegades. This adventure was celebrated by the anti-secessionist press and reviled by Confederate newspapers. The next year just before Thanksgiving day, the boat was caught in a Confederate ambush. Rather than surrendering as his captain urged and condemning the Black mariners on board to certain hanging, Smalls took charge, and salvaged the vessel for the Union cause. Consequently, Smalls was commissioned as the first Black captain in the Union navy.[16] Hopkins plunges the reader into a morass of irony with the account of the steamer. On one hand, the mention of the boat appears inconsequential: it is merely transporting the novel's villain to the plantation where he will eventually betray Hagar to slavery. But in the same paragraph, Hopkins makes two additional authorial interventions to the historic events. She writes, "No one of the proud supporters of the new government dreamed of her [the steamer's] ultimate fate ... By their reasoning, a few short months would make them masters of the entire country" (24). The leaders of the Confederacy had not anticipated their own destruction and the political resolve of an enemy which protracted defeat into victory. Most tellingly for Hopkins, the secessionists had not understood the nature of their human property which manifested itself in the slave rebellion which would bring nearly 200,000 of them into military service with Union forces.

As a serial, each installment had ended with a cliffhanger, the most spectacular and intriguing being the suicidal leap into the Potomac by the now enslaved Hagar with her infant daughter in chapter 8. Pursued by slave catchers Hagar, apparently abandoned by her planter husband, has determined that death is her final gift to the child. The novel resumes twenty years later, in 1880, its setting Washington, D.C. In a dizzying plot involving name changes, racial masquerades, coincidences, conspiracies involving a forged will and murders, and a myriad of revelations, we eventually discover that neither Hagar, her planter husband or their daughter are dead. The villain, who unmasked Hagar, also reappears with an assumed identity, necessitated by his involvement in the assassination of Lincoln. True to his malevolent nature, he is the critical agent behind a new sequence of violence. And in order to assure that his ambitions are satisfied, he has conspired with his Black factotum to kidnap two women: an aging former slave and her young, beautiful mistress. In the search for the two women, two Blacks are recruited by the chief of the secret service. As Soitos has surmised, these are the first two Black detectives in American literary fiction. The first is a young civilian woman, Venus, a maid in the household which has been devastated by the abductions. The second is Henry Smith, a veteran of the Civil War, and an agent in the secret service. Henry's appearance in the novel becomes Hopkins's device for another intervention which disrupts official memory. Soitos's interest centers on Venus, as the first Black female detective, but he notes that "... she works in close connection with the black detective Henry Smith, a veteran of the Civil War who left a leg at the Battle of Honey Hill. Smith was a member of the famous black regiment, the fifty-fourth of Massachusetts, and he talked about the Battle of Fort Wagner and the death of Colonel Robert Shaw, the white commander."[17]

In actuality, there are three battles associated with Henry Smith and instanced by Hopkins. All of them are historical and linked to the project undertaken by Hopkins and her associates in the Co-operative. In his masquerade as a pensioned off war veteran, Henry entertains his audience by recounting his experiences at the battles of Fort Wagner and Fort Pillow. Later in her narrative, Hopkins alludes to the fact that Henry was invalided at Honey Hill (239). For her own readers a generation after the war, we can assume she had quite particular objectives. Fort Wagner (July 18, 1863) is the assault most familiar in the present since it was memorialized in the film, *Glory* in 1989. Leading the second assault on the nearly impregnable fort, 116 Black soldiers were killed, another 150 wounded or captured. Their conduct was lauded as courageous in the narratives contemporary with the battle. Contradicting the imaginings of Black military service represented in American films from before *The Birth of a Nation* (1915) and long after *Gone with the Wind* (1939), *Glory* had helped to re-write that past which had been dominated by "lost cause" historical scholarship, demonized portrayals in popular literature, and burlesque characterizations in popular culture.

Fort Pillow (April 12, 1864) is another matter entirely. The battle had been immediately publicized as an atrocity; as an unforgiveable display of brutality in pro-Unionist and Black newspaper accounts, or as in secessionist newspapers, as a justifiable performance of Southern white valor.[18] Fort Pillow was a Union garrison by 1864, manned principally by Black servicemen with the Sixth United States Heavy Artillery Battery, the non-Black Thirteenth Tennessee Cavalry with supportive elements of the Union navy. They were a considerable number of civilians at the fort, including families of the Black and white soldiers. It fell to the secessionists, and afterward the Confederate forces were victorious, they undertook a massacre of their Union prisoners. It is estimated that over 300 were killed in this manner, 65 percent of the Blacks some 195, were killed. John Cimprich wrote that federal casualty figures in the battle exceeded that of the wounded, an unusual circumstance during the war, and Andrew Ward implied that the massacre was retaliation for the part played by Black artillery in the defeat of General Nathan Bedford Forrest's forces at Paducah a few weeks earlier.[19] One eyewitness testified before a Congressional investigation: "They just called them out like dogs, and shot them down. I reckon they shot about fifty, white and black, right there. They nailed some black sergeants to the logs, and set the logs on fire." In reaction, for some several weeks, Black troops resolutely refused any terms of surrender, and in victory executed defeated Confederates. As one Union general in a letter chastised General Forrest, the commander of the greys at Pillow, an oath had been taken to "show your troops no quarter ... the result of their own sense of what was due to themselves and their fellows who had been mercilessly slaughtered."[20] The third battle cited by Hopkins, Honey Hill, had seen the engagement of elements from three Black units, the 54th and 55th Massachusetts regiments, and 102nd U.S. Colored Troops. It had been a murderous defeat but that was not Hopkins's purpose in reclaiming it.

At the time that Hopkins was writing *Hagar's Daughter* the public history of Black military service in the Civil War was largely obliterated. And despite their successors' recent service in frontier wars against Native Americans and their present involvement in the wars against Spain and then Filipino nationalists, Black veterans of the Civil War were routinely marginalized or defamed. George Washington Williams, the Black historian and veteran, had attempted to rectify this in 1888 when he published *History of the Negro Troops in the War of Rebellion*. His efforts were unrewarded. By the end of the nineteenth century, according to Kirk Savage, there were only three public monuments which depicted an event which had cost nearly 37,000 Black troops their lives. In two of the monuments, Blacks were represented by seminude figures, transitioning into emancipation. In the third, the memorial to Colonel Shaw mounted in

Boston Commons, their clearly heroic figures were decorative accessories to Shaw's noble image.[21] Alessandra Lorini observes:

> National reconciliation celebrated the erasure of the abolitionist memory from the Civil War and made the reunified country a racialist democracy. The institutionalization of scientific discourses on "race" justified exclusion and segregation of the "separate but equal formula" the Supreme Court legitimized in 1896 ... The myth of a color-blind economic success was the obverse of the myth of a color-blind Constitution.[22]

It was in actuality a much more complicated reality. Financial and industrial oligarchs determined the direction of the nation, calculatedly exhibiting their patriotic beneficence in public gestures ranging from parks to imperialism. It was presumed by these same interests that the terrains of democracy could be restricted to mobs enforcing and thus advertising the entitlements of whiteness. The white democracy became the dominant national narrative, a seduction to the men and women deposited among the poor whites, the arriving European immigrants, and the managerial strata.

Hopkins and her comrades were an important component of the Black intelligentsia and community activists which strove to disrupt this fusion of white supremacy. They sought to construct a Black nation from the fragments of a community predominantly deposited in the lower rungs of peonage, contract labor, and domestic service. And in the course of her "historical fictions" Hopkins systematically interrogated several of the stratagems of survival proposed by race leaders or the lives of the aristocracy of color. In an era during which a host of assertive Black women had surfaced, Hopkins began tentatively. In *Contending Forces*, Hopkins was conciliatory toward the leading Black male and female progressives. She was not convinced that the "uplift" organizations formed by Black women nor the radicalism associated with W. E. B. Du Bois and figures like William Monroe Trotter and Mary Church Terrell were sufficiently receptive to the experienced plight of the Black majority. In the novel, though Sappho marries the "Du Boisian surrogate" (the phrase is Knadler's), her personal ordeal of rape is re-inscribed as martyrdom for the race. Her husband, Knadler observes, "... does not really interrogate the narratives that give rise to the violence, and indeed this sympathy honors rather than protests against female self-abnegation, so that it leaves Sappho's trauma unvoiced."[23]

Hagar's Daughter is Hopkins's exposition of assimilation. Treated most frequently by literary scholars as a passing novel, more significantly Hopkins renders the anti-Black attitudes and beliefs of the "near-whites" who Willard Gatewood testified had nominated themselves as aristocrats of color.[24] It is no coincidence that Hopkins situated the greater part of the novel in Washington,

D.C., since as Gatewood documents, it was the capital of the Colored aristocracy: "From Washington radiated a nationwide network of social relationships among individuals and families similar in origins, culture, color, aspirations, and life styles, who generally demonstrated a sense of *noblesse oblige* toward the black masses."[25] In the novel, Hagar and her daughter though they are of mixed ancestry, at moments when their whiteness is unchallenged, express contempt for Blacks. For instance, when her Black ancestry is exposed, Hagar muses to herself: "Her mother a slave! ... Was she, indeed, a descendant of naked black savages of the horrible African jungles?" (57) Her ignorance of the African past was identical to that of her real-life counterparts. In their schools, "The curricula devoted virtually no attention to the cultural heritage of Africa, but emphasized Anglo-Saxon or American culture."[26] Only renegades like Du Bois or radicals like Hopkins dared to contradict the national culture which demeaned Africa. The minstrel and legitimate stage, the museums, the fairs, the books and articles by educators, the popular magazines, the newspapers, the sales marketing – and every vestige of American mass culture – reiterated the sub-humanity of Blacks.

August Meier implies that for financial reasons the *Colored American Magazine* muted its criticisms of Booker T. Washington. Its subscription strategy had not been a success, and even before its eventual take-over by the Negro Business League, it had become reliant on substantial individual contributions from close associates of Washington. Hopkins's historical fiction muted this compromise, adhering to the pursuit of a radical resolution for the Black nation. Thus in 1903, her third serialized novel, *Of One Blood*, advertised a pan-African agenda. She was taking up the cause of an African diasporic internationalism. On reflection, then, it is rather remarkable that the achievements of such a stunning Black radical intellect had for so long been assigned to obscurity.

NOTES

1. Pauline Hopkins, *The Magazine Novels of Pauline Hopkins*, Oxford University Press, Oxford, 1988, 24.
2. Stephen Soitos, *The Blues Detective*, University of Massachusetts Press, Amherst, 1996.
3. Maureen Reddy, *Traces, Codes, and Clues: Reading Race in Crime Fiction*, Rutgers University Press, New Brunswick, 2003, 9, 55.
4. Neil Sargent, "Mis-Reading the Past in Detective Fiction and Law," *Law and Literature*, 22, 2, Summer 2010, 288–306.
5. Jo Tanner, *Dusky Maidens*, Greenwood Press, London, 1992, 27. Errol Hill's paper, "The Hyers Sisters," was delivered at the 4th Annual National Conference on Afro-American Theater, Baltimore, April 1987, Tanner. Ibid., 139n.21.
6. Composed in 1879, the original title was *Peculiar Sam; or, The Underground Railroad*.
7. Martha Patterson, "Remaking the Minstrel," in Carol P. Marsh-Lockett, *Black Women Playwrights*, Routledge, New York, 1998, 13.

8. Cedric J. Robinson, *Forgeries of Memory and Meaning*, University of North Carolina Press, Chapel Hill, 2007, *passim*.

9. Robert Toll, *Blacking Up*, Oxford University Press, Oxford, 1974, 248.

10. George W. Walker, "The Negro on the American Stage," *Colored American Magazine*, October 1906, 243–248.

11. Ann Allen Shockley, "Pauline Elizabeth Hopkins: A Biographical Excursion into Obscurity," *Phylon*, 33, 1, 1972, 22–26.

12. Hazel Carby, "Introduction," *The Magazine Novels of Pauline Hopkins*, Oxford University Press, New York, 1988, xxxii.

13. Ibid., xxx.

14. August Meier, "Booker T. Washington and the Negro Press: With Special Reference to the Colored American Magazine," *The Journal of Negro History*, 38, 1, January 1953, 81n.49.

15. Stephen Knadler, "Traumatized Racial Performativity: Passing in Nineteenth-Century African-American Testimonies," *Cultural Critique*, 55, Autumn 2003, 95.

16. Cedric J. Robinson, *Black Movements in America*, Routledge, New York, 1997, 78.

17. Soitos, *Blues Detective*, 67–68.

18. John Cimprich, *Fort Pillow, a Civil War Massacre and Public Memory*, Louisiana State University Press, Baton Rouge, 2005, 90–91; and John Cimprich and Robert C. Mainfort, Jr., "The Fort Pillow Massacre: A Statistical Note," *The Journal of American History*, 76, 3, December 1989, 830–837.

19. Andrew Ward, *The Slaves' War*, Houghton Mifflin, Boston, 2008, 175ff.

20. Robinson, *Black Movements in America*, 79.

21. Kirk Savage, *Standing Soldier, Kneeling Slaves*, Princeton University Press, Princeton, 1997, 188ff.

22. Alessandra Lorini, *Rituals of Race*, University Press of Virginia, Charlottesville, 1999, xv.

23. Knadler, "Traumatized Racial Performativity," 93.

24. Willard Gatewood, *Aristocrats of Color: The Black Elite, 1880–1920*, Indiana University Press, Bloomington, 1990. The phrase appeared frequently in Black newspapers in the late nineteenth century which also referred to the "400" and the "upper tens."[25] Ibid., 39.

26. Ibid., 270–271.

PART II

ON BOURGEOIS HISTORIOGRAPHY

CHAPTER 4

"The First Attack is an Attack on Culture"

This week has been a very important week for many reasons. I'm hoping at some point in the discussion to be able to allude to that just briefly and then we can perhaps talk about something related to it. Many of you know me, so, I run the risk of having already said to you what I'm about to say. So if it gets too repetitious just raise your hand and I'll move into something else. I'd like to speak for maybe thirty to forty-five minutes, and given that kind of restriction it is not possible to explore all the premises upon which I speak. So I begin with identifying two, which I want you to keep in mind as I speak about things which may seem not that particularly related – but they are.

This week you had the occasion to see Walter Rodney, C. L. R. James, and Imamu Baraka, as well as some other people from inside movements. There is a very powerful difference in what is revolution and what is organization, between, let's say the first two speakers, James and Rodney as opposed to Baraka. For many years James was associated with a sense of revolutionary theory and revolutionary organization which was identified with spontaneity. Within the understanding of spontaneity there is a basic kind of revolutionary theory which I want to use essentially as a premise. It has been looked at, thought about, thought through by other people and I wanted to quote a small section from Wilhelm Reich's *Mass Psychology of Fascism* to give you a sense of spontaneity. Reich wrote – and he was writing in the mid-1940s:

> usually an important social awareness begins to assume a more or less clear form among the population long before it is expressed and represented in an organized way. Today, 1944, the hatred of politics, a hatred based on concrete facts, has undoubtedly become general. If, now, a group of social scientists has made correct observations and formulations, that is, observations and formulations that clearly reflect the objective social processes, the "theory" must of necessity be in agreement with vital feelings of the masses of people. It is as if two independent processes moved in a convergent direction and came together at *one* point at which the social process and the will of the masses *become one* with sociological knowledge. (pp. 211–212)

That is one of the premises of spontaneity. The basic argument and belief is that organization and ideas come out not from the leadership but from the masses. Now, this is essentially the position of people like James, Reich, and Rodney, who argue that it is inappropriate for an elite to emerge with a sense of what organizations are required, what structures are required, and then begin to influence or to impose this notion on a following, on a collectivity. It is a sense of human history and human organization which is extraordinarily opposed to the ways in which we normally think of these things. The dominant paradigms of human organization, social organization, and social movements presume the extraordinary leader, the extraordinary figure out of which comes organizations, structure, and ideology. They are reversing it. I've said what I wanted to talk about today is, the first attack is an attack on culture. So keep this introductory statement in mind as I begin to look at culture in very specific terms.

I think one of the most extraordinary statements on this question and probably one of the most frequently misunderstood is an essay that Karl Marx wrote in 1843, which he called "On the Jewish Question." Marx has been interpreted to say in "On the Jewish Question," that it was important, it was necessary for human emancipation that the Jews be destroyed. It is written in some fashion in that essay but I don't believe at any time that's what Marx meant to say. He was involved in the first attack, the attack on culture. The attack on culture assumed the form of an attack on meanings of things. Marx understood that in early nineteenth century German society it was not possible for the masses of Germans to understand the Jews. He also presumed it was not necessary for them to understand the Jews. And so he used the term Jew to signify precisely its opposite; he used the term Jew to talk about the non-Jew. And in that process he began to reverse, he began to transform, he began to attack the culture which was associated, linked, and a support of the oppression that he as a Jew knew and that non-Jews would have to come to some sense of in Germany. He developed his argument in a fairly simple way. He said, let us consider the real Jew, not the Sabbath Jew, whom Bruno Bauer (the man to whom he was addressing his essay) considers, but the every day Jew. Let us not seek the secret of the Jew in his religion but let us seek the religion in the real Jew. What is the profane base of Judaism: practical needs and self-interest. What is the worldly cult of the Jew: huckstering. What is his worldly god: money. He said, further on, Judaism has been preserved not in spite of history but by history. It is from its own entrails that civil society ceaselessly engenders the Jew. What was in itself was the basis of the Jewish religion: practical needs, egos.

There is only one way in which we can begin to understand what he was saying, what he was dealing with. He was destroying that part of the culture – the German culture and Jewish culture – which argued that the Jew was significant because of selection, because of a peculiar culture, because of a peculiar national identity. Marx was denying it. He said, it is not the Jews who have made themselves, it is the society which required the Jews, which allows the Jews to maintain themselves. He was arguing then that the culture had conceptualized a people and a process in the wrong way, in an absurd way, in an irrational way, ultimately, in a very destructive way.

He goes on to say in fact, that Judaism is the ideology of civil society, not of Jews, it is the ideology of civil society. He is making the argument that in fact the Jew has become the symbol of the society, a symbol that it cannot deal with directly, which it must project on to some thing, which must – in Marx's term – alienate from itself. The society had developed a symbol for itself, but outside of itself. And it called that symbol the Jew. Marx was saying, it is no longer possible to understand German society unless you recognize it in the Jew, in its Jew.

The first attack is an attack on culture. Marx refused to accept the terms, the language, the conceptualizations of the society which he was addressing. He could not accept them because he understood them to be distortions, because he understood them to be very pointed, very clearly related to distortions, to the oppression of a people. But remember the premise, I am not necessarily saying that this was Marx's idea: Marx organized the idea.

I want to move to a second event, which has been alluded to earlier this week and which has been on people's mind for some time. And this example takes us back to what was once known as Indo-China, or Cochin-China, of the mid-nineteenth century. It takes us to North Africa, in the mid-nineteenth century. It takes us to the Caribbean in the early nineteenth century. The example has to do with French colonialism. It has to do with Haiti and what is known as Vietnam and what is known as Algeria. They are related events. They have been related through French colonialism for the last one-hundred and eighty years.

As you know, the Haitian Revolution occurred in the 1790s, achieved a form of stabilization in the 1800s. You also know that the consequences of that revolution were worldwide. Because you know that the French economy, in large measure, rested on the Haitian colony. You then should presume that French colonialism, French imperialism – being more than a political expression of the French identity, which is the way some people would so presume it – began to look for an alternative to Haiti. Haiti had been the richest colony in the modern world. The alternatives for French imperialism became in the nineteenth century South Asia and North Africa. And the French, in each instance, demonstrated the significance of the title "the first attack is an attack on culture." In each instance, they attempted to destroy the people's culture in order for those people to become appropriate citizens in the French Empire. But let me look at those same, those three dynamics, those three events in a different way.

The alternative to the imperialist attack on culture, I am arguing is the revolutionary attack on culture. And it has a peculiar kind of history as well, in terms of Haiti, Algeria, and Viet Nam.

James, as historian of the Haitian revolution, tells us something very significant but does not explore it very much. He tells us that Voodoo was the ideology of the Revolution, in Haiti, in the 1790s. Voodoo was the ideology of the Revolution. He could have gone further, as some Haitian students have done and he would have said Voodoo is the ideology of the society. We know, that from the 1760s through the 1790s the impact of Voodoo assumed, if it was merely the culture of the slaves, a disproportionate extension. Voodoo was significant in France, we know, because the bourgeoisie were purchasing the services of Haitian medicine men. Voodoo was significant in Haiti among the non-slave population, we know, because the earlier stage of the rebellion in the 1760s, under Makandel, assumed elements which were inexplicable. It was supposed to be rebellion largely organized around mass poisonings. But after measures were taken to restrict and to keep the slaves from handling any foods that Europeans were to eat, Europeans were still dying. The explanation was that they had become Voodoo, they had become accessible to the metaphysics of Voodoo.

So when James says that the ideology of the revolution was Voodoo, you must understand that that is, in itself, a statement reflecting the fundamental subversion of French culture by a Haitian culture. I say Haitian, rather than African, because you know that Voodoo, in large measure, emerges out of the synthesis of various African peoples and Indian peoples in Haiti itself, beginning in the early eighteenth century.

Now let's take a move, take that same kind of example and move it to Algeria, and move it to Indo-China, in the mid-nineteenth century. When the French began to occupy Algeria in the 1840s, the French generals began a very simple, presumably quite effective means of control. They simply destroyed, systematically, the basis of those people's capacity to survive. They destroyed their land, they destroyed their villages. In the late nineteenth century to early twentieth century, they began, now having the refuse of Europe to help them, immigrant European population. They began the systematic destruction of the Algerian cultures. Again, the first attack is an attack on culture. What emerges out of Algeria is the same thing which began to emerge out of Haiti, in the mid-eighteenth century. What emerges is what is known as a creole culture – a negation to French culture. What emerges is an Algerian culture that had never existed before. Just as in the mid-eighteenth century, what emerged out of Haiti was a Haitian culture that had never existed before.

In Vietnam, or Indo-China, what do you have? You know you have a history of successive imperialisms. From the tenth century, Christian era, to the present you know that most of those imperialist powers, most of those imperialist social forces were Asians. You know that European imperialism only appeared in South Asia in the nineteenth century. Primarily you are talking about the French. You know that Vietnam is a designation of an imperialist people, the

Vietnamese. You know that Vietnam was an Empire. An Empire of peoples coming from the north, who over three-hundred years, prior to the nineteenth century, had successively invaded this territory and brought other people, some of them earlier invaders, under control. You know that Vietnam itself is the name of the Empire which preceded the French Empire and which achieved some revitalization in the nineteenth century, between 1800–1802 and 1850. So the French began to assume some systematic power in Indo-China in the mid-nineteenth century. They began to attack the social structure, the political structure, and of course, the economic structure of the three kingdoms: Tonkin, Annam, and Cochin-China.

The result of their attack was the creation of the modern Vietnamese. A very different Vietnamese from that which was characterized by Mandarins, in the early nineteenth century, with elitist social structures, Chinese underlords. By the early twentieth century, there is a Vietnamese national movement, or nationalist movement; something which never existed before. The French had successfully destroyed the Mandarin class or alternatively successfully alienated the Mandarin class from this mass of people, of peasantry, who are in the process of emerging an identity. Their identity, their consciousness emerged as a reaction to the French. This is then, another instance, the same colonial power creating another people.

So we have instances in the nineteenth century, which become part of the history of the twentieth century, in which a colonial power successfully destroys itself by creating a people, the Haitian people, in the early nineteenth century; the Algerian people, in the late nineteenth century, and the Vietnamese people in the very [early] twentieth century.

Now, if you were to look in more detail, at specifications of these various movements, you would begin to see that there was a stage, in each of them, at which Marx's "On the Jewish Question" could be put to use. There's a stage when each of these movements must reverse the language, the symbols, must transform the culture which it is opposed to in order to emerge a very different culture than existed before. I am suggesting to you that Marx's "On the Jewish Question" fits into that development; it is an early statement of the need to reverse the ideas, to reverse the values, to reverse even the conceptualizations of movement, causality, forces, etc. I would also suggest to you that any movement which does not achieve that kind of event will not succeed. I suggest to you that that is – the failure to achieve that – is one of the things which identifies and characterizes nationalists. The *failure* to achieve that.

I don't want to move into the usual sense of what culture is, as opposed to what I think it is, because that would take a very, very long time. And I was not able to set the precedents or set the premises for that discussion. But I think you have a sense of some of the ingredients that I think are necessary. I remind you again to think about the premise that I did spend some time developing, the premise that, if you want to look at it in a phenomenological sense, the leadership always emerges after the mass; that visible figure tells you nothing about what is to become, tells you nothing about what will happen; that visible figure tells you what has already happened.

With the emergence, (we're talking about America in general), of Malcolm X – with all the machinations which might have distorted that event, in terms of electronic media, printed media, the significance of Malcolm X in the minds of non-Blacks in general – with all those machinations which might have distorted that phenomenon, the appearance of Malcolm X should have told you that there was a movement; not that there would be; not that something was about to happen, but that it was already happening. And if we move back to the short section that I read from Reich, earlier, we should also know something else about that same event. Malcolm X would not produce any element in the ideology which was not already present in the Black movement. It was not important that he say something new. It was not important that he articulate novel insights. It was important that he reflect the historical experiences, the understanding, the comprehension of the masses of Black people in this country and in the Caribbean. That is what he said, he didn't say anything new. He *did not say* anything new. It was the organized presentation which was new.

So there we have, I hope, an example, a concrete example of this premise. That the ideas, the structures, the organization of a movement, a social movement, comes from the collective. It does not come out of the individual. That sensitivity, a consciousness of that it seems to me, is an important beginning – that the first attack is the attack on culture. Thank you.

CHAPTER 5

Oliver Cromwell Cox and
the Historiography of the West

Historians have always been searching for something they could label as
the essence of the past – the principle that held everything together in
the past (or in a part of it) and on the basis of which, consequently,
everything could be understood.
— *F. R. Ankersmiti*[1]

CAPITALISM AND THE INVENTION OF THE WEST

The triumph of the West as a historical system has constituted a nearly
incontestable essentialist envelope surrounding Western literature for the past
three centuries. The telos of the narrative of the epistemic West is by now so
familiar and its logic so compelling that it can be costumed as natural history:
"the West" is conceived in a genealogy of civic virtue and moral progress from
ancient Athens to twentieth-century America.[2] With the forbearance and
confidence of modernists, we have even foresworn malice against those, like
Hegel or Marx or Adam Smith in earlier times, who might have presumed to
conclude a recitation of the triumph of Western civilization with the flowering
of Germany or England. Though a bit shortsighted, they, too, have their place in
the West's chain of being, their honored seats in the pantheon of ontologists.

Of late, however, the once faint and (by consensus) ingrate cries of the
detractors of the myth have gained in volume and sophistication. The time
when an Ishi might be installed by a proud, benevolent anthropology as a living
diorama, a museum factor in some expansive San Francisco warehouse – no
doubt in his interior being experiencing the last years of his life in some dreadful
nostalgia – is mercifully ending.[3] A naive humanism has been displaced by
conscious oppositions. An insurgency has arisen against domination and
silence, and it has struck at every cultural and ideological manifestation of the

hegemonic myth of the West. To indicate the broad diversity and vigorous authority of the present challenge we need merely to reference Hayden White's *Metahistory*, Edward Said's *Orientalism*, Michael Taussig's *Shamanism, Colonialism and the Wild Man*, Martin Bernal's *Black Athena*, Gayatri Spivak's *In Other Worlds*, or Gabriel Garda Marquez's *One Hundred Years of Solitude*.

And when we reflect on the meaning of these "deterritorializations," critiques, and defections from the Western enterprise of history and its major discursive structures (as Eric Wolf, for one, has done in his *Europe and the People Without History*), it is difficult to dismiss F. R. Ankersmit's recent observation that:

> For various reasons, we can presume that autumn has come to Western historiography ... The history of this appendage of the Eurasian continent is no longer world history ... The *meta-recits* we would like to tell ourselves about our history, the triumph of Reason, the glorious struggle for emancipation of the seventeenth-century workers' proletariat, are only of local importance and for that reason can no longer be suitable metanarratives.[4]

And with the disintegration of a grand, essentialist tradition of Western perfectibility, it becomes possible to join the practical excavation of subjugated histories to the urgencies they always possessed.

"Capitalist democracy" is one of the most powerful and enduring metanarratives of modern Western historiography. As an ideological formation it has inscribed discursive domains as distinctive as politics and science, policy, and literature.[5] As icon, its aura hovers over our institutions of knowledge and power, suffusing inquiry and decision making with the counterfeit certainties of predestination. Paradoxically, the iconic properties of capitalist democracy remain largely intact despite its disparate hybrid character-grafting discourses of commerce and property to those of moral philosophy, and in contradiction to its empirical inconsistencies. For generations, this condition of overdetermination has been due to the capacity of power to manufacture ideological negations of a more critical representation of the real.[6] More recently this achievement has prospered through technique: the seductions of information and scientific language (methodology). But consistently one of the principal domains of capitalist democracy has been the production of history, the genealogy of the West, its ideological conduit.

However, in the narratives of its victims, namely, those who inhabited the marginalized and not always remote sites of the British Empire or the French or American republics, capitalist democracy often assumed a more problematic and terrifying mien. To cite just a few select paradigmatic instances from a vast assortment of oppositional traditions which have emanated along converging fault lines of historical domination, the horrors of capitalist democracy have been rehearsed in Eric Williams's *Capitalism and Slavery*, C. L. R. James's *Black Jacobins*, Frantz Fanon's *Wretched of the Earth*, W. E. B. Du Bois's

Black Reconstruction, Walter Rodney's *How Europe Underdeveloped Africa*, and *The Autobiography of Malcolm X*. As impressive as has been David Brion Davis's apologetic trilogy of representations to establish that slavery was some anomalous alien force in the Western experience, its power to dispense comfort is largely a function of the fugitive circumstance of this oppositional literature.[7]

The subjugation of this sustained negation of "the West" was not, however, entirely complete. Because the direct representations of opposition were easily quarantined through the agencies of authorized knowledge,[8] a more subtle subterranean strategy evolved. C. L. R. James, for example, in *Mariners, Renegades and Castaways* and *Beyond the Boundary*, infiltrated the narrative codes of American and British hegemonic discourse through critiques of Melville's *Moby-Dick* and the game of cricket, respectively.[9] A second Black radical intellect who employed this approach (and with greater success) was Oliver Cox. Indeed, Cox was so adept at writing counterfeit Western discourse that it may be most helpful to explore his work in consort with that of a more obvious "outsider," the Chinese historian Ray Huang.

THE MEANING OF CAPITALISM

Oliver Cromwell Cox and Ray Huang, the principal and secondary exemplars of this paper, would appear at first glance to be a peculiar pairing for the purpose of discussing Western historiography. Cox, a historical sociologist and economist, was born in Trinidad and spent most of his active academic career in America at Black universities.[10] His most familiar work is *Caste, Class, and Race*, published more than forty years ago (1948). Huang, a professor of history, served for ten years as an officer in the Chinese Nationalist army before being trained and eventually teaching in American universities. Huang collaborated with joseph Needham on *Science and Civilization in China* and is himself the author of such works as *Taxation and Governmental Finance in Sixteenth-Century Ming China* (1972), *1587, A Year of No Significance* (1981), and, most recently, *China: A Macro History* (1988).

Nevertheless, the social experiences and intellectual endeavors of Cox and Huang display several attributes of specific significance for the task of deconstructing Western historiography: uppermost of these are the social, cultural, and ideological actualities that neither Cox nor Huang are Europeans and that both were eventually drawn into metanarratives of the West as framing devices in consequence of their professional and existential pursuits of historical originality. Perhaps of even more direct importance is that they both arrived at a moment in their intellectual development when it became necessary to reconfigure radically the episteme of the West. For our purposes here, it is particularly opportune that, in both instances, they conceptualized this task, in part, as a reconstruction of the origins of modern Western civilization and that independently they imagined that the birth of the West could be traced to the appearance of Venice as the first capitalist empire.

Neither Cox nor Huang had any illusions concerning the paradoxical nature of their chosen mission. For Cox, capitalism, the core of Western identity, had effected a most perverse consequence: Since the age of the discoveries, the world view of all other peoples has been progressively subordinated to the dominant, sophisticated view of Europeans. Hence, to know has generally come to mean knowledge from the European point of view.[11] Huang, recounting the agitated state in which he shared with Needham his own discovery of the relationship between capitalism and the stagnation of technology and science in China, put his dilemma more succinctly: There was no preconceived idea as to whether capitalism is good or bad. Taking a Chinese position, we were on the side on [sic] "nonexistence" to review something that existed.[12] There is a certain irony in Huang's humility before the West. For at this very moment, concurrent to his research on capitalism, he was embroidering the exquisitely descriptive and proprietary detail which characterizes his treatment of the imperial administration of Wan-li, the late sixteenth-century Ming emperor. An analogous aversion to a Europe-centered organization of knowledge is no less apparent in Cox, whose prodigious erudition propelled him into repeated confrontations with the most influential American and European scholars of his day.

Cox first publicly antagonized the fraternity of authorized knowledge when, in *Caste, Class, and Race*, he sought to expose the ideological constructs with which "scientific sociology" had inscribed and mystified race discourse. Between the world wars, at Chicago and then Fisk, Robert E. Park, a former publicist and confidant of Booker T. Washington, had established the "caste school of race relations."[13] Subsidized by foundations such as the Julius Rosenwald Fund, Park's taxonomy and methodology acquired professional and intellectual authority and political influence. By the mid-1930s, Park, in association with colleagues and former students (Louis Wirth, Lloyd Warner, Charles Johnson, and E. Franklin Frazier), dominated the domain of race studies.[14]

In *Caste, Class, and Race*, Cox challenges Park's assertion that, in a reiteration of the "immemorial" experience of other societies (from ancient Greece to modern India), American racism resulted from the conflict ("fundamental color antipathies") between two castes determined by "visible" differences and articulated by custom, mores, and etiquette.[15] Cox, to the contrary, argues that racism was a historically unique phenomenon linked to a "materialistic social fact": the appearance of capitalism, that is, a social organization dominated by commerce.[16] Cox maintained, for one, that capitalism was "different from any other contemporary or previously existing society"; for another, that it had "developed in Europe exclusively"; and that, finally, "In order that capitalism might exist it must proletarianize the masses of workers." Racism, Cox insisted, was an inevitable construct of the "ideology and world view" necessary for the desensitizing of the capitalist class:

> As far as ideology is concerned, the capitalists proceed in a normal way; that is to say, they develop and exploit ethnocentrism and show by any irrational or logical means available that the working class of their own race or whole peoples of other races, whose labor they are bent upon exploiting, are something apart: a) not human at all, b) only part human, c) inferior humans, and so on ...
>
> The rationalizations of the exploitative purpose which we know as race prejudice are always couched in terms of the ideology of the age. At first it was mainly religious, then historico-anthropological, then Darwinian-anthropometrical, and today it is sexual, *laissez faire*, and mystical. The intent of these rationalizations, of course, must always be to elicit a collective feeling of more or less ruthless antagonism against and contempt for the exploited race or class.[17]

Capitalism and racism were historical concomitants. As the executors of an expansionist world system, capitalists required racism in order to police and rationalize the exploitation of workers.[18] Cox insists that, by ignoring this relationship, those social scientists engaged in the study and eradication of racism could be of little value. They could never comprehend that "the white man's ideas about his racial superiority ... can be corrected only by changing the system itself."[19] Not surprisingly the book was ignored, or as Herbert Blumer, one of Park's students, put it: "it was kind of downgraded ... sort of minimized."[20]

There was much in Cox's treatment of capitalism which drew on Marx. And in an era marked by the appearance of the Cold War, Cox was subjected to a great deal of criticism. For Cox, however, Marx was another dead end in the assault on racism. Eventually, in *Capitalism as a System*, he expresses his dissatisfaction with Marx by distinguishing his own approach to capitalism on several crucial points. At one point he would declare that Marx "begins his analysis of the nature of capitalism almost where he might have ended it ... he relegates as subsidiary the very things which should have been the center of his study."[21] And emblematic of Marx's theoretical flaws were his "rigid ideas concerning the role of industrial workers in modern revolutionary movements, and ... [his] giving precedence to the more advanced capitalist nations in the succession of socialist revolutions. ..."[22]

Cox rejects the "national economy" methodology Marx employed in *Capital* which presumed an analysis of capitalism could proceed on the premise of "an essentially closed society," that is, Britain: "... [H]is approach and the particular object of study limited his chances of seeing the *capitalist system*, as distinguished from the *national society*, as the crucial entity."[23] Cox also questioned Marx's argument that capitalism was founded on "modern technology and industrialism" and that capitalism was the negation of feudalism: "[Marx's] 'primitive accumulation' is none other than fundamentally capitalist accumulation; and, to assume that feudal society dissolved before capitalist society began is to overemphasize the fragility of feudalism and to discount its uses to the development of capitalism."[24] But perhaps the most profound of Cox's differences with Marx was the former's belief that the appearance of capitalism was fortuitous.[25] It was thus in an attempt to comprehend the nature of the "simultaneous" appearances of capitalism and racism that Cox turned to the study of Venetian history.

Cox's construction of the history of Venice was substantially conceived through a literature inscribed by what is now referred to as "the myth of Venice." And his account of Venice in *The Foundations of Capitalism*, largely drawn from many of the most eminent progenitors of that myth, differs little from James Grubb's recapitulation of that narrative:

> [T]he prevailing vision of Venice has been remarkably consistent and persuasive and has been transmitted substantially unaltered in guidebooks and histories since its full articulation in the sixteenth century: a city founded in liberty and never thereafter subjected to foreign domination; a maritime, commercial economy; a unified and civic-minded patriciate, guardian of the common good; a society intensely pious yet ecclesiastically independent; a loyal and contented populace; a constitution constraining disruptive forces in a thousand-year harmony and constancy of purpose; a republic of wisdom and benevolence, provider of fair justice and a high degree of toleration.[26]

This is a Venice which approaches a caricature of history when set against the corruptions detailed in Donald Queller's *The Venetian Patriciate* and Robert Finlay's *Politics in Renaissance Venice*, or the grasping, tyrannical, and often incompetent and unlucky oligarchy described in John Norwich's *A History of Venice*.[27] Venice was an aristocratic state in which (after half a millennium) political instruments were finally incorporated that secured its ruling class from self-destruction.[28]

In contrast to later revisionists, Cox immersed himself in the myth. But his purpose was equally subversive: he employed the narrative of the Venetian miracle to reconstruct a prototype of the capitalist social order from which America acquired its ideological nature and to discover the origins of the capitalist world system whose potentialities were now, he believed, near exhaustion. Cox's conception of the demise of capitalism involved the occurrence of a radical transformation. This, he felt, was capitalism's distinctive, characterological mode of historical existence. For unlike the previous great civilizations that had "tended to moulder away," capitalism would depart from this world as it had entered: "[T]his great cultural development did not begin by adopting the features of ancient Mediterranean civilization. It was something essentially new, worthy of being called an invention-in fact, an innovation in contravention to existing models" (*FC*, 14).

Cox understood that the social and cultural origins of Venice in the fifth century A.D. were to be traced to the fugitives displaced from the Italian mainland by the successive invasions of Huns, Goths, Lombards, and Franks. Among the refugees was "an extraordinary proportion from the upper classes" as well as the educated and skilled classes (*FC*, 31). Alienated from their native lands and feudal traditions ("she had no traditionally established form of social organization"), and installed in "an interstitial power zone" between the Eastern Roman Empire and the feudal powers of Lombardy, this exceptional community proceeded to construct a new social order and a new culture and to place them under the charge of a political system consistent with a trade economy (*FC*, 32–42).

Dependent upon foreign commerce, with the sea as their only resource, over the generations the Venetian settlers transformed the production and trade of salt into a vast capitalist empire extending from Constantinople to the northern Atlantic. And as Cox painstakingly recounts their cultural and ideological achievements – the republic's displacement of the tyranny of doges, the renunciation of the hereditary principle, the establishment of elected, accountable leadership, the domination by a capitalist oligarchy of the Great Council, the legislative and administrative bodies, the confluence of free commerce and religious tolerance, the migration of foreign capital and laborers to the metropole – he deliberately draws attention to the inheritance that links Venetian and American history. Early on he postulates that "these two societies are generically related to each other as the infant is to the mature man" (*FC*, 16). And later, he observes: "Here, then, was presented a situation which later has confronted virtually every leading capitalist nation-even down to the U.S. with its factious liberated colonies and then states' rights. The Venetian solution has been uniformly followed" (*FC*, 39).

Cox declares that Venice's supersession of the Eastern Empire in the thirteenth century signaled that historical moment when the capitalist "culture had become irreversible" (*FC*, 126). Capitalist culture and the imperialist system that sustained it would subsequently be diffused throughout western Europe. But Cox is just as resolute in suggesting that the certainty which marked the future of capitalism in the thirteenth century was no more real than the contingency that enveloped its birth during the preceding centuries:

> As we have attempted to show, there were many chance occurrences leading to the rise of the new form of social organization in Venice. This type of society was not derived logically from conditions following the fall of the Roman Empire in the West ... Venice was anomalous. It started with a relatively clean slate-new people, new area, new opportunities for innovation ... The Republic did not start by

wresting rights from an established ruling power; she had no charter, no merchant guild, no bourgeois revolution, no tyrant. (*FC*, 122–123)

From the thirteenth century, Venice provided the model of future capitalist societies. And from the fifteenth century, the myth of Venice would occupy a place of privilege in capitalist discourse. And that is what is precisely demonstrated in Huang's work.

THE VIEW FROM CHINA

Huang, "the outsider," retrieves the myth of Venice so that he may have a standard by which to dissect the failures of China's several ruling classes and their dynastic administrations. Approaching the capitalist system from the vantage point of an alternative world system ("Our view of the formation of capitalism in Europe is developed from the standpoint of China"),[29] Huang uses Venice as a model of imperial administration but not merely to expose the incompetencies of China's dynastic rulers and the malfeasance of their imperial bureaucracies. Much more importantly, Venice was a corroboration, an actual existing social order, that substantiated the cosmological (ideological) structure of Chinese imperial discourse: "All boiled down, capitalism was championed in the West with a degree of sweeping thoroughness akin to what the ancient Chinese writers put down as reaching a state of sincerity from a rectification of the mind, through which one's self can be cultivated and one's household unified, and ultimately what is under the heavens put in good order."[30] Venice was "mathematically manageable," and its success, the success of capitalism at its earliest stage, stemmed from "the constitutional simplicity of the state, not from its complexities."[31] This was precisely the contrary to what Huang encounters in his reconstruction of the late Ming dynasty. In Wan-li's court, ceremony and "pomp and grandeur" had fatally delimited "the number of practical problems that could be perceived, understood, analyzed, and discharged by our literary bureaucracy that governed many millions of peasants."[32] This devotion to ritual and obsession with form had been China's legacy for millennia.[33]

But Huang's own discursive loyalties are revealed in juxtapositions that in Western moral discourse would amount to conceptual dissonance. From the vantage point of Chinese imperialist discourse – which for instance might have to accommodate the recurrence of emperors dominated by eunuch "secretaries" or their own secret services.[34] Huang apparently experienced no discomfort in characterizing Venice as a democracy and a police state: "Venice's kind of democracy had not been installed to effect democracy for its own sake. It only happened that by maintaining a monolithic order, everything was mathematically manageable."[35] Even Frederic Lane, the "doge" of American historians of Venice and a principal proponent of the myth of Venice, took pains to distinguish the aristocratic republicanism of the city-state from the more democratic Florence.[36]

Huang is drawn to Venice "as an essential clue to our understanding of contemporary China"[37] because of his own ideological location in an imperialist world-system discourse. For Huang, as the histories of Venice, the Dutch Republic, and England demonstrated, "the West" had achieved a different "organizational order" characterized by a linear progression grounded on the nature of capitalism (wide extension of credit, impersonal management, the pooling of service facilities, the inviolability of property rights, and the domination of public life by private capital).[38] And those nations that had assimilated the "organizational principle of commerce" were destined to expose the superfluous mathematics that had informed Chinese administrative and political thought.[39] That confrontation of the two organizational orders was initiated during the nineteenth century.

CONCLUSION

Huang was persuaded that commerce was the most perfect principle upon which to base the rational administration of a massive social formation. The "organizational principle of commerce" could bring mathematical manageability to any nation, whether capitalist or socialist. On that score, Huang had every reason to be confident of an accord with Marx.[40] Huang believed that capitalism was a device for state management; Cox, on the other hand, comprehended that the state had been in the service of capitalism. Finally, Cox perceived in capitalism a world system incapable of overcoming its ideological needs; for him the principle of commerce logically led not to order but to exploitation and racism.[41] The important differences between Cox and Huang are not in respect to their reconstructions of Venice nor the formative development of capitalism, but in interpretation. They differ because Huang was embedded in a world-system discourse – albeit an alternative world system – and pursued its corrective in a more rational domain.

Cox struggled against such a discourse, confident of its repressive historical consequences ("the leadership of the system ... is still able to inflict appalling punishment upon any backward nation seeking to withdraw from the system").[42] and its seductive ideological tropes ("We may eliminate, as a matter of primary consideration, discontent among workers in the advanced countries. By and large, organized labor in the leading capitalist nations has been pro-capitalist; according to its continuous preachments, the 'slaves' reside in socialist countries"[43].) The critical dialectic was the world-systemic character of capitalism. The transformation would proceed from the system's periphery, the "satellite" nations, not from its stagnant metropoles. Ironically, then, it is Cox rather than Huang (or critics of capitalism like Marx or Wallerstein[44]) who may be more properly characterized as the "outsider."

NOTES

1. F. R. Ankersmit, "Historiography and Postmodernism," *History and Theory*, XXVIII, No. 2 (1989): 148.
2. The most recent casting of this mythical system has been conveniently abbreviated by Eric Wolf, *Europe and the People Without History* (Berkeley: University of California Press, 1982), 5:

   > We have been taught, inside the classroom and outside of it, that there exists an entity called the West, and that one can think of this West as a society and civilization independent of and in opposition to other societies and civilizations. Many of us even grew up believing this West has a genealogy, according to which ancient Greece begat Rome, Rome begat Christian Europe, Christian Europe begat the Renaissance, the Renaissance the Enlightenment, the Enlightenment political democracy and the industrial revolution. Industry, crossed with democracy, in turn yielded the U.S., embodying the rights to life, liberty, and the pursuit of happiness.

3. See Theodora Kroeber, *Ishi in Two Worlds: A Biography of the Last Wild Indian in North America* (Berkeley: University of California Press, 1976).
4. Ankersmit, "Historiography and Postmodernism," 149–150.
5. See Fredric Jameson, *The Political Unconscious: Narrative as a Socially Symbolic Act* (Ithaca: Cornell University Press, 1981).
6. Eric Cheyfitz, "*Tarzan of the Apes*: US Foreign Policy in the Twentieth Century," *American Literary History*, I, No. 2 (Summer 1989): 339–360.
7. In his most recent work, Davis has completed his exoneration of "the West" (begun with *The Problem of Slavery in Western Culture* [Ithaca: Cornell University Press, 1966] and *The Problem of Slavery in the Age of Revolution, 1770–1823* [Ithaca: Cornell University Press, 1975]) from responsibility for slavery by the transfer of the origins of *white* racism to Islam: "Ironically, by enslaving or converting so many blacks and by imposing a barrier to Europe's direct knowledge of sub-Saharan Africa, Muslims contributed to Christian ignorance, mythology, and the tendency to identify blacks with Christianity's mortal and 'infidel' enemy" (David Brion Davis, *Slavery and Human Progress* [New York: Oxford University Press, 1984], 39). This in no way accounts for intra-European racism; cf. Cedric J. Robinson, *Black Marxism: The Making of the Black Radical Tradition* (London: Zed, 1983), and Michael Hechter, *Internal Colonialism: The Celtic Fringe in British National Development* (Berkeley: University of California, 1975).
8. As an example, I refer you to the treatment of Eric Williams's *Capitalism and Slavery* (Chapel Hill: University of North Carolina Press, 1944); see Cedric J. Robinson, "Capitalism, Slavery and Bourgeois Historiography," *History Workshop* 23 (Spring 1987): 122–140.
9. Earlier, and in his first subversion, James's target had been the Eurocentrism of Marxism; see his *Black Jacobins* (New York: Dial Press, 1938).
10. After obtaining his doctorate (University of Chicago, 1938), Cox received appointments at Wiley (1938–1944), Tuskegee (1944–1949), Lincoln (1949–1970), and Wayne State (1970–1974). See the excellent introduction in *Race, Class, and the World System: The Sociology of Oliver C. Cox*, ed. Herbert H. Hunter and Sameer Y. Abraham (New York: Monthly Review Press, 1987).
11. Oliver C. Cox, *The Foundations of Capitalism* (New York: Philosophical Library, 1959), 19. Subsequent references to this work will be cited as *FC* in the text.
12. Ray Huang, "The Rise of Capitalism in Venice, the Dutch Republic, and England: A Chronological Sketch," *Chinese Studies in History*, XX, No. I (Fall 1986): 10.
13. Hunter and Abraham, *Race, Class, and the World System*, xxxiv; and Louis Harlan, *Booker T. Washington: The Wizard of Tuskegee, 1901–1915* (New York: Oxford University Press, 1983), 290–291.

14. Butler Jones, "The Tradition of Sociology Teaching in Black Colleges: The Unheralded Professionals," in *Black Sociologists: Historical and Contemporary Perspectives*, James Blackwell and Morris Janowitz, eds (Chicago: University of Chicago Press, 1974), 121–163.

15. Robert E. Park, "The Nature of Race Relations," in *Race Relations and the Race Problem, A Definition and an Analysis*, ed. Edgar T. Thompson (Durham: Duke University Press, 1939).

16. Cox, *FC*, 15:

> As a form of social organization, capitalism is constituted elementally by a peculiar economic order, government, and religious structure; and these, although mutually indispensable, are yet related to each other in descending order of importance. Economically, capitalism tends to form a system or network of national and territorial units bound together by commercial and exploitative relationships in such a way that a capitalist nation is inconceivable outside this capitalist system.

17. Cox, *Caste, Class, and Race: A Study in Social Dynamics* (New York: Monthly Review Press, 1970), 485–488.

18. Hunter and Abraham give Cox the credit for the development of the world-system perspective: "… in arguing that for a capitalist nation to dominate in the world capitalist system it had to maintain uneven patterns of development, Cox was introducing a world-system perspective that predated by at least a decade the work of Immanuel Wallerstein and his followers" ("Introduction," *Race, Class, and the World System*, xxviii). Cox seems to have formed the idea from his readings of Paul Sweezy and Leon Trotsky; see *Caste, Class, and Race*, 197, 201.

19. Cox, *Caste, Class, and Race*, 462.

20. Hunter and Abraham, "Introduction," *Race, Class, and the World System*, XXXV.

21. Cox, *Capitalism as a System* (New York: Monthly Review Press, 1964), 213–214.

22. Ibid., 218.

23. Ibid., 214.

24. Ibid.

25. For a treatment of Cox and Marxism, see Hunter and Abraham, "Introduction," *Race, Class, and the World System*, xxxix–xlv.

26. James Grubb, "When Myths Lose Power: Four Decades of Venetian Historiography," *Journal of Modern History* 58 (March 1986): 43–44.

27. Queller concludes: "We are burdened with the myth of the Venetian patriciate, in part, because sycophantic fifteenth- and sixteenth-century humanists, for whom, in any case, style was more important than truth, sought to win by flattery rewards that they professed could be gained in Venice only by virtue" (*The Venetian Patriciate: Reality Versus Myth*) [Urbana: University of Illinois Press, 1986], 249).

28. I refer to the dosing (the Serrata) of the Great Council in 1297, "the most crucial event in Venetian political history," according to Robert Finlay, *Politics in Renaissance Venice* (New Brunswick: Rutgers University Press, 1980), 41. See also Stanley Chojnacki, "In Search of the Venetian Patriciate: Families and Factions in the Fourteenth Century," in *Renaissance Venice*, J. R. Hale, ed. (Totowa, N.J.: Rowman and Littlefield, 1973), 47–90.

29. Huang, "Rise of Capitalism in Venice," 17.

30. Ibid., 16–17.

31. Ibid., 25.

32. Huang, *1587, A Year of No Significance: The Ming Dynasty in Decline* (New Haven: Yale University Press, 1981), 3.

33. Huang, *China: A Macro History* (Armonk, N.Y.: M. E. Sharpe, 1989), 16.

34. Huang, *1587, A Year of No Significance*, 21ff.

35. Huang, "Rise of Capitalism in Venice," 23.

36. Frederic C. Lane, "The Roots of Republicanism," in *Venice and History: The Collected Papers of Frederic Lane* (Baltimore: Johns Hopkins University Press, 1966), 530. Lane, it might be noted, was well aware of Cox's work, viz. his "Recent Studies on the Economic History of Venice," *Journal of Economic History* XXIII, No. 3 (September 1963): 312, n. 23, where he comments: "As the birthplace of capitalism, Venice has been assigned a leading role in a semi-Marxist scheme of world history."

37. Huang, *China*, 243.
38. Huang, "Rise of Capitalism in Venice," 32.
39. Ibid., 3, "When we turn to the pages of the 'Food and Money Monographs' of the Twenty-four Dynastic Histories, we shall run into accounts that the empire builders initiated schematic designs reminiscent of the Rituals of the Zhou to bring a civilian population in the hundreds of millions as well as military personnel in line. The device started from a mathematic formula with ideal perfection, which, of course, in no way corresponded to the actual conditions in the field."
40. Cf. Alvin Gouldner, chapter 5, *The Two Marxisms: Contradictions and Anomalies in the Development of Theory* (New York: Seabury Press, 1980).
41. Marxists continue to dispute this: "The first point about capitalism is that it is uniquely indifferent to the social identities of the people it exploits ... There is a positive tendency in capitalism to undermine such differences, and even to dilute identities like gender or race" (Ellen Meiksins Wood, "Capitalism and Human Emancipation," *New Left Review* 167 January–February 1988, 5–6).
42. Cox, *Capitalism as a System*, 240–241.
43. Ibid., 239.
44. Cf. Steve J. Stern, "Feudalism, Capitalism, and the World-System in the Perspective of Latin America and the Caribbean," *American Historical Review* 93, No. 4 (October 1988): 829–872.

CHAPTER 6

Fascism and the Intersections of Capitalism, Racialism, and Historical Consciousness

This essay explores the varying responses in the U.S. to the advent in the early 1920s of Fascism in Italy and the decade of Fascist expansionism which followed. The study transduces class, race, and ethnicity, configuring in the process the analyses of the State, capitalism, and ideology.

As we shall discover, the rise of Italian Fascism occasioned a militant opposition among the Black American masses. That reaction was a singular one. Put differently – and using a phrase applied at the beginnings of the Second World War – theirs was a "premature anti-fascism," not simply anticipating but contradicting the positions other significant elements in American society assumed toward a movement which gave primacy to the interests of the State as an instrument of racial "destiny."

When we review the advent of Fascism in the twentieth century and more particularly the construction of American anti-Fascist movements, we are compelled to note the vagaries of official historiography. It is also necessary to take into account the mischief to which historical memory is vulnerable. With respect to the support of or opposition to Fascism in America, much of our received knowledge, our official memory, is erroneous, the gap between actuality and reconstruction sometimes approaching the dimensions of a vast chasm. As we shall observe, the reasons for the shoddy reconstructions of these events are numerous, their implications and consequences momentous. Nevertheless, as we attempt a recapitulation of the "forgotten" moments of that terrible time, it will not be long before it becomes evident what some of the interests behind the obfuscation have been. It will be just as evident to where we might trace the dissemblers and who they were. This, indeed, is how I propose to begin and thus establish the context for the discussion of Afro-American reactions to Fascist movements at home and abroad.

MONEY AND FASCISM

For at least half of the period of the life of Fascist regimes in Europe – from the emergence of the first Fascist government in Italy in 1922 to the defeat of Fascist powers in the Second World War two decades later – some of the most powerful elements in America and a number of popular movements in this country were demonstrably if not frankly supportive of Fascism. In a work published in 1972, the American historian John Diggins detailed the praise extended to Mussolini and his state in the popular press and the organs of corporate and finance capital in this country. Diggins has also shown that such demonstrations of affection did not stop there. The sympathies which some business interests in this country held for Mussolini and his "Corporate State" assumed financial form. "The J. P. Morgan Company," for one, "lent over one-hundred million dollars to the Fascist government in 1926."[1] Jules Archer has gone even further, maintaining that elements of the Morgan interests (the assemblage of bankers, insurance companies, utilities, railroads, steel manufacturers, and mine-owners whose interests were interlocked by Morgan's machinations into a determinant power on Wall Street) actively pursued the imposition of a Fascist administration in the U.S. in the mid-1920s.[2] Within only slightly less important circles of American capitalists, James Pool and Suzanne Pool, among others, have reconstructed similar sympathies with German Fascism.[3]

Consequently, the prestigious *Fortune* magazine, in a 1934 issue devoted entirely to an analysis of the Italian state, was less heretical than (as its editors supposed) "enlightened" when it found similarities between Mussolini, Hoover, and Roosevelt on the necessities of centralized planning of the economy. Moreover,

> *Fortune* wondered whether universal Fascism would achieve in a few decades what Christianity achieved in ten centuries. The reader was warned to "beware of glib generalities" about Fascism and to recognize in it the rebirth of such "ancient virtues" as "Discipline, Duty, Courage, Glory, and Sacrifice." (Diggins, 163)

It appeared to many powerful American businessmen that fascism was the appropriate response to domestic labor activism, the international threat of the Soviet Union, and the destructive anarchy of monopoly capitalist production, trade, and finance made evident by the world depression.

The Luce publication, however, was not the only instance of the intervention on behalf of Fascism of powerful American interests in the various organs of journalism which they either owned or controlled. Though occasionally the *New York Times* published critical accounts of Mussolini's state by "guest" authors like H. G. Wells, James Shotwell, and Cesare Rossi (an Italian exile), its regular correspondents, Arnaldo Cortesi, Edwin L. James, Arthur Livingston,

Walter Littlefield, and Anne O'Hare McCormick, constructed a routine of celebration:

> Littlefield, for example, was one of several American reporters decorated by the Mussolini government; Cortesi ... was the son of a leading journalist in Mussolini's Italy; and McCormick was a devotee who rhapsodized upon the feats of the Blackshirts and consistently defended the twists and turns of Mussolini's diplomacy, justifying the Ethiopian invasion, the Italian "volunteers" in Spain, and the Rome-Berlin Axis. (Diggins, 25)

Earlier, Herbert Croly and Horace Kallen of the "liberal" *New Republic* had found similar virtues in the regime (227–231). Mussolini himself graced the pages of the *Saturday Evening Post* with a serialized "autobiography" written in fact by the American ambassador to Italy, Richard Washburn Child.[4] And there he joined other supporters of Italian Fascism which included the movie star/humorist Will Rogers and writers Isaac Marcosson, Kenneth Roberts, and Samuel Blythe. Many of the industrialists and publishers behind these newspapers – Ochs (the *Times*), Luce (*Fortune*), Straight (*New Republic*), Curtis (*Saturday Evening Post*) – were close to the Morgan interests.[5]

In the early years, taking its leads from such financial stalwarts as Thomas Lamont (of J. P. Morgan's banking interests), Otto Kahn (of Kuhn, Loeb and Co., the investment house), Judge Elbert Gary (chairman of U.S. Steel, a Morgan "trust"), and Henry Morgenthau and Julius Basche (Wall Street), the business press found much to its liking in the Fascist State: "Favorable editorials could be read in publications such as *Barron's*, *Journal of Commerce and Commercial Bulletin*, *Commerce and Finance*, *Nation's Business* ... and the reputable *Wall Street Journal*" (Diggins, 146). Less reputable, perhaps, but equally enthusiastic and influential were the William Randolph Hearst syndicate of newspapers and the *Chicago Tribune* (after the expulsion of George Sleds from Italy), published by Colonel Robert McCormick (International Harvester), who doubled as Director of the Associated Press.[6]

This treatment of Fascism by the American press would appear to confirm the argument that the emergence of Fascism was in accord with the interests of at least some major fractions of American capital.

The First World War had proven a magnificent boon to American financial institutions; even more so after the formal entry of the U.S. into the war. In early 1917, the Allied governments had owed nearly $1.5 billion to American bankers, but "during its participation in the war the U.S. lent to Europe $9,386,311,178 ..." (Lundberg, 141). But long before these events, American bankers gave evidence of an unbecoming excitement over the opportunities that the war provided and that certainly a long war would realize. In April 1915, Thomas Lamont, speaking before the American Academy of Political and

Social Science, dangled before his listeners the prospect of the U.S. becoming the financial center of the world:

> Shall we become lenders upon a really stupendous scale to these foreign governments? Shall we become lenders for the development of private or semipublic enterprises in South America and other parts of the world, which up to date have been commercially financed by Great Britain, France, and Germany? If the war continues long enough to encourage us to take such a position, and if we have the resources to grapple with it, then inevitably we shall become a creditor instead of a debtor nation, and ... the dollar ... the international basis of exchange. (Lundberg, 139–140)

Three years later, as we have seen, Lamont (and his associates) had effectively realized this vision. Moreover, "Net corporation profits for the period January 1, 1916, to July, 1921, when wartime industrial activity was finally liquidated, were $38,000,000,000," of approximately the amount of the [U.S. Government's] war expenditures" (Lundberg, 134). Diggins acknowledges that "During the war America surpassed Germany and England and became the chief exporter to Italy; Italy in turn became America's sixth best customer" (149). After the Fascists came to power, Dante Posella remarked, American companies rushed to share "in the business revival under the thoroughly level-headed Premier Mussolini" (149).

In Italy, the Fascist movement had from its very inception in 1914 been subsidized by major Italian industrialists, arms manufacturers, and landowners.[7] This alliance was foremost in the minds of some American observers during the turmoil of the 1930s. In his *Forerunners of American Fascism*, Raymond Swing would conclude: "... if fascism follows the precedent in Europe our fascists will combine with big business in a coalition."[8] And in his personal correspondence, William Allen White would darkly muse on "a vast pretense of socialism backed by Wall Street money ..."[9] That such concerns were justified was hesitantly confirmed by a special committee of the House of Representatives in 1935. Informed by the testimony of Major General Smedley D. Butler (retired) of "an attempt to establish a fascist organization in this country," the committee refused to publicly identify the sources of the considerable funds involved. It concluded, nevertheless: "There is no question but that these attempts were discussed, were planned, and might have been placed in execution when and if the financial backers deemed it expedient."[10] The timing of the conspiracy, Jules Archer suggests, had been mortally disrupted by General Butler's disclosures.[11] On the other hand, while purportedly chronicling the "politics of upheaval" which marked the depression era in America, Arthur Schlesinger Jr. apparently had found the whole affair too distasteful to pursue.[12]

ZIONISM AND FASCISM

A second source of political and public support for Mussolini and Italian Fascism was also to be obscured for those dependent upon American historical scholarship and literature of the post-war period. But from the mid-1920s, as late as the Italo-Ethiopian War of 1935–1936, and until the very eve of the doctrinal rapprochement between the Italian and German governments,[13] some prestigious and influential Zionist and Jewish leaders in Italy, America, and Palestine had exhibited open support for Mussolini. Furthermore, as Michael Ledeen comments: "By the middle of the 1930s Mussolini was the darling of European Zionists as well as a hero to most Italian Jews."[14] In short, it seems for the first twenty years of the Fascist movement in Europe and America, a relationship of convenience and to some extent of an identity of interests and doctrine existed between Jewish nationalists and the policies of the Italian State.

The approbation and collaboration of Zionist leaders and organizations with Italian Fascism was founded on a complex correspondence of political, historical, and ideological factors. Prominent among these were: the history of Italian Jews, particularly from the Napoleonic and *Risorgimento* periods; the antagonism of the Vatican toward Zionism and the unsteady alliance between the Church of Rome and the Fascist State; the conflicting imperial ambitions of Britain and Italy in the Mediterranean area; the shared doctrinal and racial theories of Zionism and Fascism; and the conflicts of interests between Fascist Italy and Nazi Germany which dominated the relations of the two states until 1936.

In 1946, in his authoritative work, *The History of the Jews of Italy,* Cecil Roth maintained that Zionism was "one of the oldest manifestations of Jewish life in the country."[15]

> When we first hear of the Roman Jewish community, before the beginning of the Christian era, we are informed that they were in the habit of sending their yearly tribute to the Temple in Jerusalem. Later on, in imperial times and throughout the Dark Ages, they had collected their oblations for the Palestinian schools ... Throughout the Middle Ages, and throughout the Ghetto period, the intercourse continued. We know more perhaps of Palestine pilgrims from Italy than from any other land ... among the eminent Gentile precursors of Zionism in the nineteenth century, there seemed nothing incongruous in his ideas in the eyes of the Italian Jews of the old school ... (518–519)

By the beginnings of the Fascist movement during the First World War, the small Italian Jewish population numbered between 20,000 and 40,000.[16] The Jewish communities (which might or might not include a substantially assimilated element and cross-faith marriages) tended by then to be clustered in Rome and the cities further north: Florence, Bologna, Leghorn, Milan, and

Trieste in the extreme east. Paradoxically to their ties with Jewish nationalism (at least at first impression), Italian nationalism had acquired strong support among Italian Jews from the moment when at the beginnings of the nineteenth century the emancipation of West European Jews came at the hands of the otherwise imperialist Napoleonic armies (Roth, 509; Ledeen, 278–279). In the second half of the century, the struggle against the monarchy and the political and property interests of the Church washed the cleaner and more republican waters of the French Revolution against the Italian peninsula.

One consequence of the victory of liberal, anti-clerical republicanism in Italy (and Spain) in the late nineteenth century was the revitalizing of Catholic "anti-Semitism." According to Daniel Carpi, the Catholic press (*La Voce della Verità, L'Avvenire, Unità Cattolica, Civiltà Cattolica*) from this period and well into the 1930s constructed a "history" of the decline of the Church of Rome which deeply implicated Jews and Jewry: they were the hidden force behind the French Revolution and the subsequent emancipation of the Jews in Western Europe; the dominant interests in the commercial-capitalist economy which replaced agrarian-feudalism from the nineteenth century on; the basis for the materialism which had inundated European values and Western culture; the race "permeated with a revolutionary and rebellious spirit" which had eventually given rise to Bolshevism and Freemasonry; and of course they were the "murderers" of the Lord.[17] As a result, a generally sympathetic Pope Pius X reportedly told Theodor Herzl in 1904 that Zionist ambitions in the Holy Lands were out of the question: "The Jews have not recognized our Lord, therefore we cannot recognize the Jewish people" (47). In Italy, other representatives of the Catholic intelligentsia charged that the Jews had made slaves of Mazzini, Garibaldi, Cavour, Farmi, and De Pretis, the heroes of the-nationalist movement. As Catholic ideologues they insisted, in Carpi's words, that the Church assume, as the vanguard of the reaction and in defense of the Christian world, "the exalted divine task to segregate the Jews from the rest of the population ..." (45).

In the face of such sustained hostility it was natural that the revolutionary nationalism which Fascism embraced in its earliest stage would attract many Jews. Indeed, Italian Jews were among the architects of the movement. Roth recounted (509): "Half a dozen of them collaborated in its foundation, at least three were among the 'martyrs, who gave their lives on its behalf in its earliest period of struggle, and were subsequently interred in its grandiose shrines." Michael Ledeen asserts (281): "In 1922 there were nearly 750 Jews in the Fascist party; by 1928 an additional 1770 would enlist; by 1933 yet another 4800." But despite their prominence in the movement and later in the Fascist State, their influence could not deter what in retrospect seems to have been the inevitable conjoining of Mussolini's profound but frequently disguised racialism with the destructive currents of Western culture. These were to achieve their fullest fruition in Nazi Germany but not without affecting Italy.

Mussolini's association with Italian Jews had been both personal and organizational. His first biographer, the wealthy Milanese, Margherita Sarfatti, was also his "mistress" (a relationship which only ended with the introduction of racial laws in Italy in 1938). Aldo Finzi, a militarist and party enforcer, had joined the Fascist government as an assistant minister of interior; Guido Jung would serve as finance minister for a number of years; Carlo Foa and Sarfatti edited the Fascist review, *Gerarchia*.[18] His more enduring concern with Italian and European Jewry, however, was as an instrument of Italian expansion in the Mediterranean and East Africa. To Mussolini, most useful of all was the access Italian Jewry provided to Zionist organizations.

Mussolini's official attempts at rapprochement with Zionist leaders had begun almost immediately upon his assumption of government leadership: one month after his accession to power, he informed Angelo Sacerdoti, the Chief Rabbi of Rome, of his opposition to anti-Semitism; three weeks later, on December 20, he met with Zionist leaders, who pledged their loyalty to Italy and their readiness to act as agents of the Italian State through Jewish communities in the Levant; two weeks later, on January 3 of the following year, Mussolini met with Chaim Weizmann, president of the World Zionist Organization, and discussed Palestine, Zionist dependency on Britain, and the mutual interests of Zionists and Fascists in the subversion of Muslim power in the Mediterranean.[19]

In February 1928, Mussolini established the Italy-Palestine Committee (Michaelis, 10). This move was one of a series following meetings the two previous years. Lucien Steinberg remarked:

> Zionist leaders such as Chaim Weizmann, Nahum Sokolov and Nahum Goldmann were all received by him at one stage or another … [t]he Zionist-Revisionists, led by Vladimir Jabotinski … received official backing to establish a college in Italy for the purpose of training cadets for the navy of the future Jewish State, and this school was able to function right up to 1937.[20]

For the next several years, Mussolini maintained a posture consistent with his declarations to Weizmann and Sacerdoti: "You must create a Jewish state. I myself am a Zionist" (Ledeen, 292). Roth succinctly summarized:

> while at home the Fascist attitude towards the Jews was one of somewhat stiff cordiality, it was actively, and even pugnaciously benevolent towards their coreligionists abroad. This was especially the case as regards those of the Mediterranean basin, who were considered useful agents for the diffusion of Italian influence … (514)

Mussolini's long-term strategy was to employ Zionist organizations to "destabilize" the British mandate of Palestine and to enlist Jewish communities in Libya and East Africa (Italian Somalia and later Ethiopia) in the "pacification" of colonized populations. This was the design behind the policy which allowed German Jews refuge in Italy; which encouraged Jews from Central Europe to enroll in Italian institutions of higher education (as Jabotinski had years earlier); which arranged the transfer of a rabbinic school from Germany to Fiume; which tempered expressions of anti-Semitism at home; and which provided recognition to the leaders of international Zionism. Privately, though, Mussolini mused about Italian racial superiority and bemoaned the fact that "Levantine" elements in the Italian population "could not be exterminated."[21] On this score at least, according to Nissim Rejwan and others, the European Zionists concurred. Herzl, Jabotinski, Ben-Gurion, and many other leading Eurocentric Zionist activists held "Levantine" Jews and their Arab "cousins" in equal contempt.[22] But while Mussolini had insisted publicly that the racial question only applied to "colored subject peoples," his son-in-law and Foreign Minister, Galeazzo Ciano, noted in his diaries Mussolini's private disgust for America: ... country of niggers and Jews, the forces which disintegrate civilization" (Michaelis, 36).

In the U.S., the more benign facade of Italian Fascism disciplined conservative Jewish leadership. Diggins maintained that "during the twenties the synagogues remained relatively silent on the Fascist question" (202). And later,

> In the fall of 1933, editors of forty-three American Jewish publications took a poll to select twelve Christians who "have most vigorously supported Jewish political and civil rights and who have been the most outstanding in their opposition to anti-Semitism." Mussolini was one of the twelve ... he appeared to American Jews a most welcomed defender of the faith. (202–203)

Even with the invasion of Ethiopia in 1935, "American Jewry as a whole did not denounce Italian Fascism ..." (302).

For similar reasons the Federation of Italian Jewish Communities, "on the advice and at the invitation of a high-ranking Jewish officer of the Italian navy, and in agreement with the highest political authorities of the Fascist regime, at the end of 1935 sent a mission to London ... with the aim of exercising a moderating influence vis-a-vis the British government in view of the impending sanctions threatening Italy."[23] It was a last desperate attempt to deflect Mussolini from his racialist intuitions. But coterminous with his adventures in Africa and then in Spain, he had become convinced that a "Jewish-Plutocratic-Masonic clique" opposed him. Despite the public support the Zionist Revisionists had given to Italian imperialism in Africa (it appears that among Jewish nationalists, the Revisionists showed the strongest tendencies and sympathies for fascism) and the less public demonstrations of approval by the other representatives of the Zionist movement, the political potential of European Jews could not compete with the other alternatives available to Mussolini.[24] Diplomatically isolated from his other European neighbors, he now sought "to dispel German doubts about Italian loyalties."[25] From this period on, the fates of Jews in Italy would rapidly descend into a pseudo-Germanic cage of repression.[26]

It is only an apparent irony, then, that two elements of American society which would make special claims of the events of the Second World War – American capital and American Jewry – had assumed enabling postures toward one of the totalitarian states whose ambitions and ideology precipitated the conflagration. During and after the war, American industry would celebrate its part in the massive undertaking of war production and planning which provided the material basis for victory. Much less, however, would be made of the financial, industrial, commercial, and political support extended to Fascist Italy and later Nazi Germany.[27] After the war, American historiography and social theory tended to diminish if not entirely obliterate these relationships, offering in their stead as Ernst Nolte would complain, studies of the "authoritarian personality" or the "charismatic mass leader."[28] For American Jews, and particularly the Zionists, the seductions of Mussolini's support swayed judgment; for other Jews not in the Zionist cause, Fascism had other attractions.

CATHOLICS, THE ITALIAN-AMERICANS, AND THE FASCIST MOVEMENT

America held, however, other sources of support for Fascism which were either less concerned with disguising their efforts or less capable of influencing the analytical and historical reconstructions of the "age of dictators." These constituted the main demagogic and social bases for American Fascism.

Among the demagogues, perhaps the most prominent was Father Charles Coughlin, the parish priest. His broadcasts over the radio station WJR in Detroit (a station owned by the *Detroit Free Press,* that is, Edward Stair of Graham-Paige Motors, the Detroit Trust Company, First National Bank of Detroit, and the Ann Arbor Railroad), which began in 1926, would constitute the most popular program in the early history of American broadcasting-outdistancing in audience even *Amos and Andy.* A contemporary observer Herbert Flarris remarked:

> When Roosevelt defeated Hoover, Father Coughlin bad achieved national renown. He was a force to be reckoned with in American public life. He was widely quoted in the press; and as a valiant supporter of the New Deal he participated in White House councils ...
>
> ... Out of the depression's insecurity and discontent, he has formed what some believe may become the most potent political pressure-group ever to appear on the

American scene. Certainly no other American wields such complete control over his followers.[29]

In the mid-1930s Coughlin, who initially may well have tapped into the older American populist tradition as Victor Ferkis was to suggest, passed on to a fervent belief in Fascism.

> By 1936 even corporatism seemed too timid a compromise with the forces of evil. Instead of the collaboration of capital and labor, he demanded a complete purge of all money lenders ... when Mussolini was criticized in 1938 for adopting the German pogrom, Coughlin leaped to his defense. He appealed personally to Il Duce, asking the dictator to write for his weekly, *Social Justice*, an article "in which you can clarify your attitude toward the Jews ..." (Diggins, 183)

Also by 1938, Coughlin was maintaining that "Hitler and the fascists were 'the champions, of Christian social order against the forces of anti-Christian chaos,'" and by 1940 suggesting that "it would be better for the world that Germany should win the war rather than the Allies."[30] His disgust at banking, mass production, and capitalist greed had by accident and through the self-seductive powers of broadcasting transformed first into anti-communism and then into its herald, Fascism.[31]

Coughlin's base was the Catholic Church in America and its generally pro-Fascist ecclesiastical hierarchy. His was an important voice among a chorus of Catholic clergy, politicians (e.g., Al Smith, Joseph Kennedy, and James Curley), lay writers, and the newspapers and journals of the Catholic press.[32] These complemented his popularity, adding a social element which, though religiously circumscribed, substantiated his claims of a magnitude of influence superior to his contemporary but more secular rivals, Huey Long and Rev. Gerald K. Smith. But Coughlin was an Irish-Catholic. The more formidable source of American Fascism was the population of Italian-Americans.

By the beginnings of the Second World War, there were approximately 4.5–5 million Italians and Italian-Americans living in the U.S. Of these, the Italian exile Gaetano Salvemini estimated in political terms, "50 percent were indifferent, 10 percent anti-Fascist, 5 percent Fascist, while the remaining 35 percent comprised a nucleus of people 'with a mentality which has not yet clearly become Fascist and anti-democratic but which might crystallize at the first emergency'" (Diggins, 107). A not inconsiderable, or surprising number when one recalls that by 1940, a Fascist presence had been a part of the Italian-American community for nearly twenty years – predating, indeed, the March on Rome.

As was the case in Italy itself, one of the origins of Italian-American Fascism was the Italian Left which had been so violently shaken in its intellectual and politico-ideological traditions by the "slaughter of workers" during the

First World War. The vision of an international workers' movement which had informed Italian anarcho-syndicalism as well as the First and Second Communist Internationals had been shattered by the national confrontation of workers on the battlefields of Europe. Moreover, Italian national pride had plummeted because of war defeats, the post-war humiliations at Versailles, and a national economy which required millions of Italians to emigrate to the new world. Finally, once in their new "homelands" the Italian immigrants became too frequently the targets of racial arrogance and discrimination.

In the years immediate to the close of the First World War, immigration quotas designed specifically to limit further Italian immigration to the U.S. were enacted by Congress. But "so eager were Italians to get into the U.S., despite its hostility to them, that thousands rushed across the Atlantic before the new quotas went into effect."[33] "Commonly" accepted as an inferior race in a period when public discussions of sterilization would soon result in official policy (e.g., in California), when wealthy families like the Kelloggs and Harrimans assumed the role of financial patrons to the Eugenics Records Office and other racial schemes, the specter of the crush of Italian immigrants at the ports of entry merely further excited the "nativists" and their congressional agents. The quota enacted in 1921 had reduced the number of Italian immigrants to 42,000; the law signed by President Coolidge in 1924 radically reduced that figure to just over 3800. By that point, however, 1,790,000 persons of Italian birth were legally residing in the country. Nevertheless,

> Demographers and sociologists pointed out that the law's thinly veiled bigotry could only insult, humiliate, and anger those people it excluded, or virtually excluded, such as Italians. (DeConde, 179)

Since Italian-American Fascism made its first appearance while these public controversies were raging, this did appear to be the case. Diggms, for example, would conclude (80–81):

> Pressures both external and internal, then, left Italian-Americans ripe for Fascism. A nascent inferiority complex, a nostalgic nationalism, and a fear for family solidarity and community produced a quiet but true collective anxiety. Inasmuch as Fascism was an answer to these psychic tensions, the Italian-American reaction to it was more a socially conditioned reflex than a politically conscious response.

Again, however, there is strong evidence to support the notion that the phenomenon of Italian-American Fascism was not entirely spontaneous.

During this period much of the Italian population in the U.S. was naturally restricted to Italian as its primary language. The majority was drawn from this "second" wave of Italian immigration. Unlike their mid-nineteenth-century predecessors, this group clustered in urban ghettoes in the northeast and the west and small towns in contiguous agricultural regions and were largely dependent upon Italian-language newspapers and broadcasts.[34] These, in turn, were controlled by the *prominenti*, individuals like Generoso Pope, president of the Colonial Sand and Cement Co. and publisher of *Il Progresso Italo-Americano*, in New York; and, in San Francisco, A. P. Giannini (Bank of America) and the members of the Di Giorgio family (Di Giorgio Fruit Corp./Del Monte), who dominated *L'Italia* and *La Voce del Popolo*.

> In terms of circulation and financial resources the pro-Fascist press was far more important than its adversary. In New York, for example, the readership of the pro-Fascist papers outnumbered the opposition about ten to one. Newspapers sympathetic to Mussolini reflected upper-class, conservative sentiments, and they enjoyed the advertising support of large restaurants and wineries as well as manufacturers and bankers. (Diggins, 83)

The *prominenti* were more than opinion leaders, of course. As *Padroni* they had provided most of the organization for the labor recruitment which in practical terms orchestrated the second Italian immigration to America. The fees which they collected as labor contractors for American manufacturers, viticulturalists, and other interests had for many constituted the financial base which in turn allowed them to lend capital to immigrants: to support the transport of family members and inevitable costs of resettlement and survival (DeConde, 85–88). Though a few like Giannini and Pope would acquire real standing and power which rivaled the wealthiest American families, most *prominenti* remained as brokers between capital and labor (Lundberg, 40). Moreover, as the primary sponsors of organizations like the Sons of Italy, the Ex-Combattenti Society, the Fascist League of North America, the Dante Alighieri Society, and the Italian Historical Society, the *prominenti* would perform important roles as agents of the Fascist government of Italy.[35] Their capacities to orchestrate information were made abundantly clear in the 1935–1936 crisis:

> ... in the United States the campaign against Ethiopia was started as soon as the incident of Wal-Wal [December 1934] had been engineered. Most Italian language papers and all radio commentators, an army of lecturers in the English and Italian languages, all priests of the Catholic-Fascist denomination, servile correspondents from Rome, Paris and London, methodically indoctrinated day in and day out, in the course of 1935, the population of Italian origin in this country to the effect that "Mussolini was always right."[36]

The extent of the involvement of Italian authorities in the affairs of the Italian-American community is indicated by the close direction Mussolini, his

Foreign Affairs Minister Dino Grandi, and the Italian Ambassador to the U.S., Giacomo de Martino, assumed in the management and control of the Italian-language newspapers; Italian-language schools for Italian-American children;[37] and the surveillance and intervention of political activities by Italian immigrants and intervention of political activities by Italian immigrants and Italian-American citizens. In 1927 Salvemini had gotten a foretaste of the depth of the Italian government's (and its American friends') attention to anti-Fascist activities in this country. One day after his arrival in January in the U.S., the Foreign Policy Association organized a debate with Thomas Lamont, who denounced Salvemini's opposition to American, loans to Italy as irresponsible. Having already failed in its attempts to get the State Department to deny Salvemini the right to enter the country, and apparently not entirely satisfied with Lamont's performance, the Italian government then arranged a second debate with the Foreign Policy Association in April. There Salvemini was attacked for his lack of patriotism by Bruno Rosselli of Vassar College and then Count Ignazio Thaon di Revel.[38]

> In 1928 the *Nation* published an article on "Fascist Blackmail" based upon the "scores" of letters it had received from Italian workers in the industrial towns of the Northeast. The workers and their wives were warned by consular officials that unless their anti-Fascist activities ceased they would receive unpleasant news about their families back home ... The complaints eventually led to a demand for a Congressional investigation. (Diggins, 102)

When the House Un-American Activities Investigation Committee got around to inquiring into such charges in 1937–1938, the weight of testimony and documentary evidence was overwhelming. Agents of the Italian government were actively intimidating immigrants and Italian Americans. Even earlier, in 1934, some Italian consular officials had been "recalled home" as a result of State Department action (Diggins, 102–104).

But in general, the Roosevelt administration, sensitive to the numbers of Italian-American voters in its Tammany machine and other Democratic ghetto strongholds, and wary of the extent to which the *prominenti* were financially dependent upon its big business opponents, largely downplayed the extent of Fascist activity and propaganda in this country.[39] Even when Italy invaded Ethiopia in 1935, Roosevelt was willing to settle for a "moral embargo" on trade involving both countries, though he knew as well as everyone else in the government that such an act would work to the disadvantage of Ethiopia rather than Italy.[40] His second presidential campaign loomed in the near future (1936) and anything less than "neutrality" might cost him the election. He was no less cautious in 1936 when Italian "volunteers" appeared in the Spanish Civil War. According to Gabriel Jackson, Roosevelt, Claude Bowers, the American

Ambassador to Madrid, and Secretary of State Cordell Hull all favored complete noninvolvement.[41] But,

> On January 11 [1937] the government tried to inhibit the enlistment of Americans in the International Brigade by ruling American passports invalid for travel in Spain ... Thus it may be said that government-approved American participation in the Spanish Civil War in 1937 amounted to volunteer medical aid, most of which went to the Republicans, and to the sale of oil and trucks, most of which went to ... the Nationalists.[42]

With the clamor of the pro-Fascist Italian-American press and the sound of the radio priest's denunciations of neutrality acts and war sanctions ("Coughlin sided with Italy. 'After all,' he informed millions of listeners, 'Italy has at least some slight justification for her movement into Ethiopia At least Italy can truthfully charge that her territory already existing in Algeria [sic] has been invaded at least ninety times by the Ethiopians.'"[43]) resounding around him, the best Roosevelt and his political advisors could manage was political cynicism:

> ... for a while, at least, the administration gave thought to a proposal to counter the political influence of the Italian-Americans with Negro pressure, mainly by asking black groups to agitate for discriminatory embargoes against Italy. (DeConde, 221)

The Black response to Fascism, however, required little of the official encouragement or the manipulation by capital and its *prominenti* which characterized the "spontaneous" Italian-American Fascist movement.

THE BLACK RESPONSE TO THE ETHIOPIAN CRISIS

The racial hostility which had greeted Irish and Italian immigrants when they arrived in the U.S. in the nineteenth century and early twentieth century had, of course, been the unrelieved experience of Black Americans from the beginnings of the nation in the colonial era of the mid-seventeenth century. The three groups, too, shared a long history of racial violence; indeed, their dramatic translocations as emigrants from Ireland, Italy, or the deep South were immediately precipitated by periods of mass and lethal brutalities. So, too, did they share the symptoms which accompany long economic depressions: social degradation, cultural anguish, and physical debilitation. In a sense, the World Depression which in the 1920s and 1930s clawed at the securities and identities of white middle-class Americans was a too familiar terrain. And like Blacks, Italians, and the Irish poor of American were subject to lynchings, mob violence, and the most acute forms of exploitation.[44] Unlike Blacks in America, however, the Irish and the Italians could under certain circumstances take refuge in a putative racial superiority. As "Americans," for many of them it was their sole form of social mobility in the first half of the twentieth century. On the other hand, as "whites" they might also indulge in militant nationalisms: Irish, Italian, or American.

For ordinary Black men and women, the question of an historical identity was more complex. Certainly in general, Afro-Americans fixed on Africa as their historical place of origin, but the more profound and pervasive mass consciousness was as an oppressed people. The vernacular of Black Christianity provided symbols of identification with the Biblical Hebrews or the designation Ethiopians. These psychocultural materials assumed great prominence in Afro-American culture and subsequently its intellectual traditions:

> Black writing is replete with references to Ethiopia's legacy. The brilliant pan-Africanist Edward Wilmot Blyden (1832–1912) called the Ethiopians of antiquity "the most creditable of ancient peoples" and claimed that they had achieved "the highest rank of knowledge and civilization." J. A. Rogers, the lecturer, columnist, traveler, and chronicler of Negro achievements, asserted categorically that the Ethiopian royal family was the "most ancient lineage in the world." He maintained further that at least eighteen rulers of ancient Egypt were "unmixed" Negroes or Ethiopians. And W. E. B. DuBois wrote of Ethiopia as the "sunrise of human culture" and the "cradle of Egyptian civilization."[45]

"Ethiopia," then confluent with the notion of Africa, became a most ancient point of reference, a term signifying historicity and racial dignity in ways the term "Negro" could not match. Since the same symbolic complex appeared in the spiritual traditions of Afro-West Indians, it is understandable that the strength and significance of Ethiopia would grow when Afro-American and Afro-West Indian militants conjoined. Such was true of the Universal Negro Improvement Association (UNIA), whose organizational and ideological character reflected its West Indian origins and its North American experience. The UNIA's "anthem of the Negro race" was "Ethiopia, Thou Land of Our Fathers." Here again Ethiopia signified Africa as a whole.[46] And Ethiopia's importance to those in the Diaspora was enhanced by its objective status as one of the three independent Black nations.

Still, the most proximate "national" identification for Afro-Americans was not in Africa, but in the Caribbean: Haiti. Since its successful revolution at the end of the eighteenth century, Haiti had also occupied a celebratory place in Afro-American consciousness. Harvey Wish has recounted how the Haitian slave revolution inspired the insurrection led by Gabriel Prosser in 1800;[47] Arna Bontemps and Jack Conroy have recalled that among the Black emigrationists in the mid-nineteenth century, there existed a Haiti faction which "is credited with directing two-thousand settlers to that country ...";[48] and Ira Berlin records the prominence of Haiti in some of the holidays celebrated by free Blacks before the Civil War:

> In 1825, Baltimore free Negroes met at the house of a leading African Methodist minister to celebrate Haitian independence. William Watkins, the orator for the day, praised the rise of the black republic and declared it "an irrefutable argument to prove ... that the descendants of Africa never were designed by their Creator to sustain an inferiority, or even a mediocrity, in the chain of being ..." In 1859, St. Louis masons rented a train to take them into the countryside to commemorate the abolition of slavery in Saint Domingue.[49]

And the memory of Haiti had been preserved in other ways: Martin Delaney had named one of his children for Toussaint L'Ouverture and another for Faustin Soulouque, a Haitian emperor.[50]

The significations of the slave revolution in Haiti had not escaped the plantation society of the U.S. any more than they did the French and British ruling classes. Together these interests and their heirs strove to isolate Haiti politically and economically for much of the nineteenth century.[51] Of course international hostility merely exacerbated and manipulated the internal social and economic conflicts of that country so that after a century of independent Black rule Haiti was a "proper" model for colonized "natives" and their too ambitious "elites." Its government was dominated by a corrupt, racially elite caste, its economy characteristically exploitative and marginally subsistent. In 1915, Haiti was occupied by American Marines. It would be governed by American authorities for the next nineteen years. To a certain extent, this occupation served as the setting for the anti-Fascist movement among Afro-Americans. Complemented by the increased racial violence of the post-First World War period, the dislocations of the northern migrations, the Depression's aggravation of an already severe economic condition, the suppression of the mass-based UNIA, and rumblings of imperialist ambitions in Liberia,[52] this event pushed the mass of Afro-Americans and others of the African diaspora beyond the moderating intervention of established Black leadership.

The American occupation of Haiti was one of the first of the several political events in the twentieth century which dramatically exposed the differing senses of interest held by the Black middle class and the Black masses.

Brenda Gayle Plummer, one of the closest and most recent students of the American occupation of Haiti, has asserted: "Aside from the handful of intellectuals who gloried in Haiti's revolutionary past and in the unique culture of its people, most blacks looked upon the occupation as a logical consequence of that country's chronic political turbulence. Others shuddered at the lurid accounts of voodoo that frequently appeared in the popular press."[53] But as Plummer reveals in her research, this ambivalence seemed more characteristic of the Black middle class and its spokesmen than of the Black lower classes.

For the former, the occupation of Haiti was not entirely unrelated to their own ambitions: "As Harding had used the Haitian issue to appeal to black voters for support, many blacks believed that he would democratize decision making on Haiti to allow them to participate in running that country" (134). Thus, though W. E. B. DuBois immediately opposed the occupation in the pages of *The Crisis*, he did not speak for others in the NAACP executive board like James Weldon Johnson; nor did DuBois reflect the interests of career State Department figures like Lemuel Livingston (thirty-two years as consul in Cap Haitien), who at first depicted the Marines as "benefactors"; Robert Russa Moton, president of Tuskegee Institute; or Napoleon Marshall, who accepted an appointment as clerk in the treaty administration.

On the other hand, the more militant mass organization, the UNIA, whose membership contained an important fraction of West Indian immigrants to the U.S., denounced the occupation from the moment of its own inception and until the Haitian people were allowed to return to "self-rule" in 1934. The Black nationalism of the UNIA had little room for accommodating the special interests displayed by Black established leadership. In its opposition, it was joined by other volunteer organizations like the Abyssinian Baptist Church (Harlem); the Harlem Refuge Church of Christ; the National Sunday School and Baptist Youth Progressive Union Congress; and groups associated with the American Communist Party.[54] Inevitably, the established Black leadership was pushed from accommodation to protest and eventually to opposition:

> The spirit of the times made Haiti an important issue to blacks. The timing of the occupation was especially significant. The Bloody Summers of 1918 and 1919, the agitation for a federal anti-lynching bill, and the rise of militant nationalism put racism matters at the forefront. Black Americans perceived the Haitians as related to themselves, and increasingly admired the Haitian tradition of resistance to servitude and fierce independence, it is therefore not surprising that the Haitian issue was featured prominently by the NAACP. (Plummer, 131)

Still, by the time the moderate Race leaders had put opposition to the occupation of Haiti on their agenda, it had become clear to the masses of Blacks that the more responsible resistance to oppression would have to be generated from within their own ranks.

The point was perhaps brought home again in the late 1920s and early 1930s by the public charges in Britain and the U.S. that slavery was officially sanctioned in Liberia. With its government being dominated by Afro-Liberians, the social equivalents of their own petit-bourgeois leaders, it was difficult for many working-class Blacks in the Diaspora not to feel a deep resentment toward a stratum whose greed identified it with the hated plantocrats of earlier centuries and betrayed Liberia to the racist ambitions of twentieth-century imperialists.[55]

Finally, it is important to recall the part Black leadership played in the dismantling of the UNIA. An organization which had achieved unprecedented support from the Black working classes particularly in the U.S. during the mid-1920s, the UNIA had come under attack from both the State and most of the spokespersons for the Black middle classes. Here again, the Black masses were witnesses to the spectacle of collusion between private (e.g., the Firestone Rubber, Company) and public power (the trial of Marcus Garvey) and those who presumed to speak for the Black community.[56] The Italian invasion of Ethiopia, then, came on the heel of a succession of events which had effectively alienated the mediating stratum of the Black petite bourgeoisie from the bulk of Black people.

The very global character of the Black response to the invasion of Ethiopia provides support for the interpretation that it was largely spontaneous. In the U.S., mass rallies and support activities were reported in Chicago (the Negro World Alliance); New York (the Provisional Committee for the Defense of Ethiopia and the African Patriotic League); Miami (the Ethiopian Relief League); Fort Worth; Okmulgee, Oklahoma; Washington, D.C.; and Mobile (Friends of Ethiopia).[57] Letters of outrage to Black newspapers like the *Chicago Defender*, the *Pittsburgh Courier*, the *Amsterdam News*, and the *Baltimore Afro-American* were penned by Black men and women in settlements of varying size from all over the nation. Elsewhere, 100 Liberian, Ovambo, and Karro dockworkers in Southwest Africa refused to work on Italian ships; in Kenya, the Kikuyu Central Association enlisted volunteers for the campaign in Ethiopia; Egyptian doctors reported to Addis Ababa; and hundreds of West Indians from British Guiana, Cuba, and Trinidad to the Bahamas requested permission from their colonial authorities to enlist in the armies of Ethiopia.[58] In Chicago, the mass enthusiasm for enlistment in the defense forces of Ethiopia was such that Robert Abbott, the publisher of the *Chicago Defender*, found it necessary to publicly oppose such efforts three months before the actual Italian invasion:

> Don't do it, young men and women. There is too much for you to do at home! You in Dallas, Tex., who are enlisting to fight for Ethiopian independence – do you think you have independence at home? You in Miami, Fla., who in fiery words declare that Ethiopia must be kept free – do you think you are free? You, in New York and in Chicago, who have worked yourselves into a frenzy over the plight of Haile Selassie and his empire in Northern Africa [sic] – do you suppose your conditions are any better than those of the warriors of Ethiopia? If you think these things, you think without reason.[59]

Nevertheless, in Chicago, as St. Clair Drake and Horace Cayton would record:

> When the Italian legions invaded Ethiopia, the barbershops and streetcorners of the Black Belt buzzed with indignation. Haile Selassie became something of a hero to Negroes all over America. A resident of Black Metropolis [John C. Robinson]

journeyed to Addis Ababa to become the pilot of the royal family's personal airplane: his exploits were followed with interest … and in a confused, semi-superstitious sort of way people in Black Metropolis were given to prophesying that those who had sold Ethiopia out would eventually find themselves menaced by the Fascists.[60]

In turn, when the war did break out in October 1935, Abbott's paper, like all Afro-American papers in the country, followed events closely, heralding Ethiopian victories (factual and imaginary) and the eventual defeat of its armies.[61] He did not, however, succumb to voluntarism. He made that clear once again in October when he published a long interview with the Paris representative of the Ethiopian emperor headlined: "Vast Expenses Make Use of American Volunteers Impractical in Ethiopian Army."[62]

The American Communist Party was also less than totally supportive of the more militant activities of Blacks wishing to go to Ethiopia's aid. Though the Communist Party gave organizational support to public demonstrations and clothing and medical relief campaigns, it did not encourage enlistment activities.[63] The following year, with the outbreak of the Spanish Civil War, this no longer was the case. Indeed, many of the Blacks who eventually fought in Spain with the Abraham Lincoln Battalion would indicate that one of their primary motivations was to strike a blow at Mussolini. Ordinary Black workers like James Yates or professionals like the Black nurse Salaria Kea went to Spain as Black men and women and as anti-Fascists.[64] Their resolve mirrored that of Mrs. Wimley Thompson of Gallup, New Mexico. She wrote Abbott in response to his editorial opposing enlistment:

> One must remember that we didn't come into this country on our own accord, so why should we battle for something we will never receive? Justice. Ethiopia is our country and as long as there is blood in our veins we should love and respect it as such …
>
> Let every heart within a black man's body be with Ethiopia, the country which is ours.[65]

Thus in the face of a long flirtation with fascism in the American press, and the open support of Mussolini by powerful fractions of capital, elements of the international Zionist movement, proto-Fascist American demagogues like Father Coughlin, and Fascist Italian American groups, ordinary Black workers in the U.S., the West Indies, East, West, and Southern Africa mobilized in support of Ethiopia. This racial solidarity extended to Blacks on the Left who possessed reservations about the political and social character of the Selassie regime; and to those who had been disappointed by reports (not entirely attributable to Italian propaganda) that the royal family entertained an ambivalent racial identity. Ethiopia was important enough to them to absorb these contradictions, particularly in the face of the recent aggressions against Haiti and the evident designs of Western powers on Liberia. For many if not most Blacks, the historical significance of fascism was clear: at home it foreshadowed the descent of liberalism and even the faint suggestion of racial tolerance; elsewhere it meant the destruction of even the symbols of racial liberation.

Stung by the co-option of much of their leadership in the business of domination and exploitation, and effectively abandoned by the Left and the enlightened faction of American capital, they withdrew to their own council. With an immediacy which can only be understood as the result of imminent political consciousness and tradition, they mobilized to resist Fascism. The number and variety of their responses so quickly mobilized on three continents provide evidence of their historical consciousness.

W. E. B. DuBois, for one, had anticipated the deliberateness with which the Black masses would respond. In the October 1935 issue of *Foreign Affairs*, he had warned:

> The black world knows this is the last great effort of white Europe to secure the subjection of black men. In the long run the effort is vain and black men know it ... The moral of this, as Negroes see it, is that if any colored nation expects to maintain itself against white Europe it need appeal neither, to religion nor culture but only to force.[66]

In the fifty years which were to follow, it was an instruction which would be repeated in the national liberation movements of Africa, Asia, Latin America, and the Caribbean.

NOTES

1. John Diggins, *Mussolini and Fascism: The View From America* (Princeton: Princeton University Press, 1972), 32. Further references cited in the text.
2. Jules Archer, *The Plot to Seize the White House* (New York: Hawthorn, 1973); for a discussion of the Morgan banking and industrial interests, see Ferdinand Lundberg, *America's Sixty Families* (New York: Vanguard, 1938). For other accounts of the conspiracy, see Arthur Schlesinger, Jr., *The Age of Roosevelt III: The Politics of Upheaval* (Boston: Houghton Mifflin, 1960), 82–86.
3. James Pool and Suzanne Pool, *Who Financed Hitler?* (London: Futura, 1978), especially chapter 3 on Henry Ford.
4. Diggins, *Mussolini and Fascism*, 27–28. Denis Mack Smith in his biography, *Mussolini* (London: Weidenfeld & Nicolson, 1981), noted (p. 108); "Articles he wrote for American journals (or rather which were secretly written on his behalf by an American journalist in collaboration with his brother and Margherita Sarfatti) were at one point earning him $1,500 a week from the Hearst press alone."
5. Lundberg, *America's Sixty Families*, passim. Further references cited in the text.
6. Diggins, *Mussolini and Fascism*, chapter 2; see also *Chicago Defender*, September 21, 1935, p. 18.

7. Of Mussolini's wealthier supporters, Denis Mack Smith wrote (p. 117): "The Majority ... were apparently motivated by self-interest to continue backing fascism ... the years 1922–1925 were from their point of view an 'absolute paradise,' with few strikes, plenty of tax concessions for the well-to-do, an end to rent controls and generally high profits for business. Nor were they ungrateful when the threat of clawing back hundreds of millions of illicit war profits was removed." Richard Webster maintained that "Autarky and imperialism, the foundations of Fascist policy, ran like scarlet threads through the thinking of political and economic elites in liberal Italy ... And all during these years, there was a steady stream of converts to imperialism coming in from the far Left, the revolutionary syndicalists, and the Socialists ... Likewise, all major Italian business groups were expansionist ... Imperialist presuppositions reigned, and Italian heavy industry never came close to shedding its character as part of a military-industrial complex" (*Industrial Imperialism in Italy, 1908–1915* [Berkeley: University of California, 1975], 337–338). See also Daniel Guerin, *Fascism and Big Business* (New York: Pathfinder, 1973), 29–30; and Alan Milward, "Towards a Political Economy of Fascism," in Stein Ugelvik Larsen, Bernt Hagtvet and Jan Petter Myklebust, eds, *Who Were the Fascists: The Social Roots of European Fascism* (New York: Columbia University Press, 1980), 58–61.

8. *Forerunners of American Fascism* (New York: Julian Messner, 1935), 167.

9. Schlesinger, *Age of Roosevelt III*, 89.

10. House Special Committee, "Investigation of Nazi and Other Propaganda," Report No. 153, 74th Congress, 1st Session, February 15, 1935, pp. 9–10.

11. Archer reports that the Scripps-Howard press and its United Press wire service helped in the exposure of the dealings: "Following through on Butler's expose, their papers carried a story headlined: 'Liberty League Controlled by Owners of $37,000,000,000.' Directors of the League were identified as also being directors of U.S. Steel, General Motors, Standard Oil, Chase National Bank, Goodyear Tire, and Mutual Life Insurance Company ... The attacks on the League, plus Roosevelt's reelection in 1936 over its desperate and expensive opposition, destroyed the organization as an effective force of reaction in America" (Archer, *Plot to Seize*, 228–229).

12. Schlesinger, *Age of Roosevelt III*, 86.

13. See W. Walter Crotch, "Whither Mussolini?" *Current History* (February 1937), 42–47.

14. Michael Ledeen, "Italian Jews and Fascism," *Judaism* 18:3 (Summer 1969), 282. Further references cited in the text.

15. Cecil Roth, *The History of the Jews of Italy* (Philadelphia: Jewish Publication Society of America, 1946), 518. Further references cited in the text. Meir Michaelis maintains that one purpose of Roth's final chapter was to counter myths of Italian Jewish anti-Fascism constructed by such Zionists as Chaim Weizmann. See Michaelis, "The 'Duce' and the Jews: An Assessment of the Literature on Italian Jewry under Fascism (1922–1945)," *Yad Vashem Studies* 11 (1976), 15.

16. Ledeen (278) puts the figure between 40,000 and 60,000 for the period 1911–1938.

17. Daniel Carpi, "The Catholic Church and Italian Jewry Under the Fascists," *Yad Vashem Studies* 4 (1960), 43–47. Further references cited in the text.

18. Roth, *History of the Jews*, 510; Smith, *Mussolini*, 20; Ernst Nolte, *Three Faces of Fascism* (New York: Mentor, 1969), 296.

19. Lenni Brenner, *Zionism in the Age of the Dictators* (Westport: Lawrence Hill, 1983), 39–40; and Meir Michaelis, "The Attitude of the Fascist Regime to the Jews in Italy," *Yad Vashem Studies* 4 (1960), 9. Further references cited in the text.

20. Lucien Steinberg, *Jews Against Hitler* (London: Gordon & Cremonesi, 1970), 58; and Smith, *Mussolini*, 220.

21. Smith, *Mussolini*, 221. For Jabotinsky see Robert Wistrich, "Vladimir Jabotinsky: A Re-assessment," *Jewish Quarterly* 24:1 (Spring 1981), 9.

22. Nissim Rejwan, "The Two Israels: A Study in Europeocentrism," *Judaism* 16:1 (Winter 1967), 98ff.; and Kenneth Brown, "Iron and a King: The Likud and Oriental Jews," *Merip Reports* (May 1983), 6–7.

23. Michaelis, "Attitude," 19. For the presence of Jews in the Italian armed forces, see Michaelis, "Attitude," 25, and E. Brand, "The Attitude of the Italians Towards the Jews in the Occupied Territories," *Yad Vashem Bulletin* 6:7 (June 1960), 17.

24. Walter Laguer, *The History of Zionism* (New York: Schocken, 1976), 361ff.; and Nathan Weinstock, *Zionism: False Messiah* (London: Ink Links, 1979), 150–151.
25. Michaelis, "The 'Duce' and the Jews," 21.
26. Michaelis (ibid., 20) reports that according to a study by Leon Poliakov and Jacques Sabille (*Jews Under the Italian Occupation*, 1955) "the Italian authorities systematically and successfully opposed Hitler's anti-Jewish policy in all the areas under their jurisdiction, despite the official anti-Semitic policies of the Fascist Government. Furthermore, it has been proven on the basis of eye-witness reports that the Italian troops in German-occupied Poland aided the Jews in a variety of ways; in some cases they even went so far as to supply arms to Jewish partisans."
27. See Charles Higham, *Trading With the Enemy* (New York: Delacorte, 1983).
28. "It is not easy to determine precisely when the concept of fascism became a problem in post-war scholarly literature; what is certain is that for many years fascism was first regarded as self-evident and then, in the western world, as a tabu ... That the concept of fascism was accorded at most a subordinate role is obviously attributable to its unmistakably disturbing implications for western society at a time when the virtues of western democracy seemed so evident." Ernst Nolte, "The Problem of Fascism in Recent Scholarship," in Henry A. Turner, Jr., ed., *Reappraisals of Fascism* (New York: New Viewpoints, 1975), 26.
29. Herbert Harris, "That Third Party," *Current History* (October 1936), 78; for Edward Stair, see Lundberg, *America's Sixty Families*, 277; for Coughlin, see Schlesinger, *Age of Roosevelt III*, chapter 2, and Swing, chapter 2.
30. Victor Ferkis, "Populist Influences on American Fascism," *Western Political Quarterly* 10:2 (June 1957), 363.
31. See Schlesinger, *Age of Roosevelt III*, chapter 2.
32. Diggins, *Mussolini and Fascism*, 183–184; James M. Burns, *Roosevelt: The Lion and the Fox* (New York: Harcourt, Brace, 1956), 356. One defender of the Church's attitudes towards fascism and relations with fascist governments is George Q. Flynn, *Roosevelt and Romanism* (Westport: Greenwood Press, 1976), 53–55. Interestingly enough, in an earlier work, *American Catholics and the Roosevelt Presidency* (1968), though concerned with Roosevelt's first term (1932–1936), Flynn made the case for the variety of opinions among American Catholics but failed to mention once the subject of fascism.
33. Alexander DeConde, *Half Bitter, Half Sweet: An Excursion into Italian-American History* (New York: Charles Scribner, 1971), 174. Further references died in the text.
34. DeConde, *Half Bitter, Half Sweet*, 88–91; and Jeanette Sayre Smith, "Broadcasting for Marginal Americans," *Public Opinion Quarterly* 6:4 (Winter 1942), 588–603.
35. See the testimony of Carmelo Zito, editor and publisher of the anti-fascist newspaper, *Il Corriere del Popolo*, in "Un-American Activities in California," *Report of the Joint Fact-Finding Committee to the 55th California Legislature* (Sacramento, 1943), 285–288.
36. Gaetano Salvemini, *Italian Fascist Activities in the United States* (New York: Center for Migration Studies, 1977), 1967.
37. See "Un-American Activities in California," 314–319.
38. Salvemini, *Italian Fascist Activities*, xv–xvi.
39. See Diggins, *Mussolini and Fascism*, passim; "Army Office From England Upholds Duce," *Chicago Defender*, December 28, 1935, p. 4; George Flynn, *American Catholics and the Roosevelt Presidency* (Lexington: University of Kentucky Press, 1965), 10–11, 20.
40. DeConde, *Half Bitter, Half Sweet*, 218; Richard Pankhurst, "The Italo-Ethiopian War and League of Nations Sanctions," *Geneve-Afrique* 13:2 (1974), 21–22.
41. Gabriel Jackson, *The Spanish Republic and the Civil War, 1931–1939* (Chicago: Quadrangle, 1965), 256.
42. Jackson, 254–256; also Arthur Landis, *The Abraham Lincoln Brigade* (New York: Citadel, 1968), 483–484. The year previous, Salvemini asserts (202–203), two-hundred volunteers from America bad joined the Fascist army in Ethiopia.
43. DeConde, *Half Bitter, Half Sweet*, 219; also "Defenders of Black Race Rapped," *Chicago Defender*, November 23, 1935, p. 12.

44. St. Clair Drake and Horace Cayton, *Black Metropolis*, v. I (New York: Harper & Row, 1962), 83–89; and John Hope Franklin, *From Slavery to Freedom* (New York: Vintage, 1969), chapter 25; see also Gino Speranza's "How it Feels to be a Problem," in Stanley Feldstein and Lawrence Costello, eds., *The Ordeal of Assimilation* (New York: Anchor, 1974), 1867.

45. Robert Weisbord, *Ebony Kinship* (Westport: Greenwood, 1973), 89. For the most complete research on this relationship, see William R. Scott, "Going to the Promised Land: Afro-American Immigrants in Ethiopia 1930–1935" (paper delivered at 14th conference of the African Studies Association, Denver, November 1971).

46. See Yosef Ben-Jochannan, *The Saga of the "Black Marxists" Versus the "Black Nationalists"* (New York: Alkebu-Ian, 1978), 21; Weisbord, *Ebony Kinship*, 90.

47. Harvey Wish, "American Slave Insurrections Before 1861," *Journal of Negro History* 22 (July 1937); and Cedric J. Robinson, *Black Marxism: The Making of the Black Radical Tradition* (London: ZED Press, 1983), 201–202.

48. Arna Bontemps and Jack Conroy, *Anyplace But Here* (New York: Doubleday, 1966), 196.

49. Ira Berlin, *Slaves Without Masters* (New York: Pantheon, 1974), 314–315.

50. Weisbord, *Ebony Kinship*, 20.

51. Robert Lacerte, "Xenophobia and Economic Decline: The Haitian Case, 1820–1843," *The Americas* 37:4 (April 1981), 499–515.

52. Drake and Cayton, *Black Metropolis*, v. II, 732–744.

53. Brenda Gayle Plummer, "The Afro-American Response to the Occupation of Haiti, 1915–1934," *Phylon* 43 (June 1982), 125–126. Further references cited in the text.

54. Ibid., passim; and Mark Naison, *Communists in Harlem During the Depression* (Urbana: University of Illinois, 1983), 173ff.

55. P. Olisanwuche Esedebe, *Pan-Africanism* (Washington, D.C.: Howard University, 1982), 111–115; and I. K. Sundiata, *Black Scandal* (Philadelphia: Institute for the Study of Human Issues, 1980).

56. See Tony Martin, *Race First* (Westport: Greenwood Press, 1976); and Theodore Vincent, *Black Power and the Garvey Movement* (San Francisco: Ramparts, 1971).

57. See the relevant reports in the *Chicago Defender*: for activities in Chicago, see July 13, 1935 (p. 1) and September 7, 1935 (p. 2); for New York, see July 20, 1935 (p. 1) and September 14, 1935 (p. 2); for Fort Worth, Okmulgee, and Washington, see July 20, 1935 (p. 1); for Mobile, see December 21, 1935 (p. 24).

58. From the *Baltimore Afro-American*: for the dockworkers in Southwest Africa, see October 5, 1935 (p. 4); for Kenya, November 2, 1935 (p. 3); the Egyptian doctors, December 7, 1935 (p. 1). For the West Indies, see Weisbord, *Ebony Kinship*, 102–110, and the *Chicago Defender*, August 31, 1935 (pp. 13, 24) and October 26, 1935 (p. 24).

59. Robert Abbott, "Why Go to Ethiopia?" *Chicago Defender*, July 27, 1935, p. 1.

60. Drake and Cayton, *Black Metropolis*, v. I, 89. For the "Abyssinian" movement in Chicago, see Weisbord, *Ebony Kinship*, 91–94.

61. Roi Ottley, *The Lonely Warrior* (Chicago: Henry Regnery, 1955), 347–349; and Weisbord, *Ebony Kinship*, 97–98.

62. *Chicago Defender*, October 12, 1935, p. 24.

63. S. K. B. Assante, "The Afro-American and the Italo-Ethiopian Crisis, 1934–36," *Race* 15:2 (1973), 176.

64. Joseph Brandt, "Black Americans in the Spanish People's War Against Fascism," pamphlet, n.d.; Faith Berry, *Langston Hughes* (Westport: Lawrence Hall, 1983), 263; Hairy Haywood, *Black Bolshevik* (Chicago: Liberator, 1978), 467–489.

65. *Chicago Defender*, letters, August 17, 1935, p. 16.

66. W. E. B. DuBois, "Inter-Racial Implications of the Ethiopian Crisis," *Foreign Affairs*, October 1935, 88–89; and William R. Scott, "The American Negro and the Italo-Ethiopian Crisis, 1934–36," M. A. thesis, Howard University, 1966, and "Black Nationalism and the Italo-Ethiopian Conflict, 1934–1936," *Journal of Negro History* 63:2 (April 1978), 118–134.

CHAPTER 7

Ota Benga's Flight Through Geronimo's Eyes: Tales of Science and Multiculturalism

> ... all men who differ from others as much as the body differs from
> the soul ... are by nature slaves, and it is better for them ... to be
> ruled by a master. A man is thus by nature a slave if he is capable
> of becoming ... the property of another, and if he participates in
> reason to the extent of apprehending it in another,
> though destitute of it himself.
> — *Aristotle*[1]

Notwithstanding many of the premising assumptions of the current debate, multiculturalism has been an aspect of the Western social sciences since their inceptions as research disciplines in the eighteenth, nineteenth, and twentieth centuries. The modern era, too, had its progenitors since we can discern the specter of multiculturalism in the classical Greek social and moral sciences from which the modernists claimed descent. Isocrates, the fourth-century pan-Hellenic fanatic, employed a multiculturalism of difference to inspire Greeks to renounce democracy for a crusade of world domination. His contemporary Aristotle, the natural scientist, rhetorician, and political philosopher, pursued justifications of slavery, the subordination of women, and a hierarchy of distinctive constitutional orders by insinuating natural laws of multiculturalism. And his mentor Plato implicated a multiculturalist discourse in moral therapeutics ranging from cultural quarantine to eugenics.[2] In the Christian era, the examples of the perceived terrors of multiculturalism are far too numerous to detail. Any one of them would suffice: in the mid-seventeenth century, John Hare, the English "Teuton," recapitulated his diverse progenitors and anticipated their successors when he suggested that Englishmen claiming descent from the Normans reimagine themselves as Norwegians, and English laws, "devested of their French rags ... be restored into the English or Latine tongues."[3]

For millennia, as these instances suggest, premodernist multiculturalism, the preemption of multiculturalism as a construction of contamination, has preoccupied the intellectual imagination of agents of civilizations and regimes familiar with slavery, colonialism, and imperialism. Discourses in alterity thrived long before the appearance of the West as an episteme and insinuated themselves into the latter. Indeed, these premodernist discourses were the enabling practices which legislated the modernist narrative of multiculturalism which posited the West as *the* civilization, and the European white as *the* conscious agency of humanity's historical development. Consequently, the multiculturalism at the center of the current controversy, that is, anti(post) modernist multiculturalism, is a third variant, one which contests the epistemic claims of modernist multiculturalism and its progenitor, premodernist multiculturalism. And though they crudely can be arranged historically, chronology attests to their respective hegemonic moments rather than to their actual historicity. By analytic indirection, it can be surmised that Aristotle's porous defense of slavery is addressed to antecedent representatives of postmodernist multiculturalists skeptical of the naturalness of slavery and the incontestability of Greek superiority over the Other;[4] just as Hare's futile strategy of "ethnic cleansing" was a response to the historical processes of cross-cultural pollination of "English" culture to which he took offense. Whether the context was ancient, medieval, or more recent world-systems, premodernist and modernist multiculturalism are discourses intended to conceal: to conceal the prerogatives of power, conceal the humanity of the Other, and conceal the awful policing devices of subordination.

Indeed, as the more recent history of science literature has attested, research protocols such as anthropology and its derivatives, eugenics, psychometry, etc., were inspired by a desire to achieve epistemic orderings and to rationalize binaries of domination and subordination in multicultural social formations. And as Donna Haraway has demonstrated in her work on the development of biology, the natural sciences embedded identical ambitions in the pursuit of empirical discursive practices.

> Not just anything can emerge as a fact; not just anything can be seen or done, and so told. Scientific practice may be considered a kind of storytelling practice – a rule-governed, constrained, historically changing craft of narrating the history of nature. Scientific practice and scientific theories produce and are embedded in particular kinds of stories ...
>
> The primate body, as part of the body of nature, may be read as a map of power. Biology, and primatology, are inherently political discourses, whose chief objects of knowledge ... are icons (condensations) of the whole of the history and politics of the culture that constructed them for contemplation and manipulation ...

[In the natural sciences] Nature is only the raw material of culture, appropriated, preserved, enslaved, exalted, or otherwise made flexible for disposal by culture in the logic of capitalist colonialism.[5]

The question, then, is not what consequences multiculturalism might obtain for the social sciences, but rather what alternative significations of multiculturalism might presently be embraced by the social sciences and why.

For more than two-hundred years, the objective of the ensemble of race sciences and their subdisciplinary adjutants (e.g., comparative politics) was to secure fixed taxonomies, stable racial-historical and gender identities which, in turn, could be composed into a natural sociology of hierarchy. The primary colors of race – white, black, yellow, red, and brown – coordinated with an Aristotelian construction of sex differences, were to be arranged in a descending order of humanity thus justifying social privileges at home and abroad. This paradigm of multiculturalism, a concomitant to the domestic sites of Western slave economies and female subordination, and imperialism and colonialism in the outlands, pursued the appearance of a natural history. This weave of scientific difference was reprised in every furnishing of culture. The certain exactness of science was embroidered in popular culture, transmitted by lyric, limerick, and letters. And there it remains today, a haunted, majestic presence of an enduring construction of plurality and difference. Haunted, I insist, because it is no longer uncontested.

THE RIGHT MULTICULTURALISM

Louis Agassiz, the Harvard-domiciled Swiss naturalist who was one of the nineteenth century's most authorial artisans of the modernist multiculturalism's scientism,[6] was also one of the first and few of his numbers to acknowledge the audacious deceit of the project and admit defeat. Hidden away in his private notes, his secret confessional recorded his physical repulsion and fear of the dark, simian creature which inspired his professional enterprise: "he just 'knew' [Blacks] were barely higher than apes."[7] Publicly more generous at least, Agassiz first rejected civil comity with Blacks ("No man has a right to what he is unfit to use."), and then, after hearing the testaments of Black military heroism and sacrifice during the American Civil War, conceded the rights of American citizenry to this lower order.[8]

Stephen Jay Gould informs us that "For Agassiz, nothing inspired more fear than the prospect of amalgamation by intermarriage."[9] But we are no more obliged to pause and explore the admixture of circuitous subjectivity and curious logic in Agassiz's mind than we would a member of the frequent lynch mobs of the late nineteenth century. Our concern is historical. Agassiz and his coconspirators, both those performing before the public gaze of the academy and later mobbed in local secrecy among the trees, organized race-hate and practiced race-death. One conduct decoratively civil and learned, the other nakedly hysterical and compulsive, they coalesced into what Fanon would term "a mode of domination."

Intelligence, Reason, and Rationality, imagined to be superior *and* inferior, were the premodernist multiculturalist coda around which the modern social sciences grouped. The terrain, however, was inhospitable because of two features: the unstable and shifting construction of intelligence and the absence of categorical research material. Lacking any universal or culturally neutral concept of intelligence, the modernists fabricated one. Lacking the required research or experimental subjects, that is, pure-race specimens, they invented them.[10] The technical provenance of the present intelligence tests were the paraphernalia of early anthropometry: the calipers and craniometers of Victorian anthropology and their equivalents in France, Germany, Switzerland, and elsewhere. Data were characteristically inconclusive but that could be managed by fraud and finagling.[11] The psychometric provenance of the present white, Black, Hispanic/Latino, Asian, etc., experimental/tested races were the imagined Europeans, Africans, Orientals, etc., of yesteryear.[12] Undaunted by the necessity for scientistic shell games, and distracted by them from any profound investigation of the mind, the proponents of the modernist multiculturalism constructed a forgery of the mind as a predisposition toward civilization.

A counterfeit architectonic of civilization – the linear progression from hunting and gathering to urban commerce – was sutured to the forgery of the mind and encrusted with a fabricated inheritance: the birth of the West in Ancient Greece and Rome. And from the seventeenth or eighteenth centuries until now, these scrubbed-white mantras – the natural history of humankind; rationality; and the Ancient Mediterranean – were the means to drown the humanity of the Other. In Europe, George Mosse observes:

> Greek beauty provided the ideal type, which set the aesthetic criteria to which man must relate himself … Classical beauty symbolized the perfect human form within which a true soul would be bound to reside … From the eighteenth century onwards … the ideal type and countertype would not vary much for the next century and a half, nor would it matter fundamentally whether the inferior race was black or Jewish. The ideal type symbolized by a classical beauty and proper morals determined attitudes toward all men.[13]

And in American colleges and universities, well into the late nineteenth century, the classical curriculum of Greek, Latin, mathematics, natural philosophy, moral philosophy and logic concretized the premodernist multiculturalist frame in the minds of the educated. As the Yale Report of 1828 substantiated, no worthy alternative presented itself: "the single consideration that divine truth was communicated to man in the ancient languages, ought to ... give to them perpetuity."[14]

In American science in the 1820s and 1830s, phrenology and ethnology brought up the rear. Legislated by the appropriation of classical aesthetics and racial resignifications in the statistical means of craniology/craniometry and facial angles, a modernist phrenology determined the racial limits of intelligence, civilization, and moral achievement from the size of the skull and the mass of cerebral organization.[15] Championed by Charles Caldwell (*Thoughts on the Original Unity of the Human Race*, 1830) and Samuel Morton (*Crania Americana*, 1839; *Crania Ægyptica*, 1844), both American physicians and professors of anatomy, this variant of phrenology with its scientific demonstration of superior and inferior races was employed in the defense of slavery and conquest.[16] In the public debate on emancipation and abolition fueled by the Nat Turner rebellion and Native American resistance, modernist phrenology was the master-race science.[17] And under its subsequent guise as ethnology, the new American anthropology, race science confirmed the historical singularity of the white race: "Among the more important conclusions in Morton's books, noted in many journal articles in the latter half of the century, was his claim that the ancient Egyptians were not Negroes, merely dark-skinned Caucasians."[18] And with the arrival of Agassiz at Harvard in 1848, race science extended its hegemony from the modest environs of Transylvania University (Caldwell's regime in Kentucky) to the best endowed academic institutions of America.[19]

Anointed by some of the most eminent scientists and most prestigious institutions in the nation, race science hailed the inferior races, greeting the newest arrivals, the immigrant Irish, Slavs, Italians, Chinese, and Japanese, with fabulous narratives of natural baseness; and treating the already-domiciled Other, the Africans, and the Native Americans, to slavery, reservations, and segregation. So ineluctable was the march of [white] civilization that it was common and scientific knowledge that neither the Blacks nor the Indians would survive into the twentieth century, and the most benevolent fate for the lesser whites was crossbreeding with the Anglo-Saxons, the Aryans, the Nordics, or whichever "blood" group was nominated as the most superior Caucasians. As one of Morton's students, Dr. Josiah Nott declared in 1854: "No two distinctly-marked races can dwell together on equal terms. Some races, moreover, appear destined to live and prosper for a time, until the destroying race comes, which is to exterminate and supplant them."[20] And with a suddenness which appears to confirm Haraway's construction of Western science's political nature, following the abolition of slavery American ethnologists transferred their attentions almost exclusively to the Native American. St. Clair Drake reports:

> The Bureau of American Ethnology and the Smithsonian Institution did not concern themselves with Afro-Americans. Their role was to assist in forming and

carrying out an Indian policy while the Native Americans were being swept off the plains and prairies and herded onto reservations ... in collaboration with a government that was intent on stamping out the last vestiges of rebellion, abolishing treaty relations, and turning the land over to settlers, railroad and mining corporations. Blacks ... were left to the home missionary societies ...[21]

At the beginning of the nineteenth century, Thomas Jefferson had betrayed his "all men are created equal" dictum, publicizing his nightmarish vision of a land cohabited by Blacks and white.[22] And well through his century and much of our own, Americans substantiated his dreadful anticipation through slave rebellions, Indian wars, immigration riots, Civil War, the lynchings of lesser whites, Blacks, Indians, and Asians, race-inspired vigilantism, segregation, race riots, anti-immigration and anti-miscegenation laws, and the like.[23] In each instance, when the canons of race science and racism came under challenge, the modernist discourse on multiculturalism was revived. Audrey Smedley has observed of these "cycles in history" that the parallel between Samuel Morton and Arthur Jensen is instructive: "Both men published scholarly works promoting the idea of Black inferiority. In both cases, their major publications came in the wake of dramatic events that tended to advance the cause of racial equality: Morton in the wake of the abolitionist movement; Jensen following the civil rights movement of the 1950s and 1960s."[24]

In the late nineteenth and early twentieth centuries, natural and social scientists at Harvard (President Charles W. Eliot, Ernest Hooton, and Edwin Katzenellenbogen – the latter convicted of war crimes at Buchenwald), Stanford (Lewis Terman), and Yale, frequently subsidized by private research foundations like the Rockefeller Foundation (e.g., The China Medical Board) and the Kellogg Foundation (the Eugenics Records Office), espoused a modernist multiculturalist public policy in the forms of intelligence tests, eugenics, and sterilization. Terman testified that "... 1000 Harvard graduates will at the end of two hundred years have but 50 descendants, while in the same period, 1000 south Italians will have multiplied to 100,000. ..." In 1937, Hooton, the pioneer of physical anthropology in America (and president of the American Association of Physical Anthropologists) informed the *New York Times*, "I think that a biological purge is the essential prerequisite for a social and spiritual salvation." And at his trial at Dachau, Katzenellenbogen, the former Harvard Medical School faculty member, defended his participation in Nazi sterilization programs by reminding his Allied accusers that he had drafted sterilization legislation for the governor of Indiana.[25]

American anthropologists at the turn of the century, however, did not entirely confine themselves to the hallways of academia, the boardrooms of industrial capital and government. They were not above the lure of providing the public spectacles of multiculturalism. In their forays into mass opinion, they most often chose the sedate environs of museums and zoological gardens to impress their modernist constructions of multiculturalism on schoolchildren and the middling representatives of the educated. But on occasion, they employed sensationalism, the chosen discursive practice of their well-heeled sponsors. Here, the intended consumers were the mass audience. Haraway reminds us that "The relation of hoax and popular natural history is unnervingly close."[26]

One such occasion was the St. Louis World Fair of 1904 where the Fair's Anthropology Department (the first in the history of such expositions) displayed the human loot of colonialism and conquest: Igorots, Negritos, and Moros from the Philippines; Ainus from Japan; Zulus from South Africa; a Batatele prince and Batwa "Pygmies" from Leopold's Congo (including Ota Benga, the lone "Chirichiri" pygmy who was destined to be housed in the Bronx Zoo's Primate House in 1906); Geronimo, the aging (seventy-plus years) Chiricahua prisoner of war; Kwakiutl Indians from the Northwest; the Cocopas of the lower Colorado; Kiowas; Nez Perce; Seri, etc. And after a summer as public exhibits – over 18 million visitors according to the *New York Times* (December 2, 1904) – they were subjected to the "touch of the dynamometer, the pulse controller, the cephalometer, aesthesiometer, pantograph, sphygmo-graph, and tape measure."

> Anthropology Days were understood to buttress, "complement and on the whole fully conform with" the anthropometrical data "of function and structure" arrived at in the lab. The fair was built with the assumption that Caucasians were superior. Now the builders had compiled the numbers to prove it.[27]

Although the numbers were far from perfect statistical sets, they were appreciated by psychologists like Marion Mayo who acknowledged in his 1913 dissertation *The Mental Capacity of the American Negro* that his own "Negro" subjects were "a mixed and not a pure type." Mayo conceded that the scientific literature had yet to demonstrate convincingly racial inequality and that his own findings on racial "variability" were inconclusive. Nevertheless, he was persuaded that this construction of intelligence centered around the incidents of genius among race groups and, originating in Francis Galton's claims of superior mental inheritance among the English upper classes,[28] would likely settle the controversy:

> Though very little is as yet definitely known about the variability of races, there is some evidence that the European white is more variable than the negro, and that civilized peoples are more variable than primitive peoples. Also, as between the sexes, that man is more variable than woman.[29]

Within one year of Mayo's publication, "Henry Goddard's famous book *The Kallikak Family* (1914) indicted the poor for being mentally deficient and conjured up lurid scenes from the netherworld of the slums."

Once the theory of differential intelligence was accepted its implicit political applications became operational. Subjectively, psychologists were unaware of the ideological constraints upon their scientific endeavors, but their political perspective is easily discerned. Those social scientists involved in intelligence testing tended to view the propertied classes as the more naturally gifted of society whose social position was directly attributable to superior innate intellectual qualities.[30]

The Aristotelian conceits were restored in their entirety.

Race science, initially the cloistered terrain of academics and gentlemen of leisure and adventure, by the nineteenth century had transmuted into a specular entertainment in circuses, burlesque, vaudeville, and minstrelsy complementing the specular performances presented to the participants in slavery, colonialism, and wars of conquest. And now, at the beginnings of the twentieth century, with the advent of mass entertainment forms like the cinema and radio, the spectacle and incantations of modernist multiculturalism were everywhere. Still they were not sufficient to extinguish fugitive, oppositional impulses.

HOW IT ALL WENT WRONG

The discerning spectator at the "Olympic games" competition, organized for the savages by the anthropologists at the St. Louis Fair, might have been alerted by the deportments of Geronimo and the pygmies. As the sport of exhibited inferiors was now transformed (converted) to the exhibition of sport and the numerics of comparative cerebral and physiognomic structures linked with their counterparts in athleticism, movement was required. And in the regulated space of athletic performance, the inferiors located unexpected sites of dominion.

According to the sports page of the *St. Louis Post-Dispatch*, August 13, 1904, Geronimo "... leaned silently against the track-rail looking on but gave no other sign that he was at all interested;" and the pygmies, Bradford and Blume recount, "... backpedaled and did woozy figure eights on the hundred yard dash."[31] If, as Haraway assures us, "*Both* the scientist and the organism are actors in a storytelling practice," then we must surmise that the specular actors (Geronimo/ the anthropologists/the exposition's visitors) and the performers (the pygmies/ the starter with his gun) were occupying alternative yarns. Something was recognizably amiss since, in the sports-page account, the two sentences devoted to Geronimo are the only reference to someone who did not run, jump, throw, or organize the competition. He ruptures the joviality, the athleticism of the performative narrative; he disrupts the report/er. For Ota Benga, the pygmy, however, Geronimo's presence was entirely benevolent. Ota remembered Geronimo smiling to him that day; he also recalled that a few days earlier,

Geronimo had given him an arrowhead, had then chanted and danced around him. And when Ota looked into Geronimo's eyes, Ota "had the impression for a moment that he was flying. Below him was a dry red landscape of rocks, gorges, and animals he had never seen before."[32] Thankfully, the *Post-Dispatch's* reporter had been spared the full brunt of Ota's knowledge.

Ota conceived of America as the land of the dead. And until his arrival in New Orleans where he joined with some Black street musicians in an impromptu stroll and dance, he found particularly dreadful the fact that musicians read from sheets. Ota was convinced they had forgotten how to play. He had determined to remain in this metaphysical realm until he could fathom its order. And when, after twelve years, he realized "he had stopped" but could not return to Africa – the World War, its devastation of the Congo, the price of a steamship ticket – he put a bullet in his heart.[33]

Among Ota's antecedents, the other Africans in America, an identical quest, the attempt to return in the nineteenth century had presaged an anthropology distinctly subversive of the hegemonic physical anthropology. While the modernists were patrolling medical schools and graveyards for Black bodies and skulls and furtively confiscating skeletons buried in Egyptian tombs to add to their congregation of race evidence, an oppositional signification for Africa was being assembled.[34] In 1859, as St. Clair Drake reports, Martin Delaney headed the Niger Valley Exploring Party on behalf of the National Emigration Convention of Colored Men. The extraordinary impulse in Delaney, the link between he and Ota Benga, is apparent in Delaney's call seven years earlier:

> Every people should be the originators of their own designs, the projector of their own schemes, and creators of the events that lead to their destiny – the consummation of their desires ...
>
> We have native hearts and virtues, just as other nations; which in their pristine purity are noble, potent, and worthy of example. We are a nation within a nation ...[35]

An anthropology premised on the dominion of the Other, an alternative space to that of the West, would necessarily transcend the delimitations of anthropometry. An anthropology postulated on the dignity and agency of the other as "originators" would generate an interrogation of alternative histories, alternative cultures, and alternative social orders. The beginnings of such an anthropology could be found in Delaney's and Robert Campbell's *Search for a Place: Black Separatism and Africa* (1860) when they negotiated their alternative aesthetics, describing the physical beauty of their Yoruba hosts, the complexity of their language, and the intricacies of their economic institutions.[36]

The anthropology of Delaney and Campbell, of official Black envoys like George Washington Williams (Leopold's Congo and Haiti), John Henry Smyth

(Liberia), George Washington Ellis (Liberia), and Frederick Douglas (Haiti), and of Black missionaries like Henry McNeal Turner, Alexander Crummell, Edward Wilmot Blyden, and William Henry Sheppard belied the inferiorization of Africans and Africans-in-the-Americas through cultural studies.[37] In the late nineteenth century, published accounts of religious life, linguistics (e.g., Ellis' study of the Vai-speaking peoples; Sheppard's studies of Tshiluba and Tshikuba), and economics shadowed the rhetoric of skulls which sought to evacuate the workings of any creative intelligence among the Other. And following the abolition of slavery in the U.S., scholars like Williams and Sheppard turned their attention to the Black sites of the world-system cemented into the most exploitative apparatus.

In 1889, George Washington Williams, the author of the two-volume *A History of the Negro Race in America from 1619 to 1880* (1883),[38] was commissioned by the American government to investigate the conditions in Leopold's Congo. On July 18, 1890, Williams wrote an open letter to his "Good and Great Friend," King Leopold of Belgium. In his conclusion, Williams exposed the counterfeits of the West's claims to superior moral and ethical development:

> Against the deceit, fraud, robberies, arson, murder, slave raiding, and general policy of cruelty of your Majesty's Government to the natives, stands their record of unexampled patience, long-suffering and forgiving spirit, which put the boasted civilization and professed religion of your Majesty's Government to the blush.[39]

Among the twelve detailed charges Williams brought against Leopold were slavery, the prostitution of African women, forced labor, violations of international law and sovereignty, "waging unjust and cruel wars against natives," gratuitous homicide, and the encouragement of cannibalism. Each indictment destructed the pillars of the epistemic hierarchy imagined for the West. But Williams also recognized the discursive restraints insinuated into any attempt to communicate between his anthropology and the system of knowledge barricading white consciousness. Despite his reputation for eloquence, Williams repeatedly capitulated before the horrors he witnessed: "I have no adequate terms with which to depict ..."

In that same year, 1890, William Sheppard and Samuel Lapsley met with Leopold before proceeding to the Congo to cofound the American Presbyterian Congo Mission. They were together because the Presbyterian Society could not imagine a Black man heading a civilizing mission. Two years later, Lapsley, Sheppard's "white permission slip," was dead, and Sheppard began the odyssey which would lead him into the "space of death" that Leopold had commissioned around rubber extraction in his private state. And in the ninth year of his Mission, far from the racial violence at home he had sought to escape, his African communicants implored him to go and witness Leopold's culture of terror. Sheppard knew what awaited him: "It is just as if I were to take a rope and go out behind the house and hang myself to that tree"; but he went. And in the village of the Zappo-Zap, Sheppard's anthropology was transformed into a politics of outrage:

> He made note of three hundred human skeletons, the flesh of many of them having been prepared as food. He saw a spear sticking out of the blackened heart of a man who had once been a friend. He counted 81 right hands – hacked from the living and dead – from the arms of adults and children, which were to be put in a basket and delivered to Bula Mutadi [Leopold's military and civil functionaries].
>
> The Zappo-Zaps were unashamed. They held back nothing. Were they not the Force Publique, trained and corrupted first by the slave trade and now selling their skills to Leopold, who demanded they bring back either tribute or proof of corporal punishment?[40]

Sheppard's testimony joined that of Williams, bonding with the anthropological narratives woven by Delaney, Crummell, Blyden, Smyth, Turner, Ellis, and all the other Africans who dreamed of home. Williams and Sheppard had given the most exacting accounts of the human costs of the Congo rubber trade and, eventually, when those officials and their publics who could not qualify a Black anthropology, read the redacted versions published by Edmund Morel, Roger Casement, Arthur Conan Doyle, and Joseph Conrad, the crusade to rid the Congo of Leopold's rule was on. Not surprisingly, given the space dominated by *real* anthropology, when the historians reconstructed the humanitarian campaign, the contributions of Williams and Sheppard vanished.[41]

Similarly, the erasure of this alternative anthropology occurs in the dominant narratives of the rehabilitation of American anthropology. In the central space of this narrative appears, instead, the figure of Franz Boas. It is Boas who "made short work of the fabled cranial index,"[42] Boas who develops "a systematic critique of the racial, psychological, and cultural assumptions of nineteenth-century evolutionary anthropology,"[43] Boas who battled the hereditarian racists and invented cultural anthropology,[44] Boas who raised American anthropology to a science.[45] And there is much credit to be accorded to Boas for rescuing American anthropology from the likes of Daniel Brinton and William McGee. (We have already encountered McGee, the first president of the American Anthropological Association, in one of the several guises he would assume throughout his career: he was the chief of the Anthropology Department at the St. Louis Fair. And if it wasn't already obvious, as Marvin Harris ventures: "McGee was an inexhaustible mine of every error of substance and theory that it was possible to commit on the basis of the most vulgar prejudices masquerading as scientific expertise."[46]) In short, Boas is the "culture-hero" of twentieth-century American anthropology; a sort of remedial potion or antidote for the poisonous Agassiz.

Baldly put, Boas has been made to occupy the great man theory of (intellectual) history; here pinioned on Boas' training as a physicist, and substantiated by the testimony of his students (who included Alfred Kroeber, Margaret Mead, Benedict, Robert Lowie, Edward Sapir, Melville Herskovits, Clark Wissler, Ashley Montagu, Jules Henry, and Leslie Spier).[47] No Hegel/Kuhn (*The Structure of Scientific Revolutions*, 1962) paradigmatic shifts are required. Even Marvin Harris, who reconstructs the Boasian shift as a reaction to historical materialism, attributes Boas' profound recasting of anthropology to his "natural gifts, superior education," and his "puritan" devotion to facts.[48]

Notwithstanding, Boas' sustained challenge to the modernist construction of anthropology, he and those of his students who resituated "primitive" cultures within the embrace of human development obtained no clear victory. Until the present, academic anthropology and its kindred sciences (e.g., sociobiology, intelligence studies, and population genetics) have accommodated the discourses of human unity and racial hierarchy. As Stephen Jay Gould warns, the biological determinists inhabit both the ephemeral and deep structures of Western culture:

Who even remembers the hot topics of ten years ago: Shockley's proposals for reimbursing voluntarily sterilized individuals according to the number of IQ points below 100, the great XYY debate, or the attempt to explain urban riots by diseased neurology of rioters ... But I was inspired to write this book because biological determinism is rising in popularity again, as it always does in times of political retrenchment. The cocktail party circuit has been buzzing with its usual profundity about innate aggression, sex roles, and the naked ape.[49]

Undaunted by the miserable errors and chicaneries of their predecessors, the reincarnations of Agassiz and McGee are concomitants of the cultural seasons occasioned by historical, economic, and political crises. Neither the Boasians nor Gould or Noam Chomsky and his colleagues are sufficient to nullify the credibility immediately extended to determinists like Phillippe Rushton or Frederick Goodwin, to name two of the most recently celebrated.[50] Each, for a brief moment, constitutes the immediate justification for the chain-of-practices which result, for an example, in the campaigns of sterilization which still target Black and brown women in particular.[51]

No rapprochement, no real proximity occurred between Boas' destabilizing cultural anthropology and the anthropology imagined by the Other. The strategic negotiations around scientific practices between the epistemes of Boas and McGee concerned the definition of the Other as a contested site for discovery but not a locale of subjectivity. For an instance, between 1928–1933, Wissler, one of Boas' students and eventually director of the Committee for Research in Problems of Sex (Rockefeller Foundation funding), sought to interrogate the "natural" sex behaviors of the "uncivilized" (Native Americans,

Solomon Islanders). Not until 1933 did Wissler acknowledge the existence of culture among his subjects, forcing him to transfer his attention to anthropoids.[52] Herskovits, on the other hand, stood fast on the original turf, pushing "the disproof of the superiority of Euro-American culture in the realm of religion, social organization, and family life ... [to the point] that the very word 'primitive' came to be regarded as inadraissibly invidious and pejorative."[53]

Caroline Bond Day, probably the first Black Ph.D. in anthropology (trained by Hooton), and Zora Neale Hurston (Boas) aided the Boasians in their rupture of the fixed identities required by anthropometry. Day's *A Study of Some Negro-White Families in the United States* documented the vitality of mulattoes thus raising them above Hooton's sterilization threshold, while Boas sent Hurston into Harlem to collect cephalic indexes.[54] Eventually, "Papa Franz" sent Hurston off to study Black folklore, a journey from which Hurston never really returned, and further distanced his work from the subjectivity of the Other.[55] It was not as if such opportunities were frequent. Including Day and Hurston, St. Clair Drake reports, "Up to 1945 when World War II ended, only ten Afro-Americans had secured professional training in anthropology ..."[56] And until the Black studies movement, generally located from the late 1960s, most Black social scientists adhered rather closely to their disciplinary mainstreams with occasional forays into the hereditary genetics and IQ controversies. The bolder intellects, the heirs of Williams and Sheppard like Hurston, Dunham, W. E. B. Du Bois, Carter G. Woodson, Oliver C. Cox, Horace Cayton, and Drake, remained in semiquarantine in mission- and business-funded Black colleges and educational organizations.[57]

In light of the profound failures of American scientific practices and canon to achieve some internal legislative discipline over the hegemon of race, the Black studies movement began the retrieval of the anti-modernist multiculturalism deposited in the anti-colonialist studies of Williams, Sheppard, Blyden, George Padmore, C. L. R. James, Frantz Fanon, Aimé Césaire, Amilcar Cabral, Jean-Price Mars, and others. Accompanied by similar initiatives in feminist and ethnic studies, the rupture of academia's modernist discourse on multiculturalism now appears permanent. No amount of exposure, however, dissuades the conceits of fabulists.[58] They remain eminent, powerful, and committed to the Aristotelian construction of the Other. But now they are haunted by students who have encountered the anti-modernist anthropology, by colleagues whose research and publications (and classrooms) have obtained prodigious volume.

The eclipse of the racial fabulists, however, is momentary. They will continue to preserve their systems of knowledge for as long as the social order which they "legitimate" endures. And at present, not content merely to exist, drifting from one conceit to another, from one counterfeit to another, the racial fabulists and their sponsors have staked the future of higher education in their attempts to restore modernism. For the fabulists and their economic and state sponsors, the assault against anti-modernist multiculturalism is an assault against the democratization of knowledge. For them, either this Other multiculturalism or higher education must be vanquished. This is the form assumed by anti-democracy for the moment.

NOTES

1. Aristotle, *The Politics*, Book 1, 1254bl9–25.
2. Alexander Fuks, "Isocrates and the Socioeconomic Situation in Greece," *Ancient Society*, 3 (1972); Gregory Vlastos, "Slavery in Plato's Thought," in *Slavery in Classical Antiquity*, M. I. Finley, ed. (New York: Barnes & Noble, 1960); Mavis Campbell, "Aristotle and Black Slavery," *Race*, XV, 3 (1974); and Cedric J. Robinson, "Slavery and the Platonic Origins of Anti-Democracy," in press.
3. John Hare, *St. Edward's Ghost: or, Anti-Normanisme. Being a Patheticall Complaint and Motion in the Behalfe of our English Nation Against her Grand (yet neglected) Grievance, Normanisme* (1647), quoted in Hugh A. MacDougall, *Racial Myth in English History* (Montreal: Harvest House, 1982), p. 61.
4. Frank Snowden instances Ephorus, the fourth-century historian and contemporary of Isocrates and Aristotle, as one of those who "admired non-Greek peoples," *Blacks in Antiquity* (Cambridge: Harvard University, 1971), pp. 170 ff. and 318, n. 12. Notwithstanding Aristotle's direct appeal to nature, David Theo Goldberg still insists that Greek notions of inferiority were generally based on political and cultural rather than biological notions, Goldberg, *Racist Culture* (Oxford: Blackwell, 1993), pp. 21–22.
5. Donna Haraway, *Primate Visions* (New York: Routledge, 1989), pp. 4, 10, 13.
6. Audrey Smedley, *Race in North America* (Boulder: Westview Press, 1993), p. 240 ff.; Stephen Jay Gould, *The Mismeasure of Man* (New York: W. W. Norton, 1981), p. 45.
7. John Trumpbour, "Introducing Harvard: A Social, Philosophical, and Political Profile," in *How Harvard Rules*, John Trumpbour, ed. (Boston: South End Press, 1989), p. 20. Stephen Jay Gould restored and translated sections of Agassiz's correspondence which had been expurgated by Agassiz's wife and largely ignored by historians. One passage from a letter to his mother in December 1846, the year beginning his sojourn in the U.S., reads: "It was in Philadelphia that I first found myself in prolonged contact with negroes ... the feeling that they inspired in me is contrary to all our ideas about the confraternity of the human type ... In seeing their black faces with their thick lips and grimacing teeth, the wool on their head, their bent knees, then elongated hands, their large curved nails, and especially the livid color of the palm of their hands, I could not take my eyes off their face in order to tell them to stay far away." Gould, *The Mismeasure of Man* (New York: W. W. Norton, 1981), pp. 44–45. Agassiz was the principal scientific authority for polygeny – the thesis that the races had distinctive origins. Cf. Gould, p. 43; and George Frederickson, *The Black Image in the White Mind: The Debate on Afro-American Character and Destiny, 1817–1914* (New York: Harper, 1971), pp. 75, 137.
8. Stephen Bonsai, "The Negro Soldier in War and Peace," *The North American Review*, CLXXXVI (June 1907), pp. 321–322. In 1863, Agassiz, responding to questions from Dr. Samuel Gridley Howe, the radical abolitionist appointed by Lincoln to the Freedmen's Inquiry Commission authorized to recommend policy on the freed slaves, Agassiz responded: "the colored people in whom the negro nature prevails will tend toward the South, while the weaker and lighter ones will remain and die out among us." Frederickson, *The Black Image in the White Mind*, p. 161.
9. Gould, *The Mismeasure of Man*, p. 48.
10. George Stocking Jr., *Victorian Anthropology* (New York: Free Press, 1987), p. 233 ff.
11. Gould, *The Mismeasure of Man*, reports on the craniometric frauds perpetrated by Morton (p. 54 ff.); in 1906 by Robert Bennett Bean, the Virginian physician (p. 80); the IQ fakery of Cyril Burt (chapter 6); and Arthur Jensen (p. 317 ff.).

12. Jane Mercer and Wayne Curtis Brown, "Racial Differences in IQ: Fact or Artifact?," in *The Fallacy of IQ*, Carl Senna, ed. (New York: The Third Press, 1973), p. 66 ff.; and Mallory Wober, "Race and Intelligence," *Transition*, 40 (December 1971), p. 24.

13. George Mosse, *Toward the Final Solution: A History of European Racism* (London: J. M. Dent & Sons, 1978), pp. 11–12.

14. Quoted in Lawrence Levine, "Clio, Canons, and Culture," *The Journal of American History*, 80, 3 (December 1993), p. 854.

15. At its site of origin, Edinburgh (Scotland), phrenology was identified with a populist reform movement which "lobbied for changes in the provision of education, for penal reform, the more effective treatment of the insane, 'enlightened' colonial policies, and a more humane system of factory production ..." Steven Shapin, "The Politics of Observation: Cerebral Anatomy and the Social Interests in the Edinburgh Phrenology Disputes," in *On the Margins of Science: The Social Construction of Rejected Knowledge*, Roy Wallis, ed. (Staffordshire: Keele University, March 1979), p. 146.

16. Reginald Horsman, *Race and Manifest Destiny* (Cambridge: Harvard University Press, 1981), chapters 7 and 8.

17. Ibid., pp. 56–59; Smedley, *Race in North America*, p. 237 ff.

18. Smedley, *Race in North America*, p. 238.

19. Trumpbour, "Blinding Them with Science: Scientific Ideologies in the Ruling of the Modern World," in *How Harvard Rules*, ed. John Trumpbour; Smedley, *Race in North America*, pp. 241–242.

20. Nott and his coauthor, George Gliddon, from *Types of Mankind* (1854) as quoted by Horsman, *Race and Manifest Destiny*, p. 137.

21. St. Clair Drake, "Anthropology and the Black Experience," *The Black Scholar*, 11, 7 (September/ October 1980), p. 9.

22. John Miller, *The Wolf by the Ears: Jefferson and Slavery* (Charlottesville: University Press of Virginia, 1991); Winthrop Jordon, *White over Black* (Chapel Hill: University of North Carolina Press, 1969).

23. For the role of intelligence testing in the formulation of anti-immigration laws, see Gould, *The Mismeasure of Man*, pp. 226–233.

24. Smedley, *Race in North America*, p. 253, n. 7. See also Noam Chomsky, "IQ Tests: Building Blocks or the New Class System," in *Shaping the American Educational State*, Clarence Karier, ed. (New York: Free Press, 1975).

25. The quotes from Terman and Hooton, and the summary of Katzenellenbogen's testimony, are from Trumpbour, "Blinding Them with Science," pp. 224–225.

26. Haraway, *Primate Visions*, p. 279

27. Phillips Verner Bradford and Harvey Blume, *Ota Benga, the Pygmy in the Zoo* (New York: Delta, 1992), pp. 121–123.

28. "In 1869 he published *Hereditary Genius*, a landmark volume designed to convince all but the most irascible skeptics of the superior hereditary endowment of certain eminent British families." Smedley, *Race in North America*, p. 266.

29. Marion Mayo, *The Mental Capacity of the American Negro*, reprinted from the Archives of Psychology (New York, 1913), pp. 58, 69. Further on gender, Mayo quotes Dr. C. S. Myers in "Papers on Inter-Racial Problems" to the effect that: "Certainly there is not an instance of first-class musical genius ... among European women, despite centuries of opportunity." Mayo summarized the preliminary findings of R. S. Woodworth's St. Louis Fair study of "Indians, Filipinos, Africans and Ainu." R. S. Woodworth, "Racial Differences and Mental Traits," *Science* (February 1910) cited in Mayo, pp. 64–66.

30. Gilbert Gonzalez, "The Historical Development of the Concept of Intelligence," *The Review of Radical Political Economics*, 11, 2 (Summer 1979), p. 46. Goddard, in the furtherance of restrictive immigration laws and sterilization, faked data and altered photographs in his "studies" of morons. Cf. Gould, *The Mismeasure of Man*, pp. 164–171.

31. Bradford and Blume, *Ota Benga, the Pygmy in the Zoo*, pp. 253, 122.

32. Ibid., p. 212.

33. Ibid., p. 216 ff.
34. Even more macabre was the predilection among anthropometrists for weighing each other's brains. Gould reports "The dissection of dead colleagues became something of a cottage industry among nineteenth-century craniometricians." Gould describes the crisis of "small-brained men of eminence," e.g., Walt Whitman, Franz Josef Gall, Anatole France, K. F. Gauss, etc., in Gould, *The Mismeasure of Man*, 92 ff.
35. Martin Robison Delaney, "A Project for an Expedition of Adventure, to the Eastern Coast of Africa," the appendix to *The Condition, Elevation, Emigration and Destiny of the Colored People of the United States, Politically Considered* (1852), reprinted in *Apropos of Africa*, Adelaide Cromwell Hill and Martin Kilson, eds (London: Frank Cass, 1969), p. 22.
36. Drake, "Anthropology and the Black Experience," pp. 12–13.
37. For pithy biographies of Crummell, Delaney, Douglas, Turner, Smyth, and Williams, as well as excerpts of their writings on Africa, see Hill and Kilson, eds., *Apropos of Africa*, passim.
38. Subtitled *Negroes as Slaves, as Soldiers, and as Citizens; Together with a Preliminary Consideration of the Unity of the Human Family, an Historical Sketch of Africa, and an Account of the Negro Governments of Sierra Leone and Liberia*, the work cited more than 1000 of the 12,000 volumes Williams consulted, and dismissed the polygenist argument. In 1888, Williams published his *A History of the Negro Troops in the War of the Rebellion, 1861–1865, Preceded by a Review of the Military Services of Negroes in Ancient and Modern Times*. Cf. Earl Thorpe, *Black Historians* (New York: William Morrow, 1971), pp. 46–55.
39. Reprinted in Hill and Kilson, eds, *Apropos of Africa*, p. 106.
40. Bradford and Blume, *Ola Benga, the Pygmy in the Zoo*, pp. 38–52.
41. Michael Taussig, one of the more recent scholars to rehearse the holocaust of Leopold's Congo, and from whom I have borrowed the phrases "culture of terror" and "space of death," does not mention Williams or Sheppard in his otherwise extraordinary work *Shamanism, Colonialism and the Wild Man* (Chicago: University of Chicago, 1987).
42. Gould, *The Mismeasure of Man*, p. 108.
43. Stocking, *Victorian Anthropology*, p. 287.
44. Frederickson, *The Black Image in the White Mind*, pp. 330, 315.
45. Ruth Benedict, "Obituary of Franz Boas," *Science*, 97 (1943), p. 61. Benedict was one of Boas' students.
46. Marvin Harris, *The Rise of Anthropological Theory* (New York: Thomas Crowell, 1968), p. 255.
47. Cf. ibid., p. 251 for a more complete but still partial listing.
48. Ibid., pp. 257, 248–249.
49. Gould, *The Mismeasure of Man*, p. 28.
50. For Rushton's claims for craniometry, see his "Cranial Capacity Related to Sex, Rank, and Race in a Stratified Random Sample of 6,325 US Military Personnel," *Intelligence*, 16, 3–4 (July–December 1992); "Evolutionary Biology and Heritable Traits," *Psychological Reports*, 71, 3 (December 1992); "Race and Crime," *Canadian Journal of Criminology*, 32, 2 (April 1990); and Edward Reed and Arthur Jensen, "Cranial Capacity; New Caucasian Data and Comments on Rushton's Claimed Mongoloid–Caucasoid Brain-Size Differences," *Intelligence*, 17, 3 (July–September 1993). Critiques of Rushton include Zack Cernovsky and Larry Litman, "Reanalyses of J. P. Rushton's Crime Data," *Canadian Journal of Criminology*, 35, 1 (January 1993); and John Maddox, "How to Publish the Unpalatable?" *Nature*, 358 (July 16, 1992). For Goodwin, the former Director of the National Institute of Mental Health and the Alcohol, Drug Abuse, and Mental Health Administration, who compared inner-city Black youths to monkeys in the jungle, see the articles in the *Washington Post* (February 22, 1992), p. A5; (February 27, 1992), p. A4; (February 28, 1992), p. A4. For his defenders, see the *Washington Post* (March 1, 1992), p. C3; and (March 21, 1992), p. A22; and the editorial, "The Speech Police," *Wall Street Journal* (March 9, 1992), p. A14.
51. Loretta Ross, "Sterilization and 'de facto' Sterilization," *Amicus Journal*, 15, 4 (Winter 1994) p. 29; and Lynora Williams, "Violence Against Women," *Black Scholar* (January–February 1981), p. 19.
52. Haraway, *Primate Visions*, pp. 93–94.
53. Harris, *The Rise of Anthropological Theory*, p. 431.

54. Drake, "Anthropology and the Black Experience," pp. 16–17.
55. Zora Hurston, *Dust Tracks on a Road* (Philadelphia: J. B. Lippincott, 1971), pp. 170–174.
56. Drake, "Anthropology and the Black Experience," p. 5. Drake identifies Katherine Dunham, Mark Hanna Watkins, Arthur Huff Fauset, Irene Diggs, Allison Davis, Montague Cobb, Lorenzo Turner, and himself among the others.
57. For the influence of commerce on Black higher education in the U.S. and Africa, see James D. Anderson, "Philanthropic Control over Private Black Higher Education," and Edward H. Bernman, "Educational Colonialism in Africa: The Role of American Foundations, 1910–1945," in *Philanthropy and Cultural Imperialism*, Robert F. Arnove, ed. (Bloomington: Indiana University Press, 1982).
58. Fabulists like Arthur Schlesinger Jr., C. Vann Woodward, George Will, Lynne Cheney, and Eugene Genovese, have declared that anti-modernist multiculturalism is "an attack on the common American identity" (Schlesinger); "a war of aggression against the Western political tradition and the ideas that animate it" (Will); a terrorist campaign which can only be defeated "by unleashing counterterrorism against cowardly administrators and their complicit faculty" (Genovese). This mantra, Levine asserts, constitutes "a small growth industry, this jeremiad against the universities and the professoriat, this series of claims that something has suddenly turned sour in the academe, that the Pure Aims and Honest Values and True Worth of the past have been sullied and fouled by politics, by radicals disguised as professors." Levine, "Clio, Canons, and Culture," pp. 851–853.

CHAPTER 8

Slavery and the Platonic Origins
of Anti-democracy

> ... there was no action or belief or institution in Graeco-Roman
> antiquity that was not one way or other affected by the possibility
> that someone involved might be a slave.
> — *M. I. Finley*[1]

THE TWINNED DISCOURSE OF SLAVERY AND DEMOCRACY

The present essay elaborates on ancient Greek thought, and especially upon Plato's *Republic* – a conflicted text, a work that not only surreptitiously recomposed the oppositions of freedom and slavery faced by Plato and his contemporaries, but also provided a rhetorical cornice for later disputants about democracy. For the Greek philosophers of the fifth and fourth centuries, a political theory of democracy was unimaginable. T. H. Irwin tells us that "the best of them failed even to take up the task, since they thought that the Athenian democracy was theoretically indefensible." Instead, the gravity of philosophy was employed to absolve the failure. Two-thousand years later, "the loss to political theory" was still being assessed, "for the assumptions of Greek democracy are in some ways similar to, but in many important ways different from, those of what might loosely be called the modern liberal tradition."[2] M. I. Finley also argues that no democratic theory survives from fifth-century Athens,[3] a view rejected by Cynthia Farrar, who maintains that a "version of democratic theory is to be found in the ideas espoused by Protagoras, Thucydides, and Democritus."[4] In classical Athens, slavery and the discourse of democracy were twinned. As historical forces, however, they were opposed. The Athenian upper classes – the political interests most dependent on slavery – intuited that democratic values would inevitably mature in anti-slavery; the democrats were just as certain that sooner or later slavery would subvert their status as free citizens. More than two-thousand years later, again under the pall of a slave economy, an accommodation between slavery and liberty was attempted by the framers of the American Constitution. A counterfeit democratic discourse masking republicanism was substituted in order to reconcile the competing economic and moral claims of liberalism.

The monumental intelligence of Plato, the fourth-century Athenian philosopher, proved to be significant in both instances. Plato's articulation of a racial social order convalesced the proximity of slavery and liberty. No longer, perhaps, the "divine Plato" celebrated during the Italian Renaissance, his *episteme* survived to fertilize and dominate the conceits masqueraded as American democracy. Of his numerous works opposing democracy, none is more central than the *Republic*, his ingenious architecture of a Just Order. In looking at this work, I agree with Irwin and Fisher. Irwin's lament assumes a particularly greater poignancy when we resituate the Hellenic failure as a portent of the moral catastrophes that attended the antinomies of American liberty and slavery.

IDEOLOGY AND TEXTUAL INTERPRETATION

The interpretation of historical and literary texts is a daunting exercise. Evidently, the more disciplined the intelligence behind a work and urgent the anxiety surrounding its subject, the more fugitive its meaning may be. We require a method of excavation that neutralizes the encoded snares, narrative seductions, and elegant blandishments with which the text is salted. If we approach the *Republic* as the work of a political as well as philosophic imagination, Fredric Jameson might urge that we attempt to reveal the terms of Plato's ideological system, which the text represses. We should expect that these "nodal points" will be "unrealized in the surface of the text [and] the logic of the narrative."[5] Typically, the closed text obscures its ideological purpose and represses opposing discourses. But like the compulsive analysis of psychoanalytic literature, the text scatters clues about. In its repetitiveness, its silences, and its corrupted, disjunctive "speech," the text reveals what it was intended to conceal.

Jameson refers to an "ideological system," and the clearest presentation of the notion of ideology he employs is provided by James Kavanagh:

> *Ideology* ... does not primarily signify a consciously articulated set of ideas that form the explicit basis of a political "world view," but a system of unconscious or preconscious image-concepts that form the implicit basis for a "lived" relation to the real, ideology identifies a system of representations through which men and women *imagine* and *experience* as well as *think about* their relation to, and their place within, a given socioeconomic mode of production and its class structure. Indeed, strictly speaking *ideology* signifies no "thing" at all, but a *type of relation*, "indispensable in any social formation," an "imaginary" relation of individuals to their real conditions of existence.[6]

Ideology provides the inventory of the imagination, the symbolic itinerary of thought, the sensed representations of the real. These elements will constitute our interpretive "system." With it we may determine whether the rudimentary evidence of the *Republic's* partisan character is substantiated by deeper interrogation, and what germ accounts for Western civilization's recurring susceptibility to the work.

After several centuries, the interpretation of Plato has amounted to an industry. This is not quite as forbidding as it might first appear since at least one extensive division of the industry is derisive, having been devoted to preserving particular traditions in the misinterpretation of Plato.[7] Nevertheless, the boundaries are broad and, as E. N. Tigerstedt concludes, "To decide in each controversial case how Plato should be interpreted, is a matter of personal judgement and responsibility.

We are in duty bound to do our best to ascertain, in accordance with the rules of historical and philological criticism, what Plato's words mean, but we have to make sure that we have exhausted the possibilities of objective interpretation before abandoning ourselves to the lures of subjectivism."[8] So let us proceed, as Socrates might have said.

SITUATING PLATO

The first step is to situate Plato. For that we will need instrumentation. Antonio Gramsci's reconstruction of Italian history provides us with the notion of "organic intellectuals," individuals generated from particular activities of their social class whose ideas provided for their class "homogeneity and consciousness of its function ... in the economic ... social and political field."[9] Pythagoras, Plato, and Aristotle might be usefully thought of as such organic intellectuals, produced in the praxis of training the young and advising the powerful. Their class was characterized by Thomas Africa as "a leisure class [which] reflected the views of a defunct aristocracy [disdainful of] labor and commerce."[10]

On that assumption, Plato's *Republic* might simply be read as a manifesto of this "defunct aristocracy" following upon its defeats at the end of the fifth century (the oligarchic revolutions of 411 B.C. and 404 B.C.), the vanquishing and subsequent disintegration of the Athenian Empire, and the further commercialization and democratization of Athens in the first decades of the fourth century. Starting in 380 B.C. and for the next fifty years, the writings of Socrates catalogue the stasis of fourth-century Greece: "The enumeration of the evils from which Sparta was exempt is, and is meant to be, a roll of the major evils besetting the other states of the Hellenic World. These are: internal strife ... slaughter and unlawful exile of citizens ... seizure of property ... revolutionary changes of constitution ... abolition of debts ... and redistribution of land."[11]

However, as John Bremer has demonstrated, the *Republic* is no simple political tract.[12] Greek literature (and later Roman literature) was meant to be read aloud, recited in the company of friends, at public occasions (trials, legislative debates, festivals, etc.) or within the academies of Plato, Socrates, or Aristotle. In the oral culture of the Greek *poleis*, oration, recitation, and rhetoric were the commanding forms of thought and expression. The *Republic* is a masterpiece of the form. As Africa implies, such a deliberate style required the existence of leisure (which Greeks referred to as *schole*) – freedom from me preoccupations of labor, commerce, or the management of property and household affairs. In short, literature like the *Republic* or Aristotle's *Politics* emanated from an intellectual strata supported by "unfree" labor: "[T]he propertied classes in the Greek and Roman world derived their surplus, which freed them from the necessity of taking part in the process of production, not from wage labour, as in capitalist society, but mainly from unfree labour of various kinds [i.e., slavery, debt bondage, and serfdom]."[13]

The *Republic* is one of the thirty-odd survivals of Plato's didactical lectures on conduct, effective thought, and the state of Athenian (or Greek) affairs. As a cultural, historical, and literary text, its interpretation requires an interpretive system conscious of the work's hegemonic authority (the *Republic* assumes a commanding position in our own civilization). That system must also reveal the minimal "units" or *ideologemes* of its discursive structures, what Jameson terms its *pseudo-idea* systems (conceptual and belief systems, abstract value, opinion, and prejudice) and its *protonarrative* systems (social fantasy).[14]

As a dialogue, the work resonates with a particular stratagem of argumentation and demonstration. *A propos* of the employment of the binary opposition, perhaps the "signatory" logical form found in the *Republic* and Plato's truer dialogues. Only Book I of the *Republic* corresponds to the dialogic form familiar to readers of Plato. For that and other reasons, some scholars have argued that Book I was written much earlier than the rest of the work and existed for some time as "thrasymachus," an independent dialogue.[15] We must be wary of the boundaries imposed by the social and political oppositions which hover beneath the work's surface. As we shall see, Greece was racked by the opposition between poverty and riches (*penia kai ploutos*). Plato transcribed this social opposition between the few and the many into a philosophic contradiction between a chaotic injustice and moral perfection, and a political contradiction between democracy and mie by philosopher kings. He proposed an opposition between the divine orderliness that an imagined hierarchy might achieve and the messiness of actual democracy. Addressing the construction of dualities, Fredric Jameson warns that "the political imagination seeks desperately to transcend, generating the contradictories of each of these terms, mechanically generating all the syntheses logically available to it, while remaining locked into the terms of the original double bind."[16]

PLATO'S *REPUBLIC* AS A GUIDE TO POLITICAL DISCIPLINE

Keeping Jameson's remarks in mind, it is more than possible that the *Republic* is less about philosophic discovery than political discipline. Plato's choice of disputants in the first book of the *Republic* provides the initial hint of the political purpose of the work. Though largely lost on his later audiences and modern commentaries, the small group gathered at the home of Polemarchus was an unlikely social aggregate. Plato's select audience in the Academy understood this. But even for his original, intended audience Plato was satisfied to use "cultural persuasion," signification drawn upon overdetermined or prepacked symbolic materials, rather than resort to overt exposition. He counted on his audience's shared class prejudices, its shared political experiences, and its inventory of cultural-political narratives.

The aged Cephalus and his sons, Polemarchus, Lysias, and Euthydemus were *metic* manufacturers and merchants. As resident aliens in Athens they were denied the political rights and protection afforded to citizens.[17] This would have fateful consequences. They were also a family long associated with Athenian democracy. Cephalus had emigrated to Athens from Syracuse at the behest and sponsorship of his friend Pericles, the prominent Athenian democratic leader in the middle third of the fifth century. Already affluent, Cephalus indicates he had accumulated even greater wealth as an arms manufacturer (presumably with profits from the campaigns of the Peloponnesian War). However, during the oligarchic rule of the Thirty Tyrants (404 B.C.) in Athens, Polemarchus and Lysias were among the wealthy metics arrested by the extremist junta. "Lysias and his brother Polemarchus may have been among the richest men in late-fifth-century Athens, and in 404 B.C. they are certainly said to have owned the largest number of slaves which can be reliably credited to any Greek of the Classical period, but in Athens they were metics (resident foreigners) and enjoyed no political rights."[18] Polemarchus was executed by the Board of Eleven and his property (the largest Athenian manufacturing establishment mentioned in the literature) confiscated. After his own arrest, Lysias barely escaped with his life. But with the democracy restored, and upon his return from exile with the victorious *demos*, Lysias had prosecuted Eratosthenes at the court of accounting in 403 B.C. for his role in Polemarchus's execution.[19] Another (but silent) witness to the *Republic's* dialogue, Niceratus, was the son of the rather wealthy Athenian leader Nicias and had met the same fate (through association?) as Polemarchus.[20]

Among the remaining prominent participants in the dialogue were Plato's brothers, Glaucon and Adeimantus (Athenians) and the foreigner, Thrasymachus, the Chalcedonian teacher of rhetoric. Plato's family was aristocratic. His uncle Charmides and great-uncle Critias had been prominent in the extreme oligarchic rule of the Thirty Tyrants. As the discussion in the

Republic runs its course, it becomes clear that Socrates's attention is largely directed to the instruction of Glaucon and Adeimantus since the resident aliens and committed democrats alike are irrelevant to the future ideal polis.

In view of these familial identities and political persuasions, it is possible to understand how Plato's aristocratic audience accepted Socrates's obviously facile refutations of the conjectures of Cephalus, Polemarchus, and Thrasymachus. Annas concludes: "Socrates may be right, but his method of discussion and argument are not adequate to deal with someone who disagrees with him in a basic and systematic way. In Book I of the *Republic* we see the ineffectiveness of Socratic methods in dealing with the powerful claim of the moral skeptic, that there is really no reason to be just, and that one should, if one is rational and intelligent, look after one's own interest."[21] The first two were (1) supporters of the democracy; (2) metics; and (3) manufacturers whose interference in Athenian politics had been at the cost of Polemarchus's life and the loss of much of the wealth Cephalus so valued. Finally, Lysias had publicly prosecuted a representative of Athens's aristocracy. Plato's original audience would have debased Cephalus and his sons on all four accounts.[22] Finally, Thrasymachus, Socrates's most persistent and rude interrogator in the dialogues, was both foreign and so arrogant as to demand payment for his thoughts. The Academy knew on both scores that Thrasymachus the sophist was unworthy to challenge Plato's master.

The physical and temporal locations of the dialogue were also significant. Athenian law forbade metic merchants to reside in Athens. Polemarchus resided with his fellow tradesmen and manufacturers in Peiraeus, the "licentious" and prostitute-ridden seaport five miles southwest of Athens.[23] The port was thus associated with just the sort of self-indulgence and moral pollution which Socrates and Plato so frequently lamented. More importantly, in 403 B.C., it was from Peiraeus that the democratic resistance supported by metics and slaves successfully besieged Athens and fought off the army of the Thirty Tyrants and their Spartan allies.[24] The dialogue itself, Plato hinted, had taken place in the late 420s.[25] Situating the Republic at Peiraeus in the period preceding the oligarchic revolutions of 411 B.C. and 404 B.C. thus added a certain foreboding to the dialogue.

In light of this indirect evidence, one might suspect the author of the *Republic* of special pleading. Our interpretive instrument, fortunately, generates a much more profound and substantial penetration of the text. This is particularly important if we pursue the *Republic* less for its peculiar notion of a Just Order or its Pythagorean metaphysics of Absolutes than for its justification of the stratification of domination.

One rather glaring instance of an "unconscious or preconscious image-concept" in the *Republic* is Plato's evocation of Hesiod's myth of the origins of human development. Plato first advocates it as a "noble lie" ("noble falsehood" or "magnificent myth") with which to fashion the civic identity of his "republic":

"We shall," I said, "tell our citizens the following tale: 'You are, all of you in this community, brothers. But when god fashioned you, he added gold in the composition of those of you who are qualified to be Rulers (which is why their prestige is greatest); he put silver in the Auxiliaries, and iron and bronze in the farmers and other workers.'" (415a)

"In the interests of unity," Julia Annas remarks, "the citizens are to be brought to accept a story which is avowedly not true."[26] Plato's unity, his Just Order, acquires its legitimation in part through the introduction of a racial protonarrative.

THE "RACIAL" CHARACTER OF PLATO'S MYTH

Scholars disagree strongly as to whether the ruse, the noble myth, reveals a sinister intent on Plato's part. The racial character and social, imaginary of the myth itself are troubling.

The social imaginary of Plato's racial myth is a slave society, the social order long familiar to Greeks of the Classical Age and before. Classical Athens, like the other leading Greek city-states, was a slave society. Slave labor was exploited in agriculture, industry, commerce, domestic service, private and public management, entertainment, state service, and war by the *rentier* and hoplite classes, by small farmers and artisans, *metic* merchants and manufacturers, as well as by the State.[27]

The documents from the period indicate a general acceptance of slavery. "Even when crisis turned into civil war and revolution, slavery remained unchallenged."[28] For Attica, two sources from the fourth century – the census of Demetrius of Pharlerum and Hypereides – put the number of slaves at 400,000 and 150,000, respectively.[29] Finley accepts a total between 60,000 to 80,000 for the period, while the most conservative surmises are as low as 20,000.[30] Desmond Lee estimates that the total population of Plato's Athens was between 200,000 to 300,000; 60,000 to 80,000 slaves, 35,000 to 40,000 metics, and 35,000 to 45,000 male citizens.[31] Though it is not certain, the majority of slaves ware apparently non-Greeks, a good proportion of those Thracians.[32]

Gregory Vlastos has persuasively demonstrated, taking to task John Wild, that the presumption of slavery in the Just Order of the *Republic* is so unremarkable for Plato that his few references to that aspect of the economy are casual.[33] More significant, however, are Plato's justifications for slavery found scattered in his other works, particularly the *Laws* and *Timaeus*. In the *Republic*, the gold which racially distinguishes those "qualified to be Rulers" from the bronze of laborers, elsewhere in Plato are signified by *logos* (reason) and *doxa* (belief). Vlastos drew attention to the importance of the "slave metaphor" in Plato's work by asserting: "Plato uses one and the same principle to interpret (and justify) political authority and the master's right to govern the slave, political obligation and the slave's duty to obey his master." For Plato, Vlastos understood, slavery was a key to the necessary *(ananke)* order of the world:

> [H]is views about slavery, state, man, and the world, all illustrate a single hierarchic pattern; and that the key to the pattern is in his idea of *logos* with all the implications of a dualist epistemology. The slave lacks *logos*; so does the multitude in the state, the body in man, and material necessity in the universe. Left to itself each of these would be disorderly and vicious in the sense of that untranslatably Greek word, *hybris*. Order is imposed upon them by a benevolent superior: master, guardian, mind, demiurge ... In such an intellectual scheme slavery is "natural"; in perfect harmony with one's notions about the nature of the world and of man.[34]

Vlastos argued that the transference of the slave metaphor between Plato's anthropology, political theory, and ethics – logos – and his metaphysics (the Forms) and cosmology (the soul) was the elementary premise of Plato's refutation of the "contract theorists" and their "subversive view that slavery was unnatural." His attack extended to Ionian physics (with its imposition of an autonomous nature and denial of superior agency) as a consort to democratic theorists. The debate between Plato and those intent upon trivializing slavery as a mere convention concerned the economic basis of Athenian (and Greek) society. "Their conflicting idealism," Vlastos insisted, "mirrored the real contradiction in Athenian society: a free political community that rested on a slave economy."[35] No wonder, then, despite his objections to Plato's Just Order, Aristotle felt compelled to reaffirm Plato's argument, instituting natural law to justify slavery: "Therefore whenever there is the same wide discrepancy between human beings as there is between soul and body or between man and beast, then those whose condition is such that their function is the use of their bodies and nothing better can be expected of them, those, I say, are slaves by nature" (*Politics*, 125416).

So "normal" was the inferiorization and omnipresence of slaves to Plato and his contemporaries that "but for a few scattered texts in the Athenian orators and a handful of inscriptions we should have hardly any specific evidence of the central role played by slaves in production even in Attica itself."[36] S. Douglas Olson informs us that the protocols of power relations and social discourse between Athenian citizens and slaves are preserved in Aristophanes's comedies:

> The fact that mute slaves often have names while slaves with speaking parts do not ... suggests that something important is at stake here ... Silent slaves can accordingly be allowed [a name], not only for the sake of social verisimilitude but also in order that vocatives can be used against them to determine their behaviour. Servile characters who can speak (and thus potentially speak back) to their masters, on the other hand, are apparently best kept anonymous and thus prevented from wielding their names in potentially subversive ways.[37]

In the *Republic*, the determinant place of this racial fiction as a conceit in Plato's own ideology is revealed later when it rather surprisingly resurfaces as a part of Plato's *political theory!* In Book Eight of the *Republic*, we discover Plato resorting to the same mythic material as a means of explaining the beginnings of "imperfect societies" or "imperfect constitutions." Plato asserts that "change in any society starts with civil strife among the ruling class" (545d). Confronted by the self-invented paradox[38] that his perfect State has changed (a contradiction), Plato sought to escape responsibility by momentarily surrendering instruction to the Muses: "Shall we invoke the Muses, like Homer, and ask them to tell us 'how the quarrel first began'?" (545e). According to the Muses, the first instance (timarchy) of such division within the ruling class results from the trespass against the myth:

> This whole geometrical number, controlling the process, determines the quality of births, and when the Guardians ignore this and mate brides and bridegrooms inopportunely, the resulting children will be neither gifted nor lucky ... In the next generation Rulers will be appointed who have lost the true Guardian's capacity to distinguish the metals from which the different classes of your citizens, like Hesiod's, are made – gold, silver, bronze, and iron; and when iron and silver or bronze and gold are mixed, an inconsistent and uneven material is produced, whose irregularities, wherever they occur, must engender war and hatred. That, then is the pedigree of strife, wherever it happens. (546c–547a)

In similar fashion, Plato (reassuming authority for his opinions) then determines that the next degradation of society – from timarchy to oligarchy – is again a responsibility of the ruling class. Timarchy degenerates into the further concentration of wealth and the eventual disfranchisement of the poor through oligarchic legislation, armed violence, and terrorism. In time, oligarchic society, split into two factions, inevitably nurtures the seeds of its own destruction – a class of renegade, impoverished oligarchies: "This neglect [of self-discipline] and the encouragement of extravagance in an oligarchy often reduces to poverty men born for better things ... Some of them are in debt, some disfranchised, some both, and they settle down, armed with their stings, and with hatred in their hearts, to plot against those who have deprived them of their property and against the rest of society, and to long for revolution" (555de). From these embittered elites emerge the leaders of the democratic revolution (564b).

Finally, unavoidably (even for Plato), it is only in the ultimate degeneracy (from democracy to tyranny) that the demos becomes the culpable class. The *demos* reacting to the counterrevolution of the wealthy, "put forward a single popular leader, whom they nurse to greatness ... this leadership is the root from which tyranny invariably springs" (565c–d). Democracy and its issue, tyranny, spring from miscegenation and fractures of the ruling class.

Of course, Plato's political theory is a total fiction. It corresponds to neither the surviving testimony of revolutionary change in Greek societies nor to the documented reconstructions of later ancient Roman historians and modern classicists. For one instance, Solon, an oligarch credited with laying down the founding codes of Athenian democracy, indicates that it was a popular rebellion rather than factionalism in the ruling class that compelled radical changes in the Athenian *polis* at the beginning of the sixth century. In the midst of Solon's boasts, we find a rebellion: "[H]ad another than I taken the goad in hand, a wicked and avid man, he would not have been able to keep the people in check. For if I had wanted what those who were in revolt were wanting then, or again what their opponents would have Wished for them, the city would have been bereft of many men."[39]

Plato's historical environment was full of counterinstances to his political theory: the oligarchies' massacre of 700 *demos* at Aegina in the early fifth century; the oligarchic destruction of the democracies in Samos (404 B.C.) and Rhodes (391 B.C.); the aristocratic defense of Phlius (the site for Plato's *Phaedo*) in 369 B.C.; the democratic example of Plato's aristocratic contemporary Empedocles at Acragas; the *skytalismos* democratic revolt in Argos (370 B.C.); and earlier the tyrannies of the sixth century, which were "quisling" regimes for their Persian masters.[40] Modern historians like A. Fuks,[41] Finley,[42] Sealey,[43] and St. Croix confirm similar problematics in the fifth and fourth centuries for Plato's political theory. According to Paul Cartledge, the "Age of Revolution" preceding the appearances of democracy in the fifth century was conditioned by "relative overpopulation leading to settlement abroad and stimulating a decisive switch from pasturage to arable farming at home; growth of overseas trade, especially in metals and luxury goods and raw materials; decline of monarchy; full development of the *polis*; questioning of social and political values; and contrivance of new political expedients."[44]

Almost exclusively, Plato draws attention to the ruling classes in both his political theory and philosophy. It is as if the rest of Greek humanity was not real to him. For Plato, the lack of discipline within the ruling classes was a sufficient explanation for the successive appearances of imperfect constitutions – each more degraded than its predecessor. Plato's political theory thus repressed the history of popular rebellion and with it the recognition that social agency might have its genesis from the general populace. Even in his "treatment" of the degeneracy of democracy to tyranny, the *demos* is denied true agency through the selection of a demagogue. In his philosophy, "justice" (permanent order) is opposed to liberty and equality. Logically, then, he is compelled to substitute theory for the literary and cultural record that revealed the long history of popular rebellion in the Greek experience. This repression was one aspect of his political *imagination*, his *experience* of the real, his *ideology*.

One other aspect of his political theory was its manufacture of the historical origins of power. For Plato, power (rule) was identical to nobility (gold). In his presentation, the concentrations of power in Greece were totally divorced from an association with the ill-remembered centuries of tribal warfare, organized violence, pillage, exploitation of agrarian cultivators, colonization, piracy, and migration – in short, all we know of Greek dynastic history from the Dorian invasions (sometime before 1200 B.C.) to the fourth century. On the issue of these events as sources of timarchic, oligarchic, and tyrannical societies, Plato is silent. He suffocates a Thucydidean history by substituting a fabulous and theoretic construction of antecedent events. The mythical terms through which he relates to the real are ideological. Plato's contemporary, Isocrates, embellished a similar fabulous history.[45] The *Republic* is a *protonarrative* system: a "social fantasy" proceeding from the "preconstructed reality" that the aristocratic classes are the descendants of the gods.

WHY PLATO'S INFLUENCE PERSISTS

Plato's fascinating deceits in the *Republic* were inspired by the supersession of a narrow class partisanship. The deficiencies which have so frequently subverted modern Western commentaries on Plato are of a different order. Yet the two are related. If we are to understand a fundamental reason for the appreciation of Plato's work after the passage of more than two millennia, it becomes necessary to assemble Plato's moral and social philosophical thought with the historical provenance of modern Western civilization.

From the time of Aristotle to the present, the presence of slave systems, slave trades, and slave economies was nearly a constant in the historical record of the West. In Europe itself, in the eastern, Mediterranean, and western regions, large- or small-scale slave systems occur from the Roman Imperial era down to modern times.[46] During this two-thousand-year period, and beyond the European peninsula itself, Western economies have either cohered to, appropriated, or invented slave systems in Asia, Africa, or the Americas. Though, obviously, slavery was not a uniquely Western institution, the "problem" of slavery in Western culture (as David Brion Davis has supposed) manifested itself in particular forms. It concerned the contradictions between slavery and the ethical, philosophical, and social impulses coalescing into "Western humanism." The presence of slavery in Western civilization has, as Finley persuasively shows, played havoc with modern Western historiography. Assessing the most important studies of slavery in the past three-hundred years, Finley remarks, "men of firm belief were compelled to find some sort of explanation of the long survival of slavery after the triumph of Christianity."[47] For example, that discursive practice which Hayden White maintains is "inextricably bound up with modern Western culture's notions about its own identity, its status as a (or rather *the*) civilization."[48] Similarly, in the most eminently authoritative moral, theological, political, and juridical discourses spawned in the West, the rationalizations of slavery were legion. The scholastic defenders of slavery could be found in every epoch: pagan or Christian, ancient and medieval, feudal and bourgeois, the Enlightenment and its successors. In sheer number and resourcefulness, if not in conceptual consistency, the apologists – among them Plato, Aristotle, Cicero, Augustine, Aquinas, Thomas More, Las Casas, Grotius, Hobbes, and Locke – easily overwhelmed their formal opposition, just as earlier Plato had vanquished the anti-slavery Sophists.[49]

After the fourteenth century, as the more powerful European states became implicated in world-systemic slave systems, the utility of Platonic and Aristotelian thought became greater. "The *Philosophy* of Aristotle had such an authority in sixteenth- and seventeenth-century Spain, that any attack on him 'was regarded as a dangerous heresy,' and the *Politics* enjoyed a *respect casi supersticioso*."[50] David Brion Davis acknowledges that the "frigid sympathy" for the slave, which W. L. Westermann had ascribed to the Roman world, seemed all but extinguished. "Throughout Europe scholars debated the relation of slavery to divine and natural law as an exercise in dialectic; it was as if the learned volumes on law and statecraft had been produced in a different world from that which contained the Negro captives awaiting shipment at Elmina Castle, the disease and sickening stench of the slave ships, and the regimented labor of colonial plantations."[51] Davis continues that "the inherent contradiction of human slavery had always generated dualisms in thought, but by the sixteenth and seventeenth centuries Europeans had arrived at the greatest dualism of all – the momentous division between an increasing devotion to liberty in Europe and an expanding mercantile system based on Negro labor in America." Paradoxically, the unprecedented breadth of the debates around African slavery which raged in Europe and the New World in the eighteenth and nineteenth centuries concealed a deeper cultural consensus: the recession to a racialized discourse.

Vlastos concluded from his critique of Plato "that a consistent democratic philosophy would repudiate slavery altogether."[52] The abolition of slavery proclaimed in 1794 by the National Convention during the French Revolution can be read as a confirmation of that view.[53] That this was not the case with the founding of the American republic, a decade earlier, suggests (if Vlastos is correct) that something other than "a consistent democratic philosophy" informed North American republicanism. Democratic philosophy was subverted by plutocracy: the construction of a politicoeconomic order whose rulers depended on the preservation of a slave economy, the exploitation of "white" laborers (male and female), the severe restriction of women's political rights, and the expropriation of Native Americans.

During the eighteenth and nineteenth centuries, the Hellenism of the Anglo-Saxon world – as articulated in its moral and aesthetic literature and its social thought – centered on Plato, Aristotle, and Homer. Coleridge narrowed that list even further when he declared, "Every man is born an Aristotelian, or a Platonist ... They are the two classes of men, beside which it is next to impossible to conceive a third."[54] Aristotle, in particular, fell on fertile soil in the racialisms of Anglo-Saxonism in Victorian England and plantocracy in America and the British West Indies.[55] Mavis Campbell[56] discusses in detail the Aristotelian influence on George Fitzhugh,[57] George Frederick Holmes (professor of history at the University of Virginia),[58] John Calhoun,[59] and Arthur Lee.[60] The presence of Aristotle's *Politics* was so ubiquitous among the numerous defenses of slavery that Campbell suggests, "It would be too extensive a list to name, all the-nineteenth-century Southerners who were influenced by Aristotle."[61] Others argue along the same line. W. S. Jenkins says that "the Aristotelian influence upon Southern thought was strong and may be traced through much of the pro-slavery literature."[62] James Oakes similarly says: "Alfred Taylor Bledsoe, Thomas R. R. Cobb, and other pro-slavery writers ... gave prominent display to quotations from Aristotle's *Politics* ... Antebellum Southerners were apparently more receptive to Aristotle's extreme pronouncements than were the philosopher's fellow Athenians."[63]

In late eighteenth-century America, democracy was abhorrent to the most prominent and influential revolutionists.[64] As Edmund Morgan observed: "The key to the puzzle, historically [was], Virginia. Virginia was the largest of the new U.S., in territory, in population, in influence – and in slaveholding."[65] Thomas Jefferson and James Madison acquired slaves while opposing slavery, and like most in their fraternity, they fought and spoke for liberty while opposing dem-ocracy. Jefferson, intimately familiar with the "antients," was very critical of Plato. In his private correspondence, Jefferson frequently referred to Plato's "foggy brain" and his abuse of Socrates.[66] In a letter to John Adams in 1814, Jefferson commented on the *Republic*: "While wading through the Whimsies, the puerilities and unintelligible jargon of this work, I laid it down often to ask myself how it could have been, that the world should have so long consented to given reputation to such nonsense as this? ... And particularly, how could Cicero [Jefferson's favorite 'antient'] bestow such eulogies on Plato?"[67] Fitzhugh, who edited this correspondence, himself enthuses over "our Indoeuropean stock, that masterful race of tall, blue-eyed, blond-haired Northmen, whose European beginnings we have now learned to identify with the Greeks and Romans of antiquity themselves, but whose spiritual and racial unity had scarcely been established in the science of Jefferson's day."[68] Yet he, one of the most precocious intellects of his generation (he began his study of Greek, Latin, and French at age nine), reconciled these contradictions through race. However critical he was on other matters, on slavery and racial superiority

Jefferson never issues a challenge to Plato. Instead, Jefferson wholly mimicked the "antient's" construction of doctrines supportive of a racial order:

> Comparing [Blacks] by their faculties of memory, reason, and imagination, it appears to me, that in memory they are equal to the whites; in reason much inferior ... Many millions of them have been brought to, and born in America ... Some have been liberally educated, and all have lived in countries where the arts and sciences are cultivated to a considerable degree, and have had before their eyes samples of the best works from abroad ... But never yet could I find that a black had uttered a thought above the level of plain narration; never see even an elementary trait of painting or sculpture.[69]

Jefferson thus complemented the race discourse fertilizing in race science[70] and popular culture (minstrelsy)[71] of eighteenth and nineteenth centuries in Europe and America. Among the ruling classes as well as the laboring classes, the inventions of the white and Black races rationalized the suturing of liberty, freedom, domination, and oppression.[72] Winthrop Jordan provides an artifact of the moral and political system being displaced by race discourse in the eighteenth century. In the Virginia code of 1705 "negroes, mulattos, or Indians, although christians, or Jews, Moors, Mahometans, or other infidels" were barred from purchasing "christian servants." The "invention" of the idea of a race, along with the idea of ineradicable differences between races, made it possible for people who believed in "liberty" and in "freedom" to also believe simultaneously in "liberty" and "freedom" for themselves and in their right to "dominate" and to "oppress" others. The social imaginary of a slave order enveloped morality and consigned the reciprocal principles of community to a select few. Many scholars concerned with the anomaly between the American Revolution and slavery still insist the problem was reconciling natural rights philosophy and slavery: "Eighteenth-century science had concluded that Negroes were, like the whites, homo sapiens; but this conclusion did not conflict with the reality that Negroes were men, 'persons,' who were legally property ... In the colonial ideology the right of property was central."[73] Juxtaposed to the older and more local signs of difference – the racial codes assigned to previously enslaved peoples in Europe – the invented races brought to the "white" imagination a sociology of desire perhaps more accessible than Christian community. The new difference permitted suspension of the reach of the moral, gentle protocols lurking within Christianity. But simultaneously, within the embrace of the White Race, the new difference affirmed and conditioned the fraternal kinship between the superior and less-privileged strata.[74]

The constitutional debates read as if they were drawn directly from the *Republic*. This is not surprising since much of what passed for learning in the period (some of the conveners had attended British universities, others

American colleges, and quite a few were autodidacts) stressed the classics.[75] As Pierce Butler (South Carolina), one of the framers, assured a friend in October, 1787, "We tried to avoid what appeared to us the weak parts of Antient as well as Modern Republics."[76] Apparently, they believed they had discovered what Fustel de Coulanges later drew from the Greek experience, "The ruling class would perhaps have avoided the advent of democracy if they had been able to found what Thucydides calls [oligarchia isonomos] – that is to say, the government for a few, and liberty for all."[77]

Most certainly, a strong anti-democratic spirit enveloped the proceedings at Philadelphia in 1787.[78] Sherman of Connecticut abhorred direct elections: "The people" he said, "[immediately] should have as little to do as may be about the Government. They want information and are constantly liable to be misled." Elbridge Gerry (Massachusetts), who refused to endorse the Convention's agreement, suggested, "The evils we experience flow from the excess of democracy." Madison (Virginia) warned, "Democratic communities may be unsteady, and be led to action by the impulse of the moment."

At the close of the convention, George Mason, the wealthy Virginian who also opposed the final constitutional draft, reported on its handiwork: "This government will set out a moderate aristocracy: it is at present impossible to foresee whether it will, in its operation, produce a monarchy, or a corrupt, tyrannical aristocracy; it will most probably vibrate some years between the two, and then terminate in the one or the other."[79] Madison, his social and political junior, agreed: the new state was an "oligarchy" (*Federalist Paper*, No. 59). In the discussion regarding Senate terms of office, Madison suggested that long terms provided necessary "permanency": "Landholders ought to have a share in the government, to support these valuable [landed] interests ... They ought to be so constituted as to protect the minority of the opulent against the majority."[80]

Many constitutional scholars for whom Madison's words are normally authoritative routinely ignore such sentiments. They prefer the interpretation of the Constitution which ennobles its architects: "[T]here is one fundamental truth about the Founding Fathers ... they were first and foremost superb democratic politicians."[81] Over the years, then, the ignominy of the oligarchies and their governing machinery has been concealed. Indeed, a fabulist academic literature has enveloped the "Founding Fathers," nurturing a science of pseudodemocracy whose *metier* is the electoral phenomena associated with "representative democracy."[82] This counterfeit democratic tradition is openly hostile to the periodic outbreaks of what it redundantly terms "participatory" or "direct" democracy.[83] Ironically, the tradition and its techniques often parrot the corruption of philosophic instruction which Plato criticized in the *Republic*:

Suppose a man was in charge of a large and powerful animal, and made a study of its moods and wants; he would learn when to approach and handle it, when and why it was especially savage or gentle, what the different noises it made meant, and what tone of voice to use to soothe or annoy it. All this he might learn ... and then call it a science, and reduce it to a system and set up to teach it. But he would not really know which of the creature's tastes and desires was admirable or shameful, good or bad, right or wrong ... remaining quite blind to the real nature of and difference between inevitability and goodness (493b–c).

It was to this "queer" (Plato's term) procedure that Finley addressed himself in a severe critique of the pseudodemocratic subterrain he uncovered in Seymour Martin Lipset's *Political Man* (1960). Finley suggested:

> Both Plato and Lipset would leave politics to experts, the former to rigorously trained philosophers who, having apprehended the Truth, will thereafter be guided by the Truth absolutely; the latter to professional politicians (or to politicians in consort with the bureaucracy), who will be guided by their expertise in the art of the possible and be periodically checked by an election, the democratic device that gives the people a choice between competing groups of experts, and, to that extent, a measure of control ... both agree that popular *initiative* in political decisions is disastrous ... naive ideology."[84]

(Referring to Lipset's contemporaries, Quentin Skinner remarked: "[T]he operational definition of democracy supplied by Dahl and the other empirical theorists is in fact perfectly adapted to performing precisely [its] ideological task ... For its application suggests that the existence of a ruling elite may be compatible with the maintenance of a genuinely democratic political system.")[85] The elitist theory of democracy which Lipset championed did not so much appropriate Plato but rather mirrored its Platonic genealogy.

It has long been evident that the *Republic's* purpose was to mount a sustained attack on democracy. But its durability as an eminent work in modern liberal democratic society has been taken as a testament to the recognition of its literary, philosophical, ethical, and historical merits rather than its ideological prosecution. Such is not the whole explanation. In its anti-democratic plutocratic prejudice, the *Republic* provides an authority rich in intellectual stratagems a propos to the political discourse embedded in the American political order. Plato survives because if he had not existed, he would have had to be invented.

NOTES

1. M. I. Finley, *Ancient Slavery and Modern Ideology* (New York: Viking Press, 1980), 65.
2. T. H. Irwin, "Socrates and Athenian Democracy," *Philosophy & Public Affairs* 18, 2 (Spring, 1989), 205.
3. M. I. Finley, *Democracy, Ancient and Modern* (New Brunswick, N.J.: Rutgers University Press, 1985), 28.

4. Cynthia Farrar, *The Origins of Democratic Thinking* (Cambridge: Cambridge University Press, 1988), 1.

5. Fredric Jameson, *The Political Unconscious* (Ithaca, N.Y.: Cornell University Press, 1967), 48.

6. James Kavanagh, "'To the Same Defect': Toward a Critique of the Ideology of the Aesthetic," *Bucknell Review* 27, 1 (1982), 103.

7. E. N. Tigerstedt, *Interpreting Plato* (Stockholm: Almquist & Wiksell International, 1976), chapters II and III; the examples of Ronald Levinson, *In Defense of Plato* (Cambridge: Harvard University Press, 1953); Irwin, "Socrates and Athenian Democracy," page no. passim.

8. E. N. Tigerstedt, *Interpreting Plato*, 107.

9. Antonio Gramsci, *The Modern Prince and Other Writings* (New York: International Publishers, 1967), 118.

10. Thomas Africa, *Science and the State in Greece and Rome* (New York: John Wiley & Sons, 1967), 35–36. See also F. L. Vatai, *Intellectuals in Politics in the Greek World* (London: Croom Helm, 1984).

11. Alexander Fuks, "Isokrates and the Social-Economic Situation in Greece," *Ancient Society*, 3 (1972), 19.

12. John Bremer, *On Plato's Polity* (Houston, TX: Institute of Philosophy, 1984).

13. G. E. M. de Ste. Croix, *The Class Struggle in the Ancient Greek World* (Ithaca, N.Y.: Cornell University Press, 1981), 39.

14. Jameson, *The Political Unconscious*, 87.

15. "Thrasymachus." Cf. Julia Annas, *An Introduction to Plato's Republic* (Oxford: Clarendon Press, 1981), 17; George Klosko, *The Development of Plato's Political Theory* (New York: Methuen, 1986), 16.

16. Jameson, *The Political Unconscious*, 48.

17. For the relationship between citizenship and land in classical Greece, see T. E. Rihill, "EKTHMOPOI: Partners in Crime," *Journal of Hellenic Studies* CXI (1991), 104–105.

18. Ste. Croix, *The Class Struggle*, 92.

19. David Whitehead, "Sparta and the Thirty Tyrants," *Ancient Society* 13/14 (1982/83): 127ff; A. R. Burn, *The Pelican History of Greece* (Harmondsworth: Penguin, 1982), 301–302; Charles Darwin Adams, ed., *Lysias* (Norman: University of Oklahoma Press, 1970), 38ff.

20. Bremer, *On Plato's Polity*, 5–6.

21. Annas, *An Introduction*, 56–57.

22. "Aristotle's argument, which leads to the condemnation of all forms of manual labor as banausic, harmful to body and soul, is the clearest and most logical statement of a view which seems to have been commonly held by the intelligentsia of the late fifth- and fourth-century Athens." Maurice Balm, "Attitudes to Work and Leisure in Ancient Greece," *Greece & Rome* XXXI, 2 (October, 1984), 140–141.

23. The description of Peiraeus is Thomas Pangle's, cf. *The Laws of Plato* (New York: Basic Books, 1980), 381; see also, Eva Keuls, *The Reign of the Phallus* (New York: Harper & Row, 1985), 153ff.

24. For the defeat of the Thirty Tyrants, see Raphael Sealey, *A History of the Greek City States* (Berkeley: University of California Press, 1976), 379ff.

25. A. E. Taylor, *Plato: the Man and His Work* (Cleveland and New York: The World Publishing Company, 1966), 263–264.

26. Annas, *An Introduction*, 107.

27. Ste. Croix, *The Class Struggle*, 138ff; M. I. Finley, *Economy and Society in Ancient Greece* (Harmondsworth: Penguin, 1983), Part Two; Michael H. Jameson, "Agriculture and Slavery in Classical Athens," *Classical Journal* 73 (1977–1978): 122–145.

28. Finley, *Economy and Society*, 106.

29. A. H. M. Jones, *Athenian Democracy* (Oxford: B. Blackwell, 1957), 77.

30. Finley, *Economy and Society*, 102; Jones, *Athenian Democracy*, 79; Desmond Lee, "Translator's Introduction," in *Plato: The Republic* (Harmondsworth: Penguin, 1986), 26.

31. Lee, "Translator's Introduction," 26.

32. Finley, *Economy and Society*, 104; Ste. Croix, *The Class Struggle*, 227.

33. Gregory Vlastos, "Does Slavery Exist in Plato's Republic?," in Gregory Vlastos, ed., *Platonic Studies* (Princeton, N.J.: Princeton University Press, 1973), 140–146. Cf. John Wild, *Plato's Enemies and the Theory of Natural Law* (Chicago, IL.: University of Chicago, 1953), 50–51.

34. Gregory Vlastos, "Slavery in Plato's Thought," (orig. 1939) in M. I. Finley, ed., *Slavery in Classical Antiquity* (New York: Barnes & Noble, 1960), 137, 147.

35. Ibid., 138.

36. Ste. Croix, *The Class Struggle*, 171.

37. S. Douglas Olson, "Names and Naming in Aristophanic Comedy," *Classical Quarterly* 42, ii (1992), 311.

38. Plato's philosophy of knowledge founded on his theory of the Forms provided him no alternative but to presume the "imperfect societies" of his age were *derived* from an earlier, *perfect* society.

39. M. M. Austin and P. Vidal-Naquet, *Economic and Social History of Ancient Greece* (Berkeley: University of California Press, 1977), 211; Rihill, "EKTHMOPOI," 120–121.

40. Ste. Croix, *The Class Struggle*, chapter V.

41. Alexander Fuks, "Plato and the Social Question: the Problem of Poverty and Riches in the Laws," *Ancient Society* 10 (1979), 39.

42. Finley, *Democracy Ancient and Modern*, 28.

43. Sealey, *A History*, chapter V.

44. Paul Cartledge, "Hoplites and Heroes: Sparta's Contribution to the Technique of Ancient Warfare," *Journal of Hellenic Studies* 97 (1977), 21; Alexander Fuks makes similar observations in "Patterns and Types of Social-Economic Revolutions in Greece from the Fourth to the Second Century," *Ancient Society* 5 (1974), 54ff.

45. Fuks, "Isokrates and the Social-Economic Situation in Greece," *Ancient Society* 5 (1974), 21.

46. Orlando Patterson, *Slavery and Social Death* (Cambridge, MA.: Harvard University Press, 1966); David Brion Davis, *The Problem of Slavery in Western Culture* (Ithaca, N.Y.: Cornell University Press); J. Thorstein Sellin, *Slavery and the Penal System* (New York: Elsevier, 1976).

47. Finley, *Ancient Slavery*, 16.

48. Hayden White, "Between Science and Symbol," *Times Literary Supplement* 31 (January 1986), 109.

49. Cf. Davis, *The Problem of Slavery*, chapters 3 and 4.

50. Mavis Campbell, "Aristotle and Black Slavery," *Race* XV, 3 (1974), 285–286.

51. Davis, *The Problem of Slavery*, 108.

52. Vlastos, "Slavery in Plato's Thought," 148.

53. C. L. R. James, *The Black Jacobins* (New York: Vintage Books, 1963), 137ff.

54. Richard Jenkyns, *The Victorians and Ancient Greece* (Cambridge, MA: Harvard University Press, 1980), 227.

55. Jenkyns, *The Victorians*, 166–168; Campbell, "Aristotle and Black Slavery," 289ff; Eric Williams, *Capitalism and Slavery* (New York: Capricorn Books, 1966).

56. Campbell, "Aristotle and Black Slavery," 285–286.

57. George Fitzhugh, *Cannibals All! Or Slaves Without Masters*.

58. George Frederick Holmes, "*Observations on a Passage in the Politics of Aristotle Relative to Slavery*," *Southern Literary Messenger* (Vol. 16, No. 4, April 1850), 193–205.

59. On Calhoun, cf. Clement Eaton, *The Freedom-of-Thought Struggle in the Old South* (New York: Harper Torchbooks, 1964), 144, 349.

60. Ibid., Davis, *The Problem of Slavery in Western Culture*, 440.

61. Campbell, "Aristotle and Black Slavery," 295.

62. W. S. Jenkins, *Pro-Slavery Thought in the Old South* (Chapel Hill: University of North Carolina Press, 1960), 137.

63. James Oakes, *Slavery and Freedom* (New York: Alfred A. Knopf, 1990), 30–31.

64. R. R. Palmer, "Notes on the Use of the Word 'Democracy,' 1789–1799," *Political Science Quarterly* LXVIII, 2 (June 1953), 203–226.

65. Edmund S. Morgan, *American Slavery, American Freedom* (New York: W.W. Norton & Company, 1975), 5; Linda Grant DePauw, "Land of the Unfree: Legal Limitations on Liberty in Pre-Revolutionary America," *Maryland Historical Magazine* 68, 4 (1973).

66. Madison was also skeptical of Plato; Morton White, *Philosophy, The Federalist, and the Constitution* (Oxford: Oxford University Press, 1987), 113.

67. Thomas Fitzhugh, ed., *Letters of Thomas Jefferson Concerning Philology and the Classics* (University of Virginia, 1919), 36–37.

68. Ibid., 72.
69. Thomas Jefferson, *Notes on Virginia* quoted by Winthrop Jordan, *White Over Black* (Baltimore, Md.: Pelican, 1968), 436–437.
70. The term "race science" is adapted from studies of Nazi science. Michael H. Kater, *Doctors Under Hitler* (Chapel Hill: University of North Carolina Press, 1989); George L. Mosse, *Toward The Final Solution* (London: J.M. Dent & Sons, 1978). For discussions of race science, see George Stocking, Jr., *Victorian Anthropology* (New York: Free Press, 1987) and John Trumpbour, "Blinding Them With Science: Scientific Ideologies in the Ruling of the Modern World," in Trumpbour, ed., *How Harvard Rules* (Boston: South End, 1989).
71. For working-class racism and black-face minstrelsy, see David Roediger, *The Wages of Whiteness* (London: Verso, 1991); Michael Rogin, "Black Masks, White Skin," *Radical History* 54 (1992): 141–152.
72. Jordan, *White Over Black*, 94.
73. George Levesque and Nikola Baumgarten, "'A Monstrous Inconsistency': Slavery, Ideology and Politics in the Age of the American Revolution," *Contributions in Black Studies* 8 (1986–1987), 28.
74. Race science excluded women from the white race. Cf. Nancy Leys Stepan, "Race and Gender: The Role of Analogy in Science," in David T. Goldberg, *Anatomy of Racism* (Minneapolis: University of Minnesota, 1990).
75. Ferdinand Lundberg, *Cracks in the Constitution* (Secaucas, N.J.: Lyle Stuart Inc., 1980), 114ff; Stephen G. Xydis, "Ancient Greece in Emergent America," *Greek Heritage* II, 5 (1965), 84–87.
76. Lundberg, *Cracks*, 76.
77. Numa Denis Fustel de Coulanges, *The Ancient City* (Baltimore, MD: The Johns Hopkins University Press, 1980), 320.
78. William Riker, "The Heresthetics of Constitution-Making," *American Political Science Review* 78, 1 (March 1984), 6; Ellen Meiksins Wood, "Oligarchic 'Democracy,'" *Monthly Review* 41, 3 (July 1989), 48.
79. All quotes are from Lundberg, *Cracks*, 157–171.
80. Ibid., 163.
81. John L. Roche, "The Convention as a Case Study in Democratic Politics," in Leonard W. Levy, ed., *Essays on the Making of the Constitution* (New York: Oxford University Press, 1978), 179; Lundberg, *Cracks*, chapter 1.
82. Bernard Crick, *The American Science of Politics* (London: Routledge & Kegan Paul, 1959); Benjamin Ginsburg, *The Captive Public* (New York: Basic Books, 1986).
83. For a recent example, see Mostafa Rejai, *Comparative Political Ideologies* (New York: St. Martin's Press, 1984), 102.
84. Finley, *Democracy, Ancient and Modern*, 6–7.
85. Quentin Skinner, "The Empirical Theorists of Democracy and Their Critics," *Political Theory* 1, 1 (February 1983), 303.

PART III

ON WORLD POLITICS AND U.S. FOREIGN POLICY

Fascism and the Response of Black Radical *Theorists*

At the end of the war, Nazism was the damned part
of Western civilization, the symbol of evil.
— *Saul Friedlander*[1]

The purpose of this essay is to uncover a Black construction of fascism concealed by the general inattention to critical Black political thought in academic circles. In scholarship as with commonplace discourse, Black political thought like Black political activity is customarily treated as derivative (i.e., Black Democrats, Black Republicans, Black dictators, etc.). One almost needs, then, a critical theory to simply presume that a Black signification of fascism is worth investigation. Here I shall attempt not merely to rehearse the diverse resistances to fascism mounted by ordinary Blacks in the Diaspora and their leaders, but to formulate a theory of fascism from their common discourse. The final objective is to determine whether a different significance for fascism emerged from within Black historical consciousness, a meaning distinct from the hegemonic or conventional interpretations of fascism. Our objective then is an oppositional discourse which reflected whatever is generic in the Black experience of the West's contradictions.

THE MEANINGS OF FASCISM

The scholar who seizes upon the study of fascism has taken on a rather daunting task. This is not simply because by this time the preceding interrogations into the advent and characters of fascism have produced a formidable mountain of documentation. One must also contend with the fact that academic fascist studies is an industry which finds its complements of course in the mass media and entertainment industries of popular culture. But this compacted consortium is merely symptomatic of the real difficulty. The real problem is that this euphonious recital of fascism constitutes a conceit.

The dominant constructions of fascism by Western historians and social theorists as "right-wing extremism," "neurotic authoritarianism," or as a "radical resistance to modernization" are those of an ideology and "a particular political ... system of a specific geographical area in a delimited period of time."[2] In other words, according to its principal interpreters, fascism proper was restricted to Europe between the First and Second World Wars, assuming sometimes the form of state regimes (in Germany, Italy, Spain, and Portugal) and elsewhere that of more or less mass movements (in Austria, Bulgaria, Croatia, Slovakia, Hungary, Rumania, Poland, Finland, Norway, Denmark, Britain, Belgium, and France).[3] This appears to be the limit of the conceptual consensus concerning fascism.

Some scholars have attempted to distinguish between the fascisms which erupted in Central and Eastern Europe from those of Western Europe; others, to differentiate between fascist movements in agrarian societies from those in industrialized countries. There is also considerable controversy pertaining to the social base of fascism: some of its students stressing the importance of the role that industrialists and large landowners played in fascist states; others focusing on the petty bourgeoisie and the bureaucrats. Not infrequently one encounters in a single authority contradictory claims, laying the blame for fascism on practically every social category imaginable. For example, in his detailed study of Hitler's electorate, Richard Hamilton discovered that Nazi voters were industrial workers; peasants; bureaucrats; the rich, educated, and cosmopolitan; and the petty bourgeoisie.[4]

Ten years ago, in an essay devoted to what he describes as "the only genuinely novel or original form of radicalism emerging from World War I," Stanley Payne summarized the most essential of the competing treatments of the nature, meaning and causes of fascism. He began with the earliest debates on fascism: the classical, Marxist interpretation of the 1920s that fascism was "a violent, dictatorial agent of bourgeois capitalism"; the contemporary but alternative views of Benedetto Croce and Friedrich Meinecke that fascism was a "product of a cultural and moral breakdown"; of Erich Fromm, Wilhelm Reich, and Theodor Adorno that fascism was "the result of neurotic or pathological psychosocial impulses"; and of Ortega y Gasset that fascism was "the product of the rise of amorphous masses." Payne maintained that the conceptualization of fascism continued to proliferate in the post-war era: for A. F. K. Organski and Ludovico Garruccio, fascism was "the consequence of a certain stage of economic growth, or historical phases of national development"; for Hannah Arendt, Carl Friedrich, and Zbigniew Brzezinski, fascism was "a typical manifestation of twentieth-century totalitarianism"; for Ernst Nolte, Wolfgang Sauer, Henry A. Turner, and Barrington Moore, Jr., it was "resistance to modernization" while, to the contrary, A. James Gregor, Karl Bracher, and Alan Cassels argued that fascism displayed both pro- and anti-modernization impulses; and for Renzo de Felice and Seymour Lipset, fascism was "a unique radicalism of the middle classes." It should not be surprising that some of these same scholars (De Felice and Bracher, for two) eventually repudiated the coherence of any generic notion of fascism.[5]

Drawing on the work of Ernst Nolte, Payne himself concluded with some qualification that the essence of fascism was negation (anti-liberalism, anti-communism, and anti-conservatism), ideology (empire, the creation of a nationalist authoritarian state, and a multiclass integrated national economic structure), and organizational style (mystical symbolism, mass political choreography, the exaltation of male dominance, youth, violence, and personal, charismatic leadership). And based upon Eugen Weber's approach, Payne identified six "varieties of fascism": the Italian pluralistic subspecies (reiterated in France, England, Belgium, Hungary, Austria, Rumania, and "possibly even in Brazil"); the "remarkably fanatical" German National Socialism (a form adopted in Scandinavia, the Low Countries, the Baltic states, and Hungary); the Catholic and traditionalist Spanish Falangism; the semireligious Rumanian Iron Guard; the Arrow Cross Hungarian movement; and the bureaucratic fascisms of right-wing authoritarian regimes in Eastern Europe.[6] Upon reflection, then, it becomes apparent that Payne achieved merely the illusion of bringing order to the classificatory chaos of fascist studies.

Payne might have fared better if he had more seriously entertained the nugatory (what he characterized as "an extreme nominalist position"), that is the proposition that fascism was (and, perhaps, is) not a thing, not a generic political phenomenon.

The meaning of fascism – in contradistinction to the advent of fascism – is embedded in what Hayden White asserts is a specific discursive practice: namely, Western historiography.

> ... Western culture has endowed history as both a place where a distinctively human nature makes its appearance and the process by which the human species realizes its destiny. In this respect, the long debate over the question of historical knowledge seems to be inextricably bound up with modern Western culture's notions about its own identity, its status as a (or rather the) civilization, and the nature and value of that "modernity" to which, with varying degrees of pride, it lays claim.[7]

In this sense, from at least the seventeenth century, the practices of historical writing in the West have had less to do with comprehending past human societies than with the tribal desire to order them hierarchically. For this reason, White recommends an historical theory which centers on "a consideration of the rhetoric of historical discourse."

As such it becomes necessary to postulate that the meaning of fascism, the reason for the multi-iconic industries which interrogate and celebrate fascism is the historical manufacture of fascism as a negation of the Western *Geist*. The occurrence of Fascism has been taken to signify the "damned" historical identity which the West almost assumed but ultimately rejected. Fascism was made to signify the "dark" side of Western civilization. As Ernst Nolte observed:

> ... fascism is at the same time resistance to practical transcendence and struggle against theoretical transcendence ... fascism pursues its resistance to transcendence from within that transcendence and at times in the clear consciousness of a struggle for world hegemony ... Fascism represents the second and gravest crisis of liberal society, since it achieves power on its own soil and in its radical form is the most complete and effective denial of that society.[8]

For Nolte, "practical" and "theoretical" transcendence were identical to liberalism, that is with what Engels and Marx referred to as "bourgeois society" and Hayden White addresses as modern Western culture. The advent of fascism has been employed, then, as a confirmation of the existence of the epistemic West; a substantiation of the philosophic identity between Western civilization, Western culture, and human destiny.[9]

In sum, the presentation of fascism reproduces what Umberto Eco refers to as an exemplary narrative:

> ... there is a "hero" who asserts a "value" to be pursued; in order to secure and protect this value, an "interdiction" must be respected; the interdiction is violated, either by the hero under the influence of a "villain," or by the villain himself to the detriment of the hero, and a "misfortune" results; at this point a "rescuer" intervenes and engages in a struggle with the villain until victory is attained; the defeat of the villain re-establishes the compromised value.[10]

In the "exemplary" tales which constitute the interrogation of fascism, the hero is the West; the value is individual freedom (in material or spiritual terms); the interdiction is authoritarian mass movements; the villain, charismatic leaders; the misfortune, fascism; the rescuer, bourgeois democracies; the struggle, the Second World War; the moral: "The hero was imprudent, but managed to redeem himself on his own."

From the perspective of many non-Western peoples, however, the occurrence of fascism – that is militarism, imperialism, racialist authoritarianism, choreographed mob violence, millenarian crypto-Christian mysticism, and a nostalgic nationalism – was no more an historical aberration than colonialism, the slave trade, and slavery. Fascism was and is a modern social discipline which much like its genetic predecessors, Christianity, imperialism, nationalism, sexism, and racism, provided the means for the ascent to and preservation of power for elitists. And as a discipline of domination, the conditions of existence are those paradigmatic moments in the West's historical experience (e.g., the appropriation by an emergent but still amorphous elite of Christianity during the Dark Age or nationalism following the French Revolution) when the disintegration of one hierarchical social order provides the occasion for the instituting of a successor under a new regime of truth. And like Christianity and nationalism, the ethos of fascism swept through the whole of Western civilization notwithstanding the conspicuous particularities evident at specific localities. As such, for a moment it manifested itself in national or societal arenas (German national socialism, Italian fascists, Spanish Falangists, etc.) while actually composed from the ideological, political, and technological materials of a civilization. It is, then, a mistake to posit fascism as an inherent national trait or to ascribe it to a particular culture or class.

THE BLACK MASSES AND FASCISM

In the post-war period, in the wake of ideological challenges from workers' movements and renegade intelligentsias in the European metropole, and the structural breakdown and/or elasticity of war-exhausted economies and nation-states, fascist ideologies offered an apocryphal alternative to the disintegration of Europe. The adoration of war for its own sake would provide the political and moral will which would ensure the solidarity of the West. Mussolini declared: "Fascism believes neither in the possibility nor the utility of perpetual peace ... War alone brings up to its highest tension all human energy and puts the stamp of nobility upon the peoples who have the courage to meet it." And Hitler insisted: "In eternal warfare mankind has become great – in eternal peace mankind would be ruined."[11]

It was indeed, the nature of fascist war which had its most telling affect on ordinary Black men and women. By the early 1930s when it had become evident that Mussolini's war ambitions had been limited to Africa by the foreign policies and interests of the more powerful nations in Europe,[12] Blacks had already sustained crushing defeats on the international arena in Cuba, Haiti, and Liberia. In 1912, Afro-Cuban nationalists had been subjected to a near-genocidal war under the direction of U.S. officials.[13] In 1915, the U.S. had begun what was to be a nineteen-year occupation of Haiti.[14] And in 1929, the U.S. State Department had bludgeoned the corrupt Americo-Liberian elite into abject submission to American capital (Harvey Firestone).[15] In America, to further deepen these humiliations, Blacks had to contend with the spectacle of their most influential "race" leaders as collaborators:

> The diffidence of leaders like Washington in the Haitian affair; the role of figures like DuBois in the opposition to and the destruction of the UNIA's organisation

and programme; DuBois' collaboration with the War Department during the First World War ...; the collusion of Black leaders with the Liberian elite's use of forced labour, had all produced a deep resentment towards a stratum whose greed and self-deceptions led it to identifications with American imperialism at home and Black ruling-class oligarchies abroad.[16]

Deprived of radical leadership by the now decimated Universal Negro Improvement Association and the ambiguous and fluid policies of the Communist Party – the U.S., William Scott (one of the most important students of this period) writes: "aroused blacks in the the U.S. mounted a vigorous campaign between 1935 and 1936 to save the last outpost of Negro rule in the world from white domination." Often reactive to events, the resistance to Fascist Italy's African imperialism more and more took on the character of a grassroots Black nationalism.[17] And, perhaps, because it was not beholden to any established organization or fettered by established leadership, "This nationalistic attitude was prevalent in Black America, permeating every geographical section of the nation."[18]

While in the U.S., mass rallies and support groups were reported in Chicago (the Negro World Alliance), New York (the Provisional Committee for the Defense of Ethiopia and the African Patriotic League, etc.), Miami (the Ethiopian Relief League), Fort Worth, Okmulgee, Washington, D.C. (Ethiopian Research Council), and Mobile (Friends of Ethiopia), and letters to Black newspapers like the *Chicago Defender*, the *Pittsburgh Courier*, the *Amsterdam News*, and the *Baltimore Afro-American* registered a general outrage, Black protests extended well beyond the U.S.

> Elsewhere, 100 Liberian, Ovambo, and Karro dockworkers in Southwest Africa refused to work on Italian ships; in Kenya, the Kikuyu Central Association enlisted volunteers for the campaign in Ethiopia; Egyptian doctors reported to Addis Ababa; and hundreds of West Indians from British Guiana, Cuba, and Trinidad to the Bahamas requested permission from their colonial authorities to enlist in the armies of Ethiopia.[19]

From America, the British Consul-General Sir G. Campbell wrote the Foreign Office: "It seems as though the normally legal and patriotic British West Indian and British Guianan natives as well as the Afro-Americans in the community have lost their sense of perspective over the dispute ..."[20] Antifascism was thus spontaneously extended throughout the Black world. And it is a certainty that Campbell's discomfort would have been even more acute had he encountered James Moody. In June 1935, Moody, an unemployed rock driller, wrote to Franklin Delano Roosevelt, the president of the U.S.: "Now this is my point of view ... you have (1)2 million Black citizen that are classed as undesirables that voluntary want to get back to the land from which their fore-fathers had come by force which is Africa the land of the Ethiopia and it would save the government millions of dollars by sending them there."[21]

Frustrated by their own lack of resources and the shortness of the war in Ethiopia, perhaps as many as 100 African-Americans joined the International Brigades fighting for the government in the Spanish Civil War.[22] There they joined Blacks from Africa, the West Indies, Europe, and Latin America. Langston Hughes, who as a journalist spent nearly half of 1937 in Spain, reports that "some of them in the Brigades told me ... By fighting against Franco they felt they were opposing Mussolini."[23] Hughes arrived at Albacete too late to give Milton Herndon the greeting sent by his younger brother Angelo. Milton Herndon had been killed in battle on the 13th of October. But Milton's comrades remembered what he had told them: "Yesterday, Ethiopia, Czechoslovakia – today, Spain – tomorrow, maybe America. Fascism won't stop anywhere – until we stop it."[24]

THE BLACK RADICAL THEORISTS

Many of the radical Black intellectuals who witnessed the rise of fascism in Europe were convinced that whatever its origins, at some point fascism had become an instrument of capitalists with the objective of destroying working-class movements. In 1937, in his *World Revolution*, C. L. R. James while crediting the paralyzing conflict between Stalin's Communist International and the Second International for their part in the rise of Nazism, also observed that from 1931: "More and more groups of German capitalists began to see their way out in Hitler."[25] James came closest to the Euro-Marxist construction of fascism, casting his interpretation of that movement almost wholly in terms of Europe, class struggle, and the clash between capitalism on one side and, on the other, the treacherous sibling rivalry between the Second and Third Internationals. He remained true to this position long after the events leading up to the Second World War. In 1960, he wrote: "The Black Shirt Movement of Mussolini and the Brown Shirt Movement of Hitler were organized for the sole purpose of destroying the threat of a socialist society that the working class now posed, with the example of a Soviet state actually in existence."[26] He was also persuaded that "the victory of fascism in Germany [meant] ... the victory of reaction all over Central and Eastern Europe," and in Spain and France.[27] Harry Haywood, who had spent six months as a political commissar with the Abraham Lincoln Battalion in Spain, concurred: "The Spanish Civil War was a part of the worldwide drive for fascism."[28]

George Padmore and Oliver Cromwell Cox, however, saw the emergence of fascism somewhat differently. Padmore had resigned (or was expelled as his opponents would have it) from the Communist International in the mid-1930s because of his refusal to accept the new official line which distinguished between "democratic imperialists" (the U.S., Britain, and France) and "fascist imperialists" (Germany, Italy, and Japan).[29] In 1937, in his *Africa and World Peace*, Padmore had come to the resolve that fascism was a response to "the breakdown of capitalist economy": "It is exactly because of the disintegration of Capitalist-Imperialism that it became necessary for the ruling class of Germany to discard bourgeois democratic institutions and resort to open terroristic dictatorship, in order to maintain their position."[30] And ten years later, Oliver C. Cox sought to reconcile the advent of the Second World War with the notion of fascism as an expression of capitalism:

> ... the basis of many of the seeming inconsistencies in the politics of World War II lies in the fact that the capitalist alliance was interested in destroying the fascists as competitors for world markets and natural resources but in saving them as bulwarks against the proletariat.[31]

Cox described the fascist state as "a capitalist state in a certain stage of degeneration."[32] Regardless, as Scott suggested, it was the case that those Black radical intellectuals who had been influenced by Marxism held to a materialist interpretation of fascism, believing "in the primacy of class and economics over race and nationality ...,"[33] subordinating the political and historical force of Western civilization and racial ideology to (ruling) class consciousness.

The one major exception was DuBois. By asserting a cultural identity between fascism and the putative democracies ("Western Europe did not and does not want democracy, never believed in it, never practiced it and never without fundamental and basic revolution will accept it."[34]), DuBois, in the late 1920s and early 1930s anticipated by nearly thirty years Padmore's belated recognition that what fascism actually signified was "a new aggression of Europeans in Africa."[35] DuBois recalls:

> I knew that Hitler and Mussolini were fighting communism, and using race prejudice to make some white people rich and all colored peoples poor. But it was not until later that I realized that the colonialism of Great Britain and France had exactly the same object and methods as the fascists and the Nazis were trying clearly to use.[36]

Like Langston Hughes, Harry Haywood, and Milton Herndon, DuBois had been exposed to the more naked vista of fascism:

> He was in [Nazi Germany] during the frightening spectacle of the 1936 Olympic games. DuBois viewed Hitler as the latest "crude but logical exponent of white world race philosophy [that] since the Conference of Berlin in 1884" had culminated in the partition of Africa.[37]

But unlike most of his fellow radicals, DuBois insisted that the essence of fascism was racial. "The black world knows," DuBois wrote in 1935, "this is the last great effort of white Europe to secure the subjection of black men."[38] It was a construction he shared with the Black working class. And because in his early years DuBois had granted primacy to the "color line," it is not surprising that at the end of his life he would insist:

> I believe that the trade in human beings between Africa and America, which flourished between the Renaissance and the American Civil War, is the prime and effective cause of the contradictions in European civilization and the illogic in modern thought and the collapse of human culture.[39]

For DuBois, the precondition for fascism was a civilization profoundly traumatized by slavery and racism.

At the time, DuBois was in the minority among his radical colleagues, Manning Marable, one of his most sympathetic biographers, has chastised him for not being able "clearly ... to discern the broad prerogatives of industrialists and finance capitalists who supported the Nazi state" and for his "highly debatable conclusion that the majority of Germans supported 'Adolph Hitler today.'"[40] Marable, despite his obvious affection for DuBois, is more comfortable with that interpretation of fascism which envelops it in class struggle and capitalism rather than as a signifier of the West. Such an approach possesses only a tenuous relationship with the facts that the membership of the Nazi Party stood at nearly 900,000 in 1933 (by 1937, it would be 2.5 million) or that 37.2 percent of the German electorate voted for the Nazis in 1932.[41]

On the other hand, DuBois's formulation of fascism as the "logical" extension of white racism echoed that of the Black masses. And, paradoxically, it coincided with that moment when DuBois was most influenced by Marxism.[42] As a pan-Africanist, however, DuBois had gone beyond Eurocentrism, and consequently had no vested interest in subordinating his analysis of race and culture to an economic determinism. He eschewed the rationalism of historical materialism for a theory of history which granted irrationalist forces their due. Like many ordinary Black people DuBois believed that the West was pathological and fascism an expression of that nature.

NOTES

1. Saul Friedlander, *Reflections of Nazism* (New York: Harper & Row) 1984, ix.
2. Stuart Woolf, *Fascism in Europe* (London: Methuen) 1981, 1. H.R. Trevor-Roper insisted: "The public appearance of fascism as a dominant force in Europe is the phenomenon of a few years only. It can be precisely dated. It began in 1922–1923, with the emergence of the Italian fascist party which Mussolini led to power ... It came of age in the 1930s when 'fascist' parties sprung up throughout Europe and were brought to power ... under the patronage of Hitler and

Mussolini … It ended in 1945 with the defeat and death of the two dictators, the collapse or scurry of their European clients." Trevor-Roper, "The Phenomenon of Fascism," in Woolf, ibid., 19.

3. Ibid., and John Weiss, ed., *The Fascist Tradition* (New York: Harper & Row) 1967; Stein Ugelvik Larsen, Bernt Hagtvet, and Jan Petter Myklebust, eds, *Who Were the Fascists? Social Roots of European Fascism* (New York: Columbia) 1980.
4. Richard F. Hamilton, *Who Voted for Hitler?* (Princeton: Princeton University) 1982. And Istvan Deak has added domestic servants to the list: "What Was Fascism?" *New York Review of Books*, March 3, 1983, 13. Woolf, for another instance, maintains that the social base for fascism was the "urban and rural petty bourgeoisie," "rural voters," industrialists, landowners, "technocratically minded civil servants," conservatives, intellectuals, etc.
5. Payne, "The Concept of Fascism," in Larsen et al., *Who Were the Fascists?* 14–25.
6. Ibid., 20–22.
7. Hayden White, "Between Science and Symbol," *Times Literary* Supplement, January 31, 1986, 109.
8. Ernst Nolte, *Three Faces of Fascism* (London: Weidenfeld and Nicolson) 1965, 566–567.
9. On this score, the treatment of fascism coincides with that accorded to slavery, that other anomaly in the Western experience. David Brion Davis has quite unintentionally crystallized slave scholarship in the titles of his successive studies: *The Problem of Slavery in Western Culture*, *The Problem of Slavery in the Age of Revolutions*, and, ironically, *Slavery and Human Progress*. According to Davis, slavery is anti-thetical to Western culture and alien to Western civilization. By the simple device of substituting in these titles the word fascism for slavery, we come close to the conventional thrust of fascist studies by Western scholars of whatever ideological persuasion.
10. Umberto Eco, "Strategies of Lying," in Marshall Blonsky, ed., *On Signs*, 1985, 6–7.
11. Quoted in George Padmore, *Africa and World Peace* (London: Frank Cass) 1937, 73.
12. In June 1926, DuBois wrote: "In the secret Treaty of London which induced Italy to desert her allies, Germany and Austria, and to take active part with England and France, Italy was promised not only increase of territory at the expense of Austria, but the right to extend her possessions in 'Eritrea, Somaliland and Libya'; and since these extensions could not be into the ocean, they must be into Abyssinia." "African Manners," in Henry Lee Moon, ed., *The Emerging Thought of W. E. B. DuBois* (New York: Simon and Schuster) 1972, 233.
13. Lourdes Casal, "Race Relations in Contemporary Cuba," in *The Position of Blacks in Brazilian and Cuban Society*, Report No. 7, Minority Rights Group, London, 1979, 12.
14. Brenda Gayle Plummer, "The Afro American Response to the Occupation of Haiti, 1915–1934," *Phylon*, 43, June 1982.
15. I. K. Sundiata, *Black Scandal* (Philadelphia: Human Issues Institute) 1980.
16. Cedric J. Robinson, "The African Diaspora and the Italo-Ethiopian Crisis," *Race & Class*, XXVII, 2, 1985, 60. See also, Robinson, "DuBois and Black Sovereignty: The Case of Liberia," *Race & Class*, 32, 2, 1990, 39–50.
17. For examples of Black sentiment, see the dozens of letter writers volunteering their services to Ethiopia in *The Pittsburgh Courier*, July 27, 1935.
18. William R. Scott, "Black Nationalism and the Italo-Ethiopian Conflict, 1934–1936," *Journal of Negro History*, 63, 2, 1978, 119, 121.
19. Robinson, "Fascism and the Intersections of Capitalism, Racialism, and Historical Consciousness," *Humanities in Society*, 6, 4, Fall 1983, 343.
20. Campbell to Sir Samuel Hoare, F.O. 371/19125–9, J 3725, 8 August 1935.
21. Moody to Roosevelt, June 21, 1935, State Department Decennial Files, 884.5511/3.
22. Joseph Brandt, ed., *Black Americans in the Spanish People's War Against Fascism* (New York: International) n.d.
23. Hughes, *I Wonder as I Wander* (New York: Hill and Wang) 1956, 354.
24. Ibid., 377.
25. James, "After Hitler, Our Turn" in *Spheres of Existence* (London: Allison & Busby) 1980, 28.
26. James, *Modern Politics* (Detroit: Bewick) 1973, 54.
27. Ibid., 21.
28. Haywood, *Black Bolshevik* (Chicago: Liberator) 1978, 467.

29. C. L. R. James, "George Padmore: Black Marxist Revolutionary," in James, *At the Rendezvous of Victory* (London: Allison & Busby) 1984, 254–255.

30. Padmore, *Africa and World Peace*, 70.

31. Cox, *Caste, Class and Race* (New York: Monthly Review) 1970 (orig. 1948), 198.

32. Ibid.

33. Scott, "Black Nationalism," 121.

34. DuBois, *Dusk of Dawn* (New York: Harcourt, Brace) 1940, 170.

35. George Padmore, *Pan-Africanism or Communism* (London: Doubleday) 1956, 124.

36. DuBois, *The Autobiography of W. E. B. DuBois* (New York: International) 1968, 305–306.

37. Manning Marable, *W. E. B. Du Bois: Black Radical Democrat* (Boston: Twayne) 1986, 155.

38. DuBois, "Inter-Racial Implications of the Ethiopian Crisis," *Foreign Affairs*, October 1935, 88.

39. DuBois, *The World and Africa* (New York: International) 1965, 43.

40. Marable, *W. E. B. Du Bois*, 155.

41. Peter Merkl, "Comparing Fascist Movements," in Larsen et al., *Who Were the Fascists?*, 756.

42. Robinson, *Black Marxism* (London: Zed) 1983, 289ff; and Marable, *W. E. B. Du Bois*, 136.

CHAPTER 10

Africa: In Hock to History
and the Banks

The *Los Angeles Times* on Sunday (12/16/84) began a series on the African continent ("Africa – The Harsh Realities Dim Hope"), no doubt inspired by the recent attention given to famine victims on that continent by Western governments, international aid agencies, and private organizations. Unlike previous regional series by that paper (e.g., this year's series on Central America), the African series seems to be entirely the work of one reporter, Charles Powers. Unfortunately, this appears to be less a consequence of the *LA Times'* appreciation of Mr. Powers' considerable skills as a journalist than of the rather limited staffing conceded to African affairs by American newspaper publishers and the networks. Still we must be grateful for small gifts since Mr. Powers is a qualitative improvement over his predecessor, David Lamb. There are, however, certain conceptual historical and analytical lapses in Mr. Powers' articles of which the typically uninformed reader might be warned. We begin with the historical and conceptual errors since they often serve as the foundations for the analytical misdirections to be found in the first two installments of the series.

Journalists, perhaps as a consequence of their profession, possess notoriously poor senses of history. On this score, Mr. Powers is no exception. One of his unstated premises is that what is happening to the nations on the African continent is somehow unique; that the "crisis" in Africa is special to that place and this time. What we must all acknowledge at this point is that most of the nations whose political formations occurred in this century, and nearly all of those claiming independence since the Second World War are political and economic failures. Whether we address ourselves to Israel, Brazil, the Philippines, India, Indonesia, South Africa, or Chile – irrespective of the levels of external subsidization, its forms, or origins, most of the newly independent nations of the world are in crisis. The nations of Africa are the rule, not the exception.

A second, and in this instance, explicitly stated historical myth to which Powers subscribes concerns this same era, the past forty years:

The developed world seems to be losing whatever sense of guilt it once may have held regarding past exploitation of Africa and its people ... The conservatism of the Reagan Administration and the Margaret Thatcher government in Britain and increased cost-consciousness in Europe have had strong impact on international lending institutions and aid programs.

The era when "guilt" ruled Western relations with Africa was, of course, punctuated by American government's attempts on the lives of Lumumba and Nkrumah; military assaults against Egypt, Zaire, Algeria; intelligence operations against Angola, Zaire, Ghana; support of Portuguese colonialism in Angola, Mozambique, and Guinea-Bissau and numerous other transgressions – all designed by men like president Nixon who referred privately to Blacks as "jigs" or Kissinger with his racial sense of history or France's D'Estaing whose African financial empire the *Wall Street Journal* carefully detailed (see Roger Morris' *Uncertain Greatness*, or Seymour Hersh's *The Price of Power*). Powers neglects this history but he hasn't entirely failed to emulate some of its undercurrents. Those undercurrents are stored in his conceptual tools.

Powers' series is entitled "Black Africa" and the accompanying maps appear to give credence if not graphic substantiation to his inherited designation. Black Africa is a refugee term from European colonialism and its concomitant racism. "Black Africa" existed in the minds but not the realities of colonial administrators. It was the invention of racial theorists like Gobineau and Hegel and Rosenberg (and now Kissinger) who were compelled to differentiate what they understood as the "high" civilizations of Egypt and Zimbabwe from their roots in the southern Nile or among Bantu-speakers. They even invented a new race (the Hamitics) for that purpose. Powers sustains that horrific tradition to the point of absolute absurdity (he speaks of a "Muslim-Black civil war" in the Sudan).

Through similar slights of hand and of logic, Powers presumes an historical and social homogeneity among Black African nations (recall he refers to "its people"), leaping serially from one country to another to catalogue the problems to be found in what he refers to as "Black Africa," "sub-Saharan Africa," or "the region." Finally, with respect to his conceptual failings, he presumes an economic singularity and integrity to each of the countries under discussion. In his lead article his one concession to the world-system to which each is appended is a somewhat poetic flourish: "It [Africa] receives the world's news, the world's fashions and fads, the world's blows." Not until we read an entirely different article (subheaded: "History: African Triumphs Followed by Hard Truths") are we alerted to the oil crisis and the world depression of prices for African goods which have played such havoc with Third World economies in the past ten years.

In analytical terms, Powers also strikes some peculiar notes. I suppose since Africa is unique in its crises, it only follows that urbanization – a measure of economic development in every other region's history – is a measure of crisis in

Africa ("In 1960 there were three cities in Black Africa with a population of more than 500,000. Now there are 28"). Education too, we are told is deteriorating – a somewhat ironic observation for someone employed by a newspaper published in Los Angeles (or any other major American city for that matter).

The why of it all – and the solutions which follow – are, however, the most problematic arenas of Powers' analyses. Powers believes: "Africans have been failed by their leaders," and further that "There must also be a realistic appreciation of the paucity of management skills in Africa, a deficiency that will take time and dedication to overcome ... Management ability is the slow accretion of experience, painfully achieved. Most African countries have a long way to go in developing managerial talent that goes beyond the top layers of government and business." Before this, he had also declared:

Two fundamental conclusions are inescapable:

- Leftist or socialist-oriented-economies have been an abysmal failure in Africa, and the countries that have them show no sign of being able to turn themselves around. Any African students currently poring over the Marxist classics at the Sorbonne or the London School of Economics would find it instructive to view the results of the experiments in Ghana, Guinea, Tanzania, Zambia, Ethiopia, Mozambique, or Angola.
- Conversely, closed-off, oligarchical economic systems are also headed for trouble unless they can open up and allow real competition for their growing numbers of educated, talented people.

For Powers, it seems to be of little consequence that Great Britain, the oldest capitalist society in history, has experienced calamitous cycles for the past sixty years and severe "deindustrialization" for the past two decades; or that the most management-rich society, the U.S., has nevertheless seen the demise of major corporations (recall Penn Central Railroad or the 61 bank failures of the past two years) and major recessions.

The hub of Powers' analyses and solutions is the International Monetary Fund and its stratagems:

> The IMF has taken a lot of criticism in Africa over the past few years because of the conditions that it imposes for its loans. Much of the criticism seems to miss an essential point: The IMF is a lending institution. No one is forced to borrow money from the IMF. [But then in direct refutation, Powers continues.] However, the IMF is a lending agency of last resort, its stamp of approval a must for further lending or debt rescheduling on the part of other international lending agencies. And, if a country wants to borrow money from the IMF, it has to listen to what the banker has to say.

The IMF is controlled by the same bankers who have made the disastrous policies which have mired Latin America in its current fiscal depressions.

The IMF has helped to ruin Great Britain, Israel, Jamaica, and several scores of other countries as well as subsidized the management-rich but flawed policies of Citicorp, Manufacturer's Hanover, Bank of America, and Chase. And what have its successes been? In the third of his articles on Sunday, "Zaire a Case Study in IMF 'Bitter Medicine,'" Powers provides what he takes to be an example of the system working:

> Western diplomatic officials in Zaire seem pleased, but cautious. Most of them say that the Zairian government was getting the same advice [increasing taxes, cutting government expenditures, decreasing public services and the civil service] from every quarter and that, whatever one may think of Zaire's durable and often repressive president, Mobutu Sese Seko, he had the courage to follow it. Given the wretched state of his economy, he probably had little other choice.

Those who are reading Powers' series may find the remarks by Antoine Kadiga helpful. Writing in the November 1984 issue of *AfricAsia*, Kadiga observed:

> For several months, those Western media favourable to "Marshal" Mobutu Sese Seko have been trumpeting that "prosperity is once again just around the corner."
> ... The 100 illegal executions carried out by the Special Research and Surveillance Brigade of what are officially called common criminals ... marks a sinister note in the new austerity decreed by Mobutu ... they form part of a deliberate plan to reduce crime in Kinshasha above all, in order to reduce unemployment, the regime is physically liquidating those without work. Austerity Mobutu fashion.

One wonders about the moral basis of policy which allows William Colby, a former director of the CIA, to characterize the installation of Mobutu as one of its "very successful" covert operations (*Harper's*, September 1984). Is it possible that President Nyerere of Tanzania has a point when he argues: "... that the IMF is another form of modern 'colonialism,' a way of bludgeoning socialist countries into abandoning their most cherished beliefs"?

Powers, a sensitive and in some ways superior journalist, has initiated a public discussion but has barely begun an analysis of the problems which are drowning African peoples throughout the continent. He is poised between ideological satrapy and thoughtful journalism. The peoples of Africa have been betrayed but not simply by proximate "madmen and specialists" (Wole Soyinka's phrase) or by circumstance. One must inevitably turn the pages of the ledgers of the global corporations to deepen one's understanding of contemporary Africa and its troubles. Colonialism was their previous convenience. Now too often the mismanagement of ambitious soldiers and corrupt professional strata combined with woefully inadequate bureaucracies provide the political mechanisms through which Africa is bartered to non-African political and economic interests.

CHAPTER 11

The Comedy of Terror

They say this town is full of cozenage,
As, nimble jugglers that deceive the eye,
Dark-working sorcerers that change the mind,
Soul-killing witches that deform the body,
Disguised cheaters, prating mountebanks,
And many such-like liberties of sin.
— *William Shakespeare*, The Comedy of Errors

Over four-hundred years ago, William Shakespeare evoked the specter of public spellbinders: "nimble jugglers," "dark-working sorcerers," and "soul-killing witches" who "deceived the eye," "changed minds," and "deformed the body." In this, the first of his comedies, Shakespeare summoned the ghost of a corrupted city, a deformed body politic owed to "disguised cheaters" and "prating mountebanks." He was, of course, obliquely referring to Elizabethan London, a town immersed in disputatious politics, which swept over and implicated Shakespeare and others constituting England's cultural intelligentsia. And London's theater, a principal site of public opinion forming, contentious elite patronage, and artifice, translated the state's interests into beguiling entertainment. In all these matters, it is tempting to transfer Shakespeare's insights to the circumstances of present-day American politics and the dominant media and journalistic cultures that function to conceal that disturbing reality from the American public. Historically in America, national crises have tended to spawn the worst excesses in journalism and mass culture. And presently, with the formation of media conglomerates, the so-called war against terrorism has inspired a conformist and sometimes duplicitous mainstream press. As is the case with Shakespeare's outsider, Antipholus of Syracuse, it devolves on strangers to the city – in this instance the American state – to discern its eye-deceiving practices.

For months, the peoples of this America have existed under a reign of speakable terror. And it is a transparently speakable occurrence, given the tens of thousands of words and pictures that have deluged this country each day that has followed last summer. The onset was the horrifying televised spectacle on September 11, 2001: commercial flights transformed into weapons of destruction. The visual scenes were profoundly shocking, but over the next several hours, another source of unease became manifest. Scanning the sea of networks, it became evident that they disposed of only marginally competent newsgathering contrivances. They could not report on who or what occupied the World Trade Center (WTC); who was likely to be in the buildings that morning; or what had transpired on those planes with so many cell phone–bearing passengers. Instead, following the train of horrors of the first few hours, little real information was attached to the recycling images of the already obvious destruction and death.

This would prove to be the first and last of those instances of verifiable abominations, which streamed across television screens, newspaper front pages, and magazine covers over the succeeding months. Unedited and unadulterated on that first day, from that moment until now the notion of terror was reappropriated and reapportioned by the state and its diverse cast of "disguised cheaters." A raw, collectively experienced event was deliberately and cynically reconfigured into an absurd abomination of propaganda, public manipulation, and the counterfeiture of human rights. Licensed by these machinations, everything that preceded September 11 was obliterated. And in lieu of an explanatory back story, a history, the public was lured into a sycophantic chorus on "evil." The history, as usual, was well worth forgetting.

State terror – that is, a government's employment of violence against noncombatants – had been a part of American history even before the founding of the American republic. In the seventeenth, eighteenth, and nineteenth centuries, state terror was almost inextricably linked to what were termed the "Indian wars," and both a distant parliament as well as the colonial officials at hand orchestrated it. And once African slavery replaced impressed Europeans and enslaved Native Americans, Black women, children, and men, too, became the victims of colonial, then state and, eventually, federal programs of terror. By the end of the nineteenth century, when the republic was being altered into an empire, "bandits," that is, *their* patriots, in the Philippines, Puerto Rico, and Cuba were subjected to similar disciplines. Fitful (and occasionally more insistent) qualms aside, in the next century the American state extended its merciless violence onto innocent civilians in the Caribbean, Central America, Asia, the Middle East, and Africa. As the century began, so would it conclude. Just two years short of the century's end, the nastiness was visited on Europe's Yugoslavia with the destruction of power plants, bridges, hospitals, and other civilian resources.

In an earlier time, before the formulation of notions like *war crimes, crimes against humanity, the genocide convention,* and *global human rights,* later observers might have constructed the anarchy of international law as an absent brake. However, when the International Court of Justice, the world court, was established in the mid-1940s, this was no longer the case. Under the signature of President Truman, the U.S. consented to the jurisdiction of the court. For forty years, the U.S. remained within the adjudication of the International Court. But in 1986, the Reagan administration unilaterally rescinded the court's authority, preferring international anarchy to the public humiliation of a formal judgment on its conduct of foreign policy in Central America. The occasion was *Nicaragua v. United States of America*, a suit brought by the Nicaraguan government to the International Court. On June 27, 1986, the court published its findings, among them rejecting the U.S.'s assertion that it had no jurisdiction. Some of the world court's decisions doubtlessly concern state terror:

> By twelve votes to three: Decides that the United States of America, by training, arming, equipping, financing and supplying the contra forces or otherwise encouraging, supporting and aiding military and paramilitary activities in and against Nicaragua, has acted, against the Republic of Nicaragua, in breach of its obligation under customary international law not to intervene in the affairs of another State.
>
> By fourteen votes to one, Finds that the United States of America, by producing in 1983 a manual entitled *Operaciones sicológicas en guerra de guerrillas*, and disseminating it to contra forces, has encouraged the commission by them of acts contrary to general principles of humanitarian law.[1]

Mark Weisbrot recently recalled just what "principles of humanitarian law" were violated in Nicaragua: "They [the U.S. agencies and the contras] waged war not so much against the Nicaraguan army as against 'soft targets': teachers, health care workers, elected officials (a CIA-prepared manual actually advocated their assassination)... They blew up bridges and health clinics, and with help from a U.S. trade embargo beginning in 1985, destroyed the economy of Nicaragua."[2] The corporate American press said and wrote little about these actions. And when they were infrequently noted, there was nothing like the apocalyptic language of today ("threats to civilization," etc.) to suggest that an American government and its surrogates had violated the basic principles of democracy.

The court awarded Nicaragua $17 billion. And beyond U.S. shores, the decision was applauded widely. Unreported in the American press, Pope John Paul II, for one, congratulated the court on its vindication of international law. The debt was, however, "forgiven" by a new government in Nicaragua, installed as a beneficiary of the undeclared American war on that country.

What the Reagan government fomented in Nicaragua was merely a complement to the actions of preceding American governments in Central America. For thirty years, in Guatemala, El Salvador, and Honduras, U.S. officials, covert operatives, and military personnel had supported state terrorism that left hundreds of thousands dead, among them peasants, priests, nuns, unionists, political leftists, and the like. Much of this, too, was unreported, or at best misreported at the time. So a few years back, when President Clinton issued a public apology to Central Americans for (some) of the actions of his predecessors, it came somewhat as a surprise for a majority of the American public. That same public was equally bemused in 1997 when Gary Webb, then of the *San Jose Mercury News*, published the results of his investigation into the collaboration of the Central Intelligence Agency (CIA) with Central American cocaine smugglers. The CIA's inspector general eventually confirmed most of Webb's most damaging allegations, but the American press chose to misrepresent or ignore that report too.[3]

Now you may aver that all that was in the past. That was how Barbara Walters, the venerable television journalist/personality, responded to a critic of the present war on terrorism when he sought to detail the long relationship between the Taliban and various American governments. But as the ancient Greeks recognized, and I paraphrase, an unexamined past has a tendency of repeating itself.

In the second week of April of 2002, the Venezuelan military (according to the American press) sought to overthrow the elected president, Hugo Chavez. Venezuela is the third-largest exporter of oil to the U.S. and the fourth-largest economy in Latin America. Chavez, a former paratrooper, is a left-leaning populist, who himself had sought to overthrow a previous Venezuelan government in 1992. He was imprisoned, and on release began to construct a broad-based alliance against the established powers in that country. In 1998, he won the presidency by popular vote. With a new constitution in hand, Chavez began his dismantling of the economic and political structures, which had long secured the privileges of wealth in Venezuela. But according to the reports published of the coup in the *Los Angeles Times*, the *New York Times*, and the *Washington Post*, Chavez was "reckless," and provoked his own dismissal by the Venezuelan military. Now, according to the non-press, it appears that beginning in June of last year the Bush administration funded and assisted in the planning of the coup. These revelations in the London *Guardian* in large part result from the fact that the coup failed after two days.[4] But the corporate American press remained unrelievedly hostile to Chavez and loathe to acknowledge U.S. involvement in his aborted ouster. Paradoxically, while trivializing or openly denying such a possibility, some papers forwarded conceivable justifications. The *Washington Post* played the race card, describing Chavez as "dark-skinned and kinky-haired," contrasting him to one of his opponents (Rear Admiral Carlos Molina) who is opportunely "light-skinned."[5] In the *Wall Street Journal*, columnist Mary Anastasia O'Grady assured her readers that the coup had been "a spontaneous action" but, on the other hand, "Fidel Castro's handprint was all over Mr. Chavez's comeback."[6] The *New York Times* gently profiled Otto J. Reich, assistant secretary for state on Latin America, the current administration's point man in relations to the southern hemisphere. Reich, the *Times* recalled, is a former Cuban, a hardline anti-Castroist, a former lobbyist for Mobil Oil, and the aide in the Reagan State Department who (according to the General Accounting Office) had violated the law by covertly preparing pro-contra propaganda for publication in American newspapers. Yet despite his deserved reputation for lying and "nimble juggling," the *Times* published without contest Reich's declarations denying the U.S.' involvement in the coup in Venezuela.[7]

The failure of the American press to interrogate the employment of state terrorism by American governments, past and present, is merely a smidgen of the dominant practices that misinform the American people. Take, for instance, the voting debacle in Florida in 2000. Most Americans are under the impression that the presidential election was principally marred by voting machine chads and butterfly ballots. These, indeed, were at the center of the protracted drama concocted in the mainstream media in the postelection months. However, the Commission on Civil Rights and the lawsuit filed by the NAACP, *NAACP v. Katherine Harris et al.*, provide a radically different narrative. The Commission's report, "Voting Irregularities in Florida during the 2000 Presidential Election," of June 2001, based on the testimony of one hundred witnesses and the review of more than 100,000 pages of documents, concluded that "perhaps the most dramatic undercount in Florida's election was the uncast ballots of countless eligible voters who were turned away at the polls or wrongfully purged from voter registration rolls."[8]

It was not the counting of ballots but the counting of voters that was really at issue. The lawsuit brought by the NAACP and 21 Black Floridians provides further details of the diverse and heinous practices that disenfranchised thousands of Blacks and Latinos in Florida. The Florida Highway Patrol (FHP) set up numerous unauthorized (according to its commander, Colonel Hall) roadblocks, which interfered with Black motorists on the way to the polls – some of the targets were Black college students; at several polling stations in predominantly Black neighborhoods, the FHP parked unmanned patrol cars for several hours; perhaps thousands of registered Latino and Black voters were erroneously (?) purged as "felons" from the voters register;[9] in their affidavits, experienced poll workers, who had attempted to verify voter registrations, contrasted the three hours delay in 2000 to the customary ten minutes characteristic of previous elections; in the targeted counties, polling stations were closed early or closed while frustrated voters waited in line to vote; Black voter applications went unprocessed for months; and longtime voters found themselves unexpectedly declared ineligible.[10] On February 15, 2002, Florida's challenge to the lawsuit was dismissed by a district court judge; the case is currently scheduled for trial in August 2002.

Since dissembling on the part of the corporate media is now epidemic, it is nigh impossible to track the volume of nonsense served up to the American public.

In collusion with a secretive government, which now possesses legal authority for unconstitutional powers – the ACLU (American Civil Liberties Union) informs us that the U.S.A. PATRIOT (Uniting and Strengthening America by Providing Appropriate Tools Required to Intercept and Obstruct Terrorism) Act violates five of the Bill of Rights amendments – public deception and misdirection constitutes the most direct threat to public knowledge.[11] How are Americans expected to assess the meaning and significance of the war in Afghanistan when they are denied knowledge of the pre-9/11 activities of the Clinton and Bush administrations?

One of the most striking phenomena of the September attacks was the appearance of media "experts" with detailed knowledge of Osama bin Laden. Within days of the attacks, Pat Robertson recalled his meetings with bin Laden and Taliban leaders while hosting his *700 Club* on the ABC Family Channel network. And scores of retired military officers and intelligence agents were paid undisclosed but presumably handsome fees by television networks anxious to take advantage of years of (unexplained) experience in Afghan territory. Some of the experts were frauds, of course (e.g., Fox News's "Colonel" Joseph Cafasso),[12] but notwithstanding the bogeymen, an intriguing but still mostly submerged portrait emerges: once again – like Vietnam, Panama, Grenada, and so on – a cold war enterprise has produced an American invasion. And like these other instances, the official justification has more than likely served as a pretense. For what other reason, except to conceal an unacceptable truth, has the administration opposed a public investigation of the attacks on New York and Washington, D.C.? But as congresswoman Cynthia McKinney has asserted: "If the Secretary of Defense tells us that his new military objectives must be to occupy foreign capital cities and overthrow regimes, then the American people must know why."[13]

The vast majority of peoples beyond our borders recognize the American government's hypocrisy on terrorism. They were appalled at the spectacle of state terror recently unleashed by Israel on the Palestinian people and dismayed by the cynical collaboration between Israel and the U.S. While in U.S. newspapers and on U.S. screens media sorcerers wove spells of propaganda about the war against terrorism, the world media reported a very different reality: Palestinians used as human shields, peace activists in the Occupied Territories being beaten and shot by the Israeli army, humanitarian workers harassed, and emergency vehicles destroyed before they could lend aid to Palestinian victims. In Colombia, as it was in Central America, the U.S. state is providing billions in military aid, training, and equipment to a military and a paramilitary league guilty of terror. But despite the "prating mountebanks," which dominate American media with their recitations of official information, there are grounds for optimism. Surveys indicate that few Americans have real confidence in the news media (14 percent) and in major business corporations (12 percent). For the moment, however, as congresswoman McKinney stated in late March, an unelected government has seized illegal powers. That must be opposed with every democratic weapon in our arsenal.

NOTES

1. The particulars of the decision included: "Decides that the United States of America, by certain attacks on Nicaraguan territory in 1983–1984, namely attacks on Puerto Sandino on 13 September and 14 October 1983, an attack on Corinto on 10 October 1983; an attack on Potosi Naval Base on 4/5 January 1984, an attack on San Juan del Sur on 7 March 1984; attacks on patrol boats at Puerto Sandino on 28 and 30 March 1984; and an attack on San Juan del Norte on 9 April 1984; and further by those acts of intervention referred to in subparagraph (3) hereof which involve the use of force, has acted, against the Republic of Nicaragua, in breach of its obligation under customary international law not to use force against another State." *Nicaragua v. United States of America*, International Court of Justice, June 27, 1986, available at www.icj-cij.org/icjwww/idecisions/isummaries/inussummary860627.htm.
2. Mark Weisbrot, "What Everyone Should Know about Nicaragua," *Z Magazine*, November 9, 2001.
3. For an example, see James Adams's review of Webb's book, "Dark Alliance: The CIA, the Contras, and the Crack Cocaine Explosion," *New York Times Book Review*, September 27, 1998, 28.
4. See Duncan Campbell, "American Navy 'Helped Venezuelan Coup,'" *Guardian*, April 29, 2002.
5. Scott Wilson, "Clash of Visions Pushed Venezuela toward Coup," *Washington Post*, April 21, 2002.
6. Mary Anastasia O'Grady, "Venezuela Rejected a Coup, but Its Future Is No Brighter," *Wall Street Journal*, April 19, 2002.
7. Christopher Marquis, "Combative Point Man on Latin Policy: Otto J. Reich," *New York Times*, April 18, 2002.
8. U.S. Commission on Civil Rights, "Voting Irregularities in Florida during the 2000 Presidential Election," June 2001, available at www.usccr.gov/.
9. Based on a late-nineteenth-century Jim Crow law, Florida has purged some 900,000 "felons" from its voter register. In 2000, Katherine Harris, Florida's secretary of state, hired DataBase Technologies, a Georgia company, to purge felons from the Florida rolls. See Lisa Getter, "Florida Net Too Wide in Purge of Voter Rolls"; and Getter, "Thousands Were Wrongfully Called Felons: Errors May Have Affected Presidential Election," *Los Angeles Times*, May 21, 2001.
10. See *NAACP v. Katherine Harris et al.*, available at www.aclufl.org/naacp_vharris.html.
11. See Nancy Chang, "The USA PATRIOT Act: What's So Patriotic about Trampling on the Bill of Rights?" Center for Constitutional Rights, November 2001, available at www.ccr-ny.org/whatsnew usa_patriot_act.asp.
12. Cafasso served as a military consultant for Fox News for four months. His entire military career consisted of forty-four days of boot camp in 1976. See Jim Ruttenberg, "At Fox News: The Colonel Who Wasn't," *New York Times*, April 29, 2002.
13. Cynthia McKinney, "A Statement on the Events of September 11," *Black Commentator*, May 8, 2002, available at www.blackcommentator.com/rep_mckinney.html.

CHAPTER 12

Ralph Bunche and *An American Dilemma*

... This survey probably will be the most important study of the Negro
in the last twenty years. Unquestionably its findings will influence
procedure along interracial lines for certainly the next ten years and
perhaps longer ... the Carnegie report will be a guide for government
use, for private enterprise and for public opinion in all walks of life.
— *Roy Wilkins, 1939*[1]

This year marks the 60th anniversary of the publication of *An American Dilemma: The Negro Problem and Modern Democracy*. The work is well worth the attention on its own merits (or lack of same), but it is also of considerable historical significance. For one, it provided one of the seminal justifications for the Supreme Court's *Brown* decision in 1954–1955 that segregated educational systems were damaging to Black children. (Whether that was the actual reason for the ruling is debatable.) For another, it proved to be a template for integrationists in the post-war era, both in the government (e.g., Truman's executive order desegregating the armed forces in 1948) and in the social sphere. As might be anticipated, during the decade or so of Civil Rights agitation, *An American Dilemma* and its collaborators were duly pilloried by white supremacist politicians and writers as part of the "communist" conspiracy to undermine America.

According to its principal author, Gunnar Myrdal, several chapters of *An American Dilemma* were drafted by Richard Sterner, a Swedish statistician, and Arnold Rose, a graduate student. But to give some acknowledgement of the largely neglected efforts of Sterner and Rose merely disturbs a surface beneath which lies the expanse of contributors to whom *An American Dilemma* is owed. Dewey Grantham, among others, has informed us that the research which lay behind the work was contributed by Myrdal, the director of the project, with the assistance of "six top staff members ... thirty-one independent workers ... thirty-six assistants to the staff ... some fifty experts who acted as consultants ..." in addition to "a corps of secretaries and typists" who prepared some 15,000 pages.[2] The central core with which Myrdal, Sterner and Rose worked, was some 44 monographs, three of which had seen publication before *An American Dilemma* reached the book market.[3] The field research for the project was undertaken in late 1939. And given the immensity of the task – "a comprehensive study of the Negro in the United States" – it is something of a paradox that Myrdal set a deadline of September 1, 1940 for its completion.

The project was initiated and funded (some $300,000) by the Carnegie Corporation. The Carnegie foundation had been organized in 1911, and true to its benefactor, Andrew Carnegie (whose "wide sweep of ... interests included the Negro"), by the mid-1930s, the foundation had invested $2,500,000 in institutions like Hampton and Tuskegee.[4] To some at Carnegie this program appeared somewhat extravagant in the middle of the Depression years. The immediate inspiration for the "Negro study" had come from Newton Baker in 1935.[5] At a Board meeting in October 1935, Baker had questioned whether the funding for Black higher education was the most appropriate use of the Corporation's funds. And in December 1935, he wrote F. P. Keppel, the head of the Corporation (1922–1941):

> I think anybody who has read *Anthony Adverse* will share my feeling of unlimited amazement at the courage of the white people in this country who received the slaves from slave ships and undertook to make useful laborers of them. How many white civilizations could have dared to receive so many wild savages, who were practically uncaged animals, and spread them around over their farms in contact with their own families passes human comprehension. What has been done for the Negro in a hundred years is an unparalleled achievement and nothing but a theoretical democratic impatience can make us critical of it, though, of course, much more remains to be done.[6]

We owe the unearthing of this gem to Walter A. Jackson. Jackson generously characterized Baker's sentiments as "paternalistic" racism, and attributed them to Baker's "West Virginia upbringing," This construction, however, possesses a whiff of "Southern exceptionalism" (race prejudice is a southern phenomenon), conceals the perniciousness of Baker's beliefs, and fails to detect the breadth of influences which contributed to Baker's truncated sense of American history. As a member of Woodrow Wilson's war cabinet, Baker was exposed to the entirely fashionable racial conceits of an historian (Wilson) who had justified Klan violence during the Reconstruction; and government officials like Treasury Secretary William McAdoo; Postmaster General Albert Burleson; and John Skelton Williams, the Controller of the Currency, who had been the architects of the segregation of the Federal civil service and Washington, D.C.[7] It should also be remembered that as Secretary of War during the First World War, Baker had overseen a robust program of scientific racism which introduced the racial marking of intelligence testing, as well as military segregation, the execution of Black troops, and routine Negrophobic brutality.[8] It is one of history's little ironies that what would become for several decades the definitive American "Negro study" was inspired by someone who believed that slavery was an act of cultural charity by a "white civilization" toward what he termed "an infant race." A Carnegie Board member for whom higher education for Blacks was made problematic by "biological questions."

The fact that the early preference of the Carnegie Board was for a colonial administrator (Dutch, British, etc.) suggests that Baker's "paternalism" was generally shared among them. Unlike Carnegie's study of the poor whites of South Africa earlier in the 1930s,[9] the report would not engage social science research or public policy recommendations. Fortunately, Frederick P. Keppel, the head of the Board, consulted Melville Herskovits about his first candidate (Henrik Mouw, a veteran of the Dutch colonial service in the East Indies) who dissuaded Keppel from assigning the report to European colonialists. Herskovits's intervention went much further. He contacted Donald Young of the Social Science Research Council. And together "Young and Herskovits secretly collaborated on [the Carnegie project] in the hope of turning what looked like a junket into a large project that would advance social science research on blacks."[10] Their interference proved fruitful, and by the summer of 1937 the "report" had evolved into a project, and Karl Gunnar Myrdal, a Swedish economist, best known to the Rockefeller Foundation, had emerged as the leading candidate to direct the research. In their somewhat naïve anticipation of what a European would bring to the study, the Board had hoped to nominate "a man perfectly free from sentimental and social bias and from political prejudice ..."[11] Myrdal seemed ideal: a European with little experience of the U.S. or of the Black American.[12] Neither of these would serve him well. Not surprisingly, Myrdal would finally invent a mythic America, formulated precisely from his "social biases" and "political prejudices."

In late 1942, Myrdal summed up his understanding of the "American dilemma" this way:

> The "American Dilemma", ... is the ever-raging conflict between, on the one hand, the valuations ... of high national [liberty, equality, justice, and fair opportunity for everybody] and Christian precepts [the ideals of human brotherhood and the Golden Rule], and on the other hand, the valuations on specific planes of individual and group living, where personal and local interests; economic, social, and sexual jealousies; considerations of community prestige and conformity; group prejudice against particular persons or types of people; and all sorts of miscellaneous wants, impulses, and habits dominate his outlook.[13]

It is unfortunate that Baker had died in December 1937. It deprived Myrdal of a living proof that it was possible to reconcile white racism and the American creed. For Baker, what Myrdal insisted was a dilemma was merely the conceit of "a theoretical democratic impatience" incapable of acknowledging "white civilization's" burdens of superiority. On that score, Baker, was simply a clone of the dominant American culture whose legacy could be traced back to Thomas Jefferson, one of the authors of the American creed. As Samuel P. Huntington has recently observed, "The creed ... was the product of the distinct Anglo-Protestant culture of the founding settlers," and was explicitly immersed in whiteness.[14]

In 1990, Myrdal acknowledged in an interview with Walter Jackson that he wrote *An American Dilemma* under the influence of the war:

> When I was sitting there in Princeton, which was a nice place, I thought about all the youngsters, all my friends in Europe, who were either in prison or killed in war ... And here I was sitting and writing my book. It became my war work. And I think this meant much for what the book came to be.[15]

Jackson, quite rightly, took this to mean that in Myrdal's mind in 1941–1942 Nazism represented racism, and the American Creed was synonymous with democracy and the Enlightenment. What Jackson implies, then, is that Sweden, Myrdal's and Sterner's homeland, isolated but not occupied by Germany, was identified both with America and the Negro. Myrdal, who had spent ten months of 1941–1942 in Sweden, insisted that his homeland's democratic culture would sustain a powerful resistance against Nazism. In the larger scheme of things, on the global terrain, the historical preservation of democracy would have to become an American mission. But America could only defend democracy if its Creed transcended its "Negro problem." Sweden was incapable of defending itself militarily from the overwhelming might of the Nazi machine. On that score its was like that of the Negro faced with the cultural, political and economic resources of American racism. Myrdal's "war work," his imaginings about an America which would ultimately face off its own racism and Nazism, was thus signified with a vein of desperation.

Ralph Bunche, Myrdal's closest Black collaborator (we are told repeatedly) on the "Negro study," while sharing Myrdal's antipathy to fascism, had profound disagreements with Myrdal's construction of American racism and the path to its eradication. In somewhat of a paradox, it was Bunche, the political scientist, who emphasized economic class as the social agent of an anti-racist action, while Myrdal, the economist, stressed the significance of culture, ethics, and morality.

Bunche was brought into the "Negro Study," as one of Myrdal's six top staff members. He was certainly qualified for the position, but there were also aspects of Bunche's career which might have given Myrdal pause. Bunche was, it should be noted, the first Black American to earn a doctorate in Political Science; and it follows he was the first to receive such a doctorate from Harvard. Bunche's 1934 dissertation was on "French Administration in Togoland and Dahomey."

However, in the 1930s Bunche had emerged as a prominent radical scholar. His reputation had been earned as a result of published articles, public lectures, and conference presentations which excoriated the "bourgeois conservatism" of Black leaders and organizations (like the NAACP and the Urban League), denounced Western imperialism in Africa and elsewhere, exposed the racist practices embedded in Franklin Roosevelt's "New Deal," and ridiculed "Negro chauvinism." Nevertheless, Bunche was a critical resource for the "Negro Study."

Bunche was of course a specialist on African colonialism and Black America. He was also one of the best-trained and experienced, perhaps even the most qualified of the researchers brought into the project. In 1932–1933, Bunche had undertaken field research in West Africa and France.[16] Originally intending to write a dissertation on comparative racial assimilation in Brazil and the U.S., he had been discouraged from that project by Edwin Embree, head the Rosenwald Fund, his funding source, who was of the opinion that "U.S. Negroes might get 'dangerous' ideas in Brazil."[17] In 1936–1937, Bunche had returned to the African field, after first augmenting his training in field research by studying anthropological methodology with Melville Herskovits at Northwestern and then Bronislaw Malinowski at the London School of Economics, and Isaac Schapera in South Africa.[18] Bunche had also acquired substantial administrative experience. He had helped to organize the Political Science Department at Howard University, and had chaired the program from its inception in 1928. In 1935, collaborating with his fellow Howard University colleagues, Abram Harris, Jr. (head of the Department of Economics), and E. Franklin Frazier (head of Sociology) Bunche organized "the Position of the Negro in Our National Economic Crisis" conference, which in turn gave birth to the National Negro Congress (NNC).[19] Pulling together prominent Black leaders from business, the academy, the religious community, and trade unions, the NNC became a leading source of Black criticisms of the New Deal, for rejection of the conservatism of the NAACP and the National Urban League, and a champion of the Black trade union movement.[20]

The nucleus of the research team assembled by Bunche consisted of Wilhemina Jackson, a Howard student; James E, Jackson, a labor organizer; and George C. Stoney, a recent graduate of the University of North Carolina. Together they attempted to assess the political status of Southerners, both white as well as Black. Wilhemina Jackson concentrated on interviews and data collection along the corridor from Virginia to Florida; James Jackson's commission covered the territory from Virginia and to the west from Tennessee to Oklahoma and Missouri; George Stoney, the only white member of the team, focused on interviewing white officials and ordinary citizens in Alabama, Georgia, and South Carolina. His was the most daunting task, subjecting him to physical threats and verbal abuse as he toured cities, towns, and the small rural communities of his region. Nevertheless he conducted nearly half of the total interviews collected by the team. Grantham reports that "The geographical distribution of persons interviewed shows Alabama with 148, Georgia with 118, South Carolina with 92, and North Carolina with 53. There were fewer interviews in Virginia, Florida, and Texas, while Mississippi, Louisiana, and Arkansas were largely ignored, as were the border states."[21]

Their research documented vast disparities concerning political and racial attitudes in the region, corrupt voting practices which were so well established that they had assumed the status of conventions, voter registration protocols (e.g., the states with poll taxes and/or literacy tests) which excluded poor whites as well as Blacks; and generations of southerners who had never voted. For instance, in Alabama, a state with at least 18,000 Black veterans included among those exempted from poll taxes, only 1500 Blacks had participated in the 1936 election. And despite Bunche's earlier criticisms of the New Deal, he acknowledged that at least one agency, the Agricultural Adjustment Administration (AAA), had initiated some Black political participation which hadn't been seen since the Reconstruction period: "Many thousands of Negro cotton farmers each year now go to the polls, stand in line with their neighbors, and mark their ballots independently, without protest or intimidation, in order to determine government policy toward cotton production control." And even modest gains were being recorded in Black registration for the general elections: "By 1939 approximately 2100 Negroes were registered in Atlanta, as compared with fewer than 1000 in 1936. The number of Black registrants in Duval County, Florida, increased from fewer than 1500 in 1936 to more than 8000 in 1938."[22] Stoney encountered equally disparate attitudes:

> One attitude encountered fairly frequently among poor whites in the South is that the Negro, especially the Negro farm owner, is being illegally treated when he is denied the right to vote, and there is a feeling that the big whites are letting some of the better-off Negroes vote even in primary elections in a state like Georgia. In contrast to this attitude is the feeling by a great many other poor whites that the black man is unduly favored by the government benefit programs; that the Negro has no business even thinking about voting; and that in *this* region they would be scared to try. Their attitudes toward Negro voting, in contrast with their rather solemn attitudes toward the immorality of selling the vote, present an interesting moral pattern.[23]

Bunche was distressed that Myrdal's deadline had shortened the time for field research, and in his preface to his major report (finished at 5:45 am on August 31, i.e., hours before the deadline), he remarked: "The result here produced is a terribly hurried, poorly integrated, and roughly written job. There has been no opportunity to check references. There has been no time for prolonged reflection ..."[24] But despite his complaints, there were moments when his radicalism penetrated his summations of the field reports.

In the first chapter of the political status of the Negro, Bunche wrote: "It is of the greatest significance that there has never been, in democratic America, a real movement embracing and representing the masses of the population" (5). In the second chapter, "The Historical Background," Bunche commented: "Only the clever manipulation of the threat of black dominance has kept the underprivileged white masses and the privileged upper classes of the South from coming to a parting of the political ways" (10). Further on, Bunche began the chapter on the poll tax this way:

> There seems to be little room for doubt that the entrenched interests of the South in the late nineteenth century were fearful of the possible union between poor whites and Negroes, and that this possibility of a united people's movement impressed them as a revolutionary upsurge that must be crushed at all odds. The poll tax legislation lent itself admirably to this purpose. (328)

Clearly, Bunche believed that white racism was an artifice of the most powerful classes in American society. Myrdal, on the other hand, saw racism as the product of *difference:* "In all white nations which, because of the accident of ethnic homogeneity or for other causes, have not been inculcated with race prejudice, the color of the victim does not provide any excuse for white solidarity."[25] This was merely fanciful. There were and are no homogeneous white nations in the modern world (not even Sweden). In his homeland, racial prejudice had developed to the point that by the early eighteenth century, one Swedish professor, I. Nesselius, had proposed genocide against the Finns.[26] Myrdal's resistance to conceding or recognizing the historical relationship between capitalism and racism – another aspect of his "war work" – extended to his concealing the relationship between "neutral" Swedish businessmen's collaboration with Nazi war production.[27] In the stead of an historical analysis Myrdal, the economist, substituted a putative social anthropology and "white nations."

More significantly, Myrdal's prescription for the end of racism was an aristocratic program: political remedies addressed to America's elites. Concerning post-war America, in the North where economic discrimination was "the only type of discrimination which is both important and strong," Myrdal proposed: "Large-scale public intervention will be a necessity."[28] Of the three societal agencies Myrdal evoked – the trend of unionization, social legislation, and national planning – all were instruments of America's leading classes: capitalists and politicians.

In the South, the region in which Myrdal believed the dilemma between the American Creed and white racism was most acutely felt, he read the tea leaves:

> Signs of [the end of the national compromise between North and South] have been frequent during the 'thirties: a whole set of Supreme Court decisions, the New Deal in the South, the increasing activity of federal agencies to stamp out peonage, the

agitation for a federal lynching law and for an abolition of the poll tax by Congress, the repeal of the two-thirds majority rule for the nomination of the Democratic candidate for the Presidency, and so on.[29]

Here, too, national planning by an interventionist North would be required: "... things thus have to be settled by political means, Myrdal wrote."[30] Such was the domestic mission of post-war America, a nation in which, "But with few exceptions, only the liberals have gone down in history as national heroes."[31]

Bunche was clearly disposed otherwise. He was persuaded that the State was theoretically (and historically) an instrument of the most powerful economic interests in the country and that capitalism was antagonistic to an integration premised on social and political equality. "He argued in his memorandum for Myrdal that the only hope for Blacks was an alliance with the white working class. Myrdal considered this approach unrealistic because of the racism of white workers."[32] Bunche was as informed as Myrdal on racism among American white workers and the union movement, and so he was compelled to attribute the responsibility to labor bureaucrats: "[The AFL and CIO] are both weak, ridden with factional strife and disputes, controlled by a narrow-minded bureaucracy of professional labor leaders, and more often than not, socially unintelligent."[33] It was in part a contrivance so that he might preserve for the white working class some future role in anti-racism, but eventually he would be forced to abandon the position which had sustained his radicalism during the 1930s. But as we have seen it was not the last of Bunche's compromises with his earlier militancy.

As noted earlier, Bunche's hostility toward the New Deal was considerably modified in the early 1940s. Partly, this reflected the quandary which Myrdal had displayed: fascism and Nazism were far worse political regimes than an imperfect American "democracy." In 1935, Bunche had argued that fascism, imperialism and racism were intertwined:

> The doctrine of Fascism, with its extreme jingoism, its exaggerated exaltation of the state and its comic-opera glorification of race, has given a new and greater impetus to the policy of world imperialism which has already conquered and subjected to systematic and ruthless exploitation virtually all of the darker populations of the earth.[34]

Moreover, in his report to the "Negro Study" on "Programs, Ideologies, Tactics," Bunche had written: [under Fascism] the position of the Negro would be frozen permanently as an inferior racial caste."[35] Whereas Bunche had observed in 1936 that the New Deal "only served to 'crystalize [sic] those abuses and oppressions which the exploited Negro citizenry of America have long suffered under laissez-faire capitalism ...,"[36] in his report to Myrdal, Bunche included with his praise of the AAA's reviving of Black electoral participation,

Other hopeful signs involved low-income housing, black participation in the Tenant Purchase program, social security, and minimum wage and hour legislation. He interpreted the Supreme Court's decision upholding these laws along with the Labor Relations Act, as doing "more to better the condition of the Negro than the broadest conceivable decision of his equal rights."[37]

In short, Bunche was conflicted, torn between the contradictions of his radical commitment to a mass working class movement and his recognition that the State might be weaned from its co-dependence with capitalism. The New Deal had not gone far enough, as John Kirby summarizes Bunche's wartime position. But in its amelioration of the general political and economic conditions of labor, it had proceeded in the direction that Bunche had proposed nearly a decade earlier. Bunche wrote to Myrdal: "The only hope for the improvement in the conditions of the masses of any American minority group [is] the hope that can be held out for the betterment of the masses of the dominant group ... Their basic interests are identical and so must be their program and tactics."[38]

Unlike Myrdal, Bunche knew that it was labor militancy which had changed the New Deal from radical conservativism to moderate liberalism. As Howard Zinn has reported, the initial goals of the Depression-era Roosevelt reforms were "to reorganize capitalism in such a way to overcome the crisis and stabilize the system; [and] to head off the alarming growth of spontaneous rebellion in the early years of the Roosevelt administration ..."[39] Having initially, through the National Recovery Act (NRA), given control of the New Deal to industrial combines and the trade association bureaucrats, Zinn concludes that it was rank-and-file insurrections in 1934 and 1935, and the sitdown strikes of 1936 (48) and 1937 (477) which pushed the New Deal to intercede between capital and labor:

> The history of those years seems to support the argument of Richard Cloward and Frances Piven, in their book *Poor People's Movements*, that labor won most during its spontaneous uprisings, before the unions were recognized or well organized ... Their [factory workers] power during the Depression was not rooted in organization, but in disruption.[40]

And similarly, during the Second World War, it was Black militancy combined with the needs of war production and military recruitment, which compelled the State to make real and symbolic concessions to Blacks.

Bunche disagreed with Myrdal about the origins of the "Negro problem," the nature of the crisis in American society, and the means by which racial discrimination and oppression would be ended. He argued in a memorandum to Myrdal that:

> Although every American learns slogans such as "land of the free" and "land of opportunity," there are no contradictions, no inconsistencies, too serious to be

overcome by this sort of foolproof thinking. There can be no contradictions so long as one keeps the faith and utters the mumbo-jumbo of the gospel.[41]

The real contradiction was between capitalism and workers. And racism was employed by capitalism's ruling elites to estrange sectors of the laboring classes from one another, and to enlist the "white" majority of workers on the side of their own exploitation and oppression.

History has proven Myrdal mistaken. Many of Bunche's insights have endured. But because of them and their legion of colleagues, despite its nasty origins the Carnegie project has remained a magisterial enterprise. From the perspective of the present, we are bemused by its failure to interrogate whiteness; its contradictory endorsement of assimilation; its insistence that America is Black or white (Mexicans are mentioned only once – a quote from Charles Johnson's research into war-time production in California); and its overall optimism.[42] It was "war work," and from the point of view of integrationism, "Oh What A Lovely War!"

NOTES

1. Walter A. Jackson, "The Making of a Social Science Classic: Gunnar Myrdal's *An American Dilemma*," *Perspectives in American History*, New Series, 2, 1985, 249.
2. Ralph J. Bunche, edited by Dewey W. Grantham, *The Political Status of the Negro in the Age of FDR*, Chicago: University of Chicago, 1973, xii.
3. The three studies were: Melville Herskovits's *The Myth of the Negro Past* (1941); Charles S. Johnson's *Patterns of Negro Segregation* (1943); and Richard Sterner's *The Negro's Share* (1943) – all published by Harper & Brothers.
4. F. P. Keppel, Foreword, Gunnar Myrdal, *An American Dilemma*, New York: Harper & Brothers, 1944, v, I, vi.
5. Keppel's description of Baker: "He was the son of a Confederate officer, attended the Episcopal Academy in Virginia and the Law School of Washington and Lee University, and spent the greater part of his early years in the Border states of West Virginia and Maryland. His services first as City Solicitor and later as Mayor of Cleveland gave him direct experience with the growing Negro populations in Northern cities, and as Secretary of War he had faced the special problems which the presence of the Negro element in our population inevitably creates in time of national crisis." Ibid.
6. Jackson, "Making of a Social Science Classic," 228.
7. See Woodrow Wilson, *A History of the American People* (1905); and for federal segregation, "Wilson Behind Segregation," *The New York Age*, November 19, 1914, 1.
8. President Woodrow Wilson and Secretary Baker were directly responsible for the secret execution of 13, and then the public hanging of six Black "mutineers" involved in the Houston "mutiny" in 1917. See Bernard C. Nalty, *Strength for the Fight*, New York: The Free Press, 1986, 105. For the U.S. Army's mental testing, see Stephen Jay Gould, *The Mismeasure of Man*, New York: W. W. Norton, 1996 (orig. 1981).
9. See Tiffany Willoughby Herard's doctoral dissertation, "'Waste of a White Skin' or Civilizing White Primitives: The Carnegie Commission Study of Poor Whites in South Africa, 1927–1932," University of California, Santa Barbara, 2003.
10. Jackson, "Making of a Social Science Classic," 232.
11. Ibid., 231.
12. Myrdal had visited the U.S. in 1929–1930; and claimed he had never spoken with a Black American. Ibid., 234.

13. Myrdal, *American Dilemma*, xliii–xliv.
14. Samuel P. Huntington has recently reiterated the origins of the creed: "America was created by 17th- and 18th-century settlers who were overwhelmingly white, British, and Protestant. Their values, institutions, and culture provided the foundation for and shaped the development of the U.S. in the following centuries. They initially defined America in terms of race, ethnicity, culture, and religion. Then, in the 18th century, they also had to define America ideologically to justify independence from their home country, which was also white, British, and Protestant. Thomas Jefferson set forth this "creed," as Nobel Prizewinning economist Gunnar Myrdal called it, in the Declaration of Independence, and ever since, its principles have been reiterated by statesmen and espoused by the public as an essential component of U.S. identity." Huntington, "The Hispanic Challenge," *Foreign Policy*, March–April, 2004.
15. Jackson, "Making of a Social Science Classic," 255.
16. George P. Potamianos, "Visions of a Dying Africa: Ralph J. Bunche and His Second African Journey, 1936–1938," *Journal of Black Studies*, 26, 4, March 1996, 447–466.
17. Jonathan Scott Holloway, *Confronting the Veil: Abram Harris Jr., E. Franklin Frazier, and Ralph Bunche, 1919–1941*, Chapel Hill: University of North Carolina, 2002, 162.
18. Charles Henry, *Ralph Bunche*, New York: New York University, 1999, 175–176.
19. Ibid.
20. The conference precipitated a Congressional investigation of communist activities at Howard in the summer of 1935, ibid., 76ff.
21. Grantham, *Political Status of the Negro in the Age of FDR*, xiii, xv.
22. In the text, the first quote is from Bundle's report; the second quotation is Grantham's summary. Ibid., xxiv.
23. Ibid., 192–193.
24. Ibid., "Author's Preface," viii.
25. Myrdal, *American Dilemma*, v. II, 1021.
26. In the early eighteenth century, Swedish professor I. Nesselius proposed the genocide of the Finns; in 1918, Swedish military officers employed genocide against 20,000 Finns. See Kemiläinen, Aira. *Finns in the Shadow of the "Aryans": Race Theories and Racism*, Helsinki: Finnish Historical Society, 1998.
27. See Jackson, "Making of a Social Science Classic," 254; and Gerard Aalders and Cees Wiebes, *The Art of Cloaking Ownership: The Secret Collaboration and Protection of the German War Industry by the Neutrals: The Case of Sweden*, Ann Arbor: University of Michigan, 1996.
28. Ibid., 1010–1011.
29. Ibid., 1014.
30. Ibid., 1015.
31. Ibid., v. I, 7.
32. Jackson, "Making of a Social Science Classic," 250–251.
33. John B. Kirby, "Ralph J. Bunche and Black Radical Thought in the 1930s," *Phylon*, XXXV, 2, Summer 1974, 136.
34. Ralph Bunche, "French and British Imperialism in West Africa," *Journal of Negro History*, XXI, 1, January 1936, 31.
35. Ibid., 135.
36. Ralph Bunche, "A Critique of New Deal Social Planning as It Affects Negroes," *Journal of Negro Education*, IV, July 1935, 65.
37. Kirby, "Ralph J. Bunche and Black Radical Thought," 134.
38. Ibid., 132.
39. Howard Zinn, *A People's History of the United States*, New York: HarperCollins, 1995, 383.
40. Ibid., 393.
41. Jackson, "Making of a Social Science Classic," 251–252.
42. Actually there is another passing mention of Mexicans, in a chapter drafted by Rose: "Negroes, however, together with the Orientals and, to some extent, Indians and Mexicans, have not been allowed to assimilate as have European immigrants." Myrdal, *American Dilemma*, v. II, 928.

PART IV

ON REALITY AND ITS (MIS)REPRESENTATIONS

CHAPTER 13

White Signs in Black Times: The Politics of Representation in Dominant Texts

INTRODUCTION

Some fifty years ago, W. E. B. Du Bois submitted: "… somebody in each era must make clear the facts with utter disregard to his own wish and desire and belief. What we have got to know, so far as possible, are the things that actually happened in the world."[1] I refer to Du Bois' conviction as a caution. Though we may debate Du Bois' positivism, the urgency, and priority of his moral assertion must be preserved. And, I believe, it has a most specific applicability to Black theorists. We must quite self-consciously examine our wishes, our desires, and our beliefs.

While reading Stuart Hall's rather insightful observations on cultural politics, I was struck – upon transferring it to the American scene – by how acutely ideological was his insistence that we are now entering "the politics of the end of the essential Black subject." Quite suddenly, we Blacks of Afro-America have been resignified as African-Americans. Within the span of a few months, a new moment in our cultural politics has been clarioned, a moment with powerful but not entirely unambiguous implications. We are now an African people. But I am not at all certain that this present semiosis will provide transport much beyond the mere antithesis of "the unspoken and invisible 'other' of predominantly white aesthetics and cultural discourses."[2] (Consider, for a moment, the evocations of Africa in the film version of Alice Walker's *The Color Purple* or Eddie Murphy's own "Coming to America.") The reappearance of this "African-American" was always a most probable possibility and as the names of some of our institutions in the eighteenth and nineteenth centuries (e.g., the African Methodist Episcopalian Church) suggest it had ample precedents. The question we might still ponder is not why this signification has come about but why now?

THE POLITICS OF REPRESENTATION

I surmise that the present appearance of "African-American" is the Black professional intelligentsia's response to the peripheralization of the most audacious expression of Black bourgeois political ambition in American history: I refer to the 1988 presidential campaign of Jesse Jackson.

Let me immediately concede that other social groups – political progressives, factory workers, farmers, and the rural and urban underclasses – identified with Jackson's campaign. But I would also argue that the possibilities for the eventual satisfaction of their needs and aspirations within the realm of American electoral politics were always remote. Jackson's highest social vision consisted of a populist reform of the American electoral system not its revolutionary transformation. And we must admit that Jackson's broadly evangelical mission of economic justice and the rationalization of U.S. foreign policy repeatedly failed to confront or even to correspond finally with the genesis of our presently horrific and cataclysmic world. His complaints targeted the excesses of capitalist exploitation, class privilege, and racial insurgency rather than the structural transformations foregrounded by American imperial decline, militarism, deindustrialization, and the decay of the global economy.[3]

In truth, then, it was only the Black political class which could realistically anticipate a dramatic or tangible reward from Jackson's ascendancy. As either the leader of the Democratic Party, as vice president or as some other functionary in a Democratic Administration, Jackson would have served to leverage these representatives of the Black professional class into State power. Thus positioned, that class would have been provided with an unprecedented locus for social and cultural intervention.

If I am near the mark then the resolute and sudden intercession of "African-American" can be taken as an indication of the resilience with which the most privileged aspirants of this class experienced the means of the subversion and ultimate rejection of Jackson's campaign by America's political elite. The Black political intelligentsia, having largely repressed the extent and frequency with which racial discourse routinely intervenes the narrative, doctrinal, and moral conventions of this society, was undeterred. But having already foresworn race politics as too crude a political agenda for the corporate boardrooms and the sites of State power to which they aspire they have now turned to the gentility and sentimentality of ethnic politics.[4]

In their eagerness to seize upon a negotiable historical identity the broker intelligentsia has rendered meaningless the relentless litany of instances in American social, cultural, and legal history where race marked the boundaries of the polity:

It was more important, for example, to have a ratified Constitution even if it accepted the legitimacy of slavery, than to have had the sectional strife that might have meant no Constitution. It was more important to respect property rights than to distribute land and power on an equitable basis to those freed from slavery by the Civil War. And it was more important to ignore altogether the plight of the newly freed in order to get on with the "business" of industrializing America.

In the twentieth century, fighting the Great Depression meant ignoring, and then barely noticing, the plight of Black Americans, lest powerful Southern members of Congress be offended. Waging World War II was so important we could not risk the moral problems that might result from desegregating the army. We had to move slowly also in the late 1950s, lest we upset the established "Southern way of life." In the 1970s when school desegregation finally threatened the enclaves of white suburbia, the paramount value became the "local autonomy" of the suburbs.[5]

What has this to do with our heritage (or more precisely, one of our several heritages)? I think very little. Once captive in the domain of the historical systems of the West, it was not an issue of who we had been really or who we are really but what we could be made to be. And it is on this last score that either our eventual extinction or our liberation is staked.

THE GENEALOGY OF AMERICAN RACE DISCOURSE

Marx, you will recall, confronted a similar "politics of representation" in his debate with the radical, Bruno Bauer, over the emancipation of Jews in mid-nineteenth century German society. Bauer had asserted that since the source of Christian repression was the offensive religious character of the Jew, it was imperative that Jews undertake the critique and destruction of the religious basis of German society. And in his vanquishing of Bauer, Marx rebutted that it was necessary to escape from theology. Marx insisted the question which had primacy was: "what specific social element is it necessary to overcome in order to abolish Judaism?" And as Marx continued, he exhorted his readers to the realization that "Judaism ha[d] been preserved, not in spite of history, but by history;" and that "... from its own entrails ... civil society ceaselessly engenders the Jew."[6]

In our own times, however, the Bauers have reappeared as liberal and radical critics, persisting in the theoretical and historical deceptions which lead to the refabrications of racial discourse. To cite some recent examples: Michael Hunt, in his study of race consciousness in colonial America, summarized:

> They drew distinctions among the various peoples of the world on the basis of physical features, above all skin color and to a lesser extent head type ... and guided by those distinctions they ranked the various types of peoples in the world. Those with the lightest skin were positioned on the highest rung of the hierarchy, and those with the darkest skin were relegated to the lowest ...

Blacks above all others served as the anvil on which Americans forged this notion of racial hierarchy and the attendant color-conscious view of the world.[7]

George Fredrickson, disputing Winthrop Jordan's view that racism in colonial and republican America was at base a European transplant (Hunt, by the way, follows Jordan), argued:

America, I would conclude, was not born racist; it became so gradually as the result of a series of crimes against black humanity that stemmed primarily from selfishness, greed, and the pursuit of privilege.[8]

For Fredrickson, Hunt, Jordan, and a legion of such scholars, the Black is the central if not the singularly tragic character in America's racial drama.

This is precisely how Thomas Jefferson put it in his *Notes on Virginia* at the end of the eighteenth century.[9] But Jefferson was a slave holder, and a slave holder during that historical period when slavery had been transformed into the near-exclusive appropriation of African and Afro-American labor in North America. Racism as a domain entirely configured in the inferiorization of Africans and their kin had not entirely consumed Jefferson's or his class' imagination but his preoccupation with Blacks was an anticipation of that moment. As Fredrickson confirms (and keep in mind his subject is Negrophobia): "... despite the fact that Jefferson speculated in the 1780s about the possibility that Blacks were inherently inferior in some respects to whites, no one in the U.S. actually defended institutionalized inequality on the basis of racial theory until well into the nineteenth century."[10]

However, preceding this moment when Blacks assumed a privileged position in racist discourses, there was an alternative and I believe formative racist construct among the colonists. I refer you to Ben Franklin, writing in the mid-eighteenth century, some three decades before Jefferson:

The number of purely white People in the World is proportionably small. All Africa is black or tawny. Asia chiefly tawny. America (exclusive of the new Comers) wholly so. And in Europe, the Spaniards, Italians, French, Russians and Swedes, are generally of what we call a swarthy complexion; as are the Germans also, the Saxons only excepted, who with the English, make the principal Body of White People on the Face of the Earth.[11]

"And in Europe," Franklin wrote, and then indulged his desires in the ideological muck produced by centuries of crimes of greed and privilege committed by Europeans against Europeans.

Perhaps this explains how it could be that in 1664 the Maryland colony passed a law prohibiting marriage between Black male slaves and "freeborne English women." The same law, we are informed, encouraged slaveowners to facilitate such unions between white servant women and slaves for then the women, too, became slaves. "Hence," James Wright noted, "the terms of [white] servant women were bought up and the women themselves were married to slaves apparently with a view to invoking on them the penalties just recited."[12] Similarly, then, it is not so curious that in her survey of attitudes among the lower classes in eighteenth-century England, Jean Hecht found widespread hostility toward servants from the European continent concomitant with the popularity of Blacks.[13] And one more residue of this other racism was the observation of the Virginia Congressman, John Randolph, in 1816 that "You cannot make liberty out of Spanish matter."[14]

I am suggesting then that what Jefferson and his successors helped to initiate in America was not racism nor the first "rationalized racist ideology" but a new tributary of racism.[15] This new racism, however, did not replace nor displace its European antecedents – witness the survival of Polish and Irish jokes. Rather it embellished the inventory of Western racism, extending its shape, and resubstantiating its force and authority by providing simultaneously a cruder and more defensible access to whichever of its forms the occasion demanded. This new racism, initially coincident with a slave social order, by the end of the nineteenth century was being adapted to the two most urgent ideological impulses of industrial capital: the uncertain amalgamation of a white working class and the more enduring fabrication of an imperial national identity. It was in place as a social discipline when European immigrant labor flooded the factory gates of industrial America; and it was there as an historical justification when American imperialists smashed the Spanish Empire in the Philippines and the Caribbean.

I would argue then that it is mistaken to assume – as one Marxist historian, Ellen Wood, put it quite recently – that:

> The first point about capitalism is that it is uniquely indifferent to the social identities of the people it exploits ... Unlike previous modes of production, capitalist exploitation is not inextricably linked with extra-economic, juridical or political identities ... In fact, there is a positive tendency in capitalism to undermine such differences, and even to dilute identities like gender or race, as capital strives to absorb people into the labour market and to reduce them to interchangeable units of labour abstracted from any specific identity.[16]

Just how, one might ask Wood, could she justify the presumption that the human materials of capitalism - capitalists, laborers, managers, and cultural workers - could be "indifferent" to the history, culture, and politics of their social formation? For it is in precisely those realms that race consciousness is embedded. The structures of meaning are not the mirrors of production. As Hall has insisted: "... events, relations, structures do have an existence, conditions of existence and real effects, outside the sphere of the discursive; but ... it is only within the discursive, and subject to its specific conditions, limits and modalities [that] they have or can ... be constructed within meaning."[17]

Engels acknowledged, a few short years before his own death, that he and Marx were partly to blame for the conceptual rigidity displayed by later Marxists.[18] We understand that Marx's quest for the laws of capitalist development ultimately diverted him from a more richly textured sense of that "social element" with which he had countered Bauer. Ellen Wood's reference to race and gender as "extra-economic" is a direct consequence of the economism which Engels belatedly deplored.

Capitalist societies, both in America and elsewhere, were never indifferent to race or gender. As I attempted to demonstrate in *Black Marxism*, the capitalist world system was profoundly affected by race ideology. I believe that two such instances were Western imperialism and colonialism. The racist discourse of the West stamped its imprimatur on the character of capitalist expansion in the nineteenth and twentieth centuries just as surely, I believe, as the very different modality of Chinese xenophobic discourse halted that empire's overseas expansion in the early fifteenth century.[19] In turn, as I have suggested above, capitalism constructed new meanings to racist discourse. And the new meanings corresponded with new needs and new opportunities.

JESSE JACKSON AND THE GLOBAL ECONOMY

In the post-Second World War era, the imperialist international division of labor gave way to a new international division of labor and the globalization of production. Fed by the reconstructions of Europe and Japan, and under the hegemony of American-based capital, the world system thrived for nearly two decades. But beginning in the late 1960s the capitalist order started to unravel:

> Corporate profitability in the United States and in many other countries declined dramatically from the mid-1960s to the early 1970s. Plunging profitability then dampened investment, resulting in increasingly stagnant accumulation after the early 1970s. This stasis contributed to a corresponding stagnation in aggregate output. And, as corporations and their allies in the state began with intensifying vigour to take the offensive against their challengers from the mid-1970s on, both economic and political instability were amplified, leading to an increasing uncertainty of economic prospects and a heightened rabidity of neo-conservative assaults against the working majorities throughout many of the advanced capitalist countries.[20]

Stunned by falling rates of profit and spreading instability, the multinational corporations began a search for "production enclaves," sites where they could be guaranteed special privileges and higher rates of exploitation. At first, some enclaves were located in the American South. But eventually the need for enclaves linked to larger home markets lured investment and the transfer of production overseas. Production enclaves were established in Europe (Ireland, Spain, Portugal, Greece, and Yugoslavia); in Latin America (Brazil, Mexico, and Argentina); and in Asia (Hong Kong, Taiwan, Singapore, and South Korea).

And notwithstanding a short break in the early 1980s, this pattern has persisted, expanding investments in Asia (for financial services and production for re-export to the advanced countries), and in Latin America and Europe (primarily for production for their large home markets).[21] For the less developed countries the consequence has been the differentiation between a handful of "newly industrialized countries" and "75–80 developing countries ... shunted off to a side spur."[22] And among the latter, outlaw political orders and economies, characteristically military dictatorships, and the production and trade of illegal commodities, have become the rule.

But for the U.S. the acquisition of production enclaves produced massive reductions in the labor forces of the automotive, steel, chemical, ship-building, and electronic industries; further concentrations of the power of the multinationals and the banks (i.e., paper investments); and a corresponding expansion of an underground market economy.

Jackson's bid for the presidency in 1988 and his campaign for economic justice and a moral foreign policy constituted a threat to the capitalist political order.[23] This was not because of any program he espoused but because he sought to place on the public agenda the plight of American workers and farmers and the conduct of capital at home and abroad. It simply would not do to have a public debate of this character during a national election. Such an event would likely reinstitute the political instability of the pre-Reagan era. Not surprisingly, as was the case with consumerism, environmentalism, and large-scale protests against war and racism, capital resisted. And the media it dominates was its instrument.[24]

While Jackson and his advisors concentrated on matters pertaining to the reform of class privilege, the ethics of corporate capitalism and coalition-building, the most influential mainstream press marginalized his campaign. For example, one of the persistent characteristics of the *New York Times*'s treatment of the Jackson campaign was an unrelenting recodification into racial terms. Looking at the coverage in November and December 1987, the early months of the campaign, one is struck by the differences between the treatment of Jackson and his competitors.

- In November, Jackson named Willie Brown and David Austin to co-manage his campaign. Because Austin is white and a Jew, the *New York Times* used the occasion to employ racial codes ("... in a show of success already, the news conference today began on time, something rare so far for his campaign";

"The appointment of Mr. Austin, who is Jewish, appeared to be a direct attempt at addressing charges of anti-Semitism ..."); and in a stylistic practice used frequently in the next several months, an authoritative third party (in this instance the Pentagon) was cited to emphasize Jackson's status as an outsider (a new policy barring visits to armed forces overseas by candidates "unless their official duties, as members of Congress, for example, justified such a visit.")[25] In case readers missed the point the first time, the *Times* repeated the significance of a white manager to the campaign the following month.[26]

- In November and December, the paper gave prominence to Jackson supporters and benefactors who were Black – and in every instance the fact that they were Black was announced in the headline or by an accompanying photograph – but never featured the Rainbow organization's multiethnic character or the support of non-Black campaign workers.[27] Interestingly, the single exception to the *Times*'s racial construction of Jackson's support was its report of his endorsement by the [Democratic] Socialists of America.[28]

- In a December article, for an instance, while coverage of other candidates focused on policy issues (e.g., Paul Simon's advocacy of a constitutional amendment to balance the budget; George H. W. Bush's identification with the disarmament treaty; and Richard Gephardt's tendency toward protectionism in foreign trade) and the response of voters to those policy positions, when it came to Jackson the *New York Times* almost entirely concerned itself with Jackson's showing among Black and white voters.[29]

The *Times* thus helped to initiate the thematic and paradigmatic constructions which would dominate the press' treatment of the Jackson candidacy throughout the campaign season: at base, the media maintained that Jackson represented a racial political insurgency which was philosophically – whatever its politics might be – marginal to the accepted political spectrum. A race discourse contested successfully against Jackson's attempt to reorient the public agenda toward a critique of corporate and ruling class excesses. To the extent that Jackson succeeded in reaching the electorate (after all he garnered more than 7 million votes) he did so through grassroots, direct politicking.[30]

This most recent example of the appropriation of the Black subject demonstrates my earlier point: in America the politics of representation of the Black subject still obtains. But it is no longer a question of who we are (that is finally the force of Hall's intervention) but what we can be made to be. In this instance we became a distraction. And the equivalent of this strategy has routinely infected American scholarship. I have already given several such instances, but the recent work of David Brion Davis provides one more example of this pernicious practice. In his epilogue to a study which once again makes his point that the existence of the West is antithetical to racial oppression, Davis observes:

As Conor Cruise O'Brien has pointed out, the United Nations is political theater dominated by an institutional tone of "lofty morality" perfectly suited for the dramatic exploitation of guilt – in particular, "Western guilt feelings toward the non-white world." The influx of new African states enabled the nonwhite members to win hegemonic control over the "moral conscience of mankind." Unfortunately, condemnations of colonialism and apartheid as the twentieth-century equivalents of slavery sometimes served to shield forms of oppression for which whites bore no responsibility.[31]

With one swipe of his pen the historian abolishes history and historical systems of exploitation, sublimating them all to a racial psychodrama perpetrated by con men. The U.N., Davis laments, no longer commands our regard because it has been appropriated by a nest of African vipers. Fortunately, there are oppositions to what Davis and his confederates propose.

Jackson employed a cultural politics which extended the discursive meaning of the essential Black so that it encompassed class, gender, ethnic, and sexual exploitation/oppression and the domination of the Third World. He did this with a rhetorical instinct borrowed from the discursive practices of ordinary Black men and women, a practice which extends kinship ("brothers" and "sisters") to those who share the experience of social degradation regardless of their social identities.[32] This constitutes a more powerful politics of representation and resistance than ethnicity or any other cultural politics which might originate from the desires of a Black intelligentsia.

NOTES

1. W. E. B. Dubois, *Black Reconstruction in America* (New York: Meridian Books) 1964 (orig. 1935), 722.
2. Stuart Hall, "New Ethnicities," in Kobena Mercer, ed., *Black Film British Cinema* (London: Institute of Contemporary Arts) 1988, 27.
3. David Gordon, "The Global Economy: New Edifice or Crumbling Foundations?" *New Left Review*, 168, March/April 1988.
4. William J. Wilson, *The Declining Significance of Race* (Chicago: Chicago University Press) 1978.
5. Alan Freeman, "Racism, Rights and the Quest for Equality of Opportunity," *Harvard Civil Rights Civil Liberties Law Review*, 23, 2, Summer 1988, 359–360.
6. Karl Marx, "On the Jewish Question," in Robert C. Tucker, ed., *The Marx-Engels Reader* (New York: W.W. Norton) 1978, 48–50.
7. Michael Hunt, *Ideology and U.S. Foreign Policy* (New Haven: Yale University Press) 1987, 48.
8. George Fredrickson, *The Arrogance of Race* (Middletown: Wesleyan University Press) 1988, 205.
9. John Chester Miller, *The Wolf by the Ears* (New York: Meridian) 1977.
10. Fredrickson, *Arrogance of Race*, 202.
11. Benjamin Franklin, "Observations on the Increase of Mankind," in L. W. Labaree and W. B. Wilcox, eds, *The Papers of Benjamin Franklin* (New Haven: Yale University Press) 1959, 4, 234.
12. James Wright, *The Free Negro in Maryland, 1634–1860* (New York: Columbia University Press) 1921, 27.
13. J. Jean Hecht, *Continental and Colonial Servants in Eighteenth Century England* (Northampton: Department of History, Smith College) 1954, 56.

14. Hunt, *Ideology and U.S. Foreign Policy*, 59.

15. Fredrickson, *Arrogance of Race*, 201.

16. Ellen Meiksins Wood, "Capitalism and Human Emancipation," *New Left Review*, 167, January/February 1988, 5–6.

17. Hall, "New Ethnicities," 27.

18. See Engels' letter to Joseph Block in Tucker, *Marx-Engels Reader*, 760–765.

19. See Immanuel Wallerstein, *The Modern World-System* (New York: Academic Press) 1974.

20. Gordon, "Global Economy," 153.

21. See Louis Uchitelle, "U.S. Businesses Loosen Link to Mother Country," *New York Times*, May 21, 1989.

22. Gordon, "Global Economy," 156.

23. Tom Ferguson and Joel Rogers, *Right Turn* (New York: Hill & Wang) 1986.

24. Ben Bagdikian, *The Media Monopoly* (Boston: Beacon Press) 1983, 211.

25. Isabel Wilkerson, "Jackson Names 2 to Lead Campaign," *New York Times*, November 14, 1987.

26. David Rosenbaum, "Discipline Marks Jackson Campaign," *New York Times*, December 10, 1987.

27. Ronald Smothers, "Jackson Supporters Block Efforts by Black Democrats on Strategy," *New York Times*, November 16, 1987; Joyce Purnick, "Dinkins and Rangel Backing Jackson's Candidacy," *New York Times*, November 25, 1987; and Richard Berke, "Black Businessmen Donate $22,500 to Jackson," *New York Times*, December 6, 1987.

28. "Jackson to Shun Socialist Backing," *New York Times*, December 4, 1987; and "Jackson Seeking Socialist Backing," *New York Times*, December 5, 1987.

29. E. J. Dionne, Jr., "Jackson Seen as Caring But Lacking Experience," *New York Times*, December 1, 1987.

30. Andrew Kopkind, "The Jackson Moment," *New Left Review*, 172, November/December 1988.

31. David Brion Davis, *Slavery and Human Progress* (New York: Oxford University Press) 1984, 318.

32. For one, see Carol Stack's *All Our Kin* (New York: Harper & Row) 1974.

CHAPTER 14

The American Press and
the Repairing of the Philippines

The notion of journalistic "repair" comes from recent American literature on mass communications. It refers to the research findings that "journalists, like the public officials who initiate most news, possess and apply actively a set of basic assumptions about the bounds of social and political normalcy."[1] The "repairing" of the news ("news normalization"), requires journalists to refigure the narrative and thematic constructions of events. Such interventions result from the appearance of events which have intruded on the familiar themes and contours of news invented by public officials and corporate leaders and reiterated by mass media organizations. Routinely, as Philip Kuberski suggests, "[t]he demand for coherence is greater than the demand for other truths, and thus the media's search for truth is inevitably a search for an ideology of presence unthreatened by the disordering recognition [by the audience] of cultural expectations and demands."[2] The intrusive event must be refigured so that it no longer threatens to reveal ideologically unacceptable meanings of the event, or to lay bare the fact of mediation itself.

For American journalists, the phenomena associated with the deposing of Ferdinand Marcos, the Philippine dictator, in February 1986, constituted such a threat. They provide a rather clear example of some of the reasons for news repair, and the processes of news repair. As we shall see, the grounds for these processes are initially located in the history whose repression makes possible the conventions of the Philippine narrative.

I

While there were some shameful aspects to the colonization, notably the violence that accompanied the consolidation of American rule, no other country in Southeast Asia has received such a profound and mostly progressive transfusion of purely American values, attitudes, and democratic institutions. (*Time*[3])

At the end of the nineteenth century, after more than three-hundred years, Spain ceded formal control of the Philippines to the U.S. The Spanish-American War, however, was merely the final act between a make-believe empire and reality; Anglo-American commercial interests had already assumed overwhelming dominance of Philippine trade and agriculture by the 1880s.[4] There were, too, the Filipinos themselves. Their most recent revolution against Spain had begun in 1896 and would persist during the early years of American domination. Nevertheless, from 1898 to 1946, the Philippines were officially an American colony.

The architects of U.S. rule numbered among them patricians like Henry Cabot Lodge, jingoists like Albert Jeremiah Beveridge and William Howard Taft, and career militarists like Admiral George Dewey and Generals R. P. Hughes, Arthur MacArthur, and J. Franklin Bell.[5] They were bound together by a racial myth, and the conception of the nation-state as an instrument of racial destiny. Taft, the first civilian American ruler of the Filipinos, testified in Senate hearings of his native charges: "They are an agricultural people; they are a simple people; but that they regard human life with any particular sacredness I am quite sure is not true, and that they are not tender to animals is true."[6] In the same forum the military governor of the Philippines, General MacArthur, put the issue more directly. Intoxicated with the "magnificent Aryan" character and destiny of the American people, MacArthur spoke of "planting in those islands imperishable ideas." And he proudly contrasted America to "other branches of the Aryan race" which in their forays into the East were satisfied to "have simply planted trading establishments."[7] He seems to have had at his command men equal to the task ("Almost without exception," an American major reported to Washington, "soldiers and also many officers refer to the natives in their presence as 'niggers' and natives are beginning to understand what the word 'nigger' means"[8]).

For MacArthur, this "heroic age of human history" required the permanent occupation of the islands. And for much of the next half century, the pursuit of MacArthur's mission compelled American domination in the Philippines to assume varying forms and rationales: pacification campaigns (against rebellious *Filipino* nationalists and *indio* peasantries), military occupations, political and cultural tutorships of the ruling indigenous strata, and, of course, hegemonic control of the Philippines' material and human capital.

The first three years of American rule were secured by the slaughter of somewhere between 600,000 and a million Filipinos.[9] The cosmopolitan *mestizo* (planter) and *ilustrado* (bourgeois) elites, which had initially developed under Spanish hegemony, proved equally adaptable to American rule. Basically an urban class, the *ilustrado* elite was seduced into allying its professional, bureaucratic, and military services to American interests. In exchange, successive American administrations and congresses guaranteed to this elite its role in the management of the colonial state and its appropriate development through the provision of American education and training.[10] Provincial elites, initially more hostile to American rule, were also inevitably persuaded by the protected market policies enacted by the American Congress and fully in place by 1909.[11] By the opening years of the First World War, a collaboration of aristocrats and middle-class functionaries commanded the Philippines through what Philippine historian Reynaldo Ileto has characterized as a system of "compadre colonial politics."[12] For the provincial elite, the *caciques*, the rewards of collaboration included near-feudal control policed by private armies in the rural areas. Class war persisted and sharpened. In the countryside, it was inevitable that the peasant unions would evolve into resistance. These were soon complemented by organized resistance from militant trade unions and anti-imperialist intellectuals.[13] From these early 1930s roots, the *Hukbalahap* (or "Huks") would eventually constitute the anti-Japanese resistance of the 1940s, and persist as a significant factor in Filipino revolutionary nationalism until the mid-1950s.

During the Second World War, American rule of the Philippines was, of course, compromised by the expansion of the Japanese Empire. Though Japanese domination of the Philippines was not for very long or ever really complete, it did have a long-term significance. Japanese imperialism precipitated even greater resistance, pushing Filipino peasants and nationalists into new forms of armed struggle while providing some of the elite and their American rulers with a nationalist mask. With the defeat of the Japanese, however, the pretense dissolved: while pursuing a repressive campaign against Huk nationalists, General MacArthur and his staff "rehabilitated" many of the Filipino oligarchs who had collaborated with Japan so they might resume their facilitation of American domination.[14]

The peasant rebellions of the post-war years were a reaction to several events: the brutal repression of the anti-Japanese resistance; reimposition of the land-owning classes over the peasantry; the expulsion of the democratic opposition from electoral politics, and the intensification of the competition between the elites. The counter-insurgency which followed would ultimately reach far beyond the Philippines. Ralph McGehee, the former Central Intelligence Agency employee, summarized CIA operations in the Philippines in the years just before his own assignment to the islands:

> In the Philippines from 1950 through 1953, U.S. Air Force Colonel Edward Lansdale conducted a series of Agency operations to destroy the communist Huk insurgency. With a strong effort from the Agency, Philippine General Ramon Magsaysay not only successfully destroyed the Huks but also was elected President of the Philippines.

Following Lansdales's successes in the Philippines, the Agency in 1954 sent him to South Vietnam to help create the Diem regime. The burgeoning effort first to install the Catholic Ngo Dinh Diem in power and then to legitimize and extend his control over the rural Buddhist South Vietnamese was one of the Agency's most successful operations.[15]

For the next quarter of a century, the Philippines was to be both a critical site of covert operations and a pivot for the circulation of American intelligence agents in Asia. The prominences of this network ran from Japan, Taiwan and the Philippines to Indonesia, Vietnam, Thailand, Laos, and Burma, and as far west as Iran.[16]

Lansdale and his cohorts represent the imperial mechanics who helped to construct the post-war Philippines. Far more visible, however, was the parade of American political and media celebrities who stopped in the Philippines long enough for ceremonial legitimations of the Marcos regime. Though A. M. Rosenthal, the executive editor of the *New York Times*, is now appalled by the hypocrisy of one such occasion ("In 1981, Vice President Bush startled Filipinos and Americans who knew anything about the country by raising a glass to Mr. Marcos and proclaiming him an adherent of freedom"[17]), there was nothing to distinguish it from previous visitations. Vice President Mondale, Secretary of State Kissinger, and countless other American notables had circulated through the Philippines and bestowed upon Marcos the mantle of "democrat."

The Huk Rebellion was followed by other revolutionary or separatist movements: the left revolution culminating in the organization of the New People's Army in Central Luzon; and the Muslim separatist movement spearheaded by the Bangso Moro Army in Mindanao.[18] In their own right, those developments were troubling to American interests, but perhaps the most provocative event was the militant nationalism which developed within the Philippine oligarchy. This was the class which had allied with American imperialism for more than a half century, a class known locally as the "400" wealthiest and most powerful families. Now this class began to seek a separate destiny.

By the early 1970s, the Philippine oligarchy and bourgeoisie seized upon the rising rebelliousness in the islands as the occasion to assert its distinct interests. With Benigno Aquino in the lead, the oligarchs orchestrated a nationalist attack on their American benefactors and the presidency of Ferdinand Marcos:

Policies prescribed by the U.S.-dominated World Bank and International Monetary Fund (IMF) could not get through the Philippine congress ... The dockets of both houses of congress were filled with legislative proposals which categorically assailed American interests ... These developments were particularly disturbing not only to the U.S. government but also to the local American business community. The Laurel-Langley agreement [granting "parity rights" to U.S. citizens and corporations for the exploitation of Philippine natural resources and the operation of public utilities] was due to expire in 1974 but the nationalist upsurge made its renewal seem improbable. Moreover, the Philippine-U.S. military bases treaty was up for renegotiation while the Vietnam War was still in progress.[19]

Utilizing the considerable means available to them, the opposition oligarchs set the media and especially the Manila Press against Marcos, exposing corruption within his administration and his personal financial chicanery. More importantly, the oligarchs, via the media, began to attack him on an extremely volatile issue when they began to question his commitment to the basic principles of Philippine nationalism.[20]

In August 1972, the Supreme Court of the Philippines ruled that American property also fell under the laws forbidding foreigners to own land in the Philippines. One month later, Marcos declared martial law, nullifying the offending legislature and the court.

In the U.S. business press, industrialists reacted sympathetically to Marcos's declaration of martial law. Edgar Molina, vice president of Ford Motor Co, welcomed "the stability" of martial law; Robert Wales, president of Mobil Oil Philippines, pronounced: "If martial law will instill some discipline and solve the law and order problem, the temporary loss of freedom of speech is not important"; and an unidentified American oilman effused: "Marcos says, 'We'll pass the laws you need – just tell us what you want.'" And *Business Week* celebrated Marcos's victory over "the powerful family oligarchs such as the Sorianos (mining), the Aquinos (sugar), and the Laurels (banking)."[21] The *Wall Street Journal*, while conceding that Marcos's "New Society" was a public relations sham, warmed to Marcos's "liberalized requirements for foreign participation in oil exploration ventures ... [and] foreign investment..." Martial law was necessary, the *Wall Street Journal* concluded: "Politics was anarchic and violent, almost all political institutions were pervaded by corruption. Congress was more obstructive than constructive, and the press was blatantly irresponsible."[22]

During the martial law period (1972–1981), military and economic aid from the U.S. to the Philippines increased dramatically. And Ferdinand Marcos and his international banking and corporate sponsors took the occasion to invent a new Filipino elite. Not surprisingly, the capital for this elite formation was closely linked to the imposition of authoritarian rule:

there is little doubt that foreign investment increased sharply during the martial law years. Board of Investments' approvals suggest that real annual investment for the years 1973–1980 was approximately double that of 1968–1972 ... more than half took the form of official capital inflows (that is from governments, the World Bank, etc.) and only about 16 percent was private equity capital.[23]

The Marcos state employed a number of interventionist strategies for the transfer of wealth to form a new, loyalist elite. Hill and Jayasuriya describe a number of the "dubious economic projects," which included hotel and tourist-related projects as well as major industrial ventures.[24]

This induced elite, however, was less loyal to Marcos than dependent upon its American sponsors. Some of them would desert Marcos in the last hours of his rule in order to join the Aquino-Laurel forces. Juan Ponce Enrile was one of them. As defense minister for sixteen years, the Harvard-trained lawyer was a major architect of Marcos's most draconian policies and laws, and helped to create the legal apparatus of the repression.[25] During martial law, Enrile came to control the coconut industry (the Philippines' largest export) and to secure a major interest in telecommunications.[26]

In their rebellion against Marcos, it is likely that Enrile and General Fidel Ramos (West Point graduate, deputy chief of the Philippine armed forces, and a relative of Marcos) had less to fear from Marcos than had his civilian opposition. Not only could they rely on elements in the Philippine military, but as the nominal leaders of RAM, the military reform movement, they also possessed powerful allies in the Pentagon and the Reagan White House.[27] But the roles of Enrile and General Fidel Ramos were a part of the history of U.S.-Philippine relations which required "repair" by American media. This was particularly the case after November 1985 when the public pressures building against the Marcos government in both the Philippines and the U.S. signaled the possibility of a changing of the guard.[28]

II

... hard as we might wish, democracy is unlikely to appear in underdeveloped countries ... Thus while for political purposes from time to time the United States sets out to thrust democracy upon another country (Vietnam or El Salvador, for example), we should not expect much by way of positive outcomes.[29]

For the managers of American media, the unraveling of the Marcos regime made news repair imperative. The imperialist rationale that American colonialism had been in truth an instrument of Filipino liberation and democratization had disintegrated. The erratic behavior of the Marcos state betrayed even the rationale of "stability" – the lowest order of justifications produced for it over the years by American businessmen, statesmen, and intelligence operatives. In the American media, three narrative themes were used to frame and reinstitute ideological correspondence: (1) the malevolent politics of the Philippines spring from national traditions; (2) the Reagan administration removed Marcos; and (3) the Philippine Revolution was completed with the ascension of Corazon Aquino to the presidency. These constructions served to conceal a historical relationship and, perhaps more importantly, to substantiate mystifications invented for both the American and Philippine political structures.

The concealed historical impulses of American domination of the Philippines were inadmissible to those generations of Americans nurtured in the ideological environment following the Second World War. In these four decades, the ritual vanquishing of totalitarian and imperialist regimes – Nazi, Fascist, and, inevitably, Communist – has permeated American academia, literature, and popular entertainment. In this fashion, a national consciousness has been induced which corresponds with official history: the legendary maturation of the American nation from a turn-of-the-century (adolescent) flirtation with imperialism into an exemplary, tutorial democracy. In classrooms, in textbooks, in the print, and electronic media, Americans are told that the U.S. has matured into a great power, a protector of the sovereign rights and aspirations of small nations.

There was, of course, a break: the anti-Vietnam War movement. In terms of reconstituting the national consciousness, the immediate events in the Philippines had to be made to correspond with the ongoing revisions of nationalist history concerned with the American intervention in Vietnam twenty years ago and with present policies in Central and Southern America.[30] One means of achieving this was the media portrayal of Filipino political corruption as indigenous.

CORRUPTION AND TRADITION

In the margins of dispatches, editorials, and (for the most part) opinion pages, the prestigious American press systematically constructed an appropriate history and prehistory for the Marcos regime. One week before the exile of the Marcoses, in the *Christian Science Monitor*, Paul Quinn-Judge produced a typical explanation for the regime. For Quinn-Judge, the Marcos oligarchy was an entirely self-contained phenomenon.

> The [Philippine] press, monopolized by Marcos relatives or confidants, faithfully projected his views. The military enforced them. The business elite was compliant. The Roman Catholic Hierarchy was usually neutral and occasionally inclined toward the government. (February 20, 1986)

Elsewhere on the same day, the *Christian Science Monitor* gave over its opinion page to Peter Bacho (described as a lawyer teaching Philippine history at the University of Washington), who added the caveat: "Mr. Marcos did not plunder the Philippines alone. Built into the military and civilian bureaucracies are key personnel who have profited from their proximity to the presidential palace." David Newsom, director of the Institute for the Study of Diplomacy, Georgetown University (Newsom was on another day identified as the former Ambassador to the Philippines, 1977–1978), only made reference to the repressed history when he pointed to "historic ties and common interests" between the U.S. and the Philippines.

On the day following Marcos's exile, the *New York Times* was only a bit more circumspect. Reviewing the history of the regime, Eric Pace described the political phenomenon of Marcos as entirely understandable in indigenous terms, natural to the Philippines:

> Even before the Marcos era, Philippine politics were oligarchic and elitist, largely dominated by families whose influence went back for generations. Mr. Marcos was himself the son of a provincial political strongman, and in his own heyday he made power and privilege in his homeland even more dependent on personal ties ... Yet besides buttressing Mr. Marcos's rule, the Filipino web of dynastic ties eventually helped bring him down. (February 26, 1986)

Pace's "historical" account of the Marcos state was entirely oblivious of the significance of facts made evident on the same page by other reporters. Clyde Farnsworth, while assuring his readers that the Filipino economy could now be renewed, casually revealed one measure of Marcos's dependence on American dominated institutions: "The World Bank had cut back its lending to the Philippines from an annual rate of $450 million to about $200 million a year since 1983." And Eric Berg, relaying the new confidence felt by "big international banks" toward the Philippines, also passed on the news that U.S. banks held one-third of the $25 billion foreign debt of the Philippines. For Pace, however, U.S. involvement with Marcos was adequately characterized by the trivialization that "the U.S. had earlier showered him with support and compliments." *Time* magazine was content to relegate history to adjectival explicatives: Marcos was "wily," "autocratic," or (at the end) "ailing" and "unregenerate."

Of the major American newspapers, only the *Los Angeles Times* gave some hint of the extent to which successive American governments had been implicated in Philippine politics. Bob Secter's profile of Marcos (February 26, 1986) linked the Johnson administration to the corruption of Philippine politics in the early Marcos years (massive economic and military aid which "lined the pockets of friends and cronies" in exchange for support of Johnson's war in Vietnam); and identified the Nixon administration with Marcos's 1972 declaration of martial law ("hoping it would end a period of surging criminal violence and usher in a period of political and economic stability"). The immediate explanation for the *LA Times'* defection might be the size (approximately 400,000 of the country's 775,000 Filipinos) and sophistication (average income $23,680) of the Filipino community in California.[31]

But neither in the *LA Times* nor elsewhere was there any mention of the American covert operations, military and paramilitary programmes, financial and commercial machinations which had prompted, organized, and subsidized the Marcos state.

THE REAGAN ADMINISTRATION AND MARCOS

Without exception, however, the American media credited the Reagan administration with the removal of Marcos from the presidency of the Philippines. Paradoxically, the same media provided substantial evidence that the opposite was the case: the Reagan administration was a reluctant and late participant in the dissolution of the Marcos state. The public record suggests that the fate of Marcos was initiated by interests beyond the current managers of the American government and the effort to remove Marcos had begun before the Reagan administration assumed power.

By the spring of 1980, a close observer of the Philippines might have surmised that an alternative leadership structure for that country was being prepared by the same interests which had earlier promoted Ferdinand Marcos. In 1979, the State Department had interceded to gain the release of Benigno Aquino from detention; by May 1980, Aquino had been flown to the U.S. for heart surgery and subsequently provided fellowships, first to Harvard University, and then to MIT. During the final year of the Carter administration, Aquino was treated by the State Department (in the figure of Richard Holbrooke, assistant Secretary of State for East Asian and Pacific Affairs) and the *New York Times* as if he was the leader of a government in exile: Aquino was allowed to travel to Damascus to confer with leaders of the Moro National Liberation Front; encouraged to construct a nonviolent, moderate anti-Marcos coalition, and routinely briefed on American-Philippines matters by the State Department.[32]

The disaffection with Marcos within some American circles had been signaled in a three-part *New York Times* series by (senior editor) John Oakes in July 1980. Oakes compared Marcos with the Shah: "nobody seriously believes that Marcos is about to be unseated (just as few believed that the Shah would be until it happened)." Oakes also relayed the growing impatience with U.S. policy of a "rising opposition [of] middle-class intellectuals, business and professional men and women" and Catholic bishops:

> "Why do we have to fight not only our local home-grown despots but the United States Government as well?" "You confuse Marcos with the Philippines – and, in doing that, you're not going to be able to save Marcos but you're sure going to lose the Philippines."[33]

For the next three years, while the Reagan administration solicitously attended to various functionaries of the Marcos state to assure them of continued support,[34] a faction within the State Department cultivated Aquino.[35] Equally significant, when Aquino decided to return to the Philippines in August 1983, he had been assured substantial financial support from "foreign sources alone."[36]

A measure of the investment in Aquino by corporate American interests is the media attention given in America to his return from exile and subsequent assassination.[37] From January 1981 until the weeks immediate to his death on August 21, 1983, Aquino had warranted no attention in the American national press. Even his meetings with Imelda Marcos during her earlier visits to the U.S. in 1983 (May and July) had gone unreported. But Aquino's return to the Philippines marked the public launching of the plan to remove Marcos. Quite suddenly Aquino was news. In early August extensive profiles of Aquino were published in the *New York Times* (August, 12 and 20) and the *Washington Post* (August, 5, 15 and 20). And his death at Manila International Airport brought forth a media blitz. The killing of Aquino was by no means unusual in Filipino politics. The state policing apparatus established by AID in the Philippines had claimed the lives of untold thousands. As Corazon Aquino's executive secretary, Joker Arroya, observed: "When the history of the Philippines is known ... perhaps we will beat the record of Argentina in magnitude and torture."[38] Aquino had survived so long as Marcos had enjoyed unrivaled support from his corporate American sponsors. Once it became clear that Aquino had been chosen as the heir-apparent, Marcos acted to frustrate that plan by removing its key element.

The evidence for the extent to which the Reagan administration was uninvolved in this move to unseat Marcos is rather clear. Though members of the House, the Senate, and the State Department bureaucracy directly and publicly traced Aquino's assassination to Marcos, in September (and one month to the day after Aquino's death) Reagan announced that he had no intention of cancelling his November visit to Manila. Shultz, Weinberger, Bush, and others were equally adamant. Following sustained public outcry and pressure from State Department professionals and Congressional committees, the White House finally "postponed" the visit in early October. But Reagan privately wrote to Marcos that his friendship was "as warm and firm as ever."[39]

Even as late as February 1986, when the evidence of Marcos's electoral fraud was public (*Time* wrote: "What Americans saw on their television sets came as a shock") and irrefutable, Reagan could not concede:

> he said the observers had told him that "they didn't have any hard evidence beyond that general appearance." At this point he got in real trouble by adding that it was also possible that fraud "was occurring on both sides."
>
> Reagan's contentious remark was a flub, pure and simple ... [he] first made the accusation during a practice question-and-answer session with his staff before the Tuesday-night news conference. The President was corrected. But, says a Reagan aide, "he had it in his mental computer, and it couldn't be erased."[40]

For the next fifteen days, though the "White House" issued a number of pronouncements, Reagan himself was not allowed to speak publicly on the Philippines.[41] Indeed, it was not until the defections of Enrile and Ramos that the Reagan administration achieved consensus on the necessity of Marcos's removal.[42] But by eventually crediting the Reagan administration with an initiative to which it was fundamentally opposed, the American media repaired a real-world event which had required the closeting of the American president from the public arena.

CORAZON AQUINO AND THE FILIPINO REVOLUTION

There were several reasons behind the orchestration of an alternative to Marcos through the State Department. On the heels of the revolutions in Iran and Nicaragua in 1979, factions of American capital had publicly begun questioning the usefulness to "American interests" of Third World autocrats.[43] President Carter, whose waning political authority rested on his role as the restorer of legitimacy in government, was himself initially predisposed against militarist states. Post-Vietnam public opposition to military aid abroad, the defeats of the Shah and Somoza, and the vagaries of Carter's presidency were all indications of the precariousness of a strategy reliant on repressive regimes.[44] And in the Philippines, martial law had increased the ideological coherence and military effectiveness of the left insurgency, spawned unrest and corruption in the military, and inspired increasingly frequent anti-Marcos demonstrations.[45] Augmented by the pessimistic evaluations of the Marcos military by AID and Pentagon specialists, a "reform" government seemed the least costly alternative.

The existence of a guerrilla war led by the New People's Army (NPA) was reduced to a side-bar in the American press. The fact of the NPA as "a nationwide fighting force active in two-thirds of the archipelago's 73 provinces,"[46] was displaced by the "real" revolution: the triumph of Corazon Aquino. In *Time*, Roger Rosenblatt composed the journalistic conventions for the Philippines:

> Try not to forget what you saw last week ... Call that a revolution? Where were the heads stuck on pikes? Where were the torches for the estates of the rich? The rich were in the streets with the poor, a whole country up in flowers. In a short string of remarkable days a crooked election was held and exposed; a dignified woman established her stature and leadership; a despot ranted, sweated, fled; a palace changed guard – all with a minimum of blood lust ... Not since 18th century France have Americans approved so heartily of a rebellion.

And Rosenblatt equipped his readers with pithy descriptions of the *dramatis personae*: "Strong characters emerged: Vice President Salvador Laurel (crafty); General Fidel Ramos (heroic); the once-and-future Defense Minister Juan Ponce Enrile (sophisticated); White House Emissary Senator Paul Laxalt (resolute)."[47]

This neat drama is almost totally unrelated to real-world occurrences. Indeed, what remains in the relationship is restricted to an inversion of reality.

The tale, however, does possess the advantage of being memorable. And most importantly, it retrieves from the real world the unfamiliar fragments which had threatened to disrupt the news. And thus, without the slightest hint of irony, Rosenblatt could conclude with this admonishment to his audience, "Try not to forget what you saw last week. It was ourselves in eruption far away." The circle had been rounded.

The Filipino revolution which the American media permitted its audience consisted of the revolving of elites. The popular revolution, the force whose very success catalyzed the transition from Marcos, was used by the American media to legitimate the stage-play in Manila. American news-makers reconstructed the Philippines by first inventing the problem (Marcos) and then the solution (Aquino – with assistance from a recomposed Reagan administration).

NOTES

1. W. Lance Bennett, Lynne Gressett, and William Haltom, "Repairing the news: a case study of the news paradigm," *Journal of Communication* (No. 35, Spring 1985).
2. Philip Francis Kuberski, "Genres of Vietnam," *Cultural Critique* (No. 3, Spring 1986), p. 171.
3. "A test for democracy," *Time* (February 3, 1986), p. 29.
4. Jonathan Fast, "Imperialism and bourgeois dictatorship in the Philippines," *New Left Review* (No. 78, March-April 1973), p. 72.
5. Lodge and Beveridge were members of the Senate as well as historians; Taft, president of the Philippine Commission, was elected U.S. president in 1909.
6. Henry Graff (ed.), *American Imperialism and The Philippine Insurrection, Testimony Taken from Hearings on Affairs in the Philippine Islands Before the Senate Committee on the Philippines, 1902* (Boston, 1969), p. 95.
7. Ibid., pp. 136–137. Later, MacArthur's son, Douglas, would become the American Caesar in the Philippines.
8. D. H. Bain, *Sitting in Darkness: Americans in the Philippines* (Boston, 1984), p. 76.
9. Fast, "Imperialism and bourgeois dictatorship," p. 75; and John Schumacher, "Recent perspectives on the revolution," *Philippine Studies* (No. 30, 4th Quarter, 1982), pp. 445–492.
10. The educating of Filipinos in America as an aspect of cooptation begins as early as 1904 with a group of "*pensianados*" which included the Filipino jurist, Jorge Bocobo (Indiana University). Corazon Aquino's educational history merely reflects this early development. In 1946, at the age of 13, she was enrolled in Ravenhill Academy in Pennsylvania. Within days of her assumption of the Presidency of the Philippines, another private American institution, Mount Saint Vincent College (New York), purchased a full-page advertisement in *The New York Times* (February 28, 1986, p. 15) to "salute" its alumnus (BA 1953, LHD 1984).
11. Fast, "Imperialism and bourgeois dictatorship," p. 77.
12. Reynaldo Ileto, "The past in the present crisis," in R. J. May and Francisco Nemenzo (eds), *The Philippines After Marcos* (New York, 1985), pp. 7–16.
13. Benedict Kerkvliet, *The Huk Rebellion* (Berkeley, 1977), chapter 2. Kerkvliet persuasively disputes the official and left accounts which credit the development of the *Hukbalahap* movement to the PKP (the "old" Philippine Communist Party).
14. Ibid., pp. 110ff.
15. Ralph McGehee, *Deadly Deceits: My 25 Years in the CIA* (New York, 1983), p. 26; and Fast, "Imperialism and bourgeois dictatorship," pp. 85–86. McGehee's observations were "sanitized" before publication. Operations in the Philippines by the CIA and its parent organization (OSS)

were tardy because General Douglas MacArthur had jealously guarded the islands as his own preserve. See R. Harris Smith, *OSS: The Secret History of America's First Central Intelligence Agency* (New York, 1970), pp. 250–251.

16. See the testimony of Bonifacio Gillego, a 21-year veteran of Philippine military intelligence, "Among friends," *Far Eastern Economic Review* (August 5, 1972); Geoffrey Arlin, "The Organizers," *Far Eastern Economic Review* (July 2, 1973); McGehee, *Deadly Deceits*, passim; and Noam Chomsky and Edward Herman, *The Washington Connection and Third World Fascism* (Boston, 1979), Vol. I, pp. 240ff.

17. A. M. Rosenthal, "Journey among tyrants," *New York Times Magazine* (March 23, 1986), p. 73. "Vice President George Bush, on a visit to Manila in 1981, gushed effusively to Marcos that 'We love your adherence to democratic principles and to the democratic process.'" "A test for democracy," *Time* (February 3, 1986), p. 29.

18. James Goodno, "Opposition mounts in the Philippines," and Erik Guyot, "New Asian war, old Pentagon strategies," *Utne Reader* (February/March 1986).

19. Francisco Nemenzo, "The left and the traditional opposition," in May and Nemenzo, *The Philippines After Marcos*, p. 46.

20. Fast, "Imperialism and bourgeois dictatorship," p. 93.

21. "Philippines: a government that needs US business," *Business Week* (November 4, 1972), p. 42; and Henry Kamm, "Philippines president held friendly to US business," *New York Times* (November 3, 1972), pp. 53, 62. For the new sugar planters under Marcos, see Barbara Crossette, "Sugar planters look to Aquino, one of their own," *New York Times* (March 7, 1986), p. 7.

22. Peter Kann, "'Smiling martial law' leaves most Filipinos carrying on as usual," *Wall Street Journal* (March 12, 1973).

23. H. Hill and S. Jayasuriya, "The Economy," in May and Nemenzo, *The Philippines After Marcos*, pp. 142–143.

24. Ibid., pp. 145–146.

25. The immediate catalyst for the declaration of martial law in 1972 had been an attempt on Enrile's life by "leftist insurgents." Fourteen years later, Enrile acknowledged the affair had been staged by Marcos. Seth Mydans, "2 key military leaders quit and urge Marcos to resign," *New York Times* (February 23, 1986), p. 10.

26. "Defense Chief known as loyalist offers 'act of contrition,'" *New York Times* (February 23, 1986), p. 12.

27. See Paul Quinn-Judge, "Marcos's fall: how it happened," *Christian Science Monitor* (March 4, 1986), pp. 1, 18.

28. On November 3, Marcos announced a general election following meetings with Senator Paul Laxalt, one of President Reagan's closest advisors. On December 2, General Fabian Ver and 25 other defendants were acquitted of the assassination of Benigno Aquino; the next day Corazon Aquino announced her candidacy for the presidency.

29. Mostafa Rejai, *Comparative Political Ideologies* (New York, 1984), p. 106.

30. For instances of these Vietnam reconstructions, see Fox Butterfield, "The new Vietnam history," *New York Times Magazine*; and the essays by R. Betts ("Misadventure revisited") and D. Pike ("The other side") in *The Wilson Quarterly* (Summer 1983). For critiques of this revisionism, see N. Chomsky, "The Vietnam war in the age of Orwell," *Race & Class* (Vol. XXV, No. 4, 1984); and E. Herman and J. Petras, "'Resurgent democracy': rhetoric and reality," *New Left Review* (No. 154, 1985).

31. *Time* (July 8, 1985).

32. See Pamela Hollie, "Marcos foe, in US, dreams of Filipino democracy," *New York Times* (July 21, 1980); *New York Times* (November 18, 1980); *New York Times* (September 21, 1980); and Henry Kamm, "US official urges foes of Marcos to forswear the use of violence," *New York Times* (January 1, 1981).

33. J. Oakes, "The House of Marcos," *New York Times* (July 4, 1980); "How to succeed in Manila" (July 5, 1980); and "Like the Shah, President Marcos" (July 6, 1980).

34. Imelda Marcos had met with Reagan and Bush immediately after their election and before their inauguration; in Manila, Bush (1981) and Shultz (1983) had publicly pledged support for Marcos.

35. See Bain, Sitting in Darkness, pp. 411–412.

36. Ken Kashiwahara, "Aquino's final journey," *New York Times Magazine* (October 16, 1983). Kashiwahara, a brother-in-law of Aquino's and an ABC correspondent, accompanied Aquino to Manila.

37. For the corporate control of American media, see Ben Bagdikian, *The Media Monopoly* (Boston, 1983).

38. *Time* (March 10, 1986); and Chomsky and Herman, *Washington Connection and Third World Fascism*, p. 239.

39. *New York Times* (October 5, 1983). Almost simultaneously, Vice President Bush denounced accusations of Marcos's involvement in the assassination as "unfair." *New York Times* (October 7, 1983).

40. *Time* (February 24, 1986).

41. "In a speech tonight on military issues, Mr. Reagan spoke for the first time about the Philippines since a news conference two weeks ago" *New York Times* (February 27, 1986). Disingenuously *Newsweek* reported: "Shultz and other top foreign-policy advisers mounted a campaign to draw Reagan back to his basic policy of distancing himself from the faltering Marcos regime ... In a document prepared for him by the State Department later that day, Reagan seemed to change his tone" (February 24, 1986).

42. Bernard Weinraub, "US says staying on is 'futile' and offers to be "of assistance," *New York Times* (February 25, 1986).

43. Jonathan Kwitny "Anti-Mobutu feeling swells among masses living in destitution," *Wall Street Journal* (June 25, 1980).

44. Howard Zinn, *The Twentieth Century* (New York, 1984), p. 269.

45. Francisco Nemenzo, "Rectification process in the Philippine Communist movement," in Lim Joo-Jock (ed.), *Armed Communist Movements in Southeast Asia* (Aldershot, U.K., 1984), pp. 69–105; for reports on the insurgency and popular unrest, see *New York Times* (March, 10, June 7, and July 30, 1980).

46. Goodno, "Opposition mounts in the Philippines," p. 67.

47. "People power," *Time* (March 10, 1986).

CHAPTER 15

On the *Los Angeles Times*, Crack Cocaine, and the Rampart Division Scandal

The *Los Angeles Times* is one of the many big-city American dailies, which can neither be envied or admired. It would be foolhardy in the extreme to covet the awesome journalistic responsibility for recording the significant events in a metropolis as sprawling and diverse as Los Angeles. But it is regrettable that the *Times* performs that task so poorly. The result is that its readers, to the extent that they depend on the *Times* as a primary source of information on international, national, regional or city affairs, are routinely misinformed. But the litmus test for the *Times*, its most eminent counterparts in New York, Washington, Miami, Chicago, Dallas, Atlanta, and Boston or any other newspaper, must be local news.

Three years ago, the *Los Angeles Times* failed that particular trial somewhat spectacularly when it dismissed Gary Webb's investigation *(San Jose Mercury News*, August 18, 1996) into the CIA connection with the cocaine epidemic which hit Los Angeles in the 1970s. Neither the LA *Times*, the *New York Times*, or the *Washington Post* gave any credence to Webb's findings, and one or two of them launched counter-series to discredit Webb (see e.g., the LA *Times's* "Examining Charges of CIA Role in Crack Sales," October 21, 1996; and the *New York Times's* "Tale of CIA and Drugs," October 21, 1996, and the Editorial on November 5, 1996). Webb was dismissed by the *Mercury News* which apologized for sloppy editing of the original series. Nevertheless, the accusations were taken seriously by notables like Maxine Waters and Jesse Jackson. The then director of the CIA, John Deutsche appeared at a South-Central town meeting to refute the charges; and Congress, the Justice Department, and the CIA initiated investigations. In late 1998, in the midst of the media carnival around President Clinton's impeachment travesty, the third volume of the CIA's Inspector General Frederick P. Hitz was published, confirming Webb's charges that CIA officials knew that many of their Contra resources were in the narcotics trade. The IG's findings were barely reported in any of the aforementioned newspapers. The

Times, indeed, quarantined this news to Alexander Cockburn's op-ed column (10/October 22, 19/98).

Charitably, the *LA Times*'s misbehavior in the Webb affair might be attributed to outrage at being scooped on its own turf by a newspaper of the second rank. But that would hardly suffice as an excuse for its mishandling of the Bank of America scandal fourteen years earlier (the bank was laundering millions of dollars of drug money according to the *Christian Science Monitor*, August 30 and October 18, 1985). Nor would professional jealousy account for its present mischievous treatment of the scandal rocking the Los Angeles Police Department. What this story shares with the two previous debacles are drugs, law enforcement, and Central America, subjects on which the *Times* frequently flounders.

The present LAPD scandal concerns its Rampart division that polices eight square miles, west of downtown. As Scott Glover and Matt Lait of the *Times* have reported, beginning mid-September, over a dozen officers assigned to Rampart have been suspended or fired, and are under investigation for "improper shootings, evidence planting, false arrests, witness intimidation, beatings, theft, drug dealing and perjury" (*LAT* 11/November 10, /1999). So far, so good.

The principal witness against the Rampart outlaws has been one of their own: Rafael Perez. Perez, presently serving time for stealing eight pounds of cocaine from police facilities, was a member of CRASH (Community Resources Against Street Hoodlums), Rampart's anti-gang unit. In exchange for a reduced sentence, Perez has admitted and implicated other officers in "dirty" shootings, framing suspects, etc. Presently LA District Attorney, Gil Garcetti, has assigned five prosecutors to the case. Garcetti has also initiated the release of two or three inmates convicted on evidence presented by Perez and his partners; and is presently reviewing 40 or more other convictions tainted by the involvement of other policemen suspected of corruption and perjury.

Even attentive readers, however, might find the unfolding scandal difficult to follow.

The *Los Angeles Times* possesses one of the smallest "news holes" (that proportion of the paper devoted to hard news) of any major newspaper in the country. And though the story has received front-page coverage since its first appearance on September 16th, the bulk of the reportage is on the inside pages, camouflaged by a jungle of advertisements. Of the four stories printed in the first section this month: November 10th, 17th, and 20th, advertising consumes 17 of 28 pages, 16½ of 28 pages, and 23 of 34 pages, respectively. And as it has frequently done in the past with reports bringing ill-repute to Los Angeles institutions, the *Times* has sought to amend bad news with face-saving journalistic gestures.

Thus on September 23rd, just one week following the first published reports of the Rampart scandal, the *Times* published a story headlined: "In Rampart,

Support Strong" (Matea Gold and Mitchell Landsberg), documenting positive perceptions of the LAPD among Rampart residents. The import of this story seems to have been that local residents and business owners preferred the police gang to its rival gangs: "'Whatever means they used, they justified the ends,' said the community leader." Reporters Gold and Landsberg eventually seized the initiative, declaring for all concerned, "... for many neighbors, an aggressive police force is a small price to pay for safety." Perjury, drug-dealing, unwarranted shootings were obscured now by the muscular slogan "aggressive policing." But as the scandal widened, this initial effort obviously was deemed inadequate by the powers that be at the newspaper.

In any case, virtually the same story was repeated on November 10 under the headline "Crime, Poverty Test Rampart Officers' skill," this time with a by-line attributed to Anne-Marie O'Connor, Antonio Olivo, and Joseph Trevino, the last two presumably Spanish-speaking. Quite unintentionally, however, this story displayed all the inadequacies of the *Times's* reporting on drugs, Central America, and law enforcement.

The second paragraph announces the crux of the narrative concerned with law enforcement in Rampart: "A complex mix of gangs, violence and poverty in the crowded Pico-Union and Westlake districts makes policing there an unmatched challenge." Apparently LAPD officers are trained to serve and protect more sedate neighborhoods like Mulholland Drive. A different sort of rupture of the savage hood narrative, however, presents itself as an inadvertent subtext. Fully half of the informants for the story are immigrants or refugees from Central America: the police Sergeant from Mexico who resents those residents who impose Latino solidarity on him and his fellow officers (40 percent of Rampart's officers are Latino); the Honduran immigrant who was shot, paralyzed, and falsely imprisoned; the fruit seller who fled San Salvador after her mother and two sisters were killed by Death Squads; the frequently harassed Cal State Fullerton freshman who left Guatemala at the age of eight. These are the human documents of American foreign policy in Central America: the genocide in Guatemala, the dirty wars in Honduras and El Salvador; the economic colonization of Mexico. Earlier this year President Clinton publicly apologized for some of these international crimes and human rights violations. But in the context of the Rampart scandal their histories of national violation and forced evacuation have been concealed under the narrative of voluntarism. The reporters passively record Harry Pachon's assertion that "Migrants come bearing the American dream: Work hard, and with a lot of luck and skills you can make it all the way to the top." It is not clear how this ambition became uniquely American. Nor is it entirely persuasive that these refugees would assume that the U.S.-sponsored violence that victimized them in their home countries would somehow be suspended on this side of the border.

A third rupture in the reporters' justification of police misbehavior at Rampart occurs with the inclusion of Rudy de Leon in the story. De Leon is a former LAPD captain and is presently the county's law enforcement ombudsman. His explanation proceeds from this premise: "… problems often stem from inexperienced officers, most of whom grew up in more affluent neighborhoods," our reporters write. De Leon continues in his own words: "Then they graduate from the academy and go to an ethnic-minority area and walk into a house with dog feces or something in the front yard … They go home and say: 'It's a jungle out there. These people are animals.'" How this doggerel relates to the police crimes under investigation remains unexplained.

The journalists and editors of the *Los Angeles Times*, however, routinely expose synaptic breaks. On November 17th, that day's Rampart story ("Another Inmate Set to be Freed in Police Probe") is separated by one column from the story of Jay Moloney's suicide: "Onetime Superagent, Drug Abuser Is Found Hanged." The narrative is of The Fall: once an agent for notables like Spielberg, Scorsese, Mike Nichols, Letterman, and Dustin Hoffman, Moloney became addicted to cocaine, lost almost everything, and then hanged himself from a shower head at his Mulholland Drive home. Years of criminal drug abuse, and not once did he come to the attention of law enforcers – even after he publicized his addiction two years ago in *Premier* magazine!

It is well documented that the largest consumption of controlled substances occurs among the affluent in this country. William Bennett, President Bush's Drug Czar publicly announced it some years ago ("Bennett, First U.S. Drug Czar, Quits" *LAT*, November 9, 1990). We can only surmise, notwithstanding *the Los Angeles Times*'s insistence that it isn't so, that the LAPD has as much difficulty in policing Mulholland Drive as it does Pico-Union. Apparently, around Mulholland, cocaine is a supplement of creativity; at Pico-Union it merely fertilizes the jungle.

CHAPTER 16

Micheaux Lynches the Mammy

... the Aesopian mode is the zone in which minority speakers approach
the power of dominant discourse from a position of negotiation.
The speaker in this position attempts to master a language
understandable to the majority while also affirming the values and
interests of the less powerful group.
— *Clyde Taylor*[1]

The research on Oscar Micheaux, the Black filmmaker whose work began
during the silent film era, is proceeding at a vigorous pace. In the past ten years,
an Oscar Micheaux Society has come into being, producing a newsletter
documenting activities and research publications; and two of the Society's
annual film festivals have occurred. And under the auspices of prestigious
agencies like the Society for Cinema Studies in Canada, the Museum of Modern
Art in New York, the African American Film Society in Missouri, or the
Southern Historical Association, and other venues, Micheaux's life and films are
rapidly becoming a cottage industry. Part of the excitement is due to Micheaux
himself, the peripatetic producer of forty or fifty films in a thirty-year span, and
seven novels. On that score, Donald Bogle (*Toms, Coons, Mulattoes, Bucks and
Mammies*, 1973), Daniel Leab (*From Sambo to Superspade*, 1975), and Thomas
Cripps (*Slow Fade to Black*, 1977) may be credited with the most influential
efforts to initially center Micheaux in film studies.[2] Other reasons for the prolific
work on Micheaux are the maturing of Black or African-American Studies, and
the appearance of a generation or two of research scholars directly or indirectly
associated with that field. There are now enough Micheaux scholars in
American studies to stage debates over the significance of Micheaux: principally
around whether Micheaux was primarily a businessman with an erratic style or
an artist who deliberately and creatively prosecuted a Black aesthetic.[3] This
paper has much less to do with that sort of divide than with Micheaux's political
and social ideas.

About ten years ago, Micheaux's *Within Our Gates* was rediscovered in an
archive in Spain. Bearing the title *La Negra*, with Spanish-language intertitles,

the 1919 film was retranslated into English, and has inspired its own factotum (for instance, Alan Gevinson's massive catalogue of ethnicity in American film is entitled *Within Our Gates*). And I have taken *Within Our Gates* to be the most singularly political of Micheaux's films since in it he sought to respond directly to the 1915 film by D. W. Griffith and Thomas Dixon entitled *Birth of A Nation*.[4]

Much has been made of the attempts by two rival cohorts of Black leaders to produce a response to Griffith. One group drawn from prominent activists in the NAACP (W. E. B. DuBois, Mary White Ovington, and May Childs Nerney) sought to join with Carl Laemmle's Universal Studios to write and produce a film entitled *Lincoln's Dream*. Unable to meet Laemmle's condition of a matching $60,000 "nut," the project died despite the commitment of a Universal scenarist, Elaine Sterne. Meanwhile, at Tuskegee, Emmett Scott, Booker T. Washington's secretary, undertook a similar venture. After a series of fits and starts, a film partly constructed by Selig Polyscope and finished by Daniel Frohman was "completed." The premier in late November 1918 of what has been described as a disjointed menage entitled *Birth of a Race* was met with derision by *Variety* and other critics.[5] And perhaps the only saving grace from the two projects was the launching of Lincoln Motion Pictures by George and Nobel Johnson, and then Micheaux Productions by Oscar Micheaux. Both companies were constituted as independent Black enterprises committed to avoiding reliance on non-Black investors and producers. The companies differed radically, however, with respect to how they would respond to Griffith and his imitators. Since Micheaux's was by far the more arrogant and startling response, his work demands the most deliberate treatment.

Oscar Micheaux's 1919 release, *Within Our Gates*, is a stunning and enduring political statement, and a bold refutation of Griffith's imagery and social representation. Indeed, its complete deconstruction of Griffith's racial architecture was substantially more discerning than the critique which W. E. B. DuBois had mounted to Griffith's categorical portraiture in *Birth of a Nation*, or the mushy visions which fueled *Lincoln's Dream* or *The Birth of a Race*. Moreover, employing the melodrama, Griffith's favorite genre, Micheaux slyly seduced his audience while he savagely inverted Griffith's world view. Interestingly, he also employed some of Griffith's cinematic vocabulary, fades, close-ups, flashbacks, etc., to drive his narrative of romance, betrayal, race uplift, class conflicts, and social prejudices.

Among the narrative oppositions Micheaux assumed was the iconic retrieval of the mulatto. Dixon and Griffith had constructed their perverse signification of mix-racing around the characters of Lydia Brown, a mulatta, and Silas Lynch, a mulatto. In his novel, *The Clansman*, Dixon had portrayed Lydia as possessing an "animal beauty," possessing the temperament of a "leopardess," unnatural ambition, and the sexual seductiveness sufficient to ruin a nation. And as the mistress/maid of Congressman Austin Stoneman, the leader of the Radical Republicans, Lydia was "the First Lady of the Land," as Dixon described her.

No more curious or sinister figure ever cast a shadow across the history of a great nation than did this mulatto woman in the most corrupt hour of American life.

> The grim old man who looked into her sleek tawny face and followed her catlike eyes was actually gripping the Nation by the throat. Did he aim to make this woman the arbiter of its social life, and her ethics the limit of its moral laws?[6]

And among Lydia's covert agents was Lynch, as Dixon reported:

> a man of charming features for a mulatto, who had evidently inherited the full physical characteristics of the Aryan race, while his dark yellowish eyes beneath his heavy brows glowed with the brightness of the African jungle – the primeval forest.[7]

In *Birth*, Griffith slavishly followed the original, employing white performers Mary Alden and George Siegmann in brown-face to visually substantiate the freaks of nature imagined by Dixon, his collaborator. In their film, Lydia, the mulatta is a vicious mistress to an abolitionist congressman who precipitates the Civil War; and Lynch is portrayed as a lascivious, power-mad mulatto who sought to rule as dictator over the Reconstruction South while trumping his triumph with a marriage to a white woman.

Birth was premiered in February 1915. But in April of that year, William Fox's studio responded, releasing *The Nigger*, a drama concerning a Southern governor who is extorted by a whiskey-distilling political boss to oppose prohibition.[8] The boss has discovered that the governor is Black and threatens public exposure; the governor signs the prohibition legislation, then resigns, and moves to the North in order to champion his newly assigned race. Until Micheaux's intervention, however, this would be the last heroic characterization of the mulatto in American films.

In 1916, Selig Polyscope released *At Piney Ridge* in which another race-mistaken mulatto marauds through white society. He impregnates one woman, embezzles bank funds, shifts the blame for both deeds to a rival, adding the final insult that his rival is of mixed-blood. The mulatto is eventually killed by a distraught father, and while dying is told that his mother was Black. In *Pudd'nhead Wilson*, the same year, Lasky Features presented an adaptation of the novel by Mark Twain. Here a quadroon baby is switched by his mulatto mother with a white child having the same patrician father. Later the quadroon murders his uncle and tries to blame his half-brother for the deed. His original identity is revealed by fingerprint evidence and he is sent to prison. In *Bar Sinister* (1917), Edgar Lewis (the director of *The Nigger*) told the story of a mulatta who kidnaps the child of a man whose cruelty had caused the death of her husband. She raises the child as her own daughter but eventually confesses the truth. In *The Renaissance at Charleroi*, also in 1917, a wealthy aristocrat destroys the romantic liaison between a quadroon and a white man. Again that year, in *Sold At Auction*, a white child, condemned to servitude is mischievously identified by her custodian as a mulatta in order to halt a marriage to a young reporter. She is then surrendered to a prostitution ring, paradoxically auctioned to the father who had abandoned her years before, and only saved from incest by the intervention of her fiancee.

The following year, 1918, the depiction of mulattos took another turn for the worse. In *Broken Ties*, a mulatta kills her white foster father because he opposes her marriage to a white man. Her fiancé is accused of the murder but she confesses and then stabs herself to death. In *Free and Equal*, a mulatto betrays his race by succumbing to his congenital character. Trained at Tuskegee Institute, the mulatto is employed by a white philanthropist who has created a Society for the Uplift of the Negro. In gratitude the mulatto frequents brothels, seduces, and secretly marries his benefactor's daughter, and later rapes and kills a maid. At his trial, he is revealed as a bigamist and imprisoned. The philanthropist understandably renounces race equality. There was more of the same in *A Woman of Impulse* that same year. Here a mulatta stabs to death her wealthy paramour while he is assaulting another woman. The mulatta finally confesses at the trial of the other woman, thus erasing any suggestion that her action was motivated by anything other than jealousy.

Micheaux devoted much of *Within Our Gates* to the explicit publicizing and rehabilitation of the mulatto. This mission, of course, he had already undertaken in his earlier films. It could be almost plausibly argued that Micheaux's casting of light-skin players was an accident of his recruitment of actors from the professional ensembles like the Lafayette Players, the Ethiopian Art Company, the Dunbar Players, etc. But while many players in these troupes were light-complexioned, just as often prominent thespians were not.[9] Alternatively, with more plausibility, his casting decisions might be attributed to marketing considerations, that is simply employing known names from the theater and vaudeville, or deferring to assumed standards of beauty and attractiveness (for an instance the hiring of untrained Shingzie Howard).[10] Nevertheless, neither accidents of recruitment nor market strategies completely explain the fact that in *The Homesteader* (1919), *The Brute*, and *The Symbol of the Unconquered* (both in 1920), the characters his principal light-skin players portrayed were virtuous and sympathetic while there seemed to be sufficient numbers of dark-skin actors and actresses to play his villains and morally ambiguous roles.

More credible is the likelihood that Micheaux had been taken in by the caste-like definitions and social patrols established by elements of the Black middle classes in the nineteenth century. The most prominent of that strata, self-identifying as a social elite superior to both Blacks and most whites, had given inordinate value to their mixed race ancestry, taking particular pride for, as Senator Blanche Bruce's bride was described in 1878, possessing "no visible 'trace of her African ancestry.'"[11] As Henry McFarland observed of this strata in the *Philadelphia Record* in 1894:

> They have very little to do with the mass of colored citizens except in a business way or by making speeches or addresses to them. With their families and friends these leaders of their race form a society as exclusive as the most fashionable white society, and socially have almost as little to do with their brethren as if they were white, instead of almost so, as most of them are. The colored people do not feel identified with them, and although they are in a way proud of their prominence, they are not fond of them personally.[12]

Micheaux's debt to this creed of the Brown upper class was displayed in both his films and his novels. Janis Hebert commented in an analysis of *The Conquest* (1913) and *The Homesteader* (1917) that Micheaux "on the one hand views himself as being different from or 'better' than other blacks, while on the other hand he castigates the whites for impeding the progress of all African Americans."[13] Ironically, while Micheaux would advertise the social values of this upper class, he was forever disqualified from entry into their ranks by color, ancestry, wealth, or education. Nonetheless, *Within Our Gates* followed the color codes of his earlier and later films: virtue, social responsibility, race loyalty, duty, education, and professional status were reserved for his light-skin players; while darker actors portrayed the urban working class, rural sharecroppers, and social parasites (store-front preachers, gamblers, muggers, and thieves).

While the master narrative of *Within Our Gates* concerned the trials of Sylvia Landry (Evelyn Preer), a virtuous young mulatta school teacher, Micheaux also pursued a more vigorous and subversive refutation of Griffith, Dixon, and their racially bigoted confederates in film, stage, and literature. Thus while Sylvia's romantic impulses contradicted the bestial mulatta favored by Griffith and Dixon, in quite another theme Micheaux countered *Birth's* identification of whiteness with nobility. Employing the flashback toward the end of his film, Micheaux constructed Sylvia's hitherto hidden past: the legitimate child of a marriage between a Black woman and a white man, as a young woman Sylvia had experienced the lynching of her foster parents (and the attempted killing of her foster brother), and the near-rape by her own father, Armand Gridlestone! In this sequence, Micheaux portrayed the blood-lust of a white lynch mob made up of Southern patricians and farmers, women and children. And collapsing two of Griffith's most powerful depictions of Black rapists (the "Gus Chase" of Mae Marsh as Flora Cameron, and Silas Lynch's assault on Elsie Stoneman, the abolitionist senator's daughter, played by Lillian Gish), Micheaux begins the preying on Sylvia by Armand as an exterior and then moving to an interior, has Evelyn Preer re-enact the trapped Elsie's horror by almost exactly duplicating the histrionic gestures of Lillian Gish in *Birth*. Tearing at her clothes, it is only at the last moment that Armand, seeing a scar on her breast, recognizes her as his own child and, distraught, halts his attack. Micheaux had sought to rupture Griffith's Black bestiary by displaying the cruelty of whites as lynchers and rapists, but in his treatment of the *Mammy* Micheaux took his renunciation of Griffith into the realm of sublime cinematography.

In the *Mammy*, the dominant characterization of dark-skinned Black women in *Birth*, Griffith erased two or more centuries of what one Black spokesman decried as white "enforced debauchery." Countless slave women (and white indentured women) had, of course, been sexually used by their so-called masters and other males protected by race and class privilege. Griffith's asexual *Mammy* negated that very possibility. It discounted the research of Ervin Jordan, Jr. who found indirect evidence in the 1860 census confirming the account of "A Union soldier who visited the King William County, Virginia, plantation of a seventy-four-year-old farmer named Anderson Scott in 1864 [who] described it as inhabited by over 150 slaves, many with blue eyes and straight hair ... the children and grandchildren of Scott who felt little remorse about the incestuous fathering of mulatto children upon his Black daughters and granddaughters."[14] And it concealed an extraordinarily perverse moral obligation: "George Fitzhugh of Caroline County [Virginia] defended the sexual pursuit of Black women as necessary to avoid infecting White womanhood with erotic degeneracy. He praised slavery for allowing slaveowners to 'vent their lust harmlessly upon slave women' and contended that slavery protected Black women from abuse by Black men."[15]

But notwithstanding Fitzhugh's overt self-conceit, much of white Southern lore concerning ante-bellum society strove mightily to conceal the lure of, lust for, and the rape of Black women. The *Mammy* achieved this masquerade, and the *Mammy*, Cheryl Thurber assures us, was an imagined reality originating in white Southern fiction. Accordingly: "Several recent studies on slavery, notably those by Catherine Clinton, Deborah Gray White, Joan Cashin, Herbert Gutman, and Jacqueline Jones, have found little evidence for real mammies in the ante-bellum period and have even questioned the historical evidence for the existence of mammies in the period immediately after Emancipation."[16] To the contrary, in the slaveholders' households, domestic service was usually performed by young Black women. The compelling attractiveness of these Black women was memorialized by nineteenth-century American (and European) painters: Eastman Johnson recorded his father's slaves in Washington, D.C. (*Negro Life at the South*, 1859, later entitled *Old Kentucky Home*) and during the Civil War, witnessed the arrival of a "contraband" family at an army camp (*A Ride for Liberty – The Fugitive Slaves*, 1862); Richard Ansdell captured the haunting beauty of one Black woman in *Hunted Slaves* (1861); and Winslow

Homer's *At the Cabin Door* (1865/1866) depicted a handsome young Black woman forlornly watching the forced march of captured Union soldiers.[17] No matter. Griffith's *Mammy*, like her fictional predecessor, displaced the real. She became a stock character among similarly grotesque Black domestic servants in American films (and later television with characters like *Beulah*). And her important actuality in this mutilated historical memory was eventually confirmed when Hattie McDaniels received the first Oscar awarded to a Black person for her *Mammy* in *Gone With the Wind*.

In *Birth*, Griffith's *Mammy* (Jennie Lee in black-face) had defended her domestic space and the household of her patrician master, Dr. Cameron. Responding to intrusions of the Cameron domicile by Northern and renegade Black Union troops, *Mammy* had employed insults. Later, when the Camerons themselves are at risk, *Mammy* would eventually resort to physical assaults (she wrestles three Black soldiers to the ground). Micheaux, however, effaced Griffith's creature by both the display of white debauchery in the rapacious attack on Sylvia and the extraordinary sequence which was its antecedent: the white mob's week-long hunt of the Landrys; and eventually, *on a Sunday*, the lynching, and burning of Mother Landry (Mattie Edwards) and her husband.

Sylvia's foster father, Jaspar Landry, had been falsely accused of killing Philip Gridlestone, for whom he worked as a tenant farmer. The Landrys, Sylvia, Jaspar, Mother Landry, and their son, Emil, hide in the swamp, establishing a camp. And at this juncture, Micheaux begins his privileging of the *Mammy*. Accompanying the portrait of Mother Landry, Micheaux displays an intertitle:

> Meanwhile, in the depth of the forest, a woman, though a Negro, was a HUMAN BEING.

He thus extracts the *Mammy* from the lore of plantocratic apologetics, establishing her not as some fictional creature, serving the ideological functions of a fabulous Southern narrative of sexual and racial deceit, but as a mother capable of familial love and anguish. Around her are the evidence of her history: her children, her husband, and their forlorn condition. She is no longer an asexual figment of plantocratic conceit, no longer the ever-jovial and conscience-less faithful servant. Indeed, as the next intertitle establishes, her faith and her loyalty are attached to vision which far exceeds the mundane demands of social arrangement of finite duration. Thumbing her small Bible, Mother Landry implores:

> Justice! Where are You? Answer Me. How Long? Great God Almighty, HOW LONG?

And Micheaux supplies that answer. When we next see Mother and Jaspar Landry, they are being prepared for hanging. Her outer garments torn from her body, Mother Landry stands next to her husband and son. They are not resigned, however. Struggling with their tormentors, the parents manage to distract the mob long enough for young Emil to escape. Then their nooses are drawn taut. They are hung by white justice administered by the hands of women as well as men.

NOTES

1. Clyde Taylor, "The Ironies of Palace-Subaltern Discourse," in Manthia Diawara, ed., *Black American Cinema* (New York: Routledge) 1003, 184–185.
2. For a review of Micheaux scholarship, see Charlene Regester, "The Misreading and Rereading of African American filmmaker Oscar Micheaux," *Film History*, 7, 4, 1995, 426–449.
3. See Jane Gaines, J. Ronald Green, and Thomas Cripps in Manthia Diawara, ed., *Black American Cinema*.
4. See Cedric J. Robinson, "In the Year 1915: D. W. Griffith and the Whitening of America," *Social Identities*, 3, 2, 1997.
5. Thomas Cripps, *Slow Fade to Black* (New York: Oxford University) 1977, 75.
6. Thomas Dixon, *The Clansman* (Lexington: University of Kentucky) 1970 (orig. 1904), 94.
7. Ibid., 93.
8. All the following summaries are taken from Alan Gevinson's *Within Our Gates: Ethnicity in American Films, 1911–1960* (Berkeley: University of California) 1997.
9. See Anthony Hill, *Pages from the Harlem Renaissance* (New York: Peter Lang) 1996.
10. Howard volunteered this information in the documentary, *Midnight Ramble*.
11. Willard Gatewood, *Aristocrats of Color* (Bloomington: Indiana University) 1993, 3.
12. Ibid., 9.
13. The paraphrase of Hebert ("Oscar Micheaux: The Melting Post on the Plains," *South Dakota Review*, 11, 4, Winter 1973–1974, 68) is Charlene Regester's. See Regester, "Misreading and Rereading," 430.
14. Ervin Jordan, Jr., "Sleeping with the Enemy: Sex, Black Women, and the Civil War," *The Western Journal of Black Studies*, 18, 2, Summer 1994, 56.
15. Ibid., 56.
16. Cheryl Thurber, "The Development of the Mammy Image and Mythology," in Virginia Bernhard, Betty Brandon, Elizabeth Fox-Genovese, and Theda Perdue, eds., *Southern Women* (Columbia: University of Missouri) 1992, 88, 93.
17. Hugh Honour, *The Image of the Black in Western Art*, Part 1 (Cambridge: Harvard University) 1989, chapter 3. In the first year or so of the war, Lincoln ordered his officers to treat fugitive Blacks as contraband; and to return them to their masters when possible. Cf. Ira Berlin, Barbara J. Fields, Steven F. Miller, Joseph P. Reidy, and Leslie S. Rowland, "The Destruction of Slavery," in their *Slaves No More* (New York: Cambridge University) 1993.

CHAPTER 17

Blaxploitation and the Misrepresentation of Liberation

In our own time a neo-Blaxploitation has occurred which blurs the memory of Blaxploitation by rehearsing the insults of the first. The off-screen sexual gymnastics of David Alan Grier's parents in *Boomerang*; Martin Lawrence's confusion of sex with "quality time" in *Bad Boys*; Keenan Ivory Wayan's James Brown dance to ward off dogs in *Low Down Dirty Shane*; the minstrel tropes of *The Last Boy Scout, Booty Call, Senseless* (1998), Chris Rock's HBO show and dozens of similar tropes are familiar from thirty years ago. If you did not see them the first time around, the Blaxploitation films have become routine fare for the cable movie channels, particularly during Black History month. With a few exceptions, Blaxploitation was a degraded cinema. It degraded the industry which prostituted itself to political and market exigencies and constructed the genre of an urban jungle; it degraded the Black actors, writers, and directors who proved more affectionate to money than to the Black lower classes they caricatured; it degraded its audiences who were subjected to a mockery of the aspirations of Black liberationists.

The first Blaxploitation era, 1969–1975, appears precisely at that moment when Hollywood's "liberal conscience" is at its apogee.[1] In the years immediately preceding the emergence of the Black ghetto melodrama, integrationism had become the reigning ideological drama of race-theme films. Sidney Poitier was the highly successful icon of this genre, earning the highest box office, and drawing a most respectable salary which placed him among the elite of movie stars.[2] If one remained within the parameters of film production, as many film historians do, the occurrence of Blaxploitation would seem to constitute a paradox, except for the facts that Poitier's stardom and the subsequent appearance of Blaxploitation coincided with the most militant phase of Black liberationism.

Thousands of young Blacks, in colleges and high schools, had determined that integrationism, the ideology which had dominated the Civil Rights movement in the post-Second World War era, was a liberal conceit, premised on the belief that a kind of Christian forbearance would transform the hegemony of white racism. Their faith exhausted by the spectacles of bombings, beatings, insults, murders, and judicial and police injustices, many Blacks turned to the more muscular postures of Black Power, Marxism, or separationist programs. Each contained a radically different America from that inhabiting integrationism, but they were never the same alternative America. Black Power, at least in its formal expression, suggested a permanently balkanized America, disaggregated by race, religion, and ethnicity. As Carmichael and Hamilton suggested in their declaration, Black Power was merely an admission to an American apartheid in which Blacks could justifiably desire a distinct political and economic base.[3] Rather than race, religion, or ethnicity, Marxism conceptualized a class-riven society whose correction required proletarian rule; class superseded race, thus class solidarity within a militant and class-conscious working class was the ground for a true resolution. Among the separatists, America was the creation of a malevolent deity and was impervious to change.[4] The only alternative was a permanent break, a dissolution which would allow the salvation of the good. Hollywood responded by simultaneously sustaining a more muted integrationism, while conceding that Black social protest was an emergent force from a community with a historical dimension and an urgent moral impulse.

In order to understand better the filmic transmutation of Black liberation in the early 1970s, it is necessary to review briefly the stratagem employed by cultural propagandists in an earlier social crisis. In the Great Depression, the most striking project of race training in films was conducted through the genres of the jungle and plantation movies. Each of the genres had been employed during the catastrophe of immigration occurring in the teens of the present century. But then their function as narratives of whiteness had been overshadowed by the greater urgency – as proposed in the Western, the Indian, and the Civil War genres – of fabricating a nationalist mythology in popular culture.[5]

The end of the silent movies era coincided with massive economic deterioration and the emergence of extreme political oppositions. On the Right, one of the most powerful factions of American capital, the interest group coordinated by J. P. Morgan's minions, had initiated a conspiracy to "seize the White House."[6] The richly endowed plan was modeled on the emergence of the Italian Fascist movement, and sutured social materials from the American Legion, the Bonus Army, and the unemployed. On the Left, the increasing organizational impetus of communists, socialists, Black radicals, and nationalists among the more alien immigrants and Black workers was facilitated by the advance of class identity. Moreover, as the events surrounding the Scottsboro trials evidenced, the racial barriers established less than fifty years earlier had begun to disintegrate. The alleged female victims, two poor white women, had worked as prostitutes. One, indeed, had regularly serviced Black men on what she called "Negro night." The judge in the 1931 trial of the nine Black youths would have none of it:

> Where the woman charged to have been raped is, as in this case a white woman, there is a strong presumption under the law that she would not and did not yield to intercourse with the defendant, a Negro, and this is true, whatever the station in life the prosecutrix may occupy, whether she be the most despised, ignorant and abandoned woman of the community, or the spotless virgin and daughter of a prominent name of luxury and learning.[7]

The law, of course, was a fantastic artifice, a mythic concatenation of a fabulous white imaginary. The demise of the Klan in the 1920s, in a storm of sex scandals among its most prominent leaders, had exposed the hypocrisy of race patrollers like the judge. Nancy MacLean commented: "As a site of debauchery, the Imperial Palace of the Klan rivaled some of the motion picture sets its representatives so habitually rebuked."[8]

With the largest movie studios now under the hegemony of the largest fractions of capital,[9] namely the Morgan and Rockefeller groups, a significant proportion of Hollywood's productions in the 1930s provided justification for the re-establishment of overt Black repression, American colonialism, and domestic fascism. The most explicit genres were the jungle films and what Ed Guerrero has determined as the "plantation genre."[10] In both genres, the young white female serves as a besieged icon of whiteness, endangered by her own sexual desires. Concerning the first genre, Rhona Berenstein observes:

> A range of jungle films align monstrosity with darkness and position the white woman as the figure who negotiates the chasm between the white and black worlds. Her role is ambiguous. She is under threat and in need of white male care and she is liminal, aligned with and likened to monsters, blacks, and jungle creatures. The figuration of white heroines in jungle narratives underscores the slippage of race and gender traits in these pictures, and highlights the terrifying and monstrous results of transgressions of the conventional boundaries of sex, species and race.[11]

The jungle film was thus a protocol of anti-miscegenation, and like D. W. Griffith's *Birth of a Nation*, the plots of films like *Ingagi* (1930), *Trader Horn* (1931), *The Blonde Captive* (1932), *The Savage Girl* (1932), and *King Kong* (1933), all narrate the rescue of virginal white women from gorillas and Black men. Interestingly, the character's retrieval from an erotic immersion in darkness was often accompanied by the transformation of an effeminate white male into a heroically masculine figure.

In the plantation genre, the white women of films like *So Red the Rose* (1935), *Jezebel* (1938), and *Gone With the Wind* (1939) – three of the 75 major films of this genre produced between 1929 and 1941[12] – portrayed a complementary virtue of whiteness. The females' function – and invariably they were daughters of plantation-owning families – was to display the essential nobility inherent in whiteness. Typically, in the first half of the plot, their characters replicate the child-like females of Griffith's imagination, marred, however, by petulance, selfishness, self-conceit, and a passion for trivial matters. Griffith's Old South was inhabited by white women who, though young, were devoted to their families and blessed with a heightened sense of responsibility. Their successors in the 1930s were less obviously so endowed. In the end, hardship (a slave rebellion, a plague of Yellow Fever, or the ruin of the Civil War, in the aforementioned films) matures them, providing an opportunity for their noblest virtues to come to the fore.

On the other hand, the slaves of the plantation genre displayed no such depth of social or self-consciousness. The Red Summer, the judicial lynching of the Scottsboro men, the annual tabulation of actual lynchings, the constant litany of official and mob violence against Blacks were figments of reality which had no place in American films. Unlike the Blacks in the real world of the Depression years, the slaves of the plantation genre were seldom sad, rebellious, or militant. Their merriment exposed the essential and necessary paternalism of their masters; and frequently the slaves were so enthralled with slavery that they broke into song or dance. Indeed, Guerrero maintains, the only slaves who opposed slavery in the first fifty years of the cinema were the renegades depicted in *Birth of a Nation* and the short-lived rebels of *So Red the Rose*. Donald Bogle has christened the period as the Age of the Negro Servant, and has claimed "No other period in motion-picture history could boast of more black-faces carrying mops and pails or lifting pots and pans than the Depression years."[13] There was no need then for the hard justice Griffith introduced in *Birth*; and certainly no rationale for the lynching of the mammy character and her family which Oscar Micheaux dramatically presented in *Within Our Gates* (1919).

Four decades after the Depression, American film makers deployed images of Black women which adopted the ideological stratagems of the jungle films and the plantation genre. Just as the white heroine had served as a canvas upon which was inscribed the nature of her race's supposed virtues and the conflicted construct of her gender, Black women were impersonated (to use Griffith's term for acting) to display the hidden and perverse nature of Blackness, and the essentially savage erotic impulses of Black women. Shortly after the nation had been inundated by the televised scenes of freedom-seeking Black bodies being mauled by police hoses and dogs, and mobbed and spat upon by white citizens, Hollywood film makers recast the freedom movement as outlawry and, in a subgenre of Blaxploitation, Black women were portrayed as vigilantes. In the anarchy which constituted Hollywood's fabrication of Black society, all the libidinal desire and social pathology of America's urban classes was centered on the female body, the Black, as well as the white female body. The white women in these films were either masculinized degenerates or from the poor white classes; in either instance they neither expected nor deserved redemption. Remarkably, only Black women possessed the savage, primordial instinct of self-survival to resist sexual degradation and their male predators. Inhabiting a society in which the rule of law and social civility were merely superficial veneers, a world in which the quest for civil rights was at best a naive self-delusion, the Bad Black Woman's self-preservation took the form of execution and banditry.

* * *

One of the most effective and clever maneuvers of the Blaxploitation genre was the appropriation and representation of Angela Davis's public image. This manipulation, of course, was of a piece with the commercial cinema's translation of the mass Black rebellion which occurred near the end of the Civil Rights era. And in lieu of a deliberate interrogation of the political and moral dilemmas which attended the failures of an integrationist activism, independent and then established filmmakers trivialized the troubled activists of the movement into the now familiar male counter-revolutionary creatures: the male prostitute ("Sweetback"), the vigilante cops ("Gravedigger Jones" and "Coffin Ed Johnson"); the dope pusher ("Shaft"); and the gangster ("Black Caesar," etc.). The crises which communicated between American society, its dominant institutions, and the movement were masked in popular culture as ghetto epidemiology. By the era of Blaxploitation, Davis's likeness and that of Kathleen Cleaver had become two of the most familiar and alternative gender significations of revolutionary America. Film, however, transported Davis's form from a representation of a revolutionist to that of an erotic Black nationalist, largely devoid of historical consciousness. This was achieved by eviscerating the original's intellectual sophistication, political and organizational context, doctrinal commitments, and most tellingly, her critique of capitalist society and its employment of gender, race, and class.

The principal impersonations of Davis were performed by Pam Grier and Rosalind Cash, two young actresses who bore some physical resemblance to Davis. It was, however, a similarity with a difference: Grier's voluptuous figure licensed an eroticization of Davis which consisted of sexualized violence (themes of rape, castration, and the broadest contraction of the gun and the penis); Cash (*The Omega Man*, 1971, and *Melinda*, 1972), whose actual resemblance to the original was even more striking, would be penalized ironically because her own screen reticence displayed an intelligence which lent too much ambivalence and texture to the monodimensional representation of Davis. And, true to the industrial marketing strategies of American films, the roles of Grier and Cash spawned secondary and even more shallow after-images, particularly in the persons of Tamara Dobson (*Cleopatra Jones*, 1973, and *Cleopatra Jones and the Casino of Gold*, 1975) and Teresa Graves (*Get Christy Love*, 1975). Unlike the original, then, these false Angela Davises were quarantined, shut off by a cellulose barrier which invited the vicarious thrill of participation into primitive exercises depicting the cosmic contest between good and evil with nothing at risk except time and boredom.

The cinematic deceit transmuted liberation into vengeance, the pursuit of a social justice which embraced race, class, and gender into Black racism, and the politics of armed struggle into systematic assassination. The screen impostors occupied a Manichaean world in which whites were evil, corrupt, and decadent; where Black accomplices to white venality were tainted with a similarly debased nature; and the central Black protagonists were preoccupied with vigilantism. Capitalism, signified at most by skyscraper exteriors, almost entirely disappeared, constituting a normalizing space whose interstices lent marginal terrain for the practices of the drug trade and prostitution. The real world of the market, unseen and unremarked upon, hovered above the ghetto streets, the police station, the strip club, and the dealer's locales (storefront, suburban home, high rise apartment, etc.). The world in front of the camera was some sort of twisted, perverted mirror of the normal, the reasoned, the ordered, the safe, and unremarkable American landscape. The denizens dwelling in the nether world were as different from real America as gargoyles are from pigeons. The object was to exhibit these bizarre and semimythic life forms while assuring the screen audience that they inhabited a space some safe distance away.

Following the success of *Shaft* (1971), American International Pictures (AIP) began its own foray into Blaxploitation with *Slaughter* (1972) starring Jim Brown, and *Blacula* (1972) with William Marshall, Vonetta McGee, and Denise Nicholas. By then, American International Pictures had enjoyed two decades of success. AIP was begun as an independent studio by Sam Arkoff and James Nicholson in the mid-1950s. Its first film, *The Fast and the Furious* (1954) was directed by Roger Corman, whom Arkoff and Nicholson launched in a four-picture deal. And, from the beginning, AIP focused on the neglected teenage market, producing and exhibiting monster films (*The Beast with a 1,000,000 Eyes!*), adolescent rebellion films (*Hot Rod Girl*), women in prison films (*Girls in Prison* and *Reform School Girl*), teen party films (*Shake, Rattle and Rock* and *Rock All Night*), Westerns (*Apache Woman*), and horror films (*I Was a Teenage Werewolf, The She Creature, The Amazing Colossal Man,* and *Blood of Dracula*).[14] Typically, in the early years, according to Arkoff, the creation of a film began with a title (Nicholson's contribution), which inspired an ad campaign which then eventually produced a shooting script. Also typical was the use of untested film directors like Roger Corman, Francis Ford Coppola (*Dementia 13*), Woody Allen (*What's Up Tiger Lilly?*), and Martin Scorsese (*Boxcar Bertha*); young actors like Jack Nicholson, Michael Landon, Mike Connors, Peter Graves, Jayne

Mansfield, and B-grade actors like Richard Denning, Beverly Garland, and Marla English and has-beens like Chester Morris and Anna Stens. Later this impressive list of firsts, according to Arkoff, would extend to first starring roles for Charles Bronson, Melanie Griffith, Bruce Dern, Cher, Chuck Norris, Dennis Hopper, Mel Gibson, Nick Nolte, Don Johnson, and Robert De Niro.[15]

On the other hand, Pam Grier's career at AIP had begun much less auspiciously: she had been a switchboard operator. Her first film at AIP was as an extra in *Beyond the Valley of the Dolls* (1970), written by Roger Ebert, now a mandarin in film criticism! The next year, Grier began her impersonations of Angela Davis in *The Big Doll House/Women's Penitentiary I* (1971), a film which is credited with launching the women's prison genre. These appropriations of Davis continued for the next several years and included the sequel to *The Big Doll House*, entitled *The Big Bird Cage* (1972), *Hit Man* (1972), *Black Mama, White Mama* (1972) – a rip-off of *The Defiant Ones* – *Coffy* (1973), *Foxy Brown* (1974), *Friday Foster* (1975), and *Sheba, Baby* (1975). In each of these films, Grier wore Afros and revealing attire; toted pistols, revolvers, and shotguns; kick-boxed, mutilated, and "smoked" her antagonists; lectured enemies and friends on the necessity of upholding the law, protecting the community and its innocents; and eventually resorted to vigilantism. As the lone avengers against drug pushers, corrupt politicians and cops, and Black and ethnic gangsters, her characters were estranged from community or political organizations and, when they infrequently required a posse, it was only for the ultimate dispatching of the villains "with prejudice," as the CIA euphemistically had dubbed killing. *Foxy Brown*, one of Grier's best known and notorious roles of the period (she castrates her tormentor), illustrates nicely how these misrepresentations of Angela Davis transported film audiences of the mid-1970s into a counter-liberationist realm.

Foxy Brown (Grier), a young Black woman of no apparent means, lives in a comfortably furnished apartment in a Black neighborhood. Her brother (Antonio Fargas) is a cocaine dealer who has run afoul of his white mobster suppliers (Peter Brown and Kathryn Loder); her lover, Michael (Terry Carter), a federal agent, is recovering from an attempted assassination by the same mobsters. The first hint of Foxy's unusual capacity for action is her rescuing her brother from the clutches of his mobster friends. She sequesters him in her apartment and then visits her lover in the hospital, eventually bringing him, too, to her apartment. Despite her lover Michael's plastic surgery, he is recognized by the brother, who then reveals his true identity to his partners in exchange for a return to their good graces as a dealer. Michael is killed, dying in Foxy's arms, and Foxy is transformed into the avenger. She extorts the names of the killers from her brother and joins the prostitution ring directed by the mobsters. Foxy and Ann, another Black woman (Juliet Brown), are assigned as sexual toys to a corrupt judge who, in exchange, is expected to give light sentences to two mobster thugs. Instead, the two women conspire to humiliate the judge, each for her own reasons (Ann has just witnessed her husband's being beaten by her bosses). The judge in revenge hands down long sentences. Foxy's identity is discovered by the mobster chiefs who pursue and capture the two women. Foxy saves her companion, who presumably joins her husband and child, but for herself it means a period of torture and rape. Foxy escapes, killing her two keepers. In retribution, her brother is now executed by the mobsters, and Foxy persuades an organization of Black community vigilantes to join her in seeking justice and revenge. (She tells them: "You just take care of the justice, and I'll handle the revenge, myself."[16]) Together they ambush the mobsters at a cocaine drop, capture the mob boss, and Foxy castrates him. Foxy delivers the severed penis in a jar to the boss's mistress, kills the woman's bodyguards, and leaves the wounded mistress to contemplate a life with her castrated lover.

The exploitative properties of the film center on the female body and brutal violence and are established in the opening credits when, borrowing from the James Bond films, Grier dances in a kaleidoscope of colors and in various modes of undress to the funky beat of an eponymous song. In her next appearance on screen, we see her bare breasts as she dresses in order to drive to the rescue of her brother. Her naked or dressed body is constantly reprised as a source of titillation in the film as she is in bed with her lover, as she is attired for her disguise as a prostitute, as she lures the judge into his own compromise, as she is drugged and raped, etc. Voyeuristic pleasure is also provided by the naked bodies of several white women: the four prostitutes lounging in the laps of the judge's middle-aged cohorts, watching a pornographic film; and, most disturbingly, the camera conspires with the mobster killers to expose the naked body of Foxy's brother's lover moments before her jugular is severed.

The film's Blaxploitation elements are sometimes more oblique. By the time of the release of *Foxy Brown*, it had become obligatory in the form to portray the racial hierarchy of ghetto criminality: Black street dealers in the employ of white mobsters and their corrupt partners drawn from seemingly legitimate society. In this film, Fargas performed this function, effectively demonstrating his cloying subordination to the white bosses of the drug/prostitution ring. The extent of Fargas's subordination is confirmed when he violates loyalty to his own sister in order to serve his masters. It was also mandatory that there be a representation of urban anarchy: in *Foxy Brown* this was achieved quite early in the film. The opening sequence is the hunt, cornering and eventual rescue of Fargas in the stark barrenness of the city's streets at night. Shortly after, further evidence of this urban jungle is adduced with a scene ostensibly depicting Michael's release from the hospital. As he and Foxy stand at a corner in a Black neighborhood, they witness the playing out of the Black outlaw by community vigilantes. A lengthy fight takes place between the villain and his three pursuers during which a young Black woman pushing her baby's carriage is mauled. The forsaken carriage swings into on-coming traffic, only to be reclaimed at the last moment. The villain is finally hustled into a car, destined, we are assured, for a place from which he will never return. The significance of the whole altercation, which takes place in broad daylight, is brought home by the total absence of the police, the society's and the state's emblem of order. Other erasures from this imagined community are less obvious but nevertheless telling: the absence of children and oldsters, of families, churches, legitimate businesses, recreational sites, schools, and ordinary family dwellings.

Clyde Taylor has pointedly remarked that we can discern much from the comparison of a text to its subsequent adaptation.

> By lining up an adapted text diachronically behind its model, we can clearly see the differences that, when read as discursive ironies, matter in the politics of representation. Lay viewers from repressed communities are right on target in decoding the politics of adaptation by indexing what was added, changed, or left out in the transition between one telling and another.[17]

While his observations were specifically concerned with the conversion of a novel to a play, and a play to a film, it is also applicable to the transfer of social reality as text to film as text. At the time of Blaxploitation films, it was a commonplace that actual Black urban communities in all parts of the country were heavily patrolled and policed by agents deployed by federal, state, county, local, and private institutions. The external imposition of order was manifested through electronic surveillance, informants, undercover operatives, special police intelligence units, interventions of mailed correspondence, photo surveillance, foot- and automobile-patrols, frequently centralized by interagency cooperation. From within the community, moral, and civil order were maintained by church networks and the routines of daily labor, community associations, mainstream and radical political organizations, neighborhood watch groups, and a canopy of adult and youth activities. Why then would Hollywood and independent film makers construct this densely jungled urban landscape inhabited principally by predators? How might the manufacturers of such a fantastically unrealistic portrayal expect that their creation would achieve the ring of authenticity?

In the Bad Black Woman genre, the body of the Black female anoints this unreality as authentic. On the one hand, the undeniably erotic objectivity of the Black female body inscribes the mark of truth onto the social fantasy. And the narrative, filled with competing claimants for that body – lovers, rapists, and the merely obsessed (in *Foxy*, the judge is characterized by his taste for "your kind") – transports the credibility of their desires into an authentication of the world in which these denizens are imagined to exist. Unlike her white female counterpart of the jungle and plantation films, it is not the Black female who is an ambiguous figure negotiating the chasm between the white and the Black worlds. It is the chasm which is ambiguous: male desire and the resulting calumny of male domination erases the distinctions between white society and Black society. In the total absence in the genre of any allusion to actual international capitalism, a predatory fratriarchy displaces modes of production as the source of evil. Material greed, political tyranny, and the domination by capital of labor are merely vacuous surrogates for male desire.

The presence of the body in the female-centered genre permits the Black female to decompose the omnipresent, vocalized, and cartoonish Black racism which inhabits the Blaxploitation films drawing on male characters. While actual Black and non-Black revolutionaries had recited the existence of a ruling class, Blaxploitation films instructed their audiences that the subtext of the attack on bourgeois society and imperialism was really a disguised racial complaint. Liberation ideology had nothing to do with a revulsion with oppression but was fuelled by race envy. In the Bad Black Woman genre, even this masking of liberation is discarded. Black racism is displaced by female rage: Black women rage at the betrayal and abandonment by family, community, and society. These agencies have disintegrated, failing to protect her or even to provide a space for the conduct of normal life. And in the same genre, as represented in the figure of the evil white female villain, white women appear to be inspired by a similar rage. Unlike their sisters of the 1930s, the issue is not their surrender to ravishing Black males (*King Kong*) but the betrayal they sense in white male desire. The whole official rationale for the lynching of Black males collapses, revealed as an elaborate deceit to conceal the white man's hunger for the Black female body.

The subgenre of the Bad Black Woman thus negotiates its exaggerated unreality by its display of the Black female body. The false, Hobbesian depiction of the Black community, the procrustean social consciousness of its protagonists, the bluntly pathogenic and unrelievedly pure malevolence of its villains, and the outrages perpetrated on the flesh of friend and foe alike are all spun into credible artifices by the single truth of the Black woman's body. And as that body is transformed into that of the destroyer, a fascination with that violence overtakes and converges with sexual voyeurism. The pleasure of the flesh convenes with the excitement of revenge so that they might double for a notion of social justice. The enduring innocence of the avenger, beset on all sides by violence, corruption, betrayal and loss, installs the rightness of a simple, closing justice.

To paraphrase Gina Dent, the films of Blaxploitation were a historical practice.[18] Just how powerful a practice is now evident in the emergence of rap music over the past decade or so. Notwithstanding the Black bourgeois renderings of the Civil Rights and the Freedom movement era (in e.g., the television documentaries *Roots* and *Eyes on the Prize, I*), the young Black griots of the present recite history in Blaxploitation terms (Ren and Dr. Dre: "keeping a smile off a white face"), while, paradoxically, employing the racist imagery of minstrelsy (Chris Rock: "You know what the worst thing is about niggas? Niggas always want credit for shit they supposed to do ... like: "I take care of my kids." You supposed to, you dumb motherfucker!"[19]) In the early 1970s, however, a companion genre to Blaxploitation appeared, the Bad Black Woman narrative. Ironically, it borrowed more directly from reality by snatching Angela Davis from the pages of newspapers, news magazines and law enforcement dockets. On the one hand, this imagined Angela extended the life of the Black-action movie. More importantly, as the gun-toting impersonation displaced the original, it also served to rupture the transmission of Black radical thought. Between them, Blaxploitation and the Bad Black Woman narratives installed into popular culture a race-encoded critique of American society and resistance as it drew its first and later audiences further away from the reality of the liberation movement. Historical ambiguities and structural contradictions were engulfed, leaving behind an ideological apparatus ill-equipped to deal with research-based historical activity, to invite transracial resistance, or to reckon with state tyranny in Africa or the Caribbean or domestic manifestations of Black fascism.

NOTES

1. Thomas Cripps, *Making Movies Black* (New York, Oxford University Press, 1993), p. 294.
2. Ibid., 289ff.
3. Stokely Carmichael and Charles Hamilton, *Black Power* (New York, Random House, 1967).
4. Gerald Horne, *Fire This Time* (Charlottesville, University Press of Virginia, 1995), p. 5.
5. Eileen Bowser, *The Transformation of Cinema* (Berkeley, University of California, 1990), chapter 11.
6. Jules Archer, *The Plot to Seize the White House* (New York, Hawthorn, 1973) and Clayton Cramer, "An American Coup D'Etat?," *History Today* (November 1995), pp. 42–47.
7. Dan T. Carter, *Scottsboro: A Tragedy of the American South* (Baton Rouge, Louisiana State University Press, 1969).
8. Nancy MacLean, *Behind the Mask of Chivalry* (New York, Oxford University Press, 1994), p. 98.
9. Robert Stanley, *The Celluloid Empire* (New York, Hastings House, 1978).
10. Cf. Rhona Berenstein, "White heroines and hearts of darkness: race, gender and disguise in 1930s jungle films," *Film History* (No. 6, 1994), pp. 314–339; Kevin Dunn, "Lights ... camera ... Africa: images of Africa and Africans in western popular films of the 1930s," *African Studies Review* (Vol. 39, No. 1, April 1996), pp. 149–175 and Ed Guerrero, *Framing Blackness* (Philadelphia, Temple University Press, 1993).
11. Berenstein, "White heroines and hearts of darkness," p. 335.
12. The figure is from Guerrero, *Framing Blackness*, p. 19.
13. Donald Bogle, *Toms, Coons, Mulattoes, Mammies, and Bucks* (New York, Continuum, 1995), p. 36.
14. Sam Arkoff, *Flying Through Hollywood by the Seat of my Pants* (New York, Birch Lane Press, 1992).
15. Ibid., p. 5.
16. The scene takes place in the neighborhood vigilantes' headquarters, where on the doors and walls are posters of Kathleen Cleaver and George Jackson, the only instance when the film refers to originals in the actual Black movement. In a long shot of very short duration, at the far end of

a second room, a small glimpse is given of a poster of Angela Davis. But the scene is dominated by two shots of Grier in the foreground, positioned between the portraits of Cleaver and Jackson, and then another Jackson poster. The film makers thus deliberately shield their audiences from any direct exposure to what might disturb the imposture, the juxtaposition of Grier with her model. Natalie Morris, one of my students, has determined that there is also an oblique reference to George Jackson as Foxy's speech to the vigilantes appropriates the romance trope embedded in Angela Davis's *Autobiography* (New York, Random House, 1974).

17. Clyde Taylor, "The ironies of palace/subaltern discourse," in Manthia Diawara, *Black American Cinema* (New York, Routledge, 1993), p. 186.
18. Gina Dent, in discussion of her paper "Legacies," at "Unfinished Liberation" conference, March 6, 1998.
19. See Ernie Allen, Jr., "Making the strong survive: the contours and contradictions of 'Message Rap,'" in William Eric Perkins, ed., *Droppin' Science: Critical Essays on Rap Music and HipHop Culture* (Philadelphia, Temple University, 1996), p. 171; and Chris Rock, "Bring the pain," HBO, March 8, 1998 (original, 1996).

CHAPTER 18

The Mulatta on Film: From Hollywood to the Mexican Revolution

with *Luz Maria Cabral*

... the South seems to be the myth that most consciously asserts
whiteness and most devastatingly undermines it.
— *Richard Dyer*[1]

If the legal codes, prosecutions and trials hedging mixed-race persons and
marriages are any measure, the mulatto has constituted a threat to North American
racial hierarchy, property, and authority for more than three-hundred years. In
colonial Anglo-America, the designation "mulatto" first appears in a legal
document in 1644. Twenty years later it reappears in the judiciary record as a
status bounded by the moral contamination of Blackness and its association with
slavery. The year was 1662 and the grand assembly of the Virginia colony enacted
a law which proclaimed that "a child got by an Englishman upon a negro" would
follow the condition of its mother. Teresa Zackodnik comments that "Maryland
recognized earlier than Virginia the 'threat' to established order involved in
allowing mulatto children of white mothers to be free and moved in its Anti-
miscegenation Act of 1663 to enslave these children."[2] The mulatto induced
colonial legislators to assert that slavery trumped the age-old rights of paternity in
English law; and, soon afterward, by denying that baptism was a route to freedom,
Christianity, too, was vanquished as a worthy opponent by slavery. In the 1690s,
Virginia legislators described mulattos as "that abominable mixture and spurious
issue" and, in 1692, banned from the colony those men and women implicated in
interracial unions. By the end of the seventeenth century, then, the mulatto had
come to signify an abominable spiritual contamination as well as the spurious
violation of the boundaries between property and human identity. Whiteness –
the new term of self-identification – was nonnegotiable.[3]

For the next century and a half, the racial ambiguity of the mulatta was buried
under a mountain of laws, court decisions, and social practices which persisted

in the resolve to preserve the boundaries between whiteness and slavery. Nevertheless, in the cultural wars that swirled around slavery, the mulatta became a contested icon. In the three decades prior to the Civil War, the propaganda wars between the supporters of slavery and the abolitionists produced three enduring Black signs: the mulatta (and the mulatto), the tom, and the buck. Paradoxically, despite its later appropriation by the incipient American film industry as a sign of an anti-Negro cinema, the origins of the mulatta were in the abolitionist camp. From Richard Hildreth's novel *The Slave* (1836) to Dion Boucicault's *The Octoroon; or, Life in Louisiana* (an 1859 dramatization of Captain Mayne Reid's romance *The Quadroon; or, A Lover's Adventures in Louisiana*, 1856), dozens of novels and plays centered around the "mixed-race" figure who served as a fictive chiaroscuro through which the tragedy of slavery could be sentimentally experienced by white readers and playgoers.[4] Hildreth's protagonist is a male (Archy Moore), but the much more popular figure for anti-slavery writers of the antebellum period was the mulatta. Bentley argues that this preference is explained most fully by "the different *mythology* of flesh separating the bodies of men and women ... the sexual oppression that produces [the mulatta's] Europeanized 'beauty' also makes her the victim of the next cycle of abuse."[5] While mulattos like Archy Moore or Harriet Beecher Stowe's George Harris (*Uncle Tom's Cabin*) sought to resolve their "unnaturalness" through violent revolt, the imaginary poetics of novel and stage that mirrored the actual economies of race and gender stipulated that the mulatta be represented as a martyr. As Joseph Roach telescoped the trope, "a rare beauty of delicate manners and mixed race, legally exposed by the foreclosure of a mismanaged plantation, finds herself auctioned off as a slave to the highest bidder, who turns out to be the moustache-twirling villain."[6]

In the antebellum period, the control over the figure of the mulatta was clearly won by the abolitionists. But, following the Civil War and the defeat of Reconstruction, racists would revive their claim to the mulatta as an icon of propaganda. Driven by the cultural movement to replace the historical slave South with a mythical "Old South," racists transferred the moral and sexual guilt they associated with the mulatta from white males to Black women. They proclaimed in the press, novels, plays, history texts, and popular magazines that the mulatta appeared as the result of white males being submerged in a society of hypersexual and seductive Black women.[7] The vilest of these, obviously, was the mulatta since she inherited the vices of the two races, and her deviant sexuality reflected the monstrousness of her birth. The campaign to efface the virtuous mulatta of the antebellum abolitionists was not entirely successful, however. A Black middle class had developed and was now positioned to challenge white supremacy in North American historiography, the press and popular culture.

The villainization of mulattos – particularly the mulatta – in American popular culture took place in the early twentieth century. The primary vehicle for this degradation was the silent film industry, an enterprise increasingly under the control of big capital. Film was being deployed deliberately to signify and inculcate a new racial order into the imaginations of the millions of European immigrants arriving between the 1890s and the First World War. Principally a working-class entertainment, silent film consisted of elementary narratives combined with short English-text intertitles. These techniques provided the basis for language training as well as teaching ghetto audiences acceptable moral values, appropriate social behaviors, and the racial rewards of whiteness. From the mid-1890s, comedies made up one-third to one-half of the films of the largest studios, Edison and Biograph/Mutoscope. Here audiences encountered stereotypes of Blacks, Jews, Italians, Irish, Chinese, and Mexicans as a constant source of amusement. Eventually, some more controlled and reasonable sampling of caricatures was achieved, in part as a response to domestic pressure groups (e.g., the Irish associations and the Catholic Church), concerns about foreign distribution and changes in the organizational control and structure of the film studios.[8] Of equal significance were the cultural habits spawned by African slavery; what Ed Guerrero has termed "the inscriptions of slavery."[9] The "Negro comedies," an important representation of this inscription, were especially dependent on a roughhouse version of slapstick: "Early motion pictures, therefore, supported barbarism toward African-American men because the violence did not really appear to be harmful and because this use of force upheld the moral order."[10] In short, Blacks were envisioned both as a persistent threat to the stability of an exploitative social order and as a politically convenient symbolic representation of the "other" in American culture.

In the post-Reconstruction era, which began in the late 1870s, racial segregation had been instituted as a central stratagem in the attempt to acquire control over the American working classes. What had initially spurred such a program were the coalitions established between Blacks and poor whites during the Civil War; the continuing necessity for such a policy was confirmed by cross-racial coalitions between white and Black farmers, the initial impulses of the Populist Movement, and organized workers (e.g., the Knights of Labor). In the last decade of the nineteenth century, this racial separation was formalized in the Southern states as Jim Crow. This coincided with the appearance of motion pictures as a popular entertainment. At the onset of movies, the greatest racial concern of American capital was the ordinary Black working class. Consequently, films ridiculed characters who were recognizably Black. Since most American filmmakers refused to employ Black actors and actresses, the representation of Blacks was achieved by whites in burnt cork make-up, a technique borrowed from black-face minstrelsy.

Jim Crow, however, had also profoundly subverted the Black middle class's social ambitions. And, when elements of this class began to resist segregation in the first decade of the twentieth century, forging alliances with whites in the

Socialist Party and with white liberals in organizations like the National Association for the Advancement of Colored People (NAACP), they too became targets in the fledgling cinema. The renegades tended to come from the eastern branches of the Black middle class. With its variety of origins (mixed-race children of planters and slaves, slave artisans, educated free Blacks, etc.), the class had sprung up all over the country, from New York and Boston to Chicago and Atlanta, to Denver and San Francisco. But the militants had eschewed the customary clannishness of their class which was further exacerbated by Jim Crow.[11] Highly educated (several of them had graduated from Harvard or Oberlin), activists like W. E. B. Du Bois and Monroe Trotter had become public figures. At Atlanta University in the late 1890s, Du Bois had attracted some of the most eminent European and American scholars to his annual Atlanta conferences.[12] In the next decade, Du Bois was published in *The New York Times* and was among the founders of the Niagara Movement and the National Association of Colored People. Trotter had made headlines when he led a Black delegation to the White House in late 1914 to protest against the Woodrow Wilson administration's segregation of the federal civil service.[13] In 1915, for another public instance, Mary Church Terrell, a Washington, D.C. Black aristocrat, lobbied Congress against a proposed anti-miscegenation law.[14] And, since many of the most prominent families in the Black middle-class were descendants of mixed-race unions, they were attacked in film through the representation of the mulatto. The first assault came in 1915 with the exhibition of *The Birth of a Nation*.

THE NEW MYTH OF THE "OLD SOUTH"

Vanquished on the North American stage by the Black musical, black-face minstrelsy was revived in the newest mass cultural phenomenon, the silent film. But unlike the black-face minstrelsy of the nineteenth century, which featured coons and mammies, the new venue was decidedly a forum for the prosecution of the new myth of the "Old South." The two most prominent and successful representatives of "Old South" mythology were Thomas Dixon and D. W. Griffith. In 1915, they collaborated (with Woodrow Wilson) on the photo play of *The Birth of a Nation*. The villain of the piece was Austin Stoneman, the club-footed Radical Republican leader who induced the South to secede by championing the anti-slavery cause. And in his vicious campaign to humiliate the Southern plantocrats before, during, and after the Civil War, Stoneman's closest confederates were his mulatta maid/mistress Lydia and her other companion, the mulatto Lynch. By associating Stoneman *père* with mulattos such as Lydia and, later, Silas Lynch, Griffith evaded another historical truth, grafting the *blight* of miscegenation on to a powerful Northern abolitionist! In fact, most of the nearly half a million mulattos in the country residing in the South in the mid-nineteenth century were the issue principally of slave owners and female slaves. Nevertheless, since Griffith would characterize his two mulatto roles with a neurotic sexuality necessitated by plot and ideology, disclosing their relation to the ruling plantocracy would risk an unseemly speculation about the source of their sexual depravity.

The film was a phenomenal popular and commercial success. It catapulted Griffith into near-Olympian status in American cinema, bringing a productive but essentially hackneyed film producer permanent fame. *The Birth of a Nation* would influence, without any serious challenges, the representation of Black people in American film for the next six decades. As such, it became the most powerful disseminator of the "Old South" myth, providing the historical pedagogy for the millions of immigrants who now resided in the country.

The film also aroused opposition. Its exhibition sparked riots in many North American cities and towns, and in several instances its most provocative racial scenes were edited out of the film. *The Birth of a Nation* has also been credited with prompting the previously unknown NAACP – as the organization most frequently associated with the attempt to ban or censor it – on to the national stage. (It is also credited with reviving the Ku Klux Klan.) The film would be critiqued for its distortions of Reconstruction and its venomous portrayals of Blacks. And W. E. B. Du Bois, still twenty years from publishing his definitive account of Reconstruction,[15] would state in his editorial for the May 1915 issue of the *Crisis*:

> It is sufficient to add that the main incident in the "Clansman" turns on a thinly veiled charge that Thaddeus Stephens, the great abolition statesman, was induced to give the Negroes the right to vote and secretly rejoice in Lincoln's assassination because of his infatuation for a mulatto mistress. Small wonder that a man who can thus brutally falsify history has never been able to do a single piece of literary work that has brought the slightest attention, except when he seeks to capitalize burning race antagonisms.[16]

While Dixon and Griffith had taken the most minimal of precautions to avoid libel by renaming the Stevens-like character "Stoneman," they had felt nothing of the sort was necessary in the case of "Lydia."

The actual Thaddeus Stevens, one of the leaders of the Radical Republican faction in Congress, had a mulatta housekeeper, Lydia Hamilton Smith, and they were probably lovers. They had lived together for twenty years and their contemporaries considered Mrs. Smith the wife of the Congressman in all but name. But nothing in Stevens's historical record confirms the notion that Mrs. Smith had cajoled him into becoming an abolitionist or wreaking havoc on the prostrate Southern planter aristocracy. Stevens was a proud, severe, willful, and ambitious lawyer/politician who had championed causes as disparate as anti-Masonry, fugitive slaves, free schools, and railway expansion. His private life was punctuated with sexual scandals (many linking him with Black women), but a recent biographer has insisted that much of this was "baseless" rumor, the consequence of Stevens's propensity to make powerful enemies and his defense of fugitive slaves. In any case, he became the favorite villain of "Old South" propagandists who credited him as the architect of congressional policies that were meant to destroy slavery, disenfranchise the ex-Confederates, and redistribute the land holdings of the Southern planter aristocracy. As Hans Trefousse observes, Stevens intended to "Strip a proud nobility of their bloated estates, reduce them to a level with plain republicans; send them forth to labor, and teach their children to enter the workshop or handle the plough."[17] But his opposition to slavery had been exhibited as early as 1837, some ten years before his relationship with Mrs. Smith began.[18]

In the grasp of Dixon and Griffith, the fading memory of the historical Stevens was concealed behind the character assassination of Stoneman. This pathetic creature with his club-foot and ill-fitting wig is constantly being outwitted by the mulatto Lynch (whose ambitions are to rule the Reconstruction South with Stoneman's daughter as his wife and "queen") and the psychotic mulatta Lydia. As a predecessor of the twentieth-century white liberal, Stevens/Stoneman exhibits the disastrous consequences that flow inevitably from a coalition with the congenitally unstable mulatto/a. A chorus of mulatto films intended for white audiences followed Birth, and each exposed the catastrophic results of permitting the mulatto to intrude into a white American social order. The most benign of them, William Fox's The Nigger (1915), justified lynching while reassigning the mulatto away from mixed company. In Selig Polyscope's At Piney Ridge (1916), the lust-crazed mulatto is killed by a distraught white father. In Lasky Feature's Pudd'nhead Wilson, also 1916, a sociopathic, murderous quadroon is imprisoned. In Bar Sinister (1917), a mulatta kidnaps a white child. In Broadway Star Features' The Renaissance at Charleroi (1917), an octoroon woman is exposed and ridiculed. In Balboa Amusement Producing Company's Sold at Auction (1917), a white girl mistaken for a quadroon is sold into prostitution. In World Film's Broken Ties (1918), a homicidal mulatta kills her white foster father and eventually commits suicide. In Thomas H. Ince's Free and Equal (1918), an educated mulatto (Tuskegee Institute) rapes and kills before being imprisoned.[19]

Guerrero informs us that, between 1919 and 1941, more than 75 feature films were produced which took as their setting the "Old South" or the Civil War.[20] None of them involved plots in which a mulatta character was present. Griffith had employed white actors to portray Blacks and mulattos, persuading himself that Black actors and actresses were incapable of dramatic performances. In contrast, during the silent and early sound eras, Black independent films almost invariably cast Blacks in white and Black roles and utilized light-complexioned actresses in prominent and character parts. Indeed, many of these films, for example, *Within Our Gates* (1919) and *Scar of Shame* (1931), traded on the dramatic conflicts signified by their mulatta actresses. Hollywood, however, found little use for light-skinned actors and actresses. With the exceptions of *Imitation of Life* (1934) and *Emperor Jones* (1933), the mulatta was almost entirely erased from filmic North America. Light-complexioned actresses like Nina Mae McKinney, Fredi Washington, and Dorothy Dandridge were relegated to jungle movies where their mixed-race ancestry was treated with narrative indifference. This was preferable to their appearance in plantation genre films where audiences might be tempted to draw inferences about miscegenation. But suddenly, in 1943, in the midst of the Second World War and a national campaign to enlist Blacks in the war effort, the mulatta would reappear. However, she was deliberately muted by the genre: Lena Horne's performances in *Stormy Weather* and *Cabin in the Sky* were quarantined by the all-Black musical. In these films, the imagined America was entirely Black, and if the mulatta introduced a narrative or aesthetic disturbance, it was confined to Black America. And even here, the threat that a too sexualized Lena Horne might constitute for a white audience was carefully controlled. An overtly erotic scene in *Stormy Weather* with Horne in a bathtub filled with bubbles was cut before the film was released. Only in the post-Second World War era, when a small window of opportunity was provided to leftist filmmakers, were mulattos rediscovered. But even then, characteristically Hollywoodian strategies were employed. In *Pinky* (1949) and *Lost Boundaries* (1949), the mulattos were tragic and the principal roles went to white performers (Jeanne Crain in Pinky; Mel Ferrer and Beatrice Pearson in *Lost Boundaries*).[21]

THE CINEMA OF MEXICO

So much for the politico-cultural boundaries of North American cinema within which black/mulatto stereotypes were enacted. But there was another cinema, as concerned – but for different historical reasons – with images of Blackness and the mulatta; a cinema that responded to and reacted against Hollywood dominance just as, politically, the nation in which it was embedded had to confront and challenge U.S. imperial dominance. It was the cinema of Mexico, a nation in which multifaceted notions of "race" were intertwined with every aspect of daily living/politics and culture. For that reason, it is instructive to set against the Hollywood notion – and erasure – of the mulatta the conceptions expressed in Mexican films of the 1940s, a crucial period in Mexican politics and Mexican cinema.

We will concentrate here on two films in particular, Joselito Rodriguez's *Los Angelitos Negros* (1948) and Matilde Landeta's *La Negra Angustias* (1949). In both, Blackness is embroidered around the form of the mulatta, a woman whose body reveals her mixed-race ancestry, either through the birth of a dark-skinned child (in the earlier film) or through her own appearance. In *Los Angelitos Negros*, based on a play by the Cuban writer Félix B. Caignet, the mulatta character's physical appearance is entirely unremarkable, providing no apparent signs of her mixed ancestry. Nevertheless, she is completely enveloped by a radicalized context of hatred and concealed identities. *Los Angelitos Negros* recapitulates the treatment of the mulatta in American films previous to it (i.e., *Imitation of Life*, 1934) and contemporary to it (i.e., *Pinky*, *Lost Boundaries*, both 1949).

In *La Negra Angustias*, based on a novel by Francisco Rojas González, Angustias (María Elena Marqués) is brown skinned and her father is Black (both performers are darkened by make-up for their roles), yet race is a distant, almost subterranean, incidental to a film that principally explores gender in revolutionary Mexico. Indeed, Matilde Landeta significantly altered the racial materials that González had embedded in his novel. *La Negra Angustias* treks through a terrain entirely oppositional to Hollywood's explorations of the mulatta in moments of historical national conflict such as Griffith's *Birth* and Raoul Walsh's *Band of Angels* (1957). Culturally, in North American eyes, the mulatta was a figure of opprobrium, who subverted "Old South" mythical history and whose physical appearance significantly problematized the dominant racial hierarchy. She was an unnatural being, too erotic, too sexualized, too much an advertisement for a sexual congress that was supposed never to happen. In Landeta's hands, all that is swept aside – but so, too, is the awareness of a specifically Black contribution to Mexican history.

La Negra Angustias was produced during the "golden era" of the Mexican film industry. Recovering from a post-Second World War lull, Mexican film production accelerated after 1948. Surpassing Argentina, Mexico was once again the most active film-producing country in Latin America. And, despite the increase of Hollywood imports in the post-war period, Mexican filmmakers preserved a niche which provided them sanctuary. According to Emilio García Riera, North American and European films drew audiences primarily from the upper and middle classes while Mexican films secured Latin American audiences that were made up of illiterates, semi-illiterates, and minors (*"un público no pocas veces compuesto por analfabetos o semianalfabetos, de menores exigencias"*).[22]

Before the revolution (1910–1920), motion pictures in Mexico were mainly imported, most from Italy and France. Given the potential market (in 1910 Mexico City had 15 million residents), it is somewhat surprising that only a few exhibitors made the transformation to filmmakers. However, European movie companies were fiercely competitive in protecting their exports and Mexican film critics were not particularly encouraging. Far more erudite and sophisticated than their filmmaking compatriots, the critics much preferred cosmopolitan European subjects and settings to the domestic actualities, travelogues, and "propagandistic" features filmed in Mexico.[23]

The political volatility, cultural vitality, and social chaos of the revolution inspired an excitement among Mexican filmmakers. There was, of course, the fascinating spectacle of a succession of provisional governments: the embattled dictator, *don* Porfirio Díaz, resigned in 1911; his successor, Francisco Madero, was overthrown by one of his generals, Victoriano Huerta, in 1913; the next year Huerta was displaced by Venustiano Carranza (the nominal leader of a revolutionary coalition that included Francisco "Pancho" Villa and Emiliano Zapata); and, in 1920, General Alvaro Obregón staged a successful coup against Carranza. In addition, there was the drama of the two North American interventions ordered by the administration of Woodrow Wilson.

In 1914, U.S. marines seized Vera Cruz, occupying it for months, and then, in 1916, General John J. Pershing was ordered to head a punitive expedition into Mexico to hunt for Villa.[24] The Huerta coup and the subsequent assassination of Madero had pushed the revolution to the left, and filmmakers (largely residents of Mexico City) rushed to the countryside to document the hunger for land reform and the battles waged by peasants, farm laborers, small farmers, and the semirural proletariat. Carl Mora observes: "The years between 1915 and 1923 have been termed the 'Golden Age' of the Mexican silent cinema, although production was extremely modest, especially if compared with the output of the major filmmaking countries, but [it was] still impressive according to Latin American standards."[25] From 1923 until the end of the silent film (*cine mudo*) era, however, Mexico's theaters continued to be dominated by imports, but now mostly from the U.S. Moreover, from 1929 to 1934, when "talkies" acquired their dominance over the Mexican market, many talented Mexicans (on and behind the screen) migrated to the North. Not a few of them provided the cultural and technical resources with which Hollywood launched its "Hispanic" film strategy (113 films between 1930 and 1938). This was an attempt to dominate the Latin American market but, as Riera maintains (and Mora confirms), the maneuver was not particularly successful.[26] In the meantime, in the U.S., the cinematic response to the revolution was not benign: "The great majority of representations of Mexicans or Mexico ... [were] distinctly negative."[27]

In 1934, Lázaro Cárdenas was elected president of Mexico and launched the most radical social program in the country's history. Among his initiatives (which included the nationalization of oil fields and refineries claimed by American and European companies) was the organization of a state-financed film enterprise under the minister of education, Narciso Bassols. In 1934, four of the 23 films produced in Mexico were made under this arrangement, among them the radically political narratives of *Redes* (*Nets*) and *Janitzio*.[28] Mora maintains that:

> *Redes* and Janitzio can be considered as superior films that served to initiate an "Eisenstinian" current of "Indianist" films that were to be a distinguishing feature of the Mexican cinema for the next twenty years. Romanticized, and often melodramatic, such films, along with those dealing with the theme of the Revolution as in [Fernando] De Fuentes's [critical] El Compadre Mendoza [Godfather Mendoza], were to constitute a "national" style of cinema and stand in counterpoint to the horde of melodramas based mostly on French and Spanish theater pieces that Mexican filmmakers were to churn out in the following decades.[29]

In 1935, De Fuentes, paradoxically with state support, continued his critique of the revolution with *Vámonos con Pancho Villa* (*Let's Go with Pancho Villa*), but private Mexican commercial interests produced the bulk of Mexican films. Their profit-driven investments and alarm at Cárdenas's policies gave shape to the aforementioned family melodramas and the appearance of a new genre, comedia ranchera. Openly hostile to the socialist policies of Cárdenas, De Fuentes adapted the North American musical western for *Allá en el Rancho Grande (Out at Big Ranch)* in 1936 to praise the feudal patriarchalism of the grand landowner, the *charro*, who "came to represent the traditional and Catholic values in defiance of the leftist, modernizing tendencies emanating from the cities."[30]

During the Second World War, the North American film industry's share of the Latin American market was profoundly compromised by its close collaboration and identification with the military objectives of the Roosevelt administration. Argentina, Mexico's major competitor in that market, was pro-Axis and consequently lost access to raw film stock manufactured in the U.S. The subsequent decline in Argentine film production meant that it forfeited its marginal superiority over its Mexican rival. In order to ensure future access to the Mexican markets, Hollywood and its governmental regulators allocated stock and equipment to Mexican filmmakers.[31] Just as critical was the action of the new government of conservative president Manuel Ávila Camacho (1940–1946) which, in a barely concealed maneuver, subsidized the formation of the Banco Cinematográfico in 1942. The function of the bank (and its public partners, Banco Nacional de México and Nacional Financiera) was to put "private" film-making on a solid financial footing. The result was that Mexican films were unchallenged in the competition for the domestic and Latin American markets. Between 1939 (35 films released) and 1945 (82 films released), production more than doubled. In 1940 and 1941, with *Ahí Está el Detalle* (*There Is the Detail*) and *Ni Sangre Ni Arena* (*Neither Blood Nor Sand*), "Cantinflas" (Mario Moreno) became Mexico's most popular home-based international star. And while the bulk of movies remained comfortably within the political boundaries of post-Cárdenas conservatism (comedies, domestic melodramas, *comedia ranchera* musicals), some future classics were produced. During the war and the immediate post-war years, a few Mexican filmmakers began to return to the social protest "Indian" films. In 1943, for example, the classics *María Candelaria* (an adaptation of *Janitzio*) and *Flor Silvestre* (*Wild Flower*) were released, marking the first appearances of Dolores del Rio in Mexican films. The subject was repeated in 1947 with *Rio Escondido* (*Hidden River*). Borrowing from Hollywood's *film noir*, filmmakers like Alejandro Galindo and Norman Foster made crime dramas, while an established star like Pedro Infante made important films like Ismael Rodriguez's 1947 *Nosotros los Pobres* (*We the Poor*), a social drama about urban poverty.

OFF THE RADAR SCREEN?

Mexico has a substantial Black population. Yet, among Mexico's educated classes there is generally an appalling ignorance of the role and presence of Blacks in Mexican history. So, it is not entirely surprising that at the initial stages of our study of *La Negra Angustias*, Carl Mora, who has written one of the most detailed reconstructions of Mexican cinema, informed us that "the Afro-Mexican population is quite small and historically out of the national radar screen."[32] Ironically, in an interview (1995) before her death in 1999, Matilde Landeta made a similar observation to justify her casting of María Elena Marqués, a non-Black, in the title role. "Mexico doesn't have a Black population, and its absence continues in modern day."[33] Unlike elsewhere in Latin America, she asserted, in Mexico the conquering Spanish had encountered a high civilization and had enslaved these people, making the importation of Africans unnecessary (except on the coasts of Guerrero and Vera Cruz). Indeed, Landeta had seen her first "Negro" when she was sent to the U.S. at the age of twelve. That he was very Black had astonished her. One would hardly expect these cultural conceits from the director and co-writer of a film whose protagonist was an Afro-Mexican revolutionary in Zapata's army.[34]

Mexico's Black population is largely attributable to the same imperialist and commercial forces that brought Africans to the West Indies and the Americas from the sixteenth century onward. By the eighteenth century, nearly 150,000 Africans and mulattos could be found in the colony of Nueva España (present-day Mexico); and, by 1810, the Spanish census numbered 635,461 people as Africans or descendants of Africans.[35] That was a portentous year in Mexican history since it marked the beginnings of the first Mexican revolution, the war for independence. For the next eleven years, the Spanish (the rebels called them *Gachupines*) and their colonial supporters confronted rebel armies. The most prominent of the rebel leaders were Miguel Hidalgo y Costilla, José Maria Morelosy Pavón, Vicente Guerrero, and Andrés Quintana Roo. All four have states named after them, and two of them, Morelos and Guerrero, were mixed-race descendants of African slaves. Hidalgo, Morelos, and Guerrero opposed slavery and, when Guerrero became the second president of Mexico in 1829, he abolished it. This was a tribute to what was an important social base of the rebel forces. From the very onset of the rebellion, predominantly Black armies had been raised from those areas where Afro-Mexicans dominated the colonial population, and it was from the *tierra caliente*, the hot lowlands, that Guerrero waged the final campaigns that led to the Spanish surrender in 1821.[36]

Notwithstanding the amnesia or deliberate deceit of later Mexican scholars, the combatants in the independence movement were quite clear about the racial character of colonialism. For instance, Morelos, before his death in 1815, declared to the people of Oaxaca: "We call ourselves Americans, because we are all brothers ... while they (the Spanish) would have us look at one another as castes and destroy ourselves, whites against Blacks, and them against the Indians."[37] Ted Vincent informs us that one unintended consequence of independence was

> ... law #313 [which] prohibited the use of race in any government document or in church records of baptism, marriage, and death. The subsequent lack of racial counts by census takers in Mexico is one reason little is known of Black Mexico.[38]

This may be so, but it hardly explains the inability to register the persistence of substantial Afro-Mexican populations concentrated along the Caribbean coast of Vera Cruz and the Pacific coastal states of Guerrero, Michoacan, Colima, Jalisco, Nayarit, and Sinaloa (Mazatlan was once known as Mazatlan de los Mulatos).

THE MEXICAN MULATTA IN FILM

La Negra Angustias appeared in the midst of a series of films dealing with Mexican mulattas. The first was *La Mulata de Córdoba* (1945), then came *Los Angelitos Negros* (1948) and afterward *Negro Es Mi Color* (1951). Córdoba is in the state of Vera Cruz and Emilio García Riera and Fernando Macotela show how the plot of *La Mulata de Córdoba* makes use of that background:

> For this melodrama, the poet Xavier Villaurrutia adopted an old legend from colonial times to the tropical and folkloric ambiance of Veracruz. A blonde woman (played by Lina Montes) masquerades as a mulatta to be little respected and very desired by a series of lascivious young men, in the nineteenth century.[39]

Elsewhere, Riera panned the film, ridiculing the use of black make-up and finding the plot more applicable to the southern U.S. than to Mexico.[40] Among the cast was an authentic Veracruzana, Toña La Negra. Toña was a light-skinned Afro-Mexican from the Vera Cruz coast and had migrated to Mexico City to pursue a singing career. She became one of the most celebrated musicians of her time and is remembered as the greatest interpreter of the *Bolero*.[41] The equally celebrated and even more influential Afro-Cuban, Rita Montaner, played roles in both *Los Angelitos Negros* and *Negro Es Mi Color.*

Beginning her film career in 1934, Montaner was to make at least 17 films in Mexico and Cuba. And, like Toña, she had a major impact on popular culture, particularly in Cuba where she pursued the stage, recordings, and film.[42]

Los Angelitos Negros starred Pedro Infante and Emilia Guiú in the principal roles. The plot concerns a couple whose child has a dark skin. The mother, Ana Luisa (Guiú), who is extremely prejudiced, blames her husband (Infante) for the child's obvious mixed-race appearance. Earlier, for reasons of racial disgust, she had forbidden her husband to continue to associate with his Afro-Cuban musician friends. But in fact, it is Ana Luisa who has a Black mother – her nanny, Mama Mercè (Montaner) is actually her real mother. While Ana Luisa has inherited her white father's features, her baby resembles the grandmother. Ana Luisa finally learns the truth but it is too late for Mama Mercè who has died from a blow – from Ana Luisa. Riera found the film unsatisfactory. He dubbed the black make-up and the overdramatized acting of Infante and Guiú as sufficient to spoil the treatment of a serious subject.[43] Mauricio Peña, a student of Infante's films, however, considers *Los Angelitos Negros* to be the first Mexican film to treat racism against Afro-Mexicans. Peña commented, though, that the principal motive for the film's production was Infante's popularity.[44] The film was distributed in the U.S., premiering in Los Angeles in October 1950 at the Maya and Million Dollar theaters, which specialized in Latin American films.[45]

In *Negro Es Mi Color*, Montaner again plays the black-face mother of a mulatta. In this instance, the daughter Rita (played by Marga Lopez, an actress from Argentina) is light-skinned enough to pass for white, renouncing her mother and her African history. But, in the end, confronted by the constant racial prejudice directed against other Blacks, she embraces her ancestry. Apparently impressed with Hollywood's *Pinky*, director Tito Davison eschewed the excesses of earlier mulatto films from Mexico and took on racism directly by opening the film with a narration which claimed the film was not a work of fiction. Nevertheless, the setting of the film was not Mexico but an unnamed country – thus preventing its message from coming too close to home. (We can only speculate as to whether this was a factor in Riera's praise of the film.[46]) None of these films treated mulattas in a fashion that differentiated them from the standard tragic mulatta representations of Hollywood. That was left to *La Negra Angustias.*

LA NEGRA ANGUSTIAS

Apart from its other characteristics, *La Negra Angustias* distinguished itself from other Mexican films treating Blacks by its choice of setting, the Mexican revolution (1910–1917) and its choice of protagonist, a mulatta. These two points of departure not only separated it from the other few Mexican mulatta melodramas but also marked *La Negra Angustias* as a major departure from the dominant construction of the revolution found in mainstream historical texts and movies. *La Negra Angustias* referenced both a mulatta and the *soldaderas*, the women who accompanied the armies of Pancho Villa, Emiliano Zapata, and Venustiano Carranza.

Landeta based *La Negra Angustias* on the prize-winning 1943 novel of the same title by Francisco Rojas González. An anthropologist, novelist, and professor of literature, Rojas was a difficult collaborator. Their partnership had begun with the filming of *Lola Casanova* (1949), another novel by Rojas. That project resulted from the organization of TACMA studio by Landeta, Rojas, and Matilde's brother, Eduardo Landeta (a producer). They had joined forces for their mutual convenience: Rojas could realize the transformation of his work into movies, Matilde could finally direct films despite the industry's objections to female directors. Rojas and Matilde Landeta, however, had major disagreements on their second project since his vision of the protagonist, Angustias, in the original novel had offended Landeta's sense of female agency.[47] In the novel, Angustias is raped as a child after her mother has died and her father, Anton Farrera, has been imprisoned. Later, she and her father travel from Morelos to join Zapata's army in Guerrero. When her father dies, Angustias inherits the leadership of his rebel band. Elizabeth Salas admirably summarizes the remaining plot:

> As "La Coronela" she disciplines her troops whenever they assault women or villagers. She castrates one man as an example. A powerful leader, La Coronela paradoxically falls in love with an effeminate and timid teacher. At the start of the relationship, the teacher thinks that women should not meddle in men's affairs by leading them into battle. La Coronela counters with the observation that "it is only because things have been left up to men that all things are unequal." But La Coronela's true (feminine) nature emerges. She seduces the teacher, marries him, and has a child. Her husband then neglects her and has an affair with another woman.[48]

But, despite her awareness that Angustias had actually existed, Landeta recognized the essential conservatism in Rojas's account and changed many elements in the narrative.[49]

In Landeta's hands, Angustias' life paralleled that of so many *soldaderas* caught up in the maelstrom of the 1910 revolution. Like so many women of the poorer classes, Angustias had been raped and abducted. But here a rupture from convention occurred. Angustias killed her rapist and later, as a *coronela*, she ordered the castration of a bandit leader who had raped other women and briefly held her captive. Her Black father's deeds had been legendary, sufficient for a *corrido* ("Antón Farrera el mulato") to be sung in his praise, but Angustias went on to organize her own rebel group. In the film, she constantly displays the agency actual women acquired by taking up arms during the revolution. Salas recounts:

> Mexican folklore is replete with stories of women like Carmen Serdán who fought alongside their male relatives, or like Elisa Griensen, who fought without their help. … Abandoned *soldaderas* in some instances did not choose to re-attach themselves to other men, but instead realigned themselves with powerful female leaders and formed their own rebel groups. Such was the case of Margarita Neri in Guerrero, Rosa Bobadilla, Viuda de Casas in Morelos; and Juana Ramona, Viuda de Flores, "the Tigress," in Sinaloa. These women distinguished themselves as soldiers and also commanded brigades of women or men.[50]

Angustias commanded revolutionaries and encouraged other women to obtain self-respect. And in the film's ending – unlike Rojas's heroine who discovers her "female" identity in marriage, motherhood, and even spousal betrayal – Landeta's Angustias quits her philandering husband for the truer and more profound devotion of the revolution. As Riera put it, "*vuelve a ganar batallas al frente de sus hombres.*"[51]

In neither the Rojas or Landeta narratives was Blackness of primary significance in the experience of the "anguished" Black woman. Angustias' father's Africanity and her own mixed-race identity were submerged in Mexicanity, the struggles of the urban poor and rural landless for justice, and the conflict around paternalism. True to the dominant conservative creeds of the early 1940s, Rojas seems to have believed that the revolution had ended in social chaos, disturbing the rightful social order of male familial dominion. Landeta's interpretation was otherwise.[52] She championed Angustias' female agency and, nearly fifty years later recalled, at least in retrospect, that the central theme of the film was Angustias' commitment to literacy and liberation.[53] Still, it is much more likely that, in the context of Landeta's own frustrated ambitions in the Mexican film industry of the 1940s, her actual motivation was feminist.

Rojas's novel presented Landeta with a spectacular female character. The race of the character, however, meant so little to Landeta that almost fifty years later she remained misinformed about, almost indifferent to, the history of Blacks in Mexico. For Landeta there was nothing particularly troubling or essentialist in Angustias' "mulattaness," no unnaturally animalistic sexuality, no unique erotic power over men, no unbridled hunger for power, no tragedy ready to pounce on a creature reeking of social ambiguity – as there would have been for any North American filmmaker. In the post-revolutionary Mexican culture of the 1920s, 1930s, and 1940s, the "race" issue was primarily a conflict relating to light-skinned and dark-skinned mestizos (mixtures of Indians and Europeans).[54] This controversy was so overpowering, so persistent in Mexican culture in that period, that it served to obliterate the presence of Africans in Mexico's past (and present). Perhaps this explains how Landeta could almost casually reinsert Afro-Mexicans into Mexico's revolutionary past. Paradoxically, this lacuna in awareness has enabled the creation of a female Black character who is allowed a full agency and range of emotion and activity that, hitherto, most Black filmic representations had been denied.

NOTES

1. Richard Dyer, *White* (London, Routledge, 1997), p. 36.
2. Teresa Zackodnik, "Fixing the color line: the mulatto, southern courts, and racial identity," *American Quarterly* (Vol. 53, No. 3, 2001), p. 427.
3. Winthrop Jordan commented: "After about 1680, taking the colonies as a whole, a new term of self-identification appeared – *white*." Jordan, *The White Man's Burden* (Oxford, Oxford University Press, 1974), p. 52.
4. See Joseph R. Roach, "Slave spectacles and tragic octoroons: a cultural genealogy of antebellum performance," *Theatre Survey* (Vol. 33, November 1992), pp. 167–187; and Nancy Bentley, "White slaves: the mulatto hero in antebellum fiction," *American Literature* (Vol. 65, No. 3, September 1993), pp. 501–522.
5. Bentley, "White slaves," p. 504.
6. Roach, "Slave spectacles and tragic octoroons," p. 175.
7. Edward Byron Reuter, *The Mulatto in the United States* (New York, Negro Universities Press, 1969 (original 1918)), p. 131.
8. See Kevin Brownlow, *Behind the Mask of Innocence* (Berkeley, University of California Press, 1990), p. 375.
9. Ed Guerrero, *Framing Blackness* (Philadelphia, PA, Temple University Press, 1993), p. 27. Describing his research into Hollywood films between 1915 and 1975, Guerrero wrote: "By examining the depiction of slaves and slavery over the continuum of Hollywood's plantation genre, we confront a number of issues about the creation and ideological function of these representations, narratives, and images persistent so long after the abolition of slavery itself and the collapse of the antebellum South." Ibid., p. 10.
10. Gerald R. Butters, Jr., *Black Manhood on the Silent Screen* (Lawrence, TX, University Press of Kansas, 2002), pp. 27–28.
11. By the early twentieth century, the Black middle class tended to associate in exclusive clubs and resorts, select schools and churches, cultural and athletic clubs, salons and domestic parlours. See Willard B. Gatewood, *Aristocrats of Color* (Bloomington, Indiana University Press, 1990), *passim*.
12. David Levering Lewis, *W. E. B. Du Bois: biography of a race* (New York, Henry Holt & Company, 1993), pp. 217ff.
13. "Wilson behind segregation," *The New York Age* (November 19, 1914), p. 1.
14. Gatewood, *Aristocrats of Color*, p. 179.
15. W. E. B. Du Bois, *Black Reconstruction* (New York, S. A. Russell, 1935).
16. Schickel claims the film, originally entitled *The Clansman*, was retitled in early March after "Griffith dropped a love scene between Senator Stoneman and his mulatto mistress and a scene in which a black and a white engaged in a fight..." Richard Schickel, *D. W. Griffith: an American life* (New York, Limelight, 1996), p. 282.

17. Hans L. *Trefousse, Thaddeus Stevens: nineteenth-century egalitarian* (Chapel Hill, University of North Carolina Press, 1997), p. 172.
18. Ibid., p. 51.
19. For plot summaries of the "mulatto genre," see Alan Gevinson's *Within Our Gates: ethnicity in American films, 1911–1960* (Berkeley, University of California Press, 1997), *passim*.
20. Guerrero, *Framing Blackness*, p. 19.
21. Donald Bogle, *Toms, Coons, Mulattoes, Mammies & Bucks* (New York, Continuum, 2001), pp. 147ff.
22. Emilio García Riera, *Historia Del Cine Mexicano* (Mexico City, Secretaría de Educación Pública, 2000), p. 158. Carl J. Mora agrees, see Mora, *Mexican Cinema, Reflections of a Society, 1896–1980* (Berkeley, University of California Press, 1982), pp. 74–75.
23. Ibid., chapter 1. Garcia A. Gustavo maintains that the subjects of many domestic films were government officials and wealthy families strolling down the main boulevards of Mexico City. See Garcia, "In quest of a national cinema: the silent era," in Joanne Hershfield and David R. Maciel (eds), *Mexico's Cinema* (Wilmington, DE, Scholarly Resources, 1999), pp. 5–16.
24. For the early years of the revolution, see Friedrich Katz, *The Life and Times of Pancho Villa* (Stanford, CA, Stanford University Press, 1998).
25. Mora, *Mexican Cinema*, p. 20.
26. Ibid., pp. 23ff.
27. Ibid., pp. 23–24. Pancho Villa initially received favorable treatment in Hollywood. In 1914, he contracted with the Mutual Film Company for the latter to film newsreels of his battles with Huerta's troops. Mutual used the newsreels to produce a fictive narrative entitled *The Life of General Villa* (1914). In 1916, after Villa's raids in New Mexico, his Hollywood image changed dramatically. Eagle Films Manufacturing and Producing Company produced an anti-Villa tract entitled *Villa Dead or Alive*, and Feinberg Amusement Corporation added its support for the punitive expedition, *Following the Flag in Mexico*. See Katz, *Life and Times*, pp. 324–326. William Randolph Hearst, an investor in Latin American mines and a huge land-owner in Mexico, was also fairly vexed with the Mexican revolution. Hearst's own studio produced *Patria* (1915), a fifteen-part serial whose plot "depicted a Japanese-Mexican invasion of the United States and clearly was designed to capitalize on the nervousness many Americans felt over revolution in Mexico, Japanese involvement south of the Rio Grande, and United States-Japanese tensions." Mora, *Mexican Cinema*, p. 24. For Hearst's Mexican holdings, see Katz, *Life and Times*, p. 157.
28. See Mora, *Mexican Cinema*, pp. 40ff. for plot summaries of *Redes* and *Janitzio*.
29. Ibid., pp. 41–42.
30. Ibid., p. 47.
31. During the war, Hollywood's collaboration with Mexican filmmakers was managed through the US Office of the Coordinator for Inter-American Affairs (OCIAA) which "undertook the modernization of the Mexican film studios in order to develop a more authentic source of wartime propaganda for Latin American audiences." Seth Fein, "From collaboration to containment: Hollywood and the international political economy of Mexican cinema after the Second World War," in Hershfield and Maciel, *Mexico's Cinema*, p. 129. The Mexican point man for Hollywood's penetration of Mexican cinema was Miguel Alemán, Camacho's Interior Secretary and the next president of Mexico (1946–1952).
32. Personal email exchange with Luz Maria Cabral, 16 October 2001.
33. Isabel Arrendondo, "Interview with film maker Matilde Landeta," *Mexican Studies-Estudios Mexicanos* (Vol. 18, Winter 2002), p. 192.
34. Patricia Torres de San Martin maintains that both Landeta and her predecessor, the actress and director Adela Sequeyro, were children of the Mexican upper class. See Torres, "Adela Sequeyro and Matilde Landeta: two pioneer women directors," in Hershfield and Maciel, *Mexico's Cinema*, p. 38.
35. Ted Vincent, "The Blacks who freed Mexico," *The Journal of Negro History* (Vol. LXXIX, No. 3, Summer 1994), p. 258; Cedric J. Robinson, *Black Marxism* (Chapel Hill, University of North Carolina Press, 2000), pp. 129–132; and Rafael Rebollar, "La Raíz Olvidada," videotape

(D. R. Producciones Trabuco S. C., 2001). Vincent cites Joel A. Rogers's biography of Guerrero, "The Negro who freed Mexico," *Negro World* (January 4, 1930) as the inspiration for his article.

36. See Vincent, "The Blacks who freed Mexico," *passim*. Vincent relies on primary documents and a number of Mexican historical studies: Gonzalo Aguirre Beltrán, *La Población Negra de México* [Xalapa, 1991 (original 1946)]; Lucas Alaman, *Historia de México, desde los Primeros Movimientos que Prepararon su Independencia en el Año de 1808 Hasta La Epoca 2 Presente*, 5 Vols (Mexico, 1849–1852); Ubaldo Vargas Martínez, Morelos: *siervo de la nacion* (Mexico, 1977); Patrick J. Carroll, *Blacks in Colonial Veracruz: race, ethnicity, and regional development* (Austin, University of Texas Press, 1991); Patricia Seed, "Social dimensions of race: Mexico City, 1753," *Hispanic American Historical Review* (Vol. 62, No. 4, November 1982); and Patricia Seed, *To Love, Honor, and Obey in Colonial Mexico: conflicts over marriage choice 1574–1821* (Stanford, CA, University of Stanford Press, 1988).

37. Vincent, "The Blacks who freed Mexico," p. 260.

38. Ibid., p. 272.

39. Emilio García Riera and Fernando Macotela, *La Guía del Cine Mexicano de la Pantalla Grande a la televisión, 1919–1984* (Mexico, Editorial Patria, 1984), p. 210.

40. Emilio García Riera, *Historia Documental del Cine Mexicano*, Vol. IV, 1949–1951, 1972, p. 67.

41. Victor Hurtado Oviedo, "Eterna cancionera: Toña La Negra esla incesante madre lunar de los boleros," April 1998, http://www.andes.missouri.edu/andes/comen-tario/vho-lanegra.html.

42. Dani Francisco Tejera, "Rita, una sonrisa centenaria," *Cine* (Vol. VII, No. 39, September/October, 2000), http://www2.glauco.it/vitral/vitral39/cine.htm.

43. Riera, *Historia Documental del Cine Mexicano*, Vol. III, 1946–1948, 1971, n.a.

44. Mauricio Peña, "Un Tipo de Cuidado," *SOMOS* (January 2001), p. 33.

45. "Three films from Mexico slated here," *Los Angeles Times* (October 1, 1950). The two other films were *Río Escondido and El General y la Señorita*.

46. Ibid.

47. See Arrendondo, "Interview." It is not entirely clear whether Reira and Macotela approved of Landeta's vision since, following a disparaging comment on Angustias' black-face make-up, they concluded: "*pero lo que si resulto convincente fue la vehemencia feminista de la directora*" (but what is clearly evident was the feminist passion of the director). Riera and Macotela, *La Guía del Cine*, p. 215.

48. Elizabeth Salas, *Soldaderas in the Mexican Military* (Austin, University of Texas Press, 1990), p. 87.

49. Joseph Sommers, "Francisco Rojas González: exponente literario del nacionalismo mexicano," *Cuadernos de la Facultad de Filosofía, Letras y Ciencias* (Vol. 36, 1966), p. 74.

50. Ibid., pp. 41–42.

51. Riera, *Historia Documental*, p. 67. In her interview, Landeta claimed that Rojas had explained to her that, as an anthropologist, he understood that historically, when women fell in love and married, they left their previous lives to start more selfless lives of obedience to their husbands. Landeta was unconvinced – she recounted that she and her brother had taken their mother's name as a tribute to her caring for them after their father abandoned the family.

52. Landeta not too subtly critiqued Rojas by having the women of Angustias' village harass her, calling her "marimacha" (lesbian) for refusing to accept a loveless marriage. Hershfield insists that the taunt is "marimacho" and translates the term as "tomboy" in her essay "Race and ethnicity in the classical cinema," Hershfield and Maciel, *Mexico's Cinema*, p. 93.

53. Landeta referenced the film to the literacy campaign in the late 1940s. President Alemán had initiated a national education program which was dramatized in *Rio Escondido* (1947), Mexico's most internationally celebrated film of the period. Fein contrasted Alemán's politics with Cárdenas's: "If Cardenismo's populist mass-media project sought to mobilize (and incorporate) peasant and worker activism, Alemanismo's aimed to pacify proletarian and agrarian demands while expanding the state's corporatist controls." Fein, "From collaboration to containment," p. 126.

54. Ibid., 82ff. For more on this issue see the article cited by Hershfield, Alan Knight, "Racism, revolution, and indigenismo: Mexico, 1920–1940," in Richard Graham (ed.), *The Idea of Race in Latin America, 1870–1940* (Austin, University of Texas Press, 1990), pp. 72–73.

CHAPTER 19

Ventriloquizing Blackness:
Eugene O'Neill and Irish-American
Racial Performance

I created the role of the Emperor. That role belongs to me.
That Irishman, he just wrote the play.
— *Charles Gilpin*[1]

Though beyond some privileged circles Eugene O'Neill is largely a forgotten figure, he should be remembered by us all as a singular contributor to the development of American theater in the twentieth century. This assessment rests on several accomplishments: O'Neill's creation of an extensive corpus of celebrated works which included *Beyond the Horizon* (1920), "*Anna Christie*" (1921), *The Hairy Ape* (1922), *The Ancient Mariner* (1924), *Desire Under the Elms* (1924), *The Great God Brown* (1926), *Strange Interlude* (1928), *The Iceman Cometh* (1939), and *Long Day's Journey into Night* (1940). He was also one of the founders of the Experimental Theater which in the 1920s helped to transform techniques of sound and lighting, dramatic inquiries, and interior characterizations employed on the American stage. Eric Bentley, one of his severest critics, acknowledged: "At one time he performed a historic function, that of helping the American theater grow up." And N. Bryllion Fagin detailed O'Neill's oft-times contradictory endeavors: "He was a naturalist, an expressionist, a classicist, a symbolist, and even a surrealist. He used masks and choruses, pageantry and a bare stage, verse and prose, soliloquies and asides, drabness and vivid colors."[2] Because of the excitement and innovation that O'Neill brought to the theater he was awarded three Pulitzer Prizes. And in 1936 the Nobel Prize for literature was bestowed on him.[3]

More particular to our concerns is O'Neill's impact on Black participation and representation in the American theater. It was O'Neill's casting of the veteran thespian Charles Gilpin as Brutus Jones in *The Emperor Jones* in 1920 which marked the first appearance of a Black actor in a starring role on

Broadway.[4] Between 1914 and 1924, O'Neill had worked on five plays which contained or were centered on Black representations. They, too, have been largely forgotten notwithstanding that they contained Black characters unfortunately still familiar to present day audiences of film, theater, and television. The tragic mullato in *Thirst* (1914); the West Indian prostitutes of *Moon of the Caribbees* (1916); the young Black killer of *The Dreamy Kid* (1918); the corrupt Black politician of *Emperor Jones*, and the anguished Black man ensnared in a marriage to a psychotic white woman in *All God's Chillum Got Wings* (1924) are now thread-bare clichés. What did distinguish these characters is not so much their novelty in O'Neill's work but that he inserted them into American dramatic theater in a transformative moment in the country's racial regime. Lynching, segregation, and peonage were constants on the domestic front while imperialism and colonialism profoundly altered the nation's cultural infrastructure. There were, of course, precedents for this correspondence between the cultures, economies, and politics of earlier racial regimes. Indeed, O'Neill's interventions were consistent with earlier Irish and Irish-American performances of Blackness and slavery like black-face minstrelsy of the antebellum and Civil War eras.

WHITENESS AND THE IRISH

In 1972, Peter J. Gillett published a treatment of O'Neill entitled "O'Neill and the Racial Myths." Gillett began his essay:

> Until about 1940, various crushing handicaps prevented black authors from presenting the black experience cogently to a suitable public, and so the task of creating developed and truly representative black characters in works of sufficient literary merit to compel an audience fell chiefly upon white writers. Among the distinguished whites who accepted the challenge were Melville, Mark Twain, Conrad, Faulkner, and Eugene O'Neill. The challenge was a severe one for them partly because their own experience was perforce very remote from the black experience – color being a far greater barrier than, say, sex or social class …[5]

The passage is remarkable for its several suppressions of the American social and cultural past. Gillett, we suppose, is referencing Richard Wright and *Native Son* (1940), but his erasure of "cogent" Black chroniclers like Charles Chesnutt, James Weldon Johnson, Jean Toomer, Claude McKay, Zora Neale Hurston, and Langston Hughes, and academics like W. E. B. Du Bois, Charles Johnson, Rudolph Fisher, and E. Franklin Frazier is rather astounding. And if there were time and space, we might also raise some objections to the "developed and truly representative" Black characters invented by Melville, Twain, Conrad, and

Faulkner, but our more immediate concern is with Gillett's constructions of O'Neill. Our inquiry will concentrate on two conceits. Did "whiteness" distance O'Neill from the Black experience? And with special attention to Brutus Jones, were O'Neill's Black characters authentic transports of that Black experience or fabulous, imaginary conduits of racial conceits?

Whiteness, of course, has a history. At present the best evidence supports the surmise that among English-speakers whiteness began to circulate as a cultural hegemon during the second half of the seventeenth century. As Roxann Wheeler, among others, has determined, whiteness was imported from the New World colonies to the English metropole. Wheeler observes somewhat succinctly: "Similar to the emergence of *black, white* first appears as a noun in the 1670s ... in colonial contexts."[6] Whiteness was thus a concomitant with the African slave trade and the growing reliance on African and creole slave labor. That was a certainty proven by the perusal of colonial legislation and governing regulations in colonial Maryland and Virginia. Beginning in the 1660s, one can trace the steady accrual of white privilege and Black degradation in legal acts which, for instances, sought to preserve slave status for children with slave mothers and English fathers or with English mothers and slave fathers; to prohibit or mete punishments for marriage between slaves and freeborn Englishmen and women; and to alienate Africans, free or enslaved, from civil status.[7]

As a synonym for Englishness, however, whiteness excluded the Irish. The Irish were a subject people. Over the centuries, English colonial rule in Ireland had compelled a host of gestures of segregation – including the prohibition of marriages between Englishmen and Irish women in the fourteenth century – but from the late sixteenth century, Irish resistance fueled draconian measures. Edmund Spenser, the poet (*The Faerie Queene*) who was also an English landlord in Ireland, proposed a policy of genocide toward the Irish. In his 1596 *A view of the present state of Ireland*, Spenser attributed Irish resistance to English rule to their "stubborn and untamed" nature, a consequence of what he imagined was their Scythian, Gaul, Spanish, and Moorish ancestry.[8] Spenser thus provided a justification for what was already a rather common use of martial law and summary justice by English colonial authority in Ireland during the Nine Years War (1594–1603) and earlier.[9] The progression of the race-ing of the Irish achieved its ascendancy in the 1640s. The Irish Rebellion of 1641 provoked first the ministers of the Crown and later Cromwell and his soldiery into mass slaughter of Irish insurgents and civilians. And this brutal suppression acquired its own "poet," John Temple. In Temple's *The Irish Rebellion* (1646), a work which would be repeatedly reprinted in the seventeenth, eighteenth, and nineteenth centuries, the racial distinction of the Irish was documented by their savagery:

In Temple's view, the Irish violate the natural boundaries of human behavior: they do not respect those debilitated by age, gender, or physical impairment. In *The*

Irish rebellion, toddlers are constantly having their brains bashed out by the rebels and special notice is given by Temple to the suffering of aged Protestants. Temple comments that the most horrible torture meted out by the Irish was reserved for women, 'whose sex they neither pitied nor spared'.[10]

In every detail Temple's description of Irish behavior was precisely a mirror reversal of English colonial brutality. Lord Deputy Thomas Wentworth had exposed this fact when he was required at trial to defend his employment of martial law and collective punishment in Ireland in 1639, and Lord Cork and Lord Wilmot had testified to its truth in support of Wentworth. And in 1642 with respect to the last of Temple's charges, it was the Lord Justices who had rendered their opinion that Irish "women should be specifically targeted, 'being manifestly very deep in the guilt of this rebellion, and as we are informed, very forward to stir up their husbands, friends and kindred.'"[11] Clearly, English civil authorities and their military commanders – both Stuart and subsequently Parliamentary – prosecuted a racialized policy toward the Irish.

Nevertheless, Kathleen Noonan maintains that it was Temple's work which "effected a dramatic and lasting change in the image of the Irish held by the English." Building on the foundations of his predecessors like Spenser, Temple processed inchoate anti-Irish sentiment into a fixed chemistry of hatred. His treatise did not stop at chronicling the Irish uprising but concealed or misrepresented its political origins. For generations Temple's work censored from the English public the monstrous repression undertaken by the English state. And in the carefully edited instances of English and Protestant violence documented by Temple, there was the justification that it was appropriate given "the natural treachery of the Irish rooted in their racial (i.e., ethnic) identity."[12] Throughout the eighteenth century, Thomas Bartlett insists, Irish Protestants read Temple "with fascinated horror," and Irish Protestant nationalism was fueled by Temple's massacre stories, and the annual sermons memorializing October 23 (the first day of the uprising): "Indeed so well kept was the memory of 1641 in Protestant consciousness that it took very little to bring it to the fore."[13]

In the new world, the "native Irish" (i.e., Catholics), increasingly dispossessed of land, became the largest single source of indentured servants in the West Indies. Some were voluntary immigrants, but many were involuntary: convicts, rebels, "wanderers," and simply impoverished. On many of the islands, their English masters subjected Irish indentured servants to "slave-like" conditions, policing them as the "enemy within," and those suspected of indolence or insubordination were subjected to imprisonment, public flogging, deportation, and worst. And, inevitably, there was resistance. In the 1650s and in 1692, on Barbados, Irish workers participated or were suspected of participating in several slave revolts. And on St. Kitts and Montserrat in the mid-1660s, Irish servants collaborated with French forces which held the islands for a short period.[14] Toward the end of the century, as African workers came to dominate the laboring class, English planters were relieved from the burden of disciplining this recalcitrant population.

THE BLACK-FACE MASQUERADE

Prior to the American Civil War, black-face minstrelsy was predominantly (but not exclusively) an entertainment for young male workers, many of them Irish and German immigrants. And while Irish minstrel performers and composers – Eric Lott identifies Stephen Foster, Dan Emmett, Dan Bryant, Joel Walker Sweeney, and George Christy among them – may have muted some of the anti-Irish materials of black-face minstrelsy, David Roediger notes that "Irish drinking and 'thickness' drew mockery from the minstrels as did German speech."[15] The coincidence of Irish artists and Irish spectators with the blanket of blackness draped over the African and European poor in the new nationalist culture, facilitated the trope of "the plantation" as a public display of blackness with a difference. The differences marked by the comic shenanigans of the black-white Irish could now be subsumed within a white kinship when played out against the slave and the (semi-)-free Black. Black-face, as a masquerade for public revelries, ribald stage antics, or even city mobs, appropriated the class, racial, and ethnic ambiguities of blackness. Again, we need to be reminded that "Such words as *coon*, *buck*, and *Mose* had more than ambiguous or multiple meanings: they had trajectories that led from white to black ... each of them went from describing particular kinds of whites who had not internalized capitalist work disciplines and whose places in the new world of wage labor were problematic to stereotyping Blacks."[16]

It is not mere hindsight which makes Irish entertainers the most likely candidates for the lures of black-face minstrelsy. In the new American Republic, many of their contemporaries would have thought that Irishmen masquerading as Blacks was redundant. David Roediger reports that in the early decades of the nineteenth century, "... it was by no means clear that the Irish were white."[17] For most Irish-Americans this remained the case well into the twentieth century since as Noel Ignatiev observed, "... no one gave a damn for the poor Irish."[18] In the early Republic, "Nativist folk wisdom held that an Irishman was a 'nigger', inside out ... The Census Bureau regularly collected statistics on the nation's 'native' and 'foreign' populations, but kept the Irish distinct from even the latter group."[19] Between 1815–1845, nearly 1 million Irish immigrants had come to America; and in the decade following the Great Famine, between 1845–1855, that number was doubled.[20] In Southern and Northern cities, "... the Irish were thrown together with black people on jobs and in neighborhoods."[21] Consequently in New York and Boston, Irish women accounted for the majority of "mixed-race" matings with Blacks.[22] In the South, in many cases where slaves were deemed more valuable, Irish laborers were used as substitutes: "Gangs of Irish immigrants worked ditching and draining plantations, building levees and sometimes clearing land because of the danger of death to valuable slave property (and, as one account put it, to mules) in such pursuits."[23] And in the North, domestic service and prostitution became the preserves of Irish women; and young Irish men and women filled the ranks of the waning institution of indentured servitude.[24]

W. T. Lhamon makes the case that the earliest impromptu expressions of black-face minstrelsy emerged from the labor camps of slaves, free Blacks, and Irish immigrants associated with canal building in the North:

> The early canals in North America, including the Erie (1817–1825), were dug largely by unfree labor. Slaves built southern canals. Slaves working alongside indentured laborers bought from European boats docking in Philadelphia, Baltimore, and other eastern ports, shoveled canals in the mid-Atlantic and northern states. In the early days of canal work, free workers also contracted to work alongside the slaves and the indentured workers. But that changed during the years of the Erie's construction.[25]

Since waterways were the most important means of the long-distance transportation of goods in the new Republic, the building of canals (largely dependent on slave labor) was initiated in the South in the 1780s. By the early nineteenth century, canal construction had become the nation's most significant examples of capital-intensive public works. Built in the middle of the canal construction boom, the Erie Canal extended along some 363 miles; nearly a third of the 1277 miles of canals which had been dug in the U.S. by the 1830s.[26] By then the Irish immigrants were the predominant labor force among the 35,000 canallers.[27] But from the late eighteenth century and throughout the most intensive period of canal construction, immigrants and slaves were connected. "The Chesapeake and Delaware [canal directors] reported in 1826 that whites and blacks no longer worked in separate gangs 'but labour together, promiscuously' ..."; and at another canal site, "Slaves worked and lived together with little turnover for one James River Canal contractor in the 1840s and 1850s, whereas his hired white hands quickly came and went."[28] Thus it was in the work culture generated in their shanty towns, tribal villages, grog shops, family huts, and work camps, the Irish drank, sang, danced, fought, and rioted (immigrants from County Cork against Fardowners from the west coast: Corkonians versus Connaughtmen), engaged in all sorts of vices, and staged their imitations of Blacks for entertainment. Generally illiterate, their *métier* was recital and impersonation.

By the 1830s, black-face minstrel performances were an integral part of this immigrant culture:

What too often has seemed like sentimental rhyming is also a way of declaring within the surveillance of the minstrel theater the terrible exhaustion, loneliness, and privation forced on the lowest workers of the Atlantic.

It makes a gnarled sense that the cultural song and dance representing back-stooping labor of shoveling and carting dirt, of building locks and being uprooted from family and home for long periods of time, should appear at the same moment on Lake Erie and along the Atlantic coast. What looks like polygenesis, simultaneous generation of the same form in more than one place, is really the appearance of that form at about the same time at both ends of the waterway whose making matured the symbolism of the labor.[29]

By the time of its appearance in commercial settings like music halls, black-face minstrelsy was predominantly a "white" male working class entertainment – riotous, raucous, and participatory, and performed by solo entertainers. Describing an 1833 engraving of T. D. Rice's "fifty-seventh night" at the Bowery Theater (New York), Eric Lott comments: "It is a crowd of some variety, except for the almost total absence of women: workers in smocks and straw hats rub elbows with militiamen; clerks ape the betters they hope one day to become; a few respectable men intervene in scuffles that have broken out in two places on the stage ... Much of the crowd is interested in the brawl at stage left, or in conversation among themselves; some of those conversations seem concerned with the brawl, not Rice."[30] Principally famous for their "nigger dancing" and dialect singing of often ribald lyrics, the earliest black-face performers had advertised their appropriation of Black performances they had encountered on plantations and in frontier towns of the canal regions (e.g., Cincinnati, Pittsburgh, Louisville). This form acquired its theatrical structure and unambiguously racist character with the appearances of the black-face minstrel bands, the Virginia Minstrels (New York City) and E. P. Christy's Christy's Minstrels (Buffalo, New York) in 1843. By the 1850s, Lhamon insists, with the appearances of the black-face minstrel bands and the intervention of theater entrepreneurs who preferred middle- and upper-class audiences, black-face performances tended to suppress class antagonisms by stressing degrading representations of Blacks: "Thus as black gestures are taken up by white workers at first, then attended to, or policed, by more powerful whites, the uses of the tokens will alter in the transfer."[31]

Black-face minstrelsy survived into the twentieth and the twenty-first centuries. It was transferred from the stage to film in the late nineteenth century and subsequently was preserved in film, then radio and television. And presently its most celebrated performers and progenitors are Black (Eddie Murphy, Martin Lawrence, Chris Rock, Tyler Perry, etc.). There were, of course, their Black predecessors (the most famous being Bert Williams, Aida and George Walker, etc.) who began to occupy the genre in the mid-nineteenth century.

But one critical difference is that Black comedic minstrels of the earlier era fought to subvert the form, eventually generating the Black musical.[32]

EUGENE O'NEILL AND MINSTRELSY

O'Neill, however, was both an heir of the Irish-American black-face tradition and a participant. As the son of the actor James O'Neill, he was raised in the "cheap-jack" melodramatic fashion of the American theater of the turn of the century (Eugene O'Neill's characterization). And as a member of the Provincetown Players, he presumably performed in brown-face when in 1916 he performed the role of the mulatto sailor in his play *Thirst.* Notwithstanding his casting of Gilpin in 1920, as the Irish scholar Aoife Monks indicates, the racial regime of his time provided O'Neill only a slight sliver of ideological maneuverability:

> Minstrelsy was only just beginning to lose its popularity ... when O'Neill wrote his play *The Emperor Jones.* At a moment in history when the Irish American community had only tentatively become "white," O'Neill's engagement with race in *The Emperor Jones* can be read through the legacy of the minstrel tradition that he both rejected, and – unconsciously – maintained in his play and through the lens of his own Irish American ethnicity ... O'Neill, like Brutus Jones, was liminally and precariously "coloured."[33]

But while Monks dwells on O'Neill's Irish-American cultural and performative heritage and O'Neill's exploitation of the Black body, there was another register of the American racial regime which informed *The Emperor Jones.* O'Neill would signal this informing spectacle in several ways on numerous occasions. But his most indelible clue is in his preface, the setting of the play: "The action of the play takes place on an island in the West Indies as yet not self-determined by White Marines. The form of native government is, for the time being, an Empire."[34] For the moment, let's hold that evidence in abeyance.

The play consists of eight scenes. The first scene takes place in the Emperor's white palace and is followed by six scenes in the Great Forest. The final scene takes place on the edge of the Great Forest. Since the play is for the most part a soliloquy, there are only two principal characters: Brutus Jones, a former Pullman porter, convict and fugitive; and Smithers, an exploitative Cockney trader, who was once Jones's boss, then partner and now reduced to the role of a servile factor in the emperor's brutal and corrupt rule. In this first scene, the resentful Smithers enters the palace and somewhat slyly informs Jones that the island is in revolt. Jones has been deserted by his guards and his court and his rule has been reduced to his solitary presence in the palace. And it is during this conversation that Jones, sensing the end has come to his empire, recapitulates the means by which he acquired power over the island's "bush niggers," and hesitantly reveals his past.

> Maybe I goes to jail dere for gettin' in an argument wid razors ovah a crap game. Maybe I gits twenty years when dat colored man die. Maybe I gits in 'nother argument wid de prison guard was overseer ovah us when we're wukin' de road. Maybe he hits me wid a whip and I splits his head wid a shovel and runs away and files de chain off my leg and gits away safe. Maybe I does all dat an' maybe I don't. It's a story I tells you so's you knows I'se de kind of man dat if you evah repeats one word of it, I ends you' stealin' on dis yearth mighty damn quick! (122)

These lines dominate the film, *Emperor Jones* (1933), making up six of its nine reels. Jones's "confession" provided the scaffolding of a back-story written by DuBose Heyward, the author of *Porgy* (1925) and the collaborator with George Gershwin for the operetta, *Porgy and Bess* (1935). Heyward amended the original by creating several female characters: Undine (Fredi Washington), Dolly (Ruby Elzy), and Marcella (Jackie Mabley), who were not even hinted at in the play. The film starred Paul Robeson as Jones, Dudley Digges as Smithers, and Frank Wilson as Jeff, the "colored man" killed by Jones. Revisiting the romantic conflicts he had first imagined for Catfish Row in *Porgy*, Heyward invented an Undine/Bess, a sultry mulatta who preyed on men in a Harlem cabaret, trading her body for cash and a good time.[35] The possession of Undine, as Heyward imagined her, was the real center of the conflict between Jones and Jeff. And Heyward and Dudley Murphy, the film's director, undermined O'Neill's plea that the play was not about race by inserting an opening sequence which displayed African drummers and dancers fading to shout dancers in a Black church in the rural South.

Before Jones abandons the palace to pursue his planned escape through the Great Forest to the coast, he displays a pistol loaded with five lead bullets and one silver bullet. And he prompts the recollection that an important element in the mystique of his power was the myth that he could only be killed by a silver bullet. The rhythmic pounding of drums begins, in each scene increasing pace as Jones begins to spiral into an unrelieved hysteria. In each of the forest scenes, Jones experiences visitations: "formless creatures"; his dead crap-shooting victim; the chain gang; a slave auction; Africans on a slave ship; and an African witch doctor who attempts to sacrifice Jones to a crocodile god.[36] Jones fires his pistol once in every one of these scenes, expending his silver bullet on the crocodile. And in each scene his clothing is either torn away or discarded. In the final scene, Jones has been dispatched in the forest and his near naked corpse is brought before Smithers and Lem, the leader of the revolt. And Smithers delivers his eulogy: "Well, they did for yer right enough, Jonesey, me lad! Dead as a 'erring! Where's yer 'igh an' mighty airs now, yer bloomin' Majesty? Silver bullets! Gawd blimey, but yer died in the 'eight o' style, any'ow!" (153)

The island which served O'Neill's imaginary in *The Emperor Jones* was Haiti. Five years earlier Haiti had been invaded and occupied by American marines (an occupation only relinquished in 1933). During the next five years of pacification, some 3000 Haitians were killed by U.S. marines or the U.S.-commanded Haitian Gendarmerie.[37] In the twentieth century Haiti had been nominally a republic before the occupation but at the beginnings of the nineteenth century it had boasted both a monarchy (King Henri Christophe) and an empire (Jean Jacques Dessalines). In 1919 and 1920, as Mary Renda documents, O'Neill had familiarized himself with the history of the Haitian Revolution, Toussaint L'Ouverture, and Henri Christophe, and in late September 1920 had completed the play in two weeks.[38] But the more immediate influence on O'Neill was the presidency of Guillaume Sam. Sam had ruled Haiti from February to late July in 1915, inciting rebellions because of the brutality of his reign and the belief that he planned to transfer control of the country's finances to American interests.[39] The day following the massacre of more than 160 political prisoners, Sam's presidency had been ended by an avenging mob which wrested him from the French legation, executed him and then paraded his mutilated body through the city of Port-Au-Prince.[40] O'Neill maintained that Sam had made the claim about the silver bullet, but Renda attributes it to both Christophe and Sam. It is also more than possible that a third inspiration was Marcus Garvey. In early August 1920, the Universal Negro Improvement Association (UNIA) had staged a grand parade in Harlem, and Garvey had worn the regalia (minus a pistol) with which O'Neill had costumed Jones in the opening scene of his play.

Renda uncovered a further attribution to Haiti in O'Neill's stage setting: "... on an island in the West Indies as yet not self-determined by White Marines ..." Following a two-month investigation on the island, James Weldon Johnson had published a series of scathing critiques of the American occupation in *The Nation* entitled "Self-Determining Haiti."[41] The coincidence of title and language provides Renda support for her insistence that O'Neill had intended that the play mount a critique of capitalism and imperialism. She acknowledges, however, that O'Neill ultimately failed:

> Yet, while O'Neill made a point of articulating these critiques of capitalism, imperialism, and paternalism, in line with his long-standing interest in socialist and anarchist ideas, his play was not simply or even primarily written in a critical, political mode. Indeed, far from taking the side of the island's natives, the play manifested the same contempt for them that O'Neill had exhibited toward Honduran peasants in 1909. His belief, cultivated in that context, that "native" revolutions were "comic opera" affairs ultimately overshadowed the critical, political moments ...[42]

In a letter to his parents in 1909, O'Neill had characterized the Hondurans as "brainless bipeds." And in *The Emperor Jones*, in the estimation of many of his

Black critics, O'Neill's had struck a profoundly racist register. Foremost among these critics was Charles Gilpin.

As David Krasner has indicated, in his public comments Gilpin had struck an integrationist pose: "... the worthy presentation of a character by a negro actor is a credit to our race, even though the character itself is unworthy."[43] In practice, however, Gilpin had begun to censor O'Neill. Edgar M. Gray had observed that in the play the word "nigger" was employed about fifty times (*The New York News*, February 17, 1921). Gilpin changed the script during the hundreds of his performances, substituting other terms like "black baby" for "nigger," and inserting other changes to achieve "new meanings." This angered O'Neill sufficiently that after having threatened Gilpin with bodily harm ("If I ever catch you rewriting my lines again, you black bastard, I'm going to beat you up."), he eventually replaced him with Paul Robeson. And despite the rave reviews that Gilpin received from critics and reviewers in all quarters over several seasons, O'Neill spread the rumor that Gilpin frequently took the stage drunk.[44] But, as we noted in the epigram, Gilpin had already claimed ownership of Brutus Jones.

While Black critics of the time took exception to the racial construction of Brutus Jones ("clown," "buffoon," "criminal," etc.) and generally objected to the matrix of primitivism which O'Neill had employed, the broader and more historical political context of *The Emperor Jones* was largely ignored. At the time one of the most pressing issues of the American racial regime was whether Blacks and other peoples of color had the capacity for self-governance. From the presidency of William McKinley to that of Woodrow Wilson authoritative American voices had responded in the negative. In the Philippines, in the West Indies, in Liberia, in Central and South America, the American state had prosecuted imperialist appropriations whose constant accompaniment was racial arrogance. "It is our duty," declared Theodore Roosevelt, "to put down savagery and barbarism." And the same sentiment reverberated through the nation's newspapers, popular magazines, world fairs, and every imaginable conduit of mass culture. In 1915, D. W. Griffith and his collaborators had addressed that issue in *The Birth of a Nation* making the case that Reconstruction was a spectacle of Black misrule.[45] And fifteen years before the American occupation, Hesketh Prichard had raised this question with respect to Haiti in *Where Black Rules White* (1900). He had concluded: "[The Negro] has shown no signs whatever which can fairly entitle him to the benefit of the doubt ..."[46]

In the summer of 1920, just weeks before O'Neill sat down to write *The Emperor Jones*, Marcus Garvey and 20,000 of his followers had poured into Madison Square Garden in order to publicly repudiate "the White Man's Burden" and to plan for a future Africa "an immense negro republic of negroes, officered by negroes, for the negro."[47] It is a reasonable surmise that O'Neill's rejoinder to these aspirations was *The Emperor Jones*. Brutus Jones, the minstrel parody of Christophe and Garvey, spoke for O'Neill:

> You didn't s'pose I was holdin' down dis Emperor job for de glory in it, did you? Sho'! De fuss and glory part of it, dat's only to turn de heads o' de low-flung, bush niggers dat's here. Dey wants de big circus show for deir money. I gives it to 'em an' I gits de money. (*with a grin*) De long green, dat's me every time! (118)

By ridicule and grotesque caricatures black-face minstrelsy in the nineteenth century had concealed from its audiences the slaves' desires for freedom, dignity, and safety. In a period richly decorated by slave rebellions and an abolitionist which aggressively exposed the quotidian brutality of slave existence, minstrelsy had transported its audiences into a comic counterfiture. What could possibly be offensive about a social order which cultivated such lovable buffoons?

In turn, Eugene O'Neill, by masquerading himself as a brutal, egomaniacal Black ruler, had given the lie to Black self-governance. While the UNIA, in the pursuit of Black liberation, was evoking Christophe and retrieving from obscurity the Haitian revolution and its magnificent slave rebels, O'Neill had perverted this archaeology. Guillaume Sam, of course, had been a degenerate remnant of a social movement which had shocked and stunned the world a century earlier. Now the Black republic was in receivership. And consummate with the effacement of Haiti's sovereignty was the grander project of excising its history. The memory so long preserved and treasured by generations of Blacks in America and elsewhere – from the leaders of nineteenth-century slave revolts like Gabriel Prosser, Denmark Vesey, and Nat Turner to twentieth-century musicians like Duke Ellington and Charles Mingus – was denied O'Neill's audiences.[48] *The Emperor Jones* became the real, and the real was drowned out by O'Neill's voice and his tomtoms.

NOTES

1. Arthur and Barbara Gelb, *O'Neill*, New York: Harper, 1962, 450.
2. N. Bryllion Fagin, "Eugene O'Neill," *The Antioch Review*, 14, 1, Spring 1954, 15, 19.
3. See Travis Bogard, *Contour in Time: The Plays of Eugene O'Neill*, New York: Oxford University Press, 1972.
4. Susan Curtis, *The First Black Actors on the Great White Way*, Columbia: University of Missouri Press, 1998, 213–214.
5. Peter J. Gillett, "O'Neill and the Racial Myths," *Twentieth Century Literature*, 18, 2, April 1972, 111.
6. Roxann Wheeler, *The Complexion of Race*, University of Pennsylvania, Philadelphia, 2000, 98.
7. Cedric J. Robinson, *Forgeries of Memory and Meaning*, Chapel Hill: University of North Carolina Press, 2007, 33–34.
8. Kathleen M. Noonan, "'The Cruell Pressure of an Enraged, Barbarous People': Irish and English Identity in Seventeenth-Century Policy and Propaganda," *The Historical Journal*, 42, 1, March 1998, 154; for Spenser's proposal, see Nicholas Canny, "Edmund Spenser and the Development of an Anglo-Irish Identity," *The Yearbook of English Studies*, 13, 1983, 4ff.

9. Micheal O Siochru, "Atrocity, Codes of Conduct and The Irish in the British Civil Wars 1641–1653," *Past and Present*, 195, May 2007, 58.
10. Noonan, "Cruell Pressure," 161.
11. O Siochru, "Atrocity," 59, 62.
12. Noonan, "Cruell Pressure," 158n.36 and 158.
13. "Central to the Protestant perception of the rebellion was the publication in 1646 of Sir John Temple's *The Irish Rebellion*, which, through its large collection of lurid and harrowing stories of boiling, stoning, stripping, disembowelling, mutilating, hanging, whipping and drowning, would permanently sear the consciousness of Irish Protestants. At least ten editions … appeared between 1646 and 1812." Thomas Bartlett, "A New History of Ireland," *Past and Present*, 116, August, 1987, 214–215.
14. Hilary McD. Beckles, "A 'Ruthless and Unruly Lot': Irish Indentured Servants and Freemen in the English West Indies, 1644–1713," *The William and Mary Quarterly*, 47, 4, October 1990, 503–522.
15. Eric Lott, *Love and Theft*, New York: Oxford University Press, 1993, 95; and David R. Roediger, *The Wages of Whiteness*, London: Verso, 1991, 118.
16. Roediger, *Wages of Whiteness*, 100.
17. Ibid., 134.
18. Noel Ignatiev, *How the Irish Became White*, New York: Routledge, 1995, 178.
19. Roediger, *Wages of Whiteness*, 133.
20. Ignatiev, *How the Irish Became White*, 38, 39.
21. Ibid., 40.
22. Ibid., 41.
23. Roediger, *Wages of Whiteness*, 146.
24. Ibid.
25. W. T. Lhamon, *Raising Cain: Blackface Performance from Jim Crow to Hip Hop*, Cambridge: Harvard University, 1998, 62.
26. Peter Way, "Evil Humors and Ardent Spirits: The Rough Culture of Canal Construction Laborers," *The Journal of American History*, 79, 4, March 1993, 1405.
27. Way cites Harvey H. Segal's "Cycles of Canal Construction" (in Carter Goodrich, ed., *Canals and American Economic Development*, New York, 1972, 206) for the estimate that canal workers constituted 5.5 percent of the total nonagricultural work force in ten northern canal-building states in 1840.
28. Way, "Evil Humors and Ardent Spirits," 1422 and 1419, respectively.
29. Lhamon, *Raising Cain*, 66.
30. Eric Lott, *Love and Theft*, New York: Oxford University Press, 1993, 124, 126.
31. Lhamon, *Raising Cain*, 76.
32. See Robinson, *Forgeries*, chapter 3.
33. Aoife Monks, "'Genuine Negroes and Real Bloodhounds' Cross-Dressing, Eugene O'Neill, the Wooster Group, and *The Emperor Jones*," *Modern Drama*, 48 3, Fall 2005, 545.
34. Eugene O'Neill, *Four Plays by Eugene O'Neill* (introduction by A. R. Gurney), New York: Signet Classic, 1998, 111. In the text further references to the play are paginated from this edition.
35. "Will Hays, the infamous censor, demanded early on that scenes between Robeson and his leading lady, Fredi Washington, be reshot. Hays felt that Washington was too light-skinned and would be mistaken for a white woman, thus raising the specter of miscegenation. An irate Washington was smeared with dark makeup …" Jennie Saxena (with Ken Weissman and James Cozart), "Preserving African-American Cinema: The Case of *The Emperor Jones* (1933)," *The Moving Image*, 3, 1, Spring 2003, 46.
36. In the film the auction and the slave ship scenes are deleted. Ibid., 47.
37. Mary A. Renda, *Taking Haiti: Military Occupation & the Culture of U.S. Imperialism, 1915–1940*, Chapel Hill: The University of North Carolina Press, 2001, 151.
38. Ibid., 197–198.
39. "Rebels in Cape Haitien," *New York Times*, April 26, 1915, 4.
40. "Haiti Massacre: President flees; Zamor Executed," *New York Times*, July 28, 1915, 1; and "Haitians Slay Their President; We Land Marines," *New York Times*, July 29, 1915, 1. John Blassingame

uncovered overwhelming support in American newspapers (49 of 69) for the invasion of Santo Domingo and Haiti between 1904 and 1919. The most prominent exception was *The Nation*. See Blassingame, "The Press and American Intervention in Haiti and the Dominican Republic, 1904–1920," *Caribbean Studies*, 9, 2, July 1969, 27–43.

41. The articles appeared in *the Nation* on August 28, September 4 and September 11, 1920.
42. Renda, *Taking Haiti*, 205.
43. David Krasner, "Whose Role is it Anyway?: Charles Gilpin and the Harlem Renaissance," *African American Review*, 29, 3, Autumn 1995, 486.
44. Ibid., 484.
45. See Robinson, *Forgeries*, chapter II.
46. Quoted by Renda, *Taking Haiti*, 207.
47. A. B. Williams, "Clipper Ship of the African Exodus," *New York Times*, August 29, 1920, BMR4 and 19.
48. Maurice Jackson, "'Friends of the Negro! Fly with me, The path is Open to the Sea,'" *Early American Studies*, Spring 2008, 59–103.

PART V

ON RESISTANCE AND REDEMPTION

CHAPTER 20

Malcolm Little as a Charismatic Leader

"If you catch me feeling, please don't tell on me ..."
— *Sonny Terry*

In this analysis, I have attempted to deal with two simultaneous developments which are the keys to the mass charismatic event. One development is concerned with the individual phenomenon of identity as it relates specifically to political leaders – or men who *need to* lead desperately, and the other with the historical evolution of moments in the lives of members of communities where they require this particular form of leadership. I have chosen, in accordance with these interests, an analytical instrument which is bounded by the propositions which result from this conceptualization: the psychohistorical, which is closely associated with Erik Erikson's works on Martin Luther and Mahatma Gandhi. In terms of the psychological aspect, I have argued that one must become familiar with those "past moments" in the life of the individual which are really neither "past" or discretely segregated from his present. "Past moments" warrant that appellation only because they "happened," or more usefully, really began in his early years. However, like bad dreams, they return again and again to haunt him, compelling him to face dilemmas he has never satisfactorily disposed of, drawing from him a response which has already been coded into his experience (beginning, of course, with his initial confrontations). Such moments are the manifestation of private compulsion. They do not often correspond with that sense of reality the individual shares with his associates (though they might quite fortuitously) but stem from his subjective-bound, private world. They are his peculiar inheritance from childhood. Those men, whose early youths are characterized by strong ambivalence, expressive emotion deprivation, abandonment, fear of, and anger toward love-objects (e.g., parents), and who displace their private dramas into universalistic ones, seek the charismatic position. Other forms of authority have too little relevance to their needs. More than power, they must have confirmed rectitude or "righteousness," and a legitimation of their authority which transcends tradition and laws of the past. They seek absolution from their obvious guilt (certainly the resultant of the "experienced" indictments of their childhoods). One must then search that terrible period of their lives from which their personalities first emerged as integral phenomena. For it is the early authority figures and the "absoluteness" of their dominance which needs to be replicated by the charismatic leader. He requires of his followers their participation in an enormous role-reversal. In the now familiar scenario of Eric Berne's transactional analysis, they are to play Child to his role as Parent. However, his behavior is rationalized by both him and his followers in terms of the universals of justice and good in the belief system incorporated by their shared ideology and performed through the institutions they develop and sustain.

The historical component of this analysis traces the breakdown of the behavioral and normative patterns sustaining the lives of a certain proportion of a community's members. The causes of this breakdown may be a qualitative jump in the level of violence directed toward their community, physical, or social mobility experienced most heavily in individual rather than group phenomena, or events which rob the community and/or its members of the sense of power it or they have enjoyed traditionally over destiny. As a result of this breakdown, conceptualization, and cognition of reality suffer, giving rise to increased anxiety. The integration of one's life with one's understanding of reality ceases to exist. Despair, hopelessness, meaninglessness, and a sense of powerlessness invades the impacted community. Tradition has been dissolved and with it the regularity and routineness of life which allows for the expectedness and anticipation which are necessary deposits in the foundation of any enduring community. The charismatic situation then, is a converging of these two developments. The leader's search for resolution of this identity crisis and his community's search for another meaning system result in the charismatic situation. The leader offers his need-induced vision (for most do experience revelations from superior beings) as the new reality organization through his ideology, but the venture must be substantiated by an act of resolute obedience, a total submission to his will. Such an act must involve risk and a disavowal of the relevance of the laws and rules of the old regime. Just as he has sensed his marginality to them, all of his life, they must now commit themselves to a similar emotional experience. They must commit an act which shoves them to the periphery of their former world.

THE ANALYTICAL FRAMEWORK

And I remember a lone, almost ragged guitarist huddled on a side street playing and singing just for himself when he glanced up and instantly recognized the oncoming, striding figure. "Huh-ho!" the guitarist exclaimed, and jumping up, he snapped into a mock salute. "My man!"[1]

It is the nature of the phenomenon of leadership to produce great humility in any of its students for it incorporates, it seems, in compelling fashion, the total range of human experience. The leader and the led are theater, history, psychology, sociology, politics, religion – a list of analytical frameworks, constructs, and events which extends almost infinitely. Classifications which are always simplifications of reality appear even more so as organizations of this particular type of social occurrence for leadership encompasses in addition to its horizontal variety (i.e., styles) several levels of actualization and subsequent analysis (e.g., the leader may be the beloved of some of his followers, the organizational force for others, and for still others a tool through which their own interests are cynically secured). As such it is justifiable to choose from the multicharactered body of its advent any one of its variables or combination of variables to focus on but satisfaction from such stratagems is certainly more the result of energy-exhaustion than from the occasion of revealing explanations. Thus the complexity of the leadership relation justifies delimited probes but does not legitimize them as they bear fruit. Although it should be said that the more successful works on leadership have produced partial explanations, it has yet to be demonstrated whether the resultant accumulation of knowledge is additive in quantitative terms or qualitative ones. The conclusion, then, has a trite ring to it: the analyst of leadership must in the broadest sense be a student of human nature. He must be sensitive to the forms and meaning-substances of individual existence, group interaction, and community experience if he is to develop a self-satisfying *Weltanschauung* to test the validity of his later discoveries. The "agreed-upon," the "objective reality" can evolve only from such a beginning. (Quite simply, the culture of knowledge presupposes an awareness – an insight – into the culture or cultures of events it presumes to have reconstructed or explained.) Because of this logic, in this treatment of Malcolm Little, I have found it necessary to employ, within the delimitations of my circumscribed resources, the psychohistorical frameworks of Erik Erikson, Max Weber, Harold Lasswell, and their numerous successors.

The central premise of the psychohistorical approach is that certain kinds of historic occurrences (e.g., the development of institution, mass movements, ideologies, etc.) depend for their material peculiarities or idiosyncratic natures upon the psychic development of their power actors. The creative act (which may be either constructive or destructive) which results in reorganization of reality for varying numbers of people performs its art according to the intimate and often unconscious needs of the creator-leader while satisfying the requirements of the historic moment. In writing of creation I have not meant to imply that the psychohistorical approach should be restricted to or is most fully realized by a concentration on a particular kind of situation or authority. The literature on charismatic leaders has perhaps inferred such a judgment by its apparent centering on such figures as Adolf Hitler, Sigmund Freud, Martin Luther, and Jesus Christ.

Such a restriction, however, would be spurious since the psychohistorical approach is essentially a broader framework within which one can begin to understand the dynamic of decision-making as an additionally, irrational (nonmathematical) event. The creative impulse is ordered from within its creator not from without. It is more a curative than a direct application of problem and solution. The irrational process is ordered and patterned by an emphasis on the internal and individual meaning of the choice. And here I have deliberately chosen to juxtapose the terms *decision-making* and *choice* to stress their relatedness: the existential dilemma. The psychohistorical approach clearly is an instrument concerned primarily with identity and the meaning of existence as well as the anguish and pathologies which are a part of their formation and development. Thus with respect to the leader it is irrelevant whether his image is legitimized for his followers through charisma, tradition, or legal rules, he will confront such moments which resound with threats perceived as focused on his sense of personal security and continuity. Again it matters not whether he is functioning in his role as group representative, ideologue, or decision-maker; he will perforce face choices of potentially terrible consequences to his identity. With this approach the objective dimension of the decision to be made by the leader is then less significant in terms of ultimately explaining the action than the subjective interpretation (whether conscious or otherwise) of the experience by the actor.

As such the psychohistorical approach is most aptly named since it scrambles and counterposes the two "realities" of the event: the individual and historic developments. The interrupted denouement of the man Malcolm Little through the psychosocial stages of "nigger child," "Detroit Red," "Satan," "Malcolm X," and "El-Hajj Malik El-Shabazz" must be viewed against the backdrop of the American racial drama's procession through the appellations African, blacks, slaves, colored, Negro (both small and large case), Black, and finally Afro-American (soon to progress to the next stage Afroamerican) which in its turn has become increasingly responsive to the changing international postures. If this is not clear at this point, understandably so, since it is one purpose of this paper to explicate this interaction. It is sufficient to reiterate that the leader as an individual has his own psychic momentum ontogenetically discrete from that of his historic role requirements. This is a conceptualization of reality which is owed most authentically to Erikson than to any other theorist but of course must pay its dues to Freud and his passionate interdiction between Karl Marx and history as well as his own dubious efforts at political biography. Thus Erikson should be further pursued in his formulation of the research instrument and methodological prescriptions. Erikson's rationalization for the psychohistorical approach is:

> the clinician is inexorably drawn into super-personal history "itself," since he, too, must learn to conceive of, say, a "great" man's crises and achievements as communal events characteristic of a given historical period. On the other hand, some historians probably begin to suspect that they, too, are practitioners of a restorative

art which transforms the fragmentation of the past and the peculiarities of those who make history into such wholeness of meaning as mankind seeks.[2]

As a clinician and methodologist he realistically assesses the autobiography as the closest approximation to the free association familiar to psychoanalysts but realizes the delimitations:

> as to unconscious motivation, we must always remember that the autobiographer has not agreed to a therapeutic contract by which he promises to put into words all his "free associations," so that we may help him to compare them with inner and outer "reality." Memories, then, are an intrinsic part of the actuality in which they emerge. Our first concern must be with the stage of life in which a given medium was used to retell, or relive or reactivate an earlier stage for the purpose of heightening some sense of actuality in the telling.[3]

He proposes then a stratagem which he believes will be most productive in the analysis of such materials:

> One is almost embarrassed to point out what seems so obvious – namely, that in perusing a man's memoirs for the purpose of reconstructing past moments and reinterpreting pervasive motivational trends, one must first ask oneself at what age and under what general circumstances the memoirs were written, what their intended purpose was, and what form they assumed.[4]

He addends this further with a similar set of perspectives of and questions for the reviewer's relationship with the man and his events as well as for the followers of the man and the relatively passive participants in the events. These remarks are in keeping with the central identity and identification of all phenomena for Erikson summarized by his use of the term *complementarity*. In superpersonal as well as interpersonal and intrapersonal interactions, complementarity takes the form of "confirmation": Societies thus verify the new individual and are themselves historically verified.[5]

And identity developments:

> Identity formation thus goes beyond the process of *identifying oneself with* others in the one-way fashion described in earlier psychoanalysis. It is a process based on a heightened cognitive and emotional capacity to *let oneself be identified* as a circumscribed individual in relation to a predictable universe which transcends the circumstances of childhood. For this reason societies *confirm* an individual at this time in all kinds of ideological frameworks and assign roles and tasks to him in which he can *recognize* himself *and feel recognized.*[6]

and a sentiment which is echoed in his analysis of parent–child relationships as well as that between the constructs of ego and superego. The more popular version of the Lasswellian thesis of *homo politicus* is a special or delimited case of the Eriksonian one and schematically may be represented as p, d, r-P (where p = private motives, d = displacement onto public objects, r = rationalization in terms of justice, and good = "transformed into," and P = Political man). Alexander George summarily represents Lasswell's presentation as:

> a general hypothesis about the "power seeker" as a person who pursues power as a means of compensation against deprivation. Power is expected to overcome low estimates of the self, by changing either the traits of the self or the environment in which it functions.[7]

Erikson, of course, goes beyond "power seekers" and leaders and creates a perspective which is also appropriate to more ordinary role constellations and situations.

CHARISMA

It is, however, a further specialization with which I am concerned here. I am dealing with a man whose authority can best be understood as having been permitted through the agency of charisma. Thus it is to this particular phenomenon that I must now turn. Two specific definitions would seem to suffice as an introduction to the phenomenon:

> Weber borrowed this concept from Rudolf Sohm, the Strassburg church historian and jurist. Charisma, meaning literally "gift of grace," is used by Weber to characterize self-appointed leaders who are followed by those who are in distress and who need to follow the leader because they believe him to be extraordinarily qualified ... Miracles and revelations, heroic feats of valor and baffling success are characteristic marks of their stature. Failure is their ruin.[8]

and

> Charismatic authority differs from the other two types traditional and legal. Charismatic authority rests on "devotion to the specific sanctity, heroism or exemplary character of an individual person, and of the normative pattern or order revealed by him."[9]

According to Ann Ruth Willner, the phenomenon is then most accurately understood as a "relational" one between leader and led:

> As Weber repeatedly emphasized, it is not necessarily *what* the leader is but *how* he is perceived by his followers that is decisive for the validity of charisma. "What is

alone important is how the individual is actually regarded by those subject to charismatic authority."[10]

As such the independent variable is the anguished and painful condition of the community before the generation of charismatic authority. It is the nature of the dissatisfaction within the experiences of the members of a community which ultimately distinguishes charismatic leadership from popular leadership. And here I must elaborate. It is the function of the political, social, and economic institutions and systems of a society to provide order – that is, an arrangement of things into ranks, positions, sequences, and contexts. Institutions and systems are themselves the very embodiment of the rhythms, regularities, and uniformities to be found in society. They give to the past, to the present, and to the future confirmation, affirmation, and a sense of style. It is, in fact, their existence through time and space which help the individual mind to conceptualize and define these consequences. These institutions and systems thus serve the function of authoritative sources to those who live through them *by their continuity*. The members of a community "sense" themselves, locate, and identify themselves as individuals, as family, as nation, and as a people utilizing the ofttime elaborate systematizations of meaning rendered by these systems. "Reality," as well as "truth" and "validity" are clothed by these societal institutions. These are the "givens" in the experiences of all men. (And here comes to mind the "wolf children" commented upon recently by Professor Eulau, who described them as not really human; they are inhuman simply because they have no experience of the human condition which is available solely through human society. They are tragic *suggestions* of human beings.) They are the basis of all subsequent development in structure and substance. They are inevitable because of their necessity to men. These notions are not novel, of course, but merely extensions and extrapolations of Freud, Durkheim, Karl Mannheim, Michael Polanyi, Thomas Kuhn, and a whole compendium of theorists and students of perception and learning who have in one way or another exposed meaning's dependence and its arbitrariness.

It is, however, in the very nature of institutions and systems to change over time. Change can be described as growth, decay, complexification, or simplification. Such change is the resultant of a variety of possible influences: miscalculation, misdeed, genius, lack of genius (or vision or foresight), psychological vagaries, imperfect or differentiated socialization, environmental changes, etc. An example given by Kuhn in his description of Ptolemy's astronomical paradigm in its "advanced" years:

> But as time went on, a man looking at the net result of the normal research effort of many astronomers could observe that astronomy's complexity was increasing far more rapidly than its accuracy and that a discrepancy corrected in one place was likely to show up in another.[11]

The maintenance and, as well, the impermanence of such systems and institutions, being dependent upon their carriers and transmitters, that is, humans, suffer from the fluidities of human nature. Though change is thus perceived as normal, there come particular points in the life-times of all systems where they cease to discharge their functions of maintaining meaning. New phenomena thrust themselves into the old "reality," new facts or meanings emerge from the past, new challenges arrive to duel with the old "truths." These novelties become critical when they are *unanticipated*. It is thus when the old paradigm fails to explain and predict, when some significant and strategically positioned individuals in the community can no longer prepare themselves to meet the directions and substances of change and stress that a crisis of meaning which results in revolution occurs.

It is at this point that leaders contending for mass charismatic authority emerge, each seeking a relationship with other men which is absolute and irrefutable:

> By his followers, the charismatic leader is held to be uniquely capable of cognitively structuring or restructuring the world. His orientations are their orientations. For them, it is *his* normative vision of the future, and *his* prescriptions for action they accept. It therefore can be inferred that they perceive him as outstanding in wisdom, outstanding in prescience and possessing the power to bring into being goals they share.[12]

It is thus a total reorganization of meaning through total subjection which distinguishes the symbolic representativeness of popular leaders (whether they be traditional or legal) from the authority reference absoluteness of charismatic leadership. If the concept conversion seems more appropriate at this juncture, it should be recalled that Weber indeed borrowed the term from its ecclesiastical context. Freud, interpreting this process through his own analytical constructs, saw it as the acceptance and introjection by the group members of the leader as ego-ideal. The leader (as object of father) becomes the group's ideal and the energy of the group becomes committed to fulfilling his prescriptions:

> The leader of the group is still the dreaded primal father; the group still wishes to be governed by unrestricted force; it is an extreme passion for authority; in Le Bon's phrases, it has a thirst for obedience. The primal father is the group ideal, which governs the ego in the place of the ego ideal.[13]

In her paper Willner proceeds further to indicate the kinds of evidence she would require to establish the existence of the charismatic following:

> Particularly telling evidence of charismatic orientation toward a leader as was suggested in the previous section, is a dramatic revision in affect toward and

cognition of an object or a situation – a revision that is induced in followers by the leader's statements. Finally, I would add another type of indicator not suggested in the original definition – the conviction of a following that the existence or continuity of the social order they value is dependent upon the life or presence of the leader.[14]

We see then the other aspect of the confirmation theme to which Erikson is so committed. The charismatic leader confirms his own vision and identity in succeeding at gaining converts who are in fact extensions of his personality. They, in turn, are dependent upon his sustainment of sameness and continuity for their own identities. It thus becomes imperative for the maintenance and life of the movement that the leader's role should become regularized and routinized; otherwise, his death or failure would precipitate a crisis similar to that which produced the movement. This becomes an increasingly critical problem since the emergence of the movement produces strains and resistances to it analogous to the formation of antibodies in the ideological organism. As a result the leader may be killed, jailed (or may betray the movement because of personal idiosyncracies), or contested by competing authorities within or out of the movement as it gains in significance and maturity. Although the charismatic leader is the ultimate defender in affective terms to confrontations with the movement's enemies, his subleaders bear the responsibility for instrumental conservation except in those rare instances of the emergence of a total (in terms of competence) charismatic leader. It is the function of the leader to describe for his followers the objects of their hatred, the intensity with which they may hate and the forms which these hatreds may take. It is his cadres' role to bring detail to the master plan, organizing defensive machinery against the movement's enemies as well as those props needed for the preservative intensification rituals. This dichotomization is the most frequent form of role differentiation among the elite of a movement but has in the past been obviated by those charismatic leaders who also possessed organizational and bureaucratic genius (Lenin for one). Thus there are several critical dynamics in operation as the movement gropes toward institutionalization. The leader is experiencing the ambiguity of a delayed identity crisis with privatized and public dimensions, the leader-follower relationship is a dynamic of mutual and reciprocal needs:

> Ideological leaders, so it seems, are subject to excessive fears which they can master only by reshaping the thoughts of their contemporaries; while those contemporaries are always glad to have their thoughts shaped by those who so desperately care to do so.[15]

and the movement and its environmental competitors are struggling with progressively more vigor for dominance over the energies, loyalties, and imaginations of its followers.

IDEOLOGY, IDENTITY, AND ACTION

What holds these individuals together is their shared ideology for through it their experiences, their feelings, their perceptions, and their understandings take on the same proportions. The ideology is their *raison dêtre*. The moment and the man are established. The question now before us is just what he does in this moment. What act does he perform to transform moment into movement? As previously indicated, what he uniquely contributes is a *total* belief system – an ideology – which envelops some *act* or *action* by the group which is desperate, total, and frequently irreversible.

> ... ideology will mean an unconscious tendency underlying religious and scientific as well as political thought: the tendency at a given time to make facts amenable to ideas, and ideas to facts, in order to create a world image convincing enough to support the collective and the individual sense of identity.[16]

I am suggesting that additionally and unlike the "insight" (whether one conceptualizes it as revealed "hidden" meaning or meaning reorganization) available to the analysand in his "patienthood," ideology is permeated explicitly and intimately with some necessary "doing" or action. The commitment to ideological belief serves as a disavowal to continuing the meaningless wandering representative of the former fragmented life style. The act is now a compelling one for it is the key to survival in the existential dilemma for every member of the movement. That it most often entails in its possible failure a corporate, physical risk serves further to cast the commitment to act in total and absolute terms. The "sinking" and dread experienced in the former life-pattern is now understood (or better, "seen") by the follower but understanding alone does not bring with it salvation. The ideology can only *indicate* the saving act, not stand in its stead.

> Where historical and technological developments severely encroach upon deeply rooted or strongly emerging identities ... on a large scale, youth feels endangered, individually and collectively, whereupon it becomes ready to support doctrines offering a total immersion in a synthetic identity ... and a collective condemnation of a totally stereotyped enemy of the new identity.[17]

Excitement, enthusiasm, sensed spontaneity, and dynamism which are necessary concomitants to willed acts of danger settle around the movement. "An enthusiasm is kindled, a group of adherents is formed, and many are emancipated from the moral condition of their age."[18] Such occurrences are indeed appropriately characterized as "revitalization movements"[19] for a new identity has been achieved by mutual recognitions which energizes its participants into new forms of social action.

MALCOLM LITTLE

Looking now at the man Malcolm Little, despite the familiarity of the face, the figure, the gestures, and the voice to many of us, one has a sense of a vast unknown quantity. No man could be what he seemed for he seemed "the angriest Negro." He was tall, taut, brilliant, and seemingly securely buttressed against his hated object: the iniquitous white devils. But characteristic of Malcolm X was the episode reported by M. S. Handler, the *New York Times* reporter concerning their first interview:

> His views about the white man were devastating, but at no time did he transgress against my own personality and make me feel that I, as an individual, shared in the guilt. He attributed the degradation of the Negro people to the white man.[20]

Yet he was also keenly aware of his own ambivalence. Early in the *Autobiography* he tells of an episode with someone he identifies as a "little blond coed" from a New England college. After lecturing at her campus he returned to New York and found that she had followed him by plane in order to confront him:

> ... I'd never seen anyone I ever spoke before more affected than this little white college girl. She demanded, right up in my face, "Don't you believe there are any *good* white people?" I didn't want to hurt her feelings, I told her, "People's *deeds* I believe in, Miss – not their words." "What can ı *do*?" she exclaimed. I told her, "Nothing." She burst out crying, and ran out and up Lenox Avenue and caught a taxi.[21]

However this was not the end of the episode for Malcolm X for after he had returned to this country from his pilgrimage to Mecca as El-Hajj Malik El-Shabazz (which designated him a member of the tribe Shabazz and one who had journeyed to the Kaaba) he relived it again and again:

> The white people in meeting audiences would throng around me, asking me, after I had addressed them somewhere, "What can a sincere white person do?" ... It makes me think about that little coed I told you about ... I regret that I told her that. I wish that now I knew her name, or where I could telephone her, or write her, and tell her what I tell white people now when they present themselves as being sincere ...[22]

Before commenting further on the relevance of this disclosure by the man I would like to take note, briefly, of the *Autobiography* itself.

When first approached by Alex Haley (a Black freelance writer) with the idea of writing an autobiography, Malcolm X apparently realized the importance the project might have for everyone but himself. Yet as it evolved he must have come to understand what it was forcing him to acknowledge about himself:

> ... when something provoked him to exclaim, "These Uncle Toms make me think about how the Prophet Jesus was criticized in his own country!" Malcolm X

278 | *Cedric J. Robinson*

promptly got up and silently took my notebook, tore out that page and crumpled it and put it into his pocket, and he was considerably subdued during the remainder of that session.[23]

Notwithstanding the cautions of Erikson linked with the unusually "public" nature of Gandhi's work (which was a final compilation of columns written for a newspaper in the form of moral lessons for its readers) in large measure Malcolm X was freely associating in a fashion obviously similar to the nondirective interview familiar to students of Carl Rogers. Haley, frustrated by the unproductiveness of the early "visits," hit upon the stratagem of placing innocent scraps of tissue near Malcolm X since he was a habitual scribbler writing in abbreviated and short-handed form messages which could not be directly related to the conversational content of his visits. "It was through a clue from one of the scribblings that finally I cast a bait that Malcolm X took."[24]

The relationship, however, between the writer and the "analysand" was cemented for both much later:

> I don't know what gave me the inspiration to say once when he paused for breath, "I wonder if you'd tell me something about your mother?" Abruptly he quit pacing, and the look that he shot at me made me sense that somehow the chance question had hit him ... Slowly, Malcolm X began to talk ... After that night, he never again hesitated to tell me even the most intimate details of his personal life, over the next two years. His talking about his mother triggered something.[25]

It is plain that as Malcolm X remembered his experiences (some of which he claimed he hadn't thought of for years and certainly had never shared with anyone) he relived them. As Malcolm Little (and from this point the appellations will each represent specific psychosocial stages in the man's life) the child, he was "somber to grim." As Detroit Red, the hustler, pimp, dope pusher burglar, and dope "fiend," he was often exuberant.

> One night, suddenly, wildly, he jumped up from his chair and, incredibly, the fearsome black demagogue was scat-singing and popping his fingers, "re-bop-de-bop-blam-blam – " ... And then almost as suddenly, Malcolm X caught himself and sat back down, and for the rest of that session he was decidedly grumpy.[26]

It is thus with a sense of the deep emotional investment involved for the man as well as the force it brought to his reorganizations of his life that the *Autobiography* must be read. As it was being dictated from the Spring of 1963 to the Winter of 1964–1965, the man was transitioning from the troubled but passionately defensive Muslim minister Malcolm X (who had fought desperately to retain his image of Elijah Muhammed as a near-divinity despite growing awareness of the man's "immorality") to the probing, incredibly fluid "Malik" of his final days when he characterized himself as:

> I feel like a man who has been asleep somewhat and under someone else's control. I feel what I'm thinking and saying now is for myself. Before, it was for and by the guidance of Elijah Muhammad. Now I think with my own mind, sir.[27]

The *Autobiography*, then, is legitimately an extended psychoanalytic interview, a record of transference, ambivalence, and even to its most careful reader, countertransference.[28] In it we are thus in the first instance limited to recurrent themes beginning with the familiar familial triad of father–mother–child and progressing from there in metaphoric leaps to an organization of the man's life-meanings. Within the scope of this paper this will mean that I will be largely confined to detailed analysis of that period least public of Malcolm Little: his childhood, and depositing in a more generalized manner its impact on his later life. Here, then, is a brief outline of Malcolm Little's early life events as he records them:

1925 Born in Omaha, Nebraska.
1929 Home burned down probably by members of the Black Legion (an organization apparently paralleling the KKK) while firemen and policemen of Lansing, Mich. "stood around watching."
1930 Malcolm becomes at once aware of his father's brutality toward his mother and his father's interest in him (Earl Little took only his son Malcolm with him on his preaching journeys).
1931 Earl Little is murdered. His body is badly mutilated by a street-car.
1934 The Little family enters poverty and begins to disintegrate. Malcolm becomes delinquent.
1937 Louise Little (Malcolm's mother) is placed in a mental institution to remain for twenty-six years. Malcolm is sent to a detention home in Mason and enters Mason Jr. High School where he remains until 1941.
1941 Malcolm is released to his half-sister Ella Collins' custody in, Boston where he soon embarks on the hustling "scene," in which he will become known as "Big Red" or "Detroit Red."
1946 Malcolm is convicted on fourteen counts of crime (primarily burglary and possession of stolen property) and sentenced to ten years in state prison.

The narrative of the *Autobiography* begins with the construction of the heroic image of a woman, Malcolm's mother, and ironically, the last entry of intimacy in the narrative deals with a woman, "the little blond coed." Between these two revelations, Malcolm speaks again and again of his ambivalence toward women:

> "You never can fully trust any woman," he said, "I've got the only one I ever met whom I would trust seventy-five percent. I've told her that," he said. "I've told

her like I tell you, I've seen too many men destroyed by their wives, or their women."[29]

That Malcolm's mother was a powerful influence on her son is undeniable for she embodied much which would directly and indirectly return to haunt him in later life:

> Louise Little, my mother who was born in Grenada, in the British West Indies, looked like a white woman. Her father *was* white. She had straight black hair, and her accent did not sound like a Negro's. Of this white father of hers, I know nothing except her shame about it.[30]
>
> Thinking about it now, I feel definitely that just as my father favored me for being lighter than the other children, my mother gave me more hell for the same reason. She was very light herself but she favored, the ones who were darker ... She went out of her way never to let me become afflicted with a sense of color-superiority. I am sure that she treated me this way partly because of how she came to be light herself.[31]
>
> It was then that my mother had this vision. She had always been a strange woman in this sense, and had always had a strong intuition of things about to happen.[32]
>
> But the monthly welfare check was their pass. They acted as if they owned us, as if we were their private property. As much as my mother would have liked to, she couldn't keep them out. She would get particularly incensed when they began insisting upon drawing us older children aside, one at a time, out on the porch or somewhere, and asking us questions, or telling us things – against our mother and against each other.[33]

Later on in 1952 when he visited her at the mental institution (he would not see her again for a period of eleven years because he wished not to) she would deny him again:

> But she didn't recognize me at all. She stared at me. She didn't know who I was. Her mind, when I tried to talk, to reach her, was somewhere else. I asked, "Mama, do you know what day it is?" She said, staring, "all the people have gone." I can't describe how I felt. The woman who had brought me into the world, and nursed me, and advised me, and chastised me, and loved me, didn't know me. It was as if I was trying to walk up the side of a hill of feathers. I looked at her. I listened to her "talk." But there was nothing I could do.[34]

Here then was a woman who looked white but who could trust and love only those men who were dark – extending her disgust, compulsively, even to her own children. (The only other relationship which Malcolm acknowledges for his mother takes place in 1935 when she becomes involved with a lover who

Malcolm describes as "big and black and looked something like my father.")[35] That her children were named Wilfred, Hilda, Philbert, Malcolm, Reginald, Yvonne, Wesley, and Robert indicates even another kind of dominance of the setting of Malcolm's childhood for these are names taken almost exclusively from her own West Indian culture and not that of the Reynolds, Georgia culture of Earl Little.

She presented her son with a "Double-Bind" relationship of "go-away-come-here" messages which would result in an ambivalence for him as well. For Malcolm X she was an idealized figure heroic in her oppression ("she was always standing over the stove …") but one for whom he felt much guilt ("As bad as I was, as much trouble and worry as I caused my mother, I loved her,") and ambivalence ("One thing I have always been proud of is that I never raised my hand against my mother,") which he could finally only resolve by "forgetting":

> I realized that I had blocked her out of my mind – it was just unpleasant to think about her having been twenty-some years in that mental hospital … My mind had closed about our mother. I simply didn't feel the problem could be solved, so I had shut it out. I had built up subconscious defenses.[36]

Her insanity was to plague him in yet another way for all his years for it was repeated in his younger brother Reginald (with whom Malcolm was closest of all his siblings) and became a constant "danger" for Malcolm himself:

> When I discovered who else wanted me dead, I am telling you … it nearly sent me to Bellevue.[37] I didn't want Allah to "burn my brain" as I felt the brain of my brother Reginald had been burned for harboring evil thoughts about Mr. Elijah Muhammad.[38]
>
> My head felt like it was bleeding inside. I felt like my brain was damaged. I went to see Dr. Leona A. Turner, who has been my family doctor for years, who practises in East Elmhurst, Long Island. I asked her to give me a brain examination.[39]

Louise Little was also "instrumental" in the development of a style of confrontation which would characterize her son for much of his later years:

> I learned early that crying out in protest could accomplish things … I would cry out and make a fuss until I got what I wanted … So early in life, I had learned that if you want something, you had better make some noise.[40]

(It should be noted also that the dietary restrictions to which his mother was addicted – initially unexplained but later reinforced by her conversion to the Seventh Day Adventist Church – emerged again in the Lost-Found Nation of Islam and would continue with him for the remainder of his life.)

For another ten years (1937–1947) Malcolm's contact with women would be largely understood by him as negative:

I wouldn't have considered it possible for me to love any woman. I'd had too much experience that women were only tricky, deceitful, untrustworthy flesh. I had seen too many men ruined, or at least tied down, or in some other way messed up by women. Women talked too much ... I mean, I'd had *so* much experience. I had talked to too many prostitutes and mistresses.[41]

It would largely confirm the ambivalence of his early years and although he had a constant mistress for the five years of his Detroit Red period ("This fine blond" and a volume in and of itself) he would not mention love again until he spoke of his wife, Betty X. During this period, he would use and abuse or see the use and abuse of every woman he knew excepting his sister Ella.

It has been suggested that more attention should be paid to the role of West Indian culture in the socialization of the child Malcolm. It is to be recalled that two other major charismatic figures in the recent history of American Blacks came from households of West Indian heritage: Stokely Carmichael and Marcus Garvey. Richard Young (as this paper was being written a fellow seminarian and doctoral candidate in Stanford's Political Science Department) is of the opinion that such a socialization experience could serve as a "shield" against the internalization of attitudes and values concerning self which Kardiner and Ovesey investigated among Black children in their *The Mark of Oppression*. Carmichael, Garvey, and Malcolm were less "niggerized" than is usual and traditionally necessary for Black children in North America.[42] If one accepted the analysis of Melville Herskovits[43] that the cultural heritage of the African slaves was most strongly preserved in the Caribbean and Latin American areas such a speculation would clearly be in order. It would be further supported by noting Louise Little's dominance in the family and Earl Little's involvement and apparent fascination with things derived from that culture. (He was a Garveyite and married a West Indian.) The problem is, however, that there are too few cues in Malcolm's revelations around which to speculate. One can infer a more whole tradition of pride and integrity coming from the West Indian experience or a protective and innovation-producing marginality, but neither hypothesis would add much of significance to the analysis. One could go on to infinity listing those characteristics which made Malcolm Little different and unique yet more than such an index of phenomena we are searching for definitive explanations. We desire something which is more than simply a footnote to the basic proposition that this uniqueness in the individual is necessary but not sufficient in the presentiment of a charismatic leader. Having emerged from an alien or different cultural tradition is one means by which an individual may achieve societal marginality but alone it does not explain his emergence as a leader among other marginal men. Too many other options are accessible to him (defeat and acculturalization among them). Thousands of West Indian-bred Blacks have come to this country only to disappear. There are still the Nat Turners, Denmark Vesseys, Gabriel Prossers, and Martin Luther Kings to be explained who shared no such unique Caribbean-influenced socialization, yet were surely charismatic figures. The socialization factors which we are concerned with are more intimate, more individual.

Earl Little "was a Baptist minister," a dedicated organizer for Marcus Moziah Garvey's UNIA (Universal Negro Improvement Association): he, too, is described in the heroic-victim word pictures that Malcolm used for his mother. His shortened but intense, relationship with his son would set off for Malcolm a serial search and discovery which would never end. He was the child Malcolm's only respite in his turbulent first six years. He welcomed this son with open enthusiasm and a celebration that only this son could learn to find unacceptable:

Nearly all my whippings came from my mother. I've thought a lot about why. I actually believe that as anti-white as my father was, he was subconsciously so afflicted with the white man's brainwashing of Negroes that he inclined to favor the light ones, and I was his lightest child.[44]

With powerful men – Shorty, Bimbi, Elijah Muhammad, Dr. Mahoud Youssef Shawarbi, Abd ir-Rahman Azzam, Prince Faisal – Malcolm would reiterate his sense of having found a father and concomitantly his profound undeservedness. Of Elijah:

I stared at the great man who had taken the time to write to me when I was a convict who he knew nothing about ... I had more faith in Elijah Muhammad than I could ever have in any other man upon this earth ... And I worshipped him.[45]

With Dr. Azzam:

Each of them embraced me as though I were a long-lost child. I had never seen these men before in my life, and they treated me so good! I am going to tell you that I had never been so honored in my life, nor had I ever received such true hospitality ... Why, the man acted as if he were my father. His fatherly, scholarly speech. I *felt* like he was my father. He was, you could tell, a highly skilled diplomat.[46]

With Elijah Muhammad, Malcolm X had sought first a total, unrelenting kind of dependency. Muhammad was to be the perfect father, a man without imperfection. He would counsel and guide Malcolm Little into perfect submission, the perfect childhood. This meant that Malcolm X resisted and blocked out any experience which threatened to compromise his idealization. Submission, however, was an unnatural condition for Malcolm Little, and as he evolved into Malcolm X and became more convinced of his own competence, he needed less and less the authority figure he had chosen. The alienation of the two men became inevitable yet multifaceted. Muhammad was not capable of fulfilling the father-ideal any more than Malcolm Little could restrict himself to the role of dutiful son. Malcolm X at first suppressed in himself any acknowledgment of frailty in Elijah Muhammad but late in his ministry he would not only investigate and uncover compromising information but pledge his support to Mr. Muhammad's accusers. The corrosion of their relationship would be made manifest with these questions of Muhammad's sexual morality but would end with Malik accusing his once-revered leader of "religious fakery," questioning publicly the legitimacy even of his religious tenets. Malcolm Little had once again been abandoned and betrayed by the parental being.

Malcolm had experienced "abandonment" too often to accept his own worthiness. First, his own father (through his murder) and then in a seemingly endless parade, white society, hustler friends, and finally Elijah Muhammad (through his admitted corruption) betrayed and abandoned him. Yet his need for a father figure propelled him into one venture after another of total commitment without defense. Although Earl Little left to his son a bequest of revolutionary Black ideology which was acceptable to him, Malcolm was never reconciled with his violence and Christianity. Malcolm always remembered the brutality of his father toward his mother and spoke often with disdain of the hypocritical "jumping and shouting" Black congregations his father ministered to.

However, it was in his experience in Mason during his residence in the detention home there that Malcolm Little was finally to adopt the negative identity (what Erikson describes as "an identity which he has been warned *not* to become, which he can become only with a divided heart, but which he nevertheless finds himself compelled to become, protesting his wholeheartedness."[47]) which would characterize him for so many years. Malcolm had gone to Mason Jr. High School as an experiment. He was the first to do so from the detention home. He had excelled there as a student and was a "model" of rehabilitation. Along the way he had "integrated" himself cautiously but was popular with his white classmates (they elected him class president during the second semester of the seventh grade) and was beginning to trust himself. His experiences at Mason were gradually allowing young Malcolm to turn loose of the scarred image of himself which had been so systematically marked on him by his early familial and social experiences. His mother shying away from him because he was too fair, his father abandoning him with such vengeance after he had seduced the boy into loving him (for the child he had probably not simply been murdered but somehow was implicated in his own death), and white omniscient authority searching him out, indicting, and punishing him for being these experiences had stigmatized young Malcolm.

But at Mason, something very different was happening. He was being identified, *confirmed*, as someone quite different:

> "I'll never forget the day they elected me the class president. A girl named Audrey Slaugh, whose father owned a car repair shop, nominated me. And a boy named James Cotton seconded the nomination. The teacher asked me to leave the room while the class voted. When I returned I was the class president. I couldn't believe it."[48]

He was brought up sharply, however, by an interaction with a teacher whom he had come to admire. The teacher "advised" Malcolm with these remarks:

> "Malcolm, one of life's first needs is for us to be realistic. Don't misunderstand me, now. We all here like you, you know that. But you've got to be realistic about being a nigger. A lawyer – that's no realistic goal for a nigger. You need to think about something you *can* be. You're good with your hands making things ... Why don't you plan on carpentry?"[49]

Malcolm's reaction was:

> It was then that I began to change – inside. I drew away from white people. I came to class, and I answered when called upon. It became a physical strain simply to sit in Mr. Ostrowski's class. Where "nigger" had slipped off my back before, wherever I heard it now, I stopped and looked at whoever said it. And they looked surprised that I did.[50]

His next response was to travel to Boston and with quiet determination to mold himself into a hustler.

> The hustler, out there in the ghetto jungles, has less respect for the white power structure than any other Negro in North America. The ghetto hustler is internally restrained by nothing. He has no religion, no concept of morality, no civic responsibility, no fear – nothing.[51]

Without religion (that is godless), morality responsibility, and fear! What more contradictory and antagonistic role could Malcolm have chosen to that urged by his near-fundamentalist, Adventist mother, and his Christian minister father. Malcolm's naive trust and open love were now transformed into distrust and hatred. "Big Red!" what a shattering rebuke to his mother's teachings on color consciousness! "Satan!" Is there any more powerful antithesis to Christ?

It was not until prison that Malcolm Little would forge an identity which reconciled itself to the lives of his mother and father. But first he had to descend even further into his own personal hell and become Satan. His first year in prison consisted of drugs, solitary, and rebellion. His dank, foul cell, the intrusion of prison authority into every area of privacy, the impotence, and irrelevance of the concern offered by his family, his loneliness and rage, all contributed to the creation of the half-crazed, cursing, pacing animal called Satan. Malcolm plunged into the depths of desolation and hopelessness. But as it would always be, it was the word which first startled him and finally salvaged him from the bottomless inferno. The word came first in the form of an older fellow prisoner named Bimbi who possessed a following among prisoners, both Black and white, as well as a few guards. Bimbi possessed the word, he commanded other men's attention through rhetoric. For Satan this must have been startlingly familiar, addressing itself to someone worlds ago in his past:

> What fascinated me with him most of all was that he was the first man I had ever seen command total respect ... with his words. Bimbi seldom said much to me; he was gruff to individuals, but I sensed he liked me. What made me seek his friendship was when I heard him discuss religion.[52]

Malcolm identified closely with this man Bimbi and with his counsel and guidance – given in the abrupt fashion of men thrown into physical intimacy and who cover their subsequent role confusions with interactional brevity – Satan began the long journey to Malcolm X. He began to study and learn the use of language in imitation of Bimbi's didactic style. His apprenticeship went well.

Then, in 1948, he received a letter from his brother Reginald: "Malcolm, don't eat any more pork, and don't smoke any more cigarettes. I'll show you how to get out of prison."[53] Malcolm first thought it might be a "con," "shuck," or "a hype on the penal authorities."[54] But perhaps most significantly it too struck a responsive chord out of the young man's past. Had not these prescriptions, in detail, been those of his mother and her peculiar religion? Had he not heard his parents argue and fight countless times about this very same dietary law? Certainly, here was an entry for Malcolm back into the envelope of the loving, caring family, whole again! An escape from prison? It indeed was:

> It made me very proud, in some odd way. One of the universal images of the Negro, in prison and out, was that he couldn't do without pork. It made me feel good to see that my not eating it had especially startled the white convicts.[55]

Later, Malcolm X tells us that he realized that this was his "first pre-Islamic submission" – an unconscious act. Yet he was submitting to an even higher authority in his subconscious: the parental montage in Elijah Muhammad. Muhammad brought it all together. The sense of familial warmth and familiarity (the brotherhood); the deviltry of whites his mother had lived in; the churches of his parents; the Black consciousness of both parents; the "womanly" gentleness of the mother-ideal; the power of the father-ideal; and the acceptance that Malcolm Little so desperately craved. For Malcolm, the Muslim ideology put it all together again – it framed as he had not experienced it since his infant childhood, a coherence of a bewilderingly vicious universe.

> The white people I had known marched before my mind's eye. From the start of my life. The state white people always in our house after the other whites I didn't know had killed my father ... the white people who kept calling my mother "crazy" to her face and before me and my brothers and sisters, until she finally was taken off by white people to the Kalamazoo asylum ... the white judge and the others who had split up the children ... the Swerlins, the other whites around Mason ... white youngsters I was in school there with, and the teachers – the one who told me in the eighth grade to "be a carpenter" because thinking of being a lawyer was foolish for a Negro ... the judge who gave me ten years ... the prisoners I'd known, the guards and the officials ...[56]

Malcolm was humbled and "struck dumb" by what he learned from his brother Reginald and his sister Hilda concerning this new history. This "true knowledge" began driving a wedge between him and his satanic, roguish past. This true history rushed in like waves into Malcolm's brain, cleansing and tearing away those negative identities which he had constructed and clung to in desperation. He was "Paul on the road to Damascus ... in a daze."[57] Finally, he made his preparations and started off to the new world:

> I would sit in my room and stare. At the dining-room table, I would hardly eat, only drink the water. I nearly starved. Fellow inmates, concerned, and guards, apprehensive, asked what was wrong with me.[58]

His transformation was now confirmed in the eyes of his community.

THE MOMENT

When Malcolm Little emerged in this country as Minister Malcolm X, his impact derived from his acceptance among the migrant communes of the northern cities like Boston, Chicago, New York, Philadelphia, Los Angeles, known as Black ghettoes. Here, indeed, with the exception of a few ministers and ambiguously perceived politicians, lived a leaderless people. There were few national figures and none who were more than shallow symbols. The Garvey grandeur of the 1920s had been slowly corroded and finally displaced by figures like Jackie Robinson, Sugar Ray, Sugar Chile, and Joe Louis. Walter White (who was), Ralph Bunche, and Roy Wilkins were mere images speaking most directly to and for an acceleratingly emerging middle class whom E. Franklin Frazier captioned "the Black Bourgeoisie" ("White to the Blacks and Black to the Whites"). The distance between affluent Black and poor Blacks had increased following the Second World War to the point where their respective roles were parodies of the old house slave-field slave dichotomy of a century before. For the poor migrants unionism had failed, democracy had ignored them and racism had unabatingly been sustained as the supreme ethos of the land. The Black lower-class was still the actual lower caste. The promise of the preceding ten years had been political gamesmanship, the integration of the armed forces before and during the Korean War and the Supreme Court decision of 1954 were social caricatures. There was more poverty, more segregation, and more injustice than ever before following the Reconstruction period. There was anger, frustration but more importantly, an immobilizing defeat, and despair:

> A lot of times, when I'm working, I become as despondent as hell and I feel like crying. I'm not a man, none of us are men. I don't own anything. I'm not a man enough to own a store; none of us are.[59]
>
> The dark ghetto is institutionalized pathology; it is chronic perpetuating pathology; and it is the futile attempt by those with power to confine that pathology so as to prevent the spread of its contagion to the "larger community."[60]

And it was to these men and women and to this circumstance that Malcolm X appealed. His message was awe-inspiring and just as its light had blinded him with its same brilliance it lit the darkest recess of the ghetto experience. "The white man's heaven is the black man's hell."

> I want you, when you leave this room, to start to *see* all this whenever you see this devil white man. Oh, yes, he's a devil! I just want you to start watching him, in his places where he doesn't want you around; watch him reveling in his preciousness, and his exclusiveness, and his vanity, while he continues to subjugate you and me.
>
> Every time you see a white man, think about the devil you're seeing! Think of how it was on *your* slave foreparents' bloody sweaty backs that he *built* this empire that's today the richest of all nations – where his evil and his greed cause him to be hated around the world![61]

Freud, almost forty years earlier, had anticipated the psychology of a group similar to that of Malcolm's audiences:

> Inclined as it itself is to all extremes, a group can only be excited by an excessive stimulus. Anyone who wishes to produce an effect upon it needs no logical adjustment in his arguments; he must paint in the most forcible colors, he must exaggerate, and he must repeat the same thing again and again ...

What it demands of its heroed is strength, or even violence. It wants to be rules and oppressed and to fear its masters. Fundamentally it is entirely conservative, and it has a deep aversion from all innovations and advances and an unbounded respect for tradition ...

And, finally, groups have never thirsted after truth. They demand illusions, and cannot do without them. They constantly give what is unreal precedence over what is real; they are almost as strongly influenced by what is untrue as by what is true.[62]

Perhaps Freud was closer to a mob or crowd psychology than that which would most easily be identified with the group. Yet the spirit of his words clearly captures the mood of Malcolm's audiences, the structure of his logic, and the impact of his words. His words possessed the force and the certainty of a man in action. He cleaved the world in two and irresistibly and irrevocably closed the "lost-found nation" together. Black people were descendants of gods who themselves were Black. How could any force or anyone ever believe that they could remain apart from each other? In the end it would be as it was in the beginning: together! (The power surrounding the man is retained in films, records, transcribed speeches, and in the memories of those who saw him.) The response was tremendous. Thousands of Black men and women joined the temples (now mosques) in the large industrial cities of the north. In Malcolm's own estimation, the Nation itself went from 400 to 400,000 members in the twelve years of his ministry. But tens of thousands, Black and white, were galvanized by the man and his message:

Despite the fact that Malcolm began almost every sentence by saying, "The Honorable Elijah Muhammad teaches us that ..." the thousands who heard him speaking were fascinated by Malcolm, not by Elijah ... And it was at Yale that one white student cried out with guilt and jumped from a balcony while Malcolm spoke.[63] There was something about this man when he was in a room with people. He commanded the room, whoever else was present. Even out of doors; once I remember in Harlem he sat on a speaker's stand between Congressman Adam Clayton Powell and the former Manhattan Borough President Hulan Jack, and when the street rally was over the crowd focus was chiefly on Malcolm X.[64] Hundreds of Harlem Negroes had seen, and hundreds of thousands of them had later heard how we had shown that almost anything could be accomplished by black men who would face the white man without fear ... (This was during the time that the Deputy Chief Inspector at the 28th Precinct had said of me, "no one man should have that much power.")[65]

With good cause, he was described as "the only Negro in America who could either start a race riot – or stop one." (Malcolm X commented to Haley that he wasn't sure he would want to stop one.) As he was a man of tremendous energy and an insatiable reader, his wit and perception became increasingly acute until he could compete and parry with the best of scholars, debaters, and hecklers he encountered, whether on the streets or in the universities and colleges across the country. Even his death was marked by the force around him:

> "I don't know how I got up on the stage, but I threw myself down on who I thought was Malcolm – but it wasn't. I was willing to die for the man, I would have taken the bullets myself; then I saw Malcolm, and the firing had stopped, and I tried to give him artificial respiration."[66]

CONCLUSION

Yet as important as he was becoming to the lives of those before whom he spoke and for whom he spoke, they were assuming grander proportions in his life:

> Except for all-black audiences, I liked the college audiences best. The college sessions sometimes ran two to four hours – they often ran overtime. Challenges, queries, and criticisms were fired at me by the usually objective and always alive and searching minds of undergraduate and graduate students, and their faculties. The college sessions never failed to be exhilarating ... It was like being on a battlefield – with intellectual and philosophical bullets. It was an exciting battle with ideas.
>
> When I was in prison, I used to lie on my cell bunk – this would be especially when I was in solitary: what we convicts called "The Hole" – and I would picture myself talking to large crowds. I don't have any idea why such previsions came to me. But they did. To tell that to anyone then would have sounded crazy.[67]

Malcolm, then, needed them for they were the fulfillment of his vision. The tumult and excitement into which Malcolm X had succeeded in plunging the Muslim movement "confirmed" for him an identity which he could only fleetingly substantiate in private life:

> Stated another way, we Muslims regarded ourselves as moral and mental and spiritual examples for other black Americans ... I am telling the truth. I *loved* the Nation, and Mr. Muhammad. I *lived* for the Nation, and for Mr. Muhammad.[68]

Thus, for Malcolm X, his ministry and leadership became a style of life. The give and take, intellectually and emotionally, became a sustenance. He was always the master, the teacher, the listened-to, the seen, the hated one, the loved one. Though he was uncomfortable and insecure with his increasing importance in the eyes of the public (it is a possibility that he sought unconsciously to deflect fame onto Elijah Muhammad for other than ideological reasons, seeking, perhaps, a mechanism by which he could submit to his felt unworthiness without displaying it), it is obvious, too, that he was thoroughly committed to capturing and holding on to the public's attention. His public style brought him a fulfillment with which his private life could not compete. In private Malcolm X dared not tamper with the emotion or intensity of emotion which were his public sport. In the place of intimacy, Malcolm X substituted immediacy, closeness was replaced by control. He pursued his "battlefield" indefatigably in the years of his Muslim ministry consciously ignoring the administrative demands of his temple in Harlem to play for the drama of battle. When in the spring of 1964 events forced him to remove himself from the Nation, he would bitterly confide to Haley, "We had the best organization the black man's ever had – *niggers* ruined it!"[69] The bitterness of Malcolm X was understated for he clearly looked upon the Nation as his own creation despite his oft-repeated denials:

> I don't think there were more than 400 in the country when I joined, I really don't. They were mostly older people, and many of them couldn't even pronounce Mr. Muhammad's name, and he stayed mostly in the background.[70]

And as with the audiences, what the organization gave to Malcolm X was as immediate to his existence as that which he returned to it. The Nation allowed Malcolm to turn "passive into active," "to experience fate as something which he chose and in which he was active, even if this meant to have chosen or caused, invited or accepted annihilation or persecution and exile."[71] The Nation (and here is meant the ideology) transformed Malcolm Little: nigger into Malcolm X: descendant of Black gods. He could no longer be accused of being Black for he could now proclaim it. He was mascot no longer for a society ruled by powerful white figures but an emerging master reclaiming the heaven he had magnanimously relinquished (for a period) to the white devils. He, Malcolm X, an eighth grade educated Malcolm Little, could successfully match and checkmate the most powerful minds set against him. If not he could rage of the injustices committed here in the name of the Christian god until he stirred an immobilizing guilt in his antagonists. For those who had refused to acknowledge his existence, he could snatch the legitimacy from theirs. He could turn their hatred of him and the institutions by which they shamed him into fear of him. He had come "face to face" with his enemy and compelled him to acknowledge his existence by driving him before him in meek, groveling defeat. He could give no quarter for his existence was absolute in its Blackness just as his foes' was absolute in its demoniac whiteness. He forced them to declare themselves the personification of evil just as they had tried to make him believe of himself that he was manifestly unworthy. He had escaped their insane world with its insane "jumping and shouting" Christianity for the calm, self-possessing dignity of the Nation's rituals. The Nation restored to him family, literally and spiritually, with the same resoluteness which the devils had used to snatch it from him. This was the *Weltanshauung* that Malcolm X, in turn, sought to bring to his lost-found nation. In turn, he demanded from them an act which would close for eternity the dreadful turning of history against them: to become one.

NOTES

1. Malcolm X, *The Autobiography of Malcolm X*, Grove Press, New York, 1964, p. 403.
2. Erik H. Erikson, "On the Nature of Psycho-Historical Evidence: In Search of Gandhi," *Daedalus*, Summer 1968, p. 696.
3. Erik H. Erikson, "Gandhi's Autobiography: The Leader as a Child," *The American Scholar*, Autumn 1966, p. 635.
4. Erikson, "On the Nature of Psycho-Historical Evidence," p. 701.
5. Erik H. Erikson, *Insight and Responsibility*, W. W. Norton and Co., New York, 1964, p. 91.
6. Ibid., p. 90.
7. Alexander George, "Power as a Compensatory Value for Political Leaders," *Journal of Social Issues*, July, 1968, p. 29.
8. H. H. Gerth and C. Wright Mills, *From Max Weber: Essays in Sociology*, Oxford University, New York, 1958, p. 52.
9. Ann Ruth Willner, *Charismatic Political Leadership: A Theory*, Center of International Studies, Princeton University, May, 1968, p. 2.
10. Ibid., p. 4.
11. Thomas Kuhn, *The Structure of Scientific Revolutions*, University of Chicago, Chicago, 1962.
12. Willner, *Charismatic Political Leadership*, p. 7.
13. Sigmund Freud, *Group Psychology and the Analysis of the Ego*, Bantam Books, New York, 1960, p. 76.
14. Willner, *Charismatic Political Leadership*, p. 19.
15. Erik H. Erikson, *Young Man Luther*, W. W. Norton and Co., New York, 1958, p. 110.
16. Ibid., p. 22.
17. Erikson, *Insight and Responsibility*, p. 93.
18. Gerth and Mills, *From Max Weber*, p. 53.
19. Anthony Wallace, "Revitalization Movements," *American Anthropologist*, Vol. 58, 1956.
20. Malcolm X, *Autobiography*, p. xi.
21. Ibid., p. 286.
22. Ibid., p. 375–376.
23. Ibid., p. 386.
24. Ibid., p. 389.
25. Ibid., p. 390.
26. Ibid., p. 391.
27. George Breitman, *Malcolm X Speaks*, Grove Press, New York, 1965, p. 226.
28. Erikson, "On the Nature of Psycho-Historical Evidence," p. 698. It was suggested to me by Dr. Robert Dorn, a psychoanalyst teaching at UCLA, that the analytic method is unique because of the process between the analyst and analysand which sees the therapist become a focus for the patient's irrational feelings (transference). An alliance develops between patient and therapist. Dr. Dorn was suggesting that no such pact could be said to exist between a leader and his followers, a man and his biographer, or a man and himself as he writes out his thoughts and feelings. It is, of course, precisely the opposite that I am here suggesting. Let us first remember

Freud and his self-analysis as an occasion in which a man succeeded in creating an analytic relationship with himself. I am arguing also that there are indications that Haley was abused and loved by Malcolm Little in ways suggesting that he was more than biographer or friend (see the *Autobiography*, pp. 388–400). Anger and impatience with Haley was very often displacement, suspicion very often transference. There was too, shame, furtive deception, and honest love. Important, perhaps, too, Haley was several years Malcolm's senior in age, suggesting the possibility of a parental transference not uncharacteristic of Malcolm Little.

29. Malcolm X, *Autobiography*, p. 389.

30. Ibid., p. 2.

31. Ibid., p. 7. Although Malcolm X apparently associated light complexions among American Blacks with the houseslave, Uncle Tom, handkerchief head, integrationist motif (a consortium of attitudes traditional among Black rebels and strongly demonstrated in E. Franklin Frazier's analyses, e.g., *Black Bourgeoisie*), I believe that Malcolm X resolved the conflict about his own coloring by relying upon the uniquely contemporariness and violence associated with the story his mother retold to him about the violation of his grandmother. The story was apparently brutal and clear enough in its moral (the dissociation of the mother from any claim to whiteness) to serve Malcolm X for most of his life. Malcolm X continually referred to the "rapist blood within me ..." but never indicated that he felt it was anything more than an intrusion into his "natural" ancestral line. Thus he had no white lineal development.

32. *Ibid.*, p. 9. Malcolm Little would of course himself experience visions and presentiments of things to happen (p. 37). His conversion was invested with such experiences and he was more and more convinced of his early death by violence (see p. 138 of *Autobiography*). According to Wallace, "Revitalization Movements," visionary experiences are to be expected of revitalization movement leaders for they express a psychological need for justification and serve as precipitates to the act of mobilization for them. They mark the boundary between his own period of thrashing anguish and irresolute meanderings and the moment when he begins the gathering of followers. What is of significance here is that this was one source of Malcolm's self-realization of strangeness.

33. Ibid., p. 13.

34. Ibid., p. 21.

35. Ibid., p. 18.

36. Ibid., p. 393.

37. Ibid., p. 294.

38. Ibid., p. 295.

39. Ibid., p. 303.

40. Ibid., p. 8.

41. Ibid., p. 226.

42. Jessie Bernard, *Marriage and Family Among Negroes*, Prentice-Hall, New Jersey, 1966, pp. 145–149.

43. Melville Herskovits, *The Myth of the Negro Past*, Beason, Boston, 1941.

44. Malcolm X, *Autobiography*, p. 4. This is one element of the betrayal and abandonment that Malcolm Little must have felt. It is also a theme which recurs in his indictment of whites and his romanticization of the ghetto. Earl Little failed to recognize his son as an individual. Malcolm Little felt he was loved and hated not for himself but because of what he looked like. It was this failure to acknowledge the individual which is underscored by his interview with Mr. Ostrowski (see pp. 20 and 21 in the *Autobiography*) and his acceptance by Shorty and his other ghetto friends. Despite his appearance he was enveloped on the street by caring, nurturant figures (see chapter 3 of the *Autobiography*).

45. Ibid., pp. 198, 199, 196.

46. Ibid., pp. 332, 335.

47. Erikson, *Young Man Luther*, p. 102.

48. Malcolm X, *Autobiography*, p. 392.

49. Ibid., p. 36.

50. Ibid., p. 37.

51. Ibid., p. 311.
52. Ibid., p. 154.
53. Ibid., p. 155.
54. Ibid., p. 155.
55. Ibid., p. 156.
56. Ibid., p. 159.
57. Ibid., p. 163.
58. Ibid., p. 164.
59. Kenneth B. Clark, *Dark Ghetto*, Harper & Row, New York, 1965, p. 1.
60. Ibid., p. 81.
61. Malcolm X, *Autobiography*, p. 213.
62. Freud, *Group Psychology*, pp. 14–15, 16.
63. Louis E. Lomax, *To Kill a Black Man*, Holloway House, Los Angeles, 1968, p. 64.
64. Malcolm X, *Autobiography*, p. 397.
65. Ibid., p. 309.
66. Ibid., p. 435.
67. Ibid., pp. 282, 365.
68. Ibid., pp. 288, 292.
69. Ibid., p. 411.
70. Ibid., p. 410.
71. Erikson, *Insight and Responsibility*, p. 89.

CHAPTER 21

The Appropriation of Frantz Fanon

Frantz Fanon died on, reportedly, December 6, 1961.[1] His death has inspired claims and counterclaims to his legacy. Some detractors, indeed, in the name of dogma or even less attractive causes, have sought substantially to diminish his political history and contributions,[2] while, more recently, literary theorists like Edward Said, Henry Louis Gates Jr., Homi Bhabha, Abdul JanMohamed, Gayatri Chakravorty Spivak, and Benita Parry have implicated an imagined Fanon in their self-referential debates on colonial discourse.[3] Fanon's erasure in this deliberately exclusive academic terrain was inadvertently and succinctly conceded by Gates in an essay entitled "Critical Fanonism": "The course we've been plotting leads us, then, to what is, in part, Spivak's critique of Parry's critique of JanMohamed's critique of Bhabha's critique of Said's critique of colonial discourse."[4] Though, I am certain, there is much to challenge in Fanon's work, it is an ungracious conceit to employ him as merely a background device. This essay seeks to recenter Fanon in the current fashion of Fanon studies.

Fanon, the psychiatrist, revolutionary, and theorist, died of leukemia at the age of 36. In his short time, he had authored some of the most path-breaking liberationist social theory and penetrating analyses of the psycho-existential contradictions of colonialism. Drawing on his training and clinical practice as a psychiatrist, on his exposures to colonialism in the West Indies and Africa, a conflicted interval in metropolitan France, and, finally, on his familiarity with liberationist literatures and the Algerian revolutionary struggle, Fanon pioneered the psychological, social, and political investigation of anti-colonialism and what he took to be the "Negro." In this essay, I will attempt to explore two points: first, that Fanon in his revolutionary work mistook a racial subject for his own class – those he termed the "nationalist bourgeoisie"; and, secondly, of late, other representatives of that class have sought selectively to reappropriate and apportion Fanon for a post- or anti-revolutionary class-specific initiative.

THE NEGRO

A persuasive demonstration can be made that the political attributes and psychosexual characteristics which Fanon excavated and first attached to the colonized Negro were, in the light of the Algerian Revolution, eventually assigned by him to the nationalist bourgeoisie.

In *Black Skin, White Masks*,[5] written at the conclusion of his medical studies in France, Fanon dedicated himself to the "disalienation" of the Black man. More particularly, though many of his examples were Black Antilleans, Fanon was certain that his true subject (or patient) was the "colonized man," an essentially pathological personality.

White civilization and European culture have forced an existential deviation on the Negro. I shall demonstrate elsewhere that what is often called the Black soul is a white man's artifact.

> The educated Negro, slave of the spontaneous and cosmic Negro myth, feels at a given stage that his race no longer understands him ...
> ... rarely he wants to belong to his people. And it is with rage in his mouth and abandon in his heart that he buries himself in the vast black abyss ... [and] renounces the present and the future in the name of a mystical past.

Here we first encounter Fanon's antipathy to *négritude*, and are distressed by his drawing us somewhat furtively into an essentially petit-bourgeois discourse, but our more immediate concern is with his conflation of race, class, gender, and colonialism. Employing the rhetorical devices of a race discourse (e.g., "white civilization," "white man's artifact"), Fanon has for the moment abandoned his own project: "it is apparent to me that the effective disalienation of the black man entails an immediate recognition of social and economic realities. If there is an inferiority complex, it is the outcome of a double process: – primarily economic; – subsequently, internalisation ..." In his introduction, Fanon had insisted with unflinchingly male arrogance that "the black man must wage his war on both levels," but his subtextual opposition to *négritude* has drawn him, just three pages later, into prioritizing the derivative and psychological.

Furthermore, it too frequently seems of little importance to Fanon that the historical and psychological entity he sought to address slipped easily in his imagination from "the Negro" to the "Black man" to the "colonized man" to the "woman of color." At this moment of his development, however, his casualness concealed from him the specific class identity and desires of his informants.

Imitating the interior voices of his subject, Fanon recites that "the colonised is elevated above his jungle status in proportion to his adoption of the mother country's cultural standards." He then proceeds to discuss the pathetic importance attached to speaking French "correctly" ("In France one says, 'He talks like a book.' In Martinique, 'He talks like a white man'"). But, notwithstanding his observation that the colonial models which occupy the imaginations of his subjects are "his physicians, his department heads, his innumerable little functionaries," and that he is drawing on informants like M. Achille, a teacher at the Lycée du Parc in Lyon, and Aimé Césaire, the poet, playwright, and politician, Fanon appears oblivious to the petit-bourgeois fountain of these ambitions.

In his unsparing criticism of mulatto women, Fanon is similarly dazzled by color and his own weakness for the cultural discourses originating with his class. Though at times there is a suggestion of sympathy for his subjects – for example, when he writes that "all these frantic women of colour in quest of white men are waiting" – more often he seems outraged. For these women of color, Fanon reports:

> It is always essential to avoid falling back into the pit of niggerhood, and every woman in the Antilles, whether in a casual flirtation or in a serious affair, is determined to select the least black of the men … I know a great number of girls from Martinique, students in France, who admitted to me with complete candour – completely white candour – that they would find it impossible to marry Black men.

And in this chapter, he enlarges on the affidavits of these informants ("students in France") with the testimonies of a Black medical student, a customs inspector, of Mayotte Capecia, the self-consciously mulatto authoress of *Je suis Martiniquaise* and *La negresse blanche,* and Abdoulaye Sadji, an African novelist (*Nini*) and teacher. Fanon describes their behavior as "a kind of lactification" which inspires him to clinical invention. This particular Black neurosis, this "constellation of delirium," Fanon chooses to term "affective erethism." Jock McCulloch, in his study of Fanon's clinical and social theories, provides us with some sense of the seductiveness of Fanon's error:

> Affective erethism is the term Fanon coins to describe the massive sensitivity of the Negro. It is in response to this sensitivity that the Black man is drawn towards the white woman and the Black woman to the white man in a neurotic search for redemption. The gradation of Martiniquan society according to the varying tones of skin colour is the social corollary of this neurotic preoccupation with race.[6]

Once again, a class germinated and succored in a colonial web of power relations is concealed by a psychologistic discourse. Fanon even laments the absence of dream materials which prevents him from further individuating the unconscious!

Fanon had no such problem with the diseased libido of the Black male or "man of color." More certainly, he never complains of a dearth of materials. He begins his exposition with a confidently crafted interior monologue: "I marry white culture, white beauty, white whiteness. When my restless hands caress those white breasts, they grasp white civilisation and dignity and make them mine." And though his collection of informants is familiarly *classé* – Rene Maran's autobiographical novel, *Un homme pareil aux autres*, of an "extremely brown" but not Negro man ("You merely look like one"), "civilized students" – Fanon is ultimately displeased. Indeed, his displeasure is so acute that he moves to denounce himself:

> Just as there was a touch of fraud in trying to deduce from the behaviour of Nini and Mayotte Capecia a general law of the behaviour of the Black woman with the white man, there would be a similar lack of objectivity, I believe, in trying to extend the attitude of Veneuse [Maran's fictional alter-ego] to the man of colour as such.

It is at this juncture that Fanon confronts colonialism and his entire analysis ascends to a mytho-historical plane:

> In other words, I begin to suffer from not being a white man to the degree that the white man imposes discrimination on me, makes me a colonised native, robs me of all worth, all individuality, tells me that I am a parasite on the world, that I must bring myself as quickly as possible into step with the white world ... Then I will quite simply try to make myself white; that is, I will compel the white man to acknowledge that I am human.

And with the appearance of this heretofore hidden reality, *Black Skin, White Masks* sloughs off its petit-bourgeois stink: "the discoveries of Freud are of no use to us here ... the only masters are lies and demagogy." Fanon appeals to Pierre Naville's assertion that "it is the economic and social conditions of class conflicts that explain and determine the real conditions in which individual sexuality expresses itself."[7]

Lamentably, this was but an interlude. Without the experience or a consciousness of the history of liberation struggles, Fanon relapsed into the dependent discursive prism of his class: "Two centuries ago I was lost to humanity, I was a slave for ever. And then came men who said that it all had gone on far too long." This passive, grateful narrative of generous strangers is in stark contrast to the stance Fanon would assume just a few years later in *The Wretched of the Earth*. Following his immersion in the revolutionary consciousness of the Algerian peasantry, Fanon recited:

> At twelve or thirteen years of age the village children know the names of the old men who were in the last rising, and the dreams they dream ... are not those of money or of getting through their exams ... but dreams of identification with some rebel or another, the story of whose heroic death still today moves them to tears.[8]

In France, Fanon had rejected *négritude* as a fruitless nostalgia for a Black past. Enveloped in an intellectual mist manufactured by Black *évolués*, Fanon found their evocation of the past suffocating, and the quest for Black civilizations and cultures indulgent misdirection: "The discovery of the existence of a Negro civilisation in the fifteenth century confers no patent of humanity on me. Like it or not, the past can in no way guide me in the present situation."[9] And sympathetic as he was to the Vietnamese struggle for liberation, he appropriated it narcissistically and reimagined it for his own purposes: "It is not because the Indo-Chinese has discovered a culture of his own that he is in revolt. It is because 'quite simply' it was, in more than one way, becoming impossible for him to breathe." How terribly precious!

In Algeria, Fanon observed a differently constructed relationship to the past, and this new historical complex seems to have permitted him to submerge "the colonized Negro" of his French years into the cauldron of colonial political culture. The alienation, the racial envy, the compulsive acculturation, the moronic imitation, and the self-disgust which he had assigned to the colonized subject were really the characteristic apparel of a national bourgeoisie – "a bourgeoisie which is stupidly, contemptibly, cynically bourgeois," a bourgeoisie which "has totally assimilated colonialist thought in its most corrupt form."[10] Concealed during the pre-independence era, the national bourgeoisie's imaginary is unveiled once it acquires political power:

> By its laziness and will to imitation, it promotes the ingrafting and stiffening of racism which was characteristic of the colonial era. Thus it is by no means astonishing to hear in a country that calls itself African remarks which are neither more nor less than racist, and to observe the existence of paternalist behaviour which gives you the bitter impression that you are in Paris, Brussels, or London.
>
> In certain regions of Africa, drivelling paternalism with regard to the blacks and the loathsome idea derived from Western culture that the Black man is impervious to logic and the sciences reign in all their nakedness.[11]

It appears that Fanon has finally realized that the erethism, the lactification, the caressing of white breasts, the neurotic fears of niggerhood and the jungle were all merely circumstantial, occasioned by the racial artifice of the cautious master-exploiters of colonialism. The national bourgeoisie is not psychologically pathological, it is merely a class whose vocations are ambition, power, and greed.

And since, as a creature of colonialism, it has no prior existence, the national bourgeoisie, in its characteristically racial discursive practices, appropriates the histories of others: ordinarily its intelligentsia thinks in binaries of white civilization/Black primitivism, or, in rebellion, of Black civilization/ white claimants. As creatures of what Fanon termed "the organisation of the domination,"[12] they imitate the manichaeism of the hegemon's dominant culture, and rehearse the metropole's antecedent promenades of assimilation.[13]

RECOLONIZING FANON

Little if any of this Fanon, however, resurfaces in the present interrogations of colonial discourse. Small wonder, when we recall that Fanon's final prescription for the national bourgeoisie is "to repudiate its own nature." And he was quite specific:

> In an underdeveloped country an authentic national middle class ought to consider as its bounden duty to betray the calling fate has marked out for it, and to put itself to school with the people: in other words to put at the people's disposal the intellectual and technical capital that it has snatched when going through the colonial universities.[14]

While remaining alert to the snare inherent in the project, for the balance of this exercise, allow me to presume a parallel between Fanon's "underdeveloped country" and Blacks in America, between his "colonial universities" and those American institutions where the elite and their intermediaries have trained.

In his own recent ruminations on Fanon, the award-winning Black scholar, Henry Louis Gates Jr., uses his subject to question the need and the utility of a "grand, unified theory of oppression." Indeed, Gates concludes: "It's no longer any scandal that our own theoretical reflections must be as provisional, reactive, and local as the texts we reflect upon ... it requires a recognition that we, too, just as much as Fanon, may be fated to rehearse the agonisms of a culture that may never earn the title of *post*colonial."[15] Just how has Gates arrived at the certainty that Fanon has little to offer *all* victims of oppression? that theory is inevitably local? that, like Fanon's world, ours, too, is fated for permanent rupture and conflict?

At the outset (more accurately in the last note at the very end of the essay), Gates concedes a profoundly consequential flaw in his methodology: his comments refer only to *Black Skin, White Masks* since the paper was originally prepared for a Modern Language Association panel on "Race and psychoanalysis." That was disarming since, by the time I had come across this admission, I was already long prepared to make it central to a critical reading of the essay. This delayed admission then scrolls backward through the essay, insisting from the reader concession after concession. Does Gates really mean Fanon$_2$, whose last works may be "his most valuable contributions" or Fanon$_1$, the author of *Black Skin*? To which is Gates referring when he maintains that to "rehistoricize" Fanon "means not to elevate him above his localities of discourse as a transcultural, transhistorical Global Theorist, nor simply to cast him into battle, but recognize him as a battlefield in himself?"[16] It makes quite a difference since, if Gates is referring to Fanon$_2$, he is suggesting that we can dismiss Fanon's cruel critique of, and radical prescription for, the national bourgeoisie.

Again, if the mature Fanon is authentically local and provisional, then Fanon is no authority upon which to base an unease with national bourgeois intellectuals who engage in esoteric flights like Homi Bhabha's insistence that:

> The place of the Other must not be imaged as Fanon sometimes suggests as a fixed phenomenological point, opposed to the self, that represents a culturally alien consciousness. The Other must be seen as the necessary negation of a primordial identity – cultural or psychic – that introduces the system of differentiation which enables the "cultural" to be signified as a linguistic, symbolic, historic reality.[17]

Put simply, Bhabha is arguing that the Black (or Arab, Hindu, Oriental, native pre-American, etc.) imagined by whites is imaginary. They are merely useful devices for establishing European civilization as *the* civilization, European history as *universal* history. In not putting it simply, Bhabha has obscured Fanon's prior discovery of these truths (Fanon's critique of Freud, Marx, the psychological violence of colonialism, the cultural resources of anti-colonialism, etc.).[18] And, by employing a language game entirely inaccessible to most of us, he has blatantly violated Fanon's advice to the national bourgeoisie that it place its academic and technical skills at the people's disposal. Worse yet, as Abdul JanMohamed maintains, Bhabha has erased the violence, the exploitiveness, the reality of colonialism.[19] Of Bhabha's interpretation of Fanon, Benita Parry insists it "obscures Fanon's paradigm of the colonial condition as one of implacable enmity between native and invader, making armed opposition both a cathartic and a pragmatic necessity."[20]

As Gates acknowledges, Parry's Fanon is closer to the original. But he no sooner concedes this authenticity to Parry than he takes off toward its rhetorical and spiritual negation. Like John F. Kennedy, Gates seems too frequently persuaded by the most recent adviser through the door. At this juncture in the essay, it is Gayatri Spivak. And Gates' concession to Spivak reveals his most serious conceit.

Spivak resents Parry's retrieval of what Spivak terms "the native informant syndrome."

> When Benita Parry takes us – and by this I mean Homi Bhabha, Abdul JanMohamed, Gayatri Spivak – to task for not being able to listen to the natives or to let the native speak, she forgets that we are natives, too. We talk like Defoe's Friday, only much better.[21]

Gates is thrilled with Spivak's rejection of the "transparent 'real' voice of the native" which Spivak attributes to Parry. He enthuses: "I think this is an elegant reminder and safeguard against the sentimental romance of alterity. On the other hand, it still leaves space for some versions of Parry's critique ... There may well be something familiar about Spivak's insistence on the totalising embrace of colonial discourse, and Parry's unease with the insistence."[22]

And, having accomplished this miracle of reconciliation of contradictories, Gates is emboldened to conflate Fanon and Freud:

> When Fanon asserted that "only a psychoanalytical interpretation of the Black problem" could explain "the structure of the complex," he was perhaps only extending a line of Freud's ... [that] "Civilisation behaves toward sexuality as a people or a stratum of its population does which has subjected another one to its exploitation." Freud's pessimistic vision of "analysis interminable" would then refer us to a process of decolonization interminable. I spoke of this double session of paradigms, in which the Freudian mechanisms of psychic repression are set in relation to those of colonial repression; but it's still unclear whether we are to speak of convergence or mere parallelism.[23]

Here Gates compounds his negligence of Fanon$_2$, erases the contradictions and radical anticipations in Fanon$_1$, and, substituting Freud for Fanon, proceeds, through a metaphorical displacement of colonialist oppression by a therapeutic paradigm, to raise issue with the origins and purposes of the anti-colonial struggles.

The mature Fanon turned away from psychoanalysis and its preoccupation with sexuality as the explanatory paradigm for the "Black problem." Even the young Fanon, in *Black Skin*, displayed some deeper understanding of sexual repression and the rebounding dynamics of colonialism, implying neither convergence nor parallelism. Quoting a long passage from Aimé Césaire's *Discours sur le colonialisme* in *Black Skin*, Fanon recognized that eventually political and cultural repression (i.e., fascism) is transferred to the metropole because of its organization of colonial domination. Césaire's contempt for the metropole was palpable:

> And then, one lovely day, the middle class is brought up short by a staggering blow: The Gestapo are busy again ...
> ... It is savagery, the supreme savagery, it crowns, it epitomises the day-to-day savageries; yes, it is Nazism, but before they became its victims, they were its accomplices; that Nazism they tolerated before they succumbed to it, they exonerated it, they closed their eyes to it, they legitimated it because until then it had been employed only against non-European peoples ... it drips, it seeps, it wells from every crack in western Christian civilisation until it engulfs that civilisation in a bloody sea.[24]

Freud's myopia and Gates' confusions as to the origins of repression are their own. The mature Fanon was unambiguous: "when the native hears a speech about Western culture he pulls out his knife – or at least he makes sure it is within reach."[25] And the mature Fanon was equally clear about the dialectic of colonialism and liberation:

> The settler's work is to make even dreams of liberty impossible for the native. The native's work is to imagine all possible methods for destroying the settler ... for the colonised people this violence, because it constitutes their only work, invests their characters with positive and creative qualities.[26]

But in the academic terrain occupied by Gates and Spivak, the text is everything: "The Derridian *mot*, that there is nothing outside the text, is reprised as the argument that there is nothing outside (the discourse of) colonialism."[27] This is precisely the conceit to which I referred earlier. Thus, the search for the *real* Fanon takes Gates from interpretive text to the next text, from one clever exposition to its more clever critique.[28] Fanon is what occurs at whatever moment one intercepts the daisy-chain:

> If Said made of Fanon an advocate of post-postmodern counter-narratives of liberation; if JanMohamed made of Fanon a Manichaean theorist of colonialism as absolute negation; and if Bhabha cloned from Fanon's *theoria*, another Third World post-structuralist, Parry's Fanon (which I generally find persuasive) turns out to confirm her own rather optimistic vision of literature and social action.[29]

And since, for Gates, all these constructions of Fanon achieve an elegance of their own, "it may be a matter of judgment whether his writings are rife with contradiction or richly dialectical, polyvocal, and multivalent."[30] But on Gates' own claims of provisionality, from where would such a judgment originate? On what rules or laws, or accumulated experience, would it be based and evaluated? There is only the fascination of exposition. Though Fanon can never have the gravity due to the real, his reward is to become another of those intriguing texts. There is only the clever, the performative, and the elegant.

But let us be frank. Though Fanon is the signifier, the immediate objects of Gates and his fellow anti-Fanonists (Bhabha and Spivak) are Edward Said, Abdul JanMohamed, and Benita Parry. After all, Fanon is dead. But what threat, what offence are attached to Said, Parry and JanMohamed by the anti-Fanonists? What links Said, JanMohamed, and Parry, if not Fanon, or merely Fanon? If, as Madhava Prasad claims, their texts help constitute some "Fanonian tradition," the handling of that tradition makes it appear woefully mistaken if not harmless.[31] After all, how telling can a tradition be which cannot account for such things as the "incorporation of indigenous elites into the ruling consensus of the colonial state" or "the 'education' of the indigenous ruling groups in the working of the capitalist economy"?[32] Since Fanon did these things, indeed initiated his interrogation of colonialism at precisely the relationship between the apparatus of colonial racism and the native petit-bourgeoisie, there may be some question as to why Prasad assigns to him those who do not.

We can only speculate on the sources of the misdirection and concealment. Remember Said and Parry both are aggressive advocates of global theory and liberation. The one Palestinian and the other South African, they have each spent much of their lives involved in liberation movements, and not merely those which are their "own." With his study of the western "orientalist" discourses on Arab eroticism and Islamic inferiorization, Said forced this reality of bloody antagonism through the walls of the academy, and Parry has joined in the more recent inspection of academic radicalism. Prasad acknowledges that:

> Parry reads the poststructuralist privileging of "agonism and uncertainty" as a selective reading of the text that emphasises the "contemplative" mode while ignoring the uncompromising call to arms against colonial exploitation.[33]

Thus, in their attacks on the citadel we occupy and the costs our habitation sometimes incurred, they do sound like the Fanon whose attitude toward the colonized intellectual was rather extreme: "individuals without an anchor, without a horizon, colourless, stateless, rootless – a race of angels ... [who] cannot or will not make a choice."[34]

What Said, JanMohamed, and Parry now represent, and what Fanon once embodied, is the sustained attempt to locate and subsequently advertise a fixed and stable site of radical liberationist criticism and creativity.[35] Little of this project survives in a literature which posits a psycho-existential complicity between the colonized and the colonizers, which spatially and temporally domesticates all social theory, and whose mechanics recognize no voice more authentic than their own. Gates and his collaborators preserve and consume Fanon all in the same moment.

Sadly, for whatever reasons Gates requires an erasure of global theory, the project has the result of concealing the nature and possible destinies of the petit-bourgeoisie from Fanon's exposures. Fanon had made two critical correctives to class analyses of the modem world:

1. The social and cultural organization of colonial domination occurs through a racial discourse which is eventually appropriated by a native petit-bourgeoisie for its own purposes.
2. In the aftermath of an anti-colonial struggle, the petit-bourgeoisie, not the proletariat, is much more likely to inherit power from the metropole's bourgeoisie.[36]

Bound initially by the prism of his own class, Fanon had begun to imagine conceptually and theoretically the modern world outside the seductive deceits appropriated and enforced by his class. In light of the ferocious socialist orthodoxies of his day and place, Fanon (like Césaire) even had the temerity to suggest that material society (capitalism) could be profoundly (i.e., permanently) altered by ideas (racism). Analogous to Marx's proposition that, in the proletariat, the bourgeoisie had invented the instrument of its own destruction, Fanon and Césaire maintained that colonialist racialism, at the onset inspired by the material needs of capitalism, had disrupted bourgeois ideology and the modern world's social order. Still inhibited by the embedding of the European Enlightenment into their consciousness, they needed only to realize further that they were not faced with a rational order gone awry, but the exhaustion of a rationalist adventure in the wilderness of an irrational (i.e., racial) civilization. It seems more and more apparent that a metropolitan elite, whose domination and rule are increasingly disoriented by racialism, cannot hope to achieve a stable world order conspiring with a frenetic petit-bourgeois elite in the Third World. We shall have few occasions for such concerns or their implications if we are preoccupied with what he said she said.

NOTES

1. Officially, Fanon died of bronchial pneumonia, but some of the circumstances of his death (e.g., the roles of the CIA and State Department) remain disputed. Cf. Irene Gendzier, *Frantz Fanon: A Critical Study* (New York, 1973), pp. 195–196, 231–232; and Peter Geismar, *Frantz Fanon* (New York, 1971), pp. 143, 178.
2. Jack Woddis parries Fanon on behalf of Marxism in *New Theories of Revolution* (New York, 1972); and similarly for the inheritors of the Algerian National Liberation Front (FLN), see Mohamed el Mili's critique of the Fanon literature, Gendzier, *Frantz Fanon*, pp. 246–250.
3. Madhava Prasad, "The 'Other' worldliness of postcolonial discourse: a critique," *Critical Quarterly* (Vol. 34, No. 3, Autumn 1992), pp. 74–89.
4. Henry Louis Gates Jr., "Critical Fanonism," *Critical Inquiry* (Spring 1991), p. 465.
5. In the text, all references are to *Black Skin, White Masks* (New York, 1967).
6. Jock McCulloch, *Black Soul, White Artifact* (London, 1983), p. 66.
7. The excerpt is from Naville's *Psychologies, Marxisme, Materialisme* (Paris, 1948), p. 151. McCulloch (*Black Soul, White Artifact*, pp. 213–221) appropriately criticizes Fanon for failing to provide his own theory of the economic origins of colonialism in *Black Skins*, but mishandles Fanon's disagreements with Mannoni's *Prospero and Caliban* (New York, 1964), insisting that Fanon has not persuasively presented his case that Mannoni had produced an apologia for colonialism: "what evidence does Fanon produce to show the connection between economic institutions and racism?" (McCulloch, p. 216). Ironically, McCulloch later concedes the very bases for Fanon's accusations: "Fanon believes that by linking colonialism with certain qualities supposedly latent within the psyche of the Malagasy, Mannoni had played down the role of environmental factors in the development of the colonial personality ... Mannoni implies that the French presence is essential if there were to be any prospect of the Malagasy developing either socially or psychologically" (p. 220).
8. Fanon, *The Wretched of the Earth* (New York, 1968), p. 114.
9. *Black Skin*.
10. *Wretched of the Earth*.
11. Ibid.

12. "Colonialism is the organisation of the domination of a nation after military conquest." Fanon, "French intellectuals and democrats in the Algerian Revolution," in *Toward the African Revolution* (New York, 1967), p. 83. See also Cedric J. Robinson, "Fanon and the West: imperialism in the native imagination," *Africa and the World* (October 1987), p. 34.

13. For American examples of the powerless appropriating white race discourse as a means of identification with power, see David Roediger's *The Wages of Whiteness* (London, 1991) and Michael Rogin's "Black masks, White skin: consciousness of class and American national culture," *Radical History* (No. 54, 1992), for workers; and Neal Gabler's *An Empire of Their Own* (New York, 1988) and Michael Rogin's "Making America home: racial masquerade and ethnic assimilation in the transition to talking pictures," *Journal of American History* (No. 79, December 1992), for Jews.

14. *Wretched of the Earth.*

15. Gates, "Critical Fanonism," p. 470.

16. Ibid.

17. Bhabha's introduction to the 1986 edition of *Black Skin, White Masks*, quoted by Gates. Ibid., p. 461.

18. Above I have cited Fanon's dismissal of Freud. Of his many similar comments on Marxism, the following is illustrative: "In a colonial country, it used to be said, there is a community of interests between the colonised people and the working class of the colonialist country. The history of the wars of liberation waged by the colonised peoples is the history of the non-verification of this thesis." Fanon, French intellectuals, p. 82.

19. "Bhabha's unexamined conflation ['the unity of the colonial subject (both coloniser and colonised)'] allows him to circumvent entirely the dense history of the material conflict between Europeans and natives and to focus on colonial discourse as if it existed in a vacuum." Abdul JanMohamed, "The economy of Manichean allegory: the function of racial difference in colonialist literature," in Henry Louis Gates (ed.), "*Race,*" *Writing and Difference* (Chicago, 1986), p. 79.

20. Parry, "Problems in current theories of colonial discourse," *Oxford Literary Review* (No. 9, Winter 1987), p. 32, quoted by Gates, "Critical Fanonism," p. 464.

21. Maria Koundoura, "Naming Gayatri Spivak," *Stanford Humanities Review* (Spring 1989), pp. 91–92, quoted by Gates, "Critical Fanonism," p. 465.

22. Gates, "Critical Fanonism," p. 466.

23. Ibid., pp. 466–467.

24. Quoted in *Black Skin*, pp. 90–91.

25. *Wretched of the Earth*, p. 43.

26. Ibid., p. 93.

27. Gates, "Critical Fanonism," p. 466.

28. The worship of the text produces some bizarre moments. Recall that it was Spivak who, in her own defense, asserted her superiority as a native spokesperson over "Defoe's Friday," a fictional character!

29. Ibid., p. 465.

30. Ibid., p. 458.

31. According to Prasad, the ingredients of a Fanonian tradition are the "belief in the continued existence of the primary antagonism ... between coloniser and colonised," the "repressive hypothesis" of culture, a diminished capacity to recognize "the transformations in the global political economy," and an internationalist approach with a "tendency to treat cultural entities as existing prior to their encounter in the imperialist era. Globality ... [exists] between myriad discrete entities, rather than [being] a process which produces and transforms those entities." Prasad, "Other" worldliness of postcolonial discourse, pp. 87–88.

32. Ibid., p. 88.

33. Ibid., p. 79.

34. *Wretched of the Earth*, p. 218.

35. Roger Berger insists that "the significant division in African literary theory ... is to be found in what I shall call the Fanonist 'threshold' that divides 'accommodation' with existing western

textual strategies and rejection of Eurocentric methodologies in the search for an Afrocentric means of reading and understanding texts." "Contemporary Anglophone literary theory: the return of Fanon," *Research in African Literature* (Spring 1990), p. 142.

36. In the 1840s, Marx and Engels first sought to pin down the historical and political character of the petit-bourgeoisie and concluded that the class was, by its nature, reactionary. They also agreed that it was a class which would historically disappear into the proletariat. For a recent discussion, see Richard Hamilton, *The Bourgeois Epoch* (Chapel Hill, 1991), pp. 6–8.

CHAPTER 22

Amilcar Cabral and the Dialectic of Portuguese Colonialism

INTRODUCTION

In the early 1960s, Amilcar Cabral emerged from the national liberation struggle of the people of Guinea-Bissau and Cape Verde as one of the foremost revolutionary theorists in the world. With respect to Africa and the struggles against imperialism and neo-colonialism, his published thought was ranked with the works of Frantz Fanon, Julius Nyerere, Kwame Nkrumah, and Patrice Lumumba.[1] His work on revolutionary organization, on the systems and structures of imperialist exploitation, and on ideology and consciousness placed him in the forefront of radical thinkers in the twentieth century.

The circumstance of Cabral's work distinguished him from most of his African contemporaries in the post-Second World War period. The struggles in Guinea-Bissau, Mozambique, and Angola were not those of independence movements. To the contrary, like the earlier movement in Algeria, these were national liberation struggles which were consciously revolutionary. They sought not merely a national identity but more importantly the command of their national resources for all of their people. Cabral's part in his country's liberation has been put most simply by his comrade, Basil Davidson:[2]

> He raised an army, led and taught it how to fight, gave it detailed orders, supervised its every major action; but he did all this, by the habit of his practice, through a process of collective political discussion.

In addition to his roles as party organizer, commander of the army of liberation in Guinea-Bissau, and theorist of national liberation, Cabral became an international diplomat. In forums ranging from the United Nations General Assembly, the U.S., Congress, the Tricontinental Conference of Peoples of Asia, Africa and Latin America, the Frantz Fanon Center, the Institute of African Studies of the Soviet Academy of Sciences, the Conference of Non-Aligned

Countries, and the Organization of African Unity, Cabral spoke for his own people, the movements opposed to Portuguese imperialism elsewhere in Africa, and national liberation struggles the world over. He sought understanding, each time patiently explaining the tragedies of the world in which his nation existed; and he sought material and spiritual aid. From the moment on January 23, 1963 when the revolutionary movement of Guinea-Bissau and the Cape Verde struck its first official blow at Portuguese colonialism, to November 14, 1972, when the General Assembly of the U.N. recognized the African Party of Independence of Guinea-Bissau and the Cape Verde (PAIGC) as the sole representative of the people of Guinea-Bissau, Cabral was the indefatigable intruder at the threshold of international attention and opinion. Finally, on January 20, 1973, Portuguese fascism claimed a transitory victory: Cabral was assassinated. The revolution, however, had already been won.

The beginnings of Amilcar Cabral's life were as much implicated in the history of Portuguese colonialism in Africa as was the way he chose to live. In fact, one might say that the system of colonial domination historically determined the terms and the times to which Cabral was forced to respond. Moreover, he was one of those creatures – the assimilados – for whom Portuguese imperial authority had direct and conscious responsibility. In the colonial design, the *assimilados* were deliberately created to serve the Portuguese ruling class in the preservation of its system of domination and exploitation. Cabral would help to destroy that system. There was no particular irony in this, no reason for chroniclers to resort to the drama of human purpose betrayed by unanticipated and unintended deeds. Rather, Cabral's development was in the historical context of the almost inevitable collision of the contradictions of domination, the dialectic of imperialism. Profoundly influenced as he was by the peculiar system of human and material appropriation for which the Portuguese State assumed management, Cabral fought it in the armed struggles of his comrades in Guinea-Bissau, and more importantly (in his estimation), he exposed its character to the world, to his fellow Africans, and to the Portuguese people themselves. For these reasons, Cabral's life, his work, his thought form a tapestry of historical illustrations.

Cabral was born on September 12, 1924 at Bafata, a small town located at the confluence of the Colufe and Geba rivers in central Guine.[3] However, his parents, Juvenal Cabral and Dona Iva Pinhel Evora, were natives of Santiago, the largest island in the Cape Verde archipelago. Juvenal Cabral, as the names of his and his son's might imply, came from a family which had obtained elements of "classical culture" through Catholic education. Juvenal, indeed, was a school-master from a basically farming family which also "numbered teachers and priests."[4] Natives of Cape Verde, educated individuals living in a land in which even as late as the 1950 census only 2 percent of its half million people was classified as "civilized," the Cabral family bore the imprimatur of a most peculiar colonial history.

THE PORTUGUESE PRESENCE IN GUINE AND CAPE VERDE

In the mid-1920s when Cabral was born, Portuguese Guine was in the midst of the "final" phase of its colonization – what those who were to become the architects of Salazar's fascist *Novo Estado* (New State) described as "pacification." Though governments of Portugal had laid claim to some part of Guine from 1434 on, it had been only at the very end of this five-hundred-year period that Portuguese authority had been secured. In fact, in the fifteenth and sixteenth centuries, the early years of a European presence in West Africa, the obverse had been true: it was African authority which imposed itself on Portuguese traders in the form of taxes, trade, and travel restrictions.[5] Ultimately, the power relations between European imperialists and coastal African peoples began to be reversed. From the seventeenth century on, during those frequent moments when Portugal sought to realize actual sovereignty over the peoples of the area, African resistance had been persistent. Two-hundred years later, this was no less the case. The years of Cabral's childhood were scarred by recurrent campaigns of "pacification." There were several bases for this capacity of Africans to resist Portuguese ambitions in Guine for more than half a millennium.

Perhaps the most important were those which had produced of Guine a multiethnic region with a variety of political structures and economic systems. Historically, many of the peoples had been subjects of the old Sudanic empires, Ghana (fourth century to the eleventh century) and Mali (thirteenth century to seventeenth century). The rise and decline of these vast political entities had precipitated a series of counter-positions: the inventory of reactions among the African peasantry included flight, settlement, and relocation in some instances, cultural integration and resistance, political adaptation, and development in others. Meanwhile, Guine had become a region of multiples: multiple ethnic groups, multiple languages and cultures, multiple religions, multiple political systems, multiple economic structures. Its topography, too seemed to conspire in this diversity. Dominated by forests and intersected by rivers, the land had provided the sites of refuge for some, defensible space for more, while determining appropriate patterns of communication and trade. By the time that trade relations with the Portuguese began to develop in the late fifteenth century, systems of settlement and trade – and antagonisms – had been long established between the land's diverse peoples, the Felupe, Baiote, Banhum, Cassanga, Manjaco, Cobiana, Brame, Papel, Balanta, Bijago, Beafada, and Nulu on the coasts and near-hinterlands, the Mandinga and Pajadincas in the interior. Only the Fula who would occupy the eastern sections of Guine were yet to appear. By the eighteenth century, they too were in place, partially repopulating a territory upon which the Portuguese and Spanish Atlantic slave traders had preyed since the early 1500s. The sum of it all was that during the long centuries of Portuguese monarchies and the short-lived republic of the early twentieth century, the military commercial and administrative representatives of Portugal confronted a plurality of political cultural and social authorities and structures in Guine, many of them powerful enough to resist absorption into dependent relationships with indigenes or aliens.

In the early centuries, much of the hostility between Africans and Portuguese was centered around the terms of the slave trade. Separate wars were fought against the Portuguese by the Bijagos, the Papeis (sing. Pepel), the Mandingas, and detribalized slaves (grumetes[6]) in 1589, the 1620s, 1679, 1696, and 1697.[7] By the mid-eighteenth century, however, the purpose of African resistance had transferred from disputes concerning the slave trade to the opposition to conquest. For the next one-hundred and fifty years, the Portuguese as imperialists sought to discipline through war the militant states which the exchange of slaves for arms (and other goods) had done so much to develop.[8] Of this period, Basil Davidson observes:[9]

> In 1880-1882 there were campaigns against the Fula and the Beafada. In 1883–1885, the Portuguese tackled the Balante for the first time. Other campaigns followed against the Pepel (1886–1890), against the Fula at Gabu (1893), and Oinka (1897), the Bissagos (1902), the Manjak of Churo (1904–1906), the Mandinka of Bega (1907–1908), again against the Oinka (1910–1913), again against the Mandinka of Churo (1914), again against the Pepel (1915).

The most intensive campaigns of pacification were those of 1912–1925 conducted by Joao Teixeira Pinto and his Senegalese subordinate, Abdul Injai. These campaigns, however, were interrupted by Portuguese involvement in the "Great War" between the European nations, First World War. With the conclusion of this war, the "pacification" program in Guine continued, and from 1917 to 1936, the Bijagos, Papeis, and Mandingas bore the brunt of attacks from Portuguese imperial forces. For the next two decades, African resistance took the form of protest rather than armed struggle, converting sporting organizations and the only labor organization, the *Sindicato Nacional dos Empregados do Comercio e da Industria*, into proto-nationalist instruments.

In the Cape Verde islands, to which the Cabral family returned in the early 1930s, Portuguese imperialism had written a very different history. Originally, the archipelago (ten islands and several islets) had been unoccupied when first sighted by agents of the Portuguese crown in the 1450s and 1460s.[10] Situated in the Atlantic some 300 miles west of the African mainland, they were to become first a base for the trade between Europe and Africa, and ultimately once the New World was located, for the triangular trade. The islands were initially colonized by populations from both Europe – Portuguese, Genoese, Castilians, and Jews (once they were expelled from Spain),[11] and Africa – slave labor drawn

from the Balantas, the Papeis, and the Bijagos.[12] However, the redirection of
Portuguese and Spanish settlement to the New World in the early sixteenth
century was to change the social character of the islands dramatically. In the
seventeenth century, a mulatto population began to emerge, growing so rapidly
that by the middle of the century it numerically dominated the islands. Its
increase was further accelerated by the arrival of fugitives and renegades,
lancados the Portuguese called them, "men, that is who had 'gone in among' the
negroes, or had 'run away.'"[13] It was these *lancados* and their mulatto descendants
(*filhos da terra*) joined by a few officials and commercial agents who formed the
base of the scattered Portuguese or European settlements on the coast of the
mainland and upriver. Just as often, however, it was their corrupt trading
practices which precipitated the wars over trade and undermined Portuguese
domination of the exchange for slaves and gold.[14] On the islands, a plantation
system was introduced, developed by African and *mestizo* slave labor. However,
erratic rainfall, drought, poor soil, official neglect, and misadministration
limited productivity. For most of the first four-hundred years of their
colonization, the economy of the islands was dominated by their role as an
entrepot for the slaves trade to the Western Hemisphere (first to Mexico, and
finally to Peru and Brazil).[15] In the late nineteenth century, the decline of that
trade along with the recurrence of drought and famine, forced many Cape
Verdeans to emigrate. By the early twentieth century, sometimes aided by official
policy and design, Cape Verdeans could be found in substantial numbers in
Angola, Guine, Mozambique, and the Portuguese possessions in the Atlantic.
During this same period, many Cape Verdeans (especially from Brava) found
their way, through contract labor, to the U.S., working, for example, in the
cranberry farms in Massachusetts.[16]

ONE CONTRADICTION: BOURGEOISIE/PETITE-BOURGEOISIE

For most of the nineteenth century, the Portuguese bourgeoisie, which had
come to constitute the ruling class following the Napoleonic invasions and the
civil wars which had plagued Portugal for the first seventy years of that century,
was largely ambivalent about the African colonies. This was to change during
the final thirty years of the century. Spurred by the European "scramble for
Africa" in the 1880s and the emergence of an industrial and mercantile bourgeois
faction which tied its own development to protectionism, the dream of a vast
Portuguese empire was resurrected in the late nineteenth century:[17]

> Commercial and financial interests sought monopolies in the fields of transport
> and credit and favoured an induced re-routing of all colonial trade through the
> metropolis, whatever its final destination. The comprador bourgeoisie saw in the

colonies an opportunity to extend the field of its mediating functions for foreign capital. Lastly, the upper echelons of the state, army and church hierarchies viewed the colonies as a means of expanding career prospects.

Not wealthy enough in human or material resources to administer and develop its vast colonies in Mozambique, Angola, the "Coco islands" (Sao Tome, Principe), Guine, and the Cape Verdes, Portugal conceded monopolies to French and British capitalists. Portuguese monopolies, e.g., Banco Nacional Ultramarino (BNU), Campanhia Uniao Fabril (CUF), and the Companhia dos Diamantes de Angola (DIAMANG), however, were not neglected. BNU, founded in 1864 (it formed its first branch in Luanda, Angola in 1865), was to control all banking in Guine. For all the colonies, it served as the primary conduit of Portuguese and foreign capital investment. Its links with international finance included Credit Franco-Portugais, Comptoir National d'Escompte de Paris, Midland Bank Executor and Trustee Company, Westminster Bank Limited, and the Banco Hispano-Americano. With them, it integrated the interests of Portugal's powerful families and their multitude of agrarian, industrial, fiduciary, commercial, and extractive firms. CUF, founded in the early 1900s, is a near monopoly in Portugal with a conglomerate character, ranging from agriculture to textiles, copper, chemicals, steel, ship construction, and maritime carriers. A concern of the Melo family which is linked by marriage with the giants of Portuguese finance capital, the Champalimaud family, CUF brought French and West German (and concomitantly American) capital to Portugal's colonies and Portugal itself (for instance, Portugal's steel industry is, Gerard Chaliand asserts, "largely under West German control").[18] To administer the colonies, Portugal borrowed from the French the policy of "indirect rule": the employment of native authorities to manage and control the populace, and the formation of an *assimilado* class to man the civil administration, fill the ranks of noncommissioned officers, and perform the clerical duties associated with state and civilian enterprises.

The Cape Verdeans formed the largest single pool of *assimilados* (also referred to as *"civilizados"*). And while emigration to the colonies from Portugal was slight – it increased dramatically during and after the Second World War – Cape Verdeans could be found throughout "overseas" Portugal, dominating the thin strata of "civilized" natives. Cabral was one of these *assimilados*. His early education on Santiago and San Vincente was typical. Even when he secured a university scholarship to the Lisbon Higher Institute of Agronomy in 1945, it only marked him as one for whom a more advanced role in collaboration and cooptation was intended. Indeed, on the surface, Cabral seemed well along in the process of native petite-bourgeois development.[19]

There were, however, certain historical, ideological, and social conflicts which both Cabral and his generation were to confront. Ultimately, they were to prove to be significant in the transformation of at least some of the children of the colonial petite-bourgeoisie from collaborators to nationalists. For one (to be specific to the Cape Verdeans), the destructive character of Portuguese colonialism was given a most dramatic face in the years of Cabral's secondary schooling in the Cape Verdes and his training in Portugal. The islands had been again struck by drought and then famine during the years 1941–1948. Something like 50,000 Cape Verdeans were to die, more thousands to emigrate during this difficult period. Amilcar learned from his father, who had long questioned the entire agrarian system of the islands, that the catastrophy could be traced directly to agricultural techniques associated with cash crop production, the structure of large absentee landholdings, and lack of planning in irrigation and soil conservation. The island's corrupt and incompetent colonial administration, he added, as the protector of the system was directly responsible for these failures. It was, it appears, largely due to his father's influence that Cabral left for Lisbon in 1945 determined to be trained in agricultural (hydraulic) engineering.[20]

Lisbon too, had been for the moment affected by events of those years. The war had stimulated the development of anti-fascist movements especially among university students. Mario de Andrade, an Angolan, who first worked with Cabral in this period in Lisbon, recalled the significance of these movements for Carbal: "For a while (the Portuguese people) demonstrated openly. Repression speedily re-established 'order'. It was in this climate that Cabral became familiar with Portuguese resistance to Fascism. From his entry to the (Institute) he took part in the struggles for student demands."[21]

A third factor which was to have an immediate impact on the heirs of the native elite was the intensification of Portuguese colonialism proper. Following the end of the war, Portuguese emigration to the colonies – particularly Angola – was to greatly, increase. To some extent this new colonization proceeded directly from Portugal's war-time mobilization and military occupation of the colonies. But emigration was also an aspect of the plan for Portugal's post-war economic reconstruction. These colonials, of course displaced the African petite-bourgeoisie, transfiguring them into an increasingly redundant class, no longer comfortably distinct from the mass of the African populace. In the colonies, the parent generation of the petite-bourgeoisie could no longer readily justify itself nor avoid the conclusion that its situation would soon be untenable: it was being betrayed by its Portuguese masters and was obviously alienated from those it had managed, coerced and subsequently despised.[22] Cabral would write in 1966:[23]

> The colonial situation, which does not permit the development of a native pseudo-bourgeoisie and in which the popular masses do not generally reach the necessary level of political consciousness before the advent of the phenomenon of national liberation; offers the petty bourgeoisie the historical opportunity of leading the struggle against foreign domination, since by nature of its objective and subjective

position (higher standard of living than that of the masses more frequent contact with the agents of colonialism, and hence, more chances of being humiliated, higher level of education and political awareness, etc.) it is the stratum which most rapidly becomes aware of the need to free itself from foreign domination. This historical responsibility is assumed by the sector of the petty bourgeoisie which, in the colonial context, can be called *revolutionary*, while other sectors retain the doubts characteristic of these classes ...

The precision of Cabral's analysis not merely reflected his understanding of history, it was also the result of experience.

THE PETITE-BOURGEOISIE AND NATIONAL LIBERATION

The ideological history of the revolutionary sector of the petite-bourgeoisie of Portuguese Africa could be traced back quite directly to the second half of the nineteenth century. From 1870 to his death in 1890, the Angolan Joao de Fontes Pereira had in his writings challenged the foundations of Portuguese imperialism: its slavery, the hypocrisy of its "civilizing" mission, its racism, its administrative corruption and incompetence, and persistently, its discrimination against his class, "the sons of the colonies." Others followed Fontes in the first decades of the twentieth century. In Angola, Mozambique, and the Cape Verdes, petite-bourgeois nationalists continued their rhetorical offensives against the Portuguese state and its instruments, the colonists. Some of these reform nationalists went so far as to organize political parties such as the Liga Africana (1919) and the Partido National Africano (1921) in Angola. The reconstitution of the Portuguese Republic into the Estado Novo in 1926 by military coup put an end to such organizations. In post-war Lisbon, Luanda, Lorenzo Marques, and Bissau, however, nationalist elements among the petite-bourgeoisie once again emerged, encouraged by the revivification of anti-fascism in Portugal itself and the dynamic of historical events in the late 1940s. At first, their character was somewhat distinguished by the ideological weapons at their disposal. Viriato da Cruz, for instance, organized in 1948 a cultural journal, *Mensagem* (Message), which published emotionally nationalist poetry and literary essays challenging the "values of the West."[24]

In Lisbon, three African students residing at the Casa dos Estudantes do Imperio, Amilcar Cabral, Augustinho Neto, and Mario de Andrade, were allowed by state officials to organize a Center of African Studies. Neto, an Angolan, was in Lisbon studying medicine. He would within a decade become a leader of the Movimento Popular de Libertacao de Angola (MPLA) – Cabral was a co-founder – and ultimately become in 1975 head of the first independent government of Angola. Andrade, a literature student at the University of Lisbon (and later the Sorbonne in Paris), was also active in the anti-fascist movement in Portugal. Later he would head the MPLA while Neto was imprisoned by the authorities, and serve as the primary representative of all the Portuguese African national liberation movements in their attempts to secure support from the West (Sweden was the sole nation to respond). During the early l950s these three were joined in their work in Lisbon by Eduardo Mondlane and Marcellino dos Santos (both of Mozambique), Lucio Lara, Deolinda Rodrigues de Almeida (Angolan nationalists), and others.[25] Together, utilizing the short-lived Center and subsequent organizations, they set about the task of recreating themselves and establishing the political and ideological character of the national liberation movement(s) of Portuguese Africa:[26]

> ... this kernel of students in Portugal was engaged in feverish activity on two complementary levels. First came ideological and political training, extended into the absorption of knowledge in all fields, and the training was acquired in the crucible of more or less clandestine meetings, through reading Marxist works, or through personal contacts ... The second level of activity lay around the safeguarding of identity or to use Cabral's phrase the struggle for the "re-Africanization of minds." At the same time as this *group of students* became acutely conscious of their specific situation as assimilated and colonized persons, rationalized their feelings and searched for anchorage points in African culture to revive it, they were receptive to analogous experiences worked out in the universe of oppression ... the American *new negro* ... negritude.

So has written one of them, Mario de Andrade. It is he who has laid stress to the *collective* nature of their development.

Cabral, like the others, continued his professional training in Lisbon to its completion. In 1952, he returned to Guine. He and his comrades had concluded that Portuguese imperialism had to be ended but they had also been persuaded that the Marxism they had encountered in its theoretical and practical aspects in Portugal was inadequate to the task. They required further preparation, further development, further study. "The *political* plan was clear," Andrade writes. "But ... the social ground of the struggle" still had to be uncovered. Cabral's decision to return had been political:[27]

> So it is not by chance that I went to Guine. It was not material hardship ... Everything had been calculated, step by step. I had enormous potential for working in any of the other Portuguese colonies, or even in Portugal; I gave up a good position in the Lisbon agronomy centre ... It was thus to follow a calculation, the idea of doing something, to make a contribution to arousing the people for struggle against the Portuguese. And I did this from the first day I set foot in Guine.

He proceeded by employing his colonial post and his scientific training for this political purpose.

Cabral had been an outstanding student of agronomy in Portugal. He returned to Guine under contract to the Provincial Department for Agricultural and Forestry Services of Portuguese Guine, and during the next two years planned and executed the first agricultural census of the colony. The report published in 1956 remains the primary source on Guinean agriculture. Moreover, it provided Cabral with an acute understanding of the land's political economy: the derationalization of the country's economy by colonialism (he concluded only 12.21 percent of the surface area was under cultivation and that ground-nuts, a cash crop, Was transforming Guine into a monocrop economy); the techniques (slash/burn) and ethnic organization of land use ("only a quarter of the people) have almost the whole of the cultivated area" – the Balantes, the Fula, the Mandinga, and the Manjaco predominating) – all of which forged certain interdependencies (e.g., with the Fula) or hostilities (e.g., the Balantes) between the Africans of Guine and the Portuguese.[28] For his political purposes, he discovered that the Fula – Islamic, hierarchically organized and with their native authorities intimately linked to the colonial administration – were the least likely to serve as a base for the struggle, the Balantes – Islamized animists, he called them, "without any social stratification – the most likely." Later he would recall:[29]

> ... these groups without any defined organisation put up much more resistance against the Portuguese than the others and they have maintained intact their tradition of resistance to colonial penetration. This is the group that we found most ready to accept the idea of national liberation.

There were, however for the moment, other groups to which Cabral turned.

In the towns of Guine, Cabral, like his contemporary Frantz Fanon writing of Algeria, recognized two distinct groups: the African and the European, the native and the colonizer. Among the Africans, Cabral surmised three classes: the *petite-bourgeoisie* (civil servants, technical professionals, contract employees, small farmers, and the like); *wage-earners* (noncontract workers, domestic servants, factory, shop, transport, port, and farm workers); and finally the "declasses" which he divided into two categories: jobless country youths recently moved to the towns and living off their relatives, and beggars, prostitutes and the chronically unemployed. K. Opoku observes, "From Cabral's analysis of social structure, we notice that two classes, on which most analysis in modern political thought concentrates, the *bourgeoisie* and the proletariat, are missing."[30] But more of this momentarily. In his political work, Cabral first turned to his own class, the petite-bourgeoisie. "The majority took fright," Andrade tells us. Cabral however had some small success since Andrade adds, "Those rare few who responded positively were twenty years later to become the leaders of Guinea-Bissau and Cape Verde."[31] With this cadre, Cabral next sought for his revolutionary base among the wage-earners, working most closely with those workers at the experimental agricultural unit of Pessube Grange. But he was also attracting official attention:[32]

> Already in 1953 his "talking against Portuguese rule" had begun to cause him trouble with the authorities ... The governor at that time chanced to be a man of liberal inclinations. He called in Cabral and said to him, more or less in these words: "Look, never mind about my opinions. If you start making trouble for me, I shall jail you. Shut up, or leave the country."

Cabral accepted transfer back to Lisbon in 1954. The next year, he was reassigned to Africa, this time to Angola where he worked in sugar irrigation and soil studies in the Benguela district and elsewhere. For the next three years, he divided his time and energy between organizing and engineering, pursuing each in Angola, Portugal, and Guine (he was allowed to return once a year to visit his family).

The cadre which remained in Guine – including Aristides Pereira (now president of Cape Verdes), Luiz Cabral (Amilcar's brother and successor), and Abilio Duarte – continued to work focusing on wage-earners and the organization of a militant trade union, the clandestine Uniao Nacional des Trabalhadores da Guine (UNTG). Later, on September 19, 1956, during one of Cabral's authorized visits to Guine, the Cabral brothers, Pereira, Julio de Almeida, Elisce Turpin, and Fernando Fortes[33] met secretly to form the African Party of Independence (PAI). Three years later, the PAI would take its present name PAIGC, adding the initials of Guine and Cape Verdes to its acronym. But this was to come. Cabral in this meanwhile returned to Angola where he participated three months later in a similar meeting at which the MPLA took form. The PAI pressed on with its trade unionist tactic, organizing successful strikes among seamen by July 1959.

On August 3, 1959, the colonial administration struck back. It ordered its soldiers to fire on the workers striking at the Pidjiguiti quay near Bissau. Fifty were reportedly killed. Cabral would later write: "In the beginning, we thought it would be possible to fight in the towns, using the experiences of other countries, but that was a mistake. We tried strikes and demonstrations, but ... realized this would not work."[34] Cabral returned the next month to Guine and during the next several days, the PAI cadre, traumatized by the violence of the colonial administration's response, reviewed its entire political program:[35]

> Having reviewed these three past years of clandestine political work and analysed the political situation, the enlarged meeting of 19 September concluded, in the light of the Pidjiguiti experience and the nature of Portuguese colonialism that the only way to liberate the country is through struggle by all possible means including war.

Further, and just as momentous in its significance, the party decided to "without delay mobilize and organize the peasant masses who will be, as experience shows, the main force in the struggle for national liberation." The plan for the new mass movement continued, indicating that organization in the towns would remain underground, that unity was to be sought among "Africans of all ethnic groups, origins, and social strata," that larger cadres were to be developed in the country or abroad if necessary, emigres organized, and the general secretariat of Party would be transferred outside the country. Cabral took up residence in Conakry with other elements of the party secretariat. There they trained, recruited, organized, and prepared the cadres of the movement. For the next three years, this was the revolutionary project of the movement. And after several attempts to negotiate a peaceful withdrawal of the Portuguese from their land, the liberation movement moved to armed struggle. On January 23, 1963, the PAIGC attacked the military barracks at Tite.

In the previous year, 1962, while the PAIGC entered a preliminary guerrilla phase, engaging in sabotage of communications, transportation and the capturing of weapons from the Portuguese forces, Salazar's government increased the number of Portuguese troops in the country and began a campaign of destroying villages thought sympathetic to the national liberation movement. By 1963, the first year of open warfare, 10,000 Portuguese troops were in the country. Still the PAIGC claimed to have secured 15 percent of the countryside. In January of 1964, the Portuguese launched the largest counter-offensive to that date at Como island. After a seventy-five-day engagement, the Portuguese military, suffering severe losses and humiliation, cut off contact with the revolutionists. The Portuguese commander of the campaign committed suicide. In February of 1964, the first Congress of the PAIGC was held within Guine and a regular army was established of 900 soldiers. By 1965, the PAIGC claimed to have liberated 40 percent of the countryside and had initiated the establishment of People's Stores and a campaign to increase rice production in the secured areas. By 1966, with 50 percent of the interior in the hands of the revolutionary forces, and with 60 or more of the Portuguese fortified camps under attack at one time or another in the year and high casualties (1500–2000), the Portuguese military begins to emphasize the use of helicopters and other aircraft. In 1967, Portuguese casualties remain high (1905), and the PAIGC regular army absorbs the entirety of the guerrilla forces. In 1968, with 28,000 soldiers in the field, the Portuguese nevertheless move to aerial attacks and the use of chemical-biological warfare. In November 1970, desperate at this point, the Portuguese initiate the invasion of the former French Guinea, hoping to assassinate both that country's President, Sekou Toure, and Cabral. The plot fails and several members of the secret mission are captured and confess. In June of 1971, the PAIGC forces launch attacks on two major towns, Bissau and Bafata. While 30,000 Portuguese troops are in the country, the PAIGC organizes elections and establish[es] schools and hospitals in the liberated areas. In August 1971, the National Assembly of Guine is formed. In April 1972, the United Nations Special Mission travels to Guinea-Bissau and on the basis of its observations, declares that the Portuguese are no longer in control of the majority of the country. On November 14, the U.N. General Assembly votes to recognize the PAIGC as the sole, legitimate representative of the people of Guinea-Bissau. Cabral is assassinated in 1973. Guinea-Bissau becomes independent in September 1974. Through years of logistical preparation, training, and political and ideological education, the PAIGC had assumed its place in the history of African resistance to the Portuguese colonialism. Within six months of the beginning of the armed struggle, the movement controlled 15 percent of the country. Within seven years it had liberated two-thirds of the land and half the population. Within seven years, the nation of Guine was declared independent,

CABRAL'S REVOLUTIONARY THOUGHT

Cabral's development as a revolutionary theorist actually took place in these years. Events and experience compelled him to review the ideological and analytical tools with which he and his comrades had begun the struggle in order to survive. The practical experience of leading a struggle against Portuguese colonialism and its Western allies[36] brought to Cabral and the national liberation movement a clarity which transcended much of the preceding work concerned with revolution of this century. When he had finished, even the mechanics of the struggle had been overturned:[37]

> When, for instance, he was confronted with the mechanistic abstraction which argued that to wage a successful guerrilla warfare a country must be of a certain size so it could create a guerrilla base or *foco*, and further, that a mountainous topography provided the best setting for developing guerrilla warfare, he refused to be intimidated by such facile systematization ... he replied incontrovertibly, magnificently: "As for the mountains, we decided that our people had to take their place, since it would be impossible to develop our struggle otherwise. So our people are our mountains."

Cabral was not one easily persuaded by glib materialisms. At the beginning of his commitment to the liberation movement, Cabral's intellectual expression was prepossessed with the discourse and historical categories he had absorbed in Portugal from Portuguese radical Marxists.[38] This was only natural since it was in these terms – the critiques of capitalism and imperialism – that he and other Africans from the "overseas territories" had first discovered their common historical experience. Here also were the conceptual terms which had suggested the bonds between the working classes of Europe and Africa; and the language of international solidarity which punctuated efforts at practical support for the liberation movements in Africa. At this point in his development, Cabral could stridently assert the existence of an identity between imperialism and "the monopolistic stage of capitalism," or, just as unequivocally declare that "the October Revolution (was) the definitive implantation of socialism on one-sixth of the world's surface."[39] On occasion, in the early 1960s, Cabral could be just as cavalier with the history of the people of Guine: At least once he declared, "... the peasantry (of China) has a history of revolt, but this was not the case in Guinea."[40] However, the task before him and his comrades compelled their further development. As Richard Handyside has observed:[41]

> Guinea had none of the elements on which revolution in Europe and Asia had been based. There was no large proletariat, no developed working class, no large peasant mass deprived of land ... A successful revolutionary strategy for Guinea could not be based on any wholesale adoption of other revolutionary experience – what was needed was a strategy based on African conditions, on the conditions within Guinea itself.
>
> The historical and social materials immediately available to Guine's revolutionary intelligentsia conditioned the formulation of theory and program. Cabral would combine the development of revolutionary strategy and theory in his thought on the peasantry, on the culture of resistance, and on the national liberation movement.

In the very earliest texts, a certain gift for criticism, for reordering the presumptions of revolutionary theory to conform to the needs of his struggle could be observed in Cabral. In 1961, for example, he declared:[42]

> there can be no doubt that, even more than the class struggle in the capitalist countries and the antagonism between these countries and the socialist world, the liberation struggle of the colonial peoples is the essential characteristic, and we would say the prime motive force, of the advance of history in our times.

And regarding his own presumptions, he was no less critical. Following the early defeats of party work in the towns of Guine, Cabral and his colleagues came to recognize that their almost exclusive reliance on petite-bourgeois intelligentsia and urban wage-earners was mistaken and that the peasantry were the social base, the physical force of the revolution. But the peasantry, he believed, were not a revolutionary force as Fanon had surmised. The system of their exploitations was hidden from them by the mediation of traditional institutions of trade and social authority:[43]

> Among the Fula and Manjaco ... the broad mass who suffer in fact are at the bottom, tillers of the soil (the peasants). But there are many folk between them and

the Portuguese. They are used to suffering at the hands of their own folk, from the behaviour of their own folk.

The mobilization of the peasantry and their evolution into a revolutionary army would have to occur in three successive stages: political action, armed struggle, and national reconstruction. And for two years before taking to the field of armed struggle, Cabral and his colleagues engaged in preparatory political teaching in the countryside, training the revolutionary cadre which in its practice would help discover with the peasants the movement's "own formula for mobilizing for the struggle." Cabral recalled, "... we avoided all generalisations and pat phrases."[44] And in time, the peasants "came to understand that a tremendous amount of exploitation exists and that it is they themselves who pay for everything, even for the profits of the people living in the city."[45]

Cabral's attention to the less immediate but still profound aspect of revolutionary thought was just as constant, just as imaginative, and perhaps just as correct. Indeed, one of his most important contributions to revolutionary theory concerned the importance of history and culture in the projects of domination and liberation.

In colonialism (and neo-colonialism), he argued, domination takes the form of the appropriation of "the freedom of development of the national productive forces." This necessarily entails, as well the usurpation of a people's history since the mode of production, he continued, not class struggle, was the "principal factor in the history of any human group" (he would write: "(if) we can see that the existence of history before the class struggle is guaranteed, (we) avoid for some human groups is our countries ... the sad position of being peoples without any history"). The culture of the dominated is however less easily defeated or appropriated. It is the 'memory' of the historical development of the society, the dynamic synthesis ... developed and established by social conscience to resolve (the) conflicts at each stage of (the society's) evolution, in the search for survival and progress."[46] Culture contains, then, "the seed of opposition" which it is imperative for the security of colonialism to destroy. Cultural oppression, the denial of African culture, is consequently no aberration, no racial arrogance, but a necessity. Neither the British nor the French, the German nor the Spanish, the Belgian, Dutch, nor Portuguese imperialists had a choice in the matter short of the annihilation of the native population. All their acts of domination, whether in Asia, Africa, or the New World, compelled the attempt to suppress the native cultures.[47]

But cultural resistance of the African people was not destroyed. Repressed, persecuted, betrayed by some social groups who were in league with the colonialists, African culture survived all the storms taking refuge in the villages, in the forests, and in the spirit of the generations who were victims of colonialism.

In the process of this futile project, the colonial regimes created for this end and others the native petite-bourgeoisie, a deracinated, culturally alienated, and Westernized elite. The interests of these intelligentsia and their ruling classes, however, were not identical. Indeed, the interests of the two classes were opposed, each presuming for itself the right to exploit the masses to be a natural one. When inevitably the two classes clashed, as they did once again in the post-war period of Portuguese colonialism, rebellious elements of the petite-bourgeoisie had no political basis to which to turn except the people, and no ideological basis for rapprochement except that provided by the native culture. The more difficult the situation of the whole petite-bourgeoisie the more likely it was that nationalist and revolutionary nationalist elements would emerge from it. With this understanding, it becomes less possible for Cabral to overestimate the honesty of the petite-bourgeoisie as a class.

For Cabral, national liberation required the complete destruction of foreign domination. National liberation was the nation reclaiming its productive forces and its right, "the inalienable right of every people to have a history of its own." Having reacquired their freedom to choose the path of their development, the people of the nation were also responsible for the further development of their culture, integrating it with even the "positive accretion from the oppressor and other cultures." "No culture is a perfect, finished whole," Cabral warned, "Culture, like history, is an expanding and developing phenomenon." Further, he amended his remarks to a largely Black American student audience in 1970:[48]

> in the face of the vital need for progress, the following attitudes or behaviors will be no less harmful to Africa: indiscriminate compliments; systematic exaltation of virtues without condemning faults; blind acceptance of the values of the culture, without considering what presently or potentially regressive elements it contains; confusion between what is the expression of an objective and material historical reality and what appears to be a creation of the mind or the product of a peculiar temperament; absurd linking of artistic creations, whether good or not, with supposed racial characteristics; and finally, the non-scientific or a scientific critical appreciation of the cultural phenomenon.

He was not a man for compromise. "Tell no lies, claim no easy victories," he had told his PAIGC cadres in 1965.

To the petite-bourgeoisie of his own land, Cabral attempted to speak with comparable precision. In Havana in 1966, Cabral declared:[49]

> In order not to betray (the objectives of the national liberation), the petty-bourgeoisie has only one choice ... the revolutionary petty-bourgeoisie must be capable of committing suicide as a class in order to be reborn as revolutionary workers, completely identified with the deepest aspirations of the people to which they belong. This alternative – to betray the revolution or to commit suicide as a

class – constitutes the dilemma of the petty-bourgeoisie in the general framework of the national liberation struggle. The positive solution in favour of the revolution depends on what Fidel Castro recently correctly called *the development of revolutionary consciousness.*

The revolutionary petite-bourgeoisie were to be the ideological and political catalysts of the national liberation movement. Colonialism had halted the historical development of classes in Guine, resulting in the existence of no true proletariat. No factories, no centers of industrial production had arisen to expand and concentrate a proletarian class. In the absence of this social formation and in the face of the vulnerability of the towns to colonial violence, the revolutionary petite-bourgeoisie had to enlist the peasantry in the struggle. It could not accomplish this task without coming to terms with its class-specific tendency to evolve into a bourgeoisie. The revolutionary petite-bourgeoisie, itself emergent from the "reality of life in Guine," now had to choose between class illusion and national liberation. Only by arming itself with the resolve that its historical existence was transitory could it hope to succeed in the mobilization of the peasantry. The peasantry had only experienced its exploitation indirectly and was not inherently revolutionary. It would constitute the physical force of the struggle when the revolutionary petite-bourgeoisie had destroyed itself by becoming physically, ideologically, and politically integrated with it.

Cabral's revolutionary thought did not end with his considerations on history, class formation, revolutionary consciousness, national liberation, and the historical and political possibilities of the petite-bourgeoisie. Other matters pressed on him, forced by the practical considerations of maintaining and expanding the movement in Guine while securing for it broader international support. He spoke constantly to the Portuguese people, declaring that the opposition of his movement was not to them but to Portuguese colonialism. He carefully delineated the interrelationships between the nationalist liberation movements in the colonies and the struggle against dictatorship in Portugal. His teaching and practice proved his point. The struggle in Guine, as Cabral expected, spawned the revolutionary movement in Portugal. In April 1974, when the Portuguese military led the revolution against the dictatorship, many of its leaders were officers who had served in Guine. One was Major Otelo Saraiva de Carvalho, "the leader of the military planning group ... much influenced by the theories of guerrilla struggle in Guine where he had worked in psychological warfare."[50] Another, General Antonio de Spinola, who would head the first revolutionary government and whose book, *Portugal and the Future* (1974), first detailed for the Portuguese public the extent of the war and the fact that Portugal was losing it was the former governor and commander-in-chief of Guine, "... the actual 'Officers' Movement' was formed during July 1973 in Guinea-Bissau."[51]

Just as Cabral had predicted, the struggle against fascism of the Portuguese people advanced as Portugal's wars in Guine, Angola, and Mozambique compelled the Portuguese ruling class to reveal itself. As the "overseas" wars progressed, the Portuguese state began to exhaust its instruments of coercion at home and abroad. The military, which once reserved its officer corps for the sons of the ruling class *latifundia*, was forced to recruit officers from the universities and noncommissioned officers from the peasantry. It was these university-trained *milicianos* and their low-born and plebian mates who prosecuted the wars while the sons of the proper families secured military posts in Portugal or in headquarters far removed from the fighting. Saddled with an incompetent general staff whose class and racial arrogance shielded it from the realities of the wars (and the realization that they were being lost), weakened by official censorship at home which tended to demoralize a military without popular support, and threatened by the growing recognition that their professional military careers were limited by their social origins, the junior officers organized and rebelled. The Portuguese people, suddenly struck by the revelations of gross deceptions perpetuated on them and already conscious of their material, political, and social privations, responded. The coup of the Officer's Movement expanded into a democratic revolution. National liberation in Africa, following Cabral's sense of its dialectic, had precipitated the Portuguese revolution.[52]

In the field of armed struggle, Cabral's work was equally brilliant, perhaps even more so since the movement had to achieve unity amongst the myriad of social, ideological, and organizational questions extant in its social base, the peoples of Guine. We now have a better sense of these complexities with the publishing of Cabral's field notes, lectures, and seminars in *Unity and Struggle*. Cabral's records demonstrate his wit, for instance, in discussing the use of amulets by PAIGC soldiers (59–60), his severe disciplinary sense in dealing, for example, with the petty abuses of party leaders (93–98), his acutely analytical form when he reviewed Portuguese claims regarding PAIGC casualties and captured materials (191–194) and his patience in relating to elders (60). As it is the case the world over, organizations must transcend egoism, sexism, jealousies, regional and ethnic hostilities and suspicions, and dogmatism. The PAIGC was no exception and Cabral turned his attention many times to all these issues and others. He taught, he cajoled, he disciplined, and he demonstrated by his actions. These notes document Cabral's energies, his devotion to the struggle for national liberation, and everywhere the clarity of his vision.

It is now eight years since Cabral was struck down by the bullets of Portuguese agents. On that night, January 20, 1973, in Conakry, the Portuguese dictatorship sought to erase Cabral from the history of the struggle and thereby destroy the movement. But it was Cabral, not his assassins, who would have the final word:[53]

Nobody is indispensable in this struggle; we are all needed but nobody is indispensable. If someone has to go and goes away and then the struggle is paralysed, it is because the struggle was worthless. The only pride we have today, that I myself have, is the certainty that, after the work we have already done, if I were to go away, to be stopped, to die or disappear, there are those here in the Party who can carry on the Party's task. If this were not so, then what a disaster; we would have achieved nothing. For a man who has an achievement that only he can carry on has not yet done anything. An achievement is worthwhile to the extent that it is an achievement of many, and if there are many who can take it up and carry it on, even if one pair of hands is taken away.

POSTSCRIPT

On November 14, 1980, while this article was still in preparation, Major Joao Bernardo Vieira, the Prime Minister of Guinea-Bissau, affected a coup which removed the President, Luiz de Almeida Cabral, and many other senior members of the PAIGC from the government. The Lisbon-based reports on the coup which were repeated in most of the Western press ascribed the motives of Vieira and the army to "a long power struggle between the blacks of Guinea-Bissau and the mixed-race people from the Cape Verde Islands" and to the adoption of a new constitution a week prior to the coup which "eliminated the powers of the Prime Minister."[54] Not one of these reports alluded to the drought which since 1977 had reduced Guinea-Bissau from near self-sufficiency in rice and maize production to the import of more than 70,000 tons of rice this years; the mismanagement of the People's Stores which has resulted in severe shortages in fabrics and other basic commodities in the south and center of the country; the failure of Luize Cabral's government to construct an appropriate transportation infrastructure to integrate the country's economy, nor its misuse of foreign aid. Again, not one of these reports noted Vieira's promise:[55]

to check the accumulation of wealth and luxury goods by party and government officials and to return to the more spartan and politically dedicated style of leadership which characterised the PAIGC during the war.

On the other hand, Amilcar Cabral, sixteen years earlier, had confronted the issue of Guinea-Bissau after the war of liberation and had made these observations:[56]

we come to the conclusion that in colonial conditions it is the petty bourgeoisie which is the inheritor of state power (though I wish we could be wrong). The moment national liberation comes and the petty bourgeoisie takes power we enter, or rather return to history, and thus the internal contradictions break out again. ...

The petty bourgeoisie can either ally itself with imperialism and the reactionary strata in its own country to try and preserve itself as a petty bourgeoisie or ally itself with the workers and peasants ... to hope that the petty bourgeoisie will just carry out a revolution when it comes to power in an underdeveloped country is to hope for a miracle, although it is true that it *could* do this.

Cabral went on to remind his audience that the "right of all peoples to national independence" as the "judicial institution" of reference for national liberation struggles was an "imperialist initiative" designed to "create a bourgeoisie where one did not exist, in order specifically to strengthen the imperialist and the capitalist camp." He also warned the (European) Left of a tendency for quick criticism of Third World movements when the Left itself had retreated from revolution, had developed certain apathies, and been the subject of false hopes. His proscription for the tendency is instructive:[57]

the European left has an intellectual responsibility to study the concrete conditions in our country and help us in this way, as we have very little documentation, very few intellectuals, very little chance to do this kind of work ourselves, and yet it is of key importance: this is a major contribution you can make.

The revolutionary struggle continues for the people of Guinea-Bissau and Joao Vieira, the "bush" general who heads the new Revolutionary Council. The "rice coup," as it is apparently known in Bissau, has no precedent in modern African history. Though the people of Guinea-Bissau have once again disappeared from the front pages of the Western press, their struggle remains a centerpiece for Africa, the Third World and the forces of liberation the world over.

NOTES

1. For English readers, the most ready access to Cabral's thought are the several collections of his lectures, papers, party directives and field notes; see Amilcar Cabral, *Revolution in Guinea* (Monthly Review Press, New York, 1969); *idem., Return to the Source* (African Information Service, New York, 1973), and *idem., Unity and Struggle* (Heinemann, London, 1980).
2. Basil Davidson's introduction to Amilcar Cabral's *Unity and Struggle*, p. xvi.
3. The best and most recent English-language biography of Cabral is the essay by Mario de Andrade in the collection of Cabral's essays, *Unity and Struggle*, pp. xviii–xxxv. There are shorter and less intimate treatments in Gerard Chaliand's *Armed Struggle in Africa* (Monthly Review, New York, 1969); Basil Davidson's *In the Eye of the Storm: Angola's People* (Anchor, Garden City, 1973), and his *Liberation of Guine* (Penguin, London, 1969). Andrade has also published this year a full-length biography of Cabral, in French, *Amilcar Cabral* (Maspero, Paris, 1980).
4. Andrade, *Amilcar Cabral*, pp. xviii–xix; and K. Opoku, "Cabral and the African Revolution," *Presence African*, Vol. 105–106, p. 56.
5. Ronald Chilcote, *Portuguese Africa* (Prentice-Hall, Edgewood Cliffs, 1967), pp. 83–104.
6. Chilcote presumes that the term grumetes can be used interchangeably with the phrase "Christianized Africans" (*Portuguese Africa*, pp. 87–88); Walter Rodney provides a more precise

(and different) significance to the term: "... private European traders also owned slaves on the coast ... The practice probably began with the arrival of Portuguese ships in the fifteenth century, giving rise to the term *grumete* ('sailor's slave')." Rodney, "African Slavery and Other Forms of Social Oppression on the Upper Guinea Coast in the Context of the Atlantic Slave-Trade," *Journal of African History*, Vol. XII, 3, 1966, p. 438.

7. In 1589, the Papeis attacked the fort at Cacheu once it became clear to them that the Portuguese traders who had the stockade built meant to use it as a defense against the imposition of Papeis authority. In the 1620s, the Bijagos islanders repeatedly attacked Guinala, a slave port on the Ria Grande de Buba. In the 1640 and 1679 Cacheu was again a point of contention for the Papeis; in the latter instance a short war broke out when Portuguese officials and traders were accused of discriminating against their African partners. In 1696, Bibiana Vaz, a *grumete*, led a revolt in order to open trade with English and French merchants. In 1697, the Papeis continued their long period of Warfare against the Portuguese around trade restrictions and abuses in the slave trade. In the same year, the Mandingas fought to expel Europeans from Farim in northern Guine. See Chilcote, *Portuguese Africa*, pp. 93–94; and Walter Rodney, "Portuguese Attempts at Monopoly on the Upper Guinea Coast, 1580–1650," *Journal of African History*, Vol. VI, 3, 1965, pp. 307–322.

8. In 1753, the Papeis again were fighting the Portuguese, this time at Bissau. In 1792, the Bijagos attacked an English settlement at Bolama. From May 1824 to December 1825, the Papeis fought the Portuguese at Cacheu. There were three separate uprisings of the Papeis at Bissau between 1842 and 1846. Again, in 1846, the Mandingas revolted at Farim; in 1855, they attacked Geba. In 1871, the governor of Bissau was assassinated. In December 1878, the Felupes massacred a Portuguese military force near the Bolor River. See Chilcote, *Portuguese Africa*, pp. 94–95.

9. Davidson, *Liberation*, pp. 22–23.

10. Charles Verlinden, "Antonio da Noli and the Colonization of the Cape Verde Islands," in his *The Beginnings of Modern Colonization* (Cornell, Ithaca, 1970), pp. 79–97.

11. John William Blake, *Europeans in West Africa, 1450–1560*, Vol. I (Hakluyt Society, London, 1942), p. 27.

12. Chilcote, *Portuguese Africa*, pp. 90–91.

13. Blake, *Europeans in West Africa*, pp. 28–29; Rodney, "Portuguese Attempts," p. 320.

14. Ibid., and C. R. Boxer, *Four Centuries of Portuguese Expansion, 1415–1825* (Witwatersrand University, Johannesburg, 1971), pp. 24–25.

15. Philip Curtin, *The Atlantic Slave Trade* (University of Wisconsin, Madison, 1969), pp. 96–100.

16. Salahudin Omowale Matteos interview, "The Cape Verdeans and the PAIGC Struggle for National Liberation," *Ufahamu*, Vol. III, 3, Winter 1973, pp. 43–48.

17. W. G. Clarence-Smith, "The Myth of Uneconomic Imperialism: The Portuguese in Angola, 1826–1926," *Journal of Southern African Studies*, Vol. 5, 2 April 1979, p. 172. For the view that the Portuguese commitment to colonialism was fundamentally ideological rather than economic, see Thomas Henriksen, "Portugal in Africa: A Noneconomic Interpretation," *African Studies Review*, Vol. XVI, 3, December 1973, pp. 405–416.

18. See Chaliand, *Armed Struggle in Africa*, appendix.

19. In 1960 only eleven Africans from Guine had received graduate training. See Davidson, *Liberation*, p. 28.

20. Andrade, *Amilcar Cabral*, pp. xix–xx.

21. Ibid., p. xx.

22. Opoku, "Cabral and the African Revolution," p. 57. For a more general discussion of the native petite-bourgeoisie and its relationship to colonialism, neo-colonialism, see Arif Hussain, "The Educated Elite: Collaborators, Assailants, Nationalists," *Journal of the Historical Society of Nigeria*, Vol. VII, 3, December 1974, pp. 485–497.

23. Cabral, "The Weapon of Theory," in his *Revolution in Guinea* (Monthly Review, New York, 1969), pp. 108–109.

24. Davidson, *Eye of the Storm*, pp. 138–153.

25. Ibid., pp. 151–156.

26. Andrade, *Amilcar Cabral*, pp. xxiii–xxiv.

27. Ibid., p. xxv.

28. Cabral, "Agricultural Census in Guine," in *Unity and Struggle*, pp. 4–16.
29. Cabral, "A Brief Analysis of the Social Structure in Guinea," in *Revolution in Guinea*, p. 61.
30. Opoku, "Cabral and the African Revolution," p. 47.
31. Andrade, *Amilcar Cabral*, p. xxv. A nationalist petite-bourgeoisie, opposed to the PAIGC and with varying link with the Portuguese, did develop. Among the militant nationalists, some chose to participate with the Portuguese military in the struggle against the revolution. Others, and specifically the nationalist exiles residing in Senegal, organized into a Front which consistently collaborated with the Portuguese authorities; "In response to Cabral and the PAIGC ... they established their own movement based in Senegal and led by clearly identified traditional ethnic leaders and members of the urban elite who had broken with Cabral and his more radical vision ... In fact, this movement began as several parties, each with a purely ethnic base. These three parties were the largely Manjaco-based Movimento de Libertacao da Guine, the Fula-led and oriented Uniao Democratica da Guine, and the Mandinga Rassemblement Democratique de Guinee ... There was also a number of small groups founded by members of the commercial-civil service elite ... in 1962 (they) came together to found a common front ... the Frente de Luta Pela Independencia Nacional de Guinea-Bissau (FLING) ..." (Judson Lyon, "Marxism and Ethno-Nationalism in Guinea-Bissau, 1956–76," *Ethnic and Racial Studies*, Vol. 3, 2, April 1980, p. 160) Lyon's article makes the case that Cabral, "like almost all liberationists," was "blind ... to the strength of ethnic attachments" and failed to come to terms with "ethnic attachments," and failed to come to terms with "ethno-nationalism." Lyon contrasts what he takes as the PAIGC's doctrinaire importance with the "success" of FLING. He admits, though, that "FLING did nothing at all after 1963 except tend to the needs of the refugees in Senegal" (161).
32. Davidson, *Liberation*, pp. 30–31.
33. Rafael Barbosa, a former president of the PAIGC in the earliest period, is mentioned as belonging to this group by Richard Gibson (*African Liberation Movements*, Oxford University, 1972, p. 253). Gibson, apparently basing his report on American intelligence sources is contradicted by Andrade. Andrade, however, may have expunged Barbosa's name from those of founders because Barbosa defected to the Portuguese in 1969 after seven years of imprisonment (and, Gibson suggests torture).
34. David A. Andelman, "Profile: Amilcar Cabral," *Africa Report*, May l970, p. 19, cited by Report Blackey, "Fanon and Cabral: A Contrast in Theories of Revolution in Africa," *Journal of Modern African Studies*, Vol. 12, 2, 1974, p. 193.
35. Davidson, *Liberation*, p. 32.
36. The U.S. was a major contributor to the Portuguese war effort through the aid supplied by Congress and the Nixon-Kissinger administration. See Roger Morris, *Uncertain Greatness* (Harper & Row, New York, 1977), pp. 107–114; "Reagan's Kissinger: Richard Allen," *Wall Street Journal*, October 28, 1980, pp. 1 and 20; and Cabral's remarks, "The Eighth Year of Armed Struggle for National Liberation," in *Unity and Struggle*, pp. 124–125.
37. Azinna Nwafor, "Imperialism and Revolution in Africa," *Monthly Review*, April 1975, p. 30, and also Bernard Magubane, "Amilcar Cabral: Evolution of Revolutionary Thought," *Ufahamu*, Vol. 11, 2, Fall 1971, pp. 31–37.
38. Thomas Henriksen, "People's War in Angola' Mozambique, and Guinea-Bissau," *Journal of Modern African Studies*, 14, 3, September 1976, pp. 391–392.
39. Cabral, "Guinea and Cabo Verde Against Portuguese Colonialism," in *Revolution in Guinea*, p. 13.
40. Cabral, "Brief Analysis of the Social Structure in Guinea." Ibid., p. 61.
41. Handyside, "Introduction." Ibid., pp. 7–8.
42. Cabral, "Guinea and Cabo Verde," p. 14.
43. Cabral, "Unity and Struggle," in *Unity and Struggle*, p. 38.
44. Cabral, "Towards Final Victory," in The *Revolution in Guinea*, p. 159. Cabral wrote: "Remember always that the people do not fight for ideas, for things that only exist in the heads of individuals. The people fight and they accept the necessary sacrifices. But they do it in order to gain material advantages, to live in peace and to improve their lives, to experience progress, and to be able to guarantee a future to their children." Cited in Henriksen, "People's War in Angola," p. 381.

45. Cabral, Towards Final Victory, pp. 159–160.
46. The longer quote is from "The Weapon of Theory," pp. 95–96. Cabral's argument is developed there and elsewhere, especially in the essay "National Liberation and Culture," in Cabral's *Return to the Source*, PAIGC, 1973.
47. Cabral, "National Liberation," pp. 42–49.
48. Ibid., p. 51.
49. "The Weapon of Theory," p. 110. See also Henry Bienen, "State and Revolution: The Work of Arnilcar Cabral," *Journal of Modern African Studies*, Vol. 15, 4, December 1977, pp. 560–565.
50. Kenneth Maxwell, "The Communists and the Portuguese Revolution," *Dissent*, Spring 1980, p. 196.
51. Michael Harscor, *Portugal in Revolution* (Sage, Beverly Hills 1976), p. 15. For Spinola, see "A Soldier Dissents: Portugal Cannot Win in Africa," *Africa Report*, March–April 1974, pp. 37–39.
52. Kenneth Maxwell, "Portugal Under Pressure," *New York Review of Books*, Vol. XXII, 9, May 29, 1975, pp. 20–30.
53. Cabral, "Revolutionary Democracy," in *Unity and Struggle*, p. 96.
54. "Guinea-Bissau Coup Leaders to Try Cabral," *Africa Report*, January–February, 1981, p. 24; this report is a compilation of those which originally appeared in the *New York Times* (November 17, 23 and 28, 1980), the *London Times* (November 18 and 24, 1980), the *Economist* (November 22, 1980), and the London *Guardian* (November 17, 1980).
55. See Patrick Chabal's, "Coup for Continuity?," *West Africa*, January 12, 1981, pp. 52–53.
56. Cabral, "Brief Analysis of the Social Structure," pp. 69–70.
57. Ibid., p. 74.

CHAPTER 23

Race, Capitalism, and the Anti-democracy

The fear was of a Mandingo sexual encounter.
— *Sergeant Stacey Koon*

I don't want to see any white people today.
— *Herman Collins*

In the third year of the reign of King George of Avarice, under the authority of law, a high-tech Los Angeles police mob formed, and with due deliberation, secure in its corporate habits of mind and the perverse soul of the civilization which nurtured it, began the pavement lynching of Rodney King. Preserved at the height of its frenzy by an amateur video-camera operator, the naked images of "law enforcement" applying its civilizing discipline to King appeared seductively familiar to the American audience. Indeed, the images of this one brutal moment kaleidoscoped backward and forward. The scenes from this unmistakably real cop show cascaded backward to the recent and not-so-distant past as an inadvertent mimicry of the info-tech war in the Persian Gulf and prior instances of Pax Americana. And then ahead, with the less reflexive realization that this repulsive vision of muscular hatred served as well as an anticipation of an inevitable montage of public performances to be orchestrated by the powerful in America.

Among the familiar narrative oppositions, the signature of recent American military history could be discerned almost intuitively in the stark disparity in the techniques of violence, the dissimilarity of numbers, the persistence of the attack, and the presumption of moral authority which obtained between Rodney King and the uniformed predators. The videotape of the beating of King microcosmically rehearsed in specular form and ideology the political character of what Andy Rooney dubbed "the best war in modern history":[1] the "Desert Slaughter" of the Iraqi masses which the leaders of the most powerful Western/Christian/civilized nation had initiated and choreographed only a few months earlier. And in the original and its copy, in the fevered imagination of the dominant, the horror descending upon the inferior was deserved, the warrant for the act issued by natural law. White-American might was its own *raison d'être.*

The political rulers and their factoti, self-narcotized by such power and habituated by its display – in Grenada, Lebanon, El Salvador, Nicaragua, the Persian Gulf, Panama, Iraq, and the streets and courts of every American city – demonstrated their conceit and their simultaneous forfeiture of a more authentic legitimacy. Now, more than at any time in American history, societal consent had dissipated, plunging authority into that domain which the French philosopher Merleau-Ponty nominated as "contempt's radical challenge." For the increasing millions of poor and alienated the official distractions of foreign and domestic wars, the pious litanies evoking national security, the scourges of drugs and crime were wearing thin. The state was becoming a transparent instrument of partisan rule, an exposed entrenchment of the privileged. In some anguish, William Greider has proclaimed: "The decayed condition of American democracy is difficult to grasp, not because the facts are secret, but because the facts are visible everywhere."[2]

A few months following the first airing of the King tape, the congressional replica of this recurring audition of oblivious power again seized the national attention in an exhibition staged in a similarly public forum. The Senate Judiciary Committee provided the forum for the defamation of Anita Hill, the Black law professor. Unlike Rodney King, Ms. Hill had been a loyal subject to the reactionary powers that be, a willing participant in the disestablishment of institutions representing liberal democratic values and anti-racism (the Department of Education and the Equal Employment Opportunity Commission). As a Black woman in this male legislative locker room, however, she could claim no certain membership. When her professional calling caused her to balk (at first, hesitantly) at the Bush administration's counterfeiting of the Supreme Court by the cynical nomination of Clarence Thomas, she too was debased to King's disinherited status. By a conspiracy of the White House, the Justice Department, and the Senate, Ms. Hill was transformed from an admirable functionary into a political pariah with a flawed memory and an inclination toward sexual fantasies. For three memorable days, the innuendos and character assassinations bombarded the air with the same regularity with which the batons had filled the space above King's prone figure and the phosphorous munitions had rained on Baghdad. When the curtain fell, however, it was not Anita Hill but the powerful who stood in the searchlight of public humiliation.

But as it had for more than a decade, the unrelenting assault against the liberal social contract persisted. From 1980 to 1989, while Ronald Reagan occupied the White House, under the authority of law a multitrillion dollar national debt was accumulated while billions were cut from social security, unemployment insurance, food stamps, housing assistance, aid for families with dependent children, employment training, nutrition programs for poor children, low-income energy assistance, vocational education, the job corps, and compensatory education for the disadvantaged.[3] Trumpeted by a mass media, itself progressively monopolized by corporate capital, the message of limited government masked an economic revolution in the interests of the most wealthy.[4] Obliterating the historical consciousness that the anti-trust legislation of the late nineteenth century, the New Deal programs of the mid-1930s, and the Civil Rights acts of the 1960s had been necessitated by the voracious excesses of capitalism and racism, the reactionaries contained their public recitations to pseudocivic oppositions to big government, judicial activism, social engineering, and reverse discrimination (i.e., affirmative action).

In the last months of the Reagan administration, the yield from the debauchery of an unfettered capitalism and political and bureaucratic corruption surfaced with a vengeance: The junk bonds, corporate mergers, and financial mismanagement facilitated by deregulation occasioned the multibillion dollar Savings and Loan crisis. The unprecedented growth of war production and the anarchy of capitalist development submerged the economy into a depression and massive unemployment. Political and financial scandals stretched from the federal bureaucracy to Wall Street.[5] These were merely the overt concomitants to the achievement of an astounding transfer and concentration of wealth. Between 1977 and 1989, according to the Congressional Budget Office, the wealthiest 1 percent of American families amassed 60 percent of the growth in after-tax income while the poorest 40 percent of families experienced actual income declines (the "superpoor," the bottom 20 percent of families, suffered a 9 percent income loss). In the same span of time, chief-executive salaries rose from 35 to 120 times the average worker's pay, and the number of (primarily corporate) lawyers doubled to 740,000. These trends in the concentration of wealth at the top, documented by economic historians as having begun in the 1960s, accelerated in the 1980s. And they mirrored the national income disparities which had marked the late 1800s and early 1900s, a trend halted only by the Great Depression.[6] And for a final indignity, the nation became riveted in 1987 by the revelation of the existence of a secret and unconstitutional government whose activities determined foreign policy in the Middle East and Central America. Headquartered in the Central Intelligence Agency and the National Security Council, "the establishment" had financed itself through foreign potentates and tyrants, and illegal ventures in arms and drugs.[7]

The impoverishment and alienation of the electorate would take their toll on the 1988 presidential election. Only 66.6 percent of the 178.1 million eligible voters registered; and only 57.4 percent of the eligible voters participated in the election. George Bush was elected president at the behest of a minority, a mere 30 percent of those who might have voted.[8] As Reagan had before him, with the supine concurrence of the mass media, Bush pretended his minority constituted a moral mandate. And as with Reagan before him, domestic and international political extremism dominated his agenda. At the end of 1989, contravening international law, Bush ordered the invasion of Panama (Operation Just Cause) and imposed a new government on that American colony; early in 1990, ignoring both domestic and international law, Bush's CIA and its private conduits subverted the election in Nicaragua; that same year, with the complicity of the majority in the Security Council, Bush overrode U.N. regulations in order to organize the modern crusade against Iraq, the campaign which culminated in the 1991 Gulf War.

In the domestic arena, the new administration was equally cavalier with social ethics and the principles of representative government: during the first year of the Bush Administration, 24 percent of the regulations empowering the departments of Labor, Housing and Urban Development, and Education, the Occupational Safety and Health Administration, and the Environmental Protection Agency were scuttled in the sacred name of deregulation; Bush vetoed civil-rights legislation in 1990 on the basis of "quotas"; in 1991, on the most spurious grounds imaginable, the White House and the Justice Department designated and protected the Thomas nomination; in 1991 and 1992, Bush and his secretary of state, Jim Baker, refused political asylum to tens of thousands of Haitian refugees fleeing from a murderous military dictatorship, preferring to designate them "economic refugees"; and in the federal bureaucracy and the media, the Administration pursued its budgetary and ideological attack on social programs for the disadvantaged. "Twisting the data to fit a desired political conclusion" is how William Greider described the routine of the president's Office of Management and Budget, a key agency in the Executive's shenanigans in domestic affairs.[9] That came as close as any to an apt portrayal of the administration's operational sense of protocol both at home and abroad.

Though embedded in the American racial narrative, the vigilantism of Rodney King's violation extended beyond the political and ideological economies of Black oppression. Race is the signature of the beast marauding America and its empire, but only an aspect of its nature. But this was not meant to be immediately apparent to its victims, whether Black or not. Habituated by the "two nations" thesis first popularized by the Kerner Commission (the National Advisory Commission on Civil Disorders) in 1968, and supplemented by a ration of routine racial constructions in official statistics and the discursive canons of American journalism, the public perception of the increasing stratification of American society is fashioned through a racial screen.

Thus, while one-quarter of Black men in their twenties are under the control of the criminal courts, the U.S. imprisons Blacks at a rate four times that of South Africa, it is also the case that 1.2 million white males and females (56 percent of the total incarcerated; and at a rate at least twice as high as Europeans) were in prisons in 1990 and that the prison population of the country had doubled in the decade 1980–1990.[10] By 1991, based on the Sentencing Project annual report, the *Christian Science Monitor* observed, "More people, per capita, are in jail in the United States than in any other country on earth."[11] In 1985, the *Los Angeles Times* estimated that nearly one-quarter (56.1 million) of America was poor, an increase of 11 million since 1978.[12] If all Blacks were poor, one-half of the American poor would still be unaccounted for. As has been the case throughout America's history, the majority of the American poor are white but now they are absent. Andrew Hacker observes:

> Neither sociologists nor journalists have shown much interest in depicting poor whites as a "class." In large measure, the reason is racial. For whites, poverty tends to be viewed as atypical or accidental. Among blacks, it comes close to being seen as a natural outgrowth of their history and culture. At times, it almost appears as if white poverty must be covered up, lest it blemish the reputation of the dominant race.[13]

Rhetorically, in the American Empire, the stigmata of poverty, the "deviancy" of crime – and much of the political responsibilities of critical dissent – have been transferred to Blacks and other "natives."

The beating of King, was, then, a reverberation from the disintegration of civil society in America. The brutality of the racial drama was a reenactment of a multiplicity of brutalizations inaugurated by the ruling elite, historically the most constant source of anti-democratic extremism.[14] The daily occurrences of street executions, the cruel and indiscriminate arrests, and harassment conducted under the authority of law which form the immediate context for Rodney King's experience are the local reiterations of a national social agenda. Deliberately obscured, and in part negotiated into a cultural currency by the protogenocidal outrages perpetrated against Blacks, is the habituation of American society to a Hobbesian moral discipline and political order. Under the cloak of "a new world order," an amoral ruling elite has attempted to traduce the historical aspirations for democracy in America: in foreign policy substituting nationalism, militarism, and neoimperialism for international law and the community of nations; conjuring racism, sexism ("family values"), authoritarianism, and an economism of patriotism to drown out the hopes for equality, justice, and individual dignity.

However, the historical and structural forces behind the transformation of the American political order are neither psychological nor cultural. Notwithstanding the malevolent and avaricious personalities of our executive managers, the banal subordination of their bureaucratic minions, or the mean spiritedness of their functionaries, their dogmatic cultural convictions and rationally sophomoric articulations provide the surface idioms rather than the profound objectives necessitating their conduct. In the wake of the Soviet world system's collapse and the reemergence of Germany and Japan as powerful claimants to American hegemony, the modern world system is experiencing profound structural shocks and there are reasons for its political coordinators to brace for more. Utilizing the ironic voice, Noam Chomsky reports:

> As capitalism and freedom won their Grand Victory, the World Bank reported that the share of the world's wealth controlled by poor and medium-income countries declined from 23 percent to 18 percent (1980 to 1988). The Bank's 1990 report adds that in 1989, resources transferred from the "developing countries" to the industrialized world reached a new record. Debt service payments are estimated to have exceeded new flows of funds by $42.9 billion, an increase of $5 billion from 1988, and new funds from the wealthy fell to the lowest level in the decade.[15]

The social deprivations which are the concomitants to these hemorrhaging transfers of wealth constitute the circumstances which have historically spawned revolutionary movements. Presently, however, largely through the efforts of the Western intelligence community and military agencies, the preferred anti-toxin is tyranny: fascist military dictators like Saddam Hussein, Ferdinand Marcos, Anastasio Somoza, and Sese Seko Mobutu. A similar Western strategy has already made its appearance in parts of the former Soviet Union and in Eastern Europe.

In the Third World, where the instability of what Kofi Hadjor[16] characterizes as "Bonapartism" is a constant, and the loyalty of tyrants to their Western benefactors even more mercurial, U.S. power can anticipate occasions when military interventions will be necessitated. Ingratitude appears to be a dialectic of clientelism. Consider, for the moment, that after years if not decades of cultivating and hopefully assuring the loyalties of the Marcos, Noriega, and Hussein, American presidents were compelled to overthrow or destroy them. Nevertheless, such "wars" are morally ambiguous, and, of course, require major historical revision and erasure. On this last score, there are bound to be conflicts and resistance. Ronald Reagan, for instance, was so perplexed by the policy reversal involving the ejection of Ferdinand Marcos that his White House managers were forced to keep him from access to the media and the American public for weeks.[17] And though testimony and documents concerning the troubling relationship between Manuel Noriega, the CIA, and its former director George Bush were never permitted to become a part of Noriega's trial, the American public has access to some of the truth.[18] Similarly, Bush's consort with Hussein has returned to haunt him. And of course the military campaign in the Gulf, like its predecessors in Grenada and Panama, was subject to extreme press manipulation and censorship.[19] Public cynicism accrued, encouraged by the exposures of official deceits, misdeeds, and misjudgments.

In the post-Cold War era, a democratic America, that is to say, an America persistently struggling to vanquish the autocratic tendencies of its governing elites and to reverse the mean consequences of the structural "correctives" of capital, would be ill-suited as a launching site for military adventures designed to chastise former allies, recapture markets and human and material resources, and to reimpose American hegemony. Despite the deluge of pro war propaganda during the long run-up to the Gulf War, it should be recalled, substantial opposition developed to a military confrontation. Within days of the bombardment of Kuwait and Iraq, American public opinion was nearly equally divided for and against the war.[20] And earlier, several years into Reagan's poorly concealed war on revolutionary Nicaragua, the majority of Americans still consistently opposed the "secret" but official policy.[21] Alternatively, an America principally driven by nationalism, militarism, and racism, an American majority with a renewed consciousness of its external and domestic enemies, an American majority sobered through a long period of declining incomes and unsatisfied desires might be more appreciative of official alarms and remedies.

Much as during the onset of the Cold War, a radical reconstruction of American political discourse and the bounds of tolerable thought is in progress. In that previous moment, a critical segment of the American people was persuaded that in the name of anti-communism whole portions of the political spectrum would have to be sacrificed. To that end, compelled by the realization that unprincipled, fanatic communists were already within the gates, it became necessary to purge indiscriminately the deceived as well as the truly evil. The inquisition was merciless and unrelenting, and entangled industry, government, education, and entertainment; the private, the public, and the personal. Public humiliation, self-confession, denunciations of family, friends, and colleagues were a small cost when the alternative was considered.[22] That earlier repression was ultimately frustrated by Black culture and the emergence of the civil-rights movement. The first provided sanctuary for dissenters, the second, substantially but not entirely, restored a liberal discourse.[23]

In the present moment, perhaps mindful of its history, reaction has placed race in the foreground. And Rodney King was only one of its victims. Thus, in the company of such bizarre phantasmagoria as "political correctness" and "reverse discrimination" are placed the real aspirations of women, workers, the poor, and peoples of color.

Predictably, inevitably, the present machinations of power have inspired their own contradictions. On April 29, 1992, twelve years into the pageantry of the ultra-Right's usurpation of the state, the outraged and the betrayed took to the streets of Los Angeles, San Francisco, Las Vegas, and other American cities. And no one living in this America had the right to be surprised. The history of such social rebellions is as old (and current) as poverty and injustice.

338 | *Cedric J. Robinson*

The classicists inform us that in the sixth century B.C. just such insurrections initiated the process which eventually culminated in Athenian democracy. And in Europe's "Middle Ages," it took the original Inquisition centuries to suppress socialist and democratic movements. It is just as Thomas Rainboro predicted in the seventeenth century: "Either poverty must use democracy to destroy the power of property, or property in fear of poverty will destroy democracy."[24] It is this fundamental opposition which must be concealed. But it was not during the Los Angeles rebellion. The images of the betrayed coalesced; Black, Latino, and White, contradicting and marginalizing the desperate discourses on "race riot" which followed.[25] Ironically, by the very act of racial affirmation which Rodney King's assailants confidently sought in their mob identity, they provided the most certain catalyst for its negation.

NOTES

In the first passage cited in epigraph to this essay Sgt. Koon, commander of the Los Angeles Police unit which beat and arrested Rodney King, imagines the reaction of an armed female officer to King's presence. Sec Richard Serrano, "Koon Pens Blunt Book about Life in LAPD," *Los Angeles Times*, May 16, 1992, B2. In the second passage cited Herman Collins, an unemployed twenty-six-year-old Black man, comments on the acquittal of the four policemen charged in the King beating. See "The Fire This Time," *Time*, May 11, 1992.

1. John R. MacArthur, *Second Front: Censorship and Propaganda in the Gulf War* (New York: Hill and Wang, 1992), 105.
2. William Greider, *Who Will Tell the People: The Betrayal of Democracy* (New York: Simon and Schuster, 1992), 11.
3. Richard Meyer and Barry Bearak, "Poverty: Toll Grows amid Aid Cutbacks," *Los Angeles Times*, July 28, 1985; Andrew Hacker, *Two Nations* (New York: Charles Scribner's Sons, 1992), 98ff.
4. For the concentration of ownership in the media, see Ben Bagdikian, *The Media Monopoly* (Boston: Beacon Press, 1990); for the news media, sec M. Hertsgaard, *On Bended Knee: The Press and the Reagan Presidency* (New York: Farrar, Straus and Giroux, 1988).
5. For the history of the Savings and Loan crisis, see Greider, *Who Will Tell the People*, chapter 2.
6. Sylvia Nasar, "The 1980s: A Very Good Time for the Very Rich," *The New York Times*, March 5, 1992. Of course, Nasar reclaimed her loyalty to the established order by prominently displaying Paul Krugman, whose *The Age of Diminished Expectations* (Cambridge: MIT Press, 1992) maintained there was no relationship between the rich getting richer and poor more impoverished (22–23).
7. Holly Sklar, *Washington's War on Nicaragua* (Boston: South End Press, 1988).
8. See Clifford Krauss, "A Bill to Ease Voter Registration Clears House and Pressures Bush," *New York Times*, June 17, 1992, and Rosemary Keane's letter to the *Times*, July 9, 1992. Bush vetoed the 1992 bill, thus ensuring the 60 million voters – disproportionately the poor – would remain unregistered.
9. See Greider *Who Will Tell the People*, 146, and Brian Tokar, "Regulatory Sabotage," *Z Magazine*, April 1992.
10. See David Savage, "1 in 4 Young Blacks in Jail or in Court Control, Study Says," *Los Angeles Times*, February 27, 1990, and Steve Whitman, "The Crime of Black Imprisonment," *Z Magazine*, May/June 1992.
11. Cameron Barr, "U.S.: World's Lock-Em-Up Leader," *Christian Science Monitor*, March 7, 1991.
12. Meyer and Bearak, "Poverty."

13. Hacker, *Two Nations*, 100.
14. M. I. Finley, *Democracy Ancient and Modern* (New Brunswick: Rutgers University Press, 1985), 107.
15. Noam Chomsky, "The Victors II," *Z Magazine*, January 1991, 21.
16. Kofi Hadjor, *A Dictionary of Third World Terms* (New York: Penguin, 1992).
17. Cedric J. Robinson, "The American Press and the Repairing of the Philippines," *Race and Class* 27, No. 2, Autumn 1986.
18. See Mark Cook, "Scribes in the Courtroom: Controlling the Damage at the Noriega Trial," *EXTRA!*, January/February 1992, and Larry Rohter, "Noriega Sentenced to 40 Years in Jail on Drug Charges," *New York Times*, July 11, 1992.
19. See MacArthur, *Second Front*, chapter 2, and William Schaap, "The Images of War," *Lies of Our Times*, July/August 1991.
20. See MacArthur, *Second Front*, chapter 4.
21. See Sklar, *Washington's War on Nicaragua*, 190ff.
22. See Victor Navasky, *Naming Names* (New York: Penguin, 1980).
23. See Marty Jezcr, *The Dark Ages: Life in the United States, 1945–1960* (Boston: South End Press, 1982), chapters 13 and 14.
24. Quoted by Raphael Samuel, "British Marxist Historians," *New Left Review* 124, March/April 1980, 28.
25. For example, see "Race and Rage," *U.S. News and World Report*, May 11, 1992.

CHAPTER 24

David Walker and the Precepts of Black Studies

See your Declaration Americans! ! !
Do you understand your own language?
David Walker[1]

Founding texts are one convention of academic disciplines. The function of such texts is to establish the antiquity and thus a sort of historical authority for their resulting disciplines. But even more significantly, founding texts establish conceptual, discursive, and theoretical canons, transmitting sovereign structures for the epistemological, ethical, and methodological patrols which mark off special knowledge. And the names of long-dead authors function as mantra, transferring a spiritual power associated with remarkable intellects which in presumably conflicted historical moments achieved clarity, producing new knowledge, new ways of understanding. In Western political science, for examples, the works and thought of Socrates, Thucydides, Plato, and Aristotle serve these functions; just as for History, Herodotus; and for mathematics, Pythagoras and Euclid; for physics, a similar construction is attached to the moderns Isaac Newton and Albert Einstein. However, disciplinary canonization, like its counterpart in the Christian church, has its drawbacks: selection may be specious at worst, and arbitrary, dictated by fashion, ethnocentrism, nationalist fervor, and ignorance. Take for instance, the Chinese political philosopher K'ung Fu-Tzu (Confucius) who lived a hundred years before Socrates. We in the West have been led to presume that K'ung, in contrast to Socrates, made negligible contributions to the understanding of moral order and political regimes (and recall Socrates wrote nothing!). For another, Egyptian and Chinese dynastic historians, whose works predate Herodotus by centuries have also been embraced by indifference. I entreat you to approach my following remarks with the caution these last examples suggest: in the construction of knowledge there is no beginning and no end; and bounded genealogies of thought can produce as much mischief as enlightenment.

In America, in the field of *academic* Black Studies, I surmise that the preponderance of work over the past three decades has elected for singular greatness some rather constant figures: for the century now nearing its end, W. E. B. Du Bois is the dominant intellect. And for the nineteenth century, Frederick Douglass and Martin R. Delany command similar positions. Du Bois was, of course, the premier social historian, theorist, and publicist. But Delany's research in West Africa pioneered a Black ethnography just as his novel, *Blake* (along with Harriet Beecher Stowe's *Dred*), helped to establish the literary genre of Black radical fiction. And Douglass inaugurated Black constitutional studies as well as a militant Black liberalism. There were others, I might suggest, whose historical contributions respecting Black emancipation equaled or even surpassed these three: Sojourner Truth, John Brown, Harriet Tubman, Ida B. Wells-Barnett, Booker T. Washington, C. L. R. James, Oliver C. Cox, Malcolm X, Adam Clayton Powell, Jr., Ella Baker, and Martin Luther King, Jr. come to mind. Thanks to new research, some like Wells-Barnett, James, and Cox, are coming to the fore. This is the result of both their actual historical and intellectual significance, but as well the explosion of researchers in the field who are transmuting Black people from an inert subject-matter to one of the centering sites from which the modem world emerged. And one such figure to which attention has been drawn is David Walker, the nineteenth-century Boston dealer in old clothes who in 1829 and 1830 produced a messianic pamphlet which he entitled *APPEAL in Four Articles; Together with a Preamble, to the Coloured Citizens of the World, But in Particular, and Very Expressly, to Those of the United States of America.*

In some manner or other, Walker's story has been told in practically every decade since his mysterious death in 1830.[2] And a constant characteristic of the retelling is that each chronicler has sought to appropriate Walker as an intervention at a critical historical juncture. Not surprisingly, the purposes for which Walker has been employed have not always been authentic to the original. William Lloyd Garrison, while he detested the messianic and revolutionary project of the pamphlet ("We have repeatedly expressed our disapprobation of its general spirit."[3]), saw fit to reprint most of it in his new paper, *Liberator* in 1831. Walker served Garrison's objective of marking the *Liberator* as the leading abolitionist paper. Seventeen years later, in 1848, Henry Highland Garnet (reportedly, with funding assistance from John Brown) republished the *Appeal* in his effort to publicize the launching of the Free Soil Party.[4] Garnet appended to his version a brief biographical sketch of Walker, obtained from interviewing Walker's widow Elizabeth Dewson. It would be some time before historians, beginning with George Washington Williams, Carter G. Woodson, and Charles Wesley,[5] could amplify Walker's life from archives of abolitionist papers, contemporary newspapers, and court records.

In 1936, the Southern historian and populist supporter, Clement Eaton, was another chronicler who used Walker for his own ends. Eaton maintained that

"The David Walker pamphlet of 1829 was the first of these incendiary publications that caused a drastic regulation of freedom of speech and of the press."[6] Thus in contradistinction to Garrison, Garnet, and Frederick Douglass, who referenced Walker as a Black liberationist, Eaton characterized Walker as a "fanatic" and the *Appeal* as "incendiary." And no doubt, Eaton had a more contemporary figure in mind when he referred to Walker's "dangerous document," and lamented that Walker had died "unpunished in the slightest degree."[7] In 1935, one year earlier than Eaton's article, Du Bois had published his radical historical revision, *Black Reconstruction in America*. Like Walker, Du Bois had detailed the brutal horridness of slavery and the capacity of Blacks (in the Civil War which Walker had not lived to see) to fight for its destruction. And like Walker, Du Bois had become the target of friend and foe alike: reputedly for his "Black chauvinism" and his celebration of armed struggle.[8] Like Walker, Du Bois had vilified and threatened Eaton's cherished imaginings of an antebellum white Southern yeomanry hostage to a slavocracy, and Eaton feared for the worst.

Eaton reminded his readers that Walker's pamphlet, with its association with real and imaginary slave insurrections in 1829, had forced state legislatures in Georgia and North Carolina into passing repressive laws, thus "turning the South away from the liberal principles of Jefferson."[9] In Georgia, laws were enacted which quarantined vessels with Black sailors; subjected Black sailors who came on shore to immediate imprisonment; forbade the teaching of reading and writing to slaves; circumscribed the circulation of literature encouraging slave revolts; and prohibited slaves from work in printing shops. In North Carolina, meeting in secret sessions, the legislators enacted the death penalty "without benefit of clergy" for those convicted a second time for circulating publications inciting "insurrection, conspiracy, or resistance in the slaves or free Negroes." And in Virginia, again in secret sessions, the lower house had narrowly favored identical laws only to be reversed by the Virginia Senate. For Eaton, the whole spate of repressive measures undertaken by governors and legislators "was indeed unfortunate." He noted that substantial minorities among the legislators and free-speech advocates, as well, had opposed these draconian measures to no avail. Perhaps the whole debacle was, as he took pains to suggest, "the achievement of a powerful minority of proslavery men, cleverly utilizing the latent fear of servile insurrection."[10] Four years later, in his *Freedom of Thought in the Old South*, Eaton would repeat *verbatim* his condemnation of Walker ("That this publication with its doctrine of servile revolt and its instigation to commit illegal acts deserved suppression hardly admits of a doubt."), bitter that Walker's pamphlet had degraded the finer ethical impulses in white Southern culture.[11]

It may well have seemed to Eaton in 1936 that Du Bois threatened to precipitate a new repression. Du Bois had concluded his already celebrated *Black Reconstruction* with a chapter entitled "The Propaganda of History," remarking that:

... I stand at the end of this writing, literally aghast at what American historians have done to this field ...

I am not familiar enough with the vast field of human history to pronounce on the relative guilt of these and historians of other times and fields; but I do say that if the history of the past has been written in the same fashion, it is useless as science and misleading as ethics. It simply shows that with sufficient general agreement and determination among the dominant classes, the truth of history may be utterly distorted and contradicted and changed to any convenient fairy tale that the master of men wish.[12]

Du Bois had detailed how the "frontal attack on Reconstruction" had been orchestrated at Columbia University (John Burgess and William Dunning) and Johns Hopkins, and augmented by graduates from universities in Texas, North Carolina, Florida, Virginia, and Louisiana. And among the propagandists was Ulrich Phillips whom Edward Ayers as late as 1992 would characterize as "the South's foremost historian."[13] From the events of 1829 and 1830, Eaton knew well the extremes of white Southern reaction when menaced by a radical Black thinker. Even closer to his own time, at the beginnings of the twentieth century, when the threat had come from not Blacks but moderate white Southern academics, reaction had hounded from their posts intellectuals like his hero John Spencer Bassett, as well as William Trent, and Andrew Sledd.[14]

In 1965, in the turmoil following Freedom Summer, two versions of the *Appeal* were reprinted. We will concern ourselves only with that project with which the Leftist, Herbert Aptheker was associated. Aptheker's own evaluation of Walker's *Appeal* recounted some of the more passionate treatments the pamphlet had received in the previous decade, a period marked by Black integrationists. In 1950, J. Saunders Redding, in *They Came in Chains* (1950), had labeled Walker's work "scurrilous, ranting, mad"; Louis Filler, in *The Crusade Against Slavery* (1960) had denied Walker's Christian inspiration. On the other hand, in 1943, during a world war with Black militant leaders like A. Philip Randolph and aggressive Black unionism in the fore, John Hope Franklin asserted that the *Appeal* was "one of the most powerful anti-slavery tracts written." This was an assessment with which Dwight Lowell Dumond in his *Antislavery: The Crusade for Freedom in America* (1961) had agreed. Dumond maintained that Walker's writings were "precisely what would have come from a million throats could they have been articulate and have been heard."[15] And Aptheker had added to Franklin and Dumond his own estimation:

Walker's *Appeal* is the first sustained written assault upon slavery and racism to come from a black man in the United States. This was the main source of its overwhelming power in its own time; this is the source of the great relevance and enormous impact that remain in it, deep as we are in the twentieth century.

Never before or since was there a more uncompromising and devastating attack upon the hypocrisy of a jim-crow Christianity ...

Never before or since was there a more passionate denunciation of the hypocrisy of the nation as a whole – democratic and fraternal and equalitarian and all the other words.[16]

I believe that Aptheker and Dumond are right on all scores. And we will return to some of these themes when we investigate the significance of the *Appeal* for Black Studies.

More recently two historians, Wilson Jeremiah Moses and Sterling Stuckey, have sought to enlist Walker among the earliest of Black nationalists. In 1978, Moses appeared to acknowledge that his nomination of Walker as a Black nationalist elides some important issues, and eventually takes a declarative approach; "No one has yet denied that David Walker was a black nationalist, but he opposed colonization, emigration, racial separatism, and laws prohibiting intermarriage."[17] Just what sort of Black nationalist Walker could have been while denouncing emigration, colonization, and racial separatism is not clear. But in 1994, Stuckey employed a redemptive strategy which at least appeared to face the issues squarely:

While it is true that there is a certain diffuseness about Walker's formulation of the place of Africans in the world, there is nonetheless a comprehensiveness of approach, a penetration of insight and a daring of conception regarding the need for African peoples to rule themselves which mark his *Appeal* as unmistakably nationalist in ideology.[18]

Notwithstanding Stuckey's presumption, nationalism and Black nationalism are not coterminous. The domestic and international policies of most contemporary African states dramatize the differences between a state imaginary and a racial imaginary. And, of course, Walker's expressed interest in a just America, a country of Blacks and whites reconciled to providential intent was uncompromised by his assertion that Blacks were capable of self-governance.

As you can determine for yourselves, neither Moses nor Stuckey was entirely successful in prosecuting a strong claim for Walker as a Black nationalist. In each instance their integrity as historians ruptured the purity of their assertion. Moses conceded that Walker expressed a "hope that black and white Americans would eventually become a united and happy people," and Stuckey was content to pursue the softer assertion that "there is scarcely an important aspect of African American nationalism thought in the twentieth century which is not prefigured in [Walker's *Appeal*]."[19] But in an era by which time Black nationalism had emerged and persisted as the most compelling oppositional response to the continuing abuse of Black Americans and the frustrations of civil rights ambitions, its seductions are understandable. Vincent Harding, a third historian for whom Walker acquired a special prominence, avoided this conundrum by recognizing that nationalism (specifically Pan-Africanism) obtains no special or inherent privilege as "part of the stream of radical ideas in the struggle."[20] To do otherwise would risk devaluing the multitude of Black rebels, resisters, and revolutionists who from the sixteenth century to the present struggled under some ideological banner other than Black nationalism.

Aptheker observed that at least one abolitionist historian, Louis Filler, probably had denounced Walker without even having read the *Appeal*. And if that is the case we should extend some sympathy. After all it is much easier to enforce some control over Walker when you have not read him. Our concerns, however, compel us to forfeit such liberties. If we are to determine how Walker's *Appeal* can be employed as an authorizing text for Black Studies not merely reading but a close reading is required.

Walker published his pamphlet in three editions between 1829 and 1830, and Eaton had noted "These later editions were more dangerous and revolutionary than the first one."[21] Walker constructed the *Appeal* in five parts: a preamble and four chapters. Each of the four chapters constituted a thesis announced by its title. The first was entitled "Our Wretchedness in Consequence of Slavery"; the second, "Our Wretchedness in Consequence of Ignorance"; the third, "Our Wretchedness in Consequence of the Preachers of the Religion of Jesus Christ"; and the fourth, "Our Wretchedness in Consequence of the Colonizing Plan." However, the presumptive claims suggested in each of the titles were deceptive. Obviously, one of Walker's purposes in the first chapter was to denounce slavery. But his larger and more complex objective was to demonstrate that the American slavery of Africans was historically unprecedented because of the extreme juridical, ideological, political, and physical means undertaken to preserve and justify it: "... we, (coloured people of these United States) are the *most wretched, degraded,* and *object* set of beings that *ever* lived since the world began ..." (7).[22] And most telling, the slave systems created by *Christian* peoples were the most brutal and offensive to God. Surveying the conditions of slaves among the ancient Spartans, the Egyptians, and the Romans, Walker concluded that "While they were heathens, they were too ignorant for such barbarity" (17).

Among the Romans and Egyptians, Walker observed, slaves and freed slaves could obtain extraordinary political power and social privilege. And Walker declared:

Now I appeal to heaven and earth, and particularly to the American people themselves ... to show me a coloured President, a Governor, a Legislator, a Senator, a Mayor, or an Attorney at the Bar ... a man of colour, who holds the low office of a Constable, or one who sits in a Juror Box ...

... I only made this extract to show how much lower we are held, and how much more cruel we are treated by the Americans ... (8–9)

And then referencing his reader to Thomas Jefferson's *Notes on Virginia* for the assertion of Black inferiority, Walker demanded, "... show me a page of history, either sacred or profane, on which a verse can be found, which maintains, that the Egyptians heaped the *insupportable insult* upon the children of Israel, by telling them that they were not of the *human family*" (10).[23] Jefferson, Walker assured, was not some obscure crank but "was one as great characters as ever lived among the whites"; and he queried: "Do you believe that the assertions of such a man, will pass away into oblivion unobserved by this people and the world? If you do you are much mistaken ..." (15).

The proof of Black degradation, however, was not sufficient for Walker. After all he was an incendiary. And as such he taunted, cajoled, and apprenticed his Black readers in the art of insurrection:

> God will not suffer us, always to be oppressed. Our sufferings will come to an *end*, in spite of all the Americans this side of *eternity*. (15)
>
> Remember that unless you are united, keeping your tongues within your teeth, you will be afraid to trust your secrets to each other, and thus perpetuate our miseries under the *Christians*! ! ! (11)
>
> Never make an attempt to gain our freedom or *natural right*, from under our cruel oppressors and murderers, until you see your way clear – and when that hour arrives and you move, be not afraid or dismayed; for be you assured that Jesus Christ the King of heaven and of earth who is the God of justice and of armies, will surely go before you. (11–12)
>
> The man who would not fight under our Lord and Master Jesus Christ, in the glorious and heavenly cause of freedom and of God ... ought to be kept with all of his children or family, in slavery, or in chains, to be butchered by his *cruel enemies*. (12)

Walker believed in what some have called a muscular Christianity, a God of armies. But to serve that God's purpose; Blacks had to prepare and discipline themselves. Those who did not or would not ought to be butchered.

Just as "Our Wretchedness in Consequence of Slavery" was more than a litany of brutalities and horrors of slavery, Walker implanted diverse pedagogical elements into his succeeding chapters. And he possessed the practical knowledge and experience which lent impressive clarity and weight to his opinions.

Born to a free mother and slave father in Wilmington, North Carolina in 1795, Walker had lived in Charleston during the run-up to the "business" led by Denmark Vesey in 1822. And Sean Wilentz remarks that since passages in the *Appeal* place Walker in Charleston in 1821,

> The possibility that Walker was in the city a year later and the even more fascinating possibility that he, was one of Vesey's unnamed foot soldiers will forever be matters of conjecture. It is reasonable, however, to suppose that at some point during his time in the small city he met people who were connected with

the Charleston A.M.E. church, and who either knew or had known Vesey and his confederates.[24]

That the church had been central to the vast network of conspirators (131 were put on trial; and 35 hanged and 34 banished) provided concrete support to Walker's insistence on the moral defense of an insurrection against slavery, and his determination that Christianity and the Christian mission compelled Black liberation.[25] Indeed, as he maintained in a footnote to chapter one, the salvation of the world depended on the evangelical responsibility to be assumed by Blacks: "It is my solemn belief, that if ever the world becomes Christianized, (which must certainly take place before long) it will be through the means, under God of the *Blacks*. ..." (18) Moreover, the Denmark conspiracy had involved slave dock workers and free Black artisans and sailors, the same social base that Walker would employ in the distribution of the *Appeal* seven years later.[26] Finally, it is interesting that Denmark, a native of St. Thomas who had lived in Haiti, had encouraged his comrades by reading to them newspaper accounts of the Blacks of Haiti, and assuring them that Haitians stood ready to support their movement and grant them asylum. Similarly, Walker praised Haiti ("the glory of the blacks and terror of tyrants") and exclaimed: "... the one thing which gives me joy is, that they [the Haitians] are men who would be cut off to a man, before they would yield to the combined forces of the whole world ..." (21).

Contrarily, Walker had also become acutely aware of elements among the slaves and free Blacks which through ignorance or avarice (two of Walker's favorite constructions of evil) sabotaged the unity of Black liberationism. In his second chapter he recounted an incident in August 1829 concerning some 60 Maryland slaves being taken through Kentucky to Mississippi. The men had been shackled, the women and children not. Somehow the chains were filed, and the men attacked their escort, seizing a whip from one and a pistol from another. During the struggle, a slave woman had assisted the Black slave-driver, a man named Gordon, to escape. Her action eventually led to the recapture of the rebels, and the trial of six men and one woman for the murders of Gordon's two associates. Walker declared, "the actions of this black woman are really insupportable ... servile deceit, combined with the most gross ignorance; for we must remember that *humanity, kindness* and the *fear of the Lord*, does not consist in protecting *devils*" (24–25). Hers was an act of ignorance, an act uninformed by Christian reason or the authentic teachings of Jesus Christ.

But others, drawn from among Walker's own cohort of free Blacks could be guilty of avarice as well as ignorance. In 1971, the historian Donald Jacobs recalled such incidents which might have come to Walker's attention:

In 1827 a Negro was captured in Boston after escaping from Philadelphia where he had earned his livelihood stealing colored children off the streets and selling them as slaves down South: and in various northern cities there were also blacks who for the right price would reveal the whereabout of fugitive slaves recently escaped from the South.[27]

But while Jacobs excused such actions as the result of "frustration and poverty," Walker was less forgiving. Naming them "those ignorant and treacherous creatures (coloured people) sneaking about in the large cities," Walker extended to them only contempt under a ruthless political gauge:

> There have been and are at this day in Boston, New York, Philadelphia, and Baltimore, coloured men, who are in league with tyrants, and who receive a great portion of their daily bread, of the moneys which they acquire from the blood and tears of their more miserable brethren, who they scandalously delivered into the hands of our *natural enemies* ! ! ! (22–23)

Whatever their motives, these creatures conspired with tyrants. As we have seen Walker consigned such as these to be butchered by their cruel enemies.

Finally in his fourth chapter, Walker strove to expose the hypocrisy of the American Colonization Society which had been organized in 1816 by slavocrats like Henry Clay, John Randolph, and Elias Caldwell. His exposition on the Colonizing Plan as a stratagem to perfect slave control was rhetorically powerful and methodologically precise. The purpose served by transporting particularly Southern free Blacks to Africa was to separate them from the slaves whom they might contaminate with forbidden knowledge and aspirations. And over the succeeding decades Walker's arguments would be repeated by many of the Blacks (like Martin Delany and Mary Ann Shadd) and whites who opposed the scheme.[28]

Walker's immediate objective was the emancipation of Blacks, slave and free (he repeatedly scoffed at the notion that the latter were truly free). But as noted earlier, Black liberation for Walker was contextualized by his interpretation of the Gospel, that is the Christian salvation of the world. He could not, would not, and did not distinguish between the two enterprises. Black people had become the elect of God, selected to fulfill the divine mission assigned to America. For Walker, Dolan Hubbard wrote in 1986, "The fight for Black freedom was a holy crusade." And Hubbard quite astutely recognized Walker's vision: "A united Christian America, white and Black, will not only rise above the fates which pull nations down, but she will be able to spread pure undefiled Christianity to the nations of the world without compromise."[29] More than once in the *Appeal* Walker had asserted "This country is as much ours as it is the whites ..." (55). As such, when Walker prophesized that the alternative to Black emancipation was America's destruction, he was appropriating the promise of the Apocalypse described in the final book of the Protestant Bible.

However, what is most intriguing about Walker's liberationist conception was how he merged Christianity, pan-Africanism, and national birth-right. By envisioning the liberation of Blacks in America as a necessary phase to the realization of the Gospel, Walker reconceptualized a salvaged America as the Christian stronghold from which a world crusade would proceed. Blacks, the select of God, Blacks from whom "learning originated" of the arts and sciences (19), were assigned the dual responsibility of Christianizing the world while redeeming their kin: "... your full glory and happiness, as well as all other coloured people under Heaven, shall never be fully consummated, but with the *entire emancipation of your enslaved brethren all over the world*" (29). Walker tolerated no ambiguity: this was God's mission. Blacks in America could not be satisfied, would not reach "their full glory and happiness" until the world was just and fair. This was the destiny of knowledge.

Walker, thus, cannot be easily appropriated because he is nonmodern. He existed within a transhistorically moral and existential universe which can only be made to partially coincide with either Black nationalism, Black radicalism, or Black liberalism. In his understanding of the world, secular history gained no privileged status. Thus the political imaginary spawned by or concomitant with the nation-state as a form of social order was largely outside his aspirations. Secular history merely recorded injustice, merely became a narrative of flawed human societies destined for an endless succession of formation and dissolution. History was an impermanence whose glories and achievements constituted a subterranean trade of time-specific action lacking the grace of the Eternal. Nothing could be gained from history except the intelligence that God required and represented a superior destiny. God is freedom and justice.

Walker's conception of race was similarly suspended in a cosmological and providential realm, not the biological or cultural sites of modernity. The appearance, function, and mission of Blacks transcended history: Americans and other whites, Greek, Roman, Spanish, Portuguese, and English, were historical subjects, inferior categories.

One historical division was between their pre-Christian existence and their present existence as Christians who violated their divine trust. In both conditions, as heathens and Christian they had disqualified themselves as the probable agencies of God:

The whites have always been an unjust, jealous, unmerciful, avaricious and bloodthirsty set of beings, always seeking after power and authority – We view them all over the confederacy of Greece, where they were first known to be any thing (in consequence of education), we see them there, cutting each other's throats – trying to subject each other to wretchedness and misery – to effect which, they used all kinds of deceitful, unfair, and unmerciful means. We view them next in Rome, where the spirit of tyranny and deceit raged still higher. We view them in Gaul, Spain, and in Britain ... acting more like devils than accountable men. (16–17)

And what they would become, Walker was loath to venture: "... we cannot tell, it will be proved in succeeding generations" (17). He hoped, of course, that they would be reconciled to justice, reconciled to Blacks (18). Notwithstanding, in several instances Walker acknowledged the existence of "white brethren and friends" who were "engaged for good" (81–82). But greed and avarice had corrupted most Americans. Indeed, these were the only explanation he could ascertain for the Americans' brutality: "I have ... come to the immoveable conclusion, that they (Americans) have, and do continue to punish us for nothing else, but for enriching them and their country" (14).[30] Like the ancient Socrates, Walker believed that civic virtue and personal honor were compromised by greed.

The urgency of Walker's vision and mission, however, has not waned in the interval since his death. Thus, as the historical record and our memories attest, the formal organization of Black Studies as an academic discipline thirty years ago was explicitly liberationist. And implicitly when not baldly asserted, the accompanying precept of the entry of Black Studies into the Academy was that this country belongs to all regardless of origins, creed, ethnicity, gender, or any other putative disqualifiers. And Walker was determined on these questions. When he queried Americans concerning the Declaration of Independence ("Do you understand your own language?"), he was not being rhetorical but resolute. With equal force, Walker prosecuted the political, social, historical, as well as the moral power of education and the vanquishing of ignorance.

In point of fact, nearly one hundred and seventy years ago, Walker called for the, creation of Black Studies. He had been stung but not paralyzed by the slander of Blacks in Jefferson's *Notes on Virginia*. "For my own part," he wrote, "I am glad Mr. Jefferson has advanced his positions for your sake; for you will either have to contradict or confirm him by your own actions, and not by what our friends have said or done for us; for those things are other men's labours ..." (27). And his first call for action revolved around knowledge: "Men of colour, who are also of sense, for you particularly is my APPEAL designed. I call upon you therefore to cast your eyes upon the wretchedness of your brethren, and to do your utmost to enlighten them – *go to work and enlighten your brethren!*" (28), "... seek after the substance of learning," Walker pleaded.

> I would crawl on my hands and knees through mud and mire, to the feet of a learned man, where I would sit and humbly supplicate him to instill into me, that which neither devils nor tyrants could remove, only with my life – for coloured people to acquire learning in this country, makes tyrants quake and tremble on their sandy foundation. (31)

And anticipating the global significance of the national upheaval of the 1950s and 1960s to which so many Black students contributed, Walker recognized a very different import. In explication of the rationale for the policy of opposing Black learning, Walker asked: "Why, what is the matter? Why, they know that their infernal deeds of cruelty will be made known to the world" (32). The *Appeal* embodied these purposes and more.

In his "Preamble," Walker justified his writing by asserting an Aristotelian determination to observe, and thus laid down a critical methodology for Black Studies:

> Having travelled over a considerable portion of these United States, and having, in the course of my travels, taken the most accurate observations of things as they exist – the result of my observations has warranted the full and unshaken conviction, that we (coloured people of these United States) are the most degraded, wretched, and abject set of beings that ever lived since the world began ... (l)

The work was not opinion but observation, "the most accurate observation of things as they exist." Black Studies had to be empirical and not merely judgmental.

But to what purpose? Simply to confirm the conditions of Black subjugation? No. Such was of no import to Walker. In its stead he wrote: "... my motive for writing ... is, if possible, to awaken in the breasts of my afflicted, degraded and slumbering brethren, a spirit of inquiry and investigation respecting our miseries and wretchedness in this *Republican Land of Liberty!!!!!!*" (2). And we have seen what he presumed would usher from this "spirit of inquiry and investigation." Black Studies was to be emancipatory, and populist, employing inquiry for the purpose of mobilizing for deliberate and informed social action.

And thus Walker proceeded to display how the investigations of ancient and modern history, textual analysis of literature, laws, and public discourse could be employed for emancipation. From these inquiries he divined a theory of social change. Walker constructed a philosophy of history culled from Christian texts and Enlightenment authors which proposed that oppression destroyed from within those societies dependent upon violence and hypocrisy either through the appearance of a Hannibal from the midst of the oppressed, or division. To his Black readers, Walker prophesized:

> Beloved brethren – here let me tell you, and believe it, that the Lord our God, as true as he sits on his throne in heaven, and as true as our Saviour died to redeem the world, will give you a Hannibal, and when the Lord shall have raised him up, and given him to you for your possession, O my suffering brethren! remember the divisions and consequent sufferings of *Carthage* and of *Hayti* ... I charge you this day before my God to lay no obstacle in his way, but let him go. (20)

And he appended:

> ... for although the destruction of the oppressors God may not effect by the oppressed, yet the Lord our God will bring other destructions upon them – for not unfrequently will he cause them to rise up one against another; to be split and divided, and to oppress each other, and sometimes to open hostilities with sword in hand. (3)

Walker taught, no matter, then, the appearance of the thing, history demonstrated that oppression destabilized the most powerful societies because it was an offense against God. And through the dissemination of this understanding of history, he sought to free his people and salvage America.

David Walker, I am suggesting, can be taken as a founding intellect of Black Studies. He proposed it, he suggested its purposes, and he demonstrated some of the most critical practices it would be required to encompass. No theory of Black Studies can eschew his liberationist ethic, his democratic impulses, or the presumption that such knowledge signifies the termination of corruption and oppression. That someone such as David Walker, born on the margin of slavery, should achieve so exacting an intelligence suggests both the mystery and majesty of what Max Weber characterized as charisma, or what Antonio Gramsci later determined as the organic intellectual. As Aptheker claimed, the powerful rhetorical authority of Walker derived from his being Black. More importantly, as Dumond remarked, the profound gravity of Walker's symbolic force was that he spoke for the millions who could not be heard.

NOTES

1. *David Walker's APPEAL in Four Articles: Together with a Preamble, to the Coloured Citizens of the World, But in Particular, and Very Expressly, to Those of the United States of America*, with an introduction by Sean Wilentz (New York: Hill and Wang) 1995, 75.
2. See Herbert Aptheker's treatment of Walker's death in Aptheker's edition of the *Appeal: "One Continual Cry," David Walker's Appeal to the Colored Citizens of the World (1829–1830): Its Setting and Its Meaning* (New York: Humanities Press) 1965, 52–53.
3. Ibid., 51.
4. Sean Wilentz's Introduction, xxii.
5. George Washington Williams, *History of the Negro Race in American from 1619 to 1880* (New York) v. II, 1883, 553; Carter G. Woodson and Charles Wesley, *The Negro in Our History* (Washington, D.C.: Associated Publishers) 1972 (orig. 1922), 180.
6. Clement Eaton, *The Freedom-of-Thought Struggle in the Old South* (New York: Harper Torchbooks), 1964, 121.
7. Clement Eaton, "A Dangerous Pamphlet in the Old South," *Journal of Southern History*, 2, 1936, 324.
8. Among the critics of Du Bois were Benjamin Stolberg ("Black Chauvinism," *The Nation*, May 15, 1935, 570), Sterling D. Spero ("The Negro's Role," *The Nation*, July 24, 1935, 108–109), and several Howard University faculty: Sterling Brown, Ralph Bunche, Emmet Dorsey, and E. Franklin Frazier (see the letters in *The Nation*, July 3, 1935, 16–17).

9. Clement Eaton, The Freedom-of-Thought Struggle in the Old South, 118.

10. Eaton cited the work of John Spencer Bassett (Slavery in the State of North Carolina. 1899) of the University of North Carolina as the source of this suggestion.

11. Clement Eaton, *Freedom of Thought in the Old South* (Durham: University of North Carolina) 1940, 125.

12. W. E. B. Du Bois, *Black Reconstruction in America* (New York: S. A. Russell) 1935, 725–726.

13. Edward Ayers, *The Promise of the New South* (New York: Oxford University) 1992, For Du Bois, see 711–721.

14. Ayers, *Promise of the New South*, 423–426.

15. Aptheker, *One Continual Cry*, 4–5.

16. Ibid., 54.

17. Wilson Jeremiah Moses, *The Golden Age of Black Nationalism, 1850–1925* (Hamden: Archon) 1978, 39.

18. Sterling Stuckey, *Going Through the Storm* (New York: Oxford University) 1994, 88.

19. Moses, *Golden Age of Black Nationalism*, and Stuckey, *Going Through the Storm*.

20. Vincent Harding, *There is a River* (New York: Harcourt Brace Jovanovich) 1981, 85.

21. Eaton, *A Dangerous Pamphlet*, 324.

22. Pagination follows the 1995 edition of the *Appeal* by Hill and Wang.

23. Despite his naive theory of color-phobia, Winthrop Jordan's *White Over Black* (Baltimore: Penguin, 1969) remains the most compelling exposure of Jefferson's contempt for Blacks.

24. Wilentz, Introduction, x–xi.

25. Cedric J. Robinson, *Black Movements in America* (New York: Routledge) 1997, 35–36.

26. It is also significant that a number of whites were convicted in Southern courts of distributing the pamphlet. Cf. William Pease and Jane Pease, "Walker's *Appeal* Comes to Charleston: A Note and Documents," *Journal of Negro History*. LIX, 3, July 1974, 287–292; and Eaton, *A Dangerous Pamphlet*, 328–329.

27. Donald Jacobs, "David Walker: Boston Race Leader, 1825–1830." Essex Institute Historical Collections, CVII, January 1971, 96.

28. Robinson, *Black Movements in America*, 55–57.

29. Dolan Hubbard, "David Walker's *Appeal*, and the American Puritan Jeremiadic Tradition," *The Centennial Review* 30, 3, 1986, 343 and 342.

30. Perhaps too cavalierly, Harding observes: "Walker was perhaps the first writer to combine an attack on white racism and white economic exploitation in a deliberate and critical way." 86. Walker insisted that avarice corrupted Blacks as well as whites.

CHAPTER 25

The Killing in Ferguson
with Elizabeth Robinson

The killing in Ferguson, Missouri of Michael Brown by a policeman is an ordinary event in the U.S. On average over the past seven years, at least two Black men are killed every week by the police. This analysis is based on the Federal Bureau of Investigation's database which itself is an incomplete compilation of reports to that agency (e.g., the whole of Florida is absent). The actual number of such killings is certainly higher. Since the death of the unarmed Brown can hardly be taken as exceptional, what accounts for the extraordinary attention it garnered from the national and international media?

Public outrage is one factor; and the obscene display of a militarized police force, and the official refusal to reveal the circumstances were others. But none of these was unprecedented. More significant were the weeks before the Ferguson events when the same media publicized the official Israeli rationalizations for the horrific civilian deaths in Gaza. The Israeli State's stagecraft was transparent from the early days when CNN's Wolf Blitzer was transferred to Tel Aviv days before the ground invasion on Gaza was launched. Shadowing the Israeli public relations office, Blitzer and his colleagues from the other cable news organizations and networks leapt from one justification to another as the pictures and video from Gaza undermined the official narratives. First it was the murdered three Israeli teenagers; then it was the "rockets." And as the collective punishment against the innocents mounted, it became the tunnels, the annihilation of Hamas, and eventually Hamas's rejection of cease-fires. But another narrative was germinating from the attacks on U.N. refugee centers based in schools, the destruction of mosques and hospitals and the disproportion of the bodies of women and children to militants. Anti-war demonstrations were organized all over the world while the U.S. corporate media dutifully reported the White House, the Congress, and the State Department ventriloquizing Israel's "right to defend itself."

Palestinians had no such entitlement and even their right to survive was trumped by tanks, drones, fighter planes, naval bombardments, and helicopters.

The very notions of an Israeli occupation and blockade, though illegal in international law, were absent from their narratives. The Gazan tunnels were reduced to conduits for smuggling Gaza fighters into Israel with no mention of the closure of all borders including by sea by the Israeli government and its Egyptian allies. That the only means of bringing goods necessary for human survival was via those tunnels was never entertained. And then there were the casualties; the vastly greater numbers of civilians, of women, children, the elderly were minimized or covered with the fig leaf of Israeli unsupported claims of Hamas use of "human shields." In the midst of these constructions, it is not surprising that the virtual gaming world saw the emergence of games entitled "Bomb Gaza" or "Whack a Hamas."

The first attempt to retrieve some semblance of concern for human life in the American Administration and within the councils of its media sycophants was the plight of the Yazidis in Iraq. That venture faltered on the shoals of a war-mongering unpalatable to the vast majority of the American public and the transparent idiocy of Middle East policy. The appearance of concern for the Yazidis was too sudden, too obviously an attempt to rationalize a new military adventure. And though the threat of genocide had been mounting for some time, too little time had been set aside to prepare the American public for another Iraqi intervention. And the toll of similar precipitous actions was picking up. Under two successive American presidents, military operations had brought indescribable devastation to Iraq, Afghanistan, and Libya. Then occurred the outrage about the killing of Michael Brown bubbling up from the social media.

The Ferguson story incited a more heroic and noble moment of American journalism, the Civil Rights Era of the 1960s and 1970s. Here was a familiar, manageable, and seductive narrative which blew away all the ambiguities and contradictions which bedeviled contemporary America. In the past, racial oppression had been overt, publicly paraded, and advocated in schools, housing, employment, health services, electoral politics, and every other facet of American life. Now it is submerged in a "post-racial" nation where reversing the freedom movement's achievements are masqueraded in race projects like the war on drugs. Contemporary reporters adhere to the frame of reactionary politics, solemnly pronouncing the most absurd claims. Once you have feasted on WMDs in Iraq, it is no stretch really to seriously entertain the notion that the immigrant children from Central America are a terrorist threat.

Ferguson is about poverty and the lengths to which the State and its local tributaries have gone to control the poor. Militarization of the police (some $9 billion of Pentagon-originated equipment in the past twenty years) and mass surveillance (e.g., "stop and frisk" programs) are just two kinds of evidence. Inequality is increasing, consequently more severe policing is required and when reporters naively interfere (as some did in Ferguson) they will be harassed.

CHAPTER 26

On the Truth and Reconciliation Commission

The commission did not exactly "sacrifice" justice for truth, as Kader Asmal and many others suggested. It is perfectly understandable to find a lawyer, or judge, or legislator talking about sacrificing justice for truth, and implying this is a momentous decision. But for most of us we would gladly sacrifice justice for any thing of value. What more could any reasonable person demand of us after the justice of slavery, the justice of imperialism, the justice of racialism, tortures, letter bombs and murder, the justice of the greedy? Such examples of justice reveal how frequently in our actual world, justice is merely a conceit and a sham.

Truth can never be exchanged for or even equated with justice for they exist within different knowledge universes. Truth is inexhaustible, like irrational numbers, always expanding, moving, searching. Justice is fixed, always seeking to surrender the complex to the simplicity; the obscure to visibility; multiple possibilities to singular exactness. Justice seeks to tame the indeterminate, to subjugate difference to sameness. The rituals and procedures of justice are designed to give the appearances of justness by exacting revenge or manufacturing the fiction that something that has already happened can be rescinded or reversed. Justice, then, is either an intentional lie or a kindness. It routinely sacrifices truth, whether by fair or foul means. Justice, as Thrasymachus told Socrates, is whatever the powerful say it is.

And here justice was sacrificed for some kind of truth. This truth was the truth that the new South African state could afford. And the alternative was never really justice.

The presumption that the truth of apartheid is confined to South Africa nurtures in the journalist or the scholar the compulsion to manufacture a narrative whose dramatic form is adequate to the tragedies recounted before the Truth and Reconciliation Commission. Testing one's words in the theater of accounts of deeds which flirt with what was once termed the unspeakable may have its own fascinations. But everything – the theodicy of evil and forgiveness; the preservation of the deal which brought the new political landscape; the dream of a South African miracle – all conspire towards a closed text. Such a text, Umberto Eco has described, as a space of meaning so fragile that its interpretative authority requires total, uncritical acceptance of its truth claims.[1] Eco used Superman as an example of such a closed text where with the appearance of one serious inquiry the whole edifice collapses. The research and reportage of the Truth and Reconciliation Commission produce a closed text consistent with the idea that apartheid was a unique, localized, aberrant, and particularly virulent phenomenon. It is a familiar discourse. Even now, some seventy years after the advent of Nazism, it seems every year new proofs are put forward to confirm that the German people are singularly evil. And the Afrikaner is pinned to that donkey. These are modern examples of Solon's truths – the techniques used to preserve an international order by providing sacrificial lambs.

But the press reports, the journal articles, and now the books on the TRC file pass, unanimous in the declaration of the moral shame and shabby loyalties of South Africa's past.

NOTE

1. Umberto Eco, *The Role of the Reader.*

Index

NOTE: References to footnotes are signified with a lower case italicised *n*, and the footnote number. Written works are listed under their author(s).

9/11 *see* September 11th 2001
2000 Presidential Election 168

Abbott, Robert 104, 105
Abraham Lincoln Battalion 155
Abyssinian Baptist Church 103
Adams, John 139
Adorno, Theodor 150
Afghanistan 169, 355
Africa Confidential (Journal) 50–51
African Diaspora
  and emancipatory theory 6
  Ethiopia's symbolic meaning to 101
  historical 46
  and Pan-African Commonwealth 52
  and Pan-Africanism 50
  in Spanish Civil War 155
African Lakes Company 28
African Methodist Episcopalian Church
  38, 185
African Party for the Independence of
  Guinea and Cape Verde
  14, 309
"African-American" 185–195
  and black intelligentsia 186
  origin of term 185
Afro-American Studies (periodical) 5
Agassiz, Louis 112, 120, 123*n*7
Ahí Está el Detalle (There Is the Detail)
  (1936) 242
Alden, Mary 215
Alemán, Miguel 249*n*31
Algeria 7, 71, 72, 308
Algerian Revolution 296
Allá en el Rancho Grande (Out at Big Ranch)
  (1936) 242
Allen, Woody 226
The Amazing Colossal Man (1957) 226

American Civil Liberties Union
  (ACLU) 169
American Communist Party 103, 154
  on Italo-Ethiopian War 105
*An American Dilemma: The Negro Problem
  and Modern Democracy* 171–182
  authors 171
  funding 172
  Myrdal on 173
  social context 171
  structure 172
American International Pictures (AIP)
  226–227
  actors 227
  early output 226
  founding 226
  use of young directors 226
Amsterdam News 104, 154
Andrade, Mario de 314
Angola 308, 325
Ankersmiti, F.R. 75, 76
Annas, Julia 132, 133
Ansdell, Richard 218
anthropology 75, 79, 111, 113
  and Imperialism 29
  Plato's 134
  and prehistory Pan-Africanism 45
  public spectacles 115–116
  Victorian 113
Anti-Apartheid Movements 1
Anti-Miscegenation Act 1663, 233
antisemitism 48, 187
  and Catholicism 92
Apache Woman (1955) 226
Apartheid 1, 4
  dismantling of 16
  see also Truth and Reconciliation
  Commission

Aptheker, Herbert 343
  on Filler 345
  on Walker's *Appeal* 343–344
Aquino, Benigno 198, 203
  assassination 204
Aquino, Corazon 200, 205–206, 206*n*10
Archer, Jules 88, 90, 107*n*11
Arendt, Hannah 150
Argentina 242
Aristophanes 134–135
Aristotle 1, 16, 110, 123*n*4, 340
  influence on Western civilization 138
    19th century 139
  on manual labour 143*n*22
  Politics 139
  on slavery 111
Arkoff, Sam 226
Arroya, Joke 204
Asmal, Kader 356
At Piney Ridge (1916) 215, 238
Athens, classical
  as Empire 129
  political unrest in 131
  slavery in 133
Austin, David 191
Ayers, Edward 343
Azzam, Abdir-Rahman 283

Bacho, Peter 201
Bad Boys (1995) 221
Baker, Houston 54, 173
Baker, Jim 334
Baldwin, James 1
  on justice 3
Ball, John 56
Baltimore Afro-American 104
Band of Angels (1957) 240
banking
  control of Africa 160–163
  influence in Marcos' Philippines 199–200, 202
  and Portuguese colonialism 313
Baptist Youth Progressive Union
    Congress 103
Bar Sinister (1917) 215, 238
Baraka, Imamu 7, 69
Barbosa, Rafael 329*n*33
Bartlett, Thomas 254
Basche, Julius 89
Bassett, John Spencer 353*n*10
Bassols, Narciso 241
Bauer, Bruno 70, 187

The Beast with a 1,000,000 Eyes! (1955) 226
Beecher Stowe, Harriet 234
  Dred, a Tale of the Dismal Swamp
    56–57, 341
  Uncle Tom's Cabin 56–57
Belgian Congo 119, 125*n*41
Bell, Franklin J. 196
Benga, Ota 117–123
Ben-Gurion, David 94
Bennett, William 212
Bentley, Eric 251
Berenstein, Rhona 223
Berg, Eric 202
Berlin, Ira 101–102
Bernal, Martin 46
  Black Athena 76
Berne, Eric 268
Beveridge, Albert Jeremiah 196
Beyond the Valley of the Dolls (1970) 227
Bhabha, Homi 295, 301
  criticism 301
The Big Bird Cage (1972) 227
The Big Doll House (1971) 227
Bin Laden, Osama 169
Birth of a Nation (1915) 11, 223, 240, 261
  depiction of mixed race characters
    214–215, 236
  original title 248*n*16
  representation of black military service
    61–62
  responses to 214
  use of Black Face 219
Black American Negro Baptist
    Convention 30
Black Americans
  and Africa 185
  Christianity 101
  historical identity 101
  middle class 235–236, 248*n*11
  relationship with immigrant communities
    100–101
  re-signification 185
  West Indian cultural influence 282
  see also "African-American"
The Black and Green Atlantic (2009) 12
"black chauvinism" 342
Black envoys 118–119
Black Face 255–258
  in *Birth of a Nation* 219
  in cinema 257–258
  development and culture 255
  in Hollywood 235

in Mexican cinema 244–245
in modern day 257
music halls 257
in silent films 236
see also Minstrels
Black intelligentsia 63
Black internationalism
and the black radical tradition 6
culture and revolution 7
Robinson on 5–6
Black Mama, White Mama (1972) 227
Black Power 222
Black Radical Theorists 69
and *An American Dilemma* 175
and Fascism 149–159
capitalist origins 155
Black Radical Tradition 1, 4
and CLR James 48
and fascism 9
as ontological alternative 17*n*15
Robinson's impact on 2, 6–7
Black Servicemen
fictional depictions 61–62
historical neglect 62–63
Black Studies
establishment as field of study 350
founding texts 340–353
as response to race science 122
Robinson's influence on 2
Blacula (1972) 226
Blassingame, John 263–264*n*40
Blaxploitation films 11–12, 56, 221–232
and Black liberationism 221
depiction of Black urban communities 229
depiction of capitalism 226, 230
impact on Black culture 230
liberation and vengeance 226
modern era 221
politics of 230
portrayal of black women 224–225,
229–230
themes and tropes 228
Bledose, Alfred Taylor 139
Blitzer, Wolf 354
The Blonde Captive (1932) 223
Blood of Dracula (1957) 226
Blues
influence on other media 54–55
see also Jazz
Blumer, Herbert 79
Blyden, Edward Wilmot 119
Blythe, Samuel 89

Bocobo, Jorge 206*n*10
Bogle, Donald 213, 224
Bontemps, Arna 101
Boomerang (1992) 221
Booth, John 33
Booth, Joseph 30, 39
Booty Call (1997) 221
Boucicault, Dion
The Octoroon; or, Life in Louisiana 234
Bowers, Claude 99–100
Boxcar Bertha (1972) 226
Boyce Davies, Carole 17*n*9
Bracher, Karl 150
Branch, Thomas 30
Brinton, Daniel 120
Brion, David 77
British colonialism
in Africa 26–33
in Britain 30
in Ireland 253–255
Broken Ties (1918) 238
Bronson, Charles 227
Brown, Jim 226
Brown, John 29, 341
influence on African rebellions 36
Brown, Juliet 227
Brown, Michael 15, 354–355
Brown, Peter 227
Brown vs The Board of Education
(USSC decision) 171
Brown, Willie 191
Bruce, Blanche 217
The Brute (1920) 216
Bryant, Dan 255
Brzezinski, Zbigniew 150
Buchanan, John 28
Bunche, Ralph 9, 171–182
on democracy and race 177
education 174
legacy 180
vs Myrdal 177
on the New Deal 178
on racism and fascism 178–179
research 175
research team 175–176
Burgess, John 343
Burleson, Albert 172
Burns, Robert 26
Bush, George Herbert Walker 192, 332,
333–334
civil rights vetoes 334
on Ferdinand Marcos 198, 208*n*39

Butler, Pierce 141
Butler, Smedley D, Major-General 90
Bynum, Caroline Walker 16

Cabo Verde *see* Cape Verde
Cabral, Amilcar 7, 16, 39, 122, 308–329,
    308–330
  assassination 309, 325–326
  Black Intelligentsia 49
  on colonialism 322
  as critic 321
  on culture 323–324
  on culture and liberation 23
  diplomatic career 308–309
  early life 308, 309
  Marxist influence 320
  on national independence
      movements 327
  on Portuguese colonialism 314–315
  on post-war Portugal 314
  The Revolution in Guinea 329n44
  Revolutionary thought 320–326
  Robinson on 14
Cabral, Luize de Almeida 326
Cabral, Luz Maria 12
Cafasso, Joseph 169, 170n12
Caignet, Félix B. 240
Caldwell, Charles 114
Caldwell, Elias 348
Calhoun, John 139
Calvinism 25
Camacho, Manuel Avila 242
Campbell, Mavis 139
Campbell, Robert
  *Search for a Place: Black Separatism and
      Africa* 118
Cape Verde 308
  class during colonial period 313
  colonial history 311
  and slave labour 312
Capecia, Mayotte 297
capitalism
  1960s attacks on 190
  in the 1980s 333–334, 336
  in blaxploitation films 226, 230
  Chomsky on 336
  Cox on 78–79
  and deregulation 334
  and Fascism 5, 88–90, 156
  and gender 190
  post-World War II 190
  and racism 79, 177, 180, 188, 189

  in renaissance Venice 80–82, 85n36
  and slavery 76–77
Capitalism 75–84
  and democracy 76
  meaning 77–82
Carby, Hazel 58
Cárdenas, Lázaro 241–242
Carmichael, Stokely 222, 282
Carnegie, Andrew 172
Carpi, Daniel 92
Carranza, Venustiano 240, 246
Carter, Jimmy 205
Carter, Stephen
  New England White 55
Carter, Terry 227
Cartledge, Paul 136
Casement, Roger 120
Cash, Rosalind 225–226
Cashin, Joan 218
Cassels, Alan 150
Catholicism
  and Fascism 95–100, 151
  Italian vs Irish 96
  in the Philippines 203
  in the USA 108n32
  in Viet Nam 197
  and Zionism 91
Cayton, Horace 122
censorship 263n35
  of *Birth of a Nation* 237
Central Intelligence Agency (CIA)
  assassinations 166
  and drug dealing 11, 209
  drug smuggling 167
  installing Mobutu 163
  in Panama 334
  in the Philippines 197–198, 206n15
Cephalus 131
Césaire, Aimé 122, 297, 305
  Discours sur le colonialisme 302
Chaliand, Gerard 313
"charismatic leaders" *see* leaders
Chavez, Hugo 167
Checole, Kassahun 2
Cheek, L.N. 30
Cheney, Lynne 126n58
Cher 227
Chesnutt, Charles 252
Chicago Defender 104, 154
Chicago Tribune 89
Child, Richard Washburn 89
Chilembwe, John 26–33

attempts to enlist international
support 35
differing interpretations of character
35–36
lacunae surrounding 33
personality 33
as revolutionary 29
travels to US 31
China 82–83
racism 190
Chomsky, Noam 336
Christian Science Monitor 210, 335
on Ferdinand Marcos 201
Christianity
in Africa 32
and Black Americans 101
evolution of 40–41*n*13
and fascism 152
and liberationists 346, 348
and Pan-Africanism 349
as path out of slavery 233
as political revolution 37
see also Catholicism; specific churches
Christy, E.P. 257
Christy, George 255
Christy Love (1975) 226
Ciano, Galeazzo 94
Cicero 139
Cimprich, John 62
Civil Rights acts 171, 333
Bush undermining of 334
Civil War
battles 61
as setting for fiction 60
see also specific battles
Clarence-Smith, W.G. 328*n*17
class analysis
in ancient Greece 130, 133
and anti-racism 174
and corrupt voting practices 176
Fanon 304
in the Philippines 196–197
vs racial issues 14
classical literature 130
Clay, Henry 348
Clayton, Horace 104–105
Cleaver, Kathleen 225, 231*n*16
Cleopatra Jones (1973) 226
*Cleopatra Jones and the Casino of
Gold* (1975) 226
Clinton, Bill 167, 209
Clinton, Catherine 218

Cobb, Thomas R.R. 139
Cockburn, Alexander 210
Coffy (1973) 227
Colby, William 163
colonialism
Cabral on 322
and class
Fanon on 304
in Ireland 253
in the Philippines 195–198
psychological impact 295–296
in Scotland 25–26
see also Belgian Congo; British
colonialism; French colonialism;
Portuguese colonialism
"the colonised man" 295–307
The Color Purple (1985) 185
Colored American Magazine (periodical) 58
Columbia University 343
Coming to America (1987) 185
Communism
in America 103
congressional investigations 181*n*20
conspiracy theories about 171
in the Philippines 197–198
Community Resources Against Street
Hoodlums (CRASH) 11
Confucius 340
Connors, Mike 226
Conrad, Joseph 120, 252–253
Conroy, Jack 101
Coppola, Francis Ford 226
Corman, Roger 226
Cortesi, Arnaldo 88–89
Costilla, Miguel Hidalgo y 243–244
Coughlin, Charles, Father 95–96
on Italo-Ethiopian War 100
Coulanges, Fustel de 141
Cox, Oliver C. 7, 75–86, 122, 341
on capitalism 78–79
Capitalism as a System 79
Caste, Class, and Race 77, 78
criticism of 79–80
on emergence of fascism 156
on fascism 156
Marx's influence on 79, 156
on Venice 80
cranberry farms 312
craniometry 125*n*50
Cripps, Thomas 213
Croce, Benedetto 150
Croly, Herbert 89

Cromwell, Oliver 26, 29
  and Ireland 253
Crummell, Alexander 119
Cuba 153, 165
Culloden (battle) 25
culture 69–75
  Marx on 7
  and Pan-Africanism 7
  in Plato's Republic 131
  and revolution 322
Curley, James 96
Curtis, Cyrus 89

Dandridge, Dorothy 239
Davidson, Basil 308–309, 311
  Black Mother 39
  In the Eye of the Storm 327n3
Davis, Angela Y 16, 51
  and Blaxploitation cinema 225–226, 227,
    231
Davis, David Brion 137, 158n9, 192–193
  on Aristotle 138
Davison, Tito 245
Day, Caroline Bond 122
De Fuentes, Fernando 242
De Leon, Rudy 212
De Niro, Robert 227
de Rocha, Moses 39
The Defiant Ones (1958) 227
del Rio, Dolores 242
Delaney, Martin R. 348
  Blake 341
  children 102
  influence on Black Studies 341
  visits to Africa 118
Delany, Emma B. 30
Dementia 13 (1963) 226
democracy
  and American revolution 140–141
  in ancient Greece 127, 129
    destruction of 136
  and capitalism 76
  classical influence and aristocratic bias
    18n25
  decline in the US 336–338
  and fascism 157, 158n4
  in medieval Venice 82
  and mob rule 3
  Plato on 135, 142
  problems with 3
  and slavery 127–128

in the US South 176–177
Denning, Richard 227
Dent, Gina 230
Department of Education 332
Deportation
  of Blacks from Elizabethan
    England 39
  of Jews from medieval England 48
Depretis, Agostino 92
Dern, Bruce 227
Desert Storm (First Gulf War) 331, 336
  public opinion 337
Dessalines, Jean Jacques 260
detective fiction 54–65
  post-war 56
  social functions 55
Detroit Red *see* Malcolm X
Deutsche, John 209
Devil in a Blue Dress (1995) 56
Dewey, George, Admiral 196
Dewson, Elizabeth 341
Díaz, Porfirio 241
Diem, Ngo Dinh 198
Digges, Dudley 259
Diggins, John 88, 90, 94
Dixon, Thomas 214, 217, 236, 238
  The Clansman 214
Dobson, Tamara 226
Domingo, Charles 31, 38
Dorn, Richard 292n28
Douglas, Frederick 57, 119
  on David Walker 342
  influence on Black Studies 341
Doyle, Arthur Conan 120
Drake, St Clair 114–115, 122
Du Bois, W.E.B 48, 63, 122, 214, 252
  in Africa 32
  Atlanta conferences 236
  on *Birth of a Nation* 237
  Black Reconstruction in America 77,
    342, 343
  critics 352n8
  education 236
  on Ethiopia 101, 106
  on Fascism vs Imperialism 156–157
  influence on Black Studies 341
  on nature of history 22
  Pan-Africanism 157
  political pan-Africanism 48
  positivism 185
  on Treaty of London 158n12

and UNIA 153–154
on US occupation of Haiti 103
Dumond, Dwight Lowell
  Antislavery: The Crusade for Freedom in America 343
Dunbar Players 216
Dunbar, William 39
Dunning, William 343
Durkheim 273
Dyer, Richard 233

Eaton, Clement 341–342
  Freedom of Thought in the Old South 342
Ebert, Roger 227
Eco, Umberto 152, 357
Egypt 161
Einstein, Albert 340
El Salvador 166–167, 211, 332
Eliot, Charles W. 115
Elizabeth I 39, 164
Ellington, Duke 262
Ellis, George Washington 119
Embree, Edwin 175
Emmett, Dan 255
Emperor Jones (1933) 239, 259, 263n35
Engels, Friedrich 152, 190
English, Marla 227
Enrile, Juan Ponce 200, 205
Equal Employment Opportunity
  Commission 332
Erikson, Erik 267, 269, 275, 278, 292n28
  on the psychohistorical approach 270–271, 272
Ethiopia 100–106
  Jewish community 93–94
  place in spiritual tradition of West
    Indians 101
  symbolic meaning to Black Americans
    101
Ethiopian Art Company 216
ethnocentrism
  in academia 340
Euclid 340
eugenics 111
  and multiculturalism 115
Experimental Theater 251

Fagin, N. Bryllion 251
Fanon, Frantz 113, 122, 295–307, 308, 321
  abandonment of psychoanalysis 302
  background 295

Black Skin, White Masks 296, 298
  appropriation of 14
  class analysis 304
  on colonized intellectual 304
  comparison with Freud 302
  death 295
  on liberation 303
  on middle class in colonized
    countries 300
  modern application to US 300–307
  Pan-Africanism 49
  Robinson on 13–14
  Wretched of the Earth 76–77
Fargas, Antonio 227
Farnsworth, Clyde 202
Farrar, Cynthia 8, 18n25, 127
fascism
  and democracy 157, 158n4
  and Imperialism 178
  in Portugal 325
  and racism 157
Fascism 87–109
  in America 95
  and Black nationalism 154
  and Black Radical Theorist 149–159
  and Black Radical Tradition 9
  Black response 100
  and capitalism 5, 88–90, 155
  and Catholicism 95–100, 151
  as end product of colonialism 302
  Italian-American 97–98
  in Italy 222
    industrial support 90
    opposition to Nazi policy 108n26
    rise 87
  Marxist conception 9
  meanings of 149–153
  Robinson on 7
  traditional European definition 150
  US media coverage 89
  US support of 88–90
  in Western Europe vs Eastern
    Europe 150
  and Zionism 91–95
The Fast and the Furious (1954) 226
Faulkner, William 252–253
Federal Bureau of Investigation
  crime statistics 354
Federation of Italian Jewish
  Communities 94
Fein, Seth 249n31

Felice, Renzo de 151
Ferguson, Missouri 354–355
Ferkis, Victor 96
Fernand Braudel Center 5
Filipino Nationalism 197
Filipino Revolution 205–206
Filler, Louis
  Aptheker on 345
  The Crusade Against Slavery 343
film criticism and theory 11–12
  Mulatta 233–251
Finlay, Robert
  Politics in Renaissance Venice 80
Finley, Moses Isaac, Sir 3, 127, 136, 137, 142
Finzi, Aldo 93
Firestone, Harvey 153
Fisher, Randolph 252
Fitzhugh, George 139, 218
Flarris, Herbert 95
Florida
  voting irregularities in 2000 election 168
Flynn, George Q. 108n32
Foa, Carlo 93
Ford, Henry 106n3
Foreign Affairs (periodical) 106
Forrest, Nathan Bedford, General 62
Fort Pillow (battle) 61, 62
Fort Wagner (battle) 61
Fortune (magazine) 88
Foster, Stephen 255
founding texts 340
  of Black Studies 340
Fox, William 215, 238
Foxy Brown (1974) 227–229
Franklin, Benjamin 188
Frazier, E. Franklin 38, 78, 175, 252, 288
Fredrickson, George 188
Free and Equal (1918) 216, 238
Free Soil Party 341
freed slaves
  transportation to Africa 348
freedom of speech
  regulation of 342
Freedom Summer 343
French colonialism 71–75
  in Caribbean 72
  in Indo-China 72–73
  in North Africa 72
French Revolution 92, 152
Freud, Sigmund 269, 270, 273
  on mob psychology 288–289
  self-analysis 293n28

Fricker, Miranda 17n16
Friday Foster (1975) 227
Friedlander, Saul 149
Friedrich, Carl 150
Frohman, Daniel 214
Fromm, Erich 150
Fuks, Alexander 136, 144n44

Gaines, Jane 16
Galindo, Alejandro 243
Galton, Francis 116
Gandhi, Mahatma 267, 278
Garcetti, Gil 210
Garibaldi, Giuseppe 92
Garland, Beverly 227
Garnet, Henry Highland 341
Garrison, William Lloyd 341
Garruccio, Ludovico 150
Garvey, Marcus 32, 48–49, 260, 261, 282
  trial 104
Gary, Elbert 89
Gasset, Ortega y 150
Gates, Henry Louis Jr. 54–55, 295
  on Fanon 300, 302, 303
Gatewood, Willard 63–64
Gaza 354
gender
  Aristotelian conception 112
  and capitalism 190
  in *La Negra Angustias* 246–247
  Marxists on 190
Genovese, Eugene 126n58
George, Alexander and Juliet; *Woodrow*
    Wilson and Colonel House 33
Georgia
  regressive slavery laws 342
Gephardt, Richard 192
Gerarchia (journal) 93
Geronimo 116, 117–123
Gerry, Elbridge 141
Gershwin, George 259
Gevinson, Alan 214
Giannini, A.P 98
Gibson, Mel 227
Gibson, Richard 329n33
Gillett, Peter J. 252
Gilpin, Charles 251–252, 258, 261
Girls in Prison (1956) 226
Gish, Lillian 217–218
globalization 190
Glory (1989) 61
Glover, Scott 210

Goddard, Henry
  The Kallikak Family 116
Gold, Matea 211
Goldberg, David Theo 123*n*4
  Multiculturalism 7
Gone with the Wind (1939) 223
  representation of black military service
    61–62
Gould, Stephen Jay 112, 123*n*7
Grandi, Dino 99
Graves, Peter 226
Graves, Teresa 226
Gray, Edgar M. 261
Great Depression 333
  aggravation of racial tensions 102
  and cinema 222
Greece *see* Athens, classical
Gregor, A. James 150
Greider, William 332, 334
Grenada 169, 332
Gridley, Samuel 123*n*8
Grier, David Alan 221
Grier, Pam 225–226
  and Angela Davis 227
  pre-acting career 227
Griffith, D.W. 11, 214, 223, 236, 237, 238, 261
Griffith, Melanie 227
Grote, John 17–18*n*17
  A Treatise on Moral Ideals 4
Grubb, James 80
Guatemala 166–167
Guerrero, Ed 223, 235, 238–239
  Framing Blackness 248*n*9
Guerrero, Vincente 243–244
Guinea-Bissau
  colonial history 310–311
  independence movement 23, 308
    and class 315–320
  military coup 326–327
  native peoples 310
    uprisings 328*n*7, 328*n*8
  see also Portuguese colonialism
Guiú, Emilia 245
Gustavo, Garcia A. 249*n*23
Gutman, Herbert 218

Hacker, Andrew 335
Hadjor, Kofi Buenor 2, 336
Haiti 7, 71, 153
  attacks on sovereignty 262
  Black envoys to 118–119
  early political isolation 102

inspiration for *The Emperor Jones* 260
  meaning to Afro-Americans 101
  US occupation of 102–103, 260
    press support for 263–264*n*40
  Walker on 347
Haitian Revolution 48, 56, 101–102
  as inspiration for slave revolts 101
Haley, Alex 277
  The Autobiography of Malcolm X 77, 277, 278, 293*n*32, 293*n*44
  narrative 279
Hall, Stuart 185, 189–190
Hamas 354
Hamilton, Charles V. 222
Hamilton, Richard 150
Handler, M.S. 277
Handyside, Richard 321
Haraway, Donna 111–112
Harding, Vincent 344–345
  on Walker 353*n*30
Hare, John 110
Harlem Refuge Church of Christ 103
Harris, Abram Jr. 175
Harris, Katherine 170*n*9
  see also NAACP v. Katherine Harris et al.
    (court case)
Harris, Marvin 120
Hays, Will 263*n*35
Haywood, Harry 155, 156
Hearst, William Randolph 89, 106*n*3
  Mexican holdings 249*n*27
Hebert, Janis 217
Hecht, Jean 189
Henri Christophe, King of Haiti 260
Henry, Jules 121
Hepburn, John 26
Herard, Tiffany Willoughby 12, 180*n*9
Herndon, Milton 155, 156
Herodotus 340
Hersh, Seymour
  The Price of Power 161
Hershfield, Joanne 249*n*23, 250*n*52
Herskovits, Melville 121, 122, 173, 175, 282
Herzl, Theodor 92
Heyward, DuBose 259
Highlanders, destruction of 25
Hildreth, Richard 234
Hill, Anita 332
Hill, Errol 56
Himes, Chester 56
history
  Black scholasticism 22

history (*Cont.*)
  Du Bois on 22
  Pan-Africanism as 46
  ruling class control of 22, 38
  subjective interpretation of 21
  see also history, native theory of
history, native theory of 21–44
Hit Man (1972) 227
Hitler, Adolph
  and leadership 269
  on war and peace 153
Hitz, Frederick P. 209
Hobsbawm, E.J. 29
Holbrooke, Richard 203
Hollywood
  collaboration with Mexican filmmakers
      242–243, 249n31
  depiction of Mexicans 241
  depictions of Africa 185
  vs Mexican cinema 240
  and Mulatta performers 239
  see also Blaxploitation films; film criticism
    and theory
Holmes, George Frederick 139
Homer, Winslow 218–219
The Homesteader (1919) 216
Honduras 166–167, 211
Honey Hill (battle) 61, 62
Honour, Hugh 220n17
Hooton, Ernest 115
Hoover, Herbert 88
Hopkins, Pauline 5–6, 54–65
  career as stenographer 58
  Contending Forces 58, 63
    publishing 59
  early life 56
  Hagar's Daughter 54, 55
    plot 59–60, 59–61
    setting 64
  journalism 58
  musicals 56
  Of One Blood 64
  theater work 57
Hopkins, Terrance 16
Hopper, Dennis 227
Horne, Lena 239
Hot Rod Girl (1956) 226
House Un-American Activities
    Committee 99
Howard, Shingzie 216
Huang, Ray 7, 77, 82–83
  1587 - A Year of No Significance 77

China: A Macro History 77
Rise of Capitalism in Venice 86n39
Science and Civilization in China 77
*Taxation and Governmental Finace
    in Sixteenth-Century China* 77
Huerta, Victoriano 241
Hughes, Langston 156, 252
Hughes, R.P. 196
Hukbalahap 197, 198, 206n13
Hull, Cordell 100
Hume, David 26
Hunt, Michael 187, 188
Huntington, Samuel P. 181n14
Hurston, Zora Neale 122, 252
Hussein, Saddam 336

I Was a Teenage Werewolf (1957) 226
Ignatiev, Noel 255
Ileto, Reynaldo 197
Imitation of Life (1934) 239, 240
Imperialism
  attacks on culture 71
  British, in Mediterranean 91
  and capitalism 76–77
  Chinese 82
  collapse of 156
  and fascism 156, 178
  Italian 91, 94, 154
  Japanese 197
  vs rebellion 7
  Robinson on 10
  United States 90, 165, 196–198
    racialist excuses for 261
  see also United States foreign policy
In the Heat of the Night (1967) 56
Inagi (1930) 223
Ince, Thomas H. 238
Indian Journal of Political Science
      (periodical) 5
"Indian" wars 115, 165
Infante, Pedro 243, 245
Injai, Abdul 311
Injustice
  epistemic 17n16
International Court of Justice 165–166
International Monetary Fund (IMF)
      9, 162–163
Internet
  impact on information flow 18n28
Iran 198, 203, 205
Iraq 355
  see also Desert Storm (First Gulf War)

Ireland
  colonialism in 253–255
  racial identity 254
  rebellions 253
  see also Nine Years War
Irish
  exclusion from "whiteness" 253
  and "whiteness" 252–255
Irish American racial performance 251–265
Irish Americans
  and Black Americans 100–101, 255
  as labor force 256
  population centers 255–256
  second-class status 255
Irish nationalism 31–32
Israel 354
  human rights violations 169
  oppression of Palestinians 15
  as perpetrators of "terrorism" 9
Israeli Invasion of Gaza 2014, 15, 355
Italian-Americans
  fascism among 97–99
  relationship with Black Americans
    100–101
Italo-Ethiopian War 91, 94, 99, 104, 154
  African diaspora enlistment 104
  Black response 100–105
    global nature 104
Italy
  Fascism in 222
    rise of 87
    US media coverage 89
    US support for 88–90
    and Zionism 91–95
  imperialism 91, 154
  influence in Italian-American
    communities 98–99
  Jews in 91–92
  Leftism in 96–97
  World War I 97

Jackson, Gabriel 99–100
Jackson, George 231n16
Jackson, James E. 175
Jackson, Jesse 10, 186, 190–193, 209
  evangelism 186
  media coverage 191–192
Jackson, Walter A. 172
Jackson, Wilhemina 175
Jacobs, Donald 347–348
James, C.L.R. 7, 48, 69, 122, 341
  Beyond the Boundary 77

Black Jacobins 48, 76–77
  on Haitian revolution 72
  Mariners, Renegades and Castaways
    47, 77
  opposition to Haile Selassie 53n1
  Pan-Africanism 48–49
  and revolutionary theory 69
  on Western nationalism 47
  World Revolution 155
James, Edwin L. 88–89
Jameson, Fredric 128, 130, 131
Janitzio (1934) 241–242
JanMohamed, Abdul 295, 303
  on Bhabha 301
Japan 197
  CIA in 198
  reconstruction 190
Jazz 1
  see also Blues
Jefferson, Thomas 181n14
  criticism of Plato 139
  Notes on Virginia 188, 346, 350
  on race 115, 139–140, 346
  and slavery 139
Jenkins, W.S. 139
Jensen, Arthur 115
Jewish nationalism *see* Zionism
Jezebel (1938) 223
Jim Crow Laws 58, 235
  and Black middle class 235–236
  and voter suppression 170n9
John Paul II, Pope 166
Johnson, Charles 78, 252
Johnson, Don 227
Johnson, Eastman 218
Johnson, Harry 28
Johnson, James Weldon 103, 252
  on US occupation of Haiti 260
Jones, Jacqueline 218
Jordan, Ervin Jr. 218
Jordan, Winthrop 140, 188
  White Over Black 353n23
"journalistic repair" 10
JP Morgan (company)
  support for European fascism 88
Jung, Guido 93

Kadalie, Clement 31
Kadiga, Antoine 163
Kahn, Otto 89
Kallen, Horace 89
Kampingo, Wallace 35, 36

Kamwana, Elliot 31, 38
Kardiner, Abram 282
Karonga (battle) 31
Kashiwahara, Ken 208n36
Katzenellenbogen, Edwin 115
Kavanagh, James 128
Kea, Salaria 105
Kennedy, John F. 301
Kennedy, Joseph 96
Kenya 104
Kenyatta, Jomo
    Facing Mount Kenya 50
Keppel, F.P. 172, 173
    on Baker 180n5
Kerkvliet, Ben 206n13
Kerner Commission 334
King Kong (1933) 223, 230
King, Martin Luther Jr. 341
King, Rodney 331, 334, 335, 337, 338
Kiowa 116
Kissinger, Henry 161, 198
Knadler, Stephen 59
Knox, John 25
Krasner, David 261
Kroeber, Alfred 121
Ku Klux Klan 172
Kuberski, Philip 195
Kuhn Thomas 273
K'ung Fu Tzu *see* Confucius

La Negra, Toña 245
Laemmle, Carl 214
Lafeyette Players 216
Lake Nyasa 27
Lamb, David 160
Lamont, Thomas 89, 90, 99
Landeta, Eduardo 246
Landeta, Matilde 239–240, 243, 246, 249n34,
    250n52, 250n53
Landon, Michael 226
Landsberg, H.E. 211
Lane, Frederic 83, 85n36
Lansdale, Edward, Colonel 197–198
Laos 198
Lapsley, Samuel 119
Lasswell, Harold 269
    Power and Personality 33
    Psychopathology and Politics 33
The Last Boy Scout (1991) 221
Laurel, Salvador 205
Lawrence, Martin 221, 257
Laxalt, Paul 205

Leab, Daniel 213
leaders 70, 267–296
    analytical framework 268–272
    charisma 272–275
        definitions 272–273
        creation of movement 276
        and developing cultural movements
            73–74
        emergence 268, 274
        as father figures 274
        followers as extension of self 275
        function 275
        and identity 270
        ideology and action 276
        individual vs group representative 270
        Plato on 135
        psychological development 33–34
        relationship with followers 275
Lebanon 332
Lebron, Christopher J. 18n18
Ledeen, Michael 92
Lee, Arthur 139
Lee, Desmond 133
Lee, Jennie 219
Leopold II of Belgium 119
Levellers 26
Lewis, Edgar 215
Lhamon, W.T. 256
Liberator (newspaper) 341
Liberia 50, 153, 261
    Black envoys to 118–119
    imperialist ambitions 102
    slavery in 103
Libya 355
    Jewish community 93–94
Lincoln, Abraham
    on escaped slaves 220n17
Lincoln's Dream (1915) 214
Lipset, Seymour 142, 151
Little, Earl 281, 283
Little, Louise 280–282
Little, Malcolm *see* Malcolm X
Littlefield, Walter 89
Livingston. Arthur 88–89
Livingston. Lemuel 103
Livingstone, David 27
Lloyd, David 12
Loder, Kathryn 227
Lodge, Henry Cabot 196
Logan, Rayford 58
Lola Casanova (1949) 246
Long, Huey 96

Lorini, Alessandra 63
Los Angeles Police Department (LAPD) 210
  scandals 11
  see also Rampart Scandal
Los Angeles Times 11
  coverage of Africa 160–163
  on Ferdinand Marcos 202
  on increased poverty 335
  local news 209
  Ramparts Scandal 209–212
Los Angelitos Negros (1948) 12, 239–240, 244
Lost Boundaries (1949) 239, 240
Lott, Eric 255, 257
Louis, Joe 287
L'Ouverture, Toussaint 102, 260
Lowie, Robert 121
Luce, Henry 89
Lumumba, Patrice 45, 161, 308
Luther, Matin 269
Lynchings 57, 224
  depictions in film 217, 238
  increase in 58
  of Irish and Italian poor 100

MacArthur, Arthur, General 196
MacArthur, Douglas, General 197, 206n15
Macotela, Fernando 244, 250n47
Madero, Francisco 241
Madison, James 139, 141
Magsaysay, Ramon 197
Malawi 27, 28
Malcolm X 267–296, 341
  assassination 290
  on autobiography 277–278
  The Autobiography of Malcolm X 7, 277,
    278
    narrative 279
  criminal convictions 279
  different identities 278
  early life 279
  education 284–285
  emergence 74
  father 281, 283
  life as hustler 285–286
  on light complexion Blacks 293n31
  mother 280–282
  on the Nation of Islam 290
  pilgrimage 277
  psychosocial development 270
  Religion 278–279, 287, 289
  Robinson on 13
  siblings 281, 287

split with Elijah Muhammad 284, 291
  West Indian influence 282–283
  and women 282
Malinowski, Bronislaw 175
"Mammy"
  and Black Face 219
  in cinema 213–220
  historical characters 219
Mandela, Nelson 51
Mang'anja 27
Mannheim, Karl 273
Mansfield, Jayne 226–227
Maran, Rene
  Un homme pareil aux autres 298
Maravi 27
Marcos, Ferdinand 10, 336
  deposing of 195, 199–200
  seizure of power 202, 207n25
  and the United States 198–199
Marcos, Imelda 203, 207n34
Marcosson, Isaac 89
María Candelaria (1943) 243
Marqués, María Elena 243
Marquez, Gabriel Gard
  One Hundred Years of Solitude 76
Mars, Jean-Price 122
Marshall, Napoleon 103
Marshall, William 226
Martino, Giacomo de 99
Marx, Karl 190, 270, 305
  conception of fascism 152
  culture and change 7, 70
  and Hegel 40n5
  influence on Cox 79–80
  On the Jewish Question 70–71, 73
  and politics of representation 187
Marxism
  in Africa 31–32
  and Black liberationism 222
  on capitalism and freedom 86n41
  conception of fascism 9, 150
Maryland
  colonial history 253
  law banning inter-racial marriage
    188–189
  mixed race laws 233
Mason, George 141
mass surveillance 355
Massachusetts 312
Mayo, Marion
  *The Mental Capacity of the American
    Negro* 116, 124n29

Mazzini, Giuseppe 92
McAdoo, William 172
McCormick, Anne O'Hare 89
McCormick, Robert, Colonel 89
McCulloch, Jock 297–298
McDaniels, Hattie 219
McFarland, Henry 217
McGahee, Ralph 197, 206*n*15
McGee, Vonetta 226
McGee, William 120
McKay, Claude 252
McKinley, William 261
McKinney, Cynthia 169
McKinney, Nina Mae 239
McKittrick, Katherine 17*n*7
Mead, Margaret 121
media analysis 10–13, 183–264
    and Haitian occupation 263–264*n*40
    Nicaragua vs The United States 166
    terrorism 164–165
    see also propaganda
media, public trust in 169
Meier, August 59, 64
Meinecke, Friedrich 150
Melinda (1972) 225
Melville, Andrew 25
Melville, Herman 252–253
    Moby-Dick 77
Merleau-Ponty, Maurice 332
Mexican cinema 239–243
    depiction of Blacks 239, 243–244
    depiction of class 243, 249*n*23
    "Golden Age" 241
    and Hollywood 242–243, 249*n*31
    vs Hollywood 240
    Mulattas in 244–248
    during World War II 242
Mexican Revolution 240–241, 243, 249*n*27
    as movie setting 246–248
    and race 248
Mexico 312
    black population 243–244
    colonial history 243–244
    opposition to slavery 244
    and race 248
    US interventions in 241
    see also Mexican cinema; Mexican
        Revolution
Michaelis, Meir 107*n*15
    on Italian Fascism and the
        Jews 108*n*26

Micheaux, Oscar 11, 213–220, 224
    acting companies 216
    class 217
    depiction of mulatto characters
        215–216
    filmography 215–216
    recent research 213
    rediscovered works 213–214
Mill, James 26
Mingus, Charles 262
Minstrels 252
    bands 257
    and Eugene O'Neill 258–262
    evolution of racism 257
    and immigrant culture 256–257
    late 19th century 57
    pre-Civil War 255
    see also Black Face
mixed race
    depictions on film 215–216
    laws regarding 233–234
    Plato on 136
    see also Mulatta
Mobutu, Sese Seko 163, 336
Molina, Carlos 167
Moloney, Jay 212
Mondale, Walter 198
Monks, Aoife 258
Montagu, Ashley 121
Montaner, Rita 245
Moody, James 154–155
Moore, Barrington Jr. 150
Moore, Fred B. 59
Mora, Carl 241, 242, 243
moral authority
    meaning 3
    normativity of 4
    of the oppressed 3
    of protesters 18*n*18
    vs state authority 4
Morel, Edmund 120
Moreno, Mario 242
Morgan, Edmund 139
Morgan, J.P. 89, 222
Morgenthay, Henry 89
Moro National Liberation Front 203
Morris, Chester 227
Morris, Roger
    Uncertain Greatness 161
Morton, Samuel 114
Moses, Wilson Jeremiah 344

Mosley, Walter 56
Mosse, George 113
Moton, Robert Russa 103
Mouw, Henrik 173
Mozambique 308, 325
Muhammad, Elijah 283, 291
La Mulata de Córdoba (1945) 244
Mulatta 233–250
  and abolitionists 234
  actors
    lack of mainstream opportunities 239
    playing white parts 238–239
  in Cape Verde 312
  laws regarding 233–234
  in Mexican cinema 244–248
  post-Civil War 234
  in silent films 238
  villification of 234–235, 238
  see also mixed race
Multiculturalism 110–126
  classical 110
  criticisms of 126n58
  and eugenics 115
  and race science 111–112
Murphy, Dudley 259
Murphy, Eddie 185, 257
Mussolini, Benito 88
  ambitions in North Africa 94
  articles in US press 106n3
  emergence 157n2
  and Italian Jews 93
  racialism 92
  support for Zionism 93
  on the US 94
  US media coverage 89
  on war and peace 153
  wealthy supporters 107n7
Mutual Film Company 249n27
Mwase, George 35
Myrdal, Gunnar 171, 181n14
  The American Dilemma 9
  on *An American Dilemma* 173, 174
  vs Bunche 177
  on North v South in the US 177–178

NAACP v. Katherine Harris et al.
  (court case) 168
Nasar, Sylvia 338n6
Nation of Islam 289
  Malcolm X on 290
nation states

  failure of 52
  right to sovereignty 327
  as "terrorists" 165
National Advisory Commission on Civil
  Disorders *see* Kerner Commission
National Association for the Advancement
  of Colored People (NAACP) 168
  and cinema 236
  response to *Birth of a Nation* 214, 237
National Baptist Convention 38
National independence movements
  in the Philippines 205–206
  vs revolutionary movements 14
National Negro Congress (NCC) 175
National Recovery Act 179
nationalism
  Black 154
  CLR James on 47
  Filipino 197
  Indian, and Africa 31–32
  Irish 31–32
  Scottish 26
    and Africa 39
Native Americans 114, 138
  ethnologists and 114–115
  and race science 114
  at St Louis World Fair 116
  see also "Indian" wars
Naville, Pierre 298
Nazism 151, 155, 174
  Swedish collaboration 177
Needham, Joseph 77, 78
La Negra Angustias (1949) 12, 239–240, 243,
  244, 246–248
  changes to source material 246
négritude 296, 297, 298
Negro Business League 58
Negro Es Mi Color (1951) 244, 245
Negro World Alliance 154
Nemenzo, Francisco 208n45
Nerney, May Childs 214
Nesselius, I. 181n26
New Deal 333
  Bunche on 178
  racism in 175
New People's Army (NPA) 205
New Republic (periodical) 89
New York Times 208n41
  coverage of Venezuela 167
  on fascism 88
  on Ferdinand Marcos 202, 203

New York Times (Cont.)
  on Jesse Jackson 191–192
  on Malcolm X 277
news
  and fixed narratives 10
  as propaganda 10
  see also media analysis
Newsom, David 201–202
Newton, Isaac 340
Nez Perce 116
Ngoni 27
*Ni Sangre Ni Arena (Neither Blood Nor
    Sand)* (1936) 242
Nicaragua 205, 332, 334, 337
  legal action against US 166, 170n1
Nicholas, Denise 226
Nicholson, Jack 226
Nicholson, James 226
Niebuhr, H. Richard 24
Nigera 50
The Nigger (1915) 215, 238
Nine Years War 253
Nixon, Richard 161
Nkrumah, Kwame 2, 50, 308
Nolte, Ernst 95, 151
  definition of fascism 150, 152
  on Fascism and scholarship 108n28
Nolte, Nick 227
Noonan, Kathleen 254
Noriega, Manuel 336
Norris, Chuck 227
North Carolina slavery laws 342
Norwich, John
  A History of Venice 80
Nosotros los Pobres (We the Poor) (1947) 243
Nott, Josiah 114
Nyanja 27
Nyasaland
  colonized peoples 27
  establishment 28
Nyasaland Native Rising 1915, 27, 29
  competing narratives 35–37
Nyerere, Julius 38–39, 50, 163, 308

Oakes, John 203
Obregón, Alvaro, General 241
Ochs, Adolph 89
O'Connor, Anne-Marie 211
The October Revolution 321
oil industry
  in the Philippines 199
  in Venezuela 167

oligarchy 63
  in Africa, media coverage of 162
  James Madison on 81, 141
  in the Philippines 197, 199
  in Plato's Republic 129, 131–132, 135–137
Olivo, Antonio 211
Olson, S. Douglas 134
The Omega Man (1971) 225
O'Neill, Eugene 12–13, 251–265
  accusations of racism 261
  All God's Chillun Got Wings 13, 252
  cultural heritage 258
  cultural legacy 251
  depictions of Black characters 252
  The Dreamy Kid 252
  The Emperor Jones 12, 251–252, 258–262
    Black critics on 261
    film version 259
    political themes and intentions 260
    structure 258
  on Hondurans 260–261
  and Minstrels 258–262
  Moon of the Caribbees 252
  notable works 251
  parents 258
  study of Haitian Revolution 260
  Thirst 252, 258
O'Neill, James
  parents 258
O'Neill, Peter 12
Operation Just Cause 334
Oppenheimer, Franz 40n5
Organski, A.F.K. 150
Ovesey 282
Ovington, Mary White 214

Pace, Eric 202
Pachon, Harry 211
Padmore, George 53n2, 155–156
  Africa and World Peace 156
Palestine 9, 93
  human rights violations in 169
Pan-African Commonwealth 51
Pan-Africanism 32, 45–53, 157, 344–345
  and Christianity 349
  cultural 47
  in Hopkins' work 64
  Marcus Garvey 261
  political 47–50
    Western inspiration 50
  as prehistory 45–46
Panama 169, 332, 334, 336

Park, Mungo 39
Park, Robert E. 78
Parry, Benita 295, 303
  on Bhabha's interpretation of Fanon 301
  Global Theory 304
PATRIOT Act 169
Patterson, Marth 56
Pavón, José Maria Morelosy 243–244
Payne, Stanley 150, 151
Peña, Mauricio 245
Perez, Rafael 210
Perham, Margery 33, 34
Perry, Tyler 257
Pershing, John J., General 241
Philippines 10–11, 165, 195–208, 261
  banking 199–200, 202
  CIA operations in 206n15
  colonialism in
    Spanish 195–196
    United States 196–198
  martial law 199–200, 202, 207n25
  US education of political elites 206n10
  US "pacification" campaigns 196
  during World War II 197
Phillips, Ulrich 343
phrenology 114
  origins 124n15
Piess, Kathy 16
Pinky (1949) 239, 240
Pinto, Joao Teixeira 311
Pittsburgh Courier 104, 154
Pius X, Pope 92
"plantation films" 223–224
The Planter (Civil War ship) 60
Plato 110, 128, 134, 340
  brothers 131
  and class 136
  on decline of democracy 135
  on free will 134
  on inequality and class 130
  "logos" 134
  modern influence 137–142
    19th century 139
  political theory 136
  on political unrest 135
  power and nobility 137
  and race 132–133, 133–137
    breeding 135
  Republic 6, 127
    attacks on democracy 142
    character dialogues 131–133
    cultural impact 130

    interpretation 128–129
    structure 130
  Robinson on 6
  on slavery 133
  socio-historical context 129–130
  "the noble myth" 132
  theory of forms 144n38
Plummer, Brenda Gayle 102
Poitier, Sydney 56
Polanyi, Michael 273
police
  corruption scandals 11
  militarization of 355
  see also specific police departments and
    agencies
police killings 354
politics of representation 185–195
  and Marx 187
Pool, James 88
Pool, Suzanne 88
Pope, Generoso 98
Portugal
  class in the 19th century 314–315
  post-World War 2, 314
  role in slave trade 312
  socialism in 320–321
  see also Portuguese colonialism
Portuguese colonialism 308–330
  19th century 312–315
  in Angola 161
  and banking 313
  industry 313
  "pacification" of colonies 310, 311
  post-War 323
  and the slave trade 310–311
  see also Guinea-Bissau
Posella, Dante 90
Powell, Adam Clayton Jr. 341
Powers, Charles 160–162
Prasad, Madhava
  on "Fanonian tradition" 303
  on Parry 304
Preer, Evelyn 217
Presbyterianism 25–26
Price, Thomas 26
  dismissal of Mwase 37
  on the Nyasaland Native Uprising 35
Prichard, Hesketh
  Where Black Rules White 261
propaganda 222
  and 9/11, 165, 169
  anti-Irish 263n13

propaganda (*Cont.*)
and the CIA 167
Hollywood and the Mexican revolution 241
and Jesse Jackson's presidential bid 191
pro-Haitian occupation 263–264*n*40
and US occupation of Philippines 198–206
Ferdinand Marcos 203–204
Filipino revolution 205–206
and Venezuela 167
Prosser, Gabriel 101, 262
psychoanalysis
and leadership 33–34
and race 295–296, 300
Ptolemy 273
Pudd'nhead Wilson (1916) 215, 238
Puerto Rico 165
Pythagoras 340

Queller, Donald
on medieval venice 85*n*27
The Venetian Patricate 80
Quinn-Judge, Paul 201

Race & Class (periodical) 5, 10
race sciences 112, 114
and gender 145*n*74
and immigrants 114
impact on popular culture 117
and intelligence 117
origin of term 145*n*70
in revolutionary America 140–141
during World War I 172
see also An American Dilemma: The Negro Problem and Modern Democracy
racial discourse 187–190
racialism
and fascism 152
Mussolini 92
Victorian era 139
racism
and capitalism 79, 177, 188
European vs American 189
and fascism 157
in Sweden 177
as tool to divide working class 180
types 188–190
in United States
racial theory 188
theories of origin 188

radical fiction 341
Radical History Review (periodical) 5
Rainboro, Thomas 338
Ramos, Fidel, General 200, 205
Rampart Scandal 11, 209–212
Randolph, John 189, 348
Rap music 230
Reagan, Ronald 166, 208*n*41, 332–333, 337
and Ferdinand Marcos 203–205
Redding, J. Saunders
They Come in Chains 343
Reddy, Maureen 55
Reform School Girl (1957) 226
Reich, Otto J. 167–168
Reich, Wilhelm 74
Mass Psycholohy of Fascism 69
Reid, Mayne, Captain
The Quadroon; or, A Lover's Adventures in Louisiana 234
Reira, Emilio Garcia 249*n*22, 250*n*47
Rejwan, Nissim 94
Religion
and colonialism 30
David Walker on 346
and Haitian revolution 72
in Ireland 254
and Malcolm X 278–279
Marx on 187
missionaries 119
in the Philippines 198
in Scotland 25–26
in Viet Nam 198
see also Catholicism; Christianity; Protestantism
The Renaissance at Charleroi (1917) 216, 238
Renda, Mary 260
Revel, Ignazio Thaon di 99
Review (periodical) 5, 6
Revolutionary movements
vs national independence movements 14
Rhodes, Cecil 28
and the African Lakes Company 28
Rice, T.D. 257
Riera, Emilio Garcia 240, 241, 244
on *La Negra Angustias* 247
on *Los Angelitos Negros* 245
Rio Escondido (Hidden River) (1947) 243, 250*n*53
Roach, Joseph 234
Robert the Bruce (Robert I of Scotland) 26

Roberts, Kenneth 89
Robertson, Pat 169
Robeson, Paul 259, 261, 263*n*35
Robinson, Cedric J.
  African Identities 2
  An Anthropology of Marxism 2, 5
  on Black internationalism 5–6
  Black Marxism 5
    feminist critique 17*n*9
    reprints 17*n*6
  Black Movements in America 5
  on contradiction of US history 18*n*26
  and Black Radical Tradition 2, 6–7
  Bourgeois historiography 6–8
  on cinema and Hollywood 11–12
  collaboration with Elizabeth 15
  Coming to Terms 1–2
  conception of fascism 9
  Forgeries of Memory & Meaning 5, 10
    on cinema 11
  on Frantz Fanon 13–14
  impact of work 1
  on media analysis 10–13
  and moral authority of people in crisis
    3–4
  on the nature of reality 10–13
  on oppression and virtue 3
  Race & Class 13–14
  on resistance and redemption 13–16
  social ethos 17*n*15
  speaking engagements 11
  teaching and research methods 12
  television work 8
  Terms of Order 2, 5
    on charismatic leadership 13
  themes of works 5
  transdiciplinary approach 3, 5
  on U.S. Foreign Policy 8–10
Robinson, Elizabeth 2, 8, 9, 15
Robinson, Jackie 287
Rock All Night (1957) 226
Rock, Chris 221, 231, 257
Rodney, Walter 7, 69, 327*n*6
  How Europe Underdeveloped Africa 77
Rodriguez, Ismael 243
Rodriguez, Joselito 239–240
Roediger, David 255
Rogers, Carl 278
Rogers, Will 89
Rojas González, Francisco 240, 246, 247,
    250*n*51, 250*n*52

Roo, Andrés Quintana 243–244
Rooney, Andy 331
Roosevelt, Franklin D. 88, 107*n*11, 108*n*32,
    154–155
  "neutrality" doctrine 99
  reforms 179
Rose, Arnold 171–172
  on immigration and assimilation
    181*n*42
Rosenblatt, Roger 205–206
Rosenthal, A.M. 198
Rosselli, Bruno 99
Rossi, Cesare 88
Rotberg, Robert 35
  The Rise of Nationalism in Central Africa
    35
Roth, Cecil 92
  The History of the Jews of Italy 91
Russian Revolution 40*n*3
Rwanda 50

Sadji, Abdoulaye 297
Said, Edward 295, 303
  Global Theory 304
  Orientalism 76
Salas, Elizabeth 246, 247
Salazar, Antonio 310
Salvemini, Gaetano 96, 99
Sam, Guillaume 260
San Jose Mercury News 11, 167, 209
San Martin, Patricia Torres de 249*n*34
Sapir, Edward 121
Sarfatti, Margherita 93
Saturday Evening Post 89
Sauer, Wolfgang 150
The Savage Girl (1932) 223
Savage, Kirk 62
Scar of Shame (1931) 239
Schadd, Mary Ann 348
Schapera, Isaac 175
Schickel, Richard 248*n*16
Schlesinger, Arthur J. 90, 126*n*58
Scorsese, Martin 226
Scotland
  English colonialism 25–26
  influence in Central Africa 27
  religion 25
Scott, William 154
Scottish Enlightenment 25, 26
Scottish nationalism 26
  and African nationalism 39

Sealey 136
Secter, Bob 202
segregation 57
  of Jews in Italy 92
  in the military 171, 172, 288
  see also Jim Crow Laws
Selassie, Haile 53*n*1
Selig Polyscope 215, 238
Senseless (1998) 221
September 11th 2001, 164–165
  post-attack propaganda 169
Sequeyro, Adela 249*n*34
sexuality
  impact of colonialism 296–297, 298
  and Mulatta characters 237, 238, 247
Shaft (1971) 56
  success 226
Shake, Rattle and Rock (1956) 226
Shakespeare, William 164
  The Comedy of Errors 164
Shawarbi, Mahoud Youssef 283
The She Creature (1956) 226
Sheba, Baby (1975) 227
Sheppard, William Henry 119–120, 122
Shepperson, George 23–40
  ability as historian 38
  background 24
  criticism of 33–41
  Independent African 26–27
    reviews 33
  interest in Central Africa 24
  on John Chilembwe 29
  on Joseph Booth 30
  psychohistorical approach 34–35
  on Scottish vs African anti-colonialism
    42*n*78
  on task of historian 24
  teaching career 24
Shotwell, James 88
Siegmann, George 215
Simon, Paul 192
Simone, Nina 1
Skinner, Quentin 142
Slaughter (1972) 226
slave revolts 115
  19th century 262
  and the Civil War 60
  fear of 342
  in Guinea-Bissau 311
  influence on African rebellions 32–33
  Irish workers 254

moral case for 347
slavery
  abolition 138
  and American Revolution 138
  in ancient history 127, 133, 345
  in art 218
  baptism as escape from 233
  in Belgian Congo 119
  black complicity in 347–348
  and capitalism 76–77
  defences of 139
  and democracy 127–128
  depictions in cinema 224
  Egyptian 345
  in fiction 234
  French Revolution 138
  in Latin America 312
  legislation
    in Georgia 342
    in North Carolina 342
  in Liberia 103
  and Portuguese colonialism 311
  Roman 345
  and "the West" 137–138
  see also freed slaves
Sledd, Andrew 343
Sleds, George 89
Smalls, Robert, Captain 60
Smith, Adam 26, 75
Smith, Al 96
Smith, Dennis Mack 106*n*3
Smith, Gerald K. 96
Smith, Lydia Hamilton 237–238
Smyth, John Henry 118–119
Snowden, Frank 123*n*4
So Red the Rose (1935) 223
Social Identities (periodical) 6
Socialism
  in Africa, media coverage of 162
  African vs European 38–39
  black/white relations 235–236
  Cabral on 321
  Fascism as response to 155
Socrates 129, 340, 356
  in Plato's Republic 131–132
  societal virtue 350
Soitos, Stephen
  The Blues Detective 54
Sold at Auction (1917) 238
Solomon Islands 121–122
Somalia 50

Somoza, Anastasio 336
Soulouque, Faustin 102
South Africa 356
  race science in 173
Soyinka 49
Spanish Civil War 99
  international brigades 105, 155
  as part of global fight 155
Spanish-American War 196
Spenser, Edmund 253, 254
Spier, Leslie 121
Spivak, Gayatri Chakravorty 295, 303
  In Other Worlds 76
  on Parry's work 301–302
St Croix, 136
St Louis Post-Dispatch 117, 118
St Louis World Fair 1904, 116, 117–123
Stair, Edward 95
Stalin, Joseph 155
Steinberg, Lucien 93
Stens, Anna 227
Stephens, Thaddeus 237–238
Sterne, Elaine 214
Sterner, Richard 171–172
Stoney, George C. 175
Straight, Willard 89
Stuckey, Sterling 344
Sudan 50, 161
Sweden 177
Sweeney, Joel Walker 255
The Symbol of the the Unconquered
  (1920) 216

Taft, William Howard 196
Tangri, Roger 27
Tanner, Jo 56
Tanzania 163
Taussig, Michael
  Shamanism, Colonialism and the Wild Man 76, 125n41
Taylor, Charles 48
Taylor, Clyde 213, 229
Temple, John 254
  The Irish Rebellion 253, 263n13
Terman, Lewis 115
Terrell, Mary Church 59, 63, 236
terrorism 9–10, 164–172
  US hypocrisy on 169
  US sponsoring of 169
  see also War on Terror
Terry, Sonny 267

Third World News Review (TV) 8
Thirty Tyrants 131
Thomas, Clarence 332
Thomas, Darryl C. 17n9
Thompson, Wimley 105
Thucydides 127, 340
  Robinson on 3
Thurber, Cheryl 218
Tidyman, Ernest 56
Tigerstedt, E.N. 129
Toll, Robert 57
Tonga (African people) 27
Toomer, Jean 252
trade unions
  Black leaders of 175
  and Black working class 288
  and Guinea-Bissau independence 318
  in the Philippines 197
  in South Africa 31
  strikes and the New Deal 179
Trader Horn (1931) 223
Treaty of London 158n12
Trefousse, Hans 238
Trent, William 343
Trevino, Joseph 211
Trevor-Roper, H.R. 157n2
Trotter, William Monroe 63, 236
Truman, Harry S. 166
  desegregation of armed forces 171
Truth and Reconciliation Commission 15, 356–358
Truth, Sojourner 341
Tubman, Harriet 341
Turner, Henry A. 150
Turner, Henry McNeal 119
Turner, Nat 114
Turner, Nathaniel 29, 48, 56, 262
Twain, Mark 252–253
  Pudd'nhead Wilson 215

United Nations
  as inspiration for Pan-African Commonwealth 52
United States
  colonial period 54
  exceptionalism 196
  imperialism 90, 165
    and "production enclaves" 191
    racialist excuses for 261
  Italian immigrants 96
    fascism among 97–98

United States (*Cont.*)
  ghettos 98
  national identity 189
  racial discourse 187–190
  revolutionary democracy 140–141
  slavery in 139
  and World War I 89–90
United States foreign policy 8–10,
    147–182
  Afghanistan 169
  in Africa 161
  Colombia 169
  in the Congo 163
  and domestic politics 18*n*29
  El Salvador 166–167
  Guatemala 166–167
  Haitian occupation 102–103, 260
    press support for 263–264*n*40
  Honduras 166–167
  Italo-Ethiopian War 99–100
  late 20th Century 331–332
  in Latin America 211
  Liberia 153
  Mexican revolution 241, 249*n*27
  Nicaragua 166, 334
  Panama 334
  in the Philippines 196–198
    education of Filipino elites 206*n*10
    removal of Marcos 203–205
  Robinson on 8–10
  in Robinson's works 5
  Spanish Civil War 99–100
  support of Fascism 88–90
  Venezuelan coup 167–168
  see also specific conflicts and incidents
Universal Negro Improvement Association
    (UNIA) 101, 260, 283
  destruction of 104, 153–154
  and US occupation of Haiti 103
Universities Mission to Central
    Africa 27
US Office of the Coordinator for Inter-
    American Affairs (OCIAA)
    249*n*31

*Vámonos con Pancho Villa (Let's Go with
    Pancho Villa)* (1935) 242
Venezuela 167
Venezuelan coup 2002, 167
Venice 80–82
  as birthplace of capitalism 85*n*36

democracy in 82
  as model for capitalist societies 82
Vesey, Denmark 48, 262, 346–347
Vieira, Joao 327
Viet Nam 7, 71, 169
  colonial history 72
  Empire 73
Vietnam War
  press revisionism 207*n*30
  protests against 201
Villa, Francisco "Pancho" 241, 246
Villa, Pancho 249*n*27
Vincent, Ted 244, 250*n*36
Virginia
  colonial history 253
  race laws 140
  democracy and slavery 139
  mixed race laws 233
Vlastos, Gregory 133, 134, 138
Voodoo 72
  development of 72
voter suppression 168, 170*n*9

Walker, Aida 257
Walker, Alice 185
Walker, David 14, 48, 57, 340–353
  on ancient slavery 345–346
  *APPEAL in Four Articles; Together with
    a Preamble, to the Coloured Citizens
    of the World, But in Particular, and
    Very Expressly, to Those of the United
    States of America* 341
  importance to Black Studies 345
  modern reprinting 343
  structure 345
  as black nationalist 344
  on black slave traders 347–348
  calls for insurrection 350–351
  death 341
  debate over politics 342, 344
  early life 341, 346–347
  posthumous influence 341–342, 350–351
  on racial differences 349–350
  religion 346
  Robinson on 15
Walker, George 257
Walker, George W. 57–58
Wall Street Journal 167
Wallace, William, Sir 26
Wallenstein, Immanuel 16
Walsh, Raoul 240

Walters, Barbara 167
Wanyasa 27
War on Terror 164
Ward, Andrew 62
Ward, Barbara 32
Warner, Lloyd 78
Washington, Booker T. 64, 78, 214, 341
  accomodationism 59
  attitude to women 58–59
  purchase of *Colored American
    Magazine* 58
Washington, Denzel 56
Washington, Fredi 239, 263n35
Washington Post 125n50
  coverage of Marcos regime 204
  coverage of Venezuela 167
  Gary Webb revelations 209
Watch Tower movement 32
Waters, Maxine 209
Wayans, Keenan Ivory 221
Webb, Gary 11, 167, 209
Weber, Eugen 151, 274
Weber, Max 269
Weisbrot, Mark 166
Weizmann, Chaim 93, 107n15
Wells. H.G. 88
Wells-Barnett, Ida B. 341
Wentworth, Thomas 254
Wesley, Charles 341
"the West" 75–77
  vs China 83
  classicism 113–114
  definitions of fascism 151–152
  and multiculturalism 111
  and slavery 137–138, 158n9
Westerman, W.L. 138
What's Up, Tiger Lily? (1966) 226
Wheeler, Roxann 253
White, Deborah Gray 218
White, Hayden 76, 137–138, 151–152
"White Man's Burden" 173–174, 261
white privilege 253
White, William Allen 90
"whiteness"
  Franklin on 188
  and the Irish 252–255
  origin of concept 253
Wild, John 133
Wilentz, Sean
  on Walker 346–347
Wilkins, Roy 171, 287

Will, George 126n58
Williams, Bert 58, 257–258
Williams, Eric 53n1
Williams, George Washington 57, 118–119,
  122, 341
  *A History of the Negro Race in America
    from 1619 to 1880*, 119
  *History of the Negro Troops in the War of
    Rebellion* 62
Williams, John Skelton 172
Williams, Robert Gooding 14
Willner, Ann Ruth 272, 274–275
Wilson, Frank 259
Wilson, Woodrow 180n8, 236, 261
Wirth, Louis 78
Wish, Harvey 101
Wissler, Clark 121
Within Our Gates (1919) 224, 239
  rediscovery 213–214
Wolf, Eric
  Europe and the People Without History
    76, 84n2
A Woman of Impulse (1918) 216
Women's Penitentiary I (1971) *see The Big
  Doll House* (1971)
Wood, Ellen 189
Woodson, Carter G. 341
Woodward, C. Vann 126n58
World Bank 202, 336
World Trade Center 164
World War I
  and emergence of fascism 150
  impact on African colonies 31
  in Philippines 197
  and Portuguese colonialism 311
  and rise of Italian Left 96–97
  and US business interests 89–90
World War II
  impact on Africa 31
  in the Philippines 197
World Zionist Organization 93
Wright, James 189
Wright, Richard 252
Wynter, Sylvia 1, 2
  on modern political struggle 16

Yates, James 105
Yazidis 355
Yoruba 118
Young, Donald 173
Young, Richard 282

Zackodnik, Teresa 233
Zaire 163
Zambia 28
Zapata, Emiliano 241, 246
Zimbabwe 161
Zinn, Howard 179

Zionism
  attitude to "Levantine" Jews 94
  and Fascism 91–95
  reliance on Britain 93
Zulu peoples 27